Figurative Paintings

Paris and The Modern Spirit

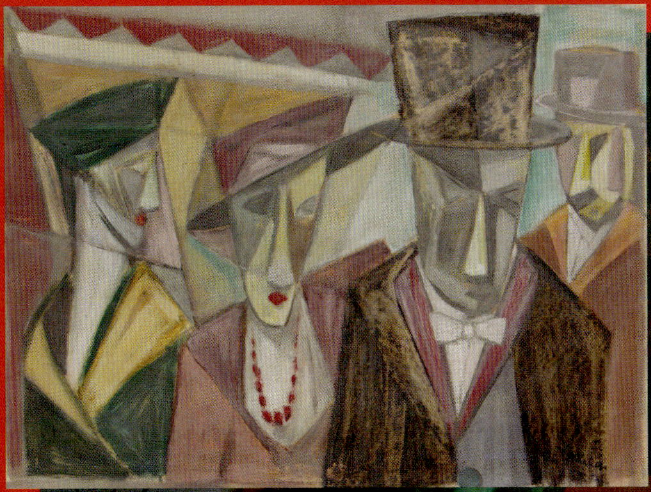

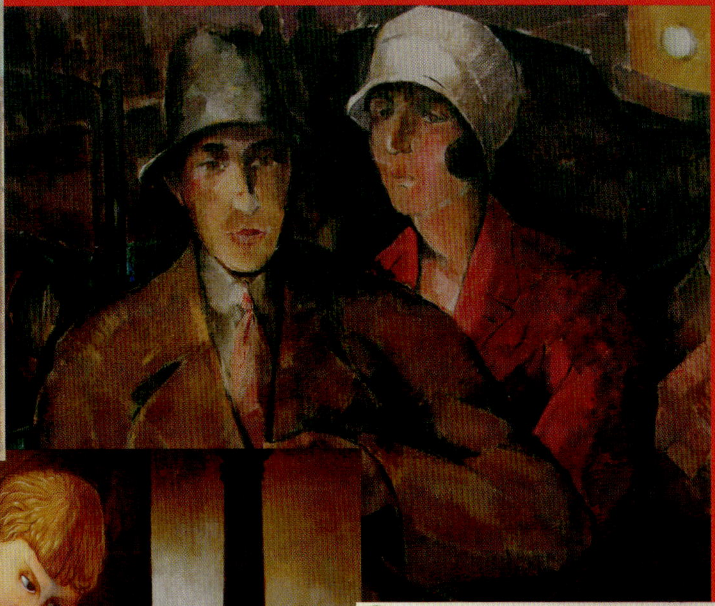

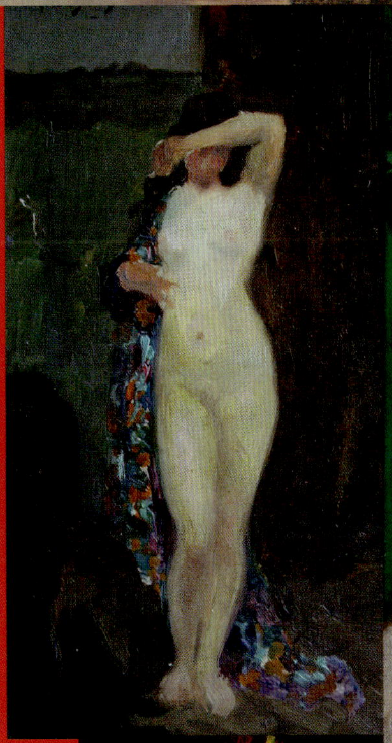

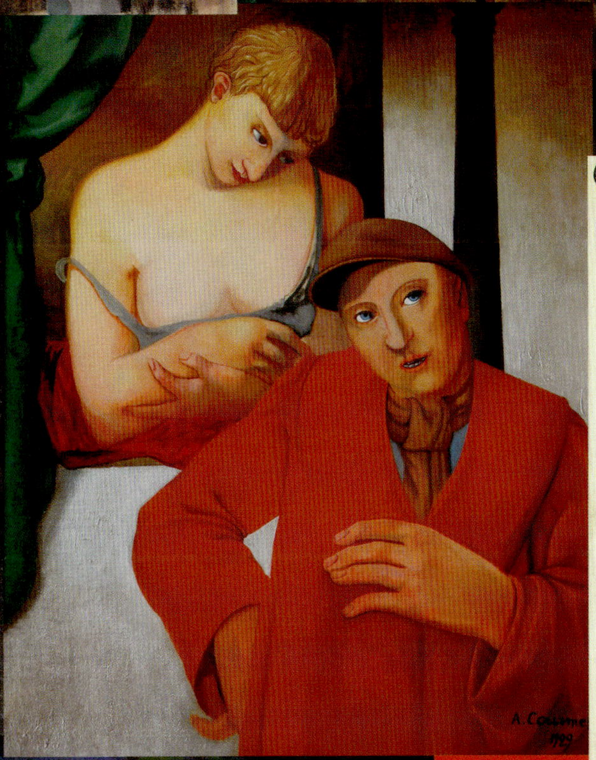

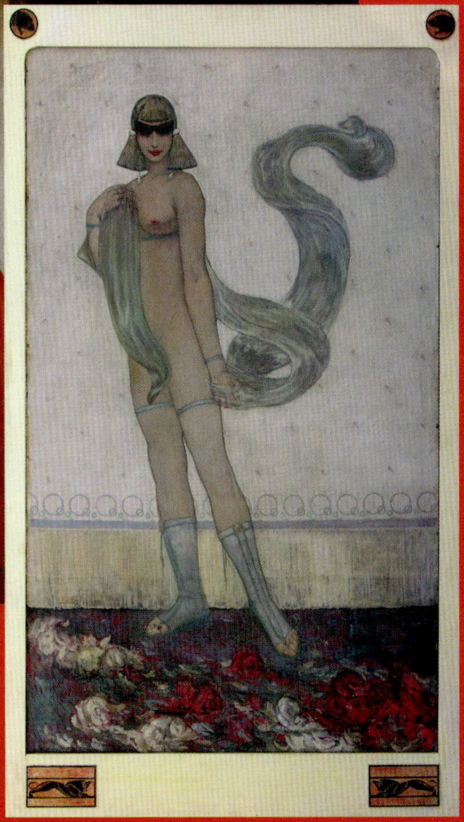

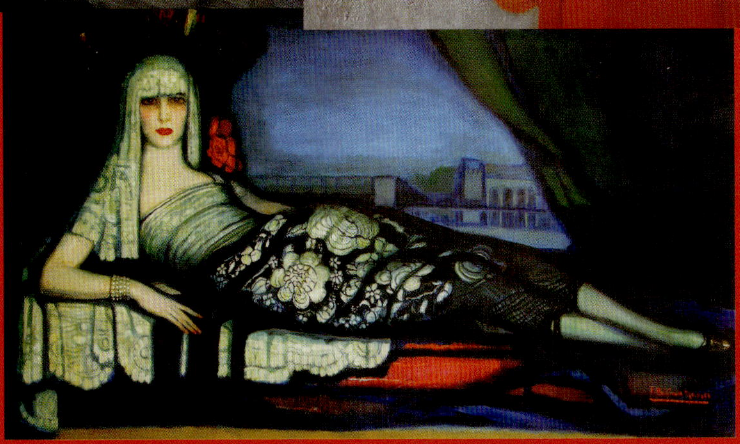

Martin Wolpert and Jeffrey Winter

Schiffer Publishing Ltd®

4880 Lower Valley Road, Atglen, PA 19310 USA

Library of Congress Control Number: 2005938061

Covers and Layout by: Bruce Waters
Type set in Benguiat heading font/Humanist 521 text font

ISBN: 0-7643-2462-4
Printed in China

Published by Schiffer Publishing Ltd.
4880 Lower Valley Road
Atglen, PA 19310
Phone: (610) 593-1777; Fax: (610) 593-2002
E-mail: Info@schifferbooks.com

Acknowledgments

We have been able to complete this book thanks to the cooperation of many collectors and dealers in California, London, New York, Paris and Brussels. Chuck and Nancy Parrish, Mark and Marina Plon, and the Scott Seligman family have been important contributors. We also particularly thank Kathleen Avery and Hillary Welde of Kathleen Avery Fine Art, Nigel Turner of Los Angeles Fine Art Gallery, Whitford Fine Art, Spencer Jon Helfen Fine Arts Gallery, Gerome Adamson of Adamson-Duvannes Gallery, Barry Friedman Ltd. and Anthony Nahas. We greatly appreciate the efforts of the many other collectors, galleries and private dealers who cooperated with us and offered their generous assistance. We also thank the many historians and authors of the fine books we have used for reference.

Brooke Doyle, with tireless dedication, put in hundreds of hours of research to bring this book to publication. She received her Bachelors Degree in Art History and Museum Studies from Beloit College in 2003 and has worked for Papillon Gallery since 2004.

We also thank Colleen Meek and Jennifer Vanderpool for their work toward the realization of this book.

We are especially grateful to Axel d'Anthes of Studio 101, Santa Barbara, California, for his assistance in proofing the French language titles and phrases in the book. Remaining errors are the responsibility of the authors.

The patience of our families for the long hours we were away working on this project deserves our praise and gratitude. Mike Iorg, wife of Martin Wolpert and co-founder of Papillon Gallery, and Ann Bridges, wife of Jeffrey Winter, along with their children, Ashley, Alex, Ariel and Amelia, have supported and contributed to this project in countless ways.

We owe our gratitude to Peter and Nancy Schiffer who agreed in one minute to publish our first book and did not hesitate to publish this second book.

And our thanks go to the artists who dedicated their lives to our collective enrichment.

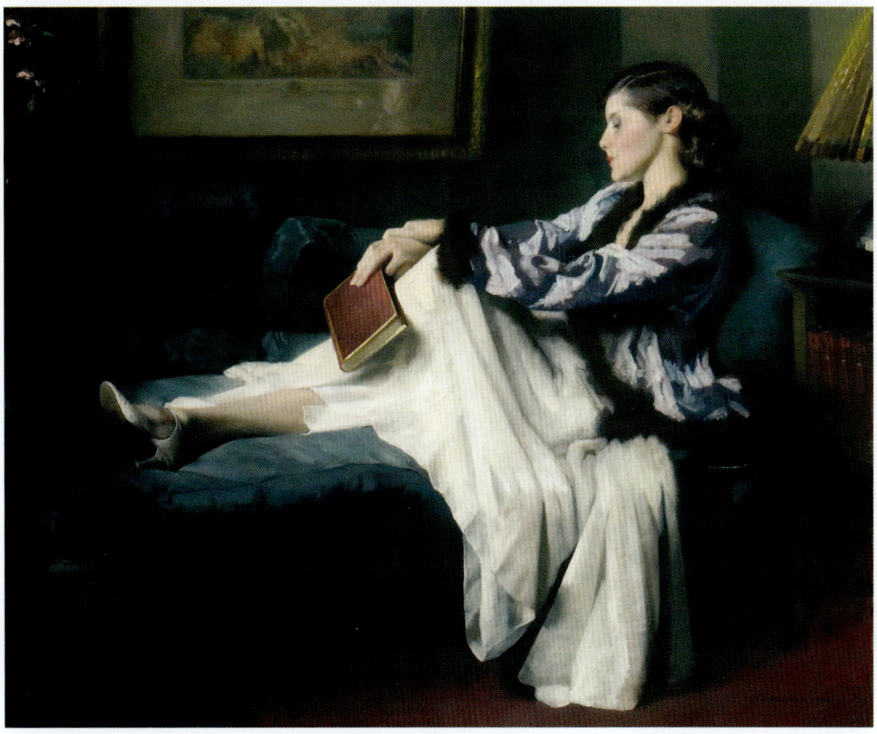

Contents

The Paris Art World, c. 1880-1950

Defining Modernism 6
Bohemian Lifestyles and the Latin Quarter 6
Art Galleries 6
The Influences of Drugs on Art and Lifestyle 7

The Belgians

Walloon Art 9

Collectors, Critics, and Art Historians

Building a Collection 11

The Artists

Pierre Abadie-Landel 13
Jacques Acrement 14
Georgette Agutte 15
Ludovic Alleaume 16
Mabel Alvarez 18
Victor Arnautoff 20
Gustave Astoy 21
Émile Baes 22
James Peter Barbarite 24
Louis Jean Beaupuy 25
Paul-Émile Bécat 26
Pierre de Belair 27
Féderico Beltran-Masses 28
Jehan Berjonneau 30
Albert Bertalan 31
René-Pierre Louis Besserve 32
Marie-Gabriel Biessy 33
Charles-Louis Bisschops 34
Roger Bissière 36
Marcel Bloch 38
Richard Bloos 39
Jean de Botton 40
Robert Bouchet 42
Abel Dominique Boyé 43
Henri Georges Bréard 44
Gaston Bussière 45
Frédéric Marius de Buzon 46
Antoine Calbet 47
Gaspar Camps 48
Ben Carré 49
Boris Chaliapin 50
Émile Chambon 51
Jean Chapin 52
Emilie Charmy 53
Roland Chavenon 58
Michael Chepourkoff 59
Édouard Chimot 60
Lev Chistovsky 61
Edythe Varian Cockroft 66
Émile Compard 67
Anna Costenoble 69
Alfred Courmes 70
Hermann Courtens 72
Albert Cresswell 73
Georges Creten 74
Claude Dalbanne 76
Georges Dayez 77
Susan Daynes-Grassot 79
Ludmilla Ferri Decler 80
Henriette Delalain 81
Edmond Delescluze 82
Herman Delpech 83
Jean-Pierre Dequene 84
Lucien Desmaré 85
Raymond Dierickx 86
Jean-Gabriel Domergue 87
Jean Dormont 89
Raphaël Dubois 90
Jean Dulac 91
Frank DuMond 92
Adrien Dupagne 93
Jean Dupas 94
Auguste Durand-Rosé 98
Charles-Auguste Edelmann 99
Francis de Erdely 100
Ivan Escribe 103
Albert Fernand-Renault 104
Gaston Simoes de Fonseca 105
Hippolyte Fournier 106
Baron Frédéric 108
Pal Fried 109
Karoly Fulop 110
Móric Gábor 112
Léon Galand 113
Richard Geiger 114
Nanette Genoud 116
Jacques Geuens 117
Robert Giron 118
Simon Glatzer 119
Nicolas Gloutchenko 120
Maurice Goossens 121
Imre Góth 122
Jean Gouweloos 123
Lucien-Henri Grandgérard 125
Marcel Gromaire 126
Nathan Grunsweigh 128
Adolfo Guiard y Larrauri 129
Paul Louis Guilbert 130
Alice Halicka 131
Jean Hanau 133
Gaston Haustrate 134
Maurice Henri Hensel 135
René Georges Hermann-Paul 136

André Hofer 137
André Louis Maxime Humbert 138
Léonie Humbert-Vignot 139
Jean Jannel 140
Romain Jarosz 142
Mainie Harriet Jellett 143
Lucien Hector Jonas 144
George M. Josimovich 145
Chrysis Jungbluth 148
Morris Kantor 150
Andrée Karpelès 151
Vital Keuller 152
Reimond Kimpe 153
Raphaël Kirchner 155
Alice Kohn 157
Richard Kollorsz 162
Peter Krasnow 163
Luc Lafnet 165
Jean Francis Laglenne 166
Anne-Marie Lagrange 167
Adolphe La Lyre 168
Bernard Lamotte 169
William Julien Émile Édouard Laparra 171
Edmond Édouard Lapeyre 172
Jean Laudy 173
Paul Lecompte 175
Mercedes Legrand 176
Pierre Lelong 178
René Lelong 179
Edmond Lempereur 180
Georges Lépine 181
Axel Linus 182
Almery Lobel-Riche 183
DeWitt McClellan Lockman 184
René Longa 185
Jean Lurçat 186
Mariette Lydis 189
Marcel-Lenoir 190
Georges Maresté 192
Mania Mavro 193
Mayo 195
Marie Ménard 197
Maurice Jean Micha 198
Maurice Millière 200
Alfred Moitroux 201
Émile-Pierre de la Montagne 202
Adrien Moreau-Neret 204
Max Moreau 203
Mela Muter 205
Charles Naillod 206
Warren A. Newcombe 207
Robert (Ernest) Noir 209
Carl (Charles) Nys 210
Jean Oberlé 211
Otis Oldfield 212
Philippe Parrot 214
Albert Joseph Penot 215
Robert Phillipp 219
Louis Picard 221
Fernand Piet 222
Edgar Pillet 223
Marcel Pouget 224
Gaston Prunier 225
Marcel Prunier 226
Jules Rambo 227
Lucie Ranvier-Chartier 228
Antoine Marie Raynolt 229
Paul Renaudot 230
Alfred Reth 232
Georges Rochegrosse 236
Vera Rockline 239
Georges Rogy 241
Walter Sauer 242
Edgar Scauflaire 243
Lucien-Victor Guirand (Guérand) de Scévola 246
Hugo Schimmel 247
Rodolphe Schönberg 248
William S. Schwartz 249
Lucien Seevagen 251
Boris Smirnoff 252
Henri Sollier 254
Simeon Solomon 255
Henri Somm (François Clément Sommier) 256
Elisabeth Sonrel 257
Jean Souverbie 259
Frantisek Srp 263
Nicolas Sternberg 264
Walter Stiner 266
Yasushi Tanaka 267
Maurice Louis Tête 269
Adrien Thevenot 270
Léon Tirode 272
André Tondu 273
Lucie Tullat 275
Milivoy Uzelac 276
Prosper Vagnier 277
Karel van Belle 278
Hugo van Beveren 280
Carlo van Her 281
Georges van Nuffel 282
Charles van Roose 283
Georges Vanzevenberghen 284
Theodoor-Joseph Verschaeren 285
Frede Vidar 286
Pierre Villain 287
Léon Voguet 288
Maurice Wagemans 289
Charles Watelet 290
Gerda Wegener 293
Muriel Wilson 296
Guy Brown Wiser 297
Edward Withers 298
Henri Achille Zo 299

Bibliography 300
Index 302

The Paris Art World, c. 1880-1950

Defining Modernism

In the middle of the 19th century intellectual and artistic communities endeavored to interpret and catalogue the times in which they lived. In art and literature the modern world was idolized and damned, analyzed and challenged. Baudelaire and Marx among other artists, writers and philosophers put forth doctrines and manifestos in which they discuss the role of religion and spirituality in contemporary society, the effects of industrialization, the politics of war, the rise of the avant-garde and new-found artistic freedom embodied in Impressionism, Postimpressionism, Symbolism, Cubism, Art Nouveau, Art Deco and Futurism.

As the 20th century began, these written formulas of modernism dominated and defined the artistic and literary communities. To be modern was to challenge traditional thinking and this became the fundamental challenge of the creative mind.

The need for new philosophies and means of expression grew as technology was altering the modes of business, industry and economy. As new technology was developing to challenge traditional values, the age of new thought began.

Towards the end of the 19th century, forward thinking itself had become institutionalized and it became more difficult for creative communities to shock their audiences. The doctrine of the avant-garde was becoming embedded in the very communities they had sought to refute.

By definition and by necessity what is modern is fluid and a well-defined context is necessary. Unlike technology, obsolescence is not inherent in art and literature; on the contrary what has proceeded is often highly recognized and revered as the building blocks of the present and what was once considered avant-garde has became 'high art.' To truly understand a painting or a novel one must understand the historic, social and geographic context of its creation.

Bohemian Lifestyles

Bohemian lifestyle in the modern age was a result of artistic communities and counter cultures converging in mid-19th century Paris where ideologies embraced freedom, intellectual curiosity and disdain for the establishment, especially the bourgeoisie. Though "Bohemia" is considered more a state of mind than a place in time, the Latin Quarter, Montmartre and Montparnasse districts of Paris were certainly its capital and their cafés, bars and restaurants became the sacred halls of this society. The artists and writers who flourished in this community are now recognized as the forerunners of modernism.

Henry Murger, an aspiring artist-turned-writer, is considered one of the first Bohemians. His seminal work, *Scènes de la Vie Bohème,* chronicled the experiences of the artist and his friends within the café culture of Paris.

One of the most prominent painters of mid-19th century Paris was Gustave Courbet, who painted ordinary people and places, and portrayed French people as a political entity. Courbet led the French Realist movement and his choice of an unglamorous lifestyle was his political statement. In his work he refuted the bourgeoisie and set out to represent the working class fairly.

Charles Baudelaire was an important figure of Bohemia as well. Born to a wealthy family, he squandered his fortune and lived in Bohemian style, fighting alongside the students in an uprising in 1848. Baudelaire was a poet, translator and critic of art and literature. His reputation rests primarily on *Les Fleurs du Mal,* which was perhaps the most important and influential poetry collection published in Europe in the 19th century. Similarly, his *Petits Poèmes en Prose* was the most successful and innovative early experiment in prose poetry of the time.

Puccini's masterpiece opera, *La Bohème,* also captured the romance and hard lifestyle of Bohemian Paris. It was first produced in Turin, Italy, in 1886 and remains to this day one of the most popular operas.

Bohemian ideals suffered greatly as World War I disrupted the tranquility that Paris had enjoyed. The tumultuous years between the world wars saw the café scene revitalized by the arrival of a new generation of free spirits. That spirit was again apparent after World War II and in the 1960s.

Art Galleries

The influences of early 20th century private Parisian art galleries on the rest of the art world cannot be over stated. Not only did they exhibit works by the giants of Modern Art, they also mounted exhibitions of emerging artists. Unlike the salons that were organized by artists themselves, private galleries were operated by professional businessmen and women with the hope of making a profit. The aesthetic choices of these merchants are responsible for bringing fresh new works to an eager public.

Often Parisian art dealers made contracts with artists to represent them exclusively, and with this arrangement often came guarantees of support. The dealers would present both solo and group exhibitions in their galleries and produce catalogs of the shows, posters and sometimes monographs on individual artists. These documents are invaluable today in understanding the art history of the early 20th century period.

Bernheim-Jeune was one of the most important Parisian galleries exhibiting young French and School of Paris artists. The gallery is still in business today at 83, rue du Faubourg Saint-Honoré and is operated by the original family. This gallery exhibited works by Delacroix, Corot and Gustave Courbet in the 19th century and in 1901 gave Vincent van Gogh his first show. In 1908 they publish the first book on Paul Cézanne's paintings. Through the first half of the 20th century the gallery hosted exhibitions of both recognized and lesser-known artists. Artists whose work is depicted in this book and who exhibited their paintings at Bernheim-Jeune include Émile Compard, Alfred Courmes, Alica Halicka, Maurice Henri Hensel, Mania Mavro, Vera Rockline, Jean Souverbie and Yasushi Tanaka.

Berthe Weill opened a new art gallery in 1917 on Rue Taitbout, close to the Paris Opera. For its opening exhibition the work of Modigliani was presented, which was the artist's first and only one-man show. Weill held exhibitions of many young women artists who were just embarking on their careers; among them were Emilie Charmy, Alice Halicka and Jacqueline Marval. In her recent book, *Women Artists and the Parisian Avant-Garde*, Gillian Perry documents all of the exhibitions at Weill's gallery.

There are many other galleries that should be remembered for exhibiting the works of new and innovative artists of the period, including Léonce Rosenberg's Galerie de l'Effort Moderne, Galerie Bing, Galerie Druet, Galerie des Quatre Chemins, Galerie Chéron, Galerie Denise René, Galerie Georges Petit and the Galerie Zborowski.

The Influences of Drugs on Art and Lifestyle

Industrialization in Europe in the late 19th century and the accompanying exuberance in art, literature, science, and medicine lead inevitably to freedom for experimentation. Fascination and curiosity for everything "new" helped to encourage an unprecedented use of narcotics and drug stimulants that played a significant role in Parisian lifestyles, Bohemian society, art and literature of the period. The use of drugs unquestionably influenced artists in this age, as can be detected in their techniques, styles, and subject matter. An understanding of this phenomenon offers additional insight into the era.

Alcohol was, of course, used heavily as well as other more mind-altering drugs that gained popularity. Opium and opium derivatives like heroin and absinthe were among the more powerful drugs used widely. They were not illegal and were commercially manufactured. Products containing opiates were marketed as pharmaceutical elixirs, and legendary "snake oil salesmen" sold a variety of concoctions containing narcotics.

Absinthe

Absinthe is a licorice-flavored liquor, sometimes containing as much as 80% alcohol. It is emerald green in color and turns cloudy and opalescent white when mixed with water. By the mid-19th century, the use of absinthe had become popular in the upper reaches of French society. Among the bourgeoisie it was fashionable, daring and unconventional. Absinthe came to be associated with the Bohemian lifestyle, providing mind-expanding effects and gaining a reputation as an aphrodisiac.

As with some other drugs, there is a ritual to drinking absinthe. A drink is prepared by pouring cold water over a cube of sugar that rests on a spoon with holes in it so the liquid can flow through into a cup containing absinthe. Water dissolves the sugar, thus diluting the absinthe. Sugar also helps to mask the bitter flavor of the absinthe.

Thujone is another toxic chemical, present in wormwood, with a similar molecular structure to THC (the active chemical in cannabis). In Pernod, wormwood oil was mixed with fennel, coriander, angelica root, hyssop, and marjoram. Similar drinks can be prepared with these drugs, sugar and water.

Myth and legend surround the history of absinthe. Dr. Pierre Ordinaire, a French doctor living in the Swiss town of Couvet, originally developed the potion with wormwood oil in 1789. He mixed his elixir with other ingredients and used it to treat a variety of ailments.

The Henroid sisters are said to have commercially exploited a similar elixir around the same time. About 1797, they sold their recipe to a Frenchman named Major Dubied, whose daughter married Henri-Louis Pernod, who opened an elixir factory in France in 1805. Soon a second factory opened as popularity for the drink grew. By the 1850s production grew sufficiently and Pernod's product was exported around the world.

Stories of absinthe use and abuse abound. Accounts of its mood-lifting sensations and myths of inspiration are due to the presence of wormwood in it. This infamous "special" ingredient in some cases leads to delirium, homicidal mania, and death. The dangers of absinthe finally led to its universal ban not long after the turn of the 20th century. The use of absinthe was made illegal in most countries by 1915, but evidence of its popularity continued into the 1930s.

Pernod, still popular in France and elsewhere, is produced today with a similar flavor to the original, though it does not contain the toxins from wormwood.

Many prominent artists, writers and poets owe at least some of their creativity to the effects of absinthe. Oscar Wilde, Edouard Manet, Baudelaire, Henri Toulouse-Lautrec and Pablo Picasso come to mind. Vincent van Gogh can be singled out in this group, since his art, life, illnesses and addictions have been the subjects of countless essays, books, movies and enormous speculation linking him to absinthe. Picasso, Manet and Edgar Degas painted now-famous images of addicts in bars stupefied by absinthe. Toulouse-Lautrec was said to have carried a cane that contained the paraphernalia to mix absinthe.

Products like Absinthe Robette and Absinthe Parisienne have been romanticized in beautiful Art Deco and Art Nouveau posters that receive continuous popularity among art collectors today.

Opium

Opium and its derivatives have been used for thousands of years for medicinal and recreational purposes. Opium's ability to induce wild fantasies and dreams of great detail made it popular among the creative society. Its use, however, went far beyond the Bohemian enclaves of artists, poets and novelists.

Opium was introduced to western culture in the mid-19th century on a grand scale through foreign travelers, sailors and Chinese immigrants. It was considered mysterious, romantic and decadent. Along with intoxication, the ritualistic nature of smoking opium was appealing and the paraphernalia, preparation and method of injecting the drug were often portrayed as glamorous. Beautiful Chinese pipes, many of carved ivory and exotic woods, were sold openly in urban areas, along with other necessary objects.

Opium became so widely accepted in the late 19th century that its use was portrayed as a popular theme in Symbolist and Art Nouveau sculpture, paintings and furniture. It is common to see carved or inlaid images of opium poppies on headboards of beds, many produced by the finest furniture artisans of the time, including Louis Majorelle and Émile Gallé. In sculpture and paintings, opium poppies are often incorporated with dreamy maidens whose eyelids are closed in states of euphoria. Novelists and poets indulged in the use of opium as well, including Baudelaire, Oscar Wilde, Edgar Allen Poe and Jean Cocteau.

Opium's popularity and enticing effects became a cause for detractors as well. Anti-opium crusaders exaggerated the manifestations of its use and linked it to white slavery and other bizarre conduct. Movies, novels, photographs and posters portrayed the seedy, dark side of the drug, which may actually have helped to spread its use.

Three of the most common opium derivatives are heroin, morphine and codeine. Morphine is still used universally as a painkiller, and codeine is widely used as a mild painkiller in pills. Heroin is the most refined, dangerous, and addictive opium derivative.

The Bayer pharmaceutical company of Germany first produced heroin as a commercial product in 1898. Clinical results were promising at first, and heroin was considered a 'wonder' drug. It was more effective than codeine in respiratory diseases, however repeated use of heroin resulted in the development of tolerance and patients soon became heroin addicts. Opium was made illegal in most of the world by the first part of the 20th century.

Cocaine

Cocaine was isolated initially from the coca plant in 1844, and cocaine products burst on the commercial market by the late 19th century as lozenges, elixirs and pills, remedies and intoxicants of all kinds. As a stimulant, cocaine is unlike most of the other drugs used recreationally in this period. It is highly addictive and produces a state of euphoria. Whether snorted or injected, extensive use of cocaine creates a sense of paranoia and sometimes psychosis.

The most notable commercial product containing cocaine was a wine which was first sold in Europe under the name Vin Mariani. It was named for its creator, Angelo Mariani, who began producing it in 1860. This wine was so popular that many notable figures, including Queen Victoria, The Pope, Thomas Edison, and many others were said to have enjoyed the product.

Vin Mariani was so successful a product that it inspired a legion of imitators. In the United States, John Styth Pemberton produced a similar drink in Atlanta, Georgia, in 1881. He enjoyed moderate success, but alcoholic products were banned in Atlanta in 1885. The enterprising Pemberton then changed the recipe, removing the alcohol, and marketed his new product under the name Coca-Cola. Other cola drinks containing cocaine were produced in Europe as well.

Cocaine is known to have been used by many artists and writers in the late 19th century, often combined with alcohol and other drugs. One of the most famous cocaine users of the time was Sigmund Freud. Sir Arthur Conan Doyle's character, Sherlock Holmes, was an intravenous cocaine and morphine user, and Jules Verne was a proponent of cocaine.

The proliferation of these and other drugs had a profound effect on the lives and works of many artists, writers and philosophers in the early 20th century. Like many of the other drugs discussed here, cocaine was almost universally banned by 1914.

The Belgians

Having discussed the influences, ideologies, and lifestyles comprising what we consider today to be modernist, we look next at some regional and artistic movements that helped to define the artistic life in this era as well.

Modern figurative painters of Belgium, whether from the north, the south, or from the capital city Brussels, have a unique style and played a significant role in modernist art. Belgium is a small country with relatively diverse cultural and strong artistic traditions. Its legacy should be brought to the attention of a wide audience. The works by artists discussed here make a strong case for the crossing influences of artists of Belgium with artists who worked in Paris.

Most Belgian artists whose work appears in this volume are known as Belgian Impressionists or Belgian Expressionists, although roots of their style and techniques are the same as their neighbors to the south in France. In the 19th century, the world was becoming a smaller place as the revolution in transportation gave the public an increased ability to travel. As transportation became easier and less expensive, artists with a natural wanderlust migrated to many European capitals to visit great museums and, more importantly, to mingle with other artists. From Belgium and the Netherlands, a train ride to Paris was just a matter of hours; even though many artists did not settle in Paris, the influences found there were contagious. Like the Eastern Europeans who came to Paris, Belgians absorbed the modernist ideals of Paris and wove it into their own tapestry of artistic tradition.

Walloon Art

Belgium has three different communities with several cultural and geographic influences to be considered. The Flemish community occupies the northern part of the country. The German speaking community is by far the smallest group in Belgium and occupies a small part of the country to the very west, in the Walloon region. The French community occupies most of the Walloon region to the South as well as the capital city, Brussels. The Walloon region includes the cities of Liège, Mons, Charleroi and Luxembourg.

Though Walloon is a separate region of Belgium, the art that originates there is often categorized under the Flemish school of art. People tend to group all Belgian art together, whether it is from the Flemish region, Brussels or the Walloon region; Belgian art is often called simply "l'École Flamande." Though it may not seem to be of great importance to those living outside of Wallonie, to classify Walloon art as Flemish does not give credit where it is due.

Prior to the exhibitions of 1911, Walloon Art was underrepresented. The Salon d'Art Moderne, comprised of contemporary works and Les Arts Anciens du Hainaut, gave more visibility and credibility to Walloon artists. The work at these exhibitions could easily be characterized as inspired by the landscape, industry and inhabitants of the region. Also, in 1911, Les Amis de l'Art Walloon was founded, comprised of six members, each representing a different section of the region. No known artistic associations of this type existed in the Flemish region.

An important advancement in the establishment of Walloon art was provided by the founding of a group called *Nervia,* in Mons, in 1928. *Nervia's* objective was to reinforce the presence of Wallonie in the art world. The group was composed of six young Walloon artists: Louis Buisseret, Anto Carte, Léon Navez, Léon Devos, and Frans Depooter, with Pierre Paulus chosen as the leader. Later, artists Rodolphe Strebelle, Taf Wallet, and Jean Winance were added to the group. These artists had a common love for classical workmanship and indifference for the avant-garde tendencies prevalent at the time. Located in the Belgian region closest to France, the group's orientation was far from the Flemish Expressionism and much closer to the art of Paris. They played an important role in maintaining the classical pictorial tradition. While *Nervia* was dedicated to exposing Walloon art to the Flemish region and the world of art, Surrealism, more specifically René Magritte and Paul De Vaux, lifted Walloon art to higher recognition. *Nervia* was active as a group until 1988.

Expressionist painting was not as widely adopted in the Wallonie region of Belgium as it was in the Flemish region. The Walloon painters generally employed a more classical and harmonious style of painting, referred to as a "Tempérament Latin." In Walloon painting the pallet tends to be lighter, the artists were said to have been draftsmen while the Flemish were more painterly. It is actually in the Germanic section of the region, the area around Liège, that Walloon Expressionism is closest to Flemish Expressionism.

Auguste Mambour was a Walloon artist who was associated with the three great Flemish Expressionists, Constant Permeke, Gustave De Smet, and Frits Van den Berghe. Mambour was awarded the Second Prix de Rome in 1923. He then traveled to the former Belgian Congo where he created art that was greatly influenced by the native African culture. But even before his sojourn in Africa the characters he painted tended to be dark African types and as for his palette he generally used cold tones such as blue bases and olive greens and blues in the background.

André de Ridder was one of the foremost proponents of Flemish Expressionism in Walloon. Charles Counhaye, from a town near Liège, was stylistically one of the closest Walloon Expressionists to his compatriots in the north. In Liège, two other painters come close to this expressionist aesthetic: Marcel Caron and Edgar Scauflaire. At times in his career Caron's work came very close to Flemish Expressionism but Scauflaire maintained a post-cubist style. In general, he used light color and shapes and planes in the manner of Georges Braque.

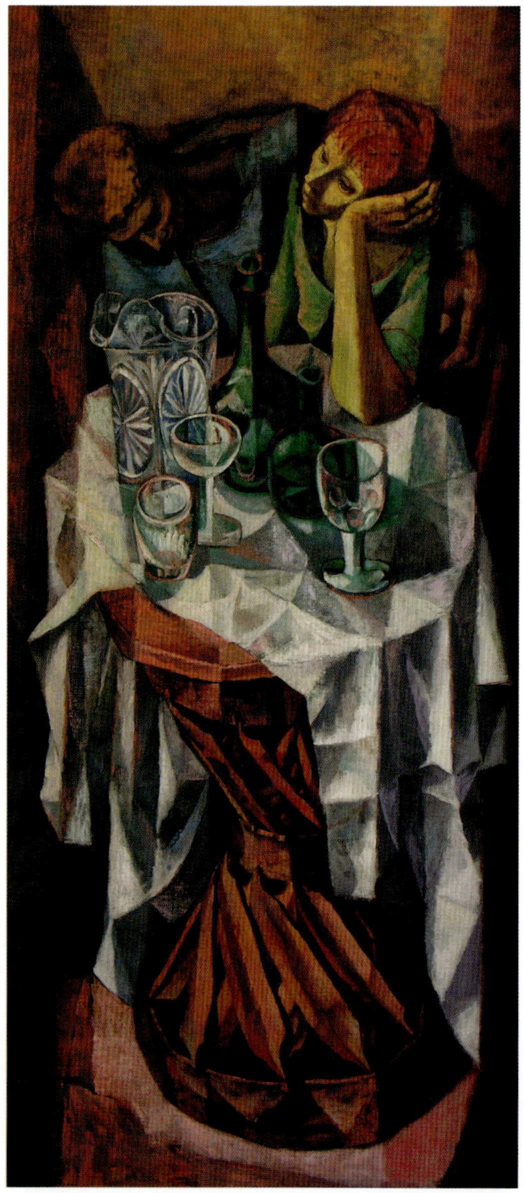

Collectors, Critics and Art Historians

In the history of modern art there are a few collectors who can be given credit for the success of emerging artists; most notably for this time period are Gertrude Stein and Peggy Guggenheim. Both avid collectors, they pursued artists in the ateliers, bars, and nightclubs of Montparnasse and their patronage launched many careers.

Critics and writers have played an important part in exposing the public to groups and individual artists. Max Jacob and André Salmon among others gave praise to what they saw as creativity unleashed. On the other hand, critics with a more traditional bent frequently panned anything they saw as out of the ordinary. Traditional art writers, along with the "establishment" seemed to throw fuel on the fires of artistic freedom. To outrage the critics became a goal in and of itself and a negative review was often worn as a badge of honor.

Art history is in a constant state of reevaluation and collecting art goes through phases and fashions as well. Today's historians, museums, dealers and collectors are constantly examining previously undocumented artists and finding their proper placement in history. The quality and validity of an artist's body of work can most often be seen more clearly in retrospect.

In this atmosphere of rediscovery the obscure, when analyzed with an open mind, reveals depth and commitment. Passion and talent, history and romance are all a part of this process.

One aspect in art collecting is regional interest, which is not a new concept in the art world though in the past few decades regionalism has become a driving force. Nationalism is one major element of this phenomenon; collectors in Eastern Europe have been actively repatriating works by Czech, Hungarian, Polish and Russian artists.

The categorization of artists has had a positive influence on the art market. It can give collectors parameters, provide historians narrow fields to investigate and auction houses take advantage as well by mounting specialized sales.

The artists added in this volume represent just a small addition to an ongoing effort. As in our first volume about this genre, many of these artists will not have familiar names though it is our goal to introduce their great talent to collectors and art historians.

Building A Collection

For those wishing to acquire fine art, either to start a serious collection or just to decorate their homes, there are some simple guidelines. First, and most important, is to identify the genre and period that appeals to you. When this is narrowed down one can begin searching for galleries and dealers that specialize in the requisite type and style of art that interests you.

Figuring out a budget can be a difficult until one has done some research, being comfortable with all acquisitions is most important. Looking at fine art as an investment can also be tricky; it has proven over time to appreciate often better than other investments. Fine art is not the most liquid of investments, and it often takes time and patience to find the most advantageous market.

Authenticity

Authenticity is a matter that should always be considered; buying from reputable galleries with a long history and loyal clientele can spare the collector a lot of aggravation. Inquiring about the reputation of a gallery among other dealers is a way to get a sense of a dealer's integrity. Having a complete description of a work of art on the bill of sale, and having copies of all the documentation on the artist and the specific work for one's files is also a necessity.

Condition

The condition of a work of art can be important; of course a work that is in fine, un-restored condition is best. It should be understood that most oil paintings that are fifty years old or older would most likely be in need of cleaning and often require minor restoration. Unlike antique furniture and other antique objects, removing the dirt and old varnish from oil paintings is proper and enhances the value. Even paintings with more than a modest amount of restoration hold their value because they are unique works and can never be replaced. Large paintings tend to have more restorations and often need to be lined with a new and heavier canvas to stabilize the original fabric; this has little or no affect on the value. Unique works on paper should be considered in the same way. Works of art done in multiples need much more consideration of condition; small flaws in an etching or lithograph can greatly affect the value. It is always interesting and informative to look at the back of an oil painting. The age becomes evident and often times there may an exhibition or auction sticker, date and title and other references to the history of the work. The condition can also be understood more from the back. This applies to works on paper as well; it is a good idea to see a work on paper out of its frame before buying.

Oil paintings on stretched canvas are most often encountered, but many artists preferred to paint with oil on a variety of other surfaces. Canvas laid down on a hard surface like wood or Masonite is not uncommon nor are paintings done directly on wood, Masonite, or cardboard. André Lhote painted many important works on paper laid on canvas; none of these variations have an effect on value. Watercolors are by nature on paper, gouaches however can be found on heavy paper or cardboard.

Market Value

Perhaps the most important and confusing part for a novice and even some more sophisticated collectors is the price of a work of art. Often it is difficult to find comparisons in this field. Auction records, if they exist at all for many artists, can be misleading. It is more practical to get a sense of prices for works from the same period and of similar subjects, sizes and quality. There is a consistency that will emerge, a price range can be established and with this kind of general research a collector can make an informed judgment of value. It will also become apparent that artists with larger amounts of documentation or that have been included in museum exhibitions will affect the value of their work. Artists that are listed in reference books are the basic criteria for establishing a value, and the more information available the better.

One of the most interesting questions for collectors is why one artist's work is worth more than another's, especially when artists worked and exhibited in such close proximity. The answer is complicated and in some instances luck has a lot to do with it.

In order for an artist to achieve recognition and commercial value several factors are necessary. Generally, it is necessary for an artist to have created a significant body of work. It is very difficult to gain widespread recognition without enough "product" to have an impact. Originality and a recognizable style distinguish an artist. Even if an artist pursues a style, or exhibits strong influences of others it is possible to create a body of work with unique qualities that sets them apart. When an artist achieves this level of distinction, the work itself becomes a signature.

The personality of the artist can be a factor; artists tend to form groups to promote their ideas, and some less gregarious artists chose not to be associated with groups. Because many groups exhibited together, it was easier to get reviewed by the press and gain attention. When an individual shows his or her work at a salon or gallery, it is easy to get lost in the crowd.

The group idea became more important in the middle of the 19th century; from the Pre-Raphaelites to the Impressionists the impact of the individual artist was facilitated by the impact of the group. This was the birth of "isms" in art.

Even in today's market for an artist to have been identified with a specific group or movement has great value. For example , an artist who was truly a Cubist must have exhibited in the Section d'Or. To some collectors a "cubist" painting done after 1914 does not carry any weight.

For this reason work from an early period of an artist's career is often used as a selling point. This of course is an arbitrary rule; one example is Piet Mondrian. His early works are representational and the value of these works pale in comparison to his abstract compositions for which he is famous. A more applicable test or standard would be to place works in the historical context of when they were created and with relationship to the development of certain styles and techniques. The closer a work is to its stylistic origins the more reasonable to assume a relationship to value. Cubism is a good example because it is indisputable that the first cubist painting was conceived in 1907. Therefore it is reasonable to conclude a cubist-style painting from 1910 will have greater value than a comparable work from 1930.

Artists also gain recognition through promotion. Self-promotion is very difficult, and there are few examples of artists becoming well known without a dealer or gallery showing the works.

To some in the art community the commercial aspect of the art world is repugnant, but without the galleries and dealers, and later the auction companies, the connection between artist and collector is difficult to accomplish.

The Artists

Pierre Abadie-Landel
1896-1972

Pierre Abadie-Landel was born on August 22, 1896, in Paris. He studied painting at l'École des Beaux-Arts in Paris until 1917.

Landel exhibited at the Salon des Artistes Français, Société Nationale des Beaux-Arts and Salon des Indépendants, where he received distinction in 1926 and 1937.

Landel was a painter and watercolorist, and worked in pastel. He used symbolist and mythological subjects to create decorative works that blended well with Art Deco interiors. Abadie-Landel died on September 23, 1972.

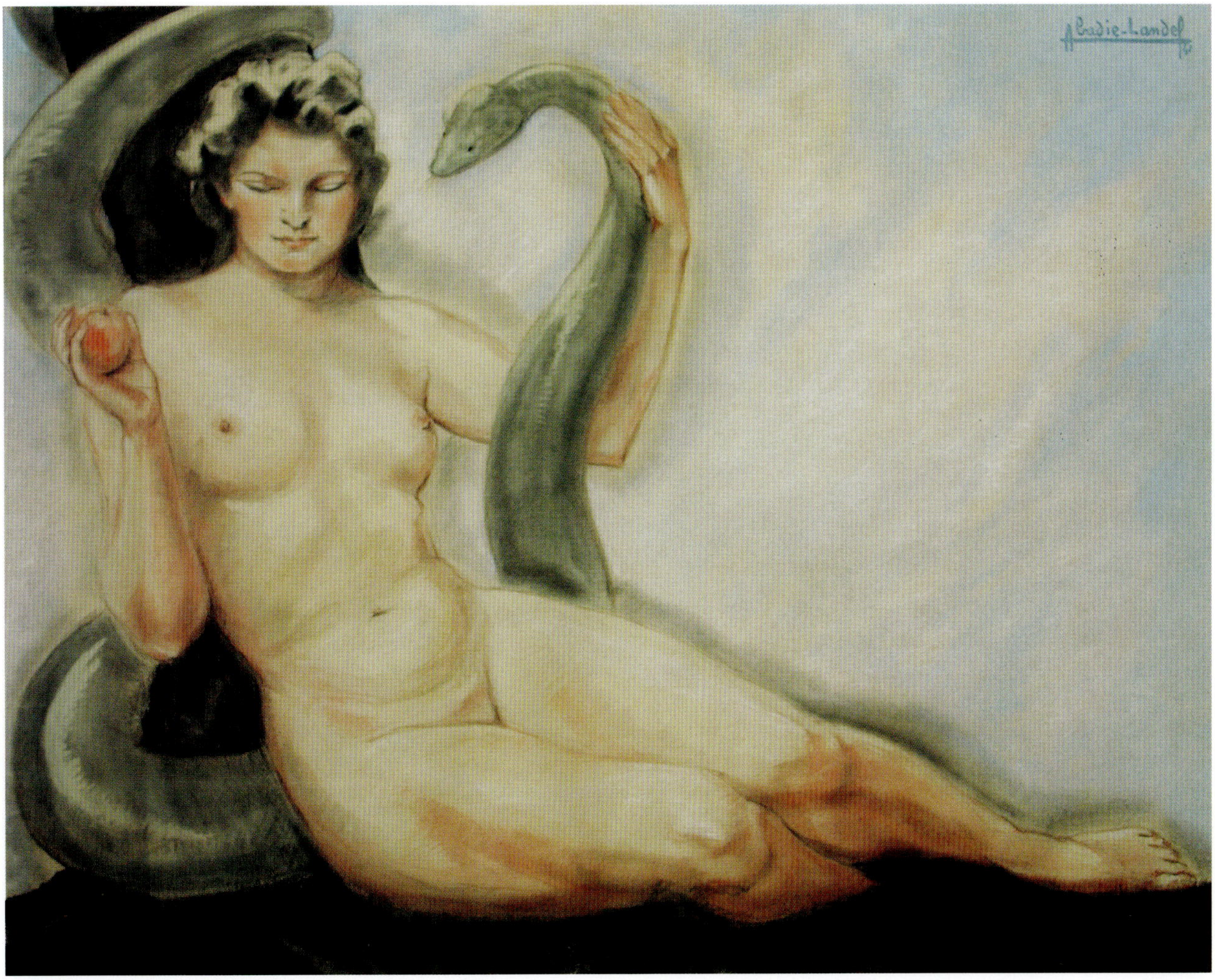

Pierre Abadie-Landel
Eve et Le Serpent, Dated 1941
Private Collection

Jacques Acremant

20th century

Limited information is available about the life of Jacques Acremant, although there is a 1947 catalog from an exhibition at Galerie Leduc, Lille in which Acremant exhibited more than sixty works, including thirty-five paintings. Philippe Kah wrote the introduction to the catalog.

Acremant exhibited in Limoges and Clermont-Ferrand as well.

He worked in a studio in the Villa du Roule in Neuilly, near Paris and illustrated several books including an edition of *La Chute de la Maison Usher*.

His paintings express the charm of café and street life in Paris. Stylistically, his work is reminiscent of Jean Dufy and other Postimpressionist artists who were more interested in conveying the emotional impact of their subject matter rather than realistic details.

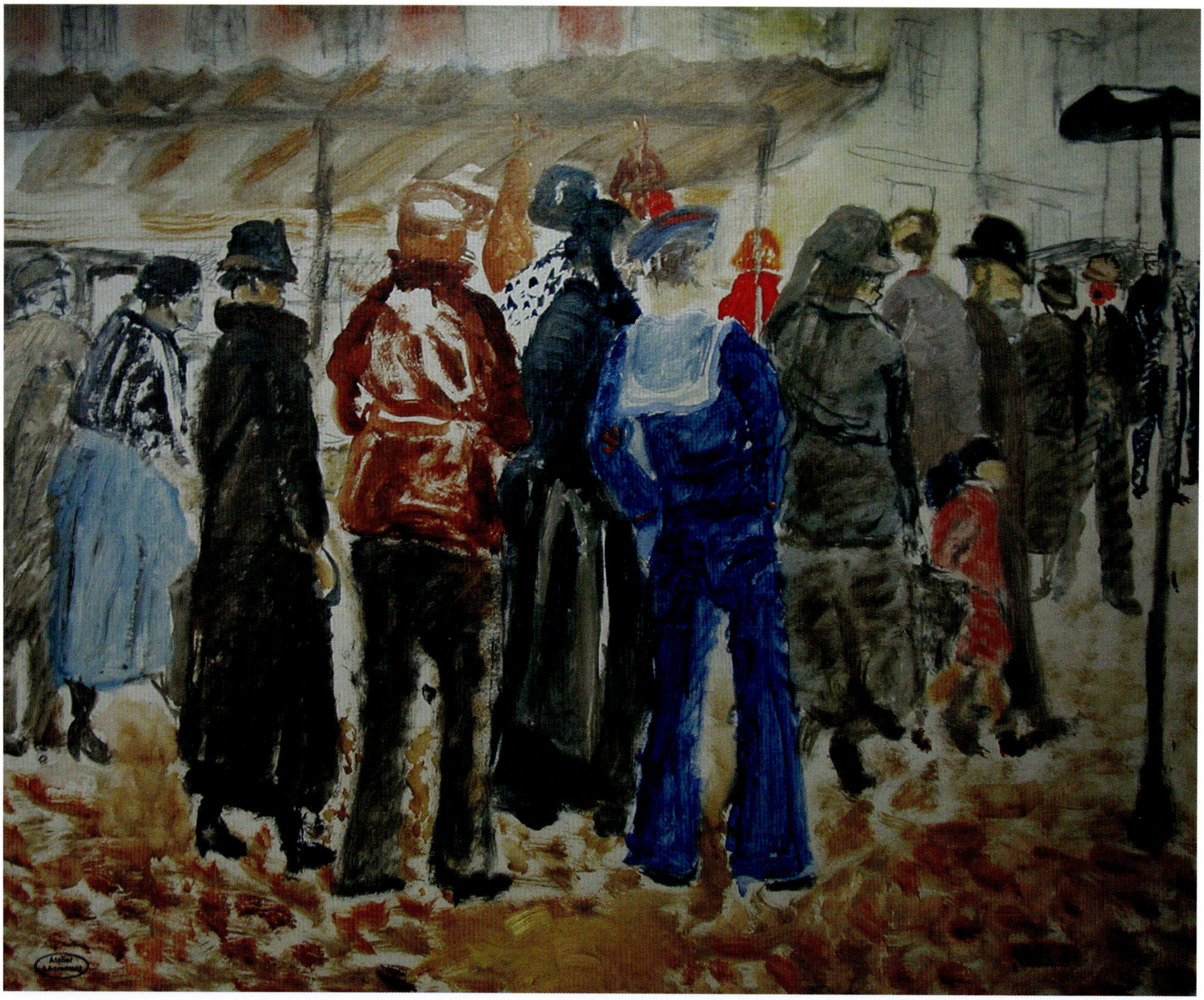

Jacques Acrement
Le Marché, c.1935
Private Collection

Georgette Agutte
1867–1922

Georgette Agutte was born May 17, 1867 in Paris. She is well known for strongly impressionistic renderings of imaginary figures, still lifes and portraits of celebrities such as Gustave Kahn.

Agutte studied at l'École des Beaux-Arts in Paris under Gustave Moreau as did Matisse and Rouault. Beginning in 1904 Agutte exhibited at the Salon des Indépendants and participated in the founding of the Salon d'Automne. In 1910 she exhibited at l'Exposition de Bruxelles and in 1922 Gustave Kahn organized a retrospective of paintings, watercolors and sculptures at the Salon d'Automne.

Agutte took her own life September 4, 1922 in Chamonix shortly after the death of her husband Marcel Sembat.

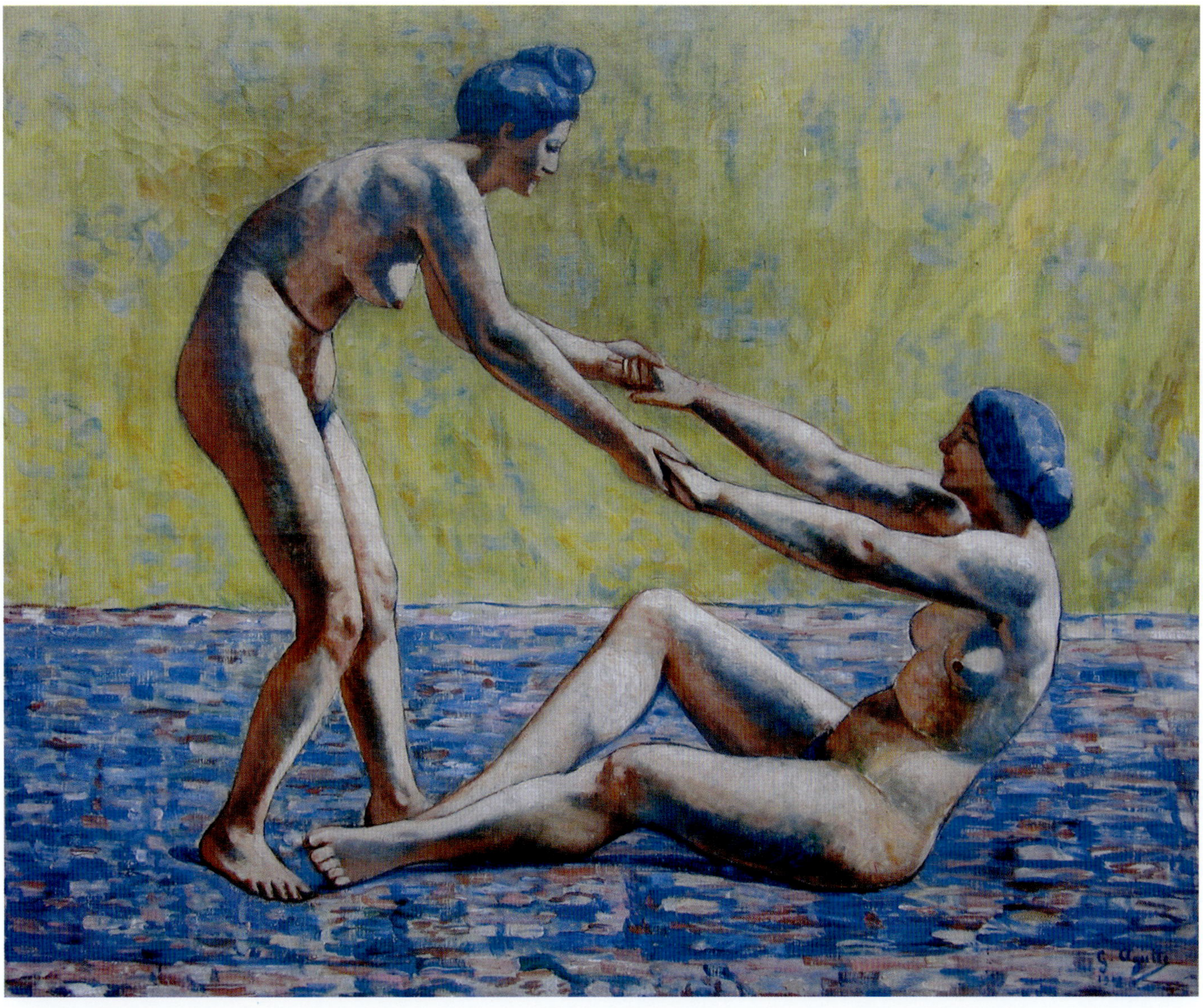

Georgette Agutte
Deux Femmes, Dated 1911
Kathleen Avery Fine Art, Palo Alto, California

Ludovic Alleaume

1859-1941

Ludovic Alleaume was born in Angers, France in 1859. He studied with Herbert and Luc-Oliver Merson at l'École des Beaux-Arts in Paris.

Alleaume exhibited consistently at the Salon des Artistes Français from 1883 until 1938, the Salon des Humoristes, Salon d'Hiver and the Société des Peintres-lithographies.

He received several awards including the Prix Bonnat and the Chevalier de la Légion d'Honneur in 1927.

In 1890 Alleaume traveled to Palestine where he completed a significant suite of drawings. Alleaume collaborated with the *Revue de Bretagne et d'Anjou*. He also created illustrations for *Monde Illustré*.

From darkly allegorical to romantic and whimsical his paintings illustrate great attention to detail, texture and mood.

Alleaume is represented in the Musée de Beaux-Arts de Rennes.

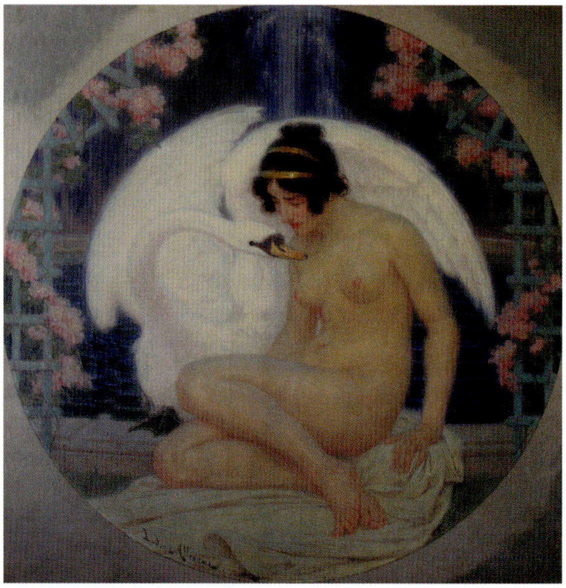

Ludovic Alleaume
Léda et le Cygne, c.1910
Christine Thorailler, Paris, France

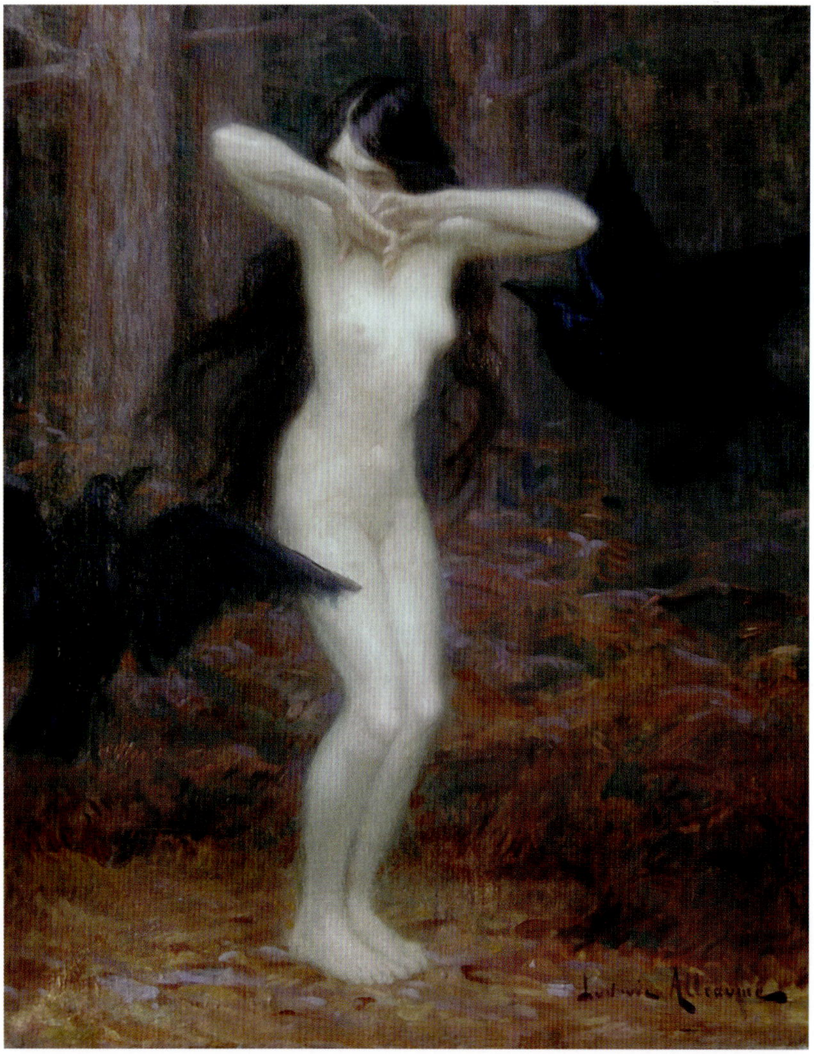

Ludovic Alleaume
Incantation, c.1910
Kiersten Warren, Los Angeles, California

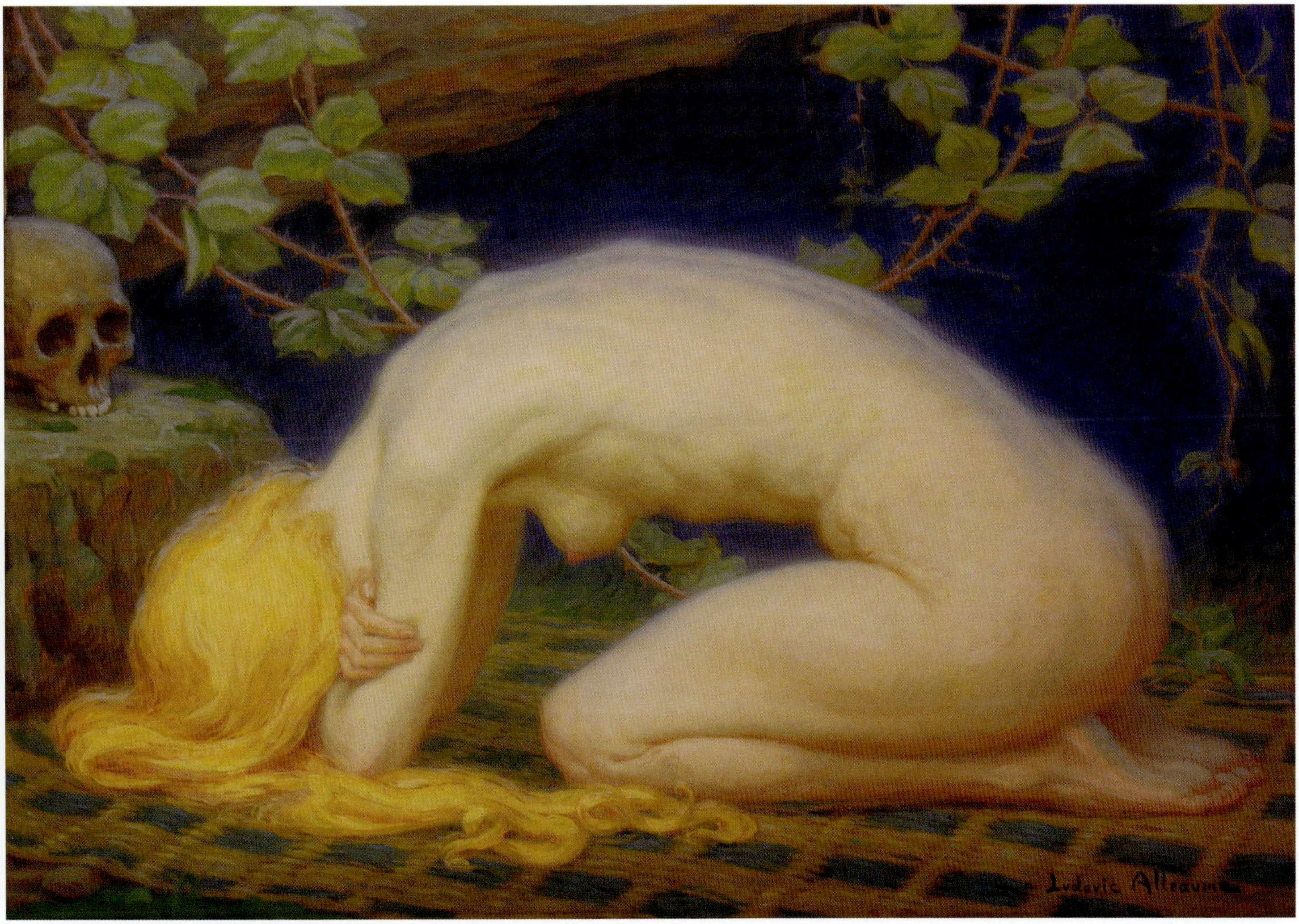

Ludovic Alleaume
Madeleine Pleurer, Exhibited 1927
Christine Thorailler, Paris, France

Mabel Alvarez

1891-1985

Alvarez was born in Hawaii and moved to Los Angeles with her family in 1909. While in high school Alvarez took many art courses and directly after went on to work for an architectural firm rendering interior designs and creating signs and advertisements.

In the article *A Quest for Excellence: Chronicling the Life of Mabel Alvarez,* Nancy Dustin Wall Moure sings the praises of Mabel Alvarez, identifying her as a strong proponent of the Los Angeles modern art movement and as "...one of Los Angeles' major figure painters."

Her drawings were shown at the 1913 Architectural Club exhibition where they were highly noted and in 1914 her high school mentor recruited Alvarez to collaborate on a commission he had received for the Panama-California Exposition murals.

Alvarez was invited to join the Modern Art Society with whom she became closely acquainted and was very active for several years. She was also a member of the California Art Club for which she raised funds and served on juries. Alvarez exhibited with the California Art Club from 1918 through 1937 and with the Los Angeles Museum's annual exhibition from 1920 through 1938.

A major influence in Alvarez's artistic career was Stanton Macdonald-Wright under whom she studied at Chouinard in 1923 and at the Art Students League in Los Angeles. She also became well acquainted with Morgan Russell in 1931 when he began teaching at Chouinard. Russell had founded the School of Synchromism and greatly influenced Alvarez's work. Upon his return to France, the two corresponded until Russell's death.

A love of travel greatly inspired Alvarez's career as well. In 1924 she traveled on the East Coast and throughout Europe after which she took an interest in Chinese paintings and Persian, East Indian and Tibetan art. Her travels took her back to Hawaii, where she took a class at the Art Academy on Oahu and taught art at a school in Honolulu. In 1940 she returned to Los Angeles where she worked through 1943 with the Red Cross and taught art to disabled war veterans. Later, in 1955 Alvarez traveled to Mexico, which gave her an invigorated new perspective of architecture, public spaces and figures.

Mabel Alvarez died March 13, 1985 at the age of 93. The Los Angeles County Museum of Art holds the painting *Arabella with Calla Lilies* in their collection and in 1999 the Orange County Museum of Art held a retrospective of her work. Several paintings have also sold at Bonhams & Butterfields, John Moran Auctioneers and Christie's Los Angeles.

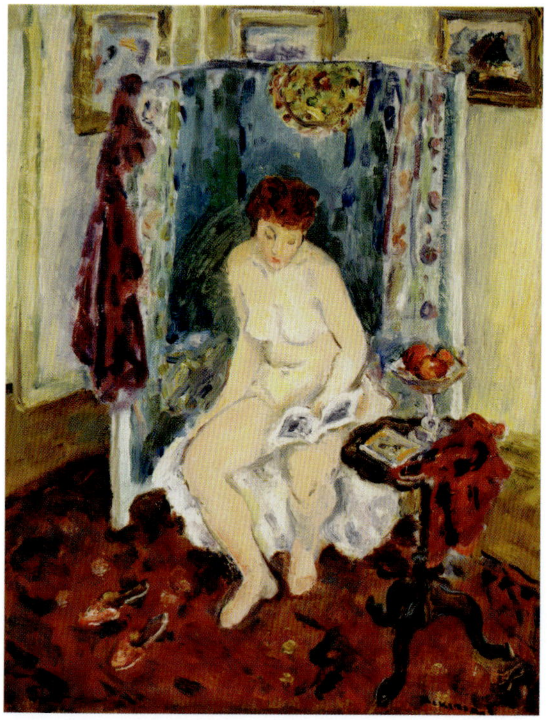

Mabel Alvarez
Seated Nude Reading, c.1930
Private Collection

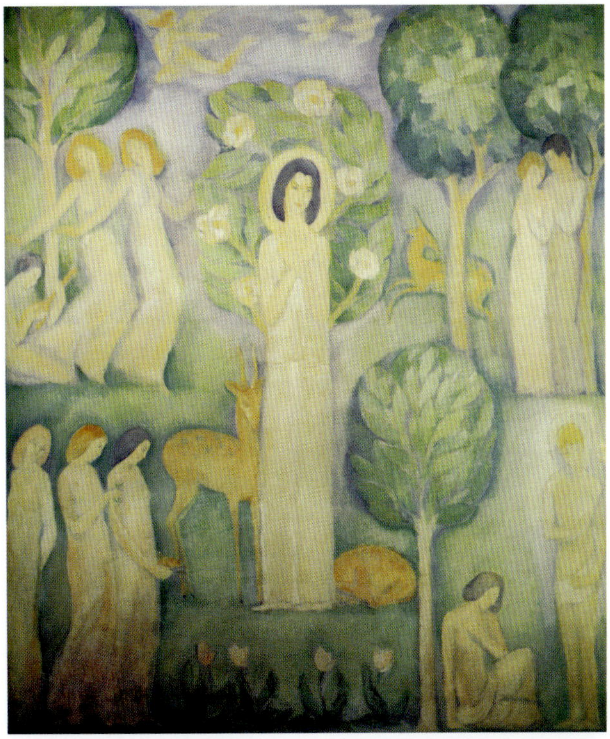

Mabel Alvarez
Dream of Youth, c.1925
Courtesy of the Jeri L. Waxenberg Collection, USA
Photo courtesy of Adamson-Duvannes Gallery, Los Angeles, California

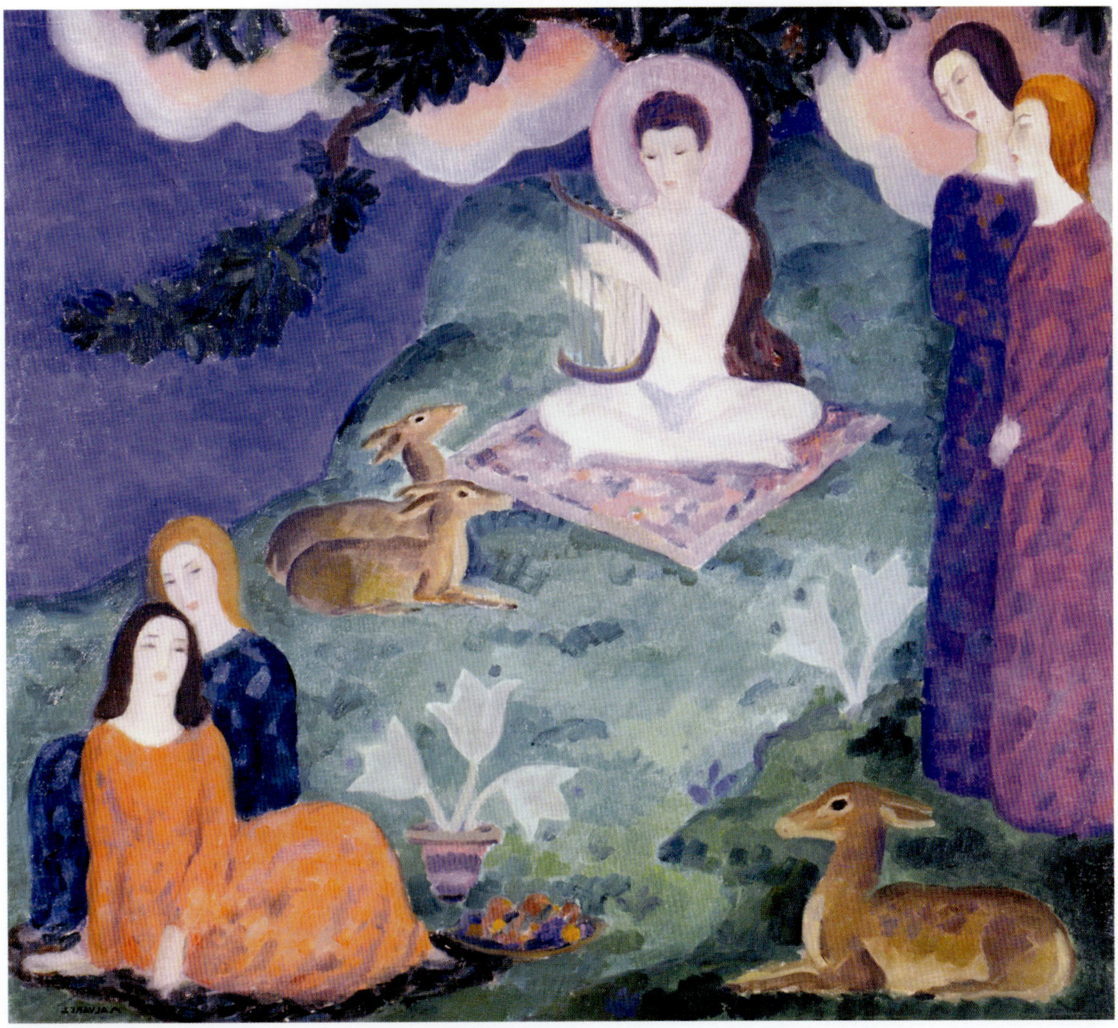

Mabel Alvarez
Adoration, (untitled) c.1925
Collection of Laura Alexakis, California
Photo courtesy of Spencer Jon Helfen Fine Arts, Beverly Hills, California

Victor Arnautoff
1896-1979

Victor Arnautoff was born in the Ukraine, Russia in 1896. After various travels and studies he came to be well respected in San Francisco as an accomplished painter, lithographer, sculptor and muralist who worked primarily in realms of Regionalism and Social Realism.

The artist traveled through China and Mexico before arriving in San Francisco in 1925. He enrolled in the California School of Fine Arts where he studied sculpture under Ralph Stackpole and painting under Edgar Walters. Arnautoff traveled again through China and Mexico with his family and from 1929 to 1931 lived in Mexico City where he worked as an assistant to painter and muralist Diego Rivera.

He returned to San Francisco where he taught at the California School of Fine Arts and from 1939 to 1963 was a professor of art at Stanford University. Arnautoff returned to Russia after the death of his wife and continued to paint and work as a mosaic muralist.

Among his most notable achievements are the murals in San Francisco at Coit Tower, George Washington High School, the Presidio and post offices in Richmond and Pacific Grove. His work is known to be fairly politically and socially conscientious, the evidence of which can be seen particularly in his murals.

The artist died March 22, 1979 in Leningrad and his work has since been represented by Spencer Jon Helfen Fine Arts.

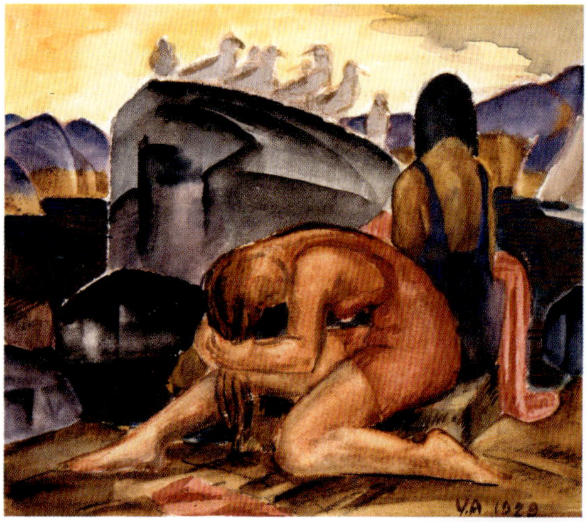

Victor Arnautoff
Bathers, Dated 1929
Photo courtesy of Spencer Jon Helfen Fine Arts, Beverly Hills, California

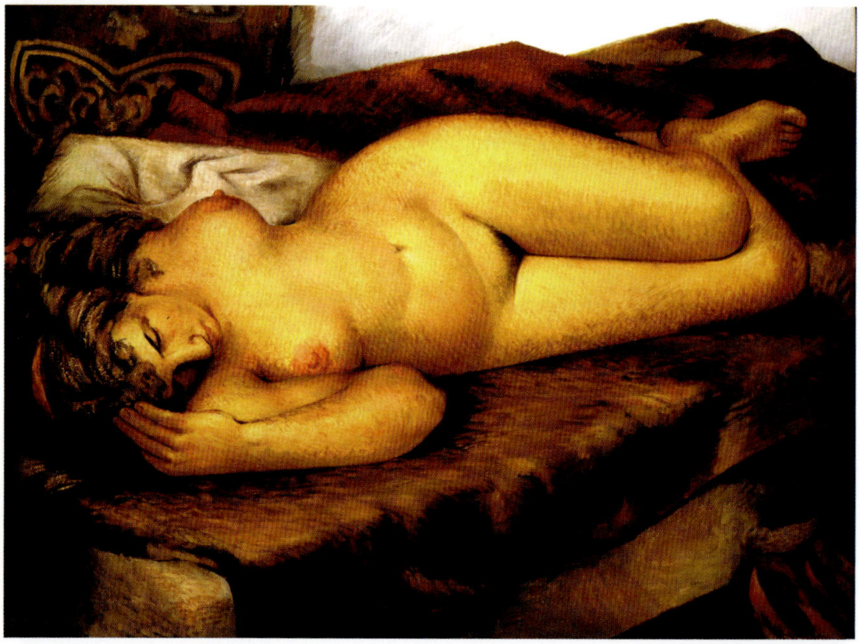

Victor Arnautoff
Lady in Repose, (untitled) c.1935
Photo courtesy of Spencer Jon Helfen Fine Arts, Beverly Hills, California

Gustave Astoy
Born 1908

Gustave Astoy, born in Madrid, Spain, was primarily a painter of nudes and landscapes. He exhibited at the Salon d'Automne between 1921 and 1924 and the Salon des Tuileries between 1924 and 1943. His nudes give the viewer a sense of quiet intimacy, with soft lines and a contemplative ambience.

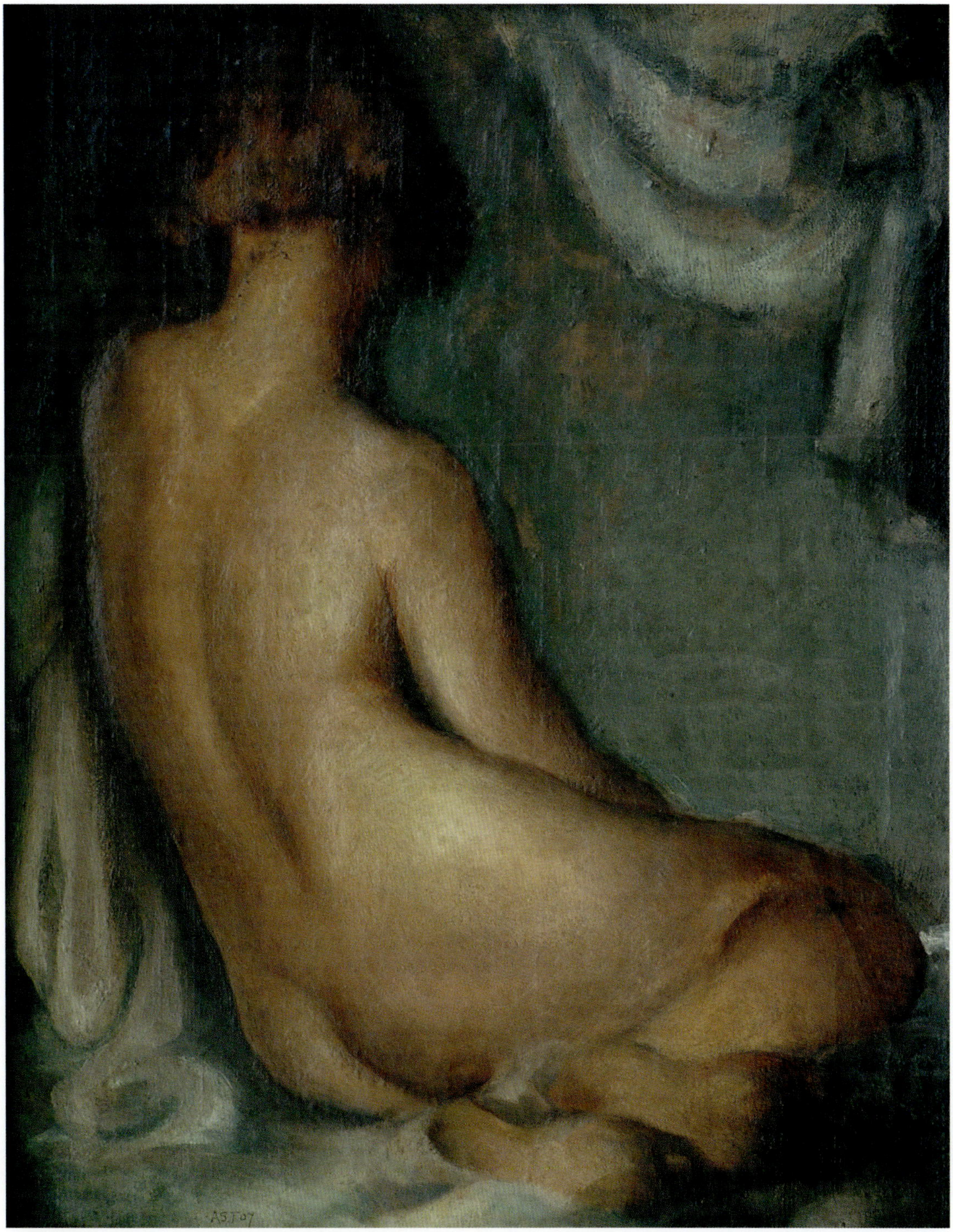

Gustave Astoy
Nu Assis, c.1935
Private Collection

Émile Baes
1879 or 1889 –1954

Émile Baes was born in Brussels in either 1879 or 1889. He studied with J. Stallaert at l'Académie des Beaux-Arts de Bruxelles and completed his education with Bonnet and Cabanel in Paris.

Baes worked as a painter, illustrator and writer. He was known for his diverse subject matter including historical paintings, portraits, nudes and landscapes. Most noteworthy among his subject matter are femme fatale figures including Salomé, Messaline and Cleopatra. The writings of Flaubert and the style and composition of Symbolism influenced the development of his work.

Baes' ouevre exemplifies the Orientalist compositional elements found in late 19th and early 20th century Parisian work. In 1903 and 1904 he exhibited at the Salon de Bruxelles and between 1928 and 1933 he exhibited at the Salon d'Automne in Paris. He exhibited at the Salon des Artistes Français from 1929 to 1938 and the Salon des Tuileries between 1933 and 1939. Baes also wrote *Les deux sadiques, Princesse d' Amour.*

He had a great consideration for the environment of his models, using highly expressive brushstrokes to create moods. Baes died in Paris in 1954.

Émile Baes
Au Bord du Mer, c.1935
Private Collection

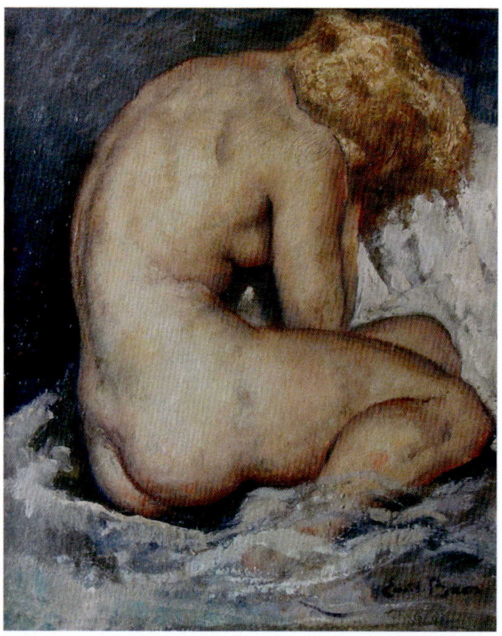

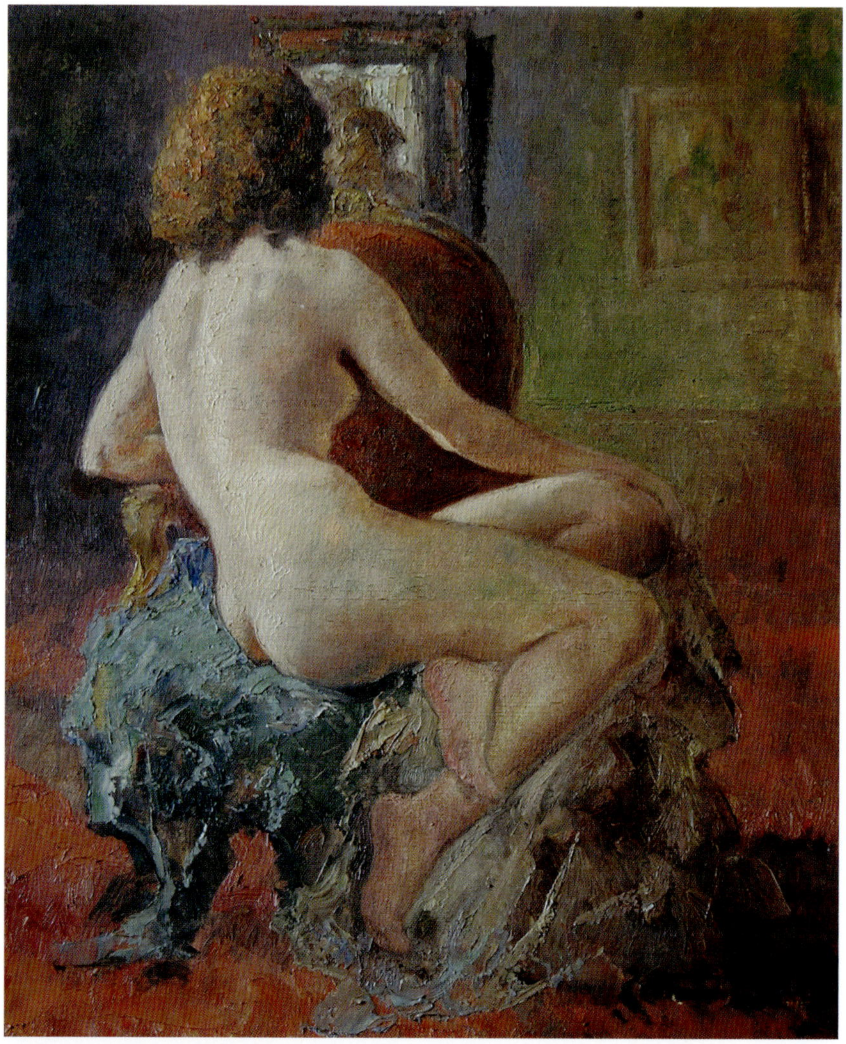

Émile Baes
Nu dans le Boudoir, 1930
Seligman Family Collection, Los Angeles, California

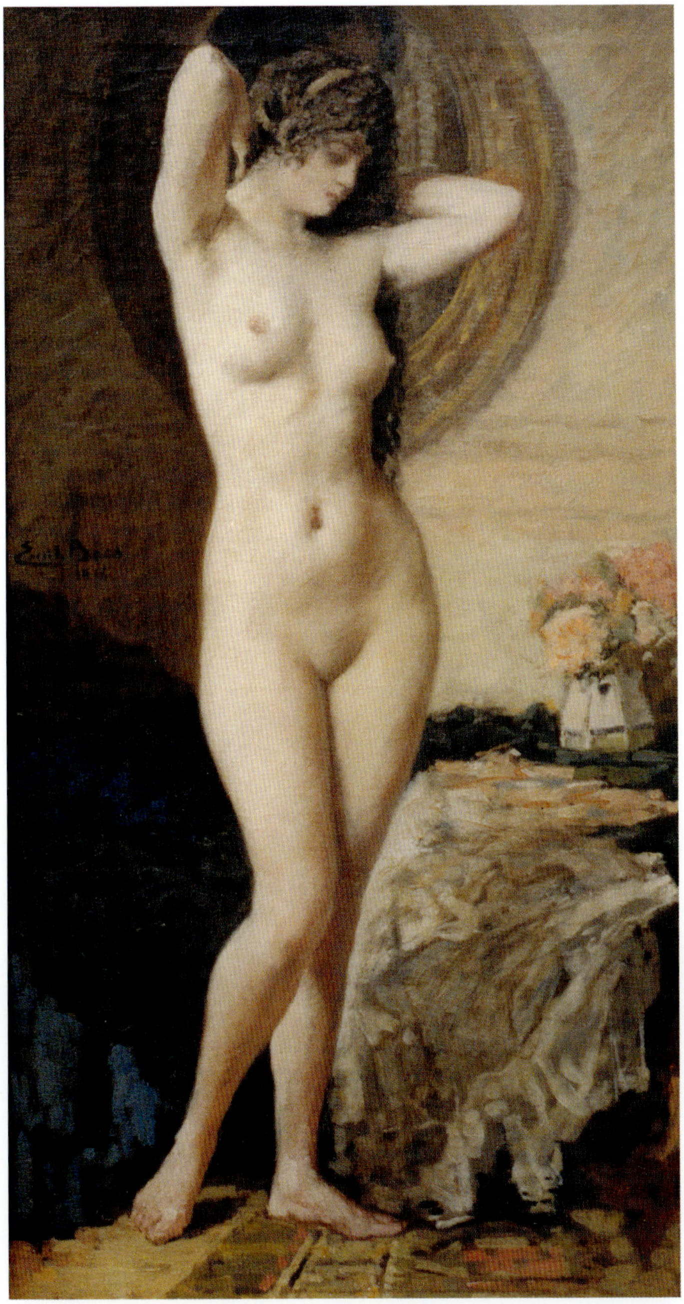

Émile Baes
Nu Jeune, c.1935
Los Angeles Fine Art Gallery, Los Angeles, California

Émile Baes
Nu dans le Miroir, c.1935
Los Angeles Fine Art Gallery, Los Angeles, California

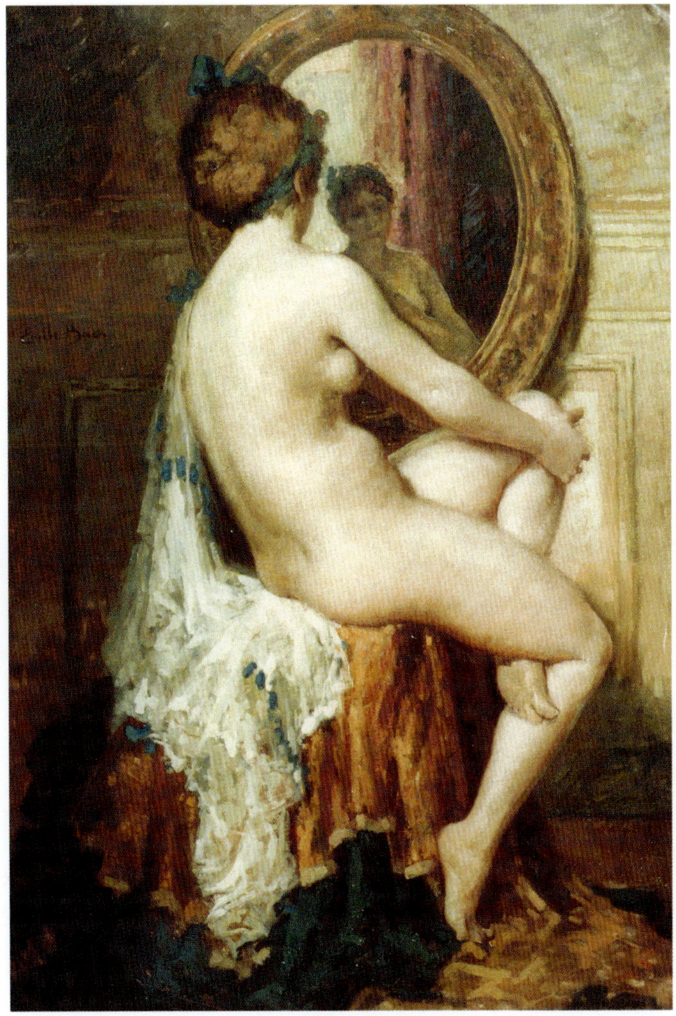

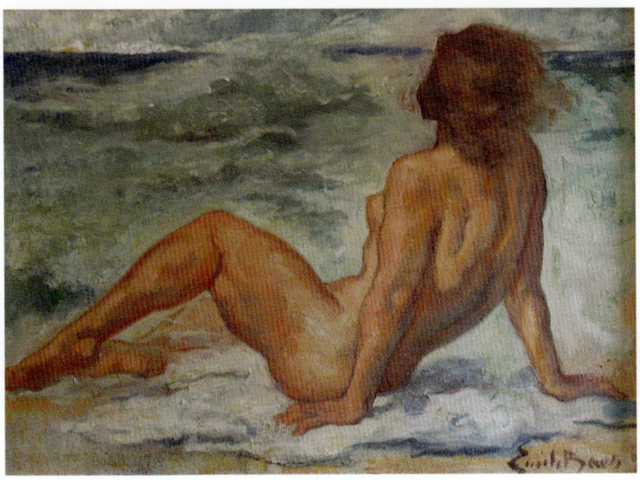

Émile Baes
Sur la Plage, c. 1940
Papillon Gallery, Los Angeles, California

James Peter Barbarite

Born 1912

James Barbarite was born in Brooklyn, New York in 1912. He studied at Cooper Union, Columbia University and later with Jonas Lie and Karl Anderson at the National Academy of Design.

From 1939 to 1942, he was a member of the Louis Comfort Tiffany Foundation in addition to the Silvermine Guild Association. He exhibited with the Milch Gallery, Brooklyn Museum, Allied Art Association, New Canaan Library and the American Watercolor Society in 1938.

Barbarite won awards from the Louis Comfort Tiffany Foundation from1939 through 1942. He won the American Prix de Rome in 1942.

In addition to his fine art career, Barbarite worked as an art educator. He taught painting at the Biarritz American University in France from 1945 to 1946. The following year he began teaching at l'Académie Royal des Beaux-Arts in Brussels, Belgium and completed his tenure in 1952.

Barbarite's sophisticated and elegant technique is embodied in his portraits. Though using a fairly realist approach he still managed to employ expressive light and color to create a beautiful sense of the fabrics in the image.

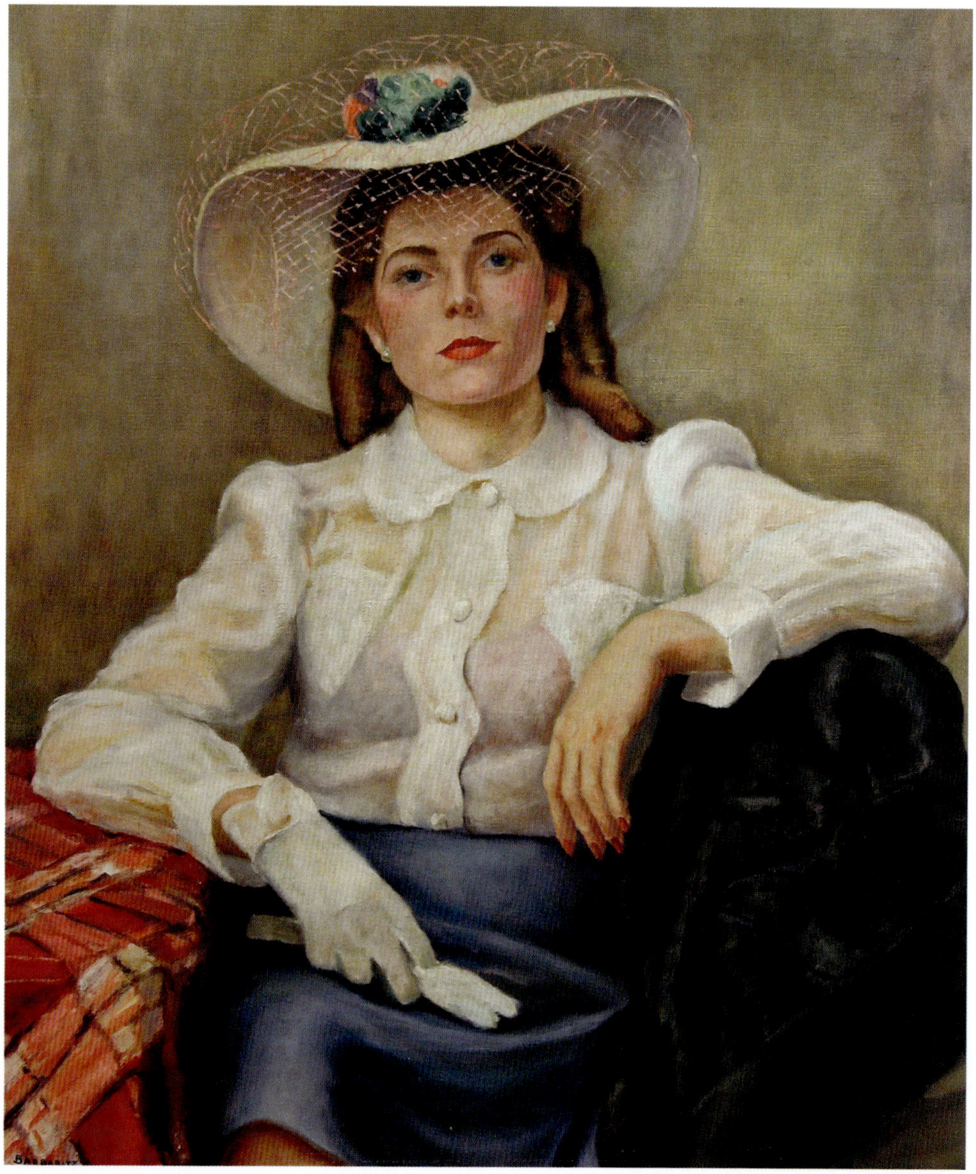

James Peter Barbarite
Woman in White, c.1940
Jeff Sagansky and Christy Welker, New York, New York

Louis Jean Beaupuy

1896-1974

Louis Jean Beaupuy was born 1896 in Elbeuf, France. He studied with Fernand Cormon at l'École des Beaux-Arts in Paris and was a member of the Salon des Artistes Français where he received an honorable mention in 1928.

From 1927 to 1929 Beaupuy exhibited at the Salon des Indépendants. Echoing an Orientalist influence, his charming models evoke a sense of warmth and repose. His soft colors and delicate brush technique add to the sensuality of his subjects. Beaupuy died in 1974.

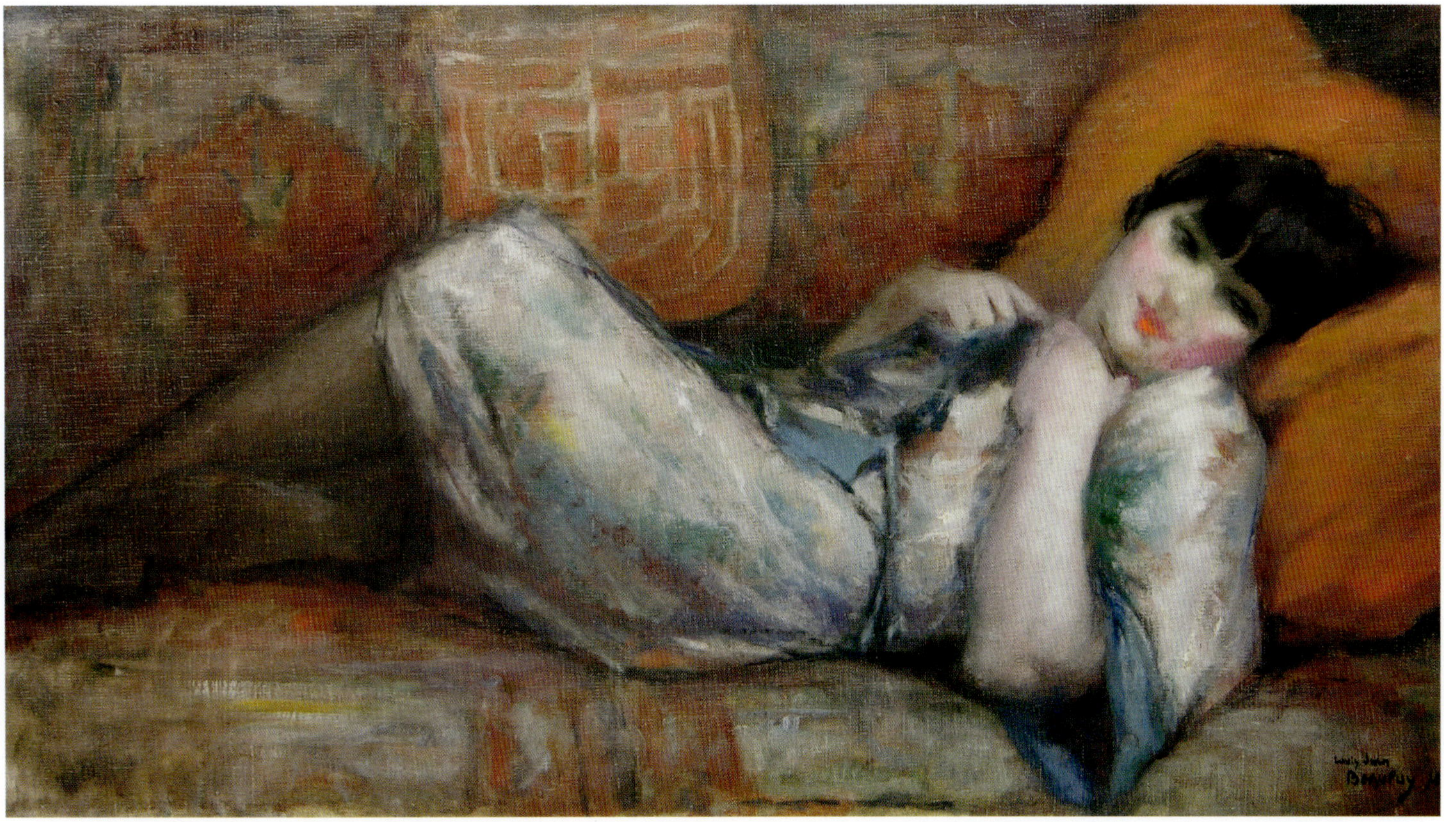

Louis Jean Beaupuy
Femme au Canapé, Dated 1928
Joel and Roya Geiderman, Beverly Hills, California

Paul-Émile Bécat

1885-1960

Paul-Émile Bécat was born February 2, 1885 in Paris. He was an accomplished printmaker, painter and extremely prolific illustrator having illustrated close to 100 books, most of which were of highly erotic content. Authors for which he illustrated works include Voltaire, Diderot, Pierre Louÿs, Baudelaire, Piron, Verlaine, Géraldy, Hélèna Varley and Brantôme.

Bécat studied at l'École des Beaux-Arts in Paris under Flammeng and Ferrier. He received the Prix de Rome, the Médaille d'Argent at the Salon des Artistes Français where he was a member, and the Prix de Robert de Rougé.

In 1950, a suite of 12 dry-point etchings by Bécat, titled *L'Art d'Aimer,* was published. Highly stylized and carefully composed, there is a sense of balance and delicacy in the moment of consideration between his models and their surroundings. Bécat died in 1960.

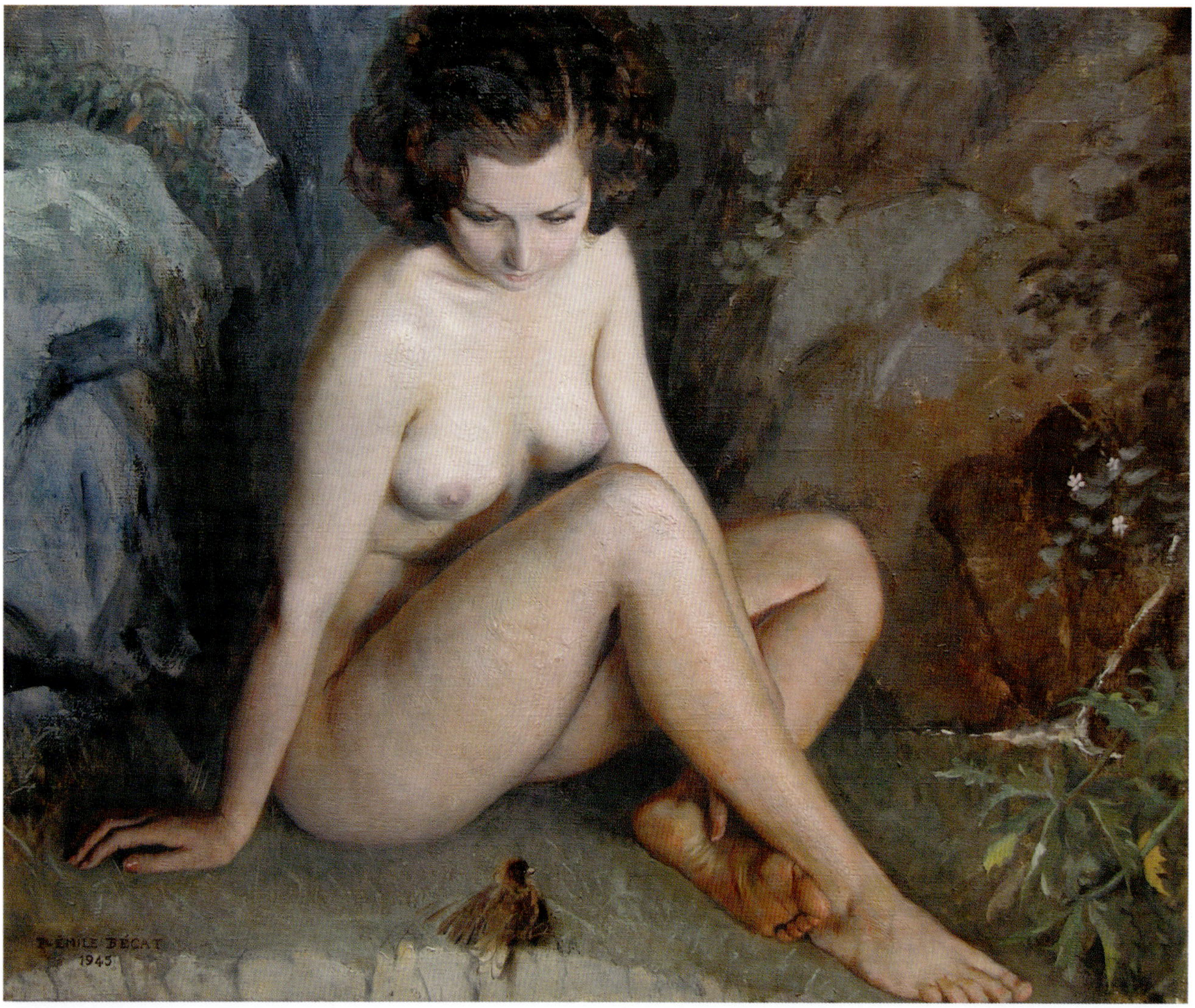

Paul Émile-Bécat
Deux Oiseaux, Dated 1945
Papillon Gallery, Los Angeles, California

Pierre de Belair

1892-1956

Pierre de Belair was born October 29, 1892 in Lyon, France and was a student of Adolphe Déchenaud, François Flameng and Jean Paul Laurens. He became member of the Société Lyonnaise des Beaux-Arts and of the Salon de la Société des Beaux-Arts, where he exhibited from 1921 to 1931.

Belair's use of composition, color and lighting carries the viewer through the mood of this period. Belair, like Gustave Florot, inspires one to imagine the romance of the soirées in Paris in the 1920s,

Belair exhibited in London, Germany and New York. He was best known as a painter, decorator and poster artist. The artist died in 1956.

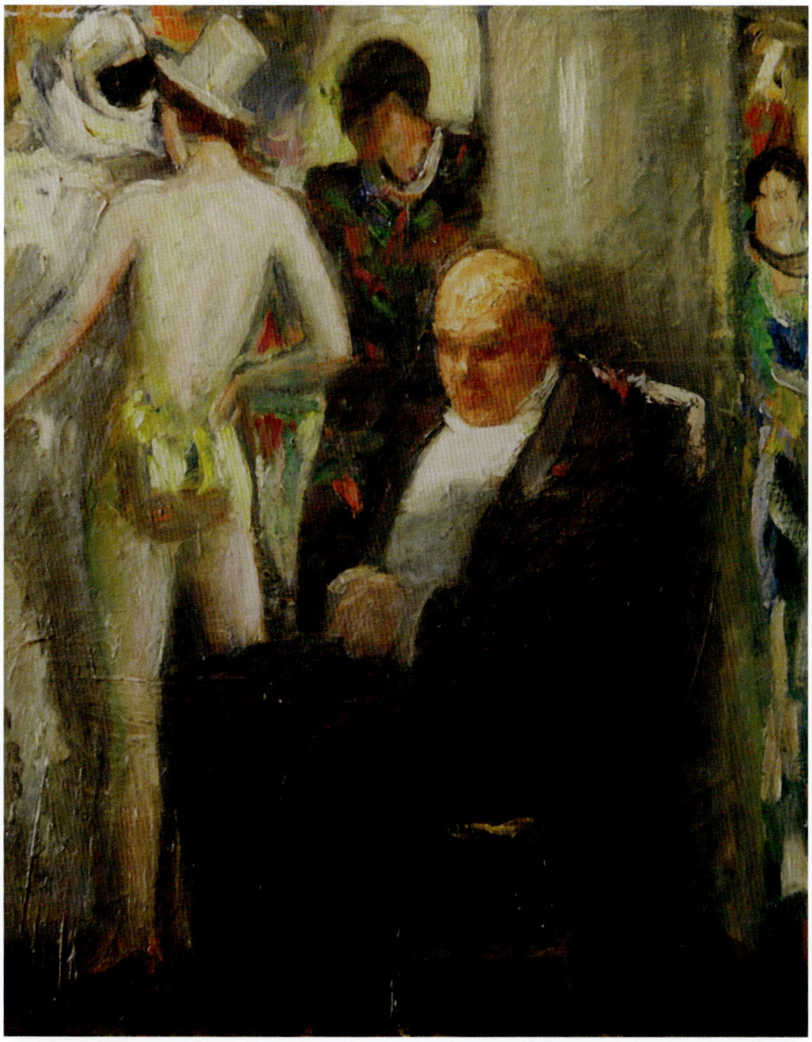

Pierre de Belair
Cabaret, c.1925
Andrew Herrera II, San Francisco, California

Pierre de Belair
Nu, c.1925
Cynthia J. Evans, Tuscany Hills, California

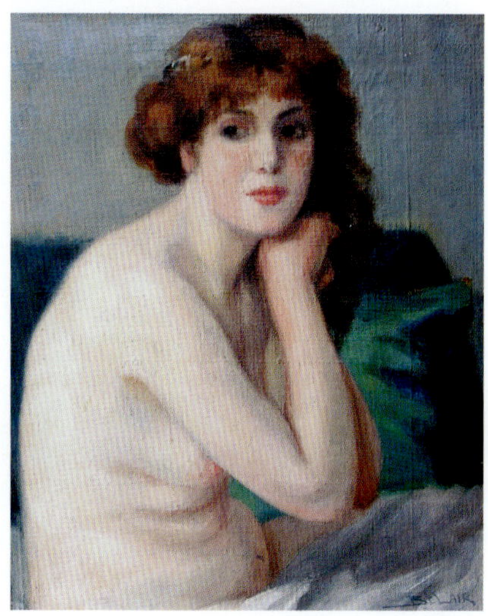

Federico Armando Beltran-Masses

1885-1949

Federico Armando Beltran-Masses was born in 1885 in Guaira de la Melena, Cuba. His father was a Spanish military envoy to Cuba and after the war between the United States and Cuba ended in 1899, the family returned to Spain.

Beltran-Masses studied with the painter Sorolla at the School of Fine Arts in Barcelona. In 1905, he traveled to Madrid to study the collection of Spanish and European art at the Prado Museum. In 1916, he moved to Paris where he received an honor from the Société Nationale des Beaux-Arts.

Commissions were received in the United States, Belgium, Italy and India and in 1919 he took charge of organizing l'Exposition Hispano-Français des Beaux-Arts. In 1920, he exhibited an exotic nude titled *Salomé* at the Venice Bienniale, which is now in the Museo Casa Lis in Salamanca, Spain.

Beltran-Masses exhibited at the Wildenstein Galleries in New York and Palm Beach, Florida in 1925. In the August 1925 issue of *International Studio Magazine* Marguerite Tjader wrote an extensive article about the artist.

The Musée des Offices de Florence bought several of his self-portraits. In 1928 he was named Commissioner General of l'Exposition International des Beaux-Arts in commemoration of the centenary of Francisco de Goya. He was a member of Royal Academy of Fine Arts in Madrid and was named both Chevalier de la Légion d'Honneur in France and Knight of the Order of Malta. In 1934 Beltran-Masses exhibited at the Royal Watercolor Society in London and in 1938 at the Burlington Galleries.

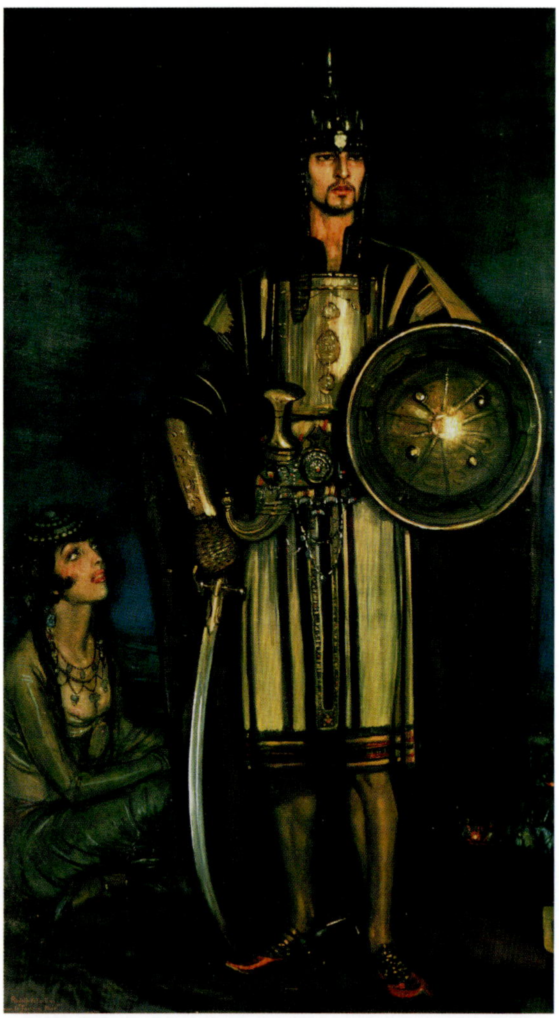

Federico Beltran-Masses
Rudolf Valentino as *Le Faucon Noir,* c.1925
Private Collection

Beltran-Masses began his career painting landscapes and figurative compositions though later in his career his focus turned to portraiture. He is best known for his portraits of royalty, society figures and movie stars like Douglas Fairbanks. He was also a dear friend to Rudolf Valentino and painted two large portraits of the actor which hung in his Hollywood home, in addition to another painting by Beltran-Masses of a famous Spanish dancer. These works were sold at auction in Los Angeles shortly after Valentino's death.

The artist developed a unique style; evident in his work is the influence of the Spanish masters with a decidedly modern flavor. He painted many large canvases often with bizarre and beautiful women; his work is distinguished by his use of shades of deep blue, which became known as "Beltran blue." Nighttime settings give his subjects an eerie contrast with star-studded skies.

Beltran-Masses died in 1949 in Barcelona, Spain and today he is considered a Spanish painter. His paintings are held by several museums, including the Musée du Jeu de Paume in Paris.

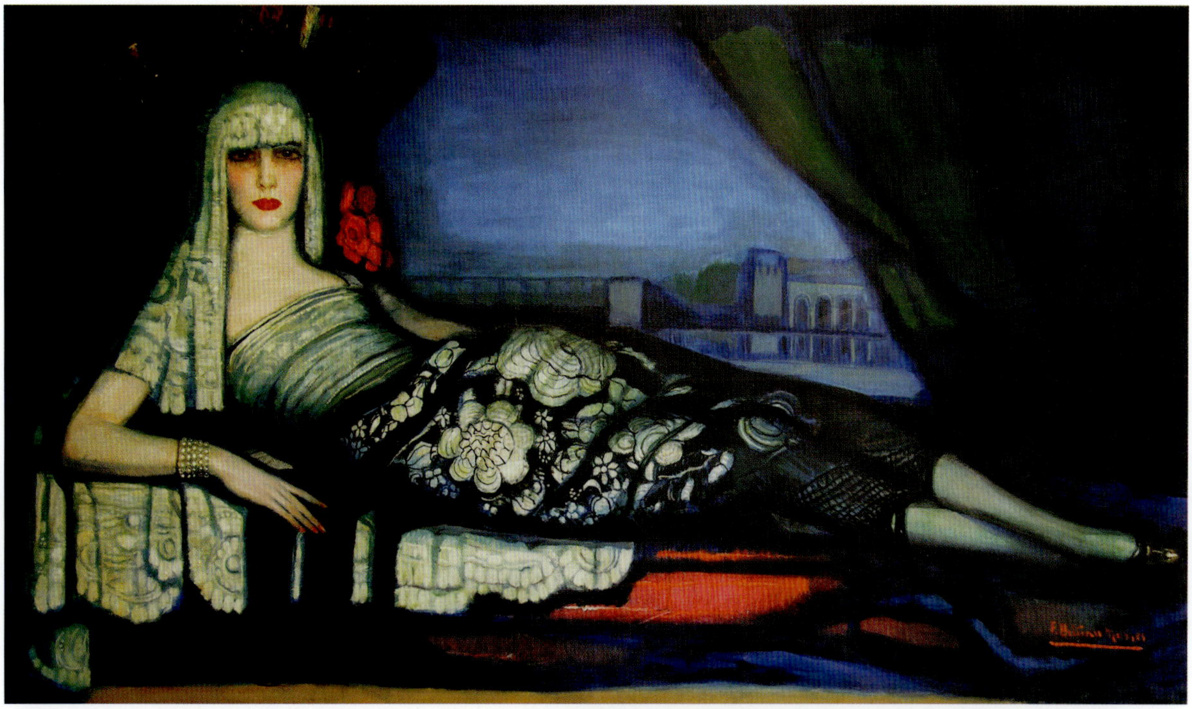

Federico Beltran-Masses
Femme dans le Chale Espagnol, c.1925
Norma Kline-Tiefel, Washington, DC

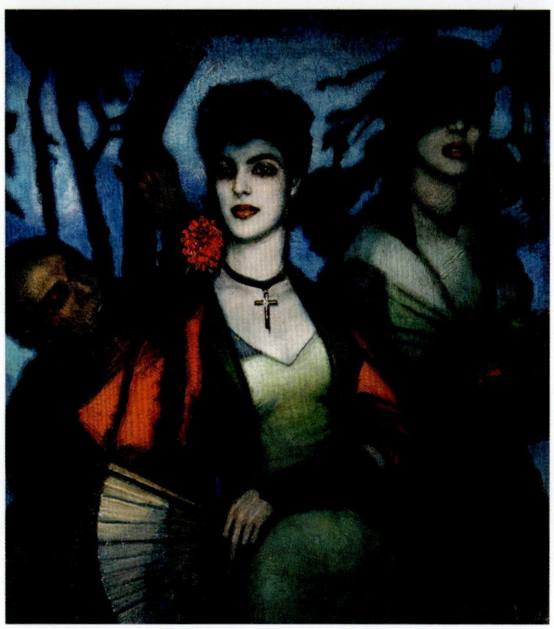

Federico Beltran-Masses
Oeillettes Rouge, c.1925
Maas Gallery Ltd, London, England

Jehan Berjonneau

1890-1972

Jehan Berjonneau was born in Montmorillon. Exhibitions include the Salon des Artistes Français, the Salon des Artistes Indépendants from 1926 to 1939, the Salon d'Automne from 1927 to 1936 and the Salon des Tuileries from 1930 to 1939. The location of his formal training is unknown.

He is best known for still lifes, landscapes and engravings though his paintings of nudes demonstrate a mastery of the human form as well. Berjonneau died in 1972.

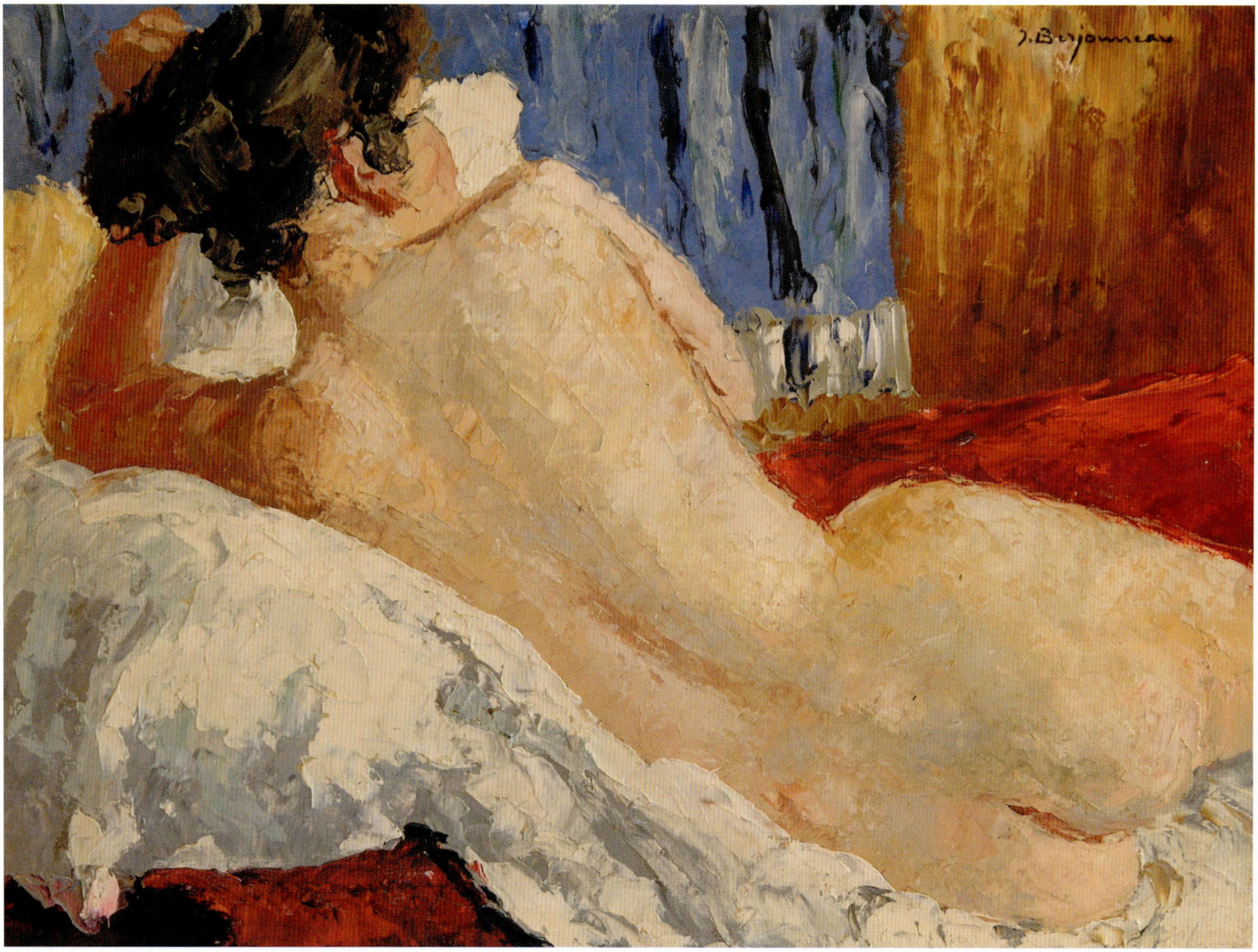

Jehan Berjonneau
Nu Allongé, c.1935
Richard Russell, Lafayette, California

Albert Bertalan

1899-1957

Albert Bertalan was born on September 21, 1899 in Jaszbereny, Hungary. He is known for painting compositions of figures in unique environments, including women by the sea among other similar subject matters.

Bertalan received a solo exhibition in Nuremberg and exhibited regularly at the Budapest Gallery of Pal Lazlo. His Parisian salon exhibitions include Salon des Indépendants in 1926 and 1930; Salon d'Automne in 1926; Salon des Tuileries in 1930. In 1928 he won the Szinvei prize.

His paintings while in Paris were very expressionistic having incorporated composition, brush technique and a unique vision; all of which now make his work very identifiable.

Many of his works have been auctioned recently in Paris and Budapest marking a renewed interest in the artist. Bertalan died in 1957 in Paris.

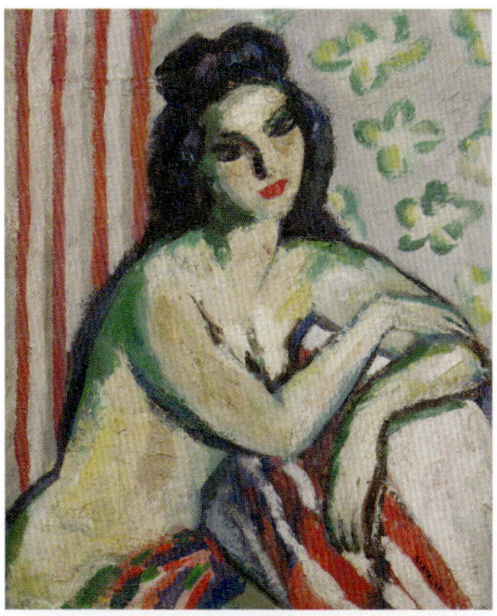

Albert Bertalan
Nu Assis, c.1935
Private Collection

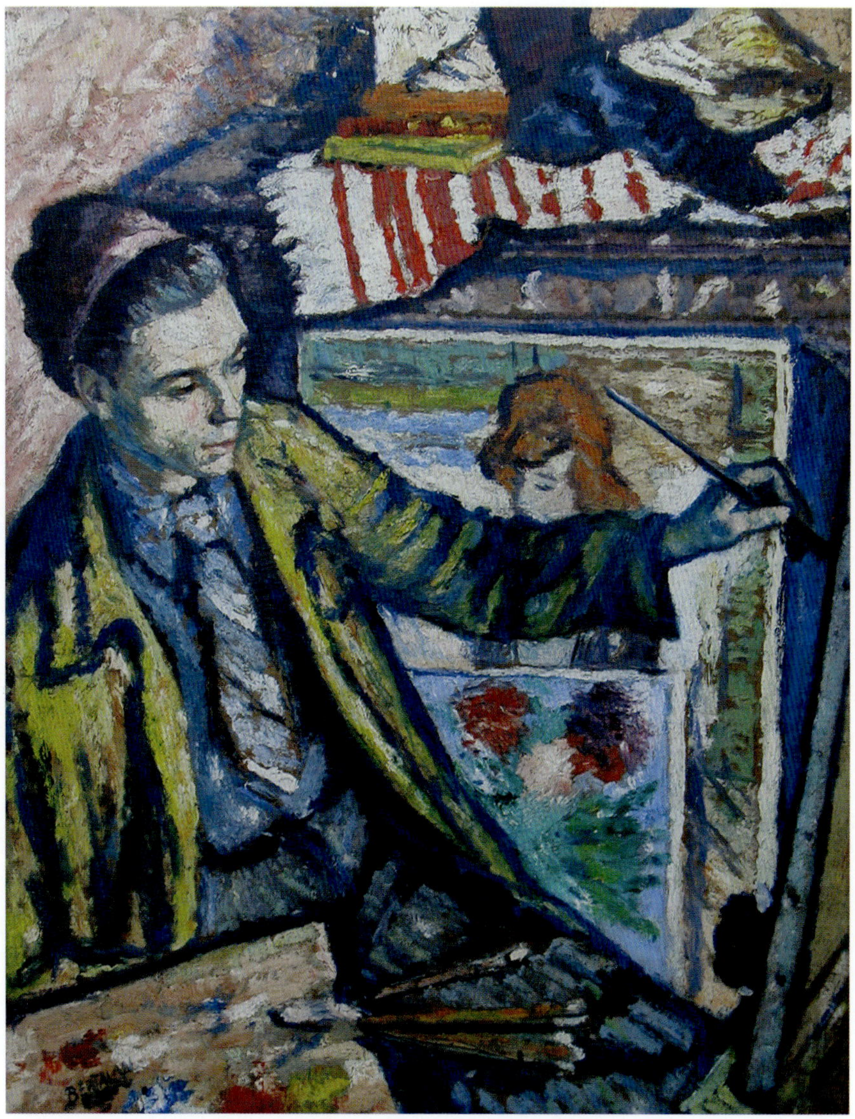

Albert Bertalan
Dans l'Atelier, c.1935
Dennis Clark, Carmel, California

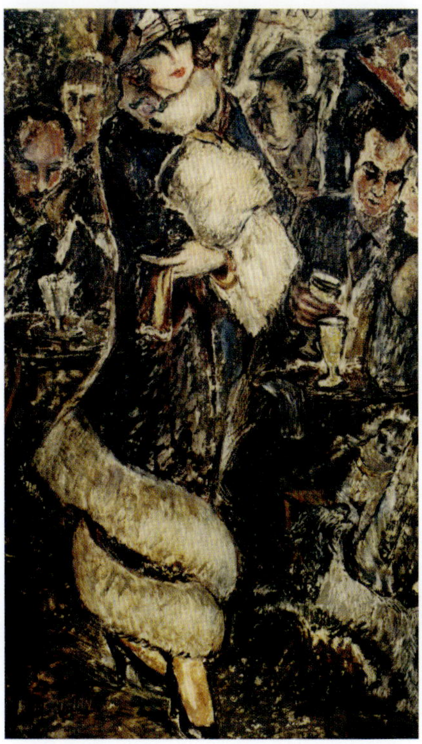

Albert Bertalan
Femme Élégante, c.1930
Los Angeles Fine Art Gallery, Los Angeles, California

René-Pierre Louis Besserve

1883–1959

René-Pierre Louis Besserve was born in 1883 in Montbéliard. He was a student at the Naval Academy before choosing a career in the arts and enrolling at the Académie Julian and later, at l'École des Beaux-Arts in Montpellier.

Besserve exhibited frequently in Paris with the Salon d'Automne between 1920 and 1938; the Société Nationale des Beaux–Arts in 1922; the Salon des Artistes Indépendants between 1926 and 1938; and the Salon des Tuileries between 1928 and 1939.

Working as an illustrator he collaborated with Juan Gris for the publication of *Cri de Paris* and contributed to several other publications such as *Rire*, *Ruy-Blas* and *Fantasio*.

Besserve is best known for his cubist and expressionistic stylizations of illustrations, posters, caricatures, nudes and landscapes.

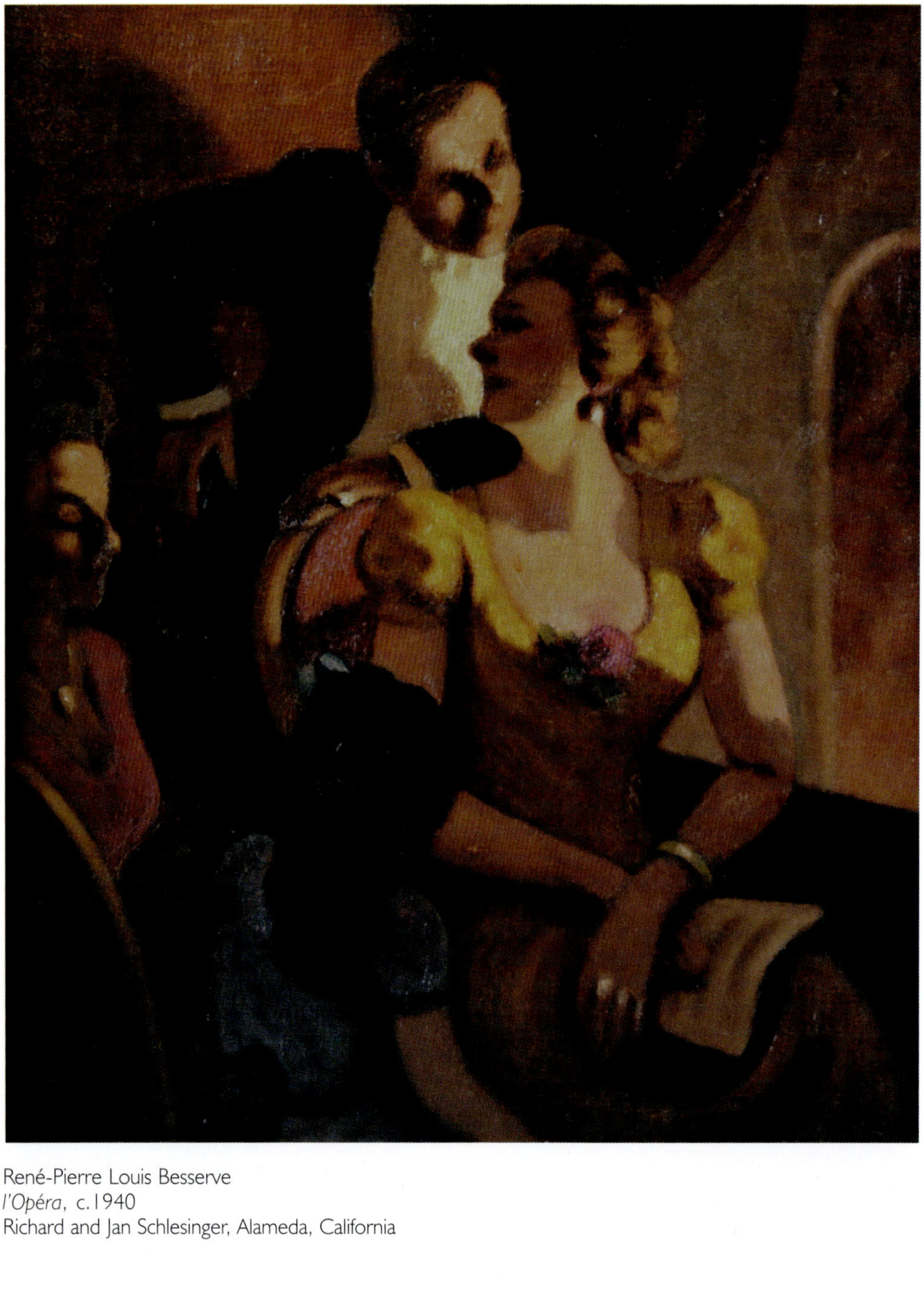

René-Pierre Louis Besserve
l'Opéra, c.1940
Richard and Jan Schlesinger, Alameda, California

Marie-Gabriel Biessy

1854–935

Marie-Gabriel Biessy was born in Saint-Pierre-du-Mont March 25, 1854. In 1876 he began his studies at l'École des Beaux-Arts in Lyon under F. Clement, and in 1879 under Carolus-Duran in Paris. He traveled extensively in the United States, England, Holland, Portugal and Senegal where he captured portraits and scenery of daily life.

Exhibitions include the Salon de Lyon, Salon de Paris and Salon de la Société Nationale des Beaux-Arts, which warranted and honorable mention in 1883 and of which Biessy became a member in 1895. An honorable mention and a Médaille de Bronze were also received at l' Exposition Universelle in 1889 and 1900. Biessy received the Chevalier de la Légion d'Honneur the same year and was awarded a gold medal at the Crystal Palace in London. Biessy also acted as Director of the Fine Arts Academy in Cairo, Egypt for some time.

Biessy's compositions are sometimes eerie with deep foggy colors that bring the viewer an unusual vision of the streets of Paris. He also employed non-traditional composition and perspective. His work can be found in museums of Bordeaux and Buenos Aires, Argentina.

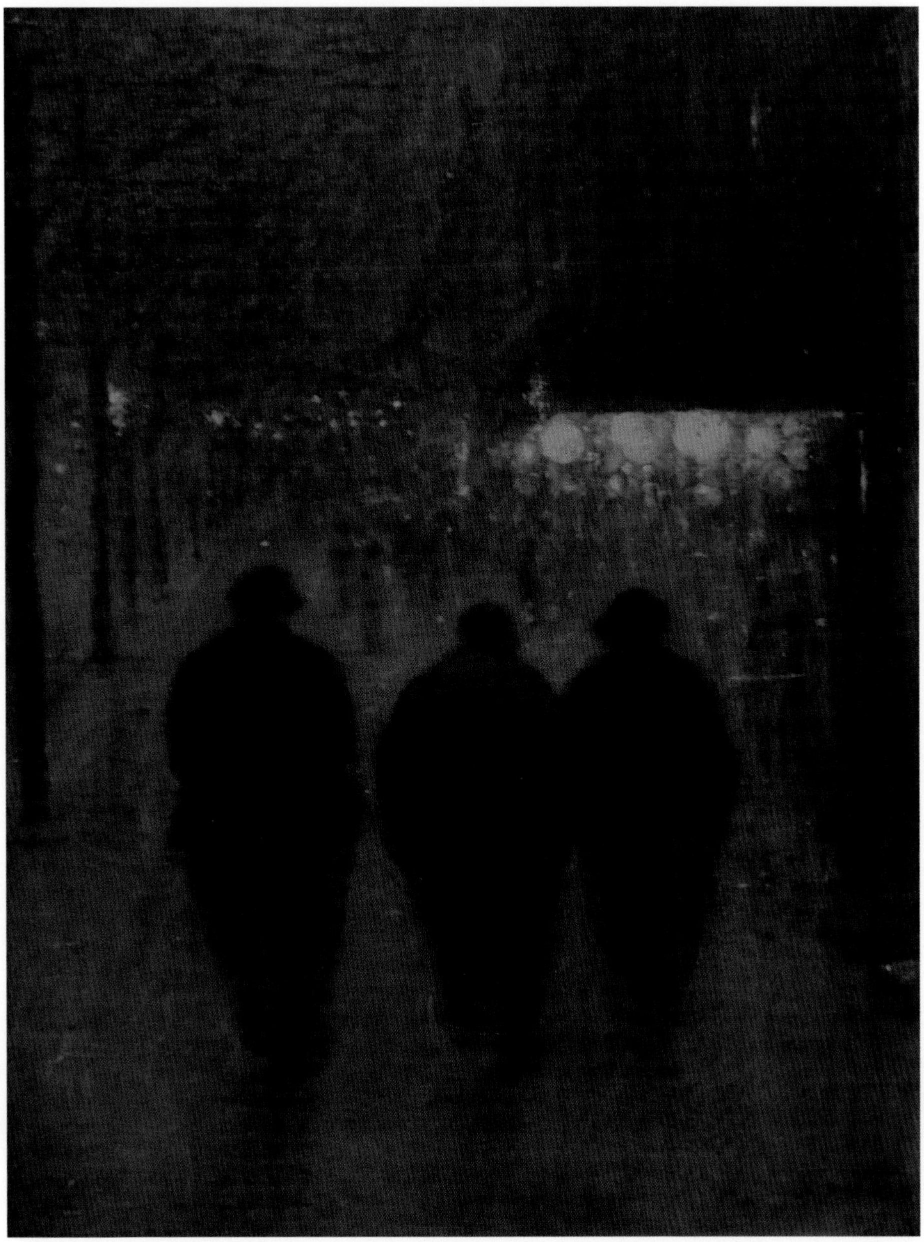

Marie-Gabriel Biessy
Dans la Rue, c.1900
Charles Tapper, New York, New York

Charles-Louis Bisschops

1894-1975

Charles-Louis Bisschops was born in Liege in 1894. He became a prolific painter of figures and portraits having studied under J. Delville and C. Montauld at l'Académie de Bruxelles. In 1912 he was awarded Le Premier Prix de Composition and in 1919 received Le Premier Prix de Peinture.

In 1931, after having traveled in Italy, Algeria and Spain, Bisschops exhibited at the Salon des Artistes Français. He continued to exhibit frequently with various Parisian Salons and the Brussels Triennial as well.

Gallery exhibitions include: Galerie Charpentier, Brussels; Salon du Printemps, Brussels; l'Académie des Beaux-Arts, Tournai; Salle Boiglet, Brussels; Sillon, Brussels; Salonnet, Brussels; Galerie de la Meuse, Liege;Galerie Kodak, Brussels; l'Essaim, Mon; and Galerie Van Looy, Brussels among many other salons in Nice, Lyon, Marseille and Liege. The Hôtel Charlier in Brussels held a retrospective of seventy paintings and fifty drawings in 1965.

Bisschops' career and style spanned five decades; his earliest paintings display the influence of the Symbolists and evolved into more an expressionistic method typical of his contemporary Belgians.

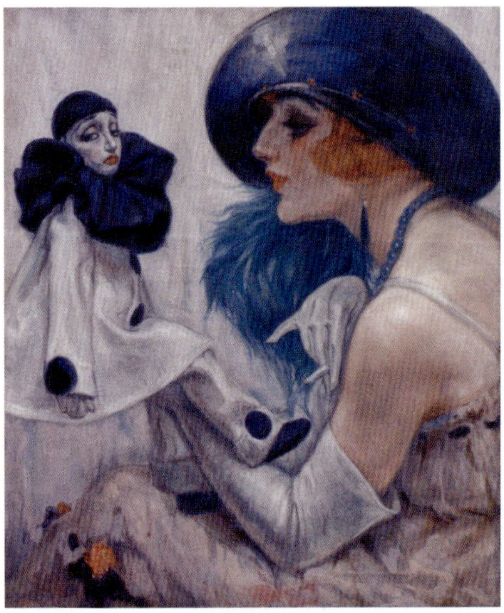

Charles-Louis Bisschops
La Poupée, Dated 1925
Private Collection

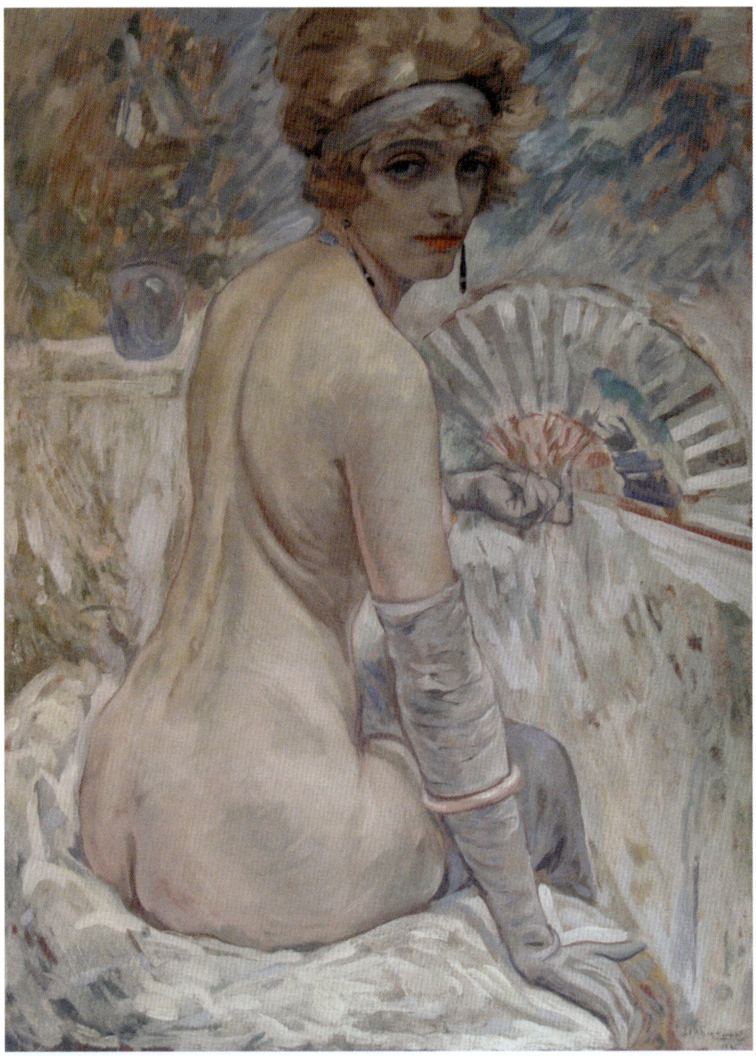

Charles-Louis Bisschops
Nu Assis, Dated 1922
Mark and Marina Plon, Henderson, Nevada

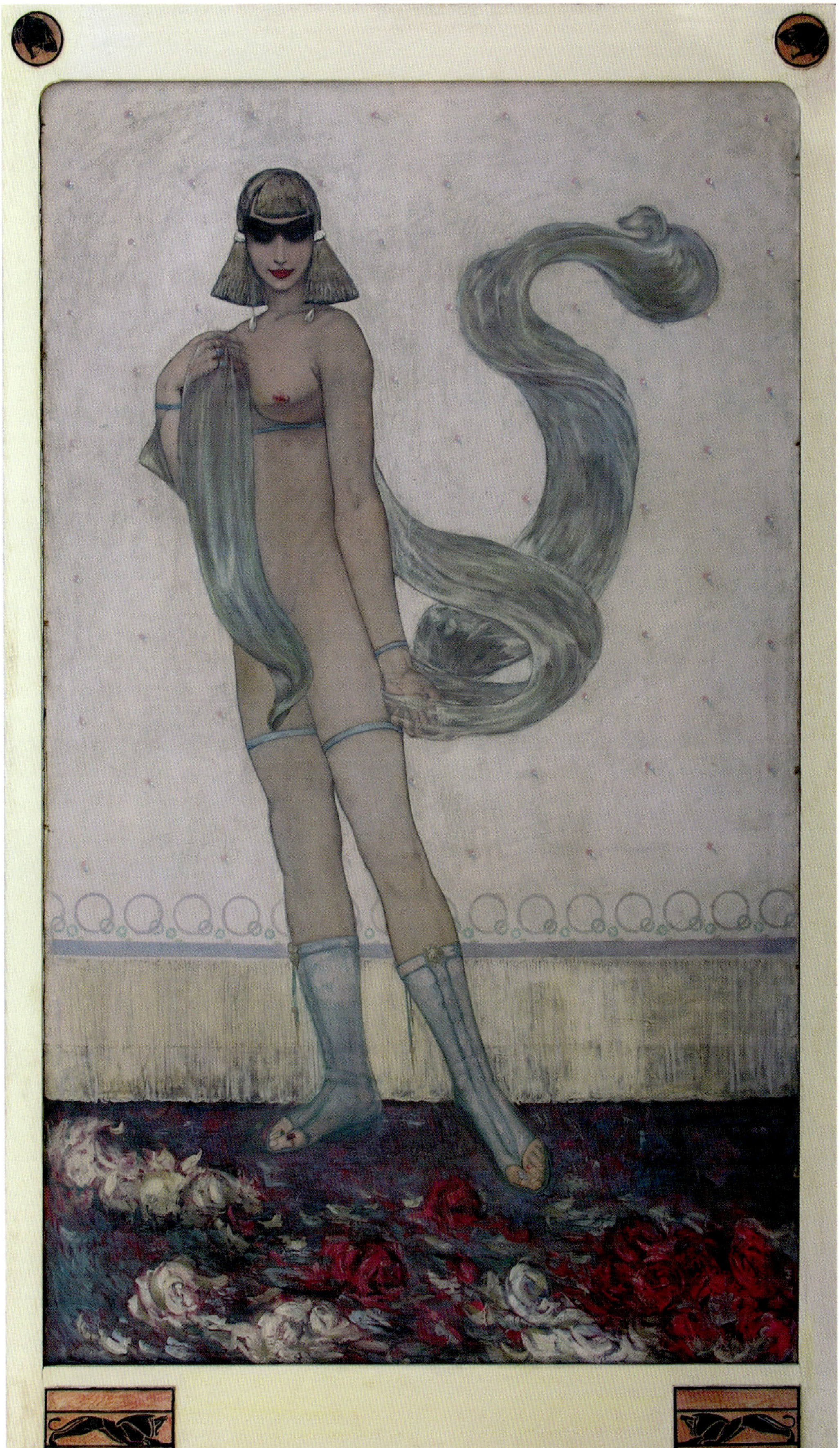

Charles-Louis Bisschops
Salomé, Dated 1913-14
Papillon Gallery, Los Angeles, California

Roger Bissière

1886-1964

Roger Bissière was born September 22, 1886 in Villeréal, Lot-et-Garonne, France. He is best known as a painter of nudes and portraits.

Bissière's artistic talents were evident as a child, but his father did not approve and intended for him to pursue a law career. At nineteen Bissière rebelled, traveling in Algiers. He eventually studied at l'École des Beaux-Arts, Bordeaux and then at l'École Nationale Supérieure des Beaux-Arts, Paris. To supplement his career Bissière wrote reviews of contemporary art for Parisian newspapers. In 1919 Léonce Rosenberg commissioned him to write the first monograph on Georges Braque's work.

Around 1910 or 1911, Bissière began participating in the Parisian Salons with his first exhibition at the Salon des Artistes Français. Other salon exhibitions include the Salon d'Automne, Salon des Tuileries, and Salon des Artistes Indépendants. In addition to the salons Bissière exhibited at the Société des Amateurs d'Art, Exposition Universelle, Petit –Palais des Maîtres d'Art Indépendant from 1895 to1937, Salon de Mai, Biennale de Venise, Biennale de Sao Paulo, and Documenta de Kassel.

Solo exhibitions include the Galerie Berthe Weil, Galerie Druet, and Galerie Drouin. The Musée National d'Art Moderne de Paris hosted a retrospective of Bissière's work, which traveled to museums in Germany, the Netherlands, and Switzerland. Subsequent exhibitions include Musée d'Art Moderne de la Ville de Paris and Musée de l'Abbaye Sainte-Croix des Sables-d'Olonne.

Bissière was a modernist and worked in the manner of Jean de Botton and Jean Souverbie. His work is now part of the permanent collections of numerous museums including Agen, Amsterdam, Bordeaux, La Chaux-de-Fonds, Saint-Étienne and Zurich. Parisian museums that have collected his work include the Musée Nationale d'Art Moderne and Musée d'Art Moderne de la Ville de Paris. Bissière died on December 2, 1964 in Boissiérettes, Lot, France.

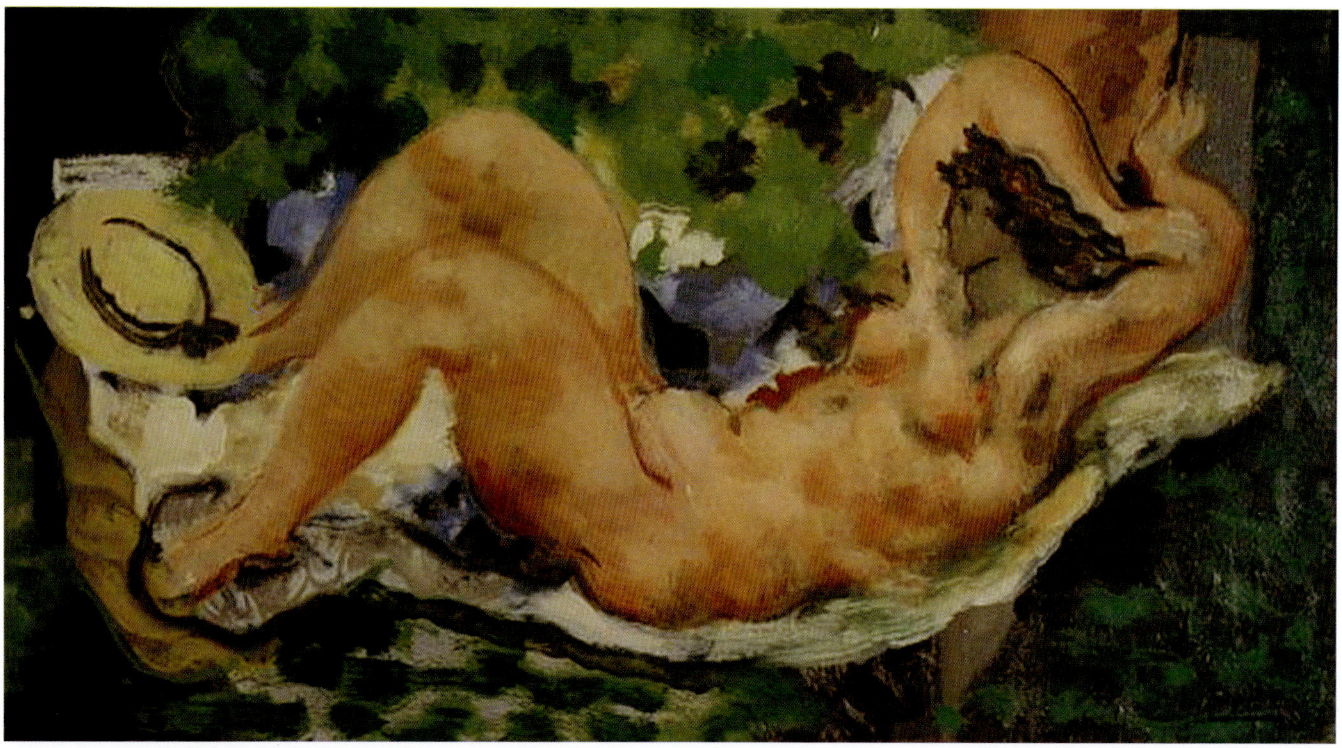

Roger Bissière
Nu Couché sur Ligne Blanc, c.1925
Private Collection
Whitford Fine Art, London, England

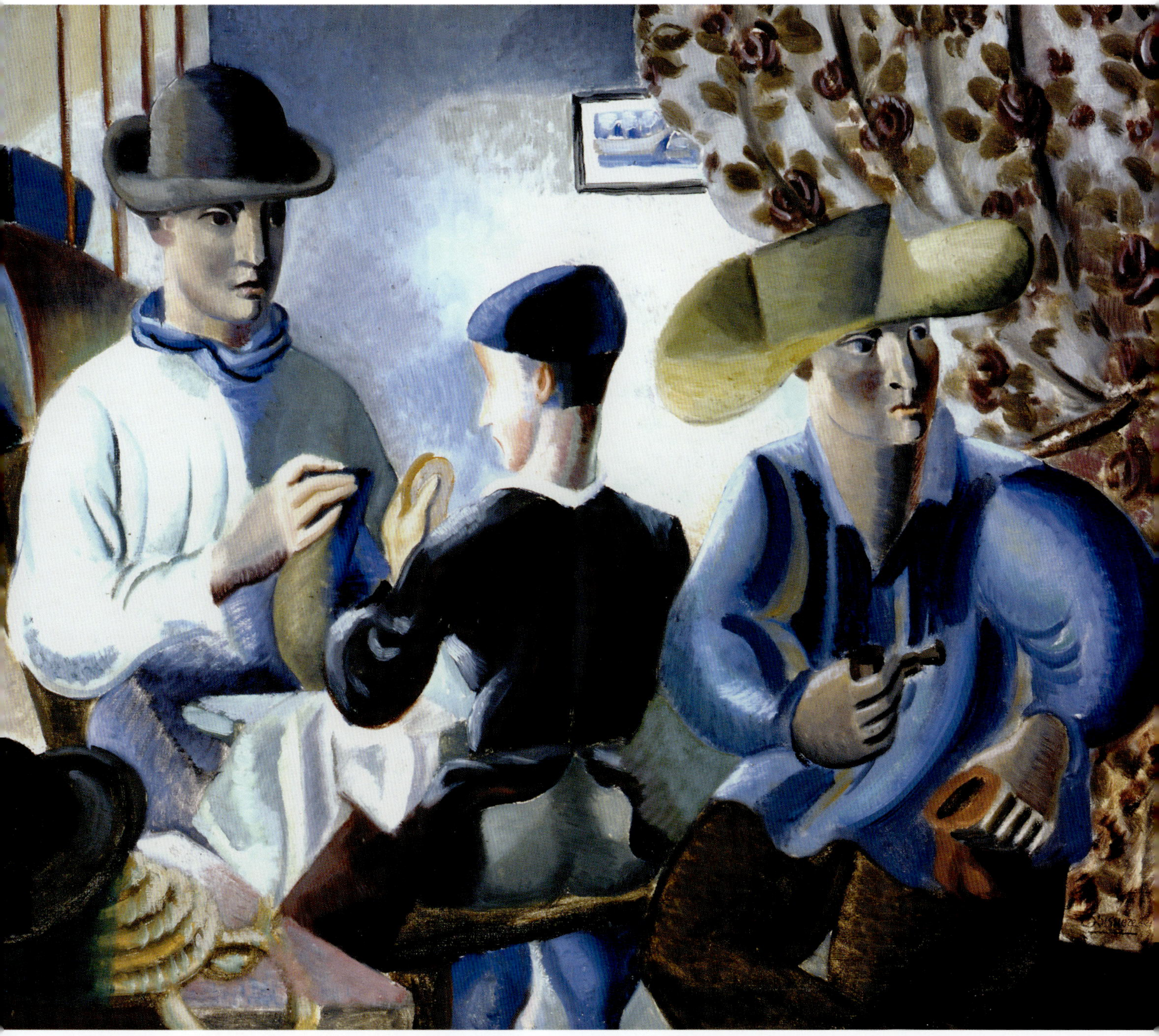

Roger Bissière, c.1925
Les Loisirs, c.1925
Montgomery Gallery, San Francisco, California

Marcel Bloch

Born 1884

Marcel Bloch was born in Paris and is best known for his portraits in oil, pastel and watercolor. He was a student of Paul Renouard and exhibited at the Salon des Artistes Indépendants for thirty years beginning in 1909. Bloch participated in various galleries in Paris and in the Salon des Artistes Français in 1921.

He was a prolific painter almost exclusively of women. He also was a fine print maker; he published many etchings in the manner of Louis Icart and Maurice Millière. The date of his death is unknown.

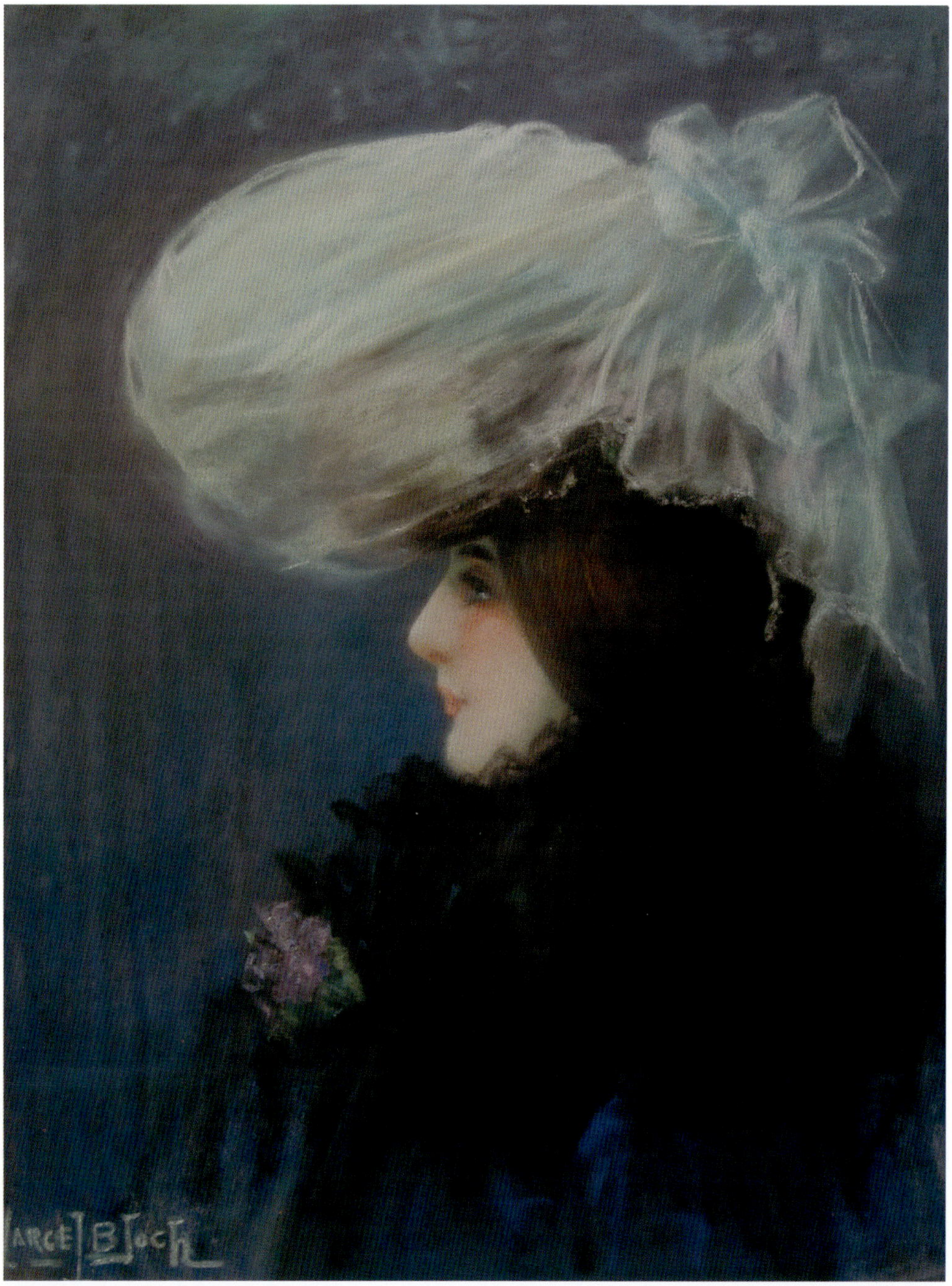

Marcel Bloch
Femme au Chapeau, c.1910
Papillon Gallery, Los Angeles, California

Richard Bloos

1878-1957

Richard Bloos was born in Dusseldorf, Germany in 1878. He was associated with Janssen, Spatz and Forberg at the Dusseldorf Academy and was greatly influenced by the work of Max Liebermann.

In 1906 Bloos settled in France and exhibited with the Salon des Artistes Indépendants in 1909 and 1910, the Salon d'Automne in 1909 and 1913 and the Salon de la Société Nationale des Beaux-Arts from 1910 to 1914.

He lived within the Montmartre and Montparnasse artist communities. The scenes of modern Parisian life inspired his figures, portraits and landscapes and his style was inspired by the techniques of the Postimpressionists.

Bloos' paintings have since been included in exhibits in Cologne, Hambourg, Paris, London, Versailles and New York. Several drawings and sketches were included in the retrospective publication *Hundert Jahre Künstlerverein Malkasten Düsseldorf 1848-1948*. A short biography on Bloos by Paul Westheim is also included in the April 1911-September 1911 volume of *Deutsche Kunst und Dekoration*.

Bloos died in 1957.

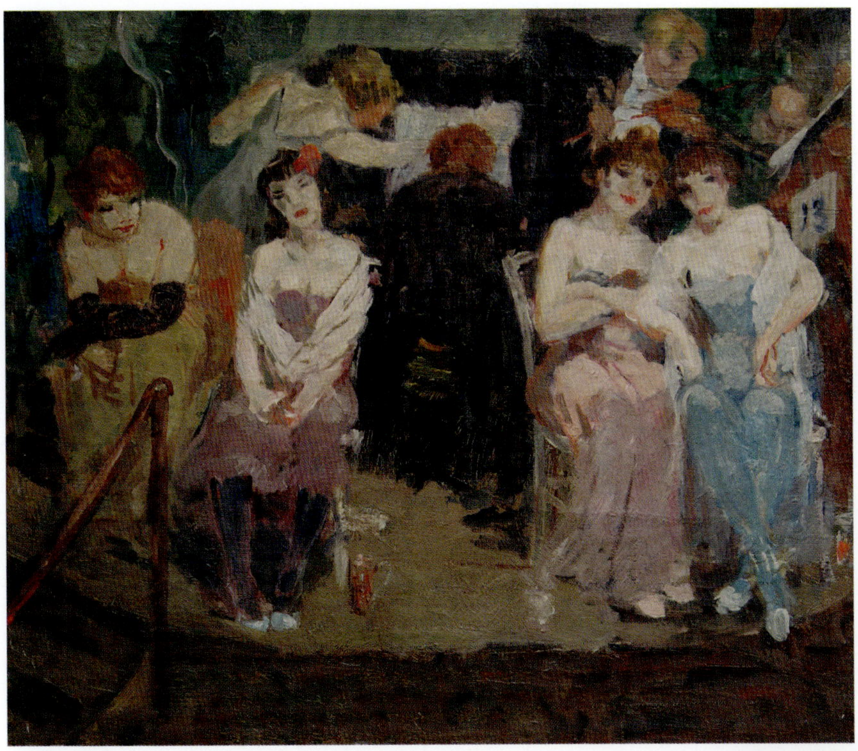

Richard Bloos
Le Répétition, Dated 1909
Papillon Gallery, Los Angeles, California

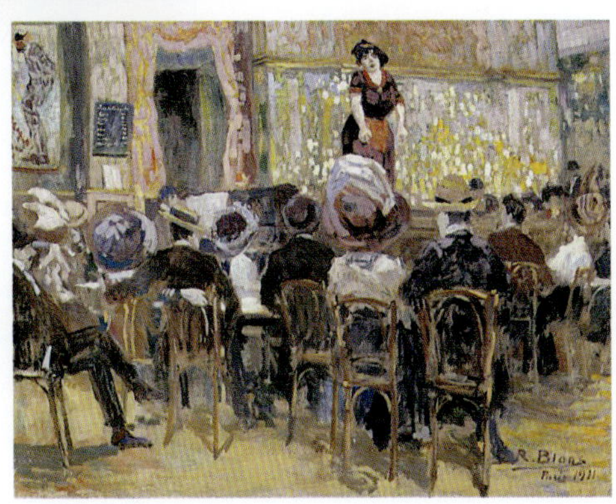

Richard Bloos
Chanteuse, Café a Paris, 1911
Kunsthandel Ivo Bouwman BV,
The Hague, Netherlands

Jean de Botton

1898-1978

Jean de Botton had a long and prolific career as painter, illustrator and muralist. His successful career started in the 1920s and continued for four decades. After earning a degree in Philosophy from the Lycée Rollins in Paris, he went on to travel extensively and become a well established artist.

Jean de Botton's early paintings display many of the characteristics of the age of Art Deco. He incorporated romantic, allegorical and historical themes with a modern technique. Jean de Botton executed many very large canvases in the 1920s in addition to many stylized portraits. As the decades passed his style changed with the times; in the 1950s and into the 1960s he painted and exhibited many abstract compositions.

Jean de Botton served on the jury of the Salon d'Automne and was a member of the Salon des Tuileries, Salon des Indépendants and Salon des Humoristes. He was Vice President of the Salon and President of the Salon France Nouvellle.

Solo Exhibitions between 1936 and 1942 include the Marie Harriman Gallery, New York; the Rockefeller Center, New York; Carol Carstairs Gallery; Leger & Co. Gallery, London; Seattle Museum; San Diego Museum; Philadelphia Art Gallery; Grace Gallery, Boston; Galerie du Livre, Casablanca; Santa Barbara Museum; Pearl Gallery, Hollywood; Vista del Arroyo, Pasadena; Francis Tayor Gallery, Beverly Hills; Courvoisier Gallery, San Francisco; and the Knoedler & Co. Gallery, New York.

Jean de Botton participated in several Carnegie Institute International Exhibitions in Pittsburg, Boston and Chicago. He participated in the Official Exhibition of French Art in Tokyo, Brussels and Anvers as well. In 1925 de Botton exhibited a mural at the Salon d'Honneur des Beaux-Arts, Paris and in 1937 at the Palace of the Navy, Paris. He also received the distinguished honor of serving as the official painter at the coronation of H.M. King George VI in 1937.

Book illustrations include *Les Fleurs du Mal* by Baudelaire, 1936; *Claude* by Fauconnier, edition Firenczi; *La Maison du Quai* by Caston Cherau, edition Firenczi; and a children's book entitled *Fou Fou Discovers America*. In 1942 de Botton designed a poster for the California National Guard as well.

The artist delivered a lecture at the San Francisco Museum of Modern Art in 1941 on the subject of Chiaroscuro and his theory of its detrimental effect on modern painting.

In June of 1944 the California Palace of the Legion of Honor held a retrospective of de Botton's paintings, frescoes, murals, drawings, tapestries and book illustrations. The same year he had written the ballet *Triumph of Hope*, which was performed at the San Francisco Opera House. Museums in Luxembourg, Versailles and Royan have collected his work.

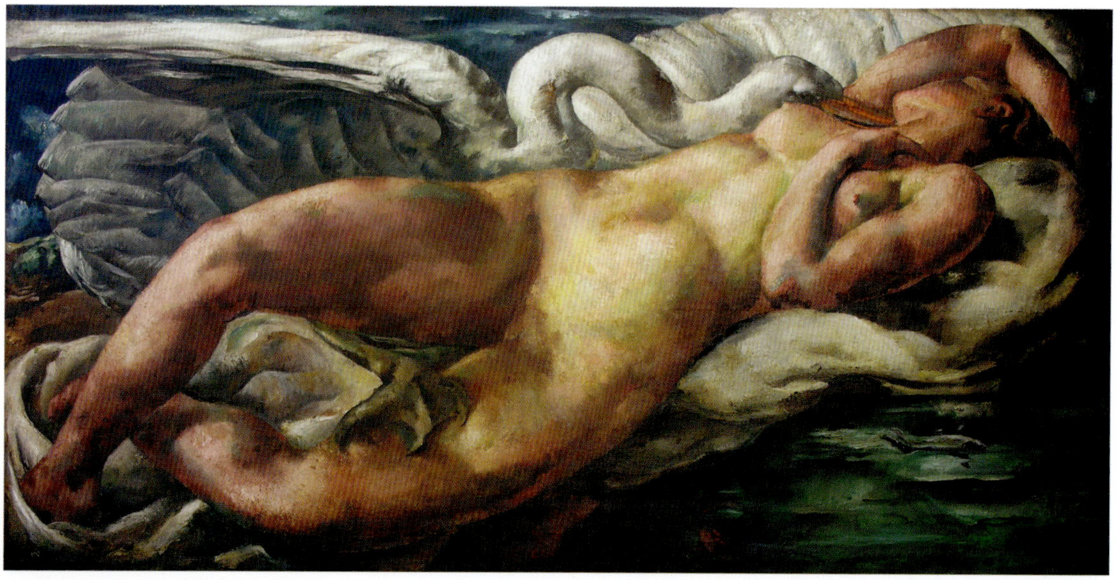

Jean de Botton
Léda et Le Cygne, Dated 1930
Papillon Gallery, Los Angeles, California

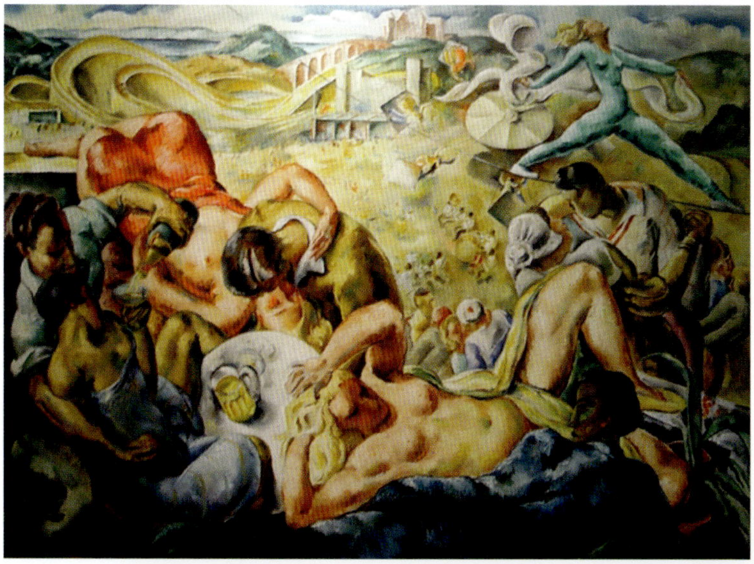

Jean de Botton
Kermesse de l'Indépendance de Belgique, c.1930
Whitford Fine Art, London, England

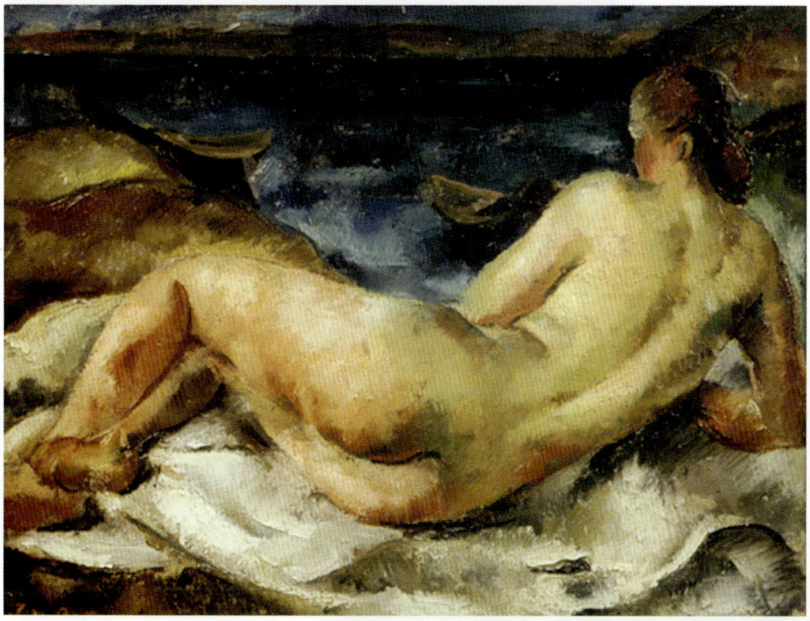

Jean de Botton
Nu sur La Plage, c.1925
Belgravia Gallery, London, England

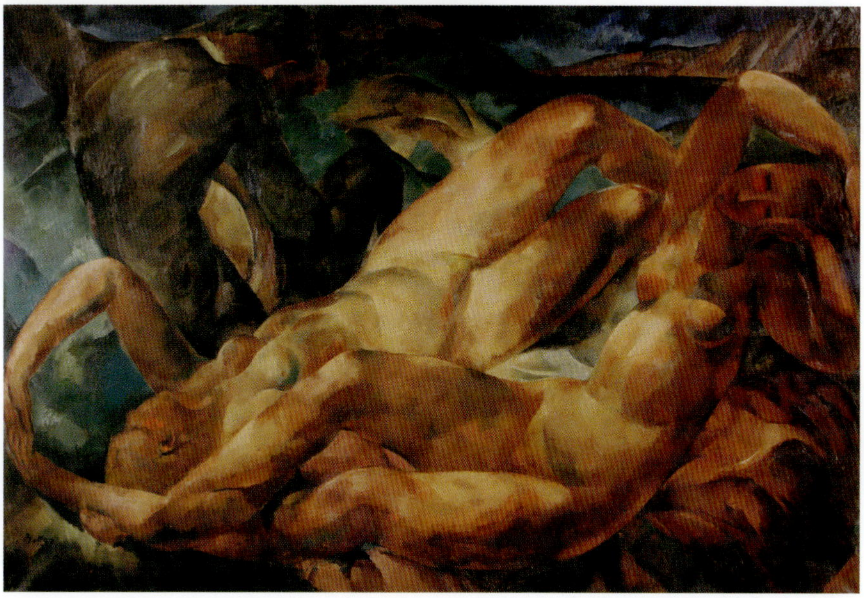

Jean de Botton
Sérénade, Dated 1926
Papillon Gallery, Los Angeles, California

Robert Bouchet
1898-1986

Robert Bouchet lived and worked in Montmartre. He began exhibiting in 1922 at the Salon des Artistes Français, as well as the Salon d'Automne and the Salon des Tuileries.

Bouchet's canvases are rich with the romance of Paris in the 1920s. His use of color and composition are typical of the Parisian Modernist School.

Bouchet was not only a painter but also gained world recognition as a guitar maker. He developed the "Méthode Bouchet," which is widely used in guitar making. Later in his life he also became an accomplished guitar player. Robert Bouchet died in 1986.

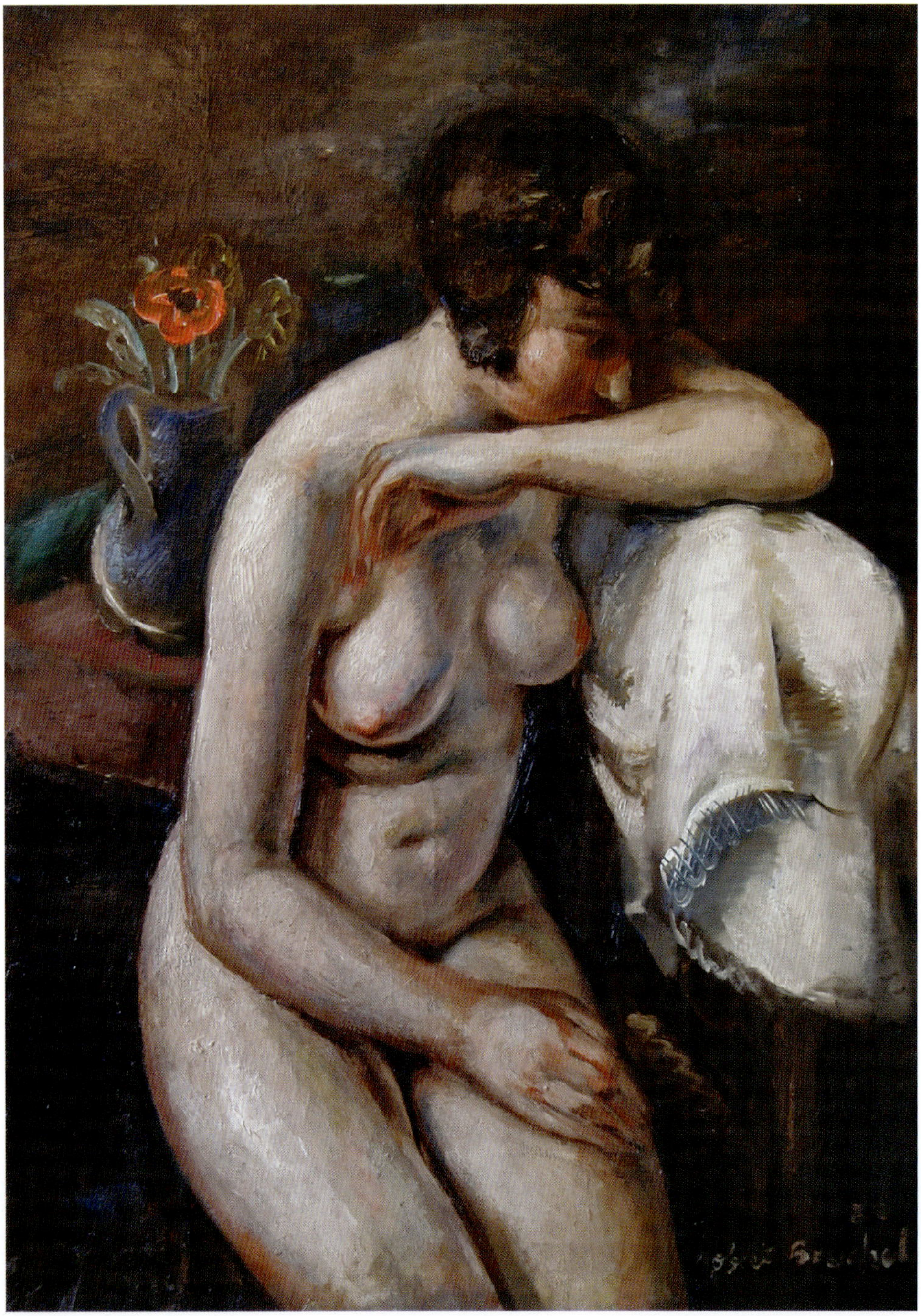

Robert Bouchet
La Modèle, Dated 1928
Papillon Gallery, Los Angeles, California

Abel Dominique Boyé

1864–1934

Abel Dominique Boyé was born in Marmande and studied under Benjamin-Constant. He was awarded the Légion d'Honneur in 1930 and received the Médaille de Troisième and Deuxième Classe.

He exhibited at the Salon des Artistes Français and is collected in the Musée d'Agen.

Boyé was a typical artist of La Belle Epoque. He incorporated beautiful women in idealistic scenes; these canvases expressed a certain charm popular in the period. Boyé died in 1934.

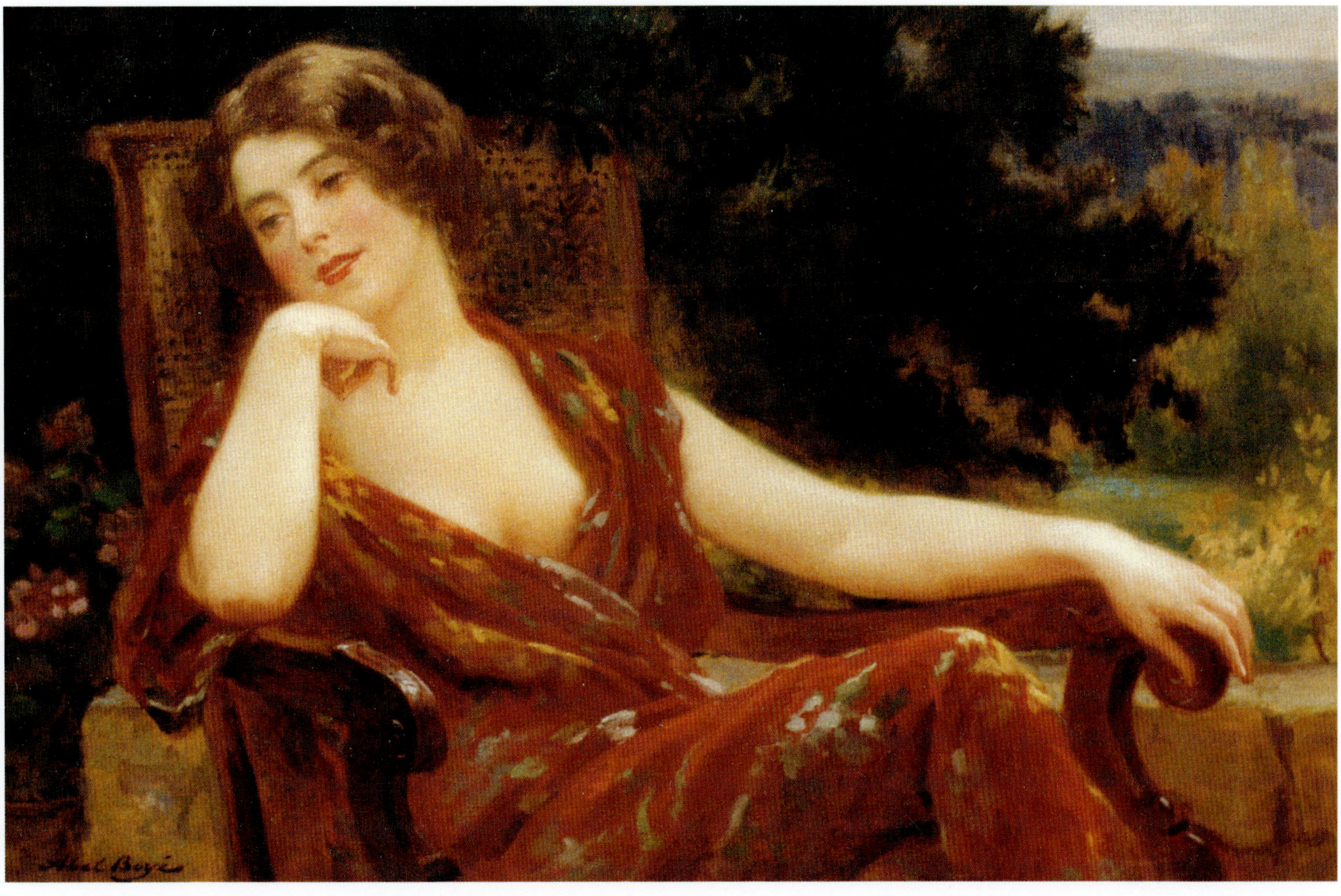

Abel Dominique Boyé
Femme Assis, c.1910
Los Angeles Fine Art Gallery, Los Angeles, California

Henri Georges Bréard
20th century

Henri Georges Bréard studied with Henri Royer and François Schommer, specializing in portraits, landscapes and caricatures. Bréard exhibited at the Salon des Artistes Français from 1911 to 1939 and received an honorable mention in 1934.

Bréard was an accomplished artist in the manner of the salon painters of the previous generation and his clever style and impeccable technique made his boudoir paintings widely popular. Exact dates of his birth and death are unknown.

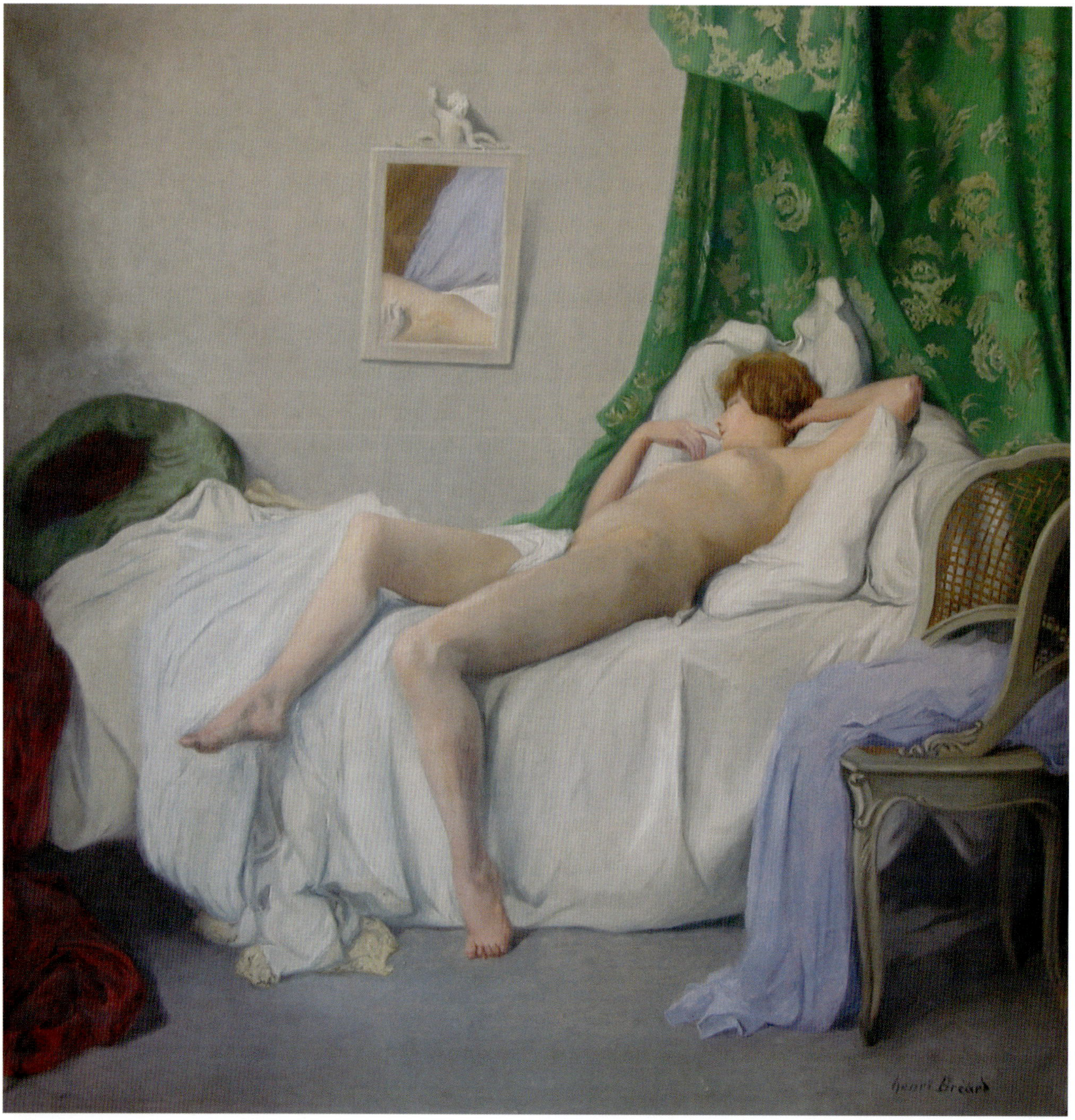

Henri Georges Bréard
Nu Allongé, c.1930
Seligman Family Collection, Los Angeles, California

Gaston Bussière
1862-1928

Born April 24, 1862 Bussière studied painting and engraving under Cabanel and Puvis de Chavannes in Paris. He exhibited at l'Exposition Universelle in Paris in 1900 where he received a Médaille de Bronze. He was also awarded the Légion d'Honneur in 1917. Bussière participated frequently with the symbolist Salon de la Rose-Croix for two years

Bussière was influenced by the operas of Berlioz and Wagner and created illustrations inspired by the stories. Notable illustrations include *Hélène de Troie* in 1895, *Les Filles du Rhin* in 1906 and many others. In 1897 he also illustrated *The Splendors and Miseries of Courtesans* by Balzac.

Bussière was an outstanding and accomplished artist. Many of his subjects are enticing and romantic in the tradition of the Art Nouveau artists. His canvases are filled with passion and beauty.

The artist died in Paris in 1928.

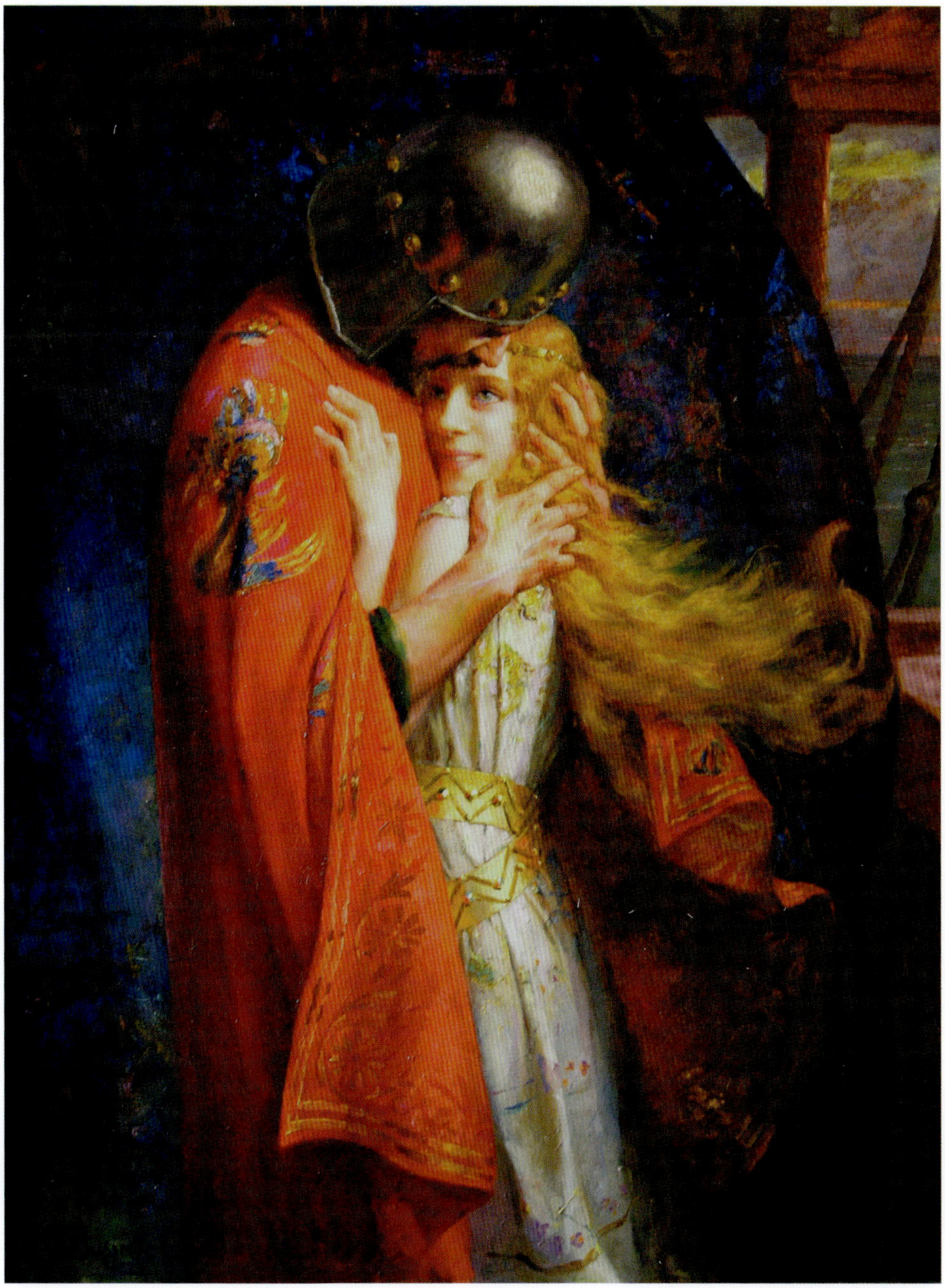

Gaston Bussière
L'Héro, Dated 1922
Bill and Jo LaMond, Los Angeles, California

Frédéric Marius de Buzon

1879–1958

Frédéric Marius de Buzon was born on September 18, 1879 in Bayon (Gironde). He was a student of Maignan and Cormon and exhibited in the Salon des Artistes Indépendants, Salon d'Automne and Salon de Tuileries among others.

The artist's public decorative works include decorations at the Palais d'Eté in Algiers, l'Exposition des Arts Décoratifs in Paris in1925, and the Palais des Délégations Financières in Algeria. De Buzon received awards and medals including the Prix Maguelonne-Lefebvre-Glaize in 1910, the Médaille d'Or et Hors-Concours in 1922, and the Prix de Rosa Bonheur in 1923.

Known for his orientalist portrayals of North Africa, he also painted many genre scenes of life in France. He was a talented and prolific artist whose career spanned several decades.

He is represented in the collections of the Musée de Bordeaux, Pau, Bayonne, Tunis and Algiers. Buzon died on November, 26 1958 in Algeria.

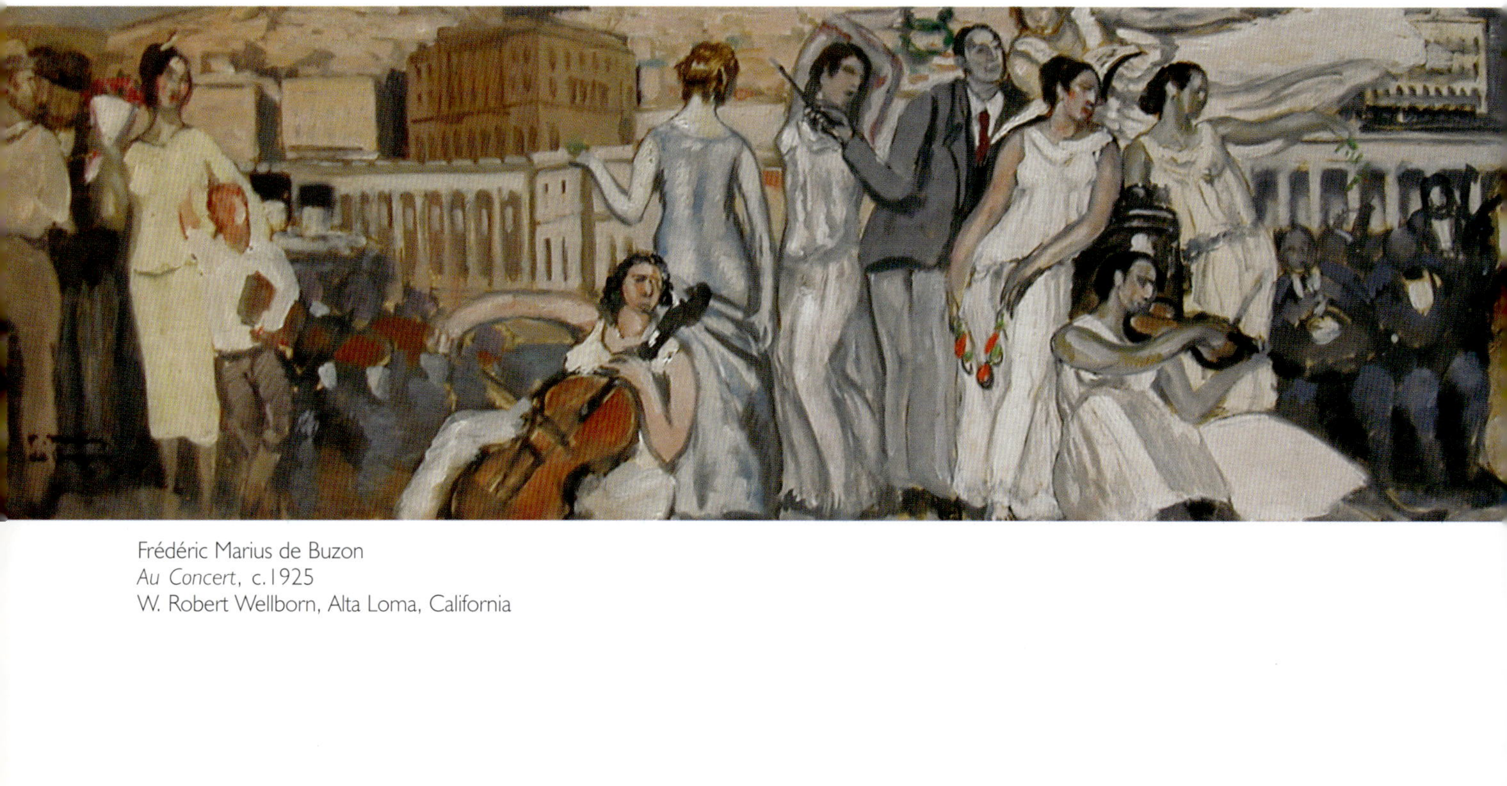

Frédéric Marius de Buzon
Au Concert, c.1925
W. Robert Wellborn, Alta Loma, California

Antoine Calbet

1860-1944

Antoine Calbet was born in Engayrec, Lot-et-Garonne August 16, 1860. He was a student of Alexandre Cabanel and began exhibiting in 1881. He was a member of the Salon des Artistes Français and in 1900 received both the Médaille d'Argent and the Chevalier de la Légion d'Honneur.

Calbet was well known as an illustrator and worked on such publications as *Aphrodite* and *Léda* by P.Louys, *L'Écran* by P. Bourget, *Lorely* by J. Lorrain.

Calbet's depictions of nymphs frolicking in the forests were popular themes in the age of the Symbolists. At the turn of the 20th century in Paris, in the galleries and salons his style and subjects were all the rage. These fantasy paintings blended perfectly with the Art Nouveau furniture and the object d'art collections of this unique and special time. Calbet died in Paris in 1944.

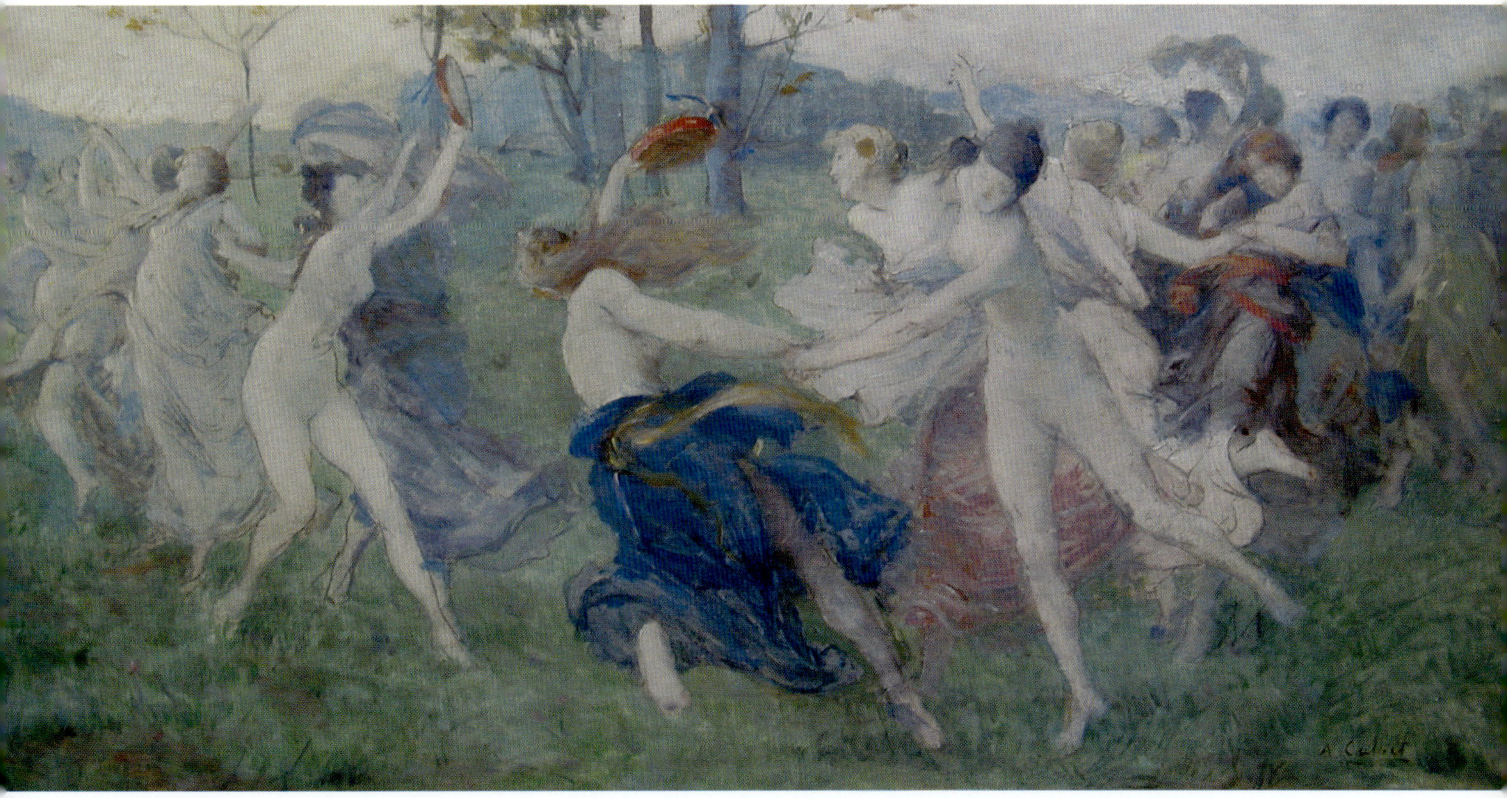

Antoine Calbet
La Danse Païenne, c.1910
Kathleen Avery Fine Art, Palo Alto, California

Gaspar Camps
20th century

Gaspar Camps was known best as a Spanish graphic artist. He was influenced greatly by Alphonse Mucha and for a time emulated his work. The artist eventually moved to Paris and began creating posters that reflected the styles of the Byzantine tradition. Camps worked primarily at the Sirven printing plant in Toulouse.

The Bibliothèque Nationale in Paris has a collection of 176 of his advertising images that he produced in Toulouse from 1915-1935.

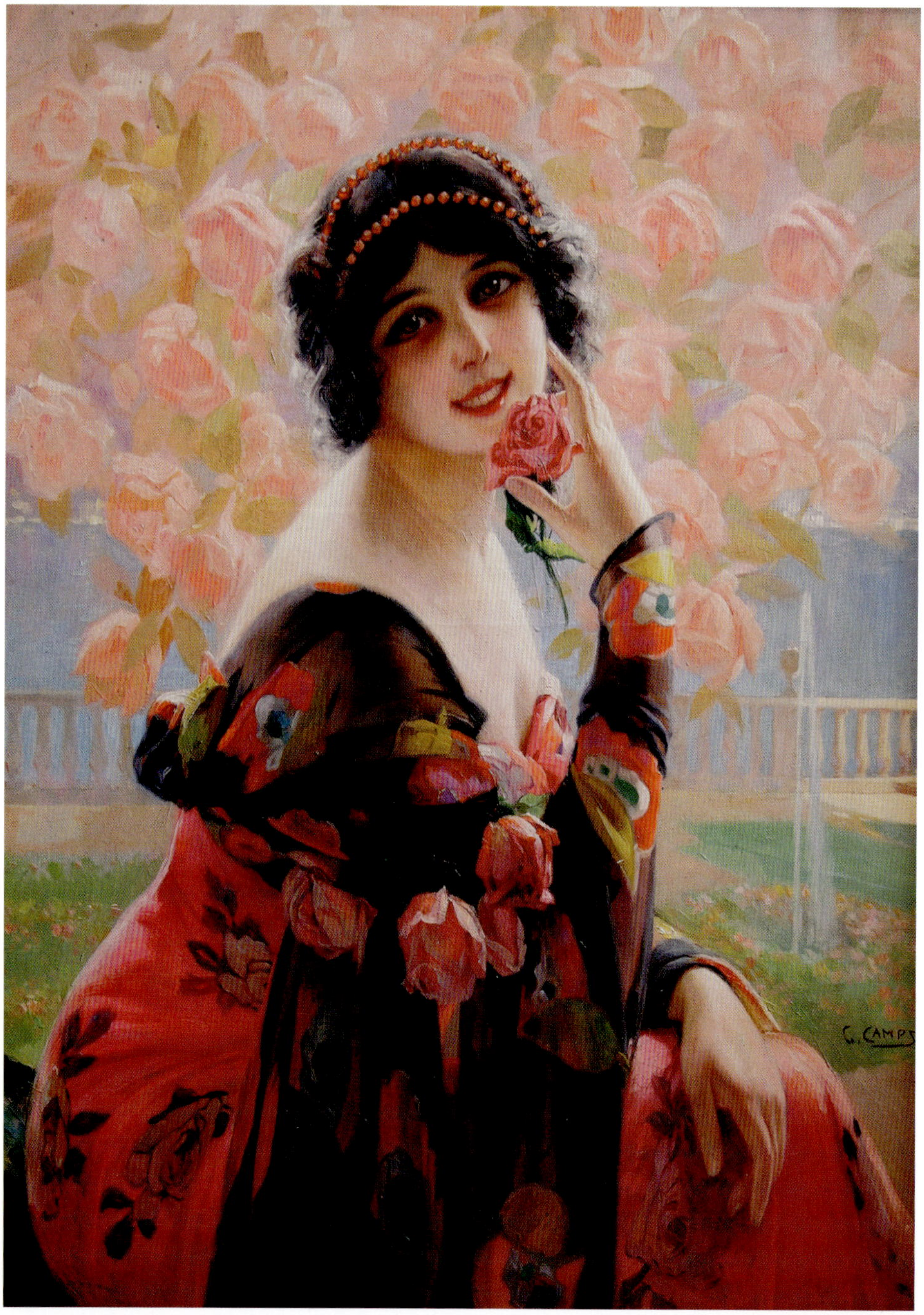

Gaspar Camps
Femme avec des Fleurs, c.1900
Julia Evershade and Mark Smith, Los Angeles, California

Ben Carré

1883-1978

Ben Carré was born in Paris in 1883. He had a long and successful career in fine art and film in both France and the United States.

His career started at the age of thirteen when he was hired to design and paint sets for the Paris Opera, Comédie Française and Convent Garden. He eventually gained the title of Art Director for Gaumont Studios where he became an innovator with the use of color in his sets.

In 1912 he joined Éclair Studios in New York and subsequently he moved to Hollywood to work for Samuel Goldwyn. Carré went on to work with such prominent studios as Warner Brothers, Metro and Fox and went on to become a founding member of the Academy of Motion Picture Arts and Sciences. He contributed to such films as *The Phantom of the Opera*, *The Jazz Singer*, *North by Northwest*, *Singing in the Rain* and *The Wizard of Oz*.

Carré's style closely resembles paintings of the English and French Symbolists. He was a masterful technician and created many formidable canvases.

In addition to his extremely active career in film Carré was associated with the Painters and Sculptors Club of Los Angeles. In 1978 the Telluride Film Festival was dedicated to the artist who is now credited as being the first motion picture Art Director.

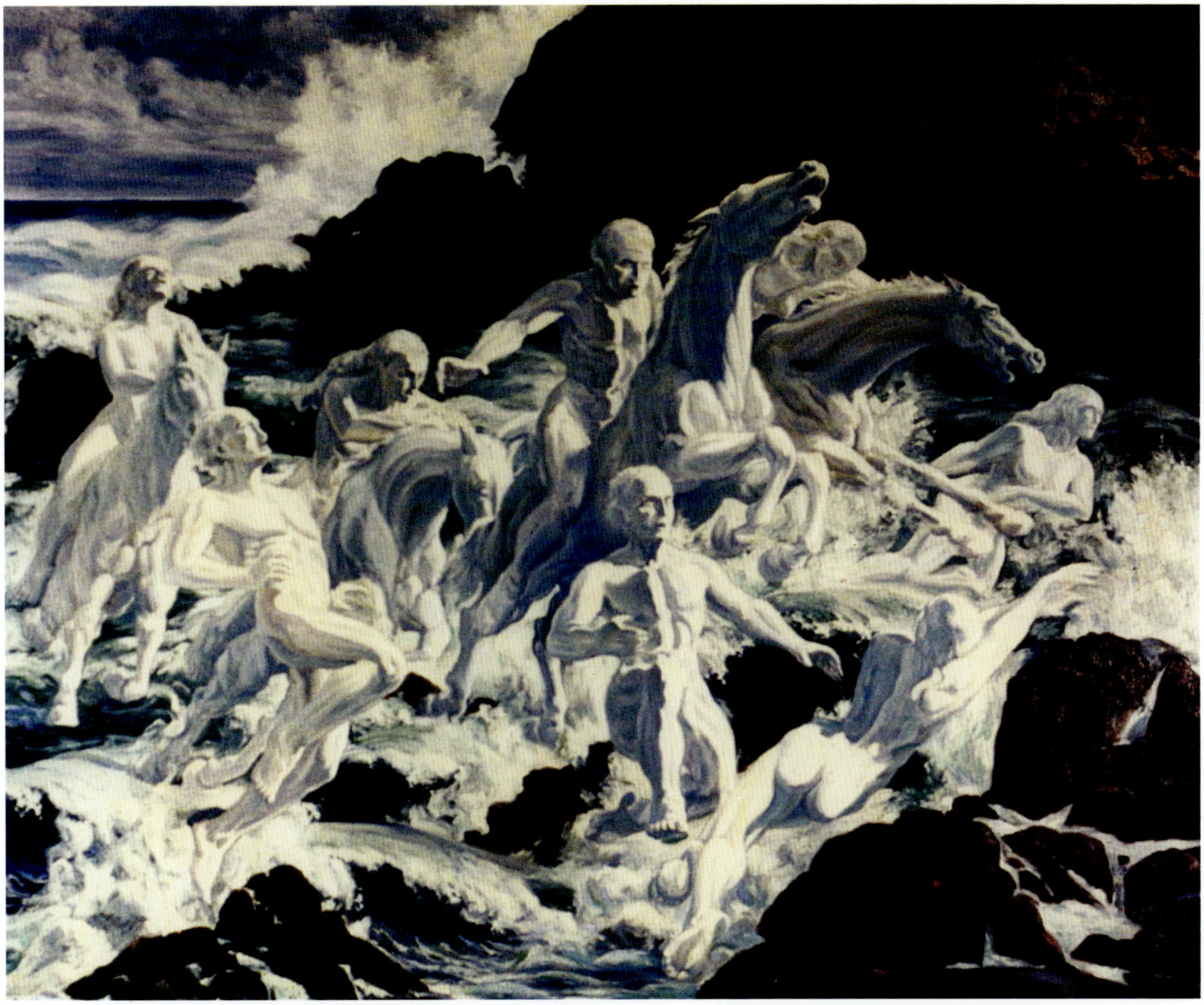

Ben Carré
Rushing Tide, c.1930
Mr. and Mrs. Mark H.L. Morris, Los Angeles, California
Photo courtesy of Adamson-Duvannes Gallery, Los Angeles, California

Boris Chaliapin

1904-1979

Boris Chaliapin was born to legendary opera singer Feodor Chaliapin in Moscow in 1904. Forced to find artistic freedom in the West, Chaliapin relocated to Paris in the mid-1920s. He received some training while in Paris and had his first exhibition in London at the Covent Garden Theater in 1927.

Chaliapin's taste was rooted in realism and the avant-garde atmosphere, though some of his earlier non-illustrative works express an influence of Surrealism that often accompanies hyperrealism.

Chaliapin's arrival in New York was met with almost instant success and he received a commission to paint a portrait of Nehru for *Time Magazine*. This was the beginning of a career with the magazine that lasted over 40 years, during which time he created approximately 400 covers.

One of Chaliapin's most famous portrait is that of Martin Luther King Jr. for a *Time* cover in 1957. This work now is in the National Portrait Gallery.

Chaliapin's work has been included in many exhibitions including the National Academy of Design 75 year retrospective of *Time Magazine* covers.

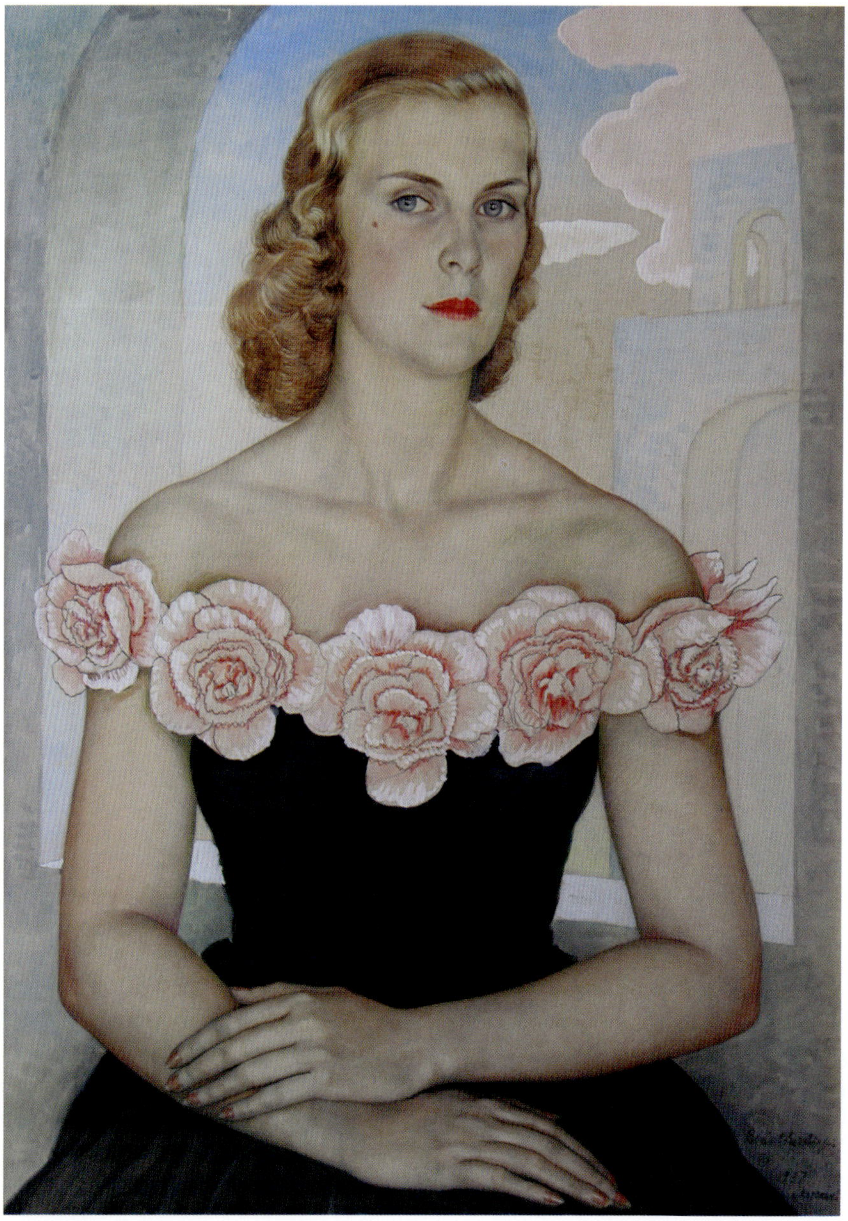

Boris Chaliapan
Portrait de Femme, Dated 1937
Kenton and Tessa Nelson, Pasadena, California

Émile François Chambon

1905-1993

Émile François Chambon was born in 1905 in Geneva, Switzerland. Between 1919 and 1921, Chambon studied at l'École des Beaux-Arts de Genève. Chambon lived for three years in Paris and then traveled throughout Europe from 1931 to 1939. During his travels, Chambon participated in numerous group exhibitions. He received solo exhibition in Geneva and other Swiss cities between 1929 and 1970, and in Paris in 1962.

Between 1951 and 1952 Chambon painted a fresco for the Collège Moderne. In 1956 he created a tapestry for the Palais de Justice and from 1963 to 1964 he created another for Hospice de Prieuré. Chambon's work is part of the permanent collections of museums in Aaran, Berne, Geneva, Lausanne and Thoune. He is best known as a painter and fresco artist. Chambon also created the under-paintings for tapestries.

Chambon is often compared to the artist Balthus because of the surreal quality of his paintings; however they do not venture far into the bizarre. Chambon's work has charm and a fine painterly quality; his compositions are left open to interpretation by the observer. Chambon died in 1993.

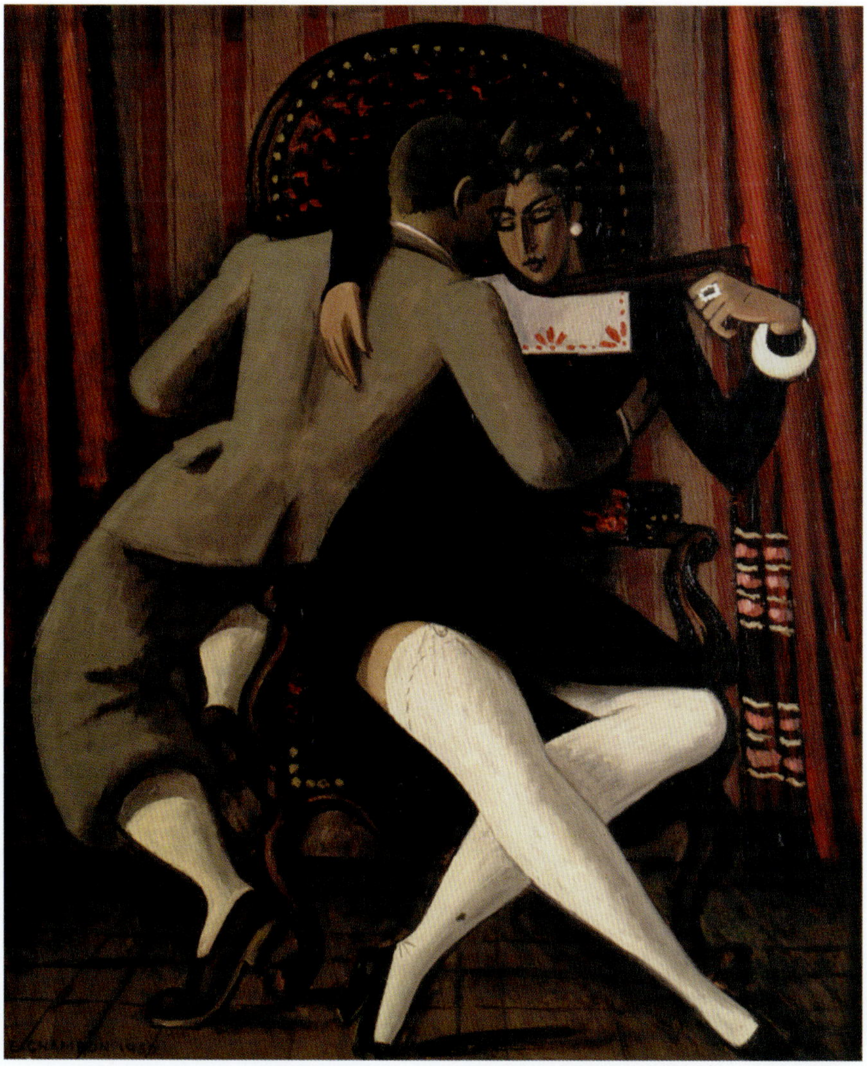

Émile François Chambon
Le Couple, Dated 1950
Primavera Gallery Inc. New York, New York

Émile François Chambon
Jeune Femme au Tricot Jaune, c.1950
Primavera Gallery Inc. New York, New York

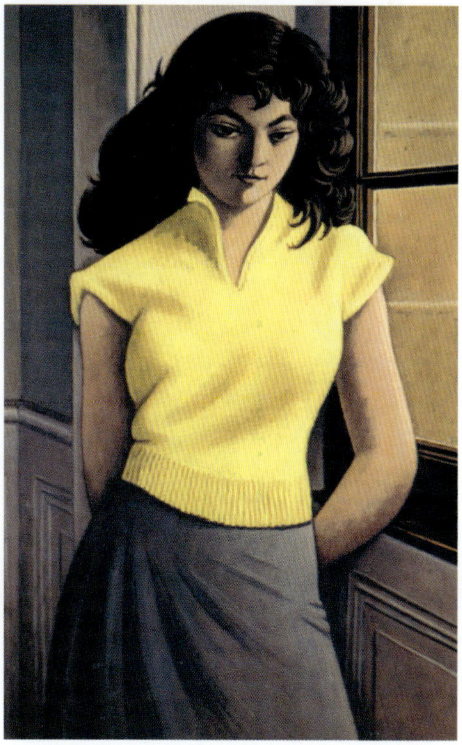

Jean Chapin

Born 1896

Jean Chapin was born on February 21, 1896 in Paris, France. He studied at l'École Boulle and also attended l'Académie de la Grande Chaumière in Paris.

Chapin's first paintings date to 1913, though his work was interrupted by World War I. Chapin exhibited in Paris between 1926 and 1955 when he retired. He exhibited at the Salon des Artistes Indépendants and became member in 1919. He also showed work at the Salon d'Automne, Salon de la Société Nationale des Beaux-Arts, Salon des Tuileries and Salon de la Marine.

Chapin's style leans towards Expressionism; he uses bold colors and composition to bring his subject to the attention of the viewer. His brush strokes give the paintings a very modern and rich texture. The date of the artist's death is not known.

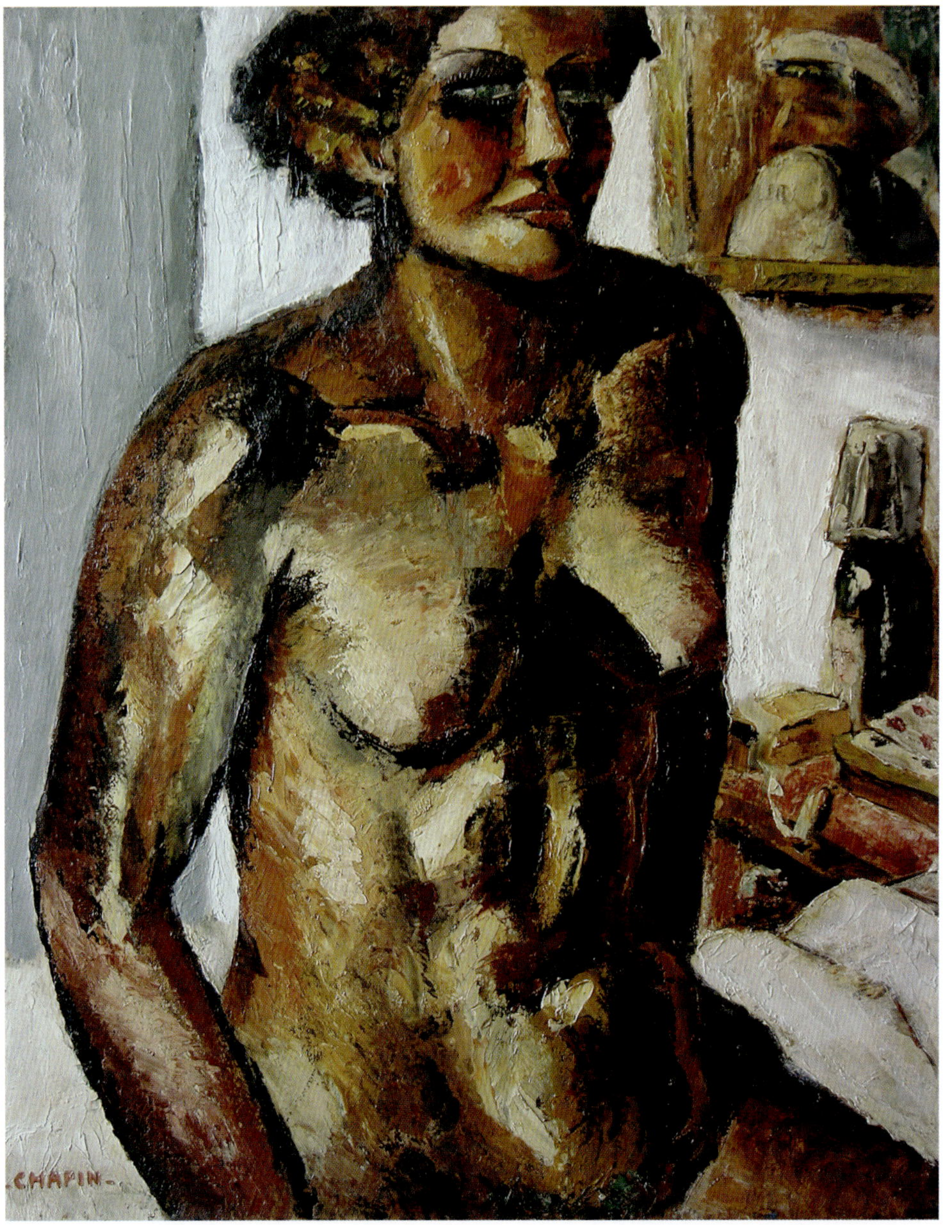

Jean Chapin
Partir du Marin, c.1930
Papillon Gallery, Los Angeles, California

Emilie Charmy
1877-1974

Emilie Charmy was a prolific painter in France during the early and mid 20th century, despite the marginalization of education and resources for women artists at the time. Along with Jacqueline Marval, Charmy was a formidable Postimpressionist and a bold and imaginative artist in the truest spirit of the avant-garde. It is hard to imagine that art historians and museums have cruelly ignored female artists of this caliber.

In the late 19th century enrollment was closed to women at l'École des Beaux-Arts so Charmy first received private lessons from artist Jacques Martin in Lyon. Martin encouraged her singing career as well, which warranted a performance opportunity in New Orleans; however her brother forbade it. In 1902 she moved to St. Cloud on the outskirts of Paris with her brother where he encouraged Charmy to continue painting. They eventually moved to Paris where Charmy settled into what would become her home and studio for the following seventy years.

In 1904 Charmy exhibited for the first time at the Salon des Indépendants and in 1905 at the Salon d'Automne, where the term "les fauves" was first used by critic Louis Vauxcelles to describe the bright boldness and freedom of Fauvism. Charmy's work at the time encompassed mostly still-lifes. She quickly gained recognition and acclaim among her peers including the reputable dealer Berthe Weill, who helped launch Charmy's career.

An admirer, Georges Bouché, was so struck by Charmy's work he insisted on meeting the artist; though he had been under the assumption she was a man due to her artistic mastery. The two became well acquainted, eventually married and had a son, Edmond. Charmy and Bouche lived independently from each other for quite sometime as she was extremely committed to and focused on her career.

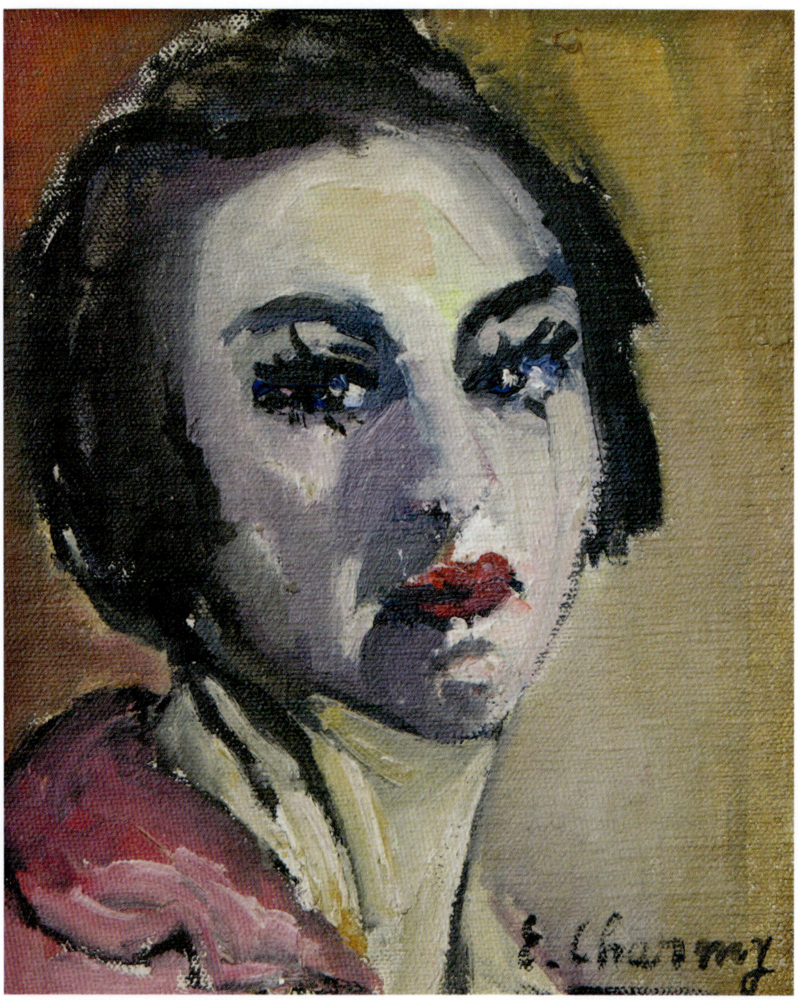

Emilie Charmy
Autoportrait, c.1930
Papillon Gallery, Los Angeles, California

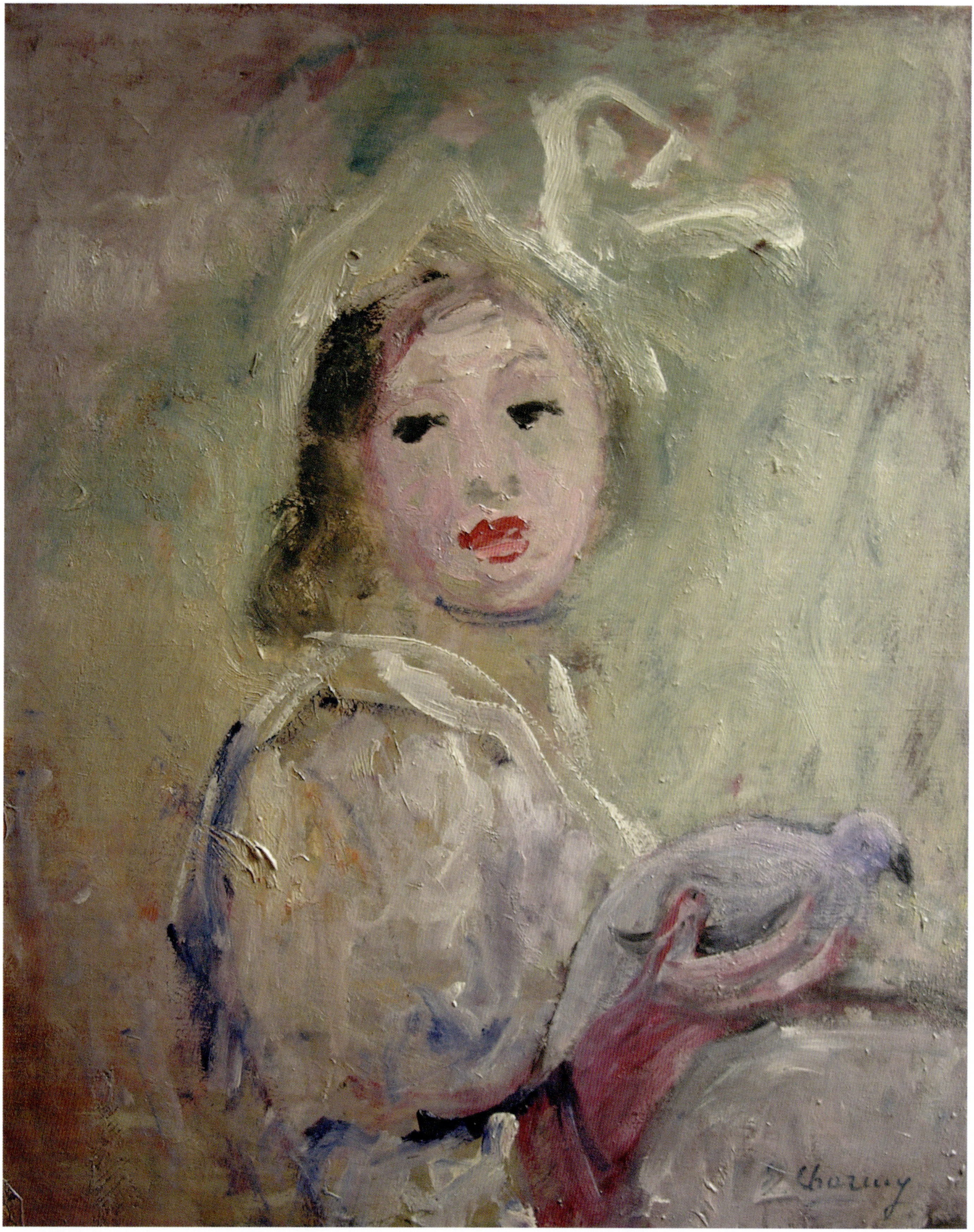

Emilie Charmy
Jeune Femme avec un Oiseau Bleu, c.1910
Ernie and Ronna Vigil, Aptos, California

Charmy's fame and exposure grew as she had several solo exhibitions and participated in a group show at the esteemed Galerie d'Oeuvres d'Art as well as the 1913 Armory Show. Charmy was made an official member of the Salon d'Automne in 1910. She attracted the attention of patron Compte Etienne de Jouvencel who arranged an exhibition for Charmy at the Galerie Styles alongside her male contemporaries Ingres, Delacroix, Corot, Manet, Renoir, Matisse, Cézanne, Derain, Rouault and Picasso.

The oeuvre in which Charmy worked ranged from still lifes, figures and nudes to political portraiture. Though most of the subject matter had been deemed 'feminine' her technique, stylization and aesthetic demand is highly masculine. She was acclaimed by critic Louis Vauxcelles in 1921 as 'one of the most remarkable women [artists] of our time.' She became identified with and established alongside Suzanne Valadon, Jacqueline Marval, Marie Blanchard, Marie Vassiliev and Sonia Delaunay.

Charmy is represented in the Musée d'Art Moderne in Paris, the Georges Pompidou Centre at Beaubourg, the Musée de l'Orangerie, the Tel-Aviv Museum and the Musée des Beaux-Arts in Lyon.

She painted well into her seventies and died in 1974 at the age of ninety-four. In 1980 her son, Edmond Bouché, wrote of her life and work for an exhibition by the Patrick Seale Gallery in London. In recent years, the Kunsthaus Bühler Gallery in Stuttgart, Germany has presented a large number of Charmy's paintings. Gill Perry speaks highly of Charmy's talent and status as well in *Women Artists and the Parisian Avant-Garde*.

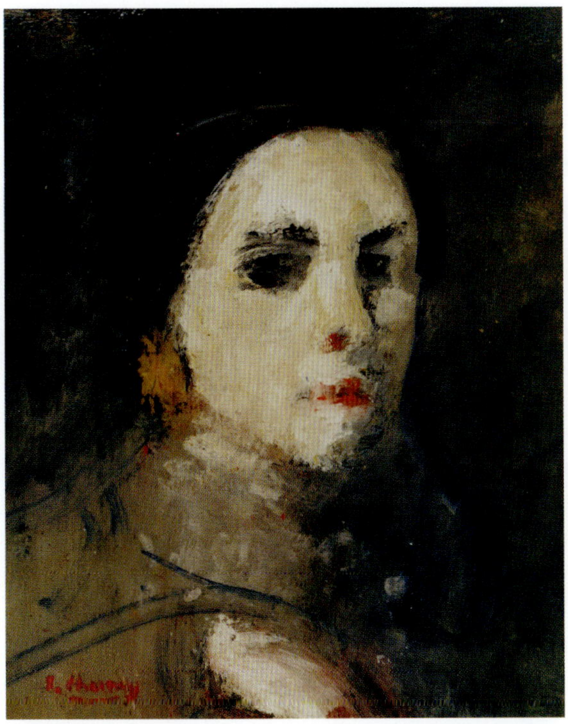

Emilie Charmy
Autoportrait, Dated 1940
Kunsthaus Bühler, Stuttgart, Germany

Emilie Charmy
Autoportrait, Dated 1942
Kunsthaus Bühler, Stuttgart, Germany

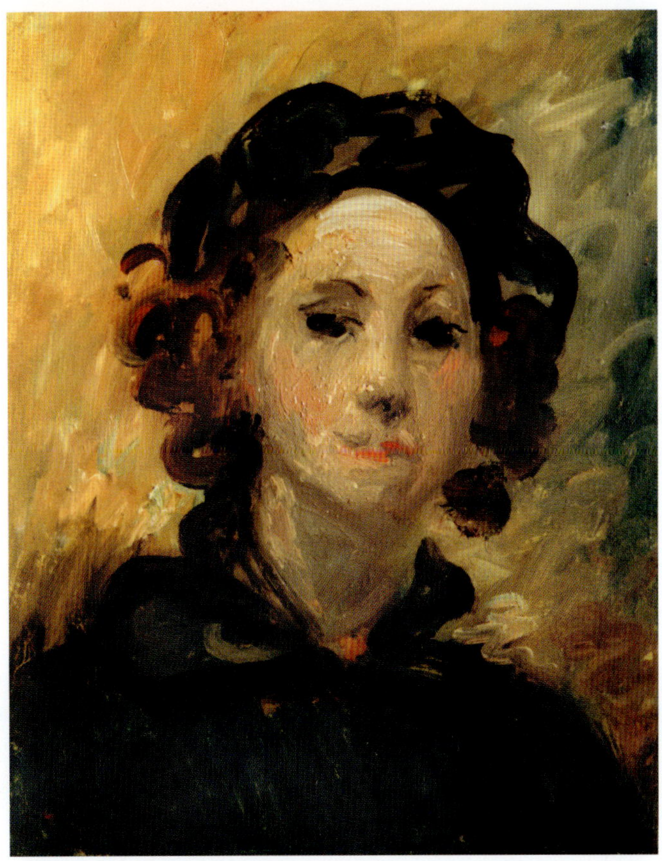

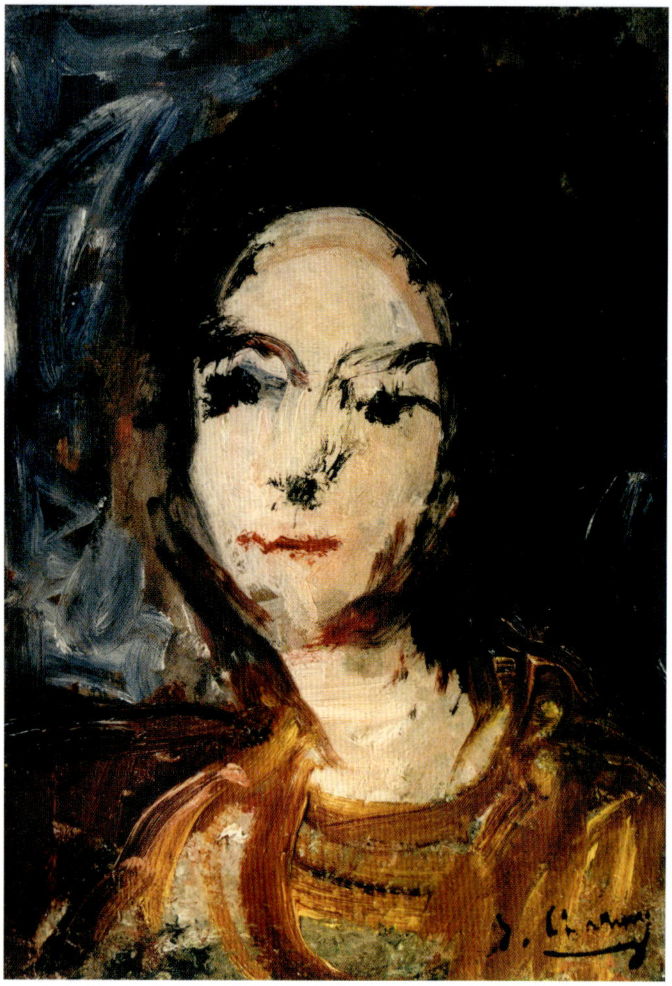

Emilie Charmy
Portrait d'une Femme, c. 1935
Kunsthaus Bühler, Stuttgart, Germany

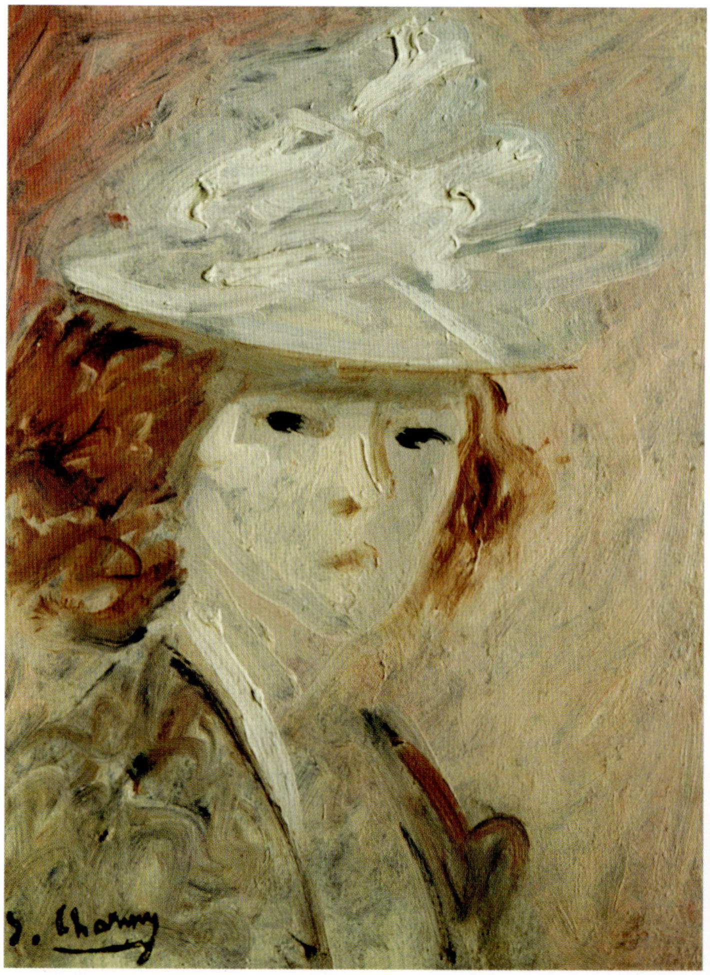

Emilie Charmy
Femme au Chapeau Blanche, c.1935
Kunsthaus Bühler, Stuttgart, Germany

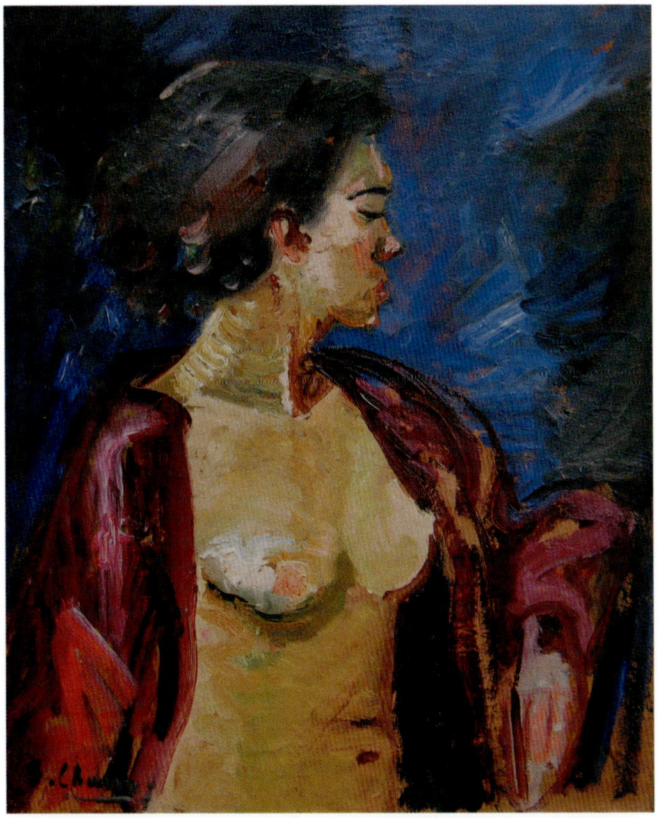

Emilic Charmy
Femme au Robe Rouge, c.1930
William A. and Sandra Royall, Richmond, Virginia

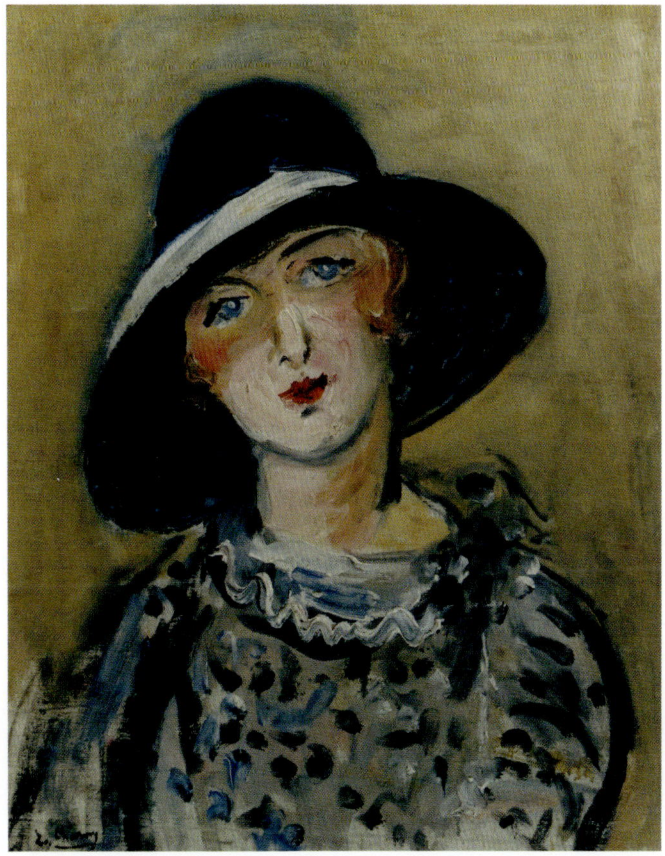

Emilie Charmy
Femme au Chapeau Bleu, c.1920
Kunsthaus Bühler, Stuttgart, Germany

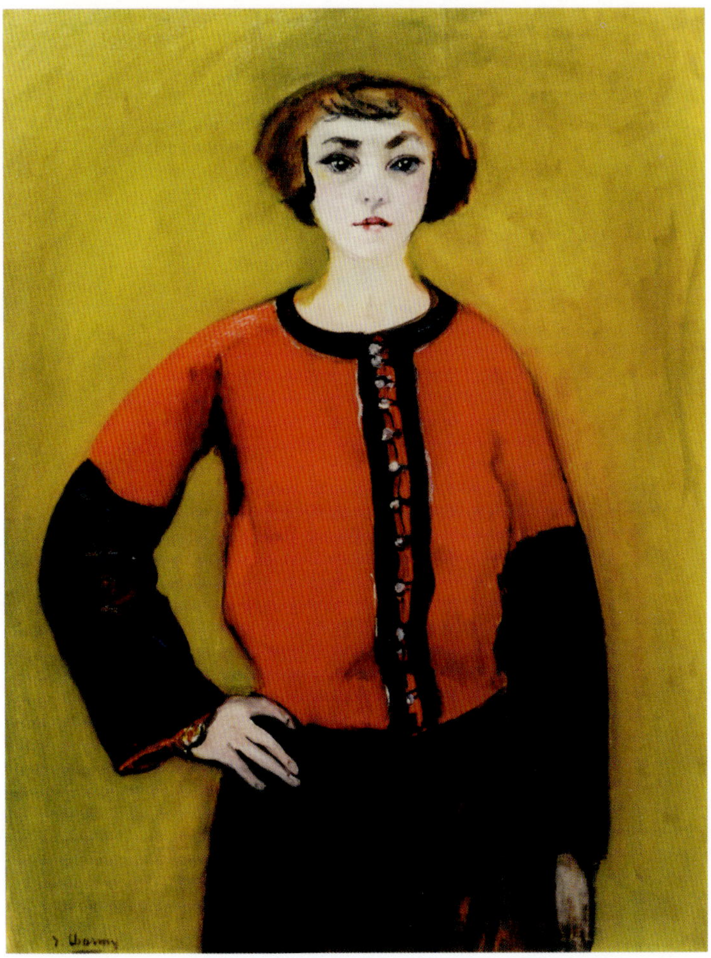

Emilie Charmy
Autoportrait, c.1921
Kunsthaus Bühler, Stuttgart, Germany

Roland Chavenon

Born 1895

Roland Chavenon was born in Paris and exhibited widely during the early part of the century among the ranks of Paul Cézanne. His credits include exhibits with Salon d'Automne from 1919, Salon des Indépendants until 1929 and the Salon des Tuileries. In 1922 Paul Sentenac wrote of Chavenon's life and work in *L'Art d'Aujourd'hui*.

Chavenon's early work was in the style of the Postimpressionists; he painted still lifes, portraits and landscapes. Later he incorporated the discipline of the Cubists and created colorful and highly decorative paintings. The Grenoble and Nantes museums have collected his work.

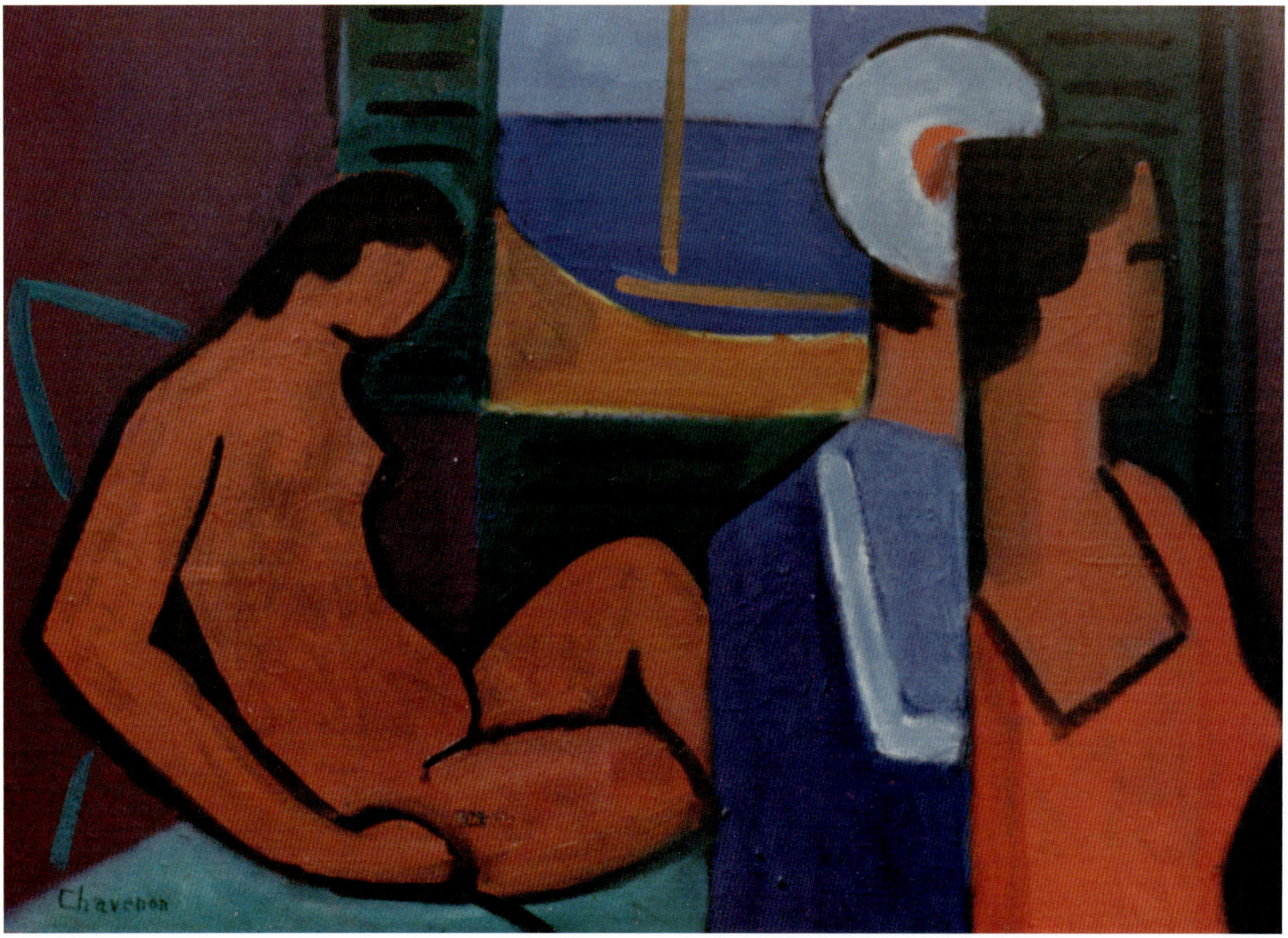

Roland Chavenon
Deux Femmes et le Marin, c.1930
Private Collection

Michael Gabriel Chepourkoff

1899-1955

Michael Gabriel Chepourkoff was born in Lugansk, Russia, in 1899. He studied at the Imperial Academy in St. Petersburg before moving to California in 1923. He attended the University of California at Berkley where he earned a masters degree. Chepourkoff was a student of George Luks.

The artist worked primarily as a sculptor in metal, but also did etchings and was an accomplished painter. He received the Wheeler Memorial Medal Design award in 1929.

Chepourkoff lived and exhibited in the San Francisco area for many years. He exhibited with the San Francisco Art Association in the late 1930s and received several awards. His works were exhibited at the Golden Gate International Exposition in 1939-1940 and the Dorian Gallery in 1940. He also participated in exhibitions at the San Francisco Museum of Art.

Though it is not known if Chepourkoff lived or worked in Paris, he was highly influenced by Parisian modernists. With his use of rich colors and qualities of the Futurists and the Cubists he created strong and decorative works.He is represented in the San Francisco Museum of Art.

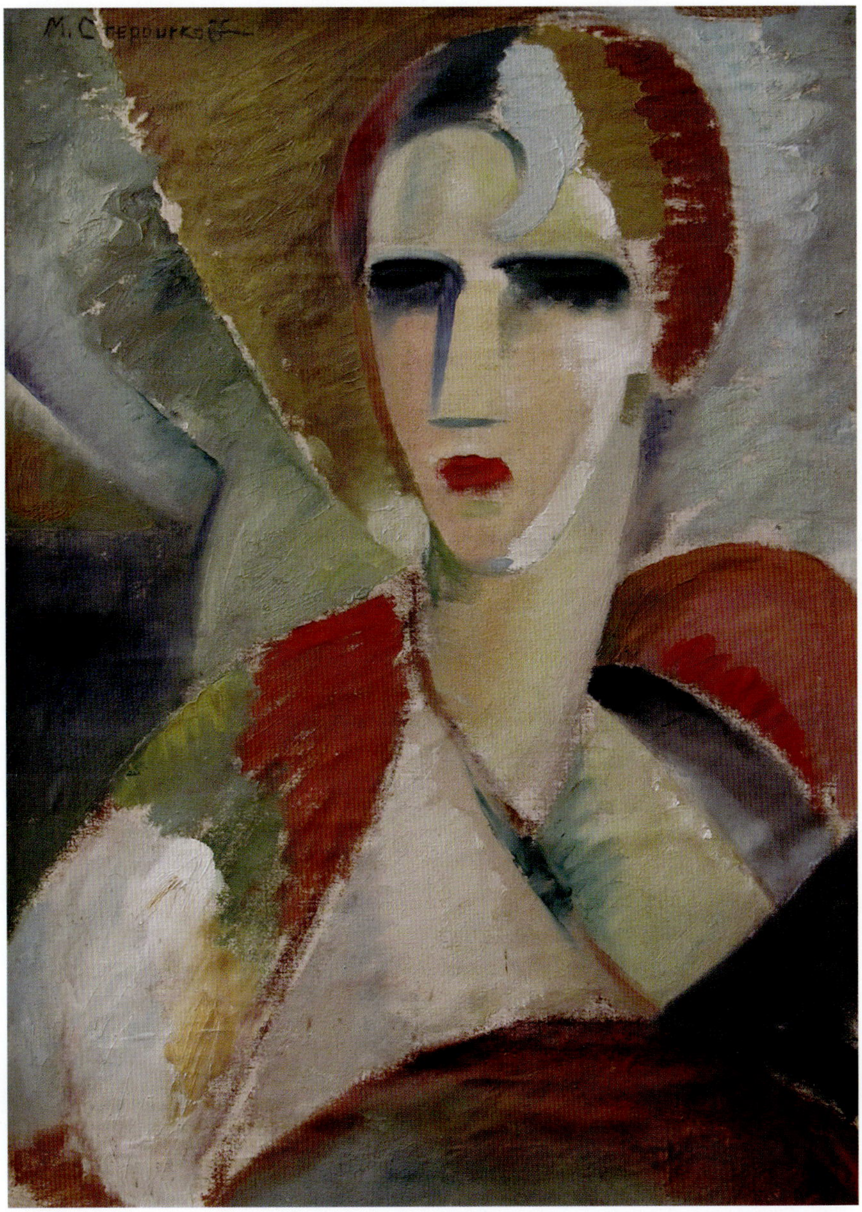

Michael Gabriel Chepourkoff
Femme Cubiste, c. 1930
Private Collection

Édouard Chimot

1890-1959

Édouard Chimot was born in 1890 in Lille, France. Chimot was a painter and watercolorist and also worked in pastel. Chimot's subjects were always sensual women, often quite erotic including many lesbian images.

He studied at l'École des Beaux-Arts de Roubaix and de Tourcoing and l'École des Arts Décoratifs in Nice. Chimot was most successful as an illustrator. He illustrated many literary works including *l'Enfer* by H. Barbusse and *Le Spleen de Paris* by Baudelaire.

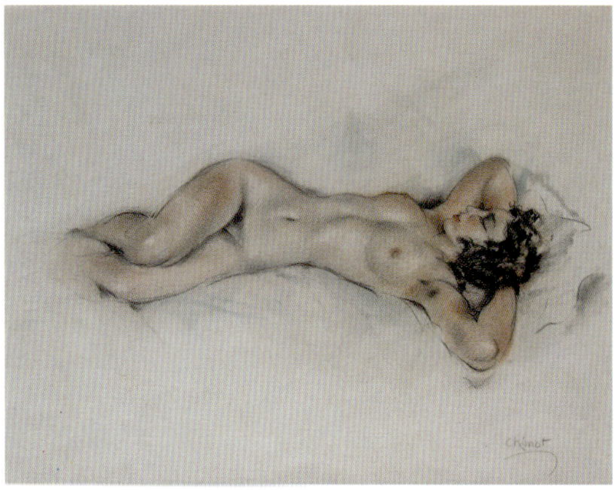

Edouard Chimot
Nu Allongé, c.1924
Seligman Family Collection,
Los Angeles, California

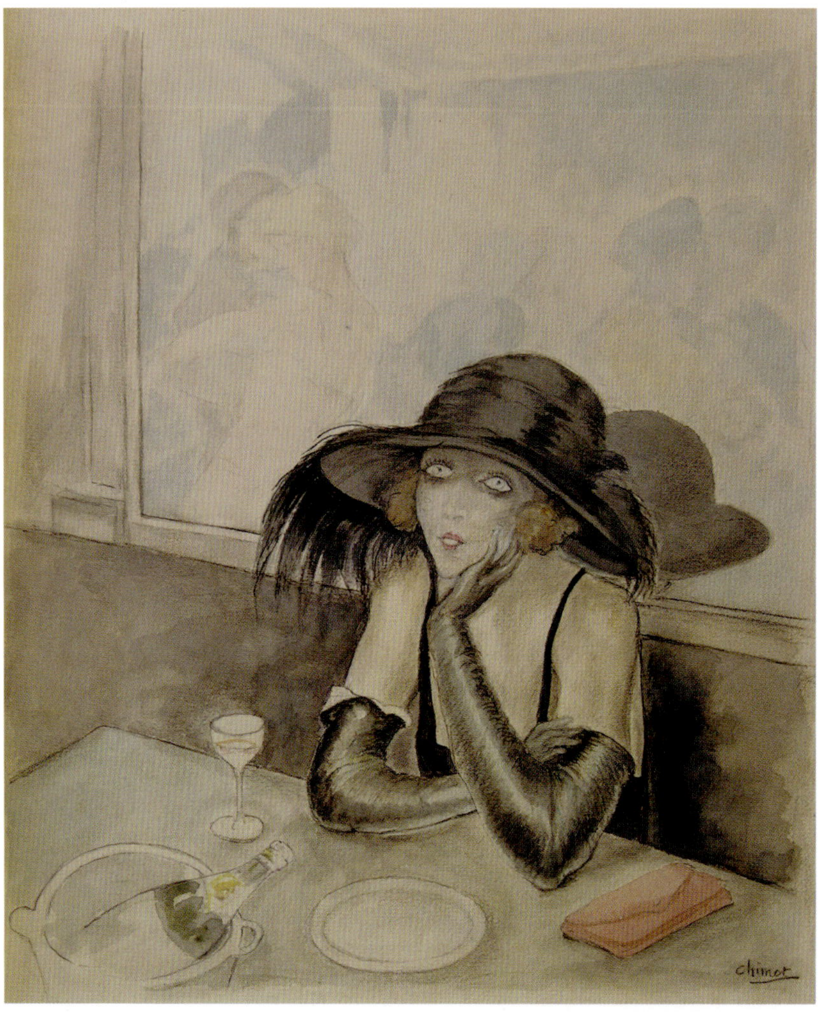

Edouard Chimot
Au Bar, c.1925
Private Collection

Lev Chistovsky
1902-1969

Lev Chistovsky is presumed to be of Russian descent. His name is sometimes written Tchistovsky in Western documentation, which is a common variation in transliteration.

The artist lived in Paris in the 1930s and was certainly classically trained; the quality of his work suggests a strong Beaux-Arts influence. He was very prolific and produced a significant number of watercolors and is known to have completed at least one large format oil painting.

His watercolors are of such rare excellence that they are immediately recognizable. Many are masterfully composed paintings of luscious nudes in decadent interiors. They are executed with great skill and capture a quality of realism that is extremely rare and difficult to achieve using watercolor as a medium; his oils display the same proficiency.

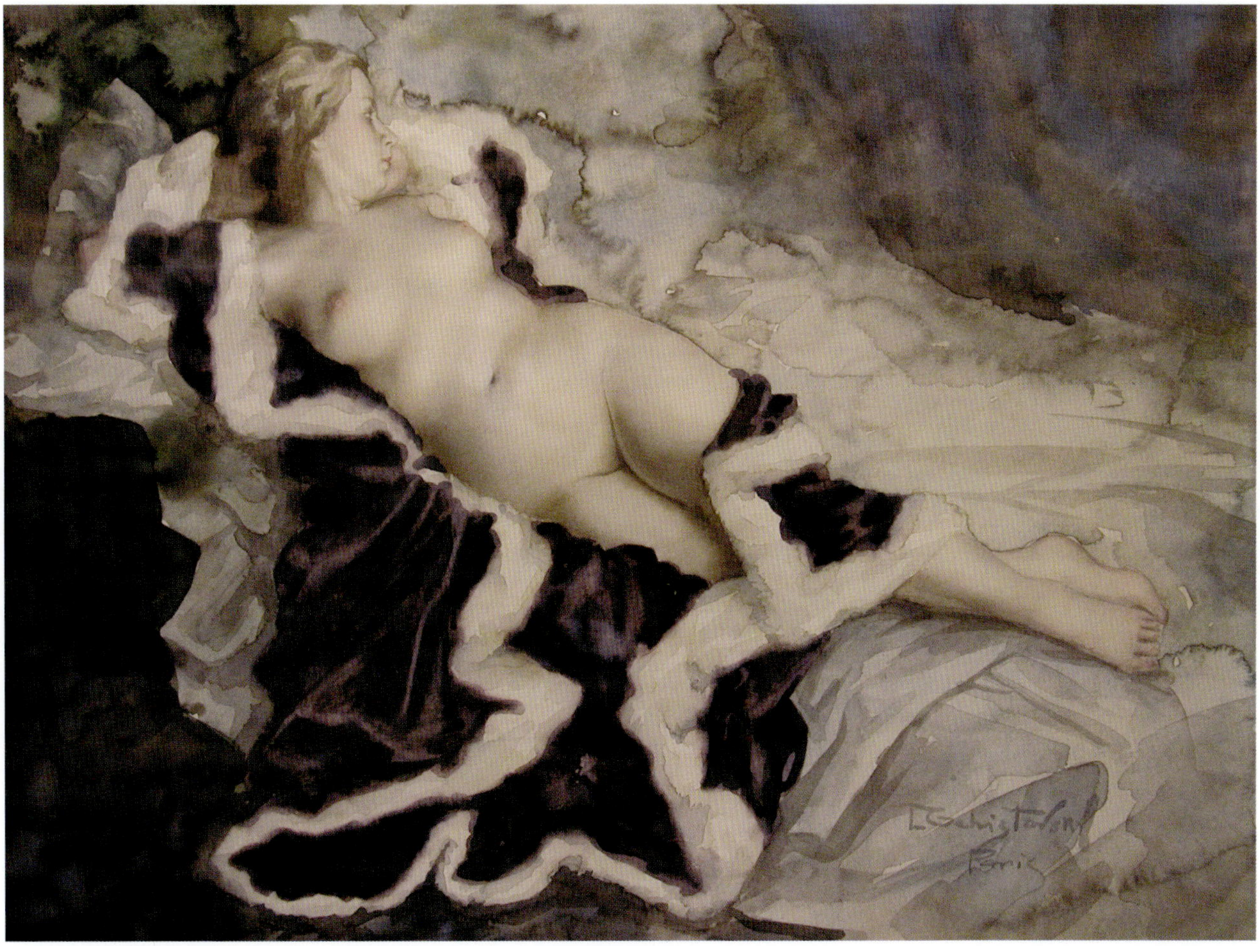

Lev Chistovsky
Repose, c.1935
Berensen Art Consultants, Montreal, Canada

Chistovsky's works are frequently dated and inscribed "Paris," and his address in Paris has also been found on the verso of some works. There is no reference to him in any biographical dictionaries and it is therefore unlikely he exhibited in salons or galleries. One may speculate that he sold his works directly to collectors possibly at street fairs or in the plaza in Montmartre. He may have also received commissions to paint works for specific clients. He produced at least one etching for L'Estampe Moderne, one of the most prestigious publishers of fine prints in Paris.

Chistovsky's work has come to the particular attention of collectors of 20th century Russian art. In large part because of the significant economic and political changes in Eastern Europe and Russia, auction houses mounting specialty sales have recently been quite successful in marketing works by heretofore unknown artists like Lev Chistovsky.

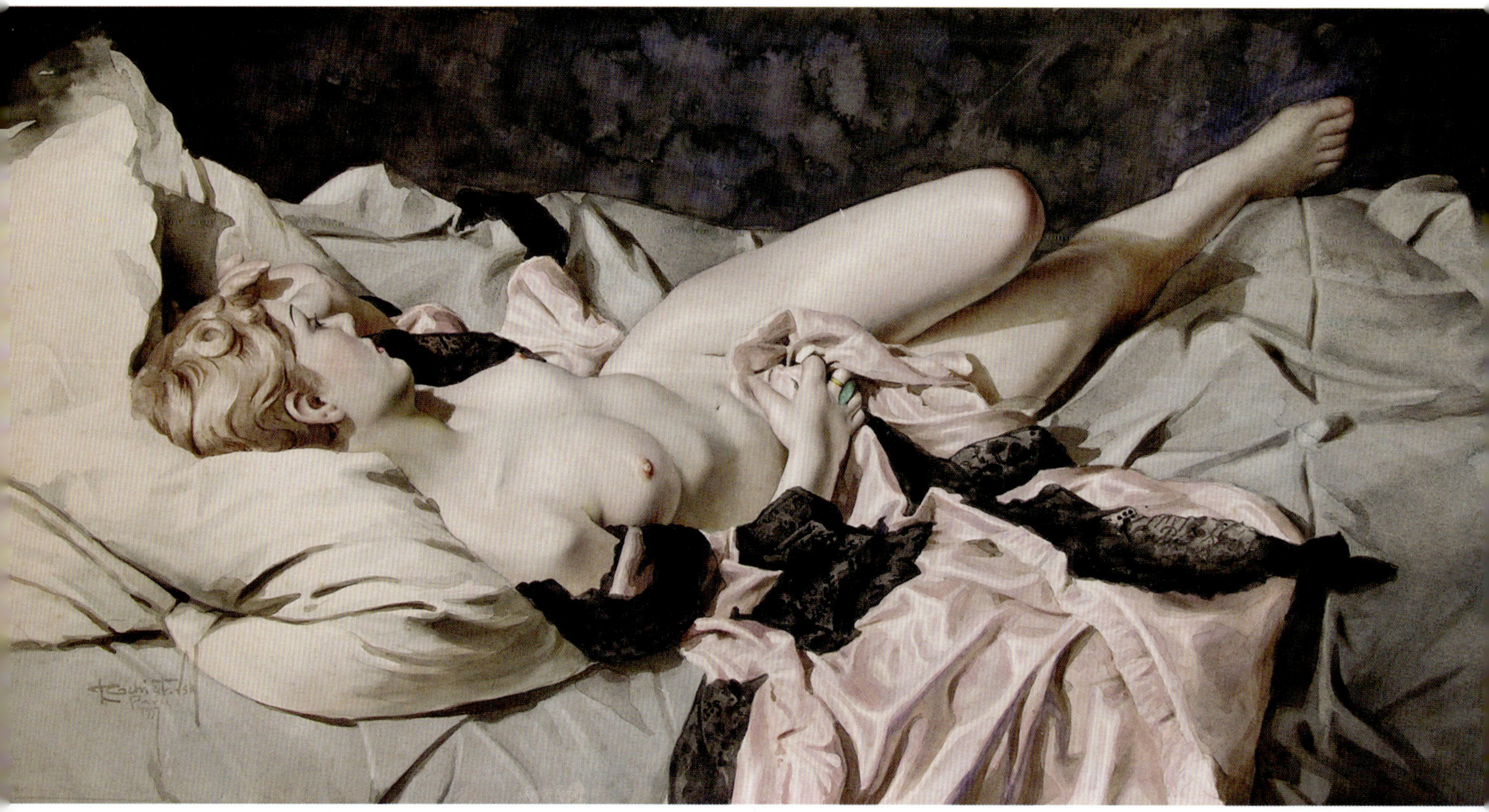

Lev Chistovsky
Nu Allongé, Dated 1937
Jeffrey Winter Fine Arts, Long Beach, California

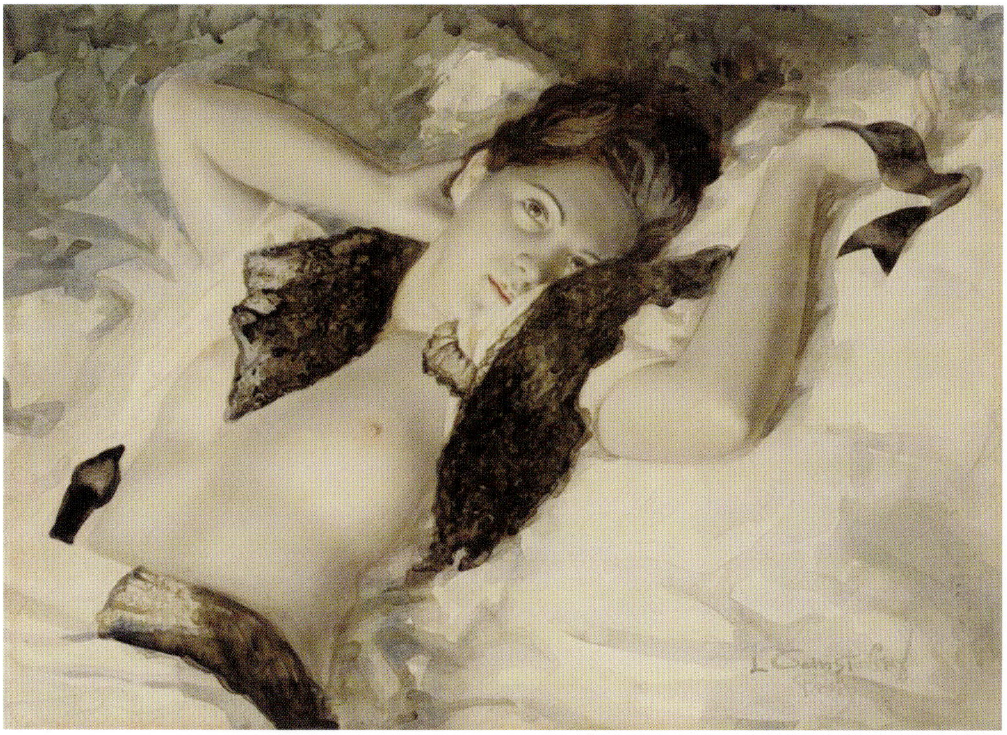

Lev Chistovsky
Nu avec l'Écharpe Noir, c. 1935
Private Collection

Lev Chistovsky
Nu avec l'Éventail, Dated 1937
Private Collection

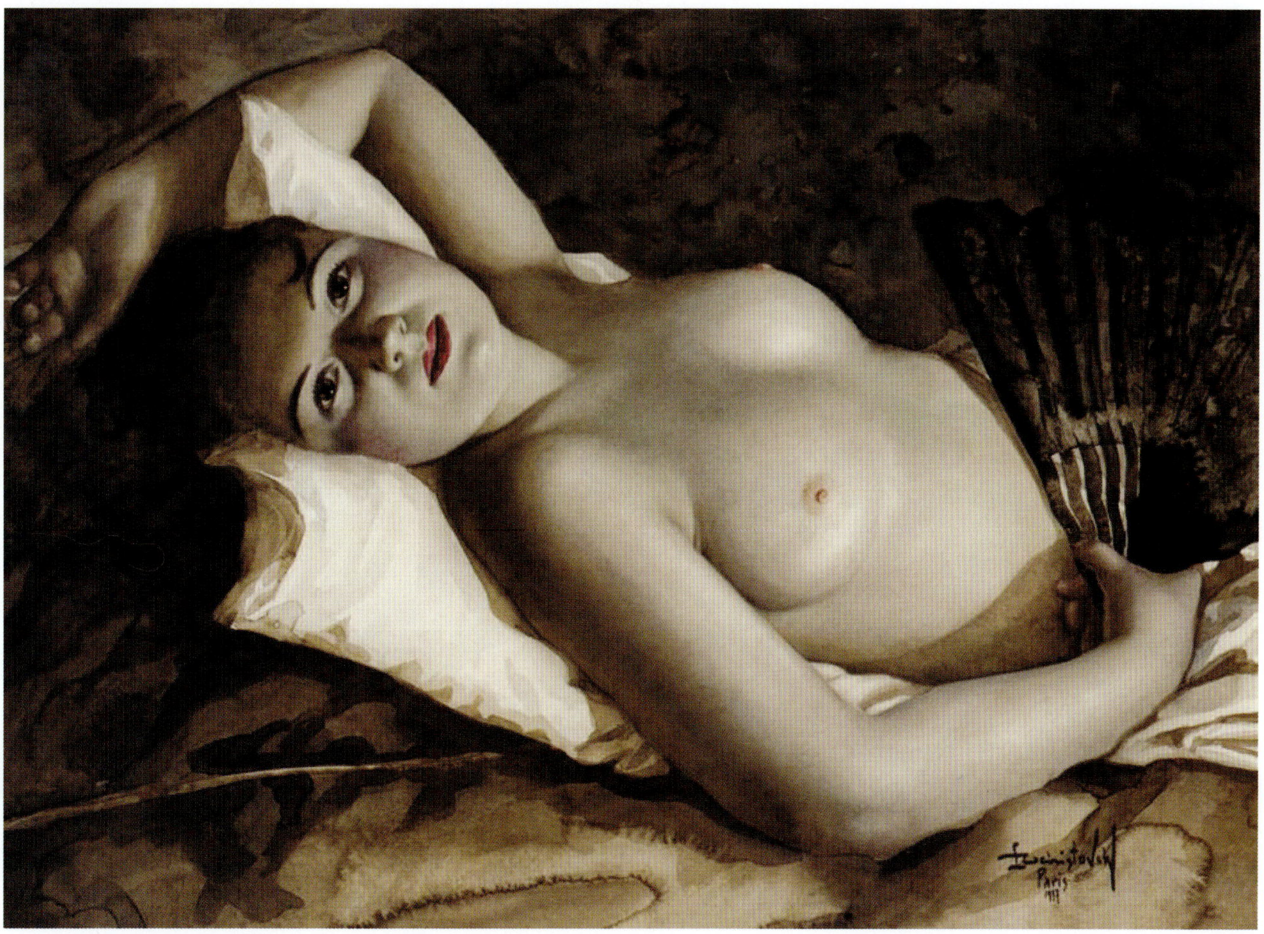

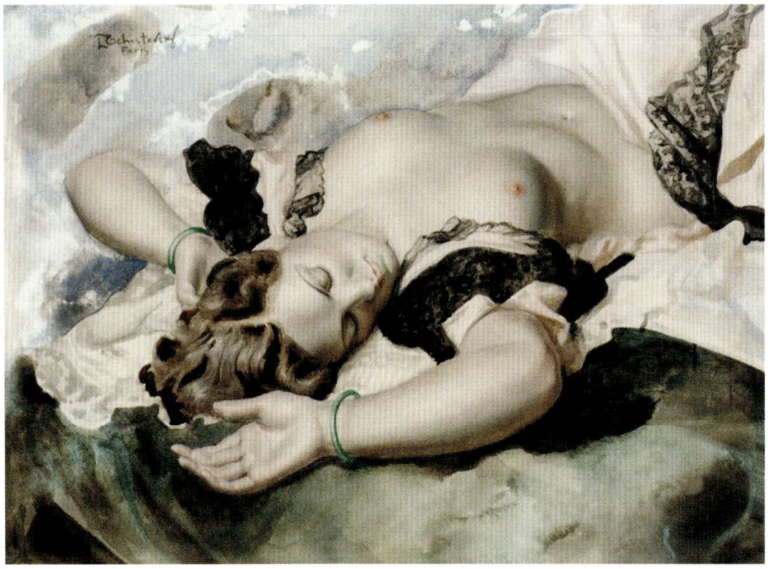

Lev Chistovsky
Nu avec le Bracelet de Jade, c. 1935
Private Collection

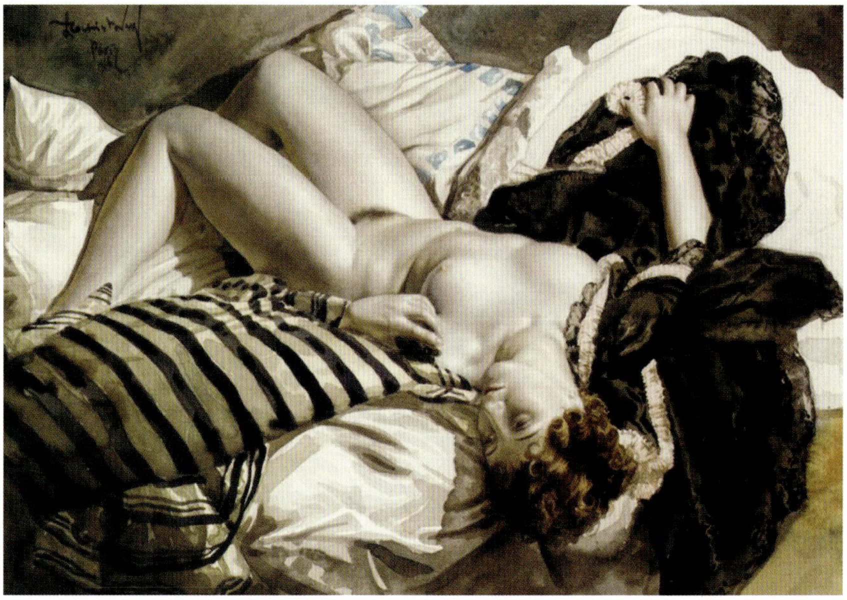

Lev Chistovsky
Nu Allongé, Dated 1934
Private Collection

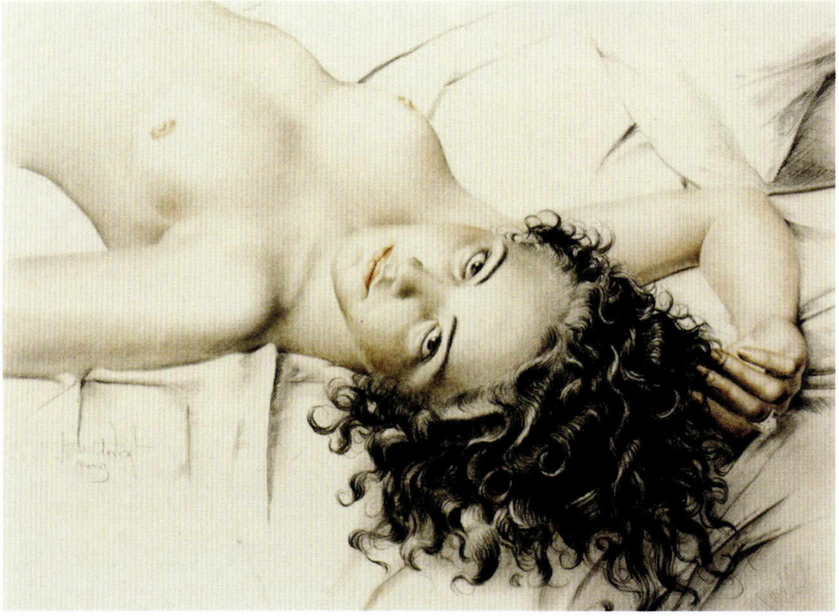

Lev Chistovsky
Nu Allongé, c. 1935
Private Collection

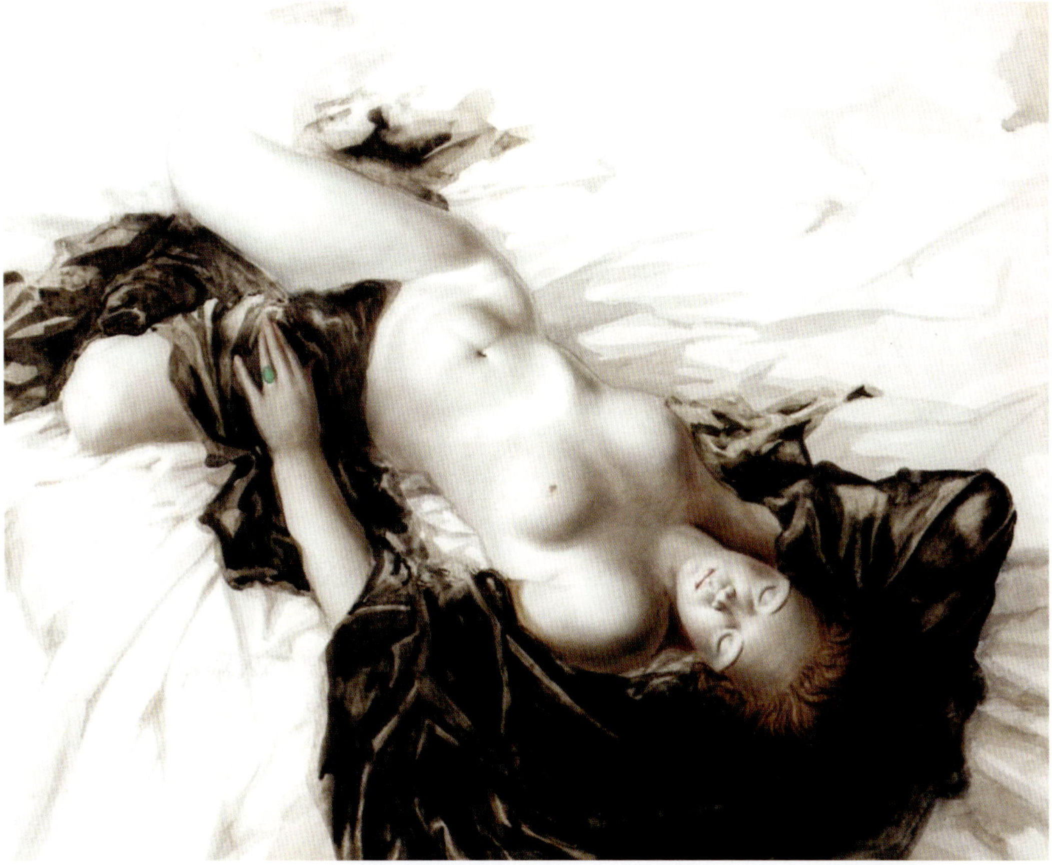

Lev Chistovsky
La Réveureuse, c. 1935
Private Collection

Lev Chistovsky
Coquette, c. 1935
Private Collection

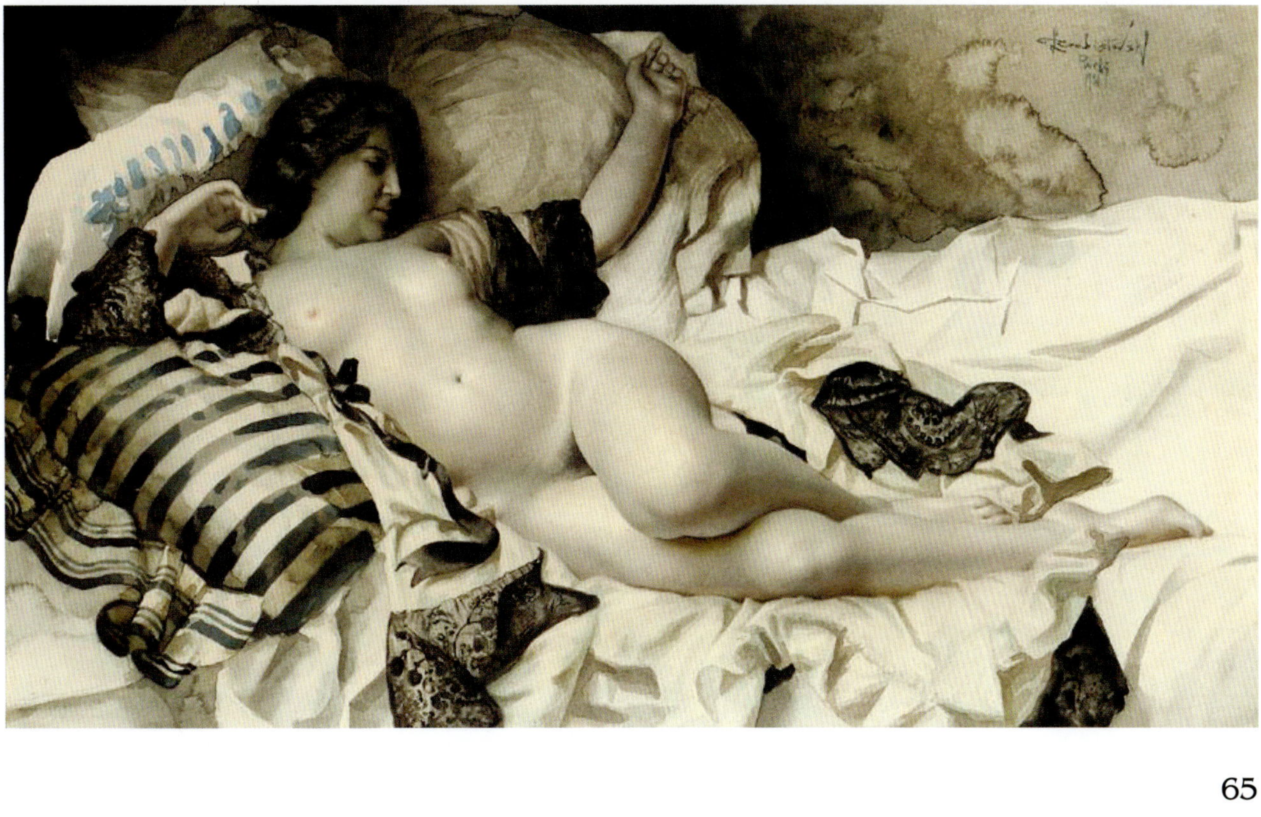

Edythe Varian Cockcroft

1881-1962

Edythe Varian Cockcroft (also known as Edythe Varian Wyland) was born in Brooklyn, New York in 1881. She was a painter, designer and craftsperson who worked in Paris, Brittany and Haiti. Stylistically her work is associated with Postimpressionism and it is rumored she was friends with Renoir and Gauguin.

Cockcroft exhibited at the Salon de la Société Nationale des Beaux-Arts in 1911 and the Salon d'Automne in 1910 and 1911. She was a member of the National Association of Women Painters and Sculptors, where she received an award in 1916. She also won awards from the International Art Union in Paris and the Wolfe Art Club in New York City.

Cockcroft was very expressionistic, using deep and opulent colors and fine composition. She was a fairly prolific artist and painted a wide variety of subjects. Cockcroft died in New York in 1962.

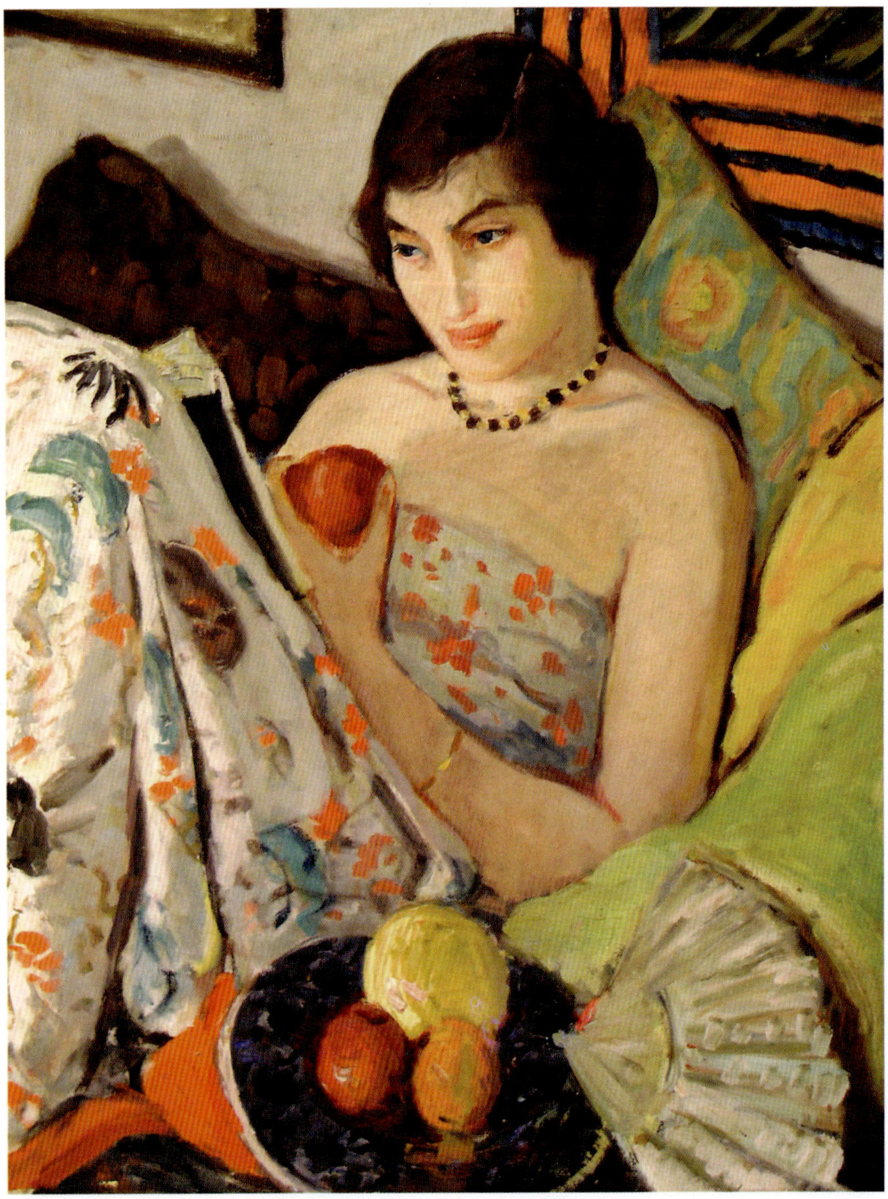

Edythe Varian Cockcroft
Femme avec un Livre, c. 1915
Bob Thompson and Marilyn Vantosh, Parkton, Maryland

Émile François Jacques Compard
1900-1977

Émile François Jacques Compard was born on October 13, 1900, in Paris. He was encouraged from an early age by the collector Richard Goetz, who later introduced him to Félix Fénéon. Fénéon owned the Galerie Bernheim-Jeune where Pierre Bonnard was also represented. Compard studied at l'Académie Julian from 1916 to 1920 and at the Araujo atelier from 1920 to 1922. In 1961 Compard created a series of humorous drawings about his time spent at l'Académie Julian.

In 1922 Compard married Simone Dangla and had a son, François. He later divorced and remarried Anna Sophie Johanesson with whom he had two children, Anne-Marie and Eric.

During his time spent in Faouët and the Port Doëlan, he came to know and befriend many artists working at the time, including Pierre Bonnard and Pierre Tal Coat, both of whom had a great impact on Compard's work. Compard also frequented the restaurant Chez Mélanie and created a series of portraits of the owner, her husband, and their famous patrons.

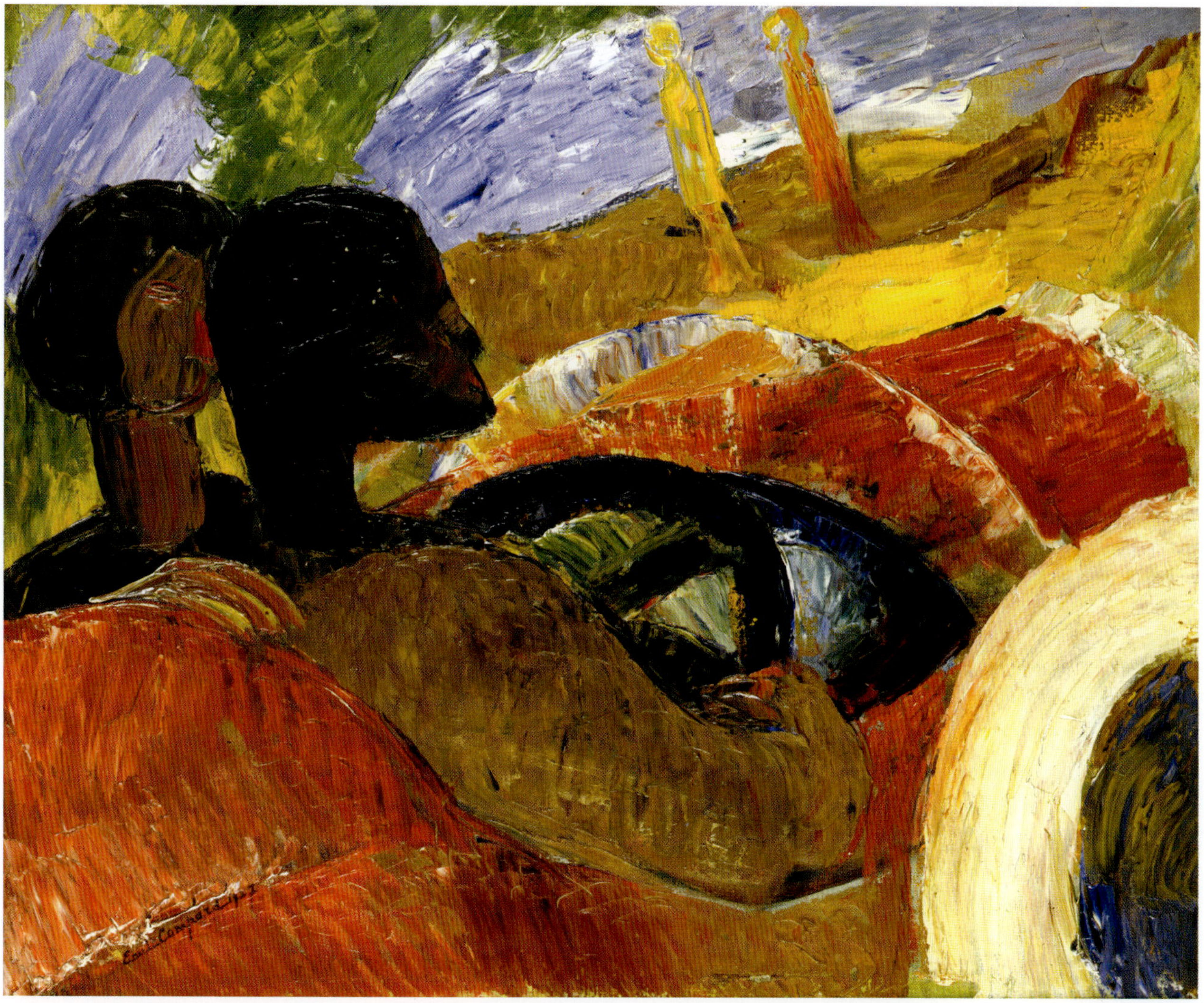

Émile François Jacques Compard
Couple dans la Voiture, Dated 1927
Galerie 1900-2000, Paris, France

Compard exhibited frequently at the Salon de la Société Nationale des Beaux-Arts, Salon des Indépendants, Salon des Tuileries and the Salon d'Automne, of which he was a member. Other exhibitions include the Salon de la Jeune Peinture Contemporaine; Galerie d'Art du Montparnasse; Galerie A. Fabre; Galerie Renaissance; and in 1937 l'Exposition Universelle. Compard's work was exhibited in New York, Berlin, Munich, Dusseldorf and Stockholm.

Having worked under cubist influence and encouraged by Félix Fénéon and Pierre Bonnard, Compard came to experiment with non-figurative content. Compard was also greatly influenced by Taoist teachings and turned to the metaphysical in his work.

A collection of his work has been exhibited in a retrospective, *Émile Compard 1900-1977* at the Musée du Faouët in Morbihan, in the south of Brittany. Compard died in 1977.

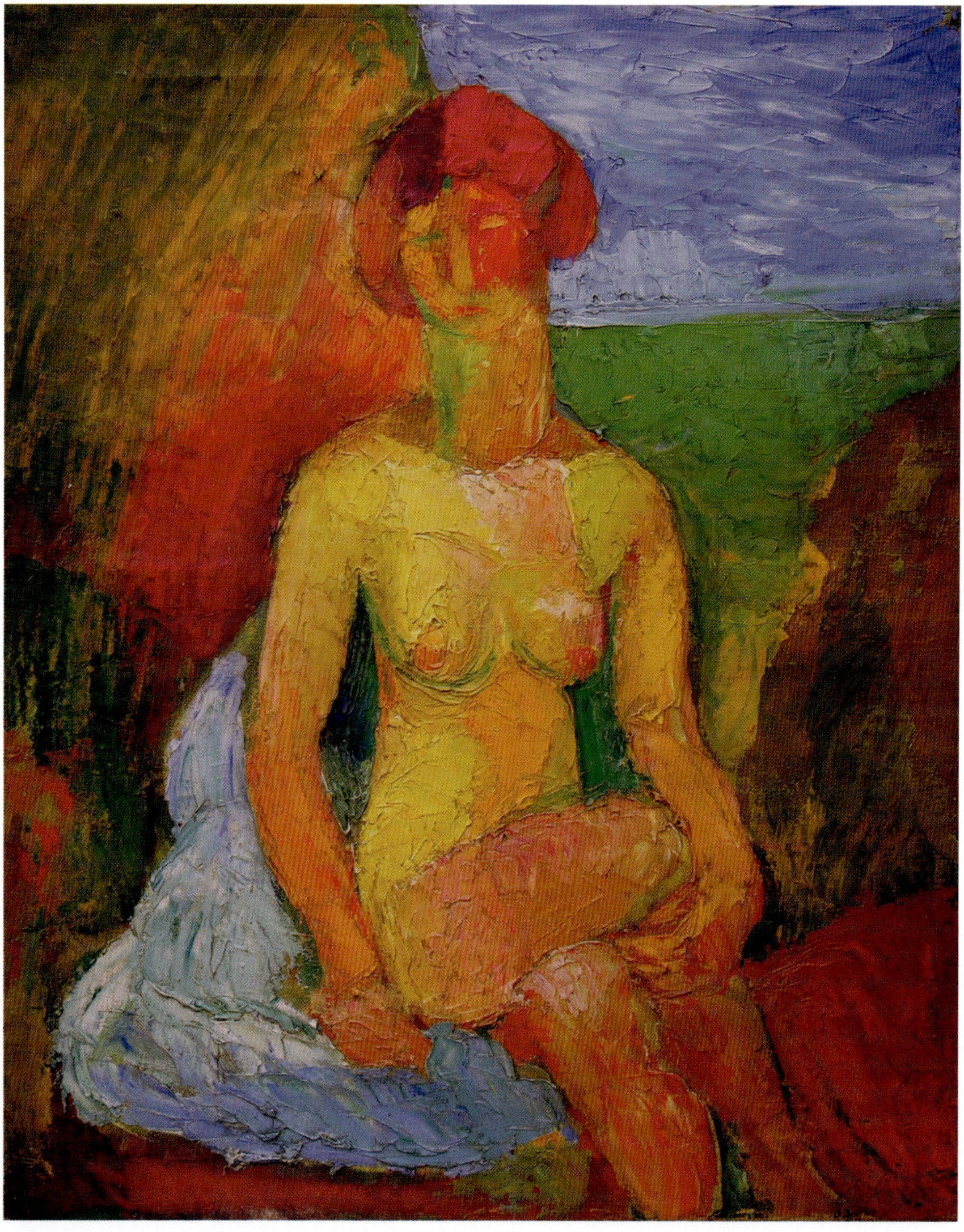

Émile François Jacques Compard
Nu Fauviste, c.1925
Jeffrey Winter Fine Arts, Long Beach, California

Anna Costenoble
1866-1930

Anna Costenoble was a graphic artist and painter born in Danzig, Germany in 1866. As of 1883 she was a student of Karl Gussow and later studied in Munich. In 1888 the artist moved to Berlin. Costenoble exhibited with the Vienna Secession in 1899 and the Berlin Secession in 1900, 1901 and 1908. In 1907 She illustrated the book *Penthesileia* by Frölich and Kaufmann.

In 1898 with the exhibition of a series of paintings, *Tragedy of the Woman*, in Dresden she received great public recognition, though critics did not agree with this acclaim. In response to the critics' negative sentiment she published several original etchings in the Vienna Secession newspaper in 1899 and the Bildner Kunst newspaper in 1905.

In the exhibitions of the Secessionists Costenoble was among some of the foremost artists in the world at the turn of the 20th century. This was the era of giants like Klimt, Schiele, Moser and Kokoschka; as a woman artist working during this period there must have been significant amazement, perhaps outrage at the subjects she chose. Her talent was indisputable, her creativity exceptional and she painted very large canvases that could not be ignored. Though Costenoble maintained a successful career her work is still fairly obscure. Costenoble died in Berlin in 1930.

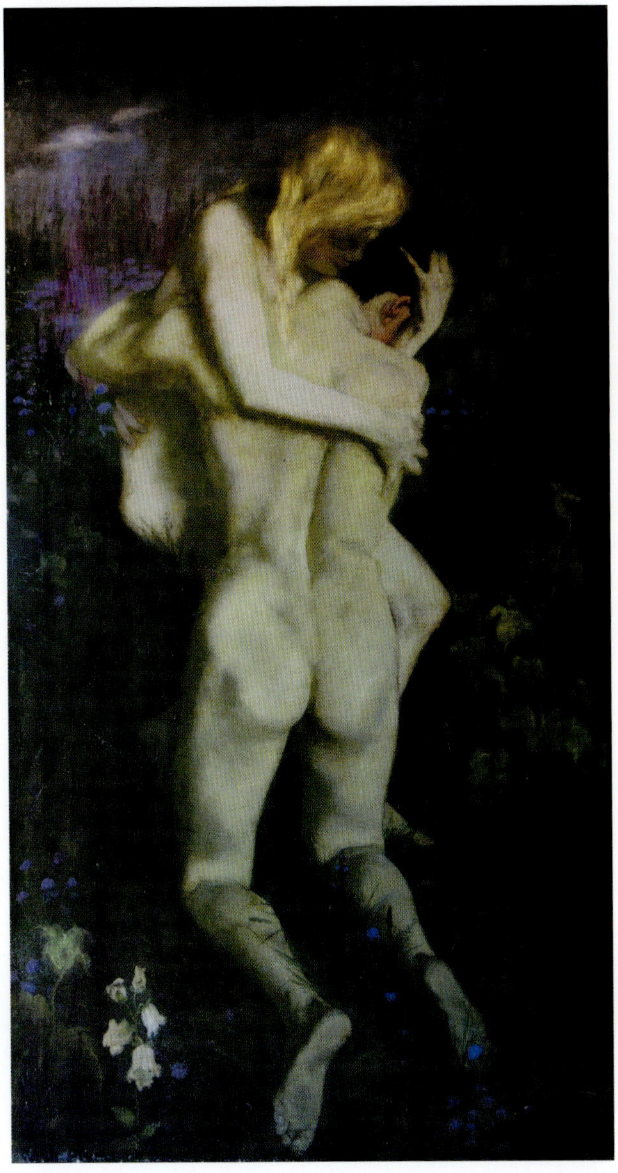

Anna Costenoble
Tristan and Isolde, Exhibited in1900
Papillon Gallery, Los Angeles, California

Alfred Courmes

1896-1993

Alfred Courmes was born in Bormes-les-Mimosas, France, in 1896 and was educated in Monaco. Following World War I, Courmes studies with Roger de La Fresnaye and may have been La Fresnaye's only student. From 1920 to 1925 Courmes lived in Lavandou in the Provence region of France. In 1922 he exhibited at the Société Lyonnaise des Beaux-Arts. Three years later he traveled to Paris to exhibit at the Salon d'Automne, Salon des Tuileries and the Salon des Indépendants. In 1926 he painted what is now a famous portrait of Peggy Guggenheim.

In 1927 Courmes moved to Ostende, Belgium. There he befriended James Ensor, Felix Labisse and the well-known Belgian artist Constant Permeke. The development of Courmes' style over several decades can be attributed to these friendships in addition to regular visits to museums in Brussels and Amsterdam. It was within these institutions Courmes was exposed to Classical as well as Surrealist and Belgian Expressionist works which greatly impacted his own artistic endeavors.

Also in 1927, Courmes exhibited his first solo show at the Galerie Montparnasse, and in 1930 he moved to Paris. In 1935 he exhibited at the prestigious Galerie Bernheim-Jeune and in 1936 received the Prix Guillaume. Courmes was commissioned to create the decorations for the pavilion of Manufacture de Sèvres for the 1937 l'Exposition Internationale de Paris and in the same year exhibited at the Galerie des Beaux-Arts, Paris.

In 1938 Courmes was commissioned to paint a complex, large-scale mural for the dining room at the French Embassy in Ottawa, Canada. It measured thirty meters long and four meters high and accommodated two hundred and twenty-five people.

After the liberation of France, Courmes exhibited with the Surrealists at the Salon d'Automne; he also exhibited at the Salon des Indépendants. In 1946 he exhibited at l'Exposition Surréaliste de Mai with Clovis Trouille and René Magritte.

Courmes continued to exhibit regularly showing at the Salon de Mai in 1957 and the Biennale de São Paulo, Brazil in 1965. In 1971 he had an exhibition in Bordeaux titled *Les Autres*. In 1972 he participated in an exhibition at the Grand Palais, in Paris, and in 1977 he had a solo exhibition at Galerie Jean Briance in Paris. Between 1982 and 1989 Courmes had solo exhibitions at the Musée de Grenoble, Galerie Jean Briance, FIAC, Galerie Berggruen, Musée de Roubaix and the Centre Georges Pompidou.

In 1973 Jean-Marc Campagne published a beautifully illustrated monograph on Courmes' life and work. Courmes continued to exhibit well into the 1980s and was awarded the Chevalier de la Légion d'Honneur in 1991. His creativity and imagination never diminished. In recent years the full extent of his contribution to the art of the 20th century is being realized. In 1997 his work was included in an exhibition at the Centre Georges Pompidou, in Paris, called *Made in France 1947-1997, 50 Ans de Creation en France*. In 2003 the Musée Arts et Histoire in his hometown of Bormes-les-Mimosas exhibited *Alfred Courmes et Son Pays*. The exhibition traveled to Belgium and is complemented by a large color catalogue. In 2004 a new, heavily illustrated book was published on Courmes' life's work.

The Montreal Museum included Courmes' work in the 1991 exhibition *The 1920's, The Age of Metropolis*.

His work is included in many Paris museum collections, including the Musée Carnavalet as well as the Musée des Années Trente. Additionally, his work is represented in the Musée National d'Art Moderne and the Musée National de la Cooperation Franco-Américaine holds his famous portrait of Peggy Guggenheim. He is also represented in museums in Grenoble, Poitiers, Roubaix, Issoudun and Algiers.

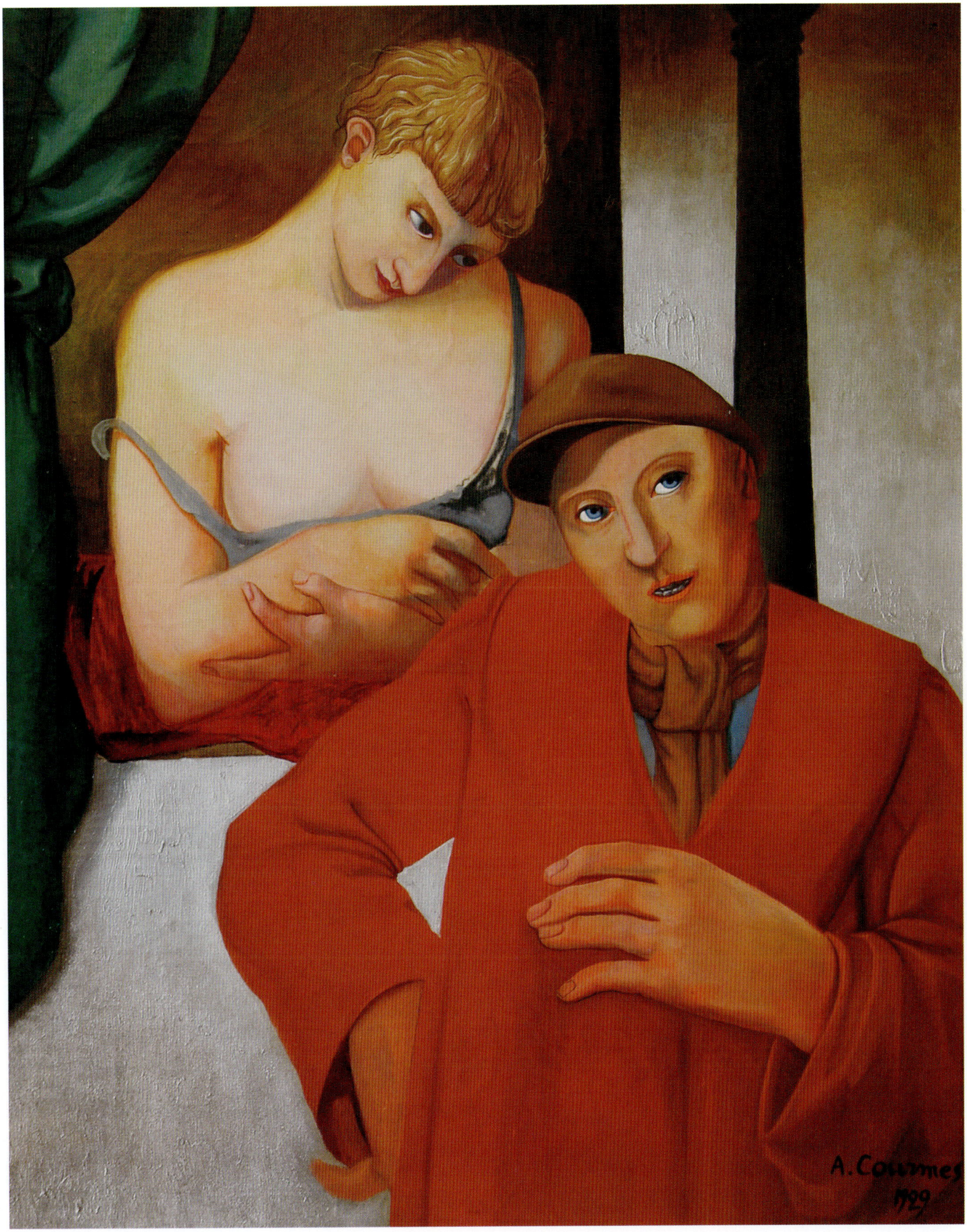

Alfred Courmes
Au Balcon, Dated 1929
The Parrish Collection, San Francisco, California

Hermann Courtens
1884-1956

Hermann Courtens was born in Saint-Josse-ten-Noode, Brussels, Belgium in 1884. He was the son of Franz Courtens and Isidore Verheyden and his son was the esteemed sculptor, Alfred Courtens.

Courtens is best known for his paintings of figures, genre scenes and still lifes. He exhibited at the Salon de la Société des Beaux-Arts and in 1941 C. Conrardy wrote a catalog essay about Courtens' work for an exhibition held at La Petite Galerie in Brussels. Courtens was a professor at the Institute Supérieur des Beaux-Arts as well. Courtens died in 1956 in Ixelles, Brussels.

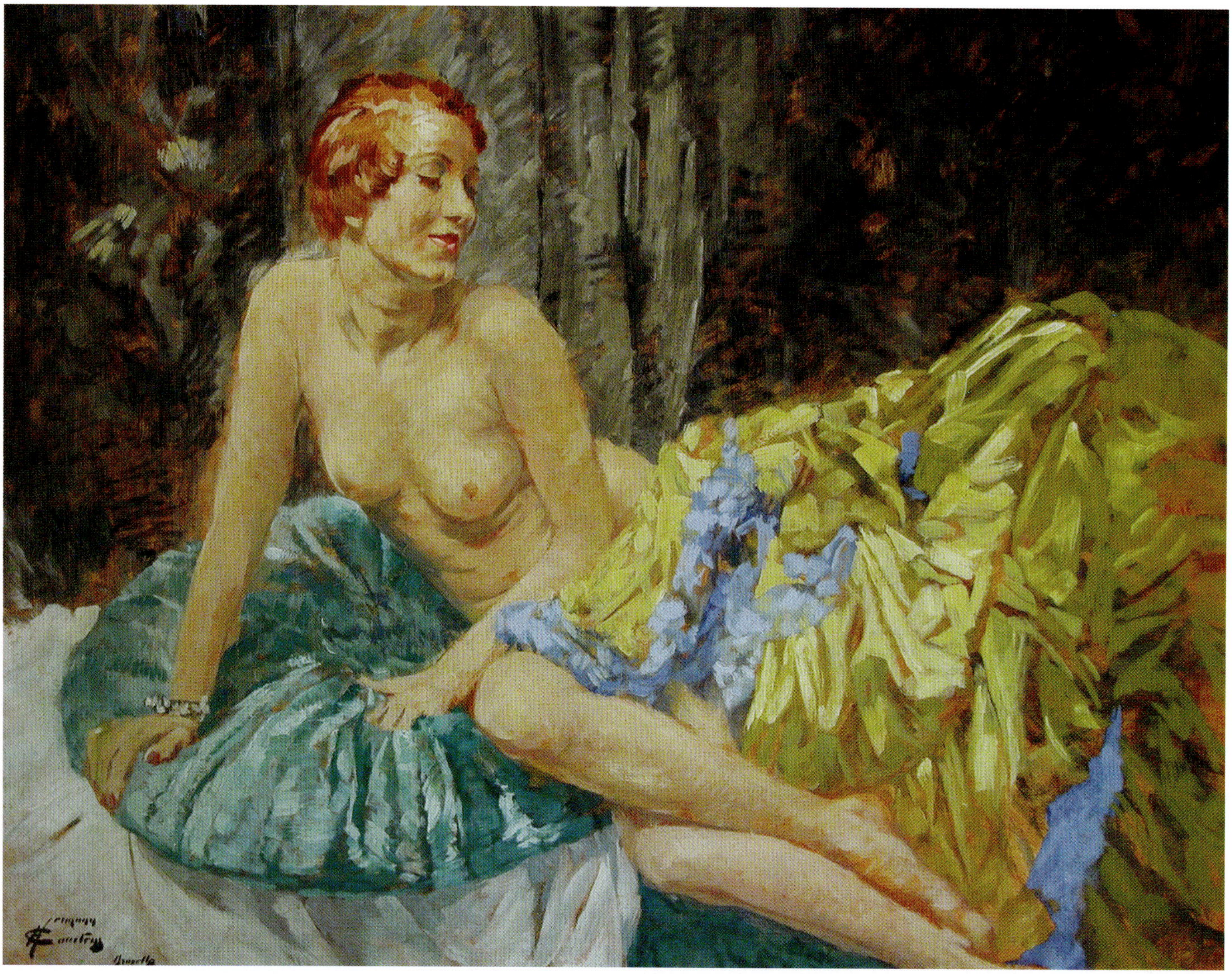

Hermann Courtens
Femme en Repose, c.1925
Ron and Barbara Sickmen, New York, New York

Albert Cresswell

1879-1936

Albert Cresswell was born in Paris in 1879. He was a student of Boulanger, Lefebvre and Olivier-Merson. Cresswell was a member of the Société des Artistes Français where he exhibited from 1880 to 1929. In 1892 he was awarded an honorable mention and the Médaille de Troisième Classe in 1907.

Cresswell was an artist of La Belle Époque and created fantastic paintings that graced many homes in France. The artist died in 1936.

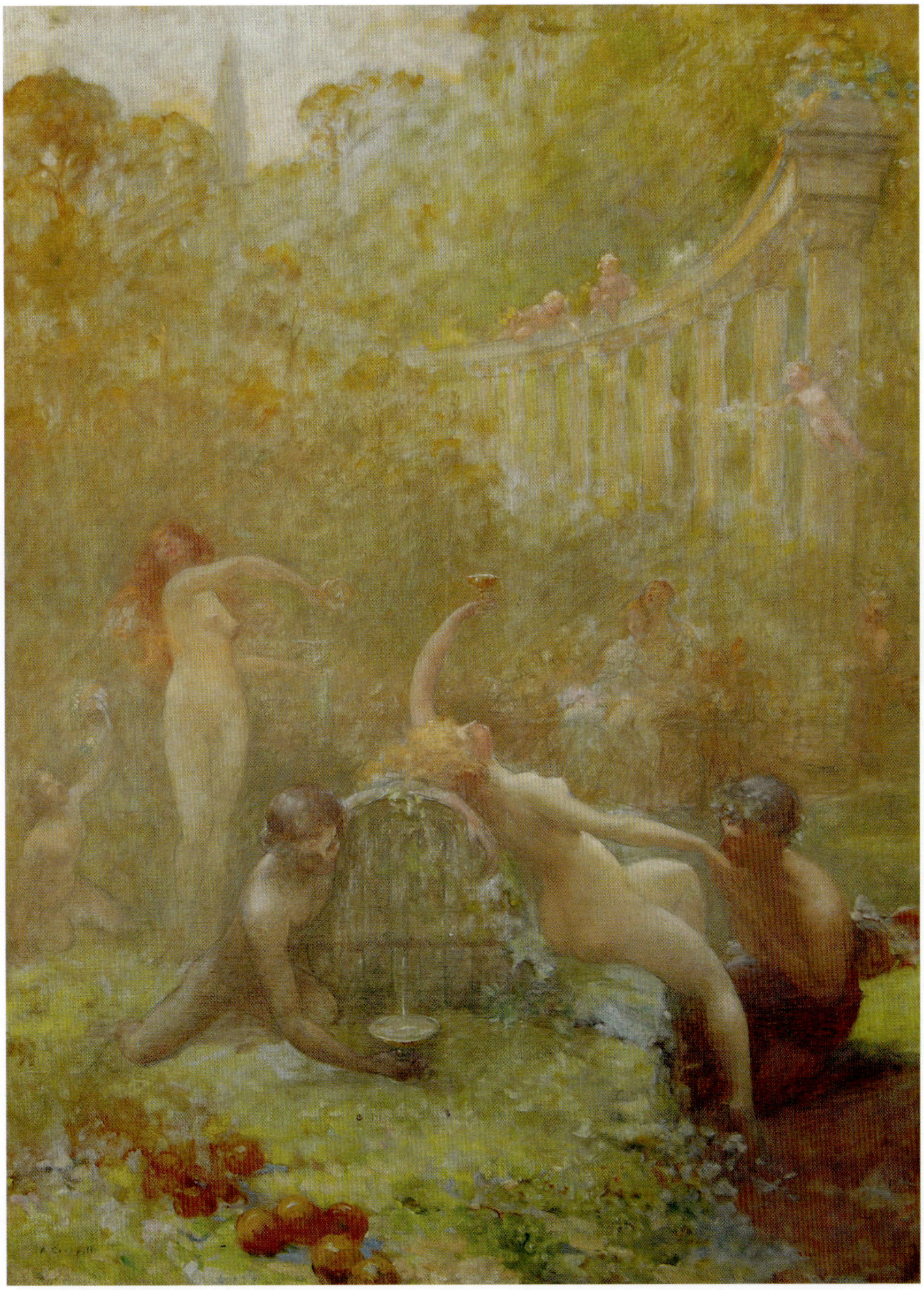

Albert Cresswell
Bacchanale, c.1900
Bill and Jo LaMond, Los Angeles, California

Georges Creten
1887-1966

Georges Creten was born on March 14, 1887 in Saint-Gilles, Brussels, Belgium. Creten first studied painting under his father Eugène Creten, and at the age of fifteen under Gustave and Julien Dillens. In 1910 he joined the group of avant-garde artists and began exhibiting in 1913 at the Salon du Printemps. Between 1910 and 1920 Creten worked to define his style and create an independent oeuvre of paintings.

He exhibited at the Salon de l'Art Contemporain in Anvers in 1924. Creten was also a founding member of the artist collective *l'Art Vivant* and exhibited with the group in 1931 at the Galerie Giroux in Belgium and the Palais des Beaux-Arts. Other notable exhibitions include solo showings at Galerie Le Centaure in 1922, 1926, 1930; Galerie Manteau in 1923, 1933; Galerie Le Cheval de Verre in 1949, 1952, 1957 and Galerie La Sirène in 1953. Collective exhibitions include the Venice Biennial in 1924; l'Art Belge au Jeu de Paume in Paris, 1928; the Carnegie Institute in Pittsburg, 1935; *Compagnons de l'Art* at the Palais des Beaux-Arts in Brussels, 1938; Unesco in Paris, 1946; and l'Exposition Universelle in Brussels, 1958.

He became best known for his figures, portraits and nudes in addition to still-lifes and landscapes. Creten also found inspiration through his travels in Egypt, Rome, Venice and Florence where he took delight in the festivals and architecture.

Creten's work may be found in the permanent collections of museums in Brussels, Gent and Ixelles. Verviers. R. de Bendère has discussed his work in *Artistes d'Aujourd'hui* and he is included in dictionaries of Belgian artists as well. Jean Mogin also wrote of his life and work in the published book of monographs, *Creten-George*, in 1959.

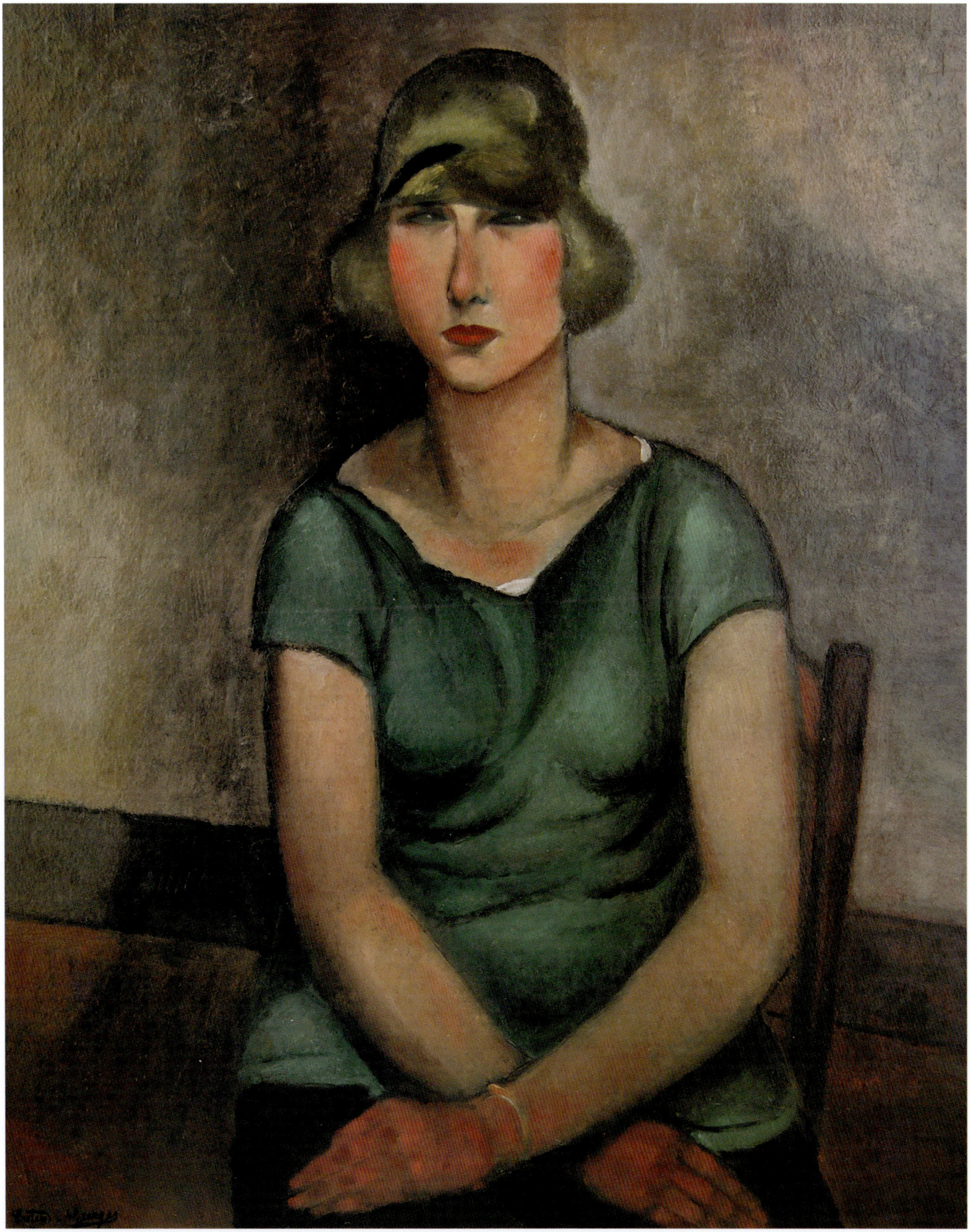

Georges Creten
Femme au Chemise Vert, Dated 1925
Papillon Gallery, Los Angeles, California

Claude Dalbanne

1877-1964

Claude Dalbanne was born in 1877. In Paris he studied with Jean-Paul Laurens at l'Académie Julian. Dalbanne became affiliated with the avant-garde group *Ziniars* and exhibited with the Salon d'Automne.

Upon arriving in Lyon he became curator of the Musée Gadagne and was extremely active in the city's artistic community. Dalbanne wrote editorials for the review *Promenoir* and continued to exhibit with the *Ziniars*.

Galleries with which Dalbanne participated include Galerie St-Pierre-Alfred Poyet, Galerie Bellecour, Galerie Les Archers and the Salon du Sud-Est Lyon. Dalbanne's work has been collected by the Musée des Beaux-Arts and the Musée Paul Dini Villefranche-sur-Saône. He has also been noted in several catalogues and dictionaries of Lyonnaise artists. Claude Dalbanne died in 1964.

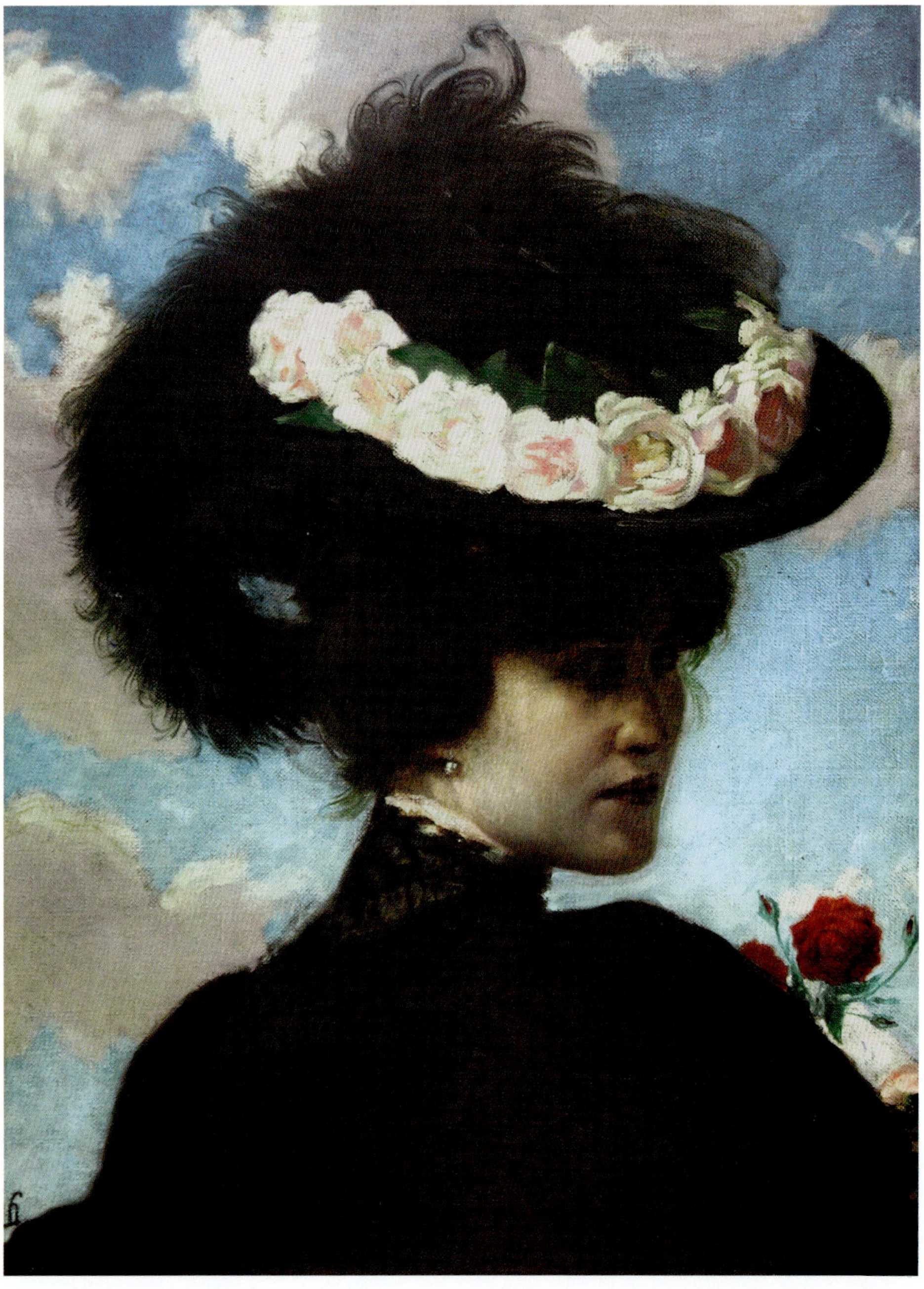

Claude Dalbanne
Femme au Chapeau, c.1900
Jennmaur Gallery, San Francisco, California

Georges Dayez

1907-1991

Georges Dayez was born on July 29, 1907. His father Jules was a commercial printer. In 1909, the Dayez family moved to Vaires-sur-Marne. Dayez's father fought with the French army during World War I, while the family hid in Bayeux.

Dayez received a traditional French education through which he was introduced to drawing, painting and fine art . He completed the first part of his baccalaureate in 1924. Much to his father's dismay, Dayez interrupted his studies to pursue oil painting. In 1925 he worked with his father in a print shop and took an evening drawing class taught by the sculptor Henry Arnold. His classmates included such emerging painters and sculptors as Brayer, Humblot, Adam, Corbin, and Raymond Martin. Dayez could not afford tuition at the academies of Montparnasse, so Lucien Simon let Dayez audit his class during 1926.

Dayez completed his mandatory military service from 1927 to 1929. He was given special permission to attend a night class at Robert Wlérick's studio where he met Édouard Pignon and was allowed a leave of absence to paint in Brittany. Discharged from military service in 1929, Dayez moved to his first studio on the heights of Belleville in Paris. Pignon moved to nearby Billancourt and the two young artists painted, studied and visited museums together. In 1931, Dayez and Pignon traveled around the Côte d'Azur. The following year, both artists exhibited in the Salon des Indépendants. Dayez and Pignon joined Henri Barbusse, painters Hélion and Herbin, sculptor Adam, the October Group, as well as the writers Dabit and Nizan, and the poets Aragon and Eluard to form l'Association des Ecrivains et Artistes Révolutionnaires (A.E.A.R.). The goal of the organization was to create an art form that conveyed the struggles of the working class and to address the rise of fascism and the threat of war. With the onset of World War II, Dayez joined the French 58th Infantry Division and was stationed north of Metz.

In 1941, Dayez met French artist André Lhote who greatly influenced the development of his work. Beginning in 1944 Dayez exhibited regularly in the Parisian Salons. He showed in the Salon d'Automne and the Salon des Artistes Indépendants. He exhibited in the first Salon de Mai in 1945 and became a member of the committee in 1950. During the 1950s, he exhibited at the Musée de Grenoble and Museum of Modern Art in San Francisco as well as another exhibition in Munich. Dayez received numerous solo exhibitions of his work during the 1950s and 1960s in New York, Lausanne, Nancy, Oslo, Amsterdam, Lyon, Avignon, Milan and Madrid among other cities.

During the 1951-52 academic year, Dayez taught at l'Académie d'André Lhote. In 1967 he was named a professor at l'Atelier de Lithographie de l'École des Beaux-Arts de Paris. Dayez traveled extensively during this period. He visited Italy, Greece and the United States. He made a sojourn to Argenteuil, the birthplace of Georges Braque whose work Dayez greatly admired.

Dayez was by and large influenced by the discipline of the Cubists. In his long and prolific career he painted figures and abstract compositions in his own unique translation of the modernist methods that preceded him. Against the tide of Abstract Expressionism after World War II Dayez pursued his vision steeped in the Cubist tradition and had remarkable success.

Jacques Duchateau wrote the catalog essay for the 1967 exhibition *Dayez* at the Musée de Pooches, Paris. In 1991 a large illustrated book was publish on Dayez, written by Jean Lescure and George Schwab. Dayez's work is found in the collections of numerous museums, including La Chaux-de-Fonds, Göteborg, Tolède, Le Havre, Luxembourg, Finlande, Paris, Skoplje and Tokyo. Dayez died in 1991.

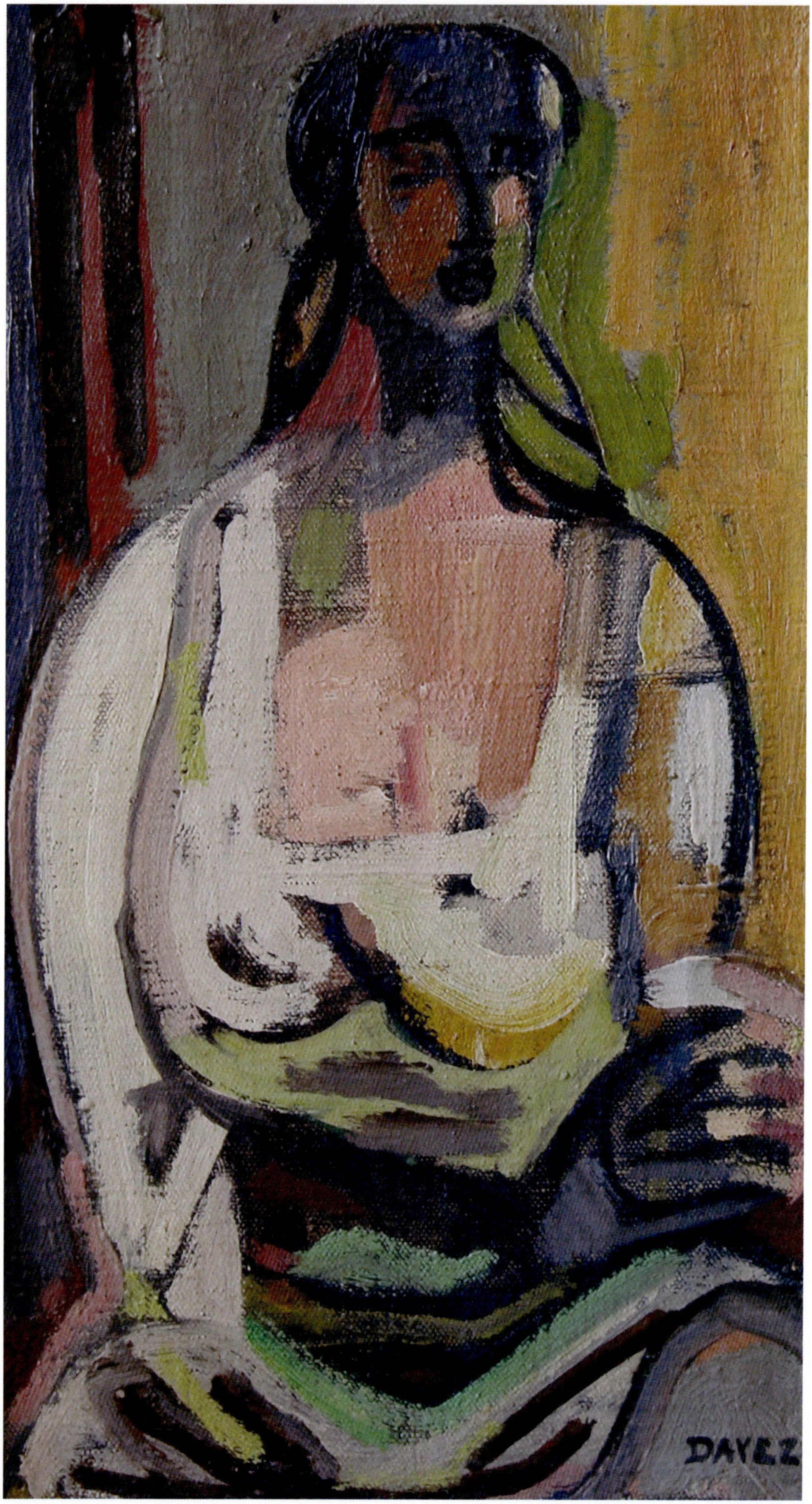

Georges Dayez
Femme Assis, c.1940
Martin and Marsha Brander, Brentwood, California

Suzanne Daynes-Grassot

1884-1976

Suzanne Daynes-Grassot was born in Paris in 1884. Her father Victor Daynes was a painter and she grew up surrounded by many artistic influences. She studied with Jean Béraud and painted many portraits of theater performers, but is best known for her nudes.

In 1904 she received critical acclaim for a portrait of her grandmother, a Vaudeville comedian. She was awarded the Prix Armand Berton in 1930 and exhibited at the Salon Société Nationale de Beaux-Arts until 1935. She also exhibited at the Salon des Artistes Indépendant and the Salon d'Hiver.

In 1910 the Museum of Buenos Aires purchased one of Daynes-Grassot's paintings and in 1925 The Tokyo Museum purchased another of her works. Daynes-Grassot is represented in several other museums, including the Musée d'Art Moderne in Paris. Dealers and collectors in New York and Canada own works by Daynes-Grassot.

Daynes-Grassot's long and successful career included exhibitions at the Salon d'Automne, Salon des Indépendants and l'Union des Femmes Peintres et Sculpteurs.

Daynes-Grassot was a prolific artist who utilized the techniques of Impressionism and Postimpressionism to create a very unique body of work.

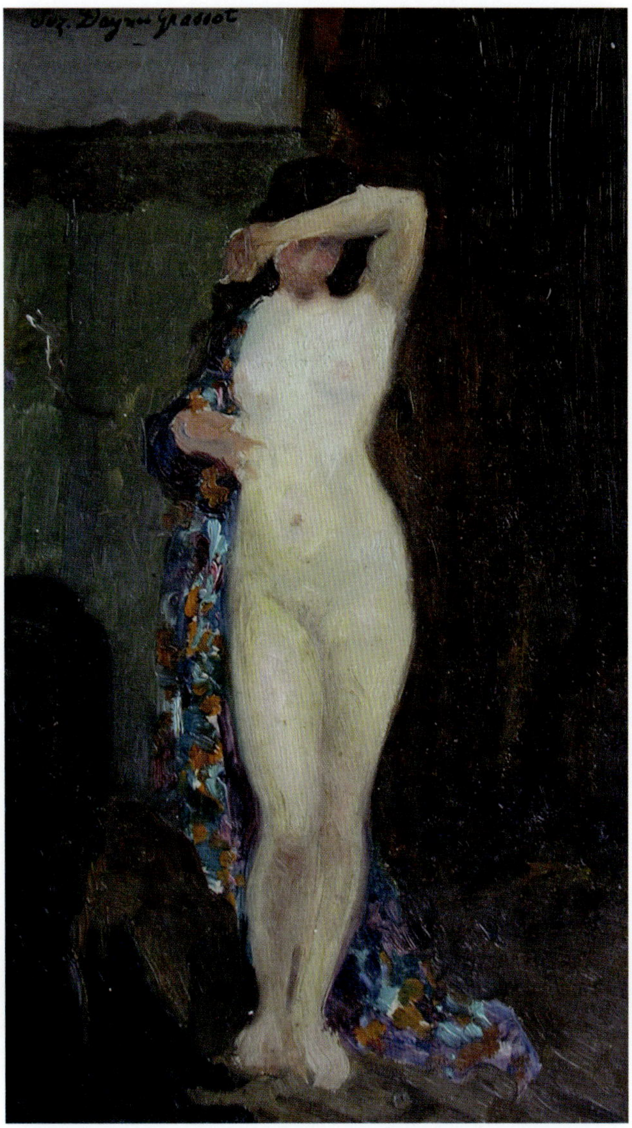

Suzanne Daynes-Grassot
Jeune Femme au Robe, c.1910
Ann Bridges, Long Beach, California

Ludmilla Ferri Decler

20th century

Ludmilla Ferri Decler was born in Warsaw, Poland. She was a member of the Salon d'Automne where she exhibited in 1928. In 1927 and 1929 she exhibited at the Salon des Indépendants as well.

Like many of the School of Paris artists Decler showed a fascination with Parisian café life. She painted in a modern style and captured the essence of the age.

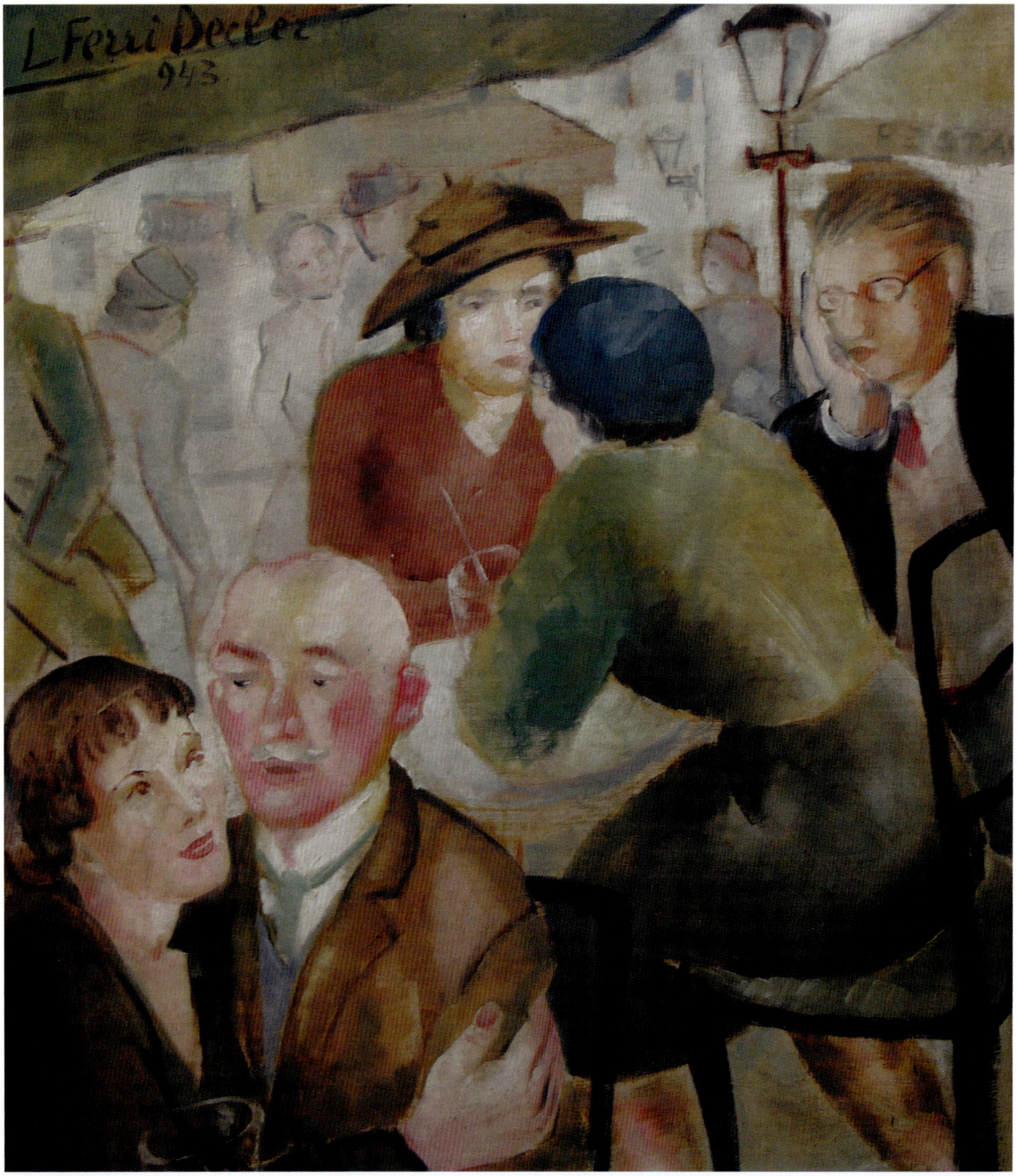

Ludmilla Ferri Decler
Au Café, Dated 1943
Eric Van Vredenburgh Ltd., London, England

Henriette Delalain

Born 1885

Henriette Delalain was born on April 20, 1885 in Paris. She studied with Marcel Baschet and Henri Royer. Delalain is noted for her portraits, nudes and genre scene paintings. She exhibited at the Salon des Artistes Français beginning in 1908. Delalain received an honorable mention in 1922 and the Médaille de Troisième Classe in 1923. She also exhibited regularly at the Salon d'Automne.

Delalain worked with rich colors, influenced by the Postimpressionists. She painted her subjects in elaborate interiors.

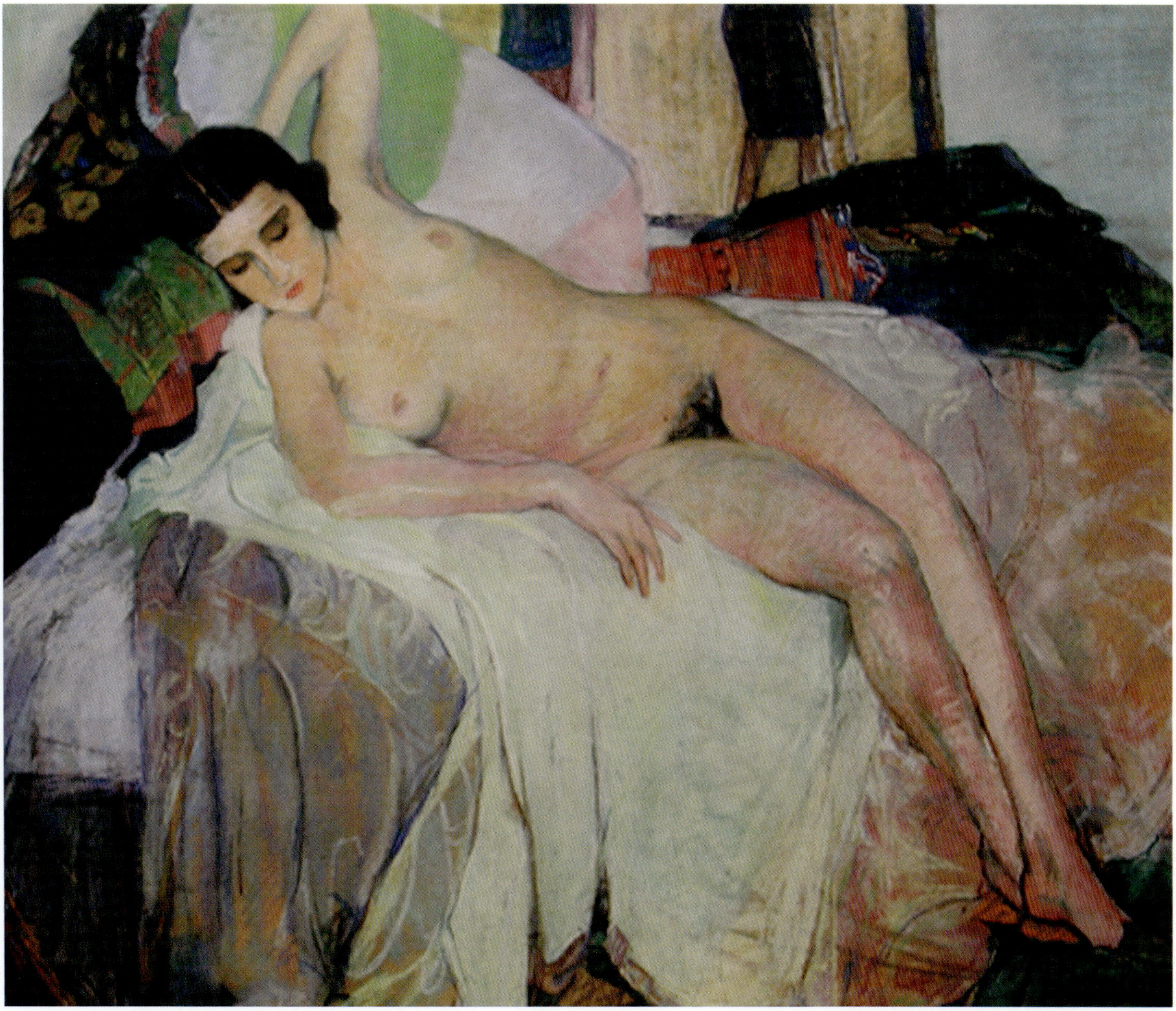

Henriette Delalain
Nu Allongé, c.1925
Private Collection

Edmond Delescluze

1905-1993

Born in Brussels in 1905, Edmond Delescluze was best known as a decorative painter, engraver, ceramicist and painter of figures, landscapes and seascapes. He was a student of Delville, Montald and Fabry at l'Académie de Bruxelles.

Delescluze married Suzanne Fabry who was also a painter.

Between 1940 and 1958 he worked as a set and costume designer. Like his father, Jean Delescluze, Edmond worked for the Théatre Royal de la Monnaie in Brussels. In 1947 Delescluze was awarded the Grand Prix de Maquette de Théâtrales for the set designs of *Le Libertin* and *Jeanne au Bûcher*.

Exhibitions include l'Exposistion Universelle de Bruxelles in 1958. The artist died in 1993.

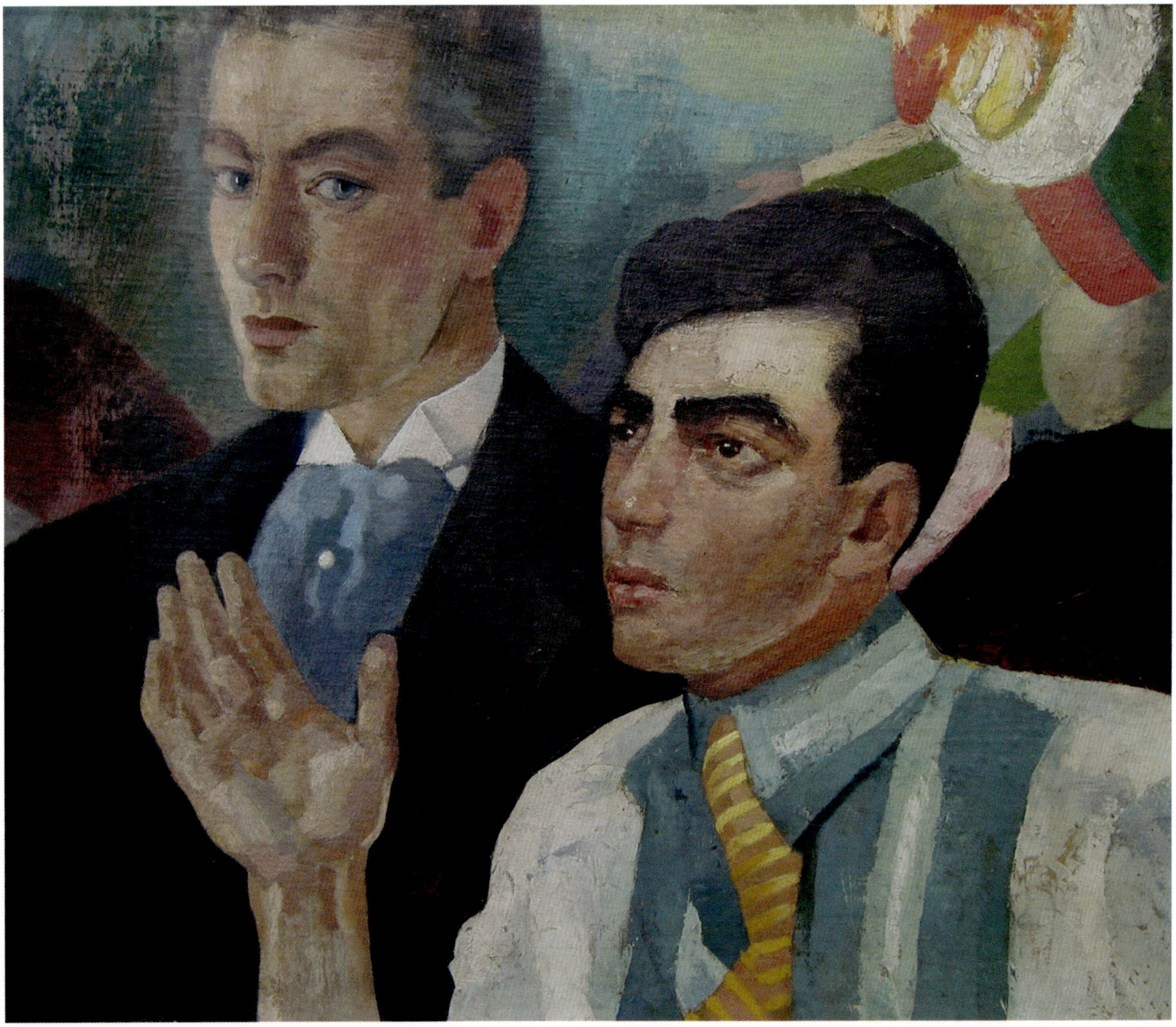

Edmond Delescluze
Bal des Hommes, c.1925
Kathleen Avery Fine Art, Palo Alto, California

Herman Delpech

Born 1865

Herman Delpech was born in 1865 in Bordeaux, Gironde. Delpech is best known for his genre and landscape compositions. He regularly exhibited at the Salon des Artistes Français and received the Médaille de Troisième Classe in 1914.

Delpech worked in the typical stylization of La Belle Époque with whimsical and romantic subjects. He also displays exquisite attention to detail and fine painterly quality typical of the Beaux-Arts tradition. Delpech's painting *Une ménagère*, 1892 is part of the permanent collection at the museum in Cognac.

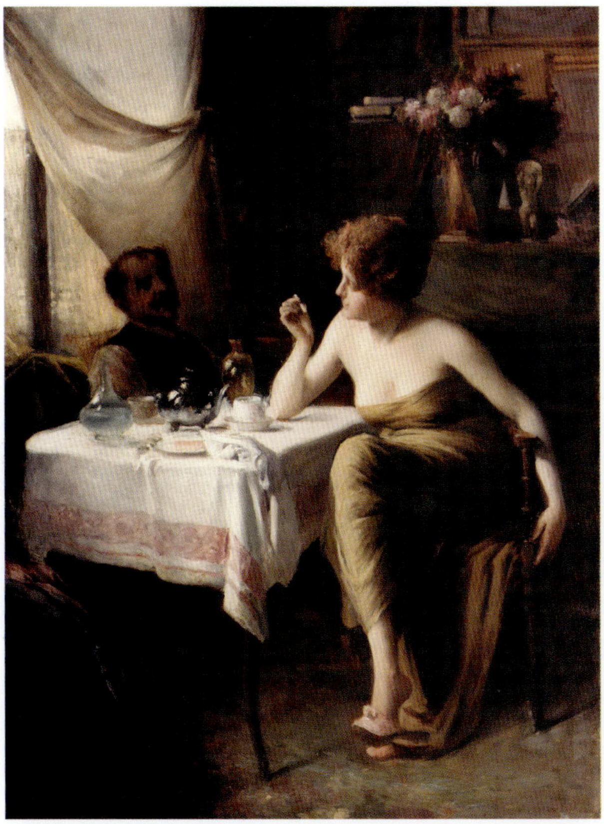

Herman Delpech
Á la Table, c.1900
Los Angeles Fine Art Gallery, Los Angeles, California

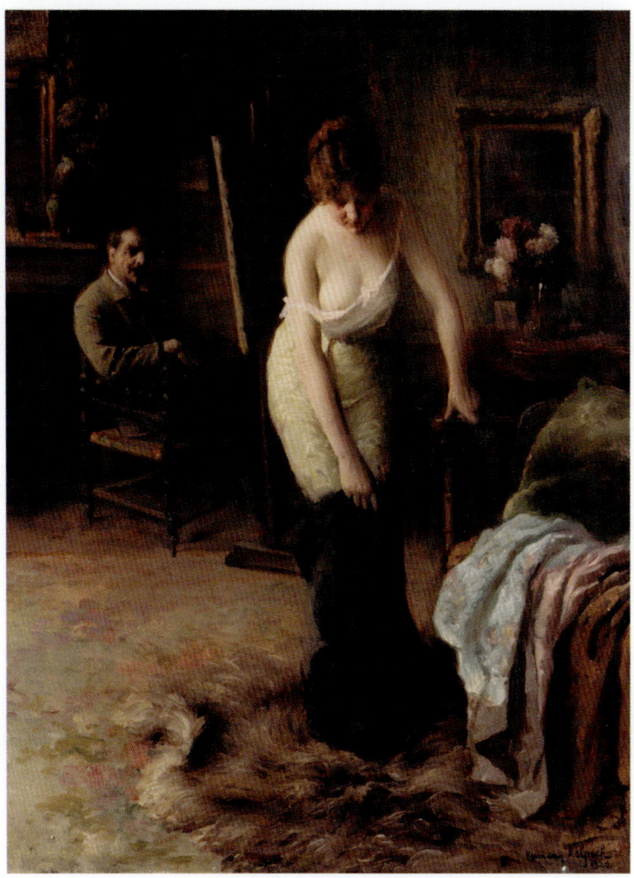

Herman Delpech
Le Voyeur, c.1900
Los Angeles Fine Art Gallery, Los Angeles, California

Jean-Pierre Dequene

1905-1954

Jean-Pierre Dequene was born May 20, 1905 in Mons, Belgium. He studied with Émile Motte, A. Duriau and C. Caty at l'Académie des Beaux-Arts de Mons and was a student at the Atelier of M. Gillis

Dequene painted portraits, nudes and still lifes and worked as an illustrator and muralist as well, signing his work "P. Dequene." His style is characteristic of other Belgian modernists, specifically the Belgian Expressionists. His works are highly detailed and exhibit some elements of Surrealism.

Dequene was a member of the group *Les Loups* (The Wolves) and exhibited in Paris at the Salon d'Automne and Salon des Artistes Indépendants. He created a decorative mural for l'Université du Travail in Charleroi. The artist is represented in museum collections in Brussels, Mons and Tournai.

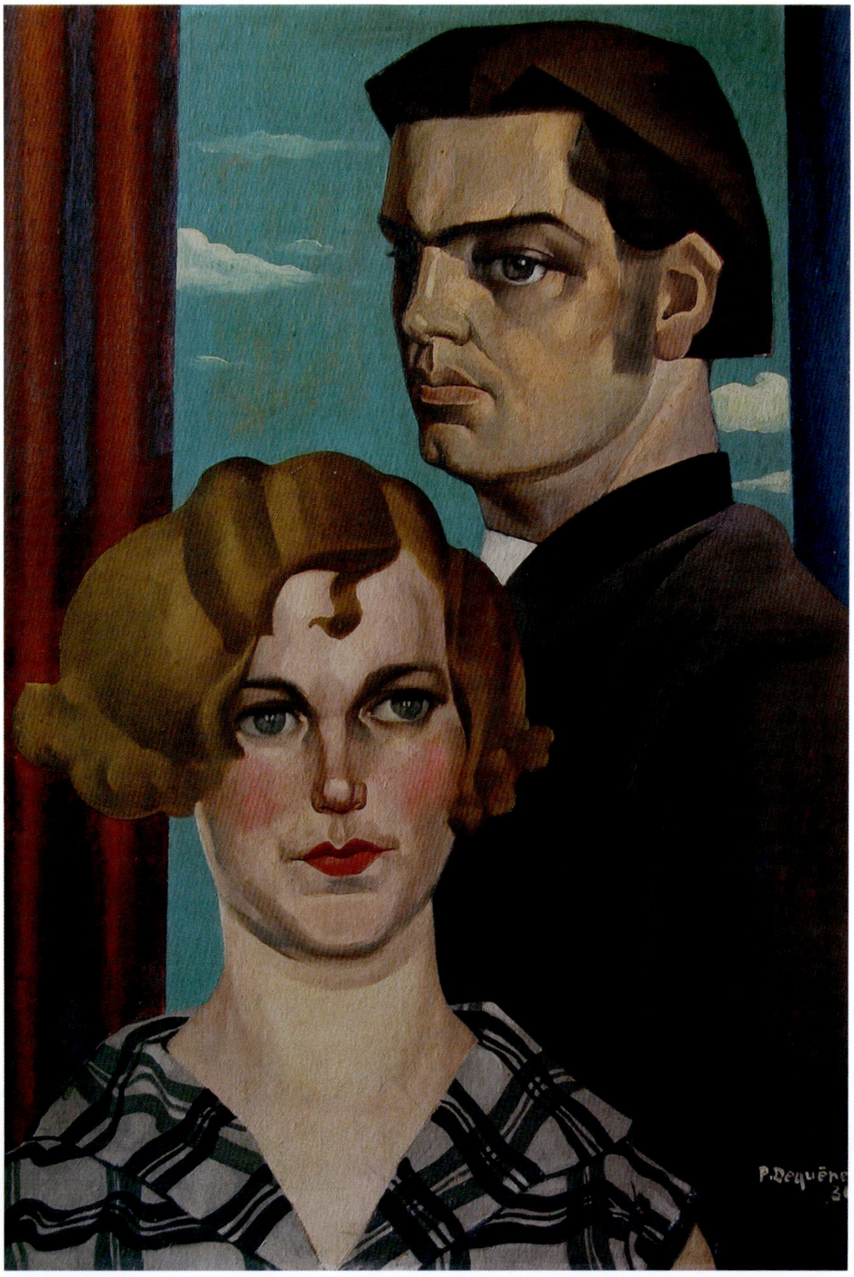

Jean-Pierre Dequene
Le Couple Belge, Dated 1930
Oviatt Investment Group, Los Angeles, California

Jean-Pierre Dequene
Jeune Femme au Chapeau, c.1930
Ron and Barbara Sickmen, New York, New York

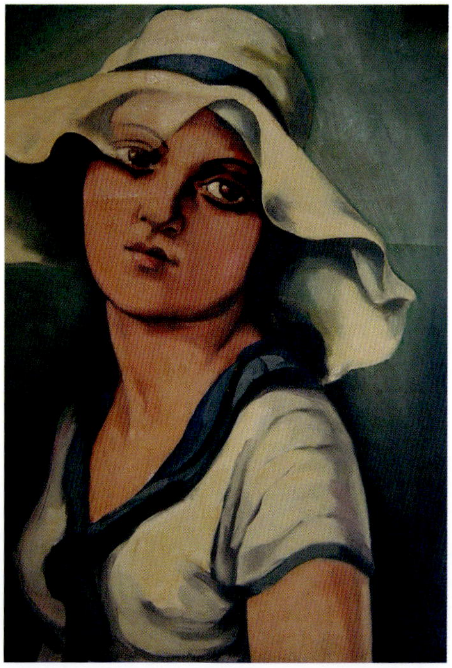

Lucien Desmaré

1905-1961

Lucien Desmaré was born in Schaerbeek, Belgium. He was best known as an illustrator, decorator and painter of landscapes and portraits. He received the Grand Prix d'Art Décoratif in the province of Brabant in 1935.

Desmaré's genre scenes, often in very large formats, capture the warmth and vogue fashion of his subjects and illustrate the romance of the bar and café culture of Europe between the wars. Desmaré died in 1961 in Brussels.

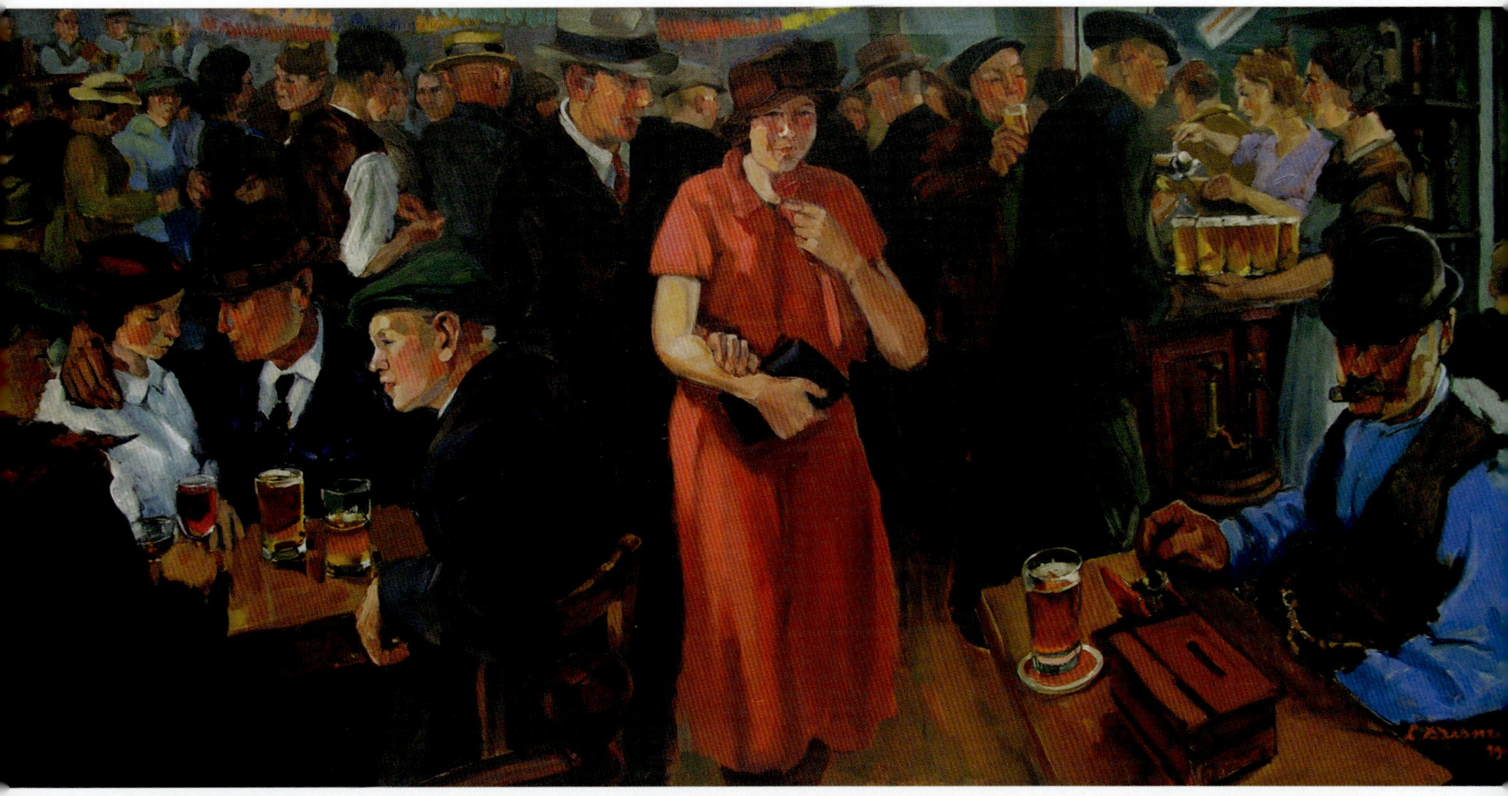

Lucien Desmaré
Au Bar, Dated 1936
The Parrish Collection, San Francisco, California

Raymond Dierickx
1904-1978

Raymond Dierickx was born in Uccle, Belgium, in 1904. He was the son of Joseph Dierickx and the nephew of Omer Dierickx, both accomplished and successful artists.

Beginning in 1920, Dierickx studied with Delville and Fabry at l'Académie de Bruxelles. His first exhibition was in 1926 at Galerie G. Giroux which was known for showing Belgian Modern artists including James Ensor and Rik Wouters.

Dierickx participated in l'Expositions Internationales de Liege in 1930 and an international exhibition in Brussels in 1935. He also participated in an exhibition of Belgian art in Oslo, Norway in 1938.

Dierickx began teaching at l'Académie d'Ixelles in 1932. His work is represented in museums in Ixelles, Mons, and Reims.

Dierickx's paintings are typical of the Belgian Expressionists. His splendid use of color and lyrical, intriguing subjects are typical in Belgian Modern Art.

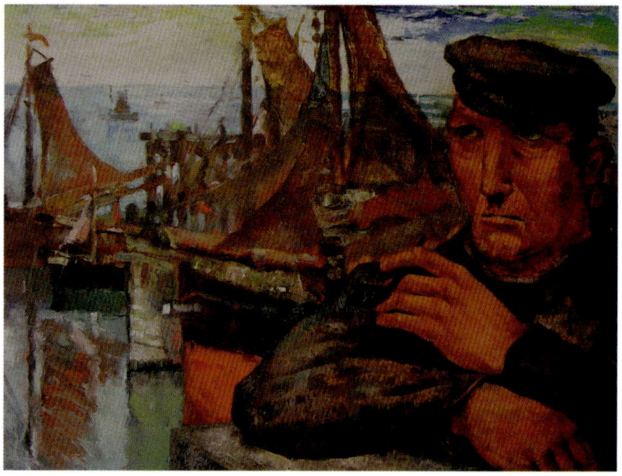

Raymond Dierickx
Au Port, c.1925
Papillon Gallery, Los Angeles, California

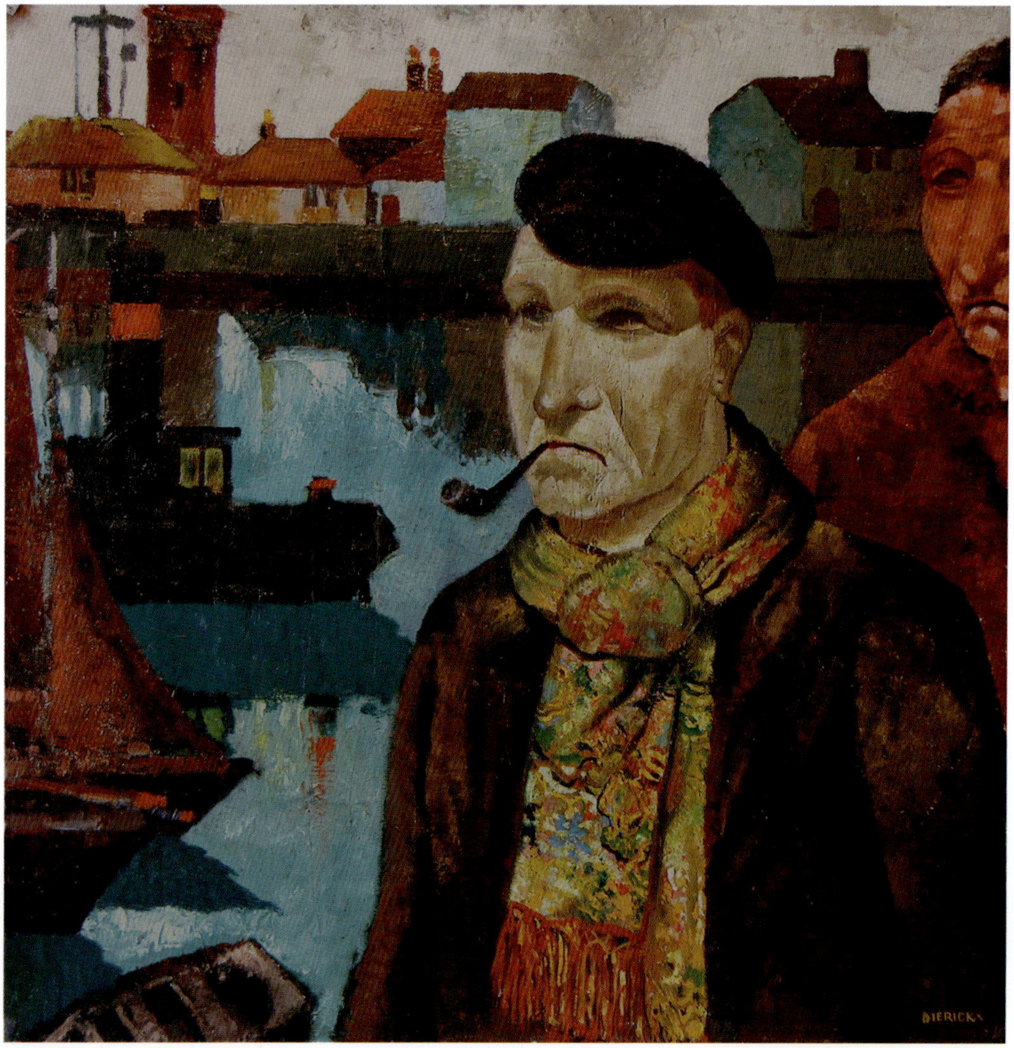

Raymond Dierickx
Le Marin, c.1925
The Parrish Collection,
San Francisco, California

Jean-Gabriel Domergue
1889-1962

Jean-Gabriel Domergue was born March 4, 1889 in Bordeaux, France. He studied at l'École des Beaux-Arts under many well-established artists of the time including Jules Lefebvre, Tony Robert-Fleury, Jules Adler, Fernand Humbert and François Flameng.

In 1906, at the age of seventeen, the artist debuted at the Salon des Artistes Français. He received an Honourable Mention two years later and in 1920 he received a Médaille d'Or. Additional notable expositions include the Royal Academy in London and the Carnegie Institute in Pittsburg. In 1933 Domergue was named Chevalier de la Légion d'Honneur and became a member of l'Académie des Beaux-Arts.

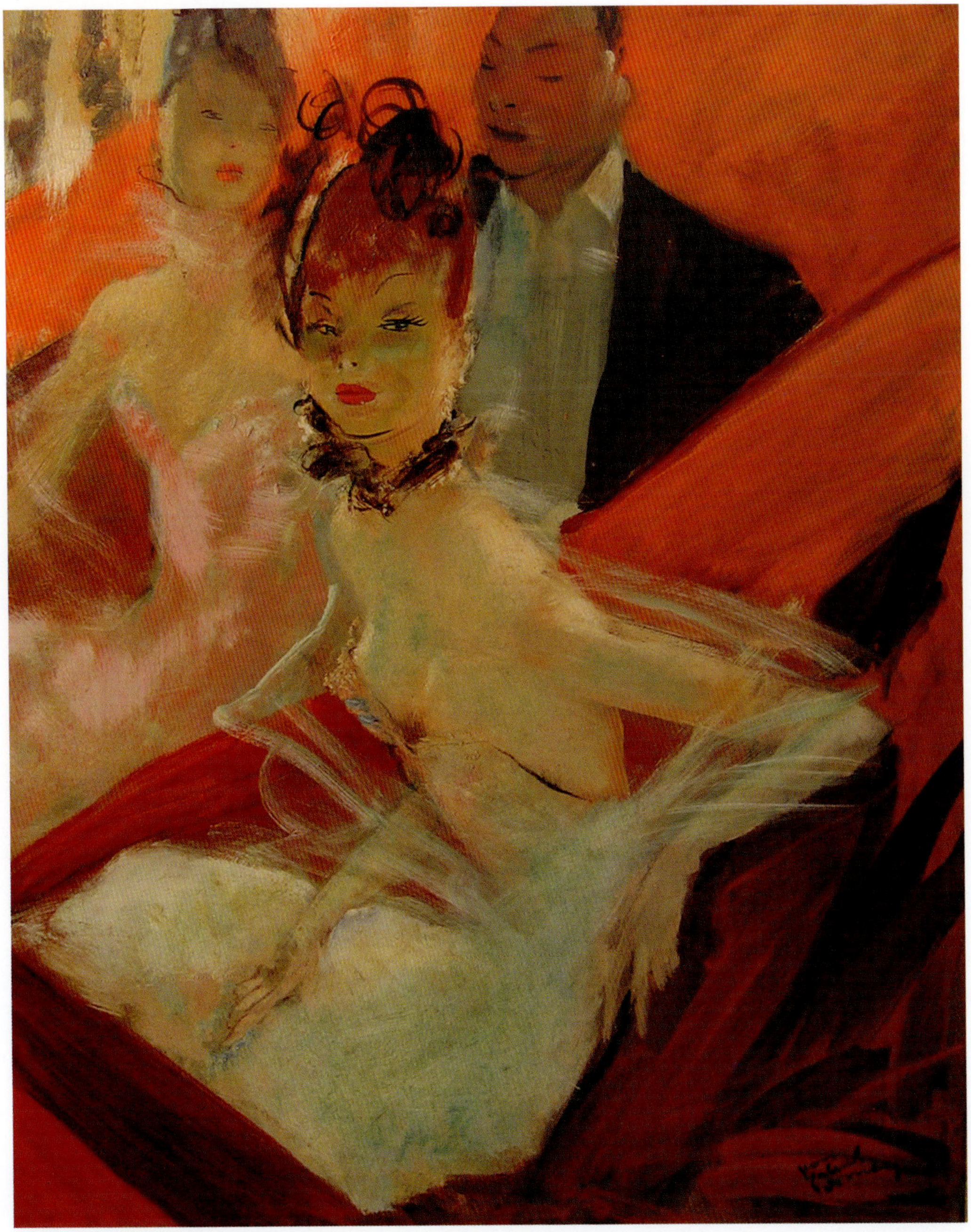

Jean-Gabriel Domergue
La Loge, c.1940
Galerie Delorme, Paris, France

Domergue was an extremely prolific artist and illustrator, creating covers for such publications as *La Parisienne*. He did illustrations for the American magazine *Esquire* in 1940 and 1936 he illustrated a book titled *Le Mariage de Loti*. In 1948 he illustrated *Quand on parle d'Amour ou le Vrai dialogue sentimental* with original hand colored lithographs. Like his contemporary Louis Icart, who was also a fine painter, he published many beautiful etchings. His subjects were most often portraits and models in extravagant and en vogue fashions. Many of his finest paintings portray elegant men and women in nightclubs, at the opera and at the races. He also created theatre bills, costumes, tapestries and sets for *l'Opéra* and other festive balls and galas.

Domergue's early work exhibits the influence of the Postimpressionists though in the early 1920s his style took on unique characteristics. He began to represent his models with long slender bodies and with elongated arms and necks, all characteristics that became his hallmark. His paintings are colorful and have a joyous exuberance.

In 1955 he was named curator of the Musée Jacquemart-André in Paris where he organized several well-attended exhibitions on van Gogh, Toulouse-Lautrec, Baudelaire, Morisot and Goya. In 1927 Domergue purchased an elaborate villa in Cannes that he later bequeathed to the city. A highly illustrated book on the artist was published in 1984; written by Gérard-Louis Soyer and preface by Madame Alix Grés.

Domergue's paintings were so popular they spawned a whole industry of imitation artists and outright copies. Many artists who emulated or copied his style also imitated his signature, which requires the collector to have proper authentication of his work. The artist died in 1962 in Paris.

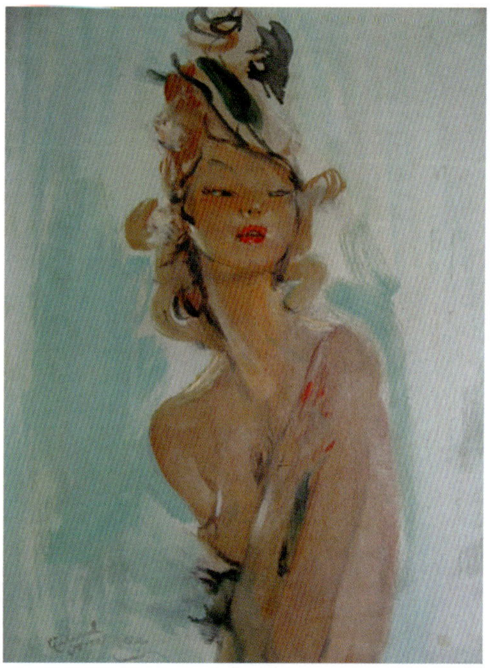

Jean-Gabriel Domergue
Vanita, c.1940
Galerie Delorme, Paris, France

Jean-Gabriel Domergue
Modèle Nu Assis, c.1940
Galerie de Souzy, Paris, France

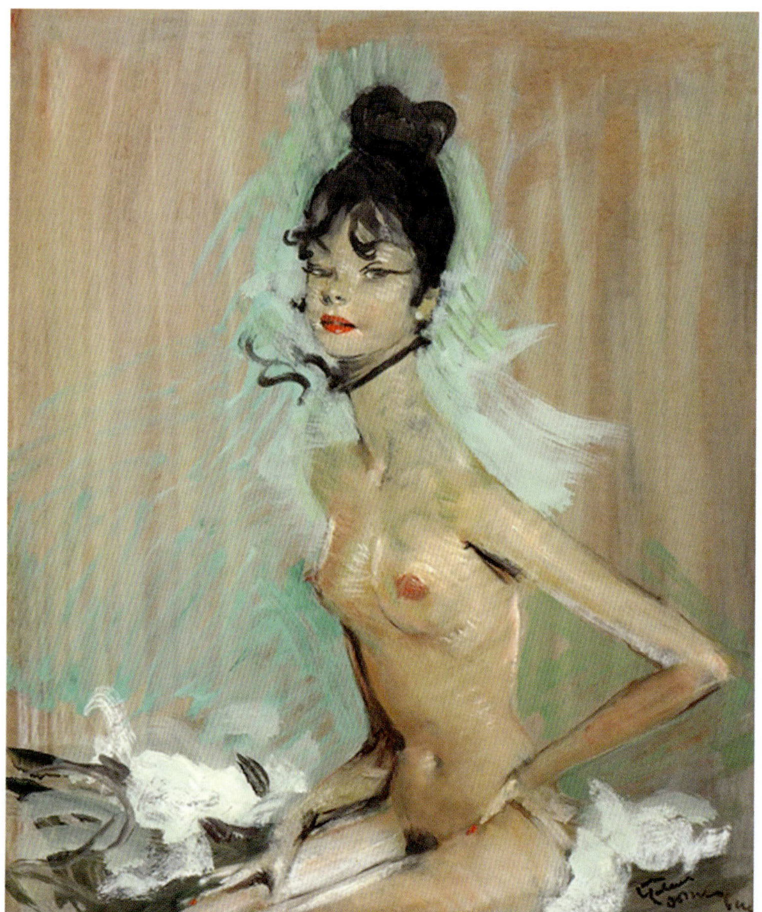

Jean Dormont

Born 1914

Jean Dormont attended l'Académie des Beaux-Arts in Mons, Belgium under the instruction of Louis Buisseret and Léon Navez. Dormont's paintings have a mystical quality that gives his subjects an inviting presence consistent with the Belgian modernist sensibility. The date of his death is unknown.

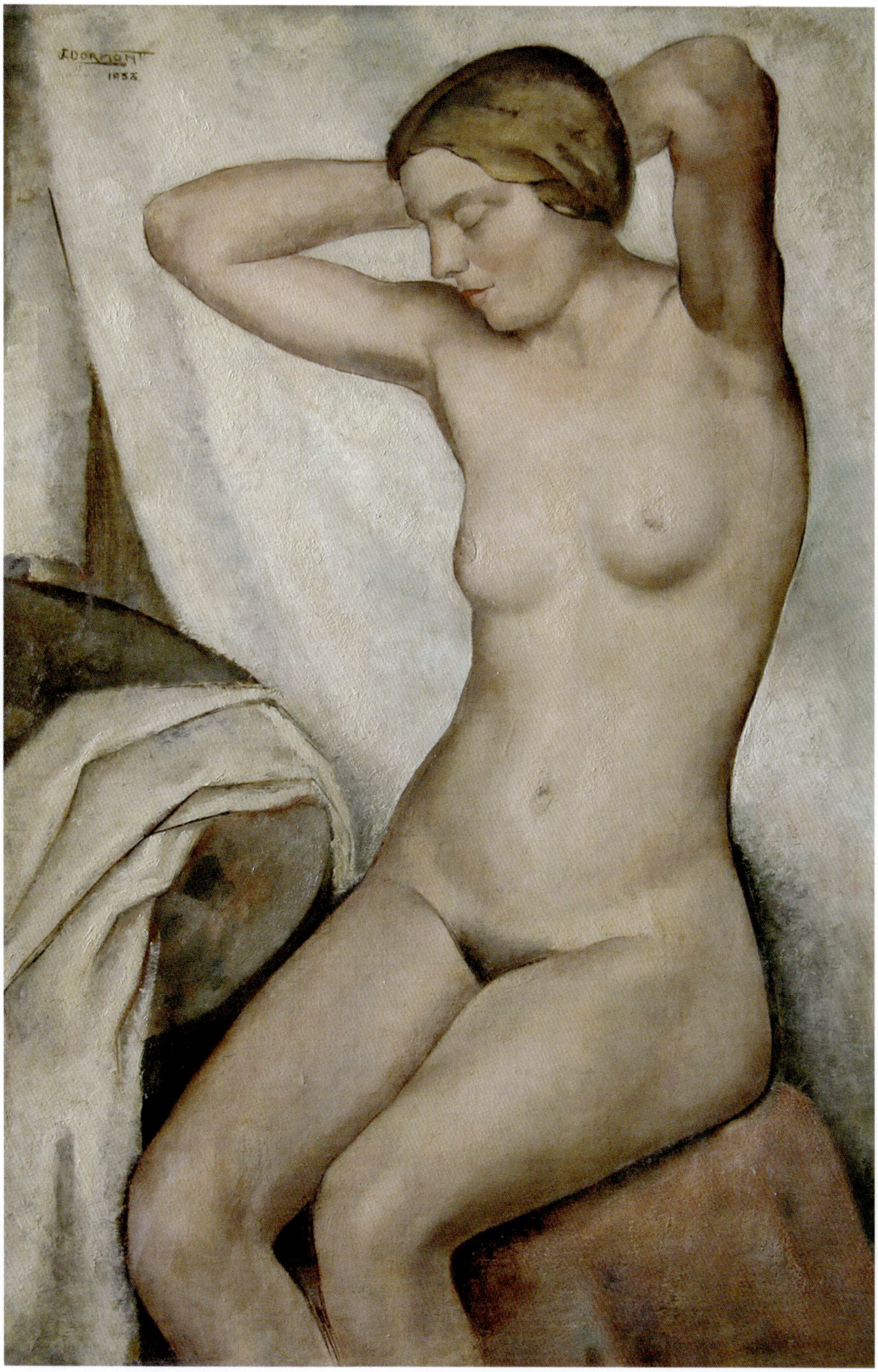

Jean Dormont
Nu Assis, Dated 1937
José and Carolyn Quant, Anaheim, California

Raphaël Dubois

1888-1962

Raphaël Dubois was born in 1888 in Liege, Belgium. He studied with Evariste Carpentier at l'Académie de Liege. During his subsequent studies with C. Mauclair, Dubois became largely influenced by the Impressionists.

Dubois is recognized for his paintings of religious subject matter, genre scenes, landscapes and still lifes. Dubois' first solo Paris exhibition was held at Galerie Le Studio and in 1911 and he exhibited at the Salon d'Automne in 1912. After World War I, he moved to Montparnasse. Between 1930 and 1939, Dubois lived in Nice.

Dubois painted bold and expressive canvases that were rich in color. His style and technique are in the tradition of Belgian Impressionists, though intensely personal.

Publications on Dubois' work include a 1921 catalog from an exhibition at Galerie Breckpot in Brussels. Charles Conrardy published a monograph on the artist titled *Le Peintre Raphaël Dubois* in 1946. Dubois' work is mentioned in S. Goyens de Heusch's 1988 book *L'impressionisme et le fauvisme en Belgique*.

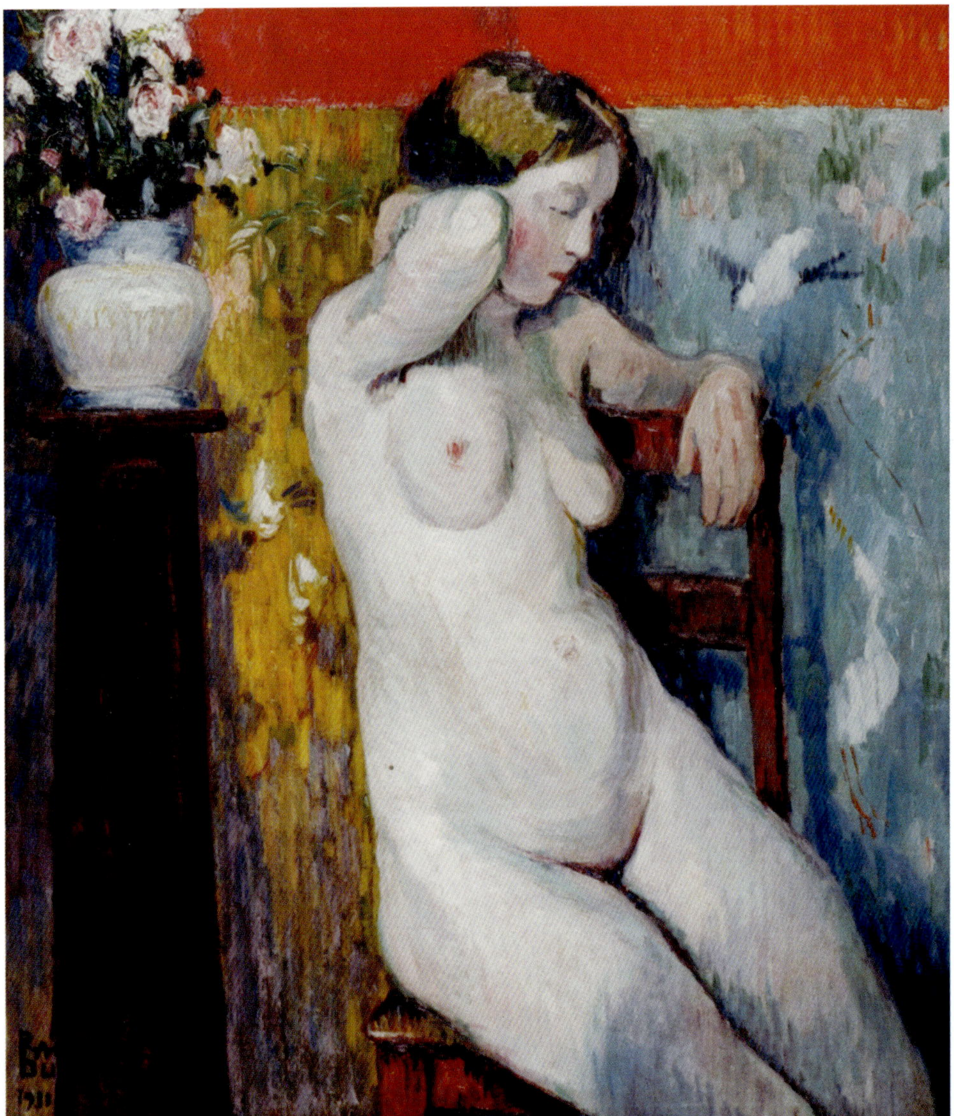

Raphaël Dubois
Nu Assis, Dated 1931
Los Angeles Fine Art Gallery, Los Angeles, California

Jean Dulac

1902-1968

Jean Dulac was born February 12, 1902 in Bourgoin, France. He was an extremely prolific painter and sculptor and enjoyed a long successful career. The artist specialized in nudes and painted many Montmarte street scenes. His canvases are rich in color, sensual and exhibited the sensitivities of a sculptor.

Dulac began his formal training in 1915 at l'École National des Beaux-Arts in Lyon under Louis Prost. In Paris he studied in the ateliers of Coutan and the sculptor Landowski.

Dulac received the Prix de Paris and in 1930 he began exhibiting at the Salon des Artistes Français and the Salon d'Automne. From 1946 to 1968 he chaired the Lyon Salon de la SLBA and was a member of their jury.

He illustrated *The Beloved Vagabond* (1922) by William J. Locke and *Nous Deux* (1929) by Marcel Valotaire.

The artist is represented in museums in Bourgoin, Germany, Belgium, Canada, Chile, the United States, Great Britain, Mexico and the Musée des Beaux-Arts de Lyon.

Jean Dulac died in 1968.

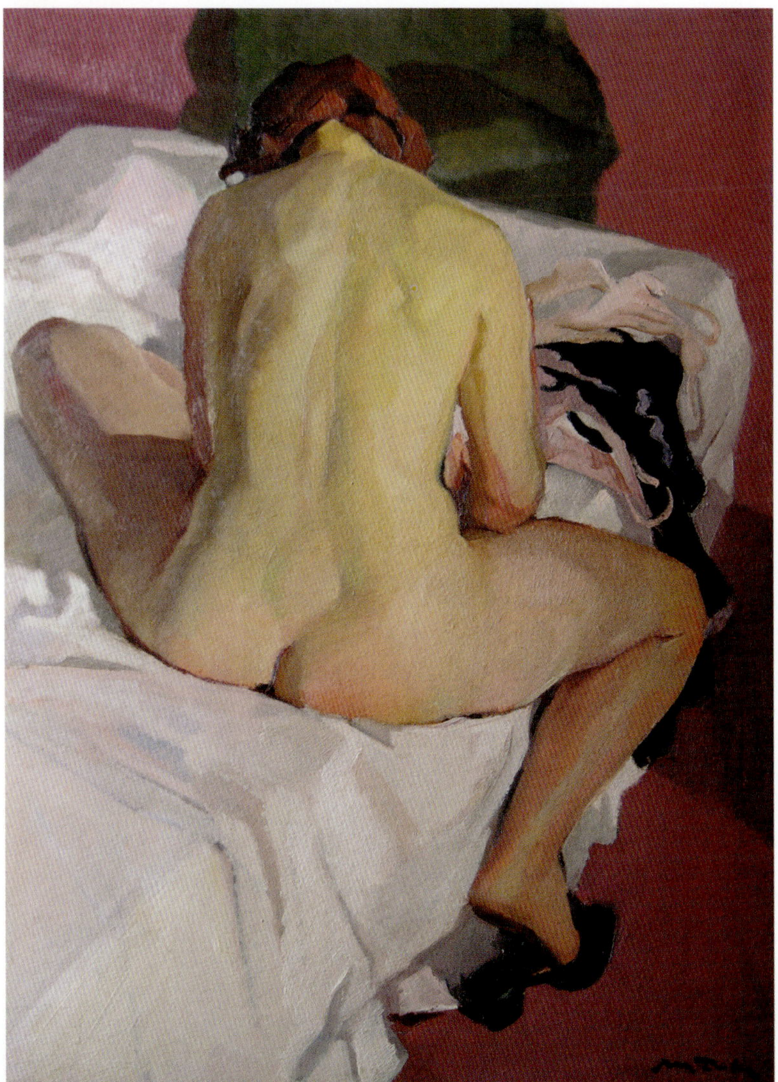

Jean Dulac
Le Boudoir Rose, c.1940
Kim Harman, Wilmington, Delaware

Frank Vincent DuMond

1865-1951

Frank Vincent DuMond was born in Rochester, New York. He studied with William Sartain and J.C. Beckwith at the Art Students League. In Paris he studied with Gustave Boulanger, Jules-Joseph Lefebvre and Benjamin Constant at l'Académie Julian.

In the tradition of many the great French painters of the 1890s DuMond's early paintings are Art Nouveau with symbolist subjects. His later works were typically American; he painted landscapes, flowers, fishing scenes and portraits, and he also worked as an illustrator. Dumond exhibited at the Paris Salons from 1889 through 1892 and was a member of the Salon des Artistes Français where he received a medal in 1890.

In 1892 he exhibited at the Cotton State Exposition in Atlanta, Georgia where he received a silver medal. That same year he exhibited at the Mechanics Charitable Exposition in Boston and was awarded the gold medal. The following year, he participated in the Worlds Columbian Exposition in Chicago. In 1901 he was awarded two silver medals at the Pan-American Exposition and three years later he received a silver medal at the St. Louis Exposition. He painted a fifteen-foot mural for the Court of the Universe at the Panama-Pacific Exposition in San Francisco in 1915 titled *Conquest of the Pacific Coast*.

DuMond exhibited work at the Corcoran Gallery of Art from 1907-1908 as well as in 1912, 1919 and 1926. Later in his career, DuMond received solo shows at galleries and schools in New York City and New England.

DuMond's work is included in the permanent collections of numerous museums including; Florence Griswold Museum in Old Lyme, Connecticut; Lyman Allyn Museum in New London, Connecticut; and the New Britain Museum of American Art. Other institutions that own DuMond's work are the San Francisco Public Library; Liberty Tower & Hotel des Artistes in New York City; Lotos Club; organizations in Portland, Oregon; Denver, Colorado; Richmond, Indiana and Lake Forest, Illinois. DuMond died in 1951.

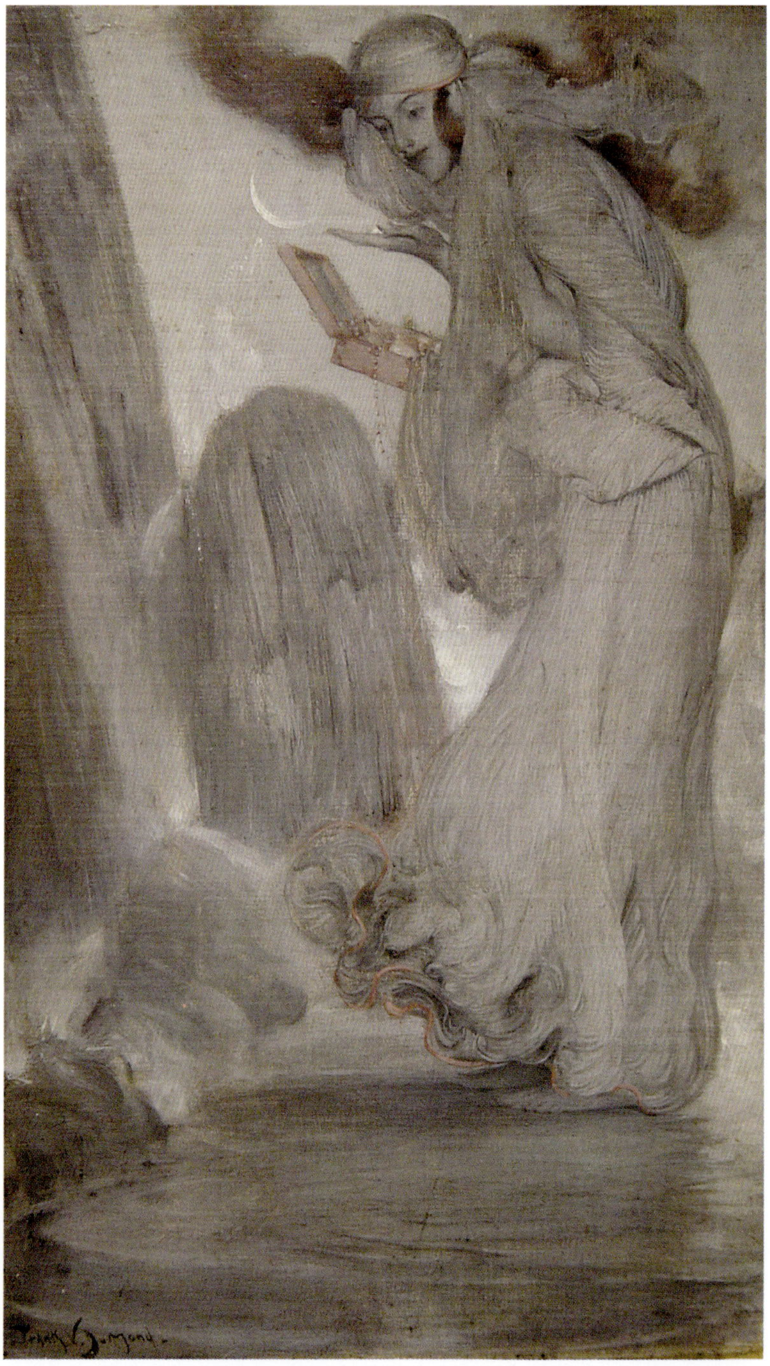

Frank Vincent DuMond
The Gift, c.1900
Papillon Gallery, Los Angeles, California

Adrien Dupagne
20th century

Adrien Dupagne was born in Liège, Belgium and exhibited frequently at the Salon d'Automne in Paris, beginning in 1928. He is best known for his female figures and nudes.

Realism with a modern flare best describes the works of Dupagne. His canvases are filled with atmosphere and the distinct personalities of his subjects.

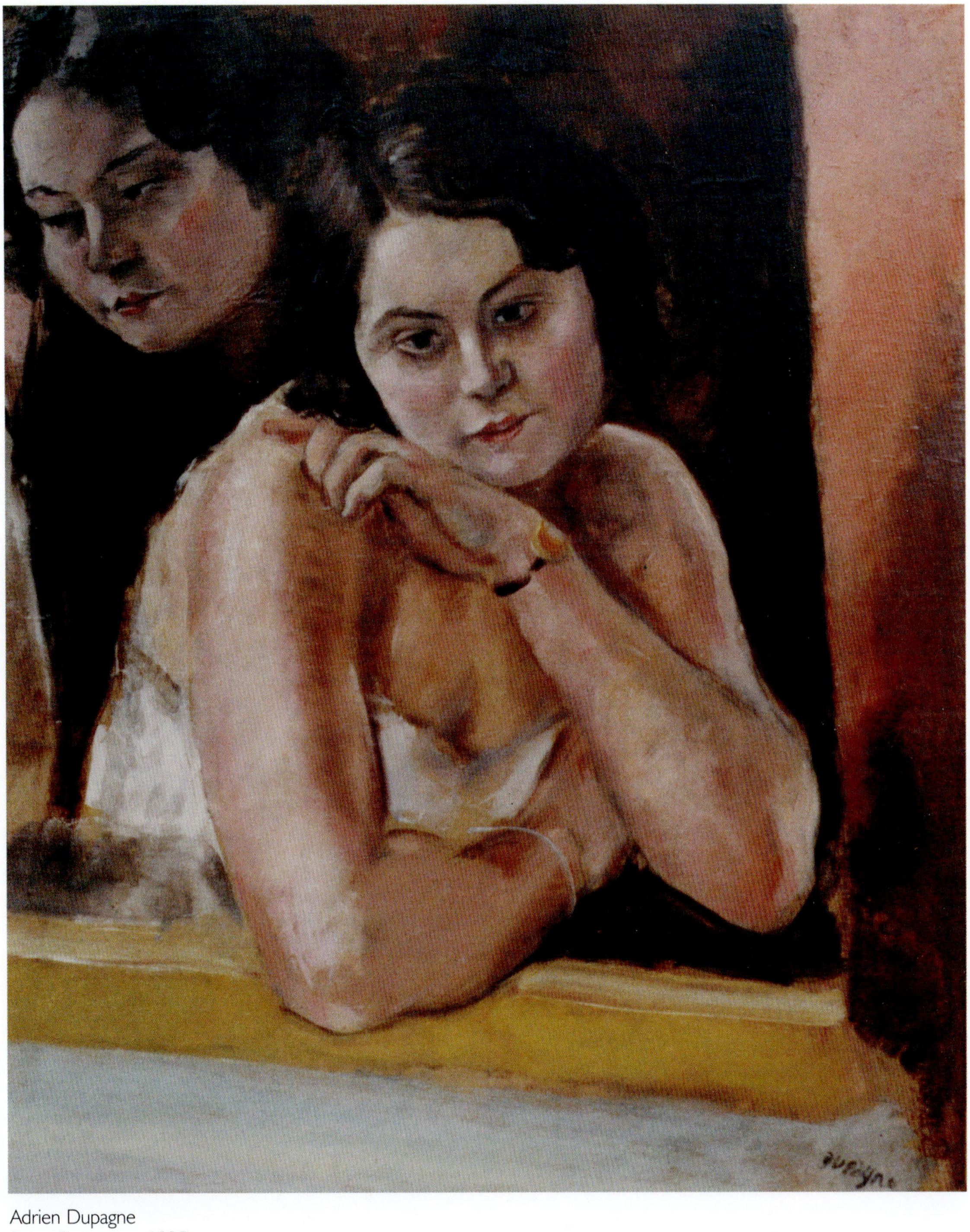

Adrien Dupagne
Deux Femmes, c.1935
Martha Wright, Cherry Hill, New Jersey

Jean Dupas
1882-1964

Jean Dupas was born in Bordeaux in 1882. He studied with Carolus-Duran and Albert Besnard at l'École des Beaux-Arts de Bordeaux.

Dupas was awarded the prestigious Grand Prix de Rome in 1910. He exhibited at the Salon de la Société des Artistes Français and received several awards at the salon, including a Médaille d'Or in 1922. In 1925 Dupas received international fame when he was asked by Émile-Jacques Ruhlmann to decorate his pavilion at the Exposition Internationale des Arts Décoratifs et Industriels in Paris. He was awarded the Légion d'Honneur in 1926.

Dupas worked as a ceramicist with René Buthaud in the Sèvres porcelain factory in the early 1920s, though Dupas' interests soon turned to other art forms including poster design, painting under glass, tapestry, mosaics and lacquer. Dupas executed many works throughout France includ-

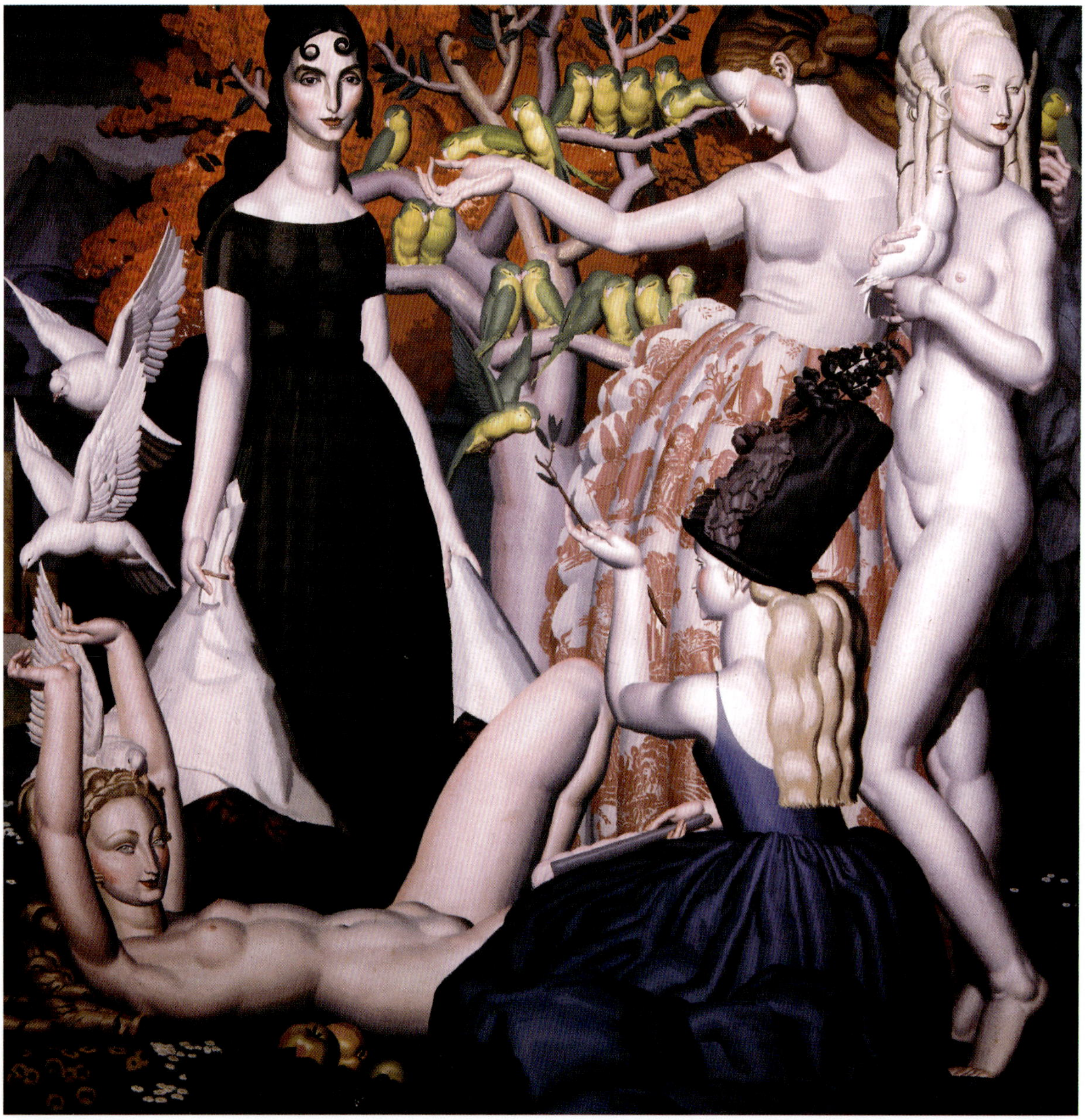

Jean Dupas
Les Perruches, c.1925
Xavier Roberts Collection, Atlanta, Georgia

ing a large composition called *La Vigne et le Vin* for the Bordeaux wine pavilion. He also painted several decorative panels including *Les Perruches* for the Hotel du Collectionneur and an allegorical image for the Palais de la Laine. In 1926 he worked with Ruhlmann and Janniot to design the interior of the tearoom for the *Ile de France*, the first ocean liner built after World War I.

In 1928 Dupas painted a fresco for the Church of the Saint-Esprit in Paris. After this commission Dupas concentrated on poster design. He created numerous posters for stores in England and the United States. In 1935 Dupas created a large stained glass window for the main lounge of the steamship *Normandy*; the commission was an honor that confirmed his importance in the world of Art Deco. Additionally, in 1941 he was elected to the Académie des Beaux-Arts.

Dupas' mannerist style can be classified as neo-classical, typical of other Bordeaux modern artists. His works evoke the art of Ingres and Raphaël. With his portrayal of sophisticated women and allegorical fantasies, Dupas' works convey the optimism, elegance and decadence of the Art Deco style. As in the paintings of Delorme and Despujols, Dupas' paintings also express utopian ideals and romance. Though Dupas has been extremely well known to collectors and dealers in Art Deco for many years, his contribution to modern art remains grossly under-appreciated.

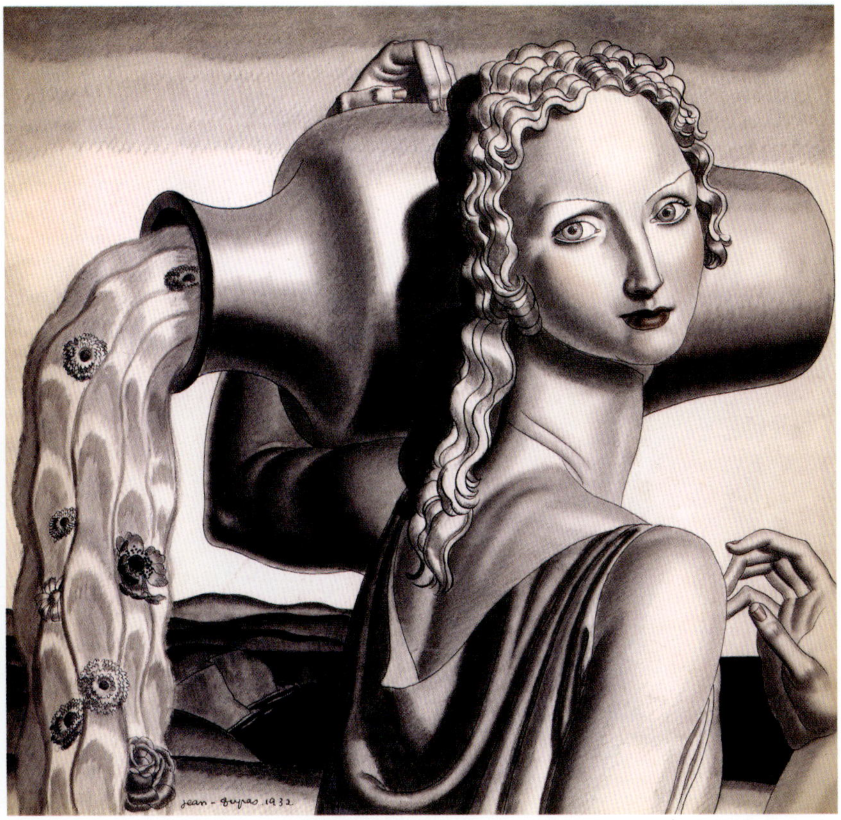

Jean Dupas
Un Vase de l'Eau, Dated 1932
Barry Friedman Ltd., New York, New York

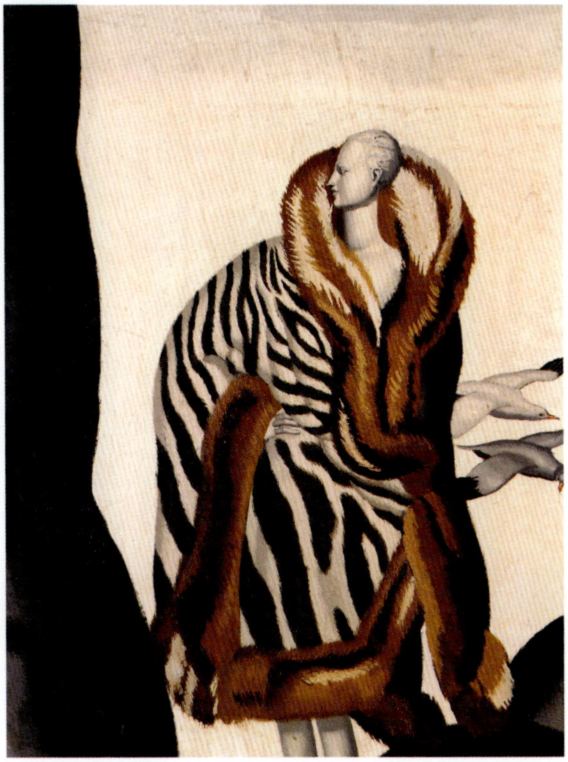

Jean Dupas
Femme Élégante, c.1920
Barry Friedman Ltd., New York, New York

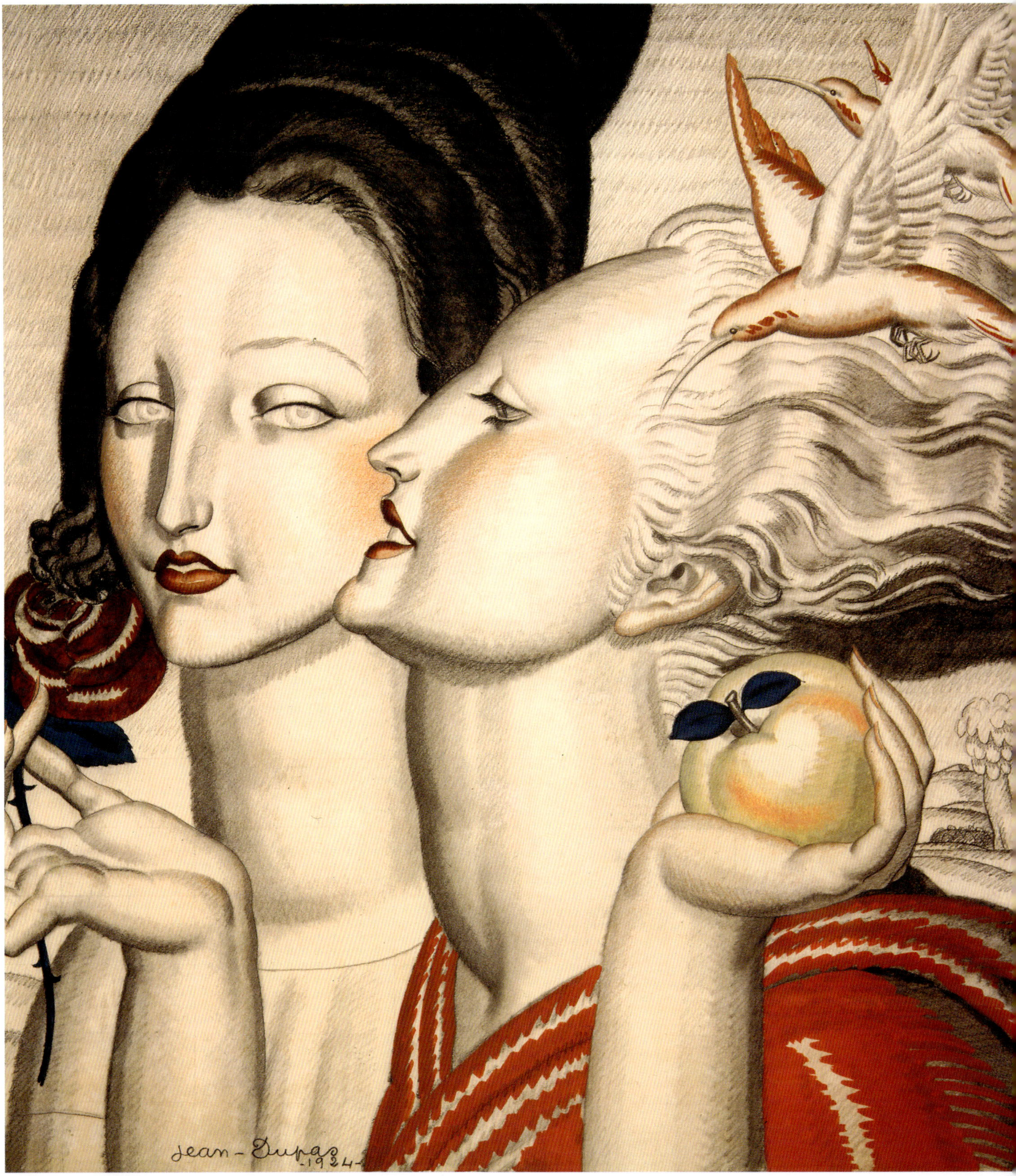

Jean Dupas
Deux Femmes, Dated 1924
Barry Friedman Ltd., New York, New York

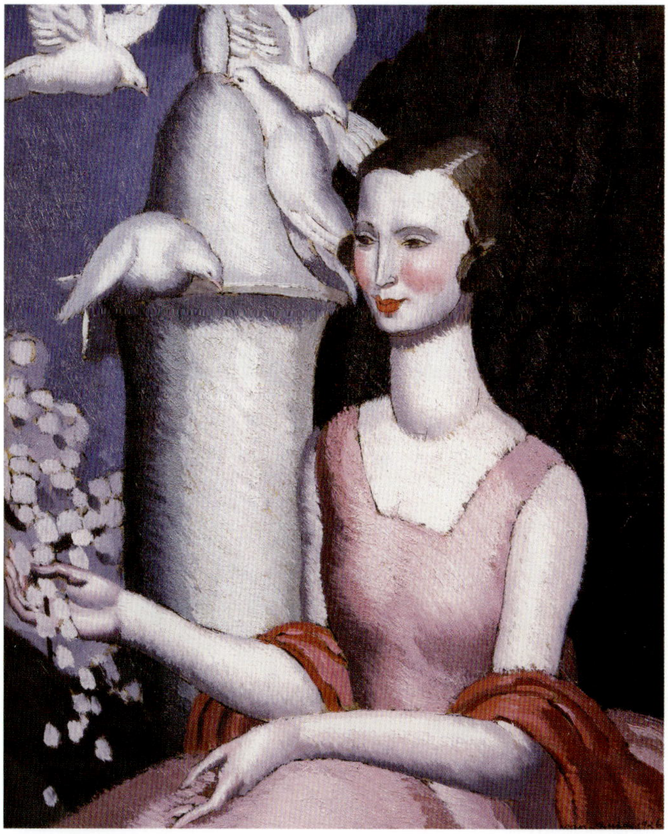

Jean Dupas
Femme Assis, c.1925
Barry Friedman Ltd., New York, New York

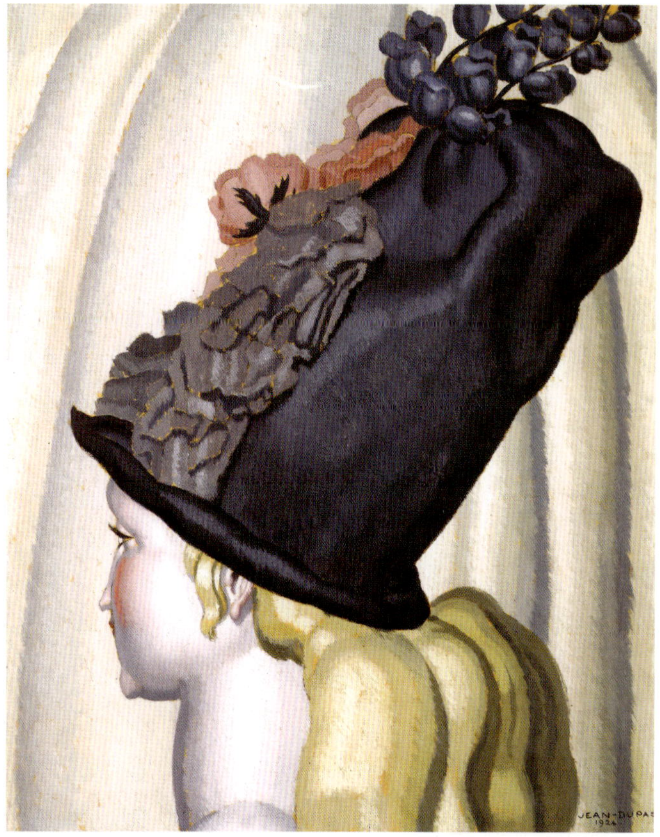

Jean Dupas
Femme au Chapeau, Dated 1924
Barry Friedman Ltd., New York, New York

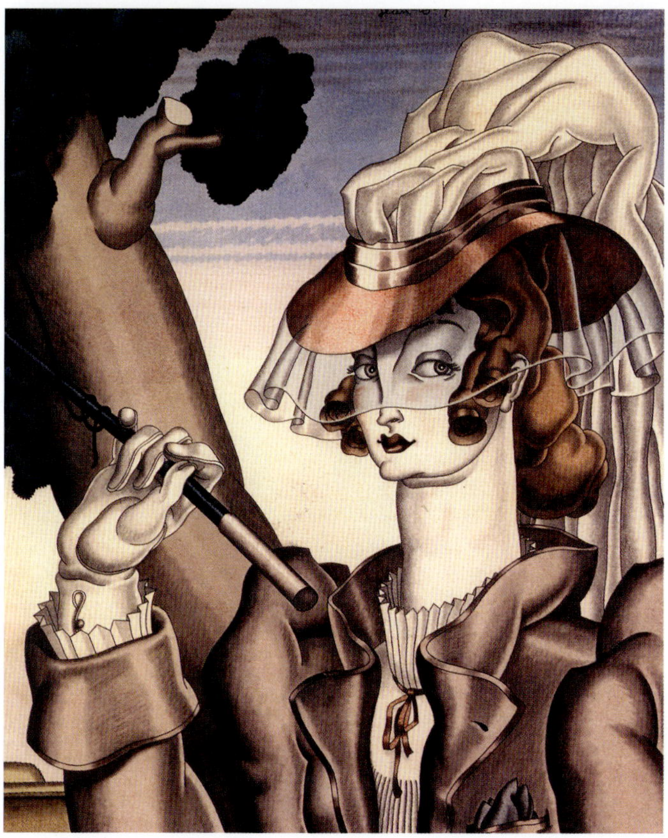

Jean Dupas
Femme au Chapeau, c.1940
Barry Friedman Ltd., New York, New York

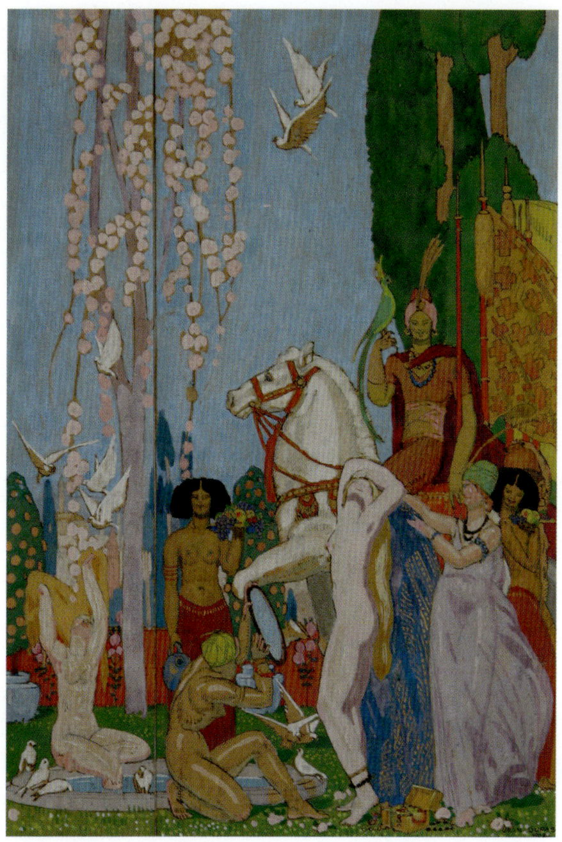

Jean Dupas
La Célébration, Dated 1918
Papillon Gallery, Los Angeles, California

Auguste Durand-Rosé

1887-1962

Auguste Durand-Rosé was born in Marseille in 1887. He exhibited at the Salons des Artistes Indépendants, Salon des Tuileries and the Salon d'Automne where he was a member in 1937. He exhibited in a number of group shows in France, Brussels, Prague and at the Carnegie Foundation in Pittsburg.

Durand-Rosé's paintings are rich in texture and color. He gives subtle expression to his subjects with his use of posture and composition.

Durand-Rosé died in 1962 in Paris. The Musée Cantini in Marseille holds one of his works in their collection.

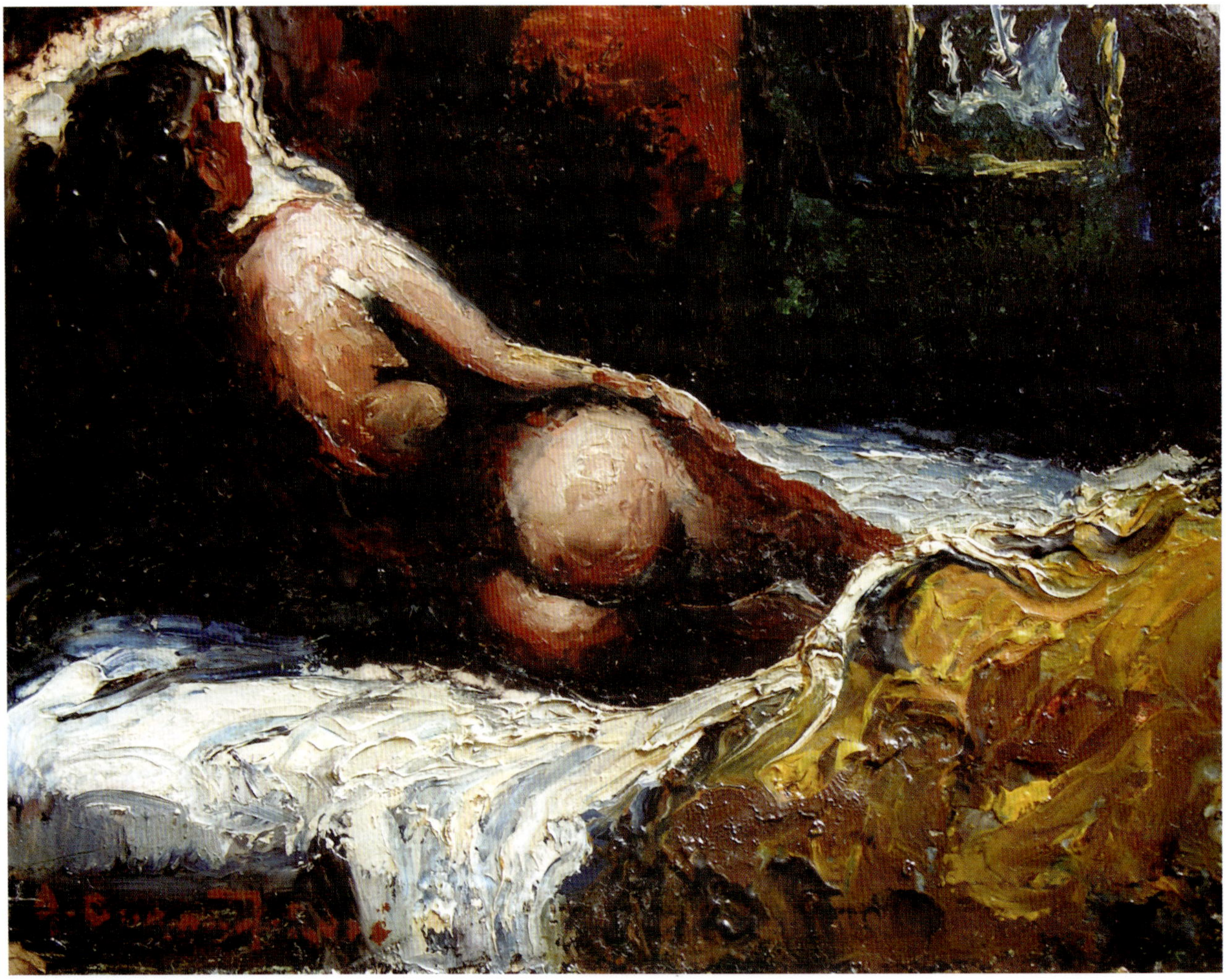

Auguste Durand-Rosé
Nu Allongé, c.1930
Papillon Gallery, Los Angeles, California

Charles-Auguste Edelmann

1879-1950

Charles-Auguste Edelmann was born in 1879 in Soulot-sous-Forêts. He was a student of J.L. Gérôme and Ferdinand Humbert at l'École des Beaux-Arts in Paris and became a member of the Salon des Artistes and of the Salon d'Automne where he exhibited in 1928.

Edelmann captured the essence of the café life in Paris between the wars. His colorful compositions are clever and express the romance of the period.

Edelmann illustrated several books by Balzac, Musset, Courteline, Oscar Wilde and Kessel. He died in Paris in 1950.

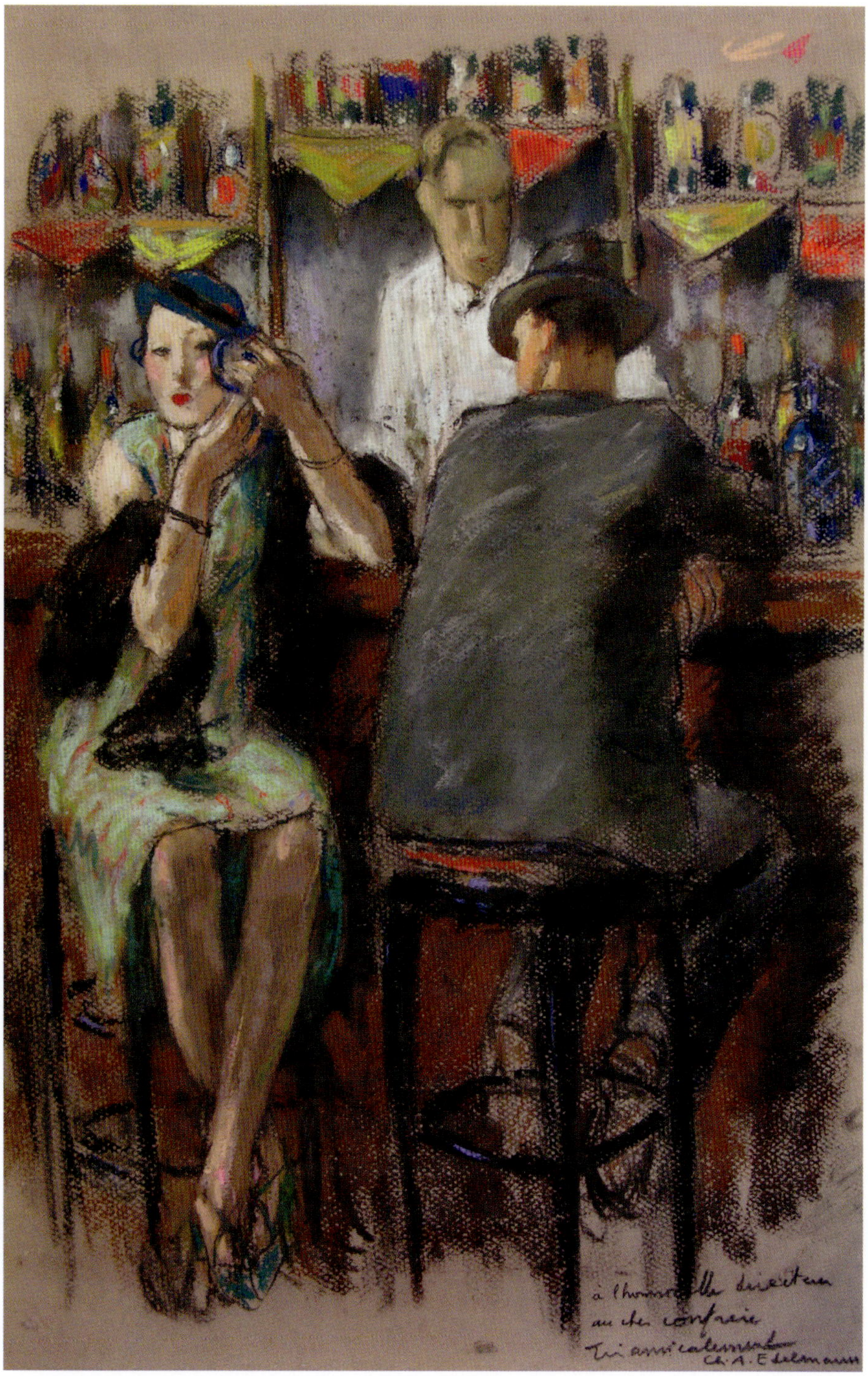

Charles-Auguste Edelmann
Au Bar, c.1925
Ernie and Ronna Vigil, Aptos, California

Francis de Erdely

1904-1959

Francis de Erdely was born in Budapest, Hungary in 1904 where he studied at the Royal Academy of Art. De Erdely continued his studies at the Academy of San Fernando in Madrid and later at the Sorbonne and l'École du Louvre in Paris. De Erdely lived abroad in Brussels, Amsterdam, Vienna and Prague. De Erdely exhibited in Budapest and received awards as early as 1925.

He abandoned war-torn Europe and moved to New York in the late 1930s where he began a new, successful career in the United States. In 1939 he exhibited in New York City and in 1941 he showed at the Pennsylvania Academy of Fine Art in Philadelphia. Between 1940 and 1944 he exhibited at the Detroit Institute of Art. During the following decades he exhibited widely including shows at the Corcoran, Carnegie Institute, de Young Museum and Los Angeles County Museum of Art.

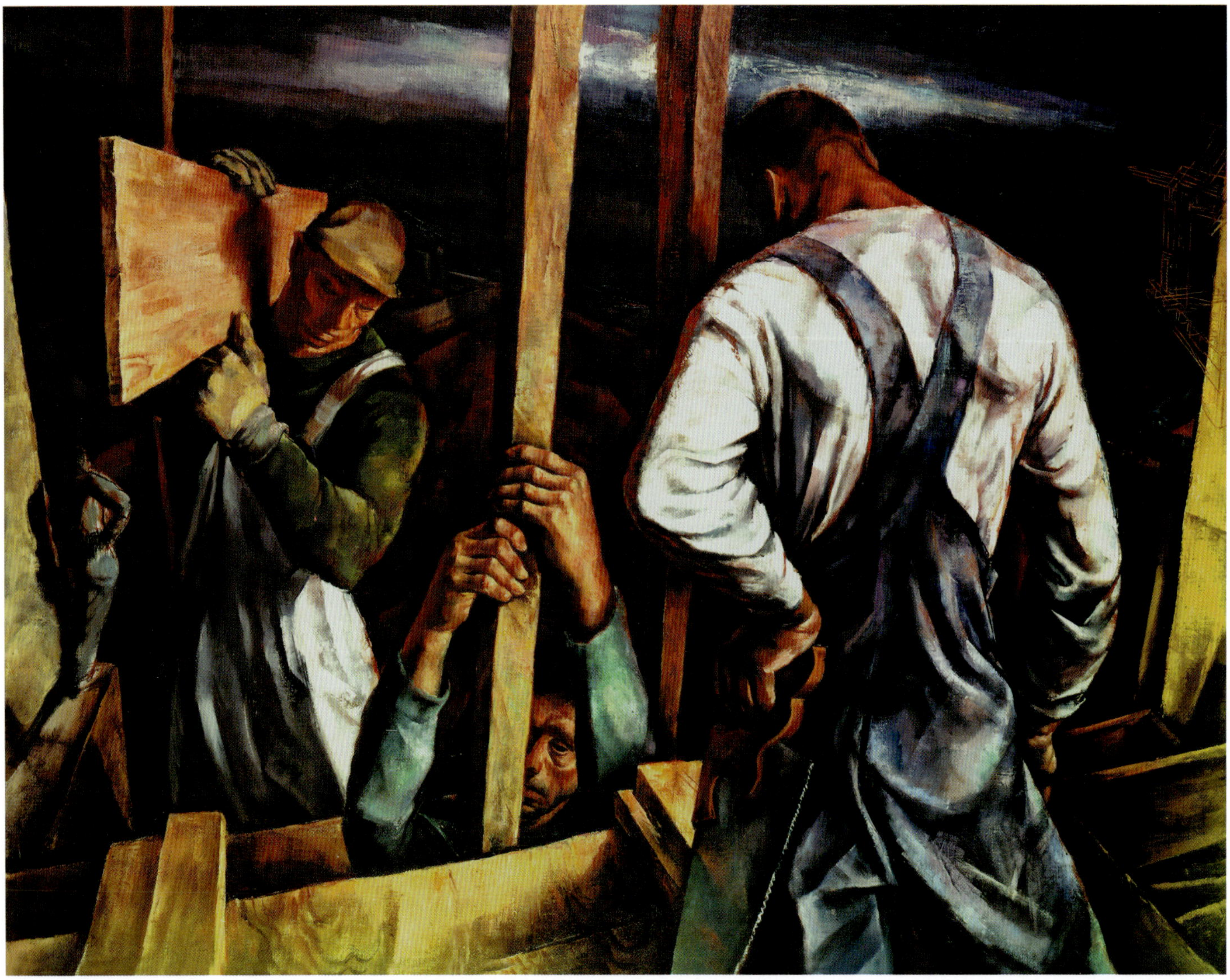

Francis de Erdely
The Builders, Exhibited in 1939
Michael Loren and Gloria Aronson, Leucadia, California

De Erdely was also an influential teacher. He first taught at the Netherlands Art Academy in The Hague and then at the Pasadena Museum School. From 1945 until his death in 1959 he taught at the University of Southern California. His influence on the art community of Southern California cannot be overstated. De Erdely was both a successful artist and respected teacher.

De Erdely was a modernist with roots in the techniques of the Cubists and the traditions of Cézanne. In character with his Eastern European upbringing, De Erdely's subjects are often filled with angst, yet ultimately his works are a celebration of the human experience. He was an innovative artist, brilliant draftsman and sophisticated colorist. De Erdely was a master of expressive subject matter and composition.

The artist was a tall, imposing figure. He often wore a black cape and a large brimmed hat; his friends described him as an eccentric bohemian. De Erdely frequented the coffee houses and Jazz clubs that populated Los Angeles after World War II.

De Erdely's work is in the collections of the Los Angeles County Museum of Art, de Young Museum, Cranbrook Academy, and National Gallery of Victoria in Melbourne, Australia.

Francis de Erdely
Table for Two, c.1945
Michael Loren and Gloria Aronson, Leucadia, California

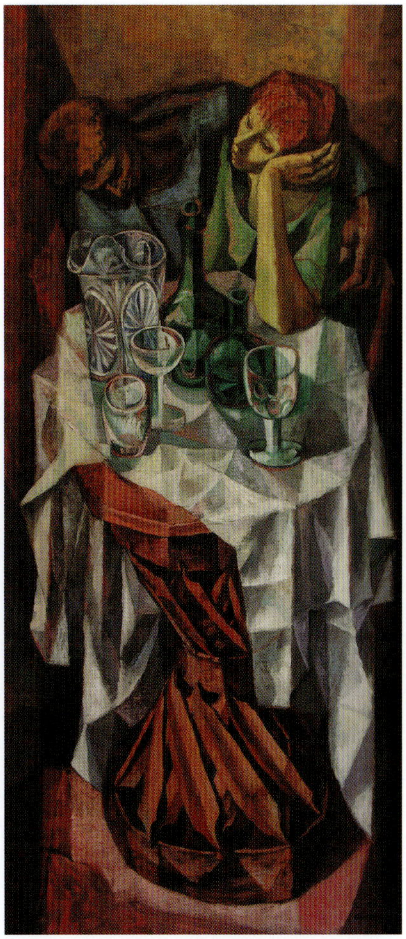

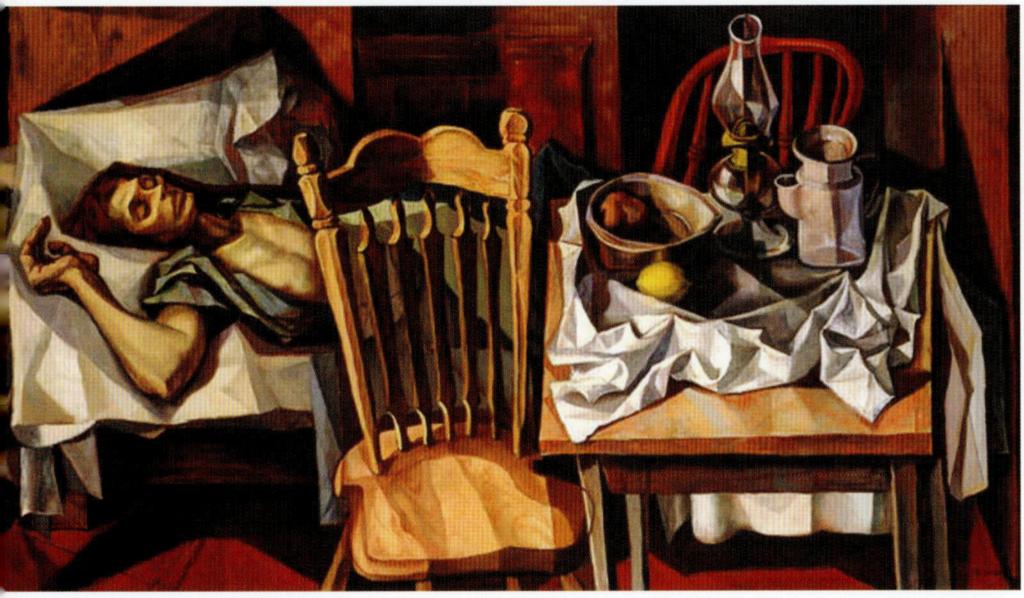

Francis de Erdely
Servants Quarters, c. 1940
Collection James and Martha Newkirk, California
Photo courtesy of Spencer Jon Helfen Fine Art, Los Angeles, California

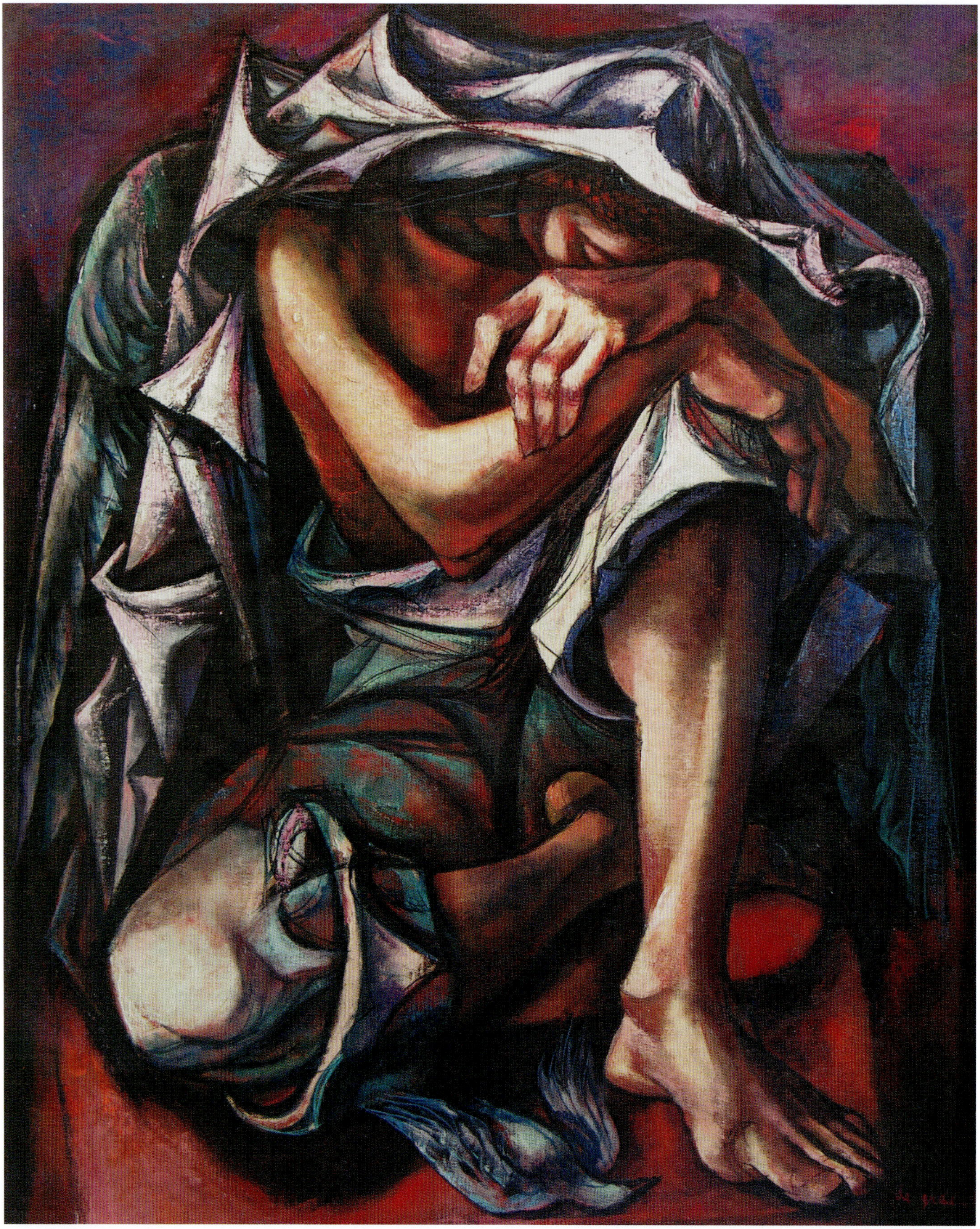

Francis de Erdely
Blue Bird, c.1945
Private Collection

Ivan Marie Laurent Escribe

1913-1991

Ivan Marie Laurent Escribe was born in Briatexte, France in 1913. He studied with P.A. Laurens as well as Aubry and L. Roger. In 1934 he debuted at the Salon des Artistes Français.

Escribe painted intriguing scenes of bars and restaurants in a modern style. He also painted highly detailed still lifes. The artist died in 1991.

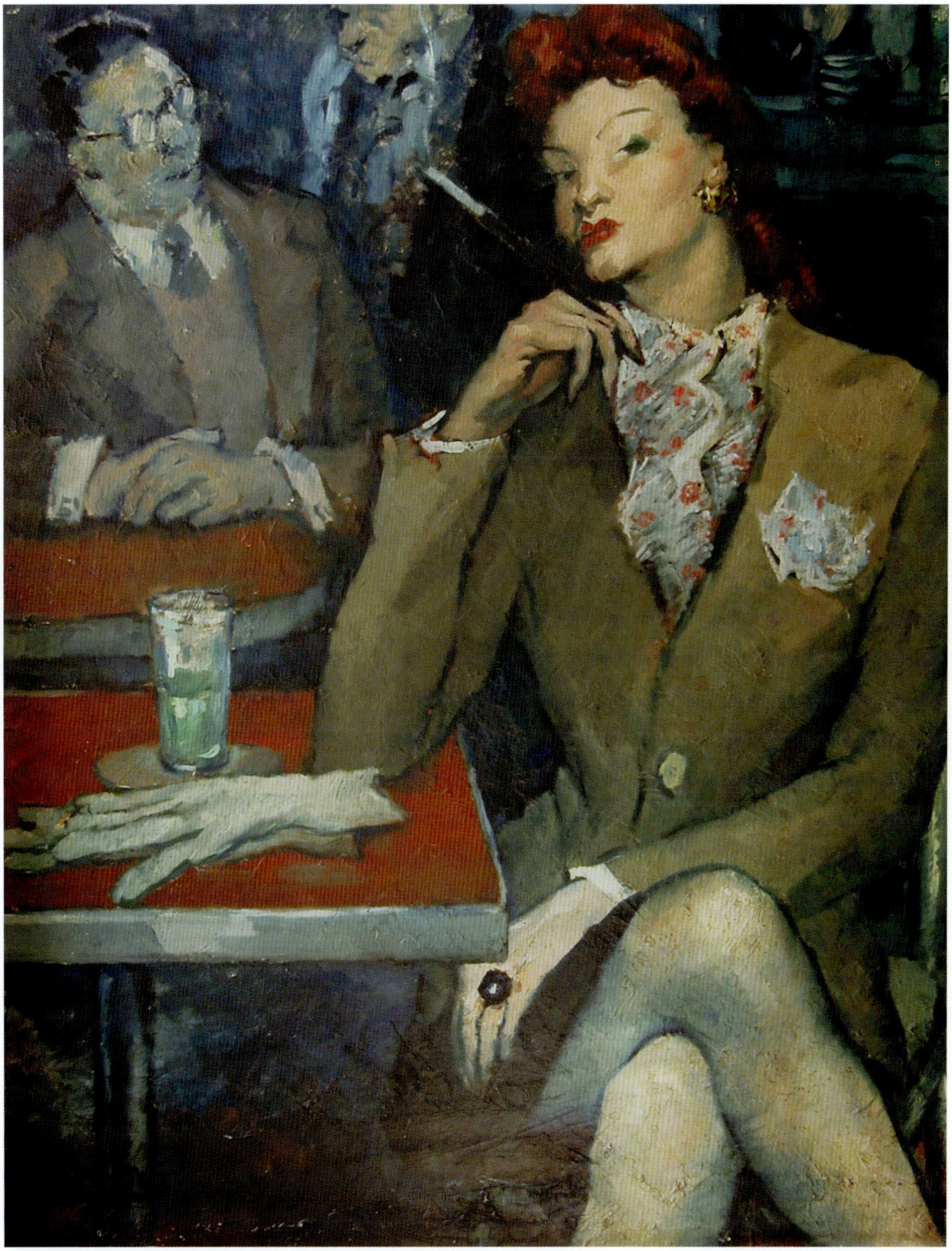

Ivan Marie Laurent Escribe
Femme au Café, c.1940
Jeff Sagansky and Christy Welker, New York, New York

Albert Fernand-Renault

Born 1887

Albert Fernand-Renault was born 1887 and was a student of Fernand Cormon at l'École des Beaux-Arts. He enjoyed much success after World War I and received both the Médaille d'Argent in 1928 at the Salon des Artistes Français and the Médaille d'Or in 1931.

Fernand-Renault painted large bold canvases of idealized utopian subjects that were fashionable with Art Deco designers of the period. Stylistically his brush technique is closest to the Postimpressionists.

Fernand-Renault is thought to have died sometime after 1940 and it is possible that he may have disappeared during World War II.

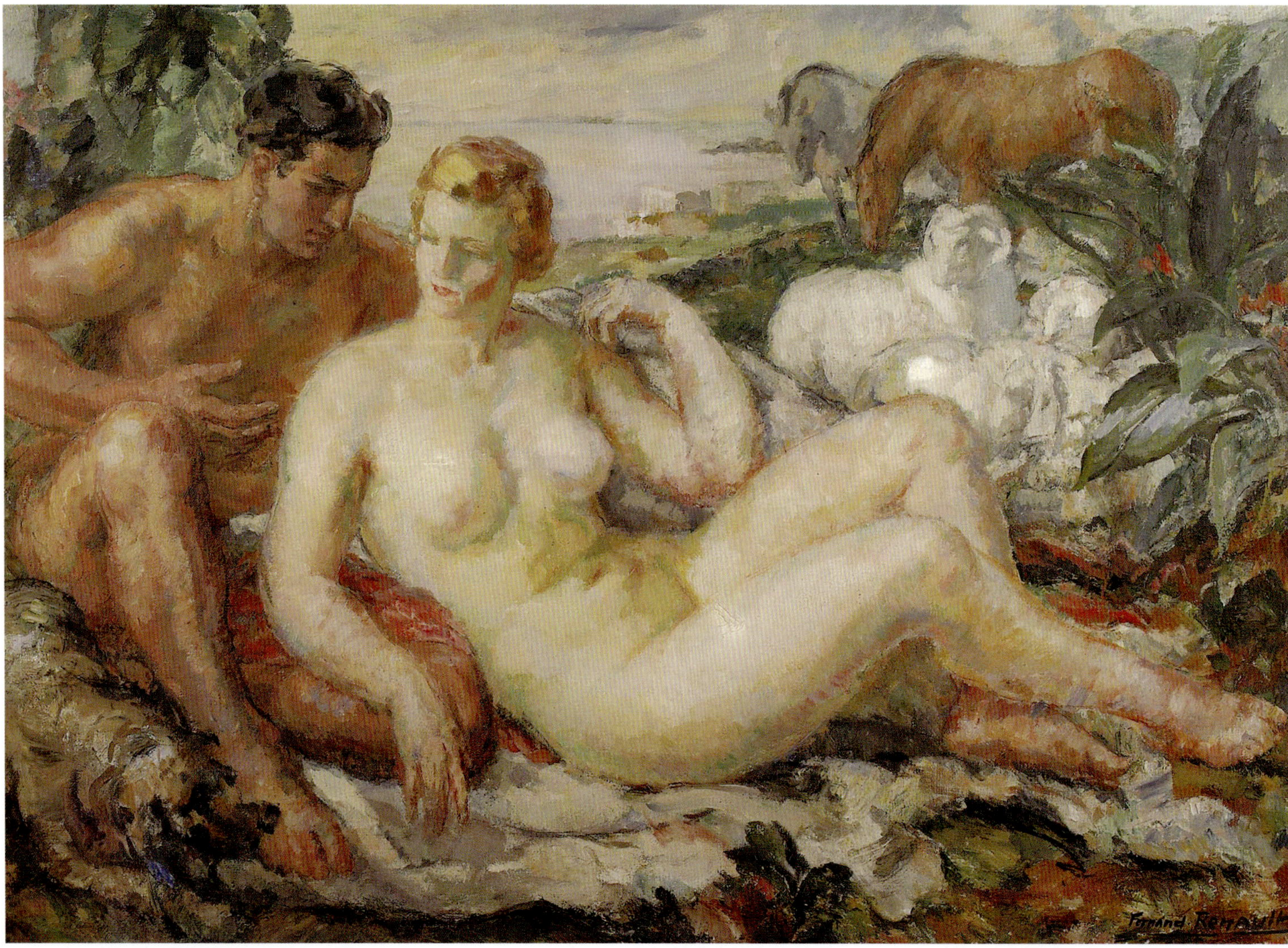

Albert Fernand-Renault
Pastorale, Exhibited 1935
Private Collection, Paris, France

Gaston Simoes de Fonseca

Born 1874

Gaston Simoes de Fonseca was born October 16, 1874 in Rio de Janeiro. He established himself in Paris as a painter and illustrator and exhibited at the Salon des Artistes Français in 1913 and 1914 where he received the Médaille de Bronze. From 1937 to 1943 Simoes de Fonseca exhibited at the Salon des Indépendants. He was awarded the Chevalier de la Légion d'Honneur in 1929.

His works have since been exhibited in Paris and New York and have sold at auction by Sotheby's and Swann Galleries.

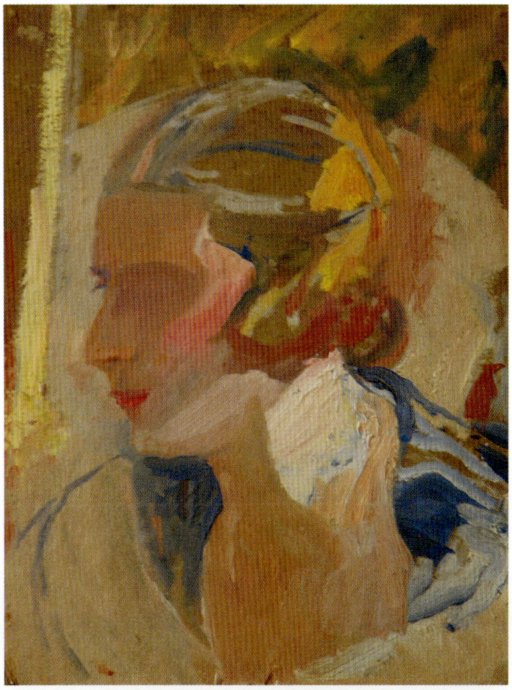

Gaston Simoes de Fonseca
Portrait d'une Femme, c.1920
Private Collection

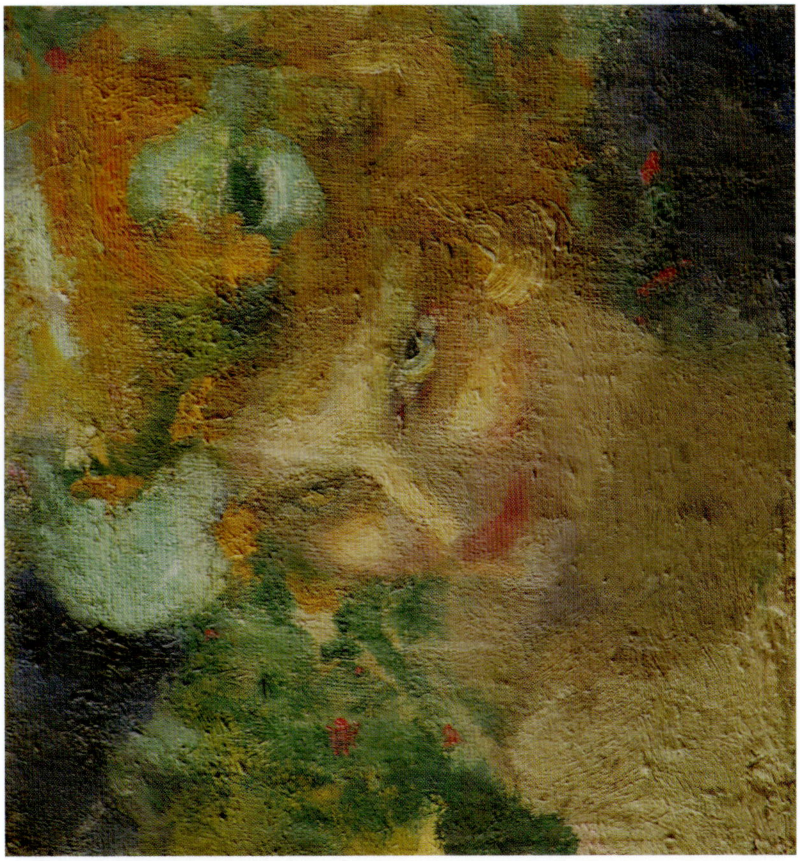

Gaston Simoes de Fonseca
Portrait d'une Femme, c.1920
Jeffrey Winter Fine Arts, Long Beach, California

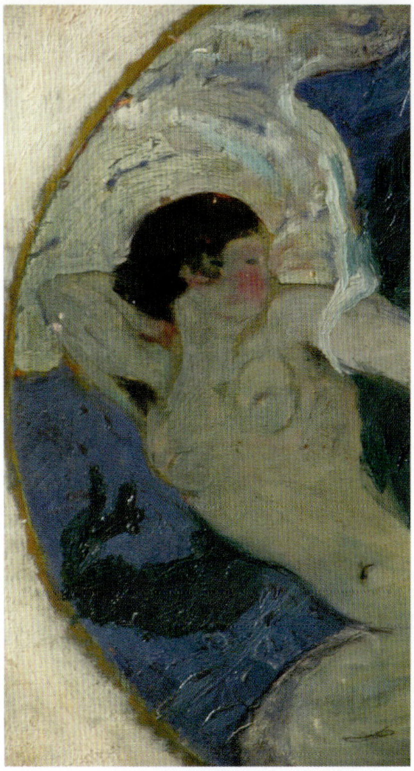

Gaston Simoes de Fonseca
Nu Symboliste, c.1920
Jeffrey Winter Fine Arts, Long Beach, California

Hippolyte Fournier
1852-1926

Hippolyte Fournier was born March 4, 1852 in Rablay, Maine-et-Loire, France. He was a student of Jean-Paul Laurens at l'Académie Julian.

Fournier exhibited at the Salon des Artistes Français. He first exhibited his paintings in 1881 and continued to exhibit regularly at this salon. He received a medal at the l'Éxposition Universelle of 1889 and again in 1890. He was awarded a bronze medal at l'Exposition Universelle de 1900 and continued to exhibit until 1910.

Fournier was a painter in the tradition of the Paris Salons. Classically instructed he employed his obvious talent to construct intriguing scenes of beauty and used large canvases to create an inviting mood for the viewer.

Like many other artists in the last decades of the 19th century he experimented with composition and subtle use of light and shadow. His choice of subjects, especially his nudes, captivated the public's imagination and ultimately proved to be commercially successful. The Musée d'Angers holds one of his paintings. Fournier died January 12, 1926.

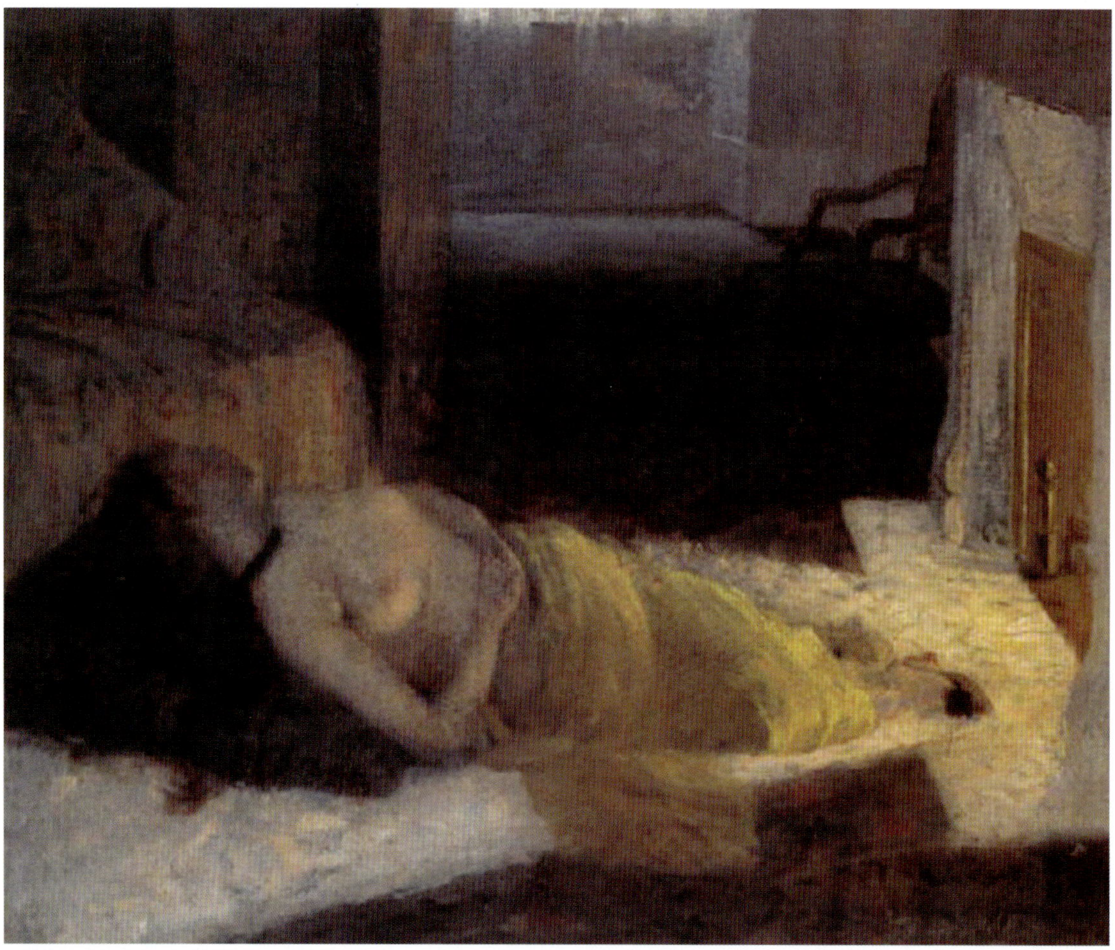

Hippolyte Fournier
Nu Allongé, c.1900
Private Collection

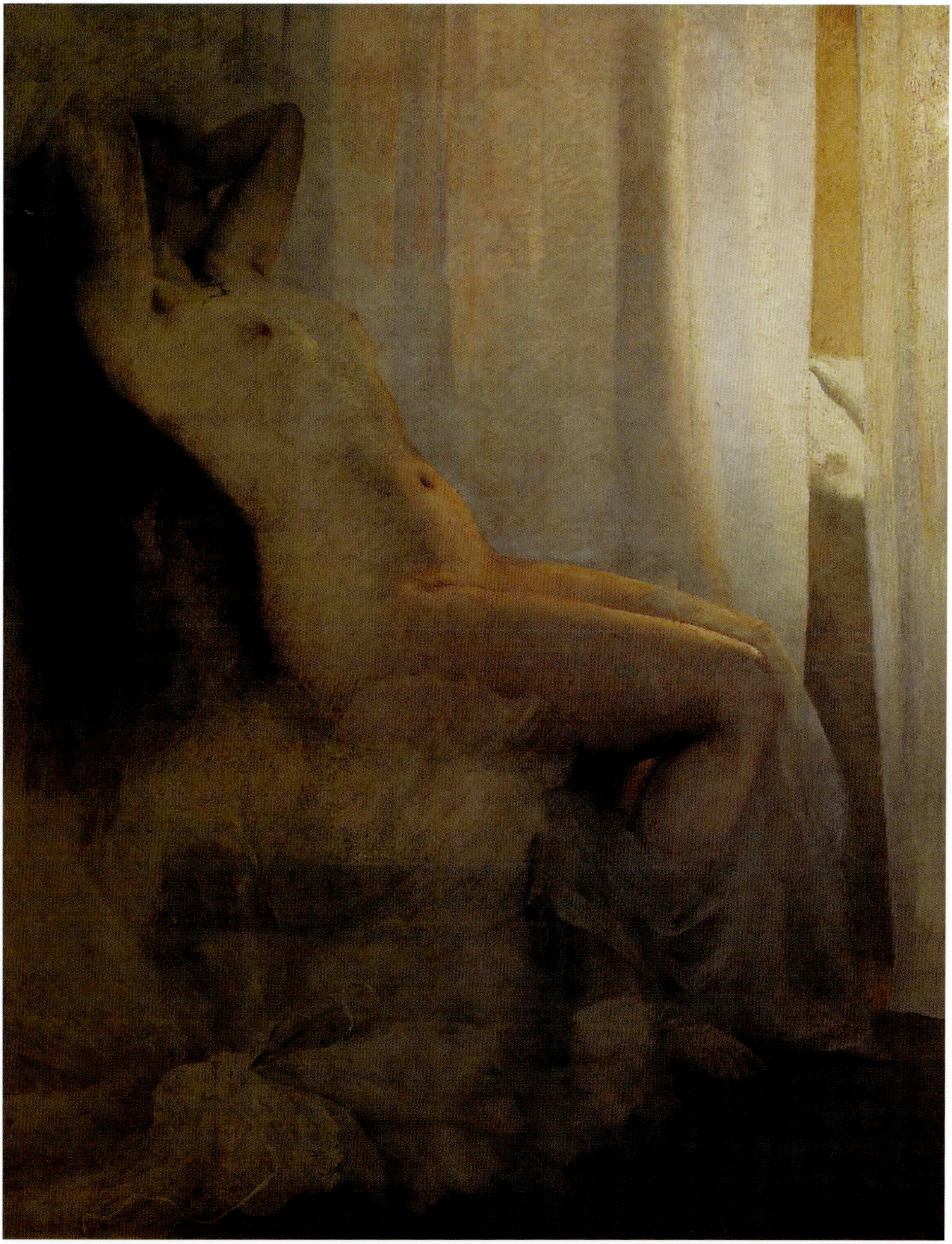

Hippolyte Fournier
Le Soir, Paris, Dated 1889
Private Collection, Paris, France

Baron Léon Henri Marie Frédéric

1846-1940

Baron Léon Henri Marie Frédéric was born on August 16, 1856 in Brussels, Belgium. He was the brother of well-known painter Georges Frédéric and a student of Jules van Kersblick and Jean François Portaels at l'Académie des Beaux-Arts de Bruxelles.

In 1876 he moved to Italy and traveled for two years, visiting Rome, Florence, Venice and Naples. Returning to Belgium in 1878, Frédéric exhibited at the Salon de Bruxelles and then the Cercle d'art l'Essor. Subsequent to these exhibitions, Frédéric showed work in Gent, Liège, Munich, Nice and Paris and received a medal at the 1891 Berlin exhibition. In 1899 Frédéric exhibited at Schaerbeek. That same year he received a bronze medal at the Paris International Exhibition and a gold medal the following year. In addition to these acknowledgements, Frédéric was honored with the Chevalier de l'Ordre de Léopold and named a member of l'Académie Royale de Belgique.

Frédéric was a masterful technician of realistic painting, but his canvases far surpassed mere technical skill. His subjects have a quality beyond reality that is alluring and mysterious and many of his works are symbolic to the point of the bizarre.

While living and traveling in Italy, Frédéric painted local landscapes and villages. In 1883 he traveled to Nafraiture in Ardennes forest, which became his principle source of inspiration. At that time he also traveled in England, Germany and the Netherlands. Beyond natural landscapes, Frédéric also painted religious and symbolic paintings. He is known as a Symbolist painter and was greatly interested in social justice and the idealistic objectives shared by other artists and intellectuals of his era. Frédéric died in 1940.

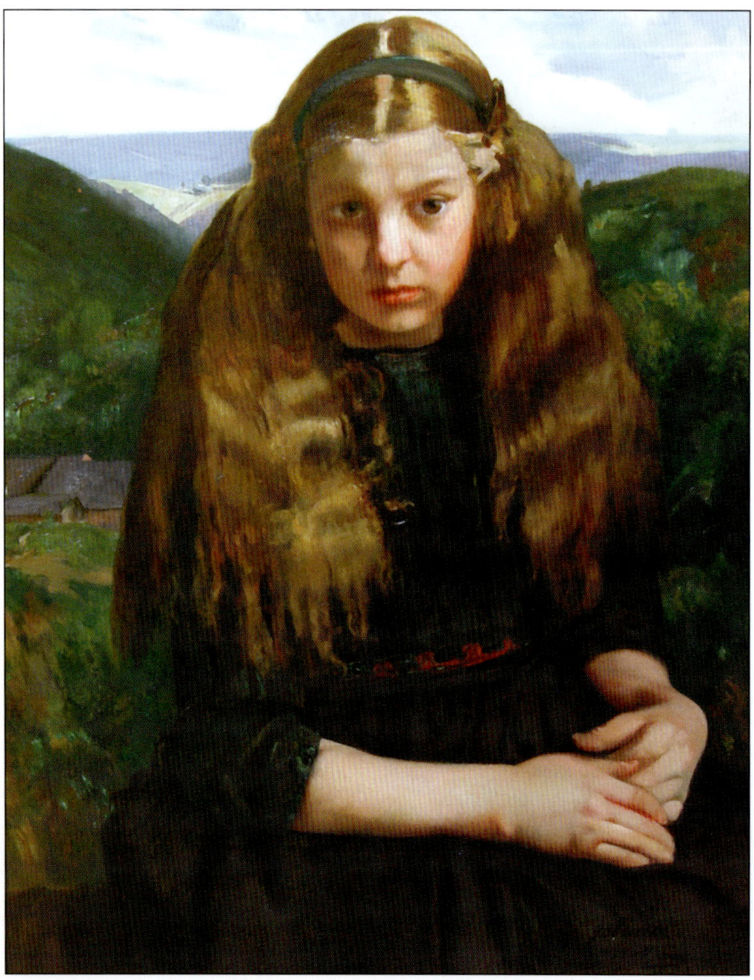

Baron Léon Henri Marie Frédéric
Jeune Femme Assis, Dated 1902
Los Angeles Fine Art Gallery, Los Angeles, California

Pal Fried
1893-1976

Pal Fried was born in 1893 in Budapest. He studied at the Hungarian Academy under the instruction of Hugo Pohl and in Paris under Claude Monet and Lucien Simone. He excelled in portraits of high society Parisian women, ballerinas, nudes, Oriental and western scenes, and seascapes in oil and pastels. His work is often signed *Fried Pal*.

Fried traveled in Africa and Spain experimenting with light and movement in his work. He exhibited in Müücsarnok, Budapest and in 1947 moved to the United States where he taught in New York at the Academy of Arts. He later worked in Hollywood in the 1950s and 1960s painting portraits of high-profile celebrities including the Gabor sisters and Marilynn Monroe. He painted many scenes of fashionable women with Parisian landmarks in the background. His work was extensively collected by Frances Wilke Haussner and hung in the famed Haussner Restaurant in Baltimore, Maryland.

Pal Fried was a highly prolific artist and his career spanned more than five decades. He painted beautiful women in a realistic style that became his hallmark. Stylistically his work evolved with the times, his early paintings display a mood and depth lacking in his later work but his success never faded. Pal Fried died March 6, 1976 in New York City.

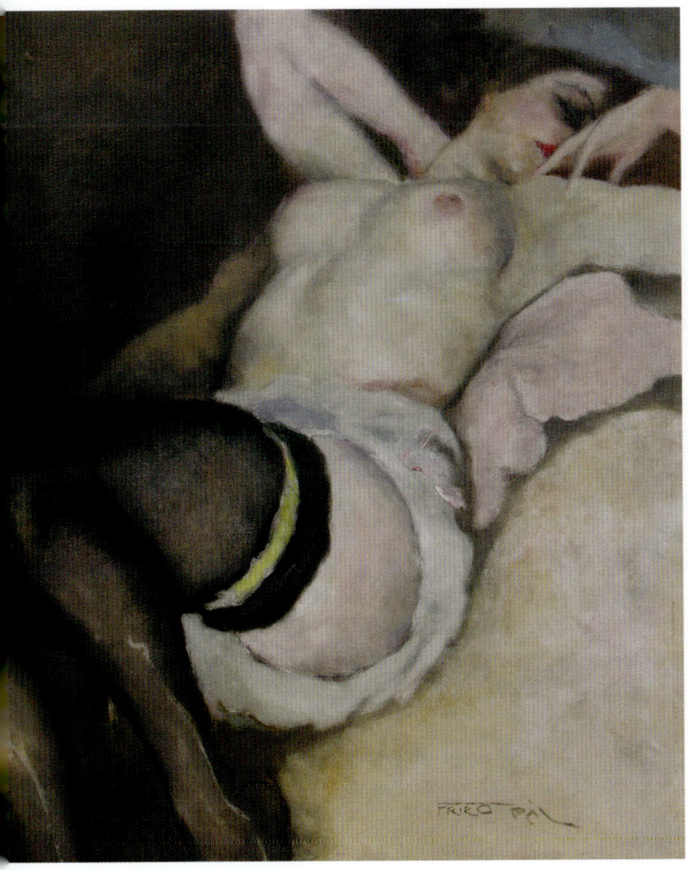

Pal Fried
Vamp, c.1930
The Parrish Collection, San Francisco, California

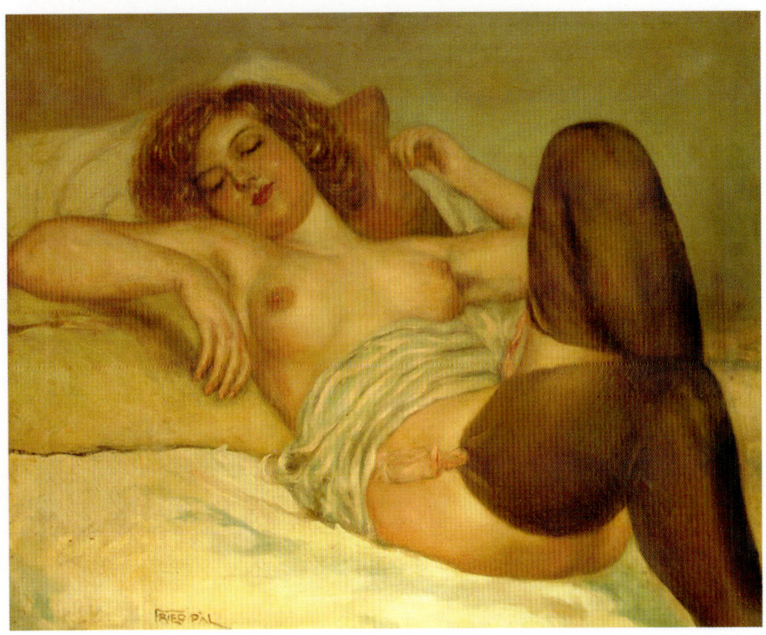

Pal Fried
Cinderella, c.1935
Jozef Koenen, Venlo, The Netherlands

Karoly Fulop
1893–1963

Karoly Fulop was born in 1893 in Czabadka, Hungary and is known as a painter, watercolorist and sculptor of ceramics, wood, and bronzes. He studied art in Budapest, Munich and Paris. Fulop was an artist of unique and curious influences who incorporated icons from his Catholic background with symbolist images from the Modern European avant-garde art movements. His paintings, watercolors and sculptures are reminiscent of the decorative qualities found in work from the Byzantine Empire. The ornate onion domes and architectural style from Byzantium can still be seen in many buildings around Budapest. The influence of the Vienna and Hungarian Secessionist movements are also evident in Fulop's work.

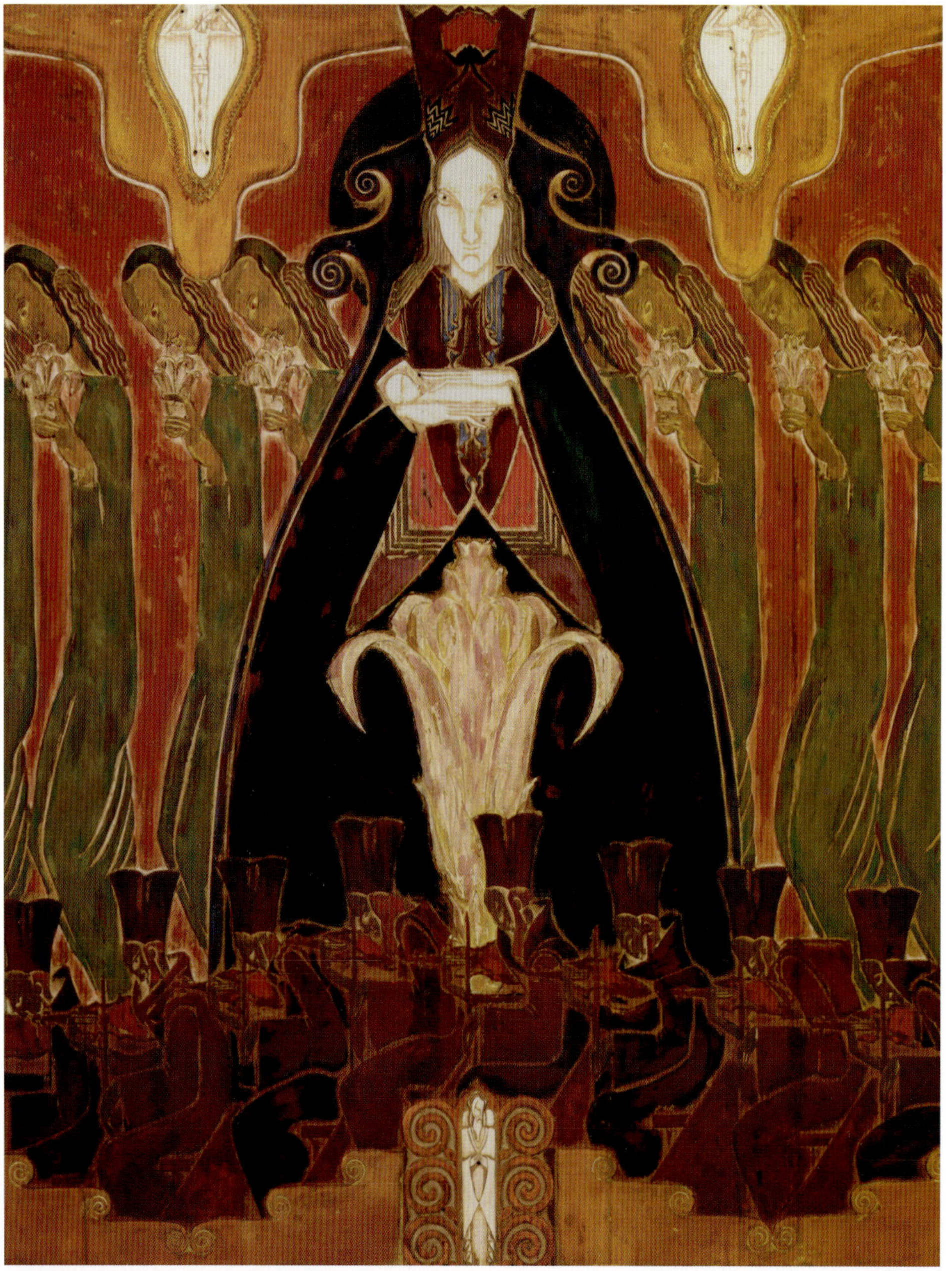

Karoly Fulop
Madonna and Child, c.1930
Mark McDonald, Hudson, New York

The artist's earliest works portrayed the romantic themes of medieval stories. His travels further influenced the subject matter of his paintings. In New York he created sculptures with musical and nautical themes. In California he incorporated the Spanish missions in his work; the image of the bell ringers was a reoccurring theme.

Fulop moved to New York in 1920 and eventually to Los Angeles in the 1930s. He opened a school of decorative arts in his L.A. studio. While living in Los Angeles he maintained a studio in Paris and spent time on the East Coast. He exhibited at the Whitney Studio Club in New York in 1921, at the Babcock Galleries in New York around 1930, and at the Stendahl Galleries in Los Angeles in 1930. He also exhibited at the Doll and Richards Galleries in Boston. He participated in a group exhibition at the Grand Central Galleries in New York.

In California he exhibited at the Pacific International Exposition in San Diego in 1935 and the Golden Gate International Exposition: Treasure Island in San Francisco in 1939. Fulop's work was included in the Los Angeles County Museum of Art 1980 exhibition *Painting and Sculpture in Los Angeles: 1900-1945*. He also gained fame for the murals he designed for the Philadelphia Public Library.

Fulop won a First Prize in 1937 at the Los Angeles County Museum of Art as well as an award at the New York World's Fair in 1939. Additionally, he won the Mr. and Mrs. Irving T. Snyder Prize at the San Diego Museum.

Fulop's work is represented in the collections of the Los Angeles County Museum of Art, the Fine Arts Gallery in San Diego, the Palace of the Legion of Honor in San Francisco and the Cleveland Museum of Art. He died in Los Angeles on April 7, 1963.

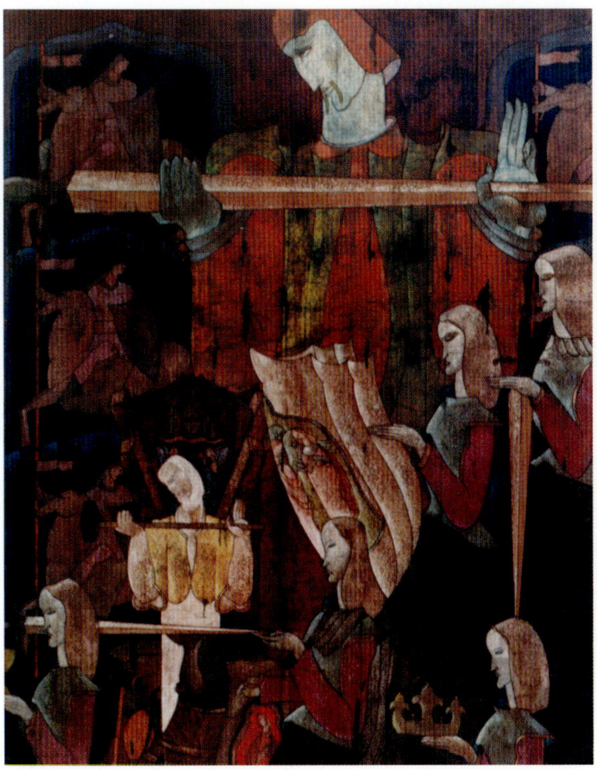

Karoly Fulop
Procession, c.1935
Julia Evershade and Mark Smith,
Los Angeles, California

Karoly Fulop
Procession, c.1935
Collection of Tim Fredrickson, California
Photo courtesy of Spencer Jon Helfen Fine Arts, Beverly Hills, California

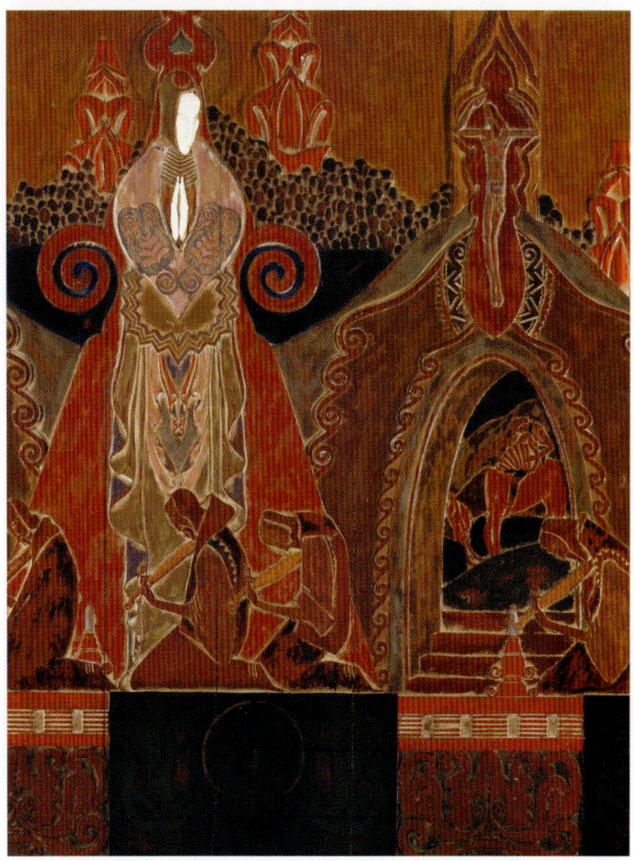

Móric Gábor

1889-1986

Móric Gábor was born in Kisújszállás, Hungary, and studied at the Budapest Academy of Fine Art under Bertalan Székely and Pál Szinyei-Merse. In 1907 and 1908 he studied at l'École des Beaux-Arts in Paris and exhibited in Austria, Germany and Belgium as well.

Gábor's work combines the influence of the Hungarian and Parisian modern painters. The main figures in his work seem separate from their background; his use of color, composition and shading give his subjects unusual depth. Gábor died in 1986 in Budapest. He is represented in the Budapest Museum of Fine Arts.

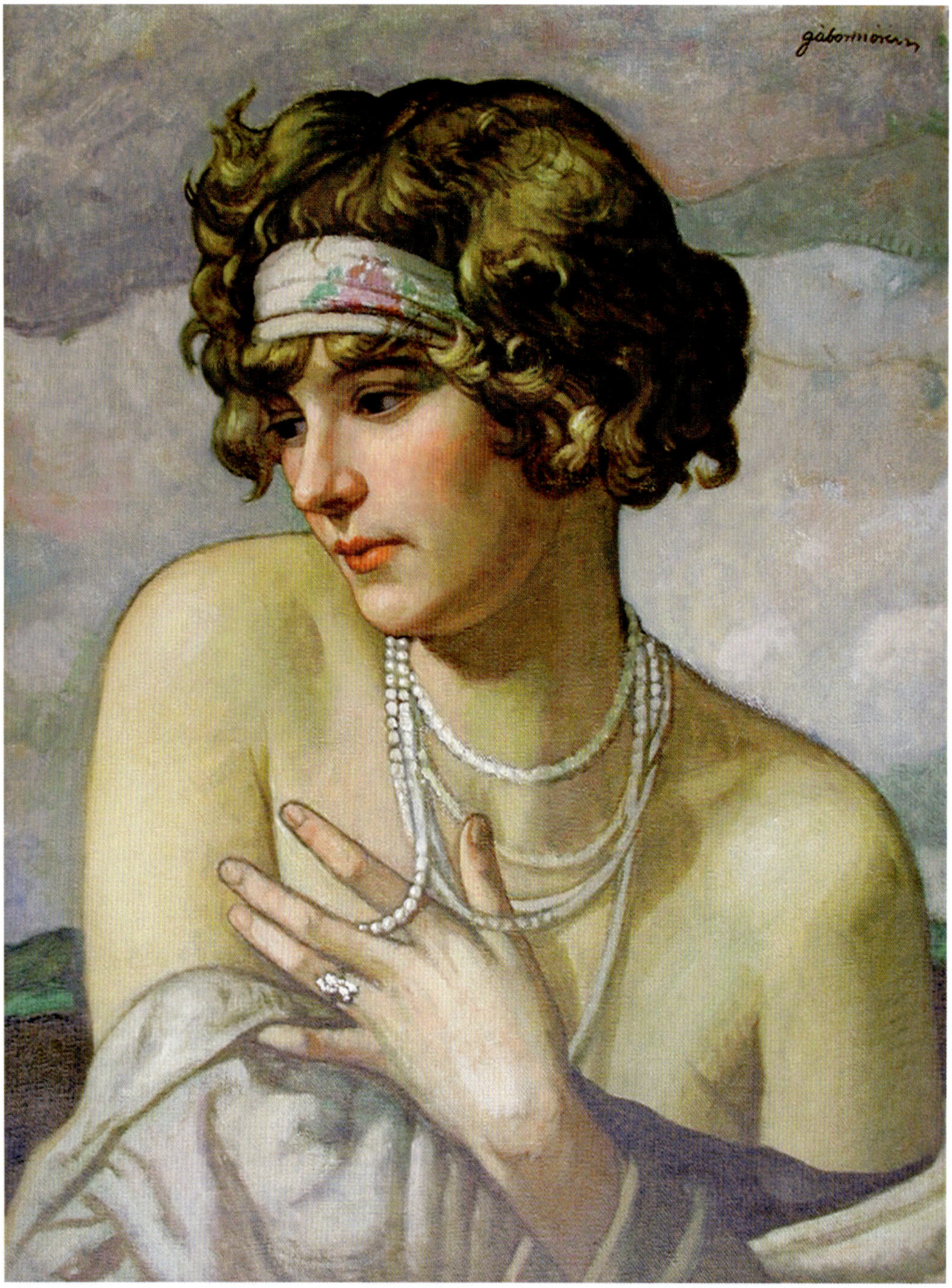

Móric Gábor
Jeune Femme, c. 1925
Private Collection

Léon Galand

1872-1960

Léon Galand was born in Montpellier where he studied under E. Michel, Delaunay, Moreau, Cormon and Blanc. He exhibited regularly at the Salon des Artistes Français where he was a member and received an Honorable Mention in 1903.

Though he later became best known for his nudes Galand was an established painter and draftsman of portraits, dancers, landscapes, marine scenery, still lifes and frescos. In 1941Galand received a retrospective of his work at the Galerie Raphaël Gérard in Paris. Several periodicals published Galand's work including *L'Illustration, Le Monde Illustré, Le Midi Illustré, Comoedia, Les Beaux-Arts* and *Match*.

Galand received the Deuxième Prix de Rome, the Troisième Médaille, Médaille d'Or and the Légion d'Honneur. The Museum of Montpellier, the City of Paris, the Faculté of Montpellier and several private collectors have acquired the work of Galand. In 1942 Marcel Claivé published an illustrated catalog and editorial exploration of Léon Galand's life and work. Galand died in 1960.

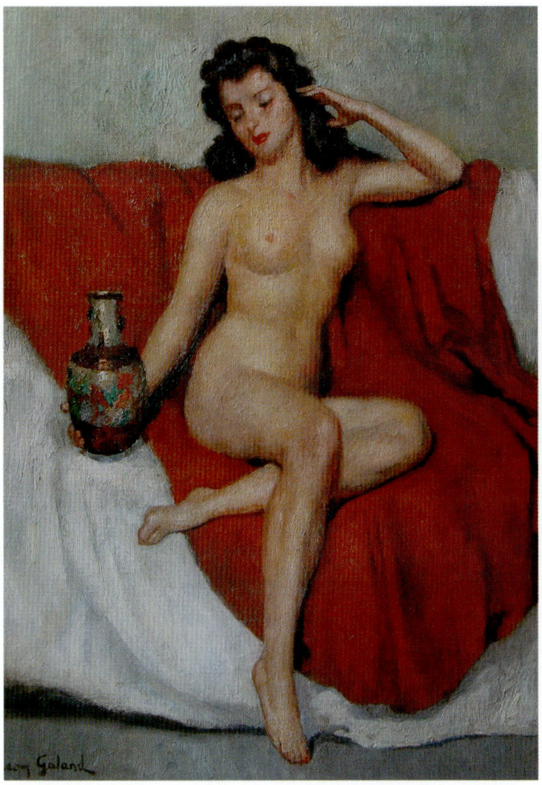

Léon Galand
Nu Assis, c.1940
The Parrish Collection, San Francisco, California

Léon Galand
Au Miroir, c.1940
Tracey Jacobs, Los Angeles, California

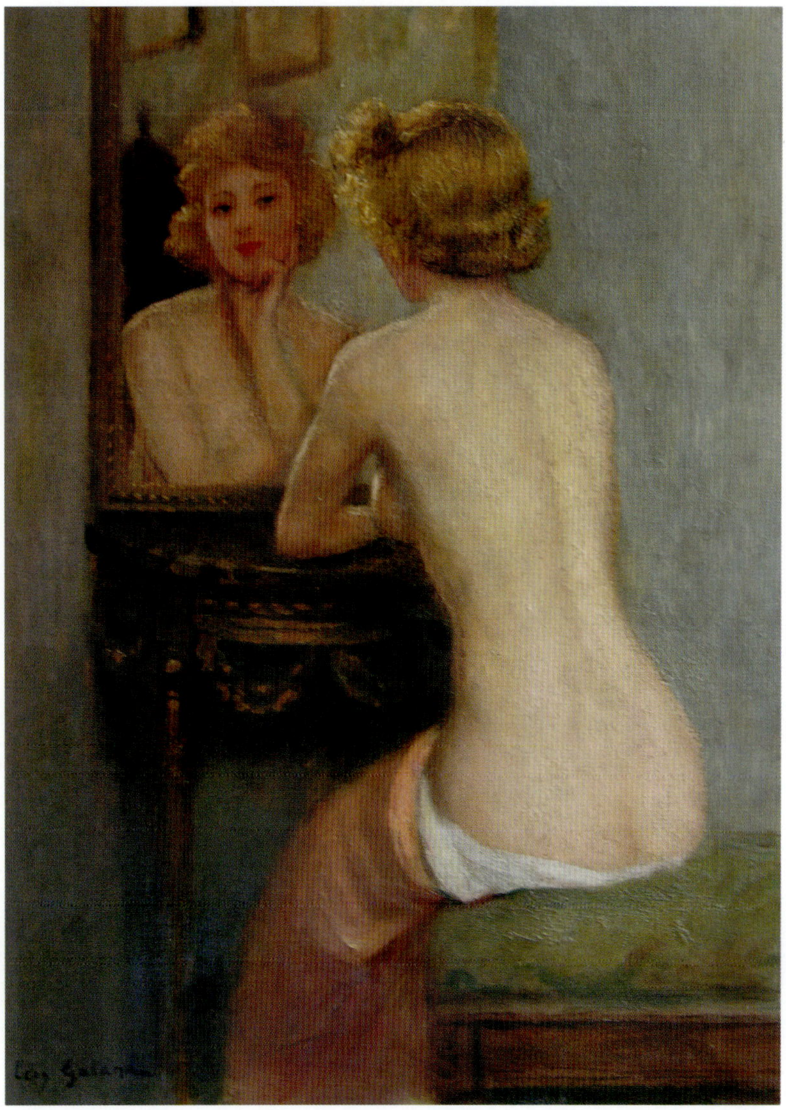

Richard Geiger
1870-1945

Richard Geiger was born in Vienna, Austria, on June 29, 1870. Geiger's oeuvre includes genre scenes, figures, nudes, and portraits. He also painted many costume party and carnival scenes. He worked in Vienna and Paris from the 1900s though the 1930s.

Though no known exhibition record exists, he was an extremely prolific artist and his paintings surface in Europe and America. His most popular subjects were scenes of stage actors in costumes of the Comedia del Arte.

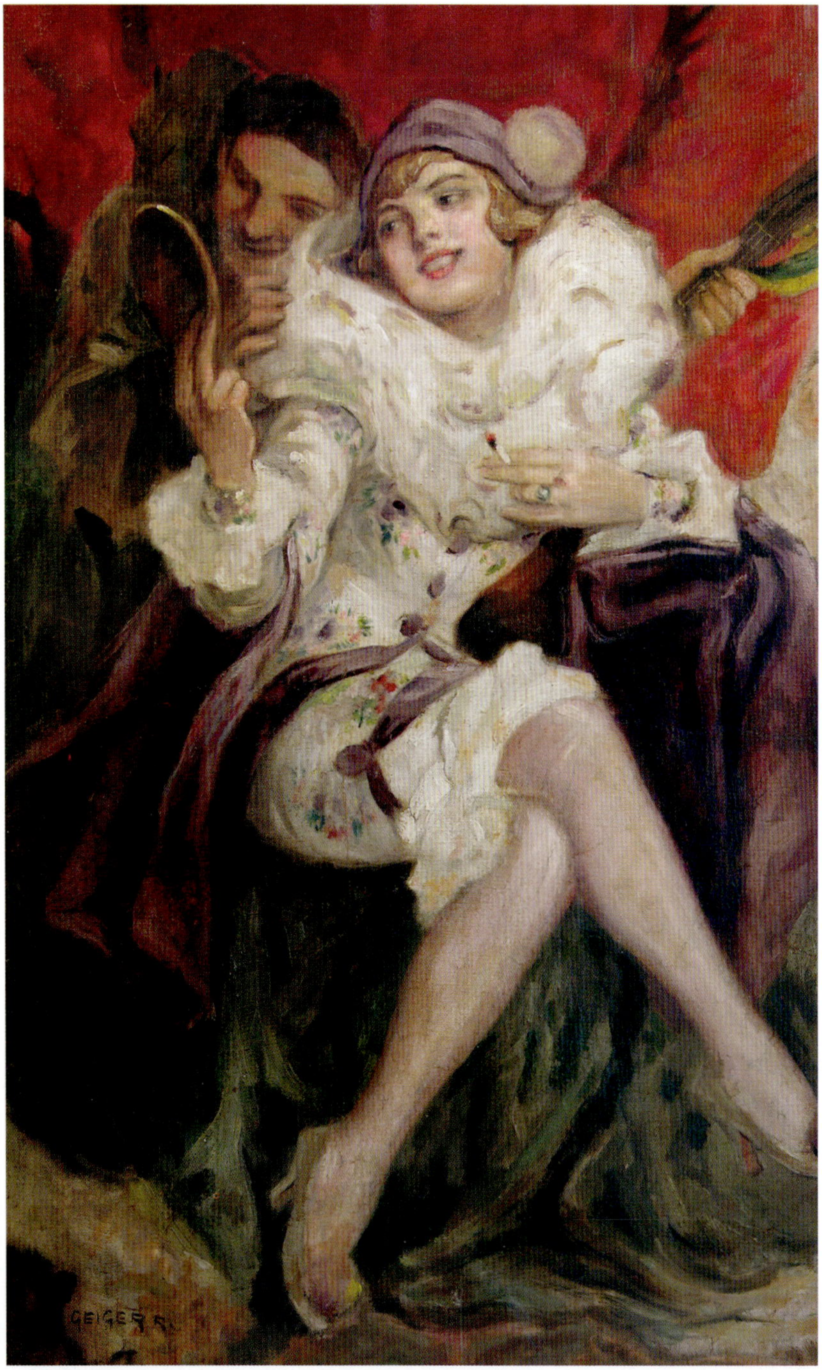

Richard Geiger
Le Miroir, c.1935
Julia Evershade and Mark Smith, Los Angeles, California

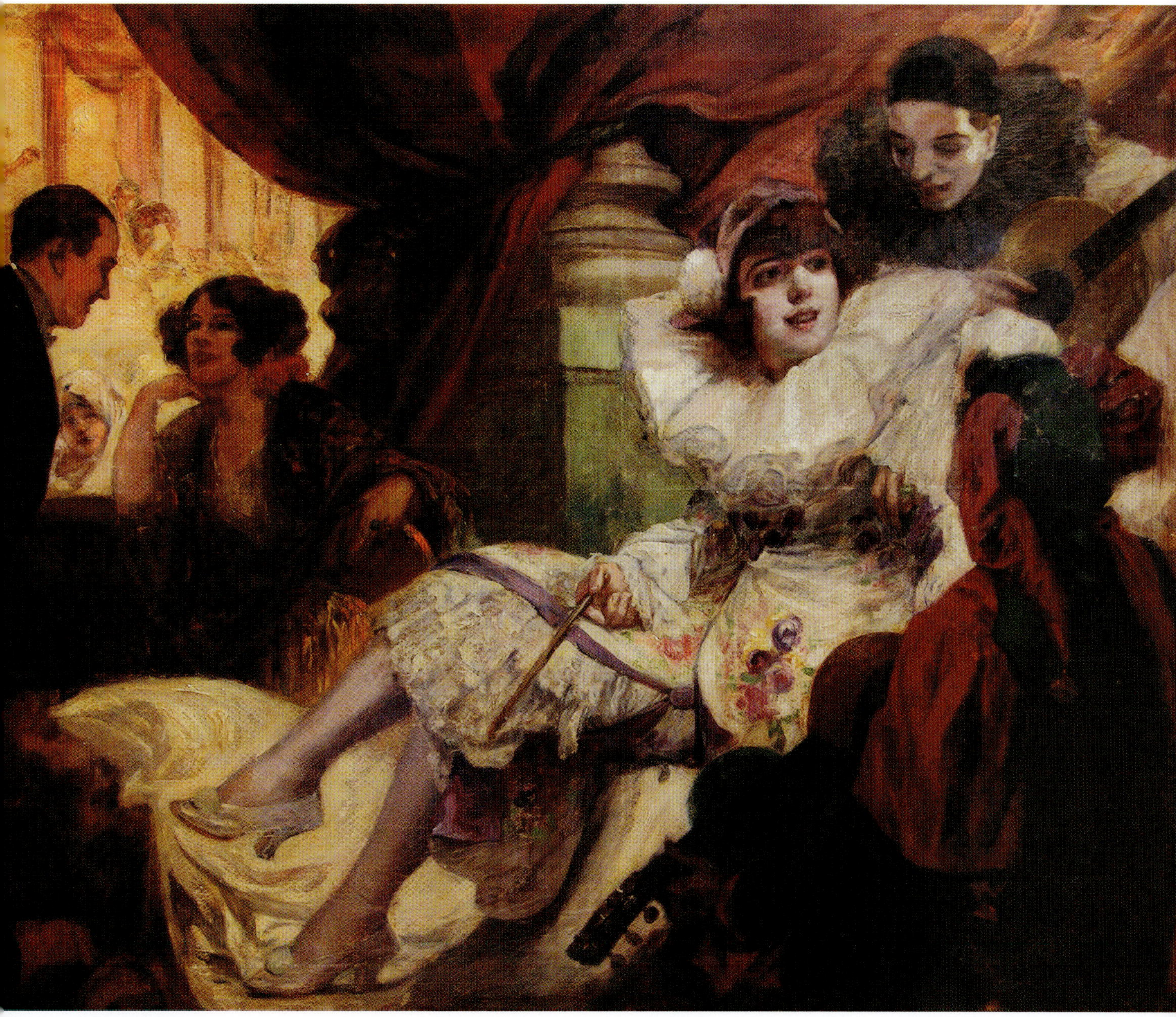

Richard Geiger
Au Cirque, c.1935
Julia Evershade and Mark Smith, Los Angeles, California

Nanette Genoud
1907-1987

Nanette Genoud was a Swiss painter of figures and nudes. In 1991 her painting *Nu dans l'Atelier*, dated 1936, was exhibited in Amsterdam. There was a major exhibition of her work at the Salon Wolfson in Zurich in 1953 for which a well known poster was published. She was also known as a print maker working in lithography and etchings and illustrated several books with original prints.

Genoud painted colorful and appealing works which employed techniques of the Postimpressionists. Her nudes are sensual and inviting; like many of the women artists of her time she brought certain sensitivity to her canvases.

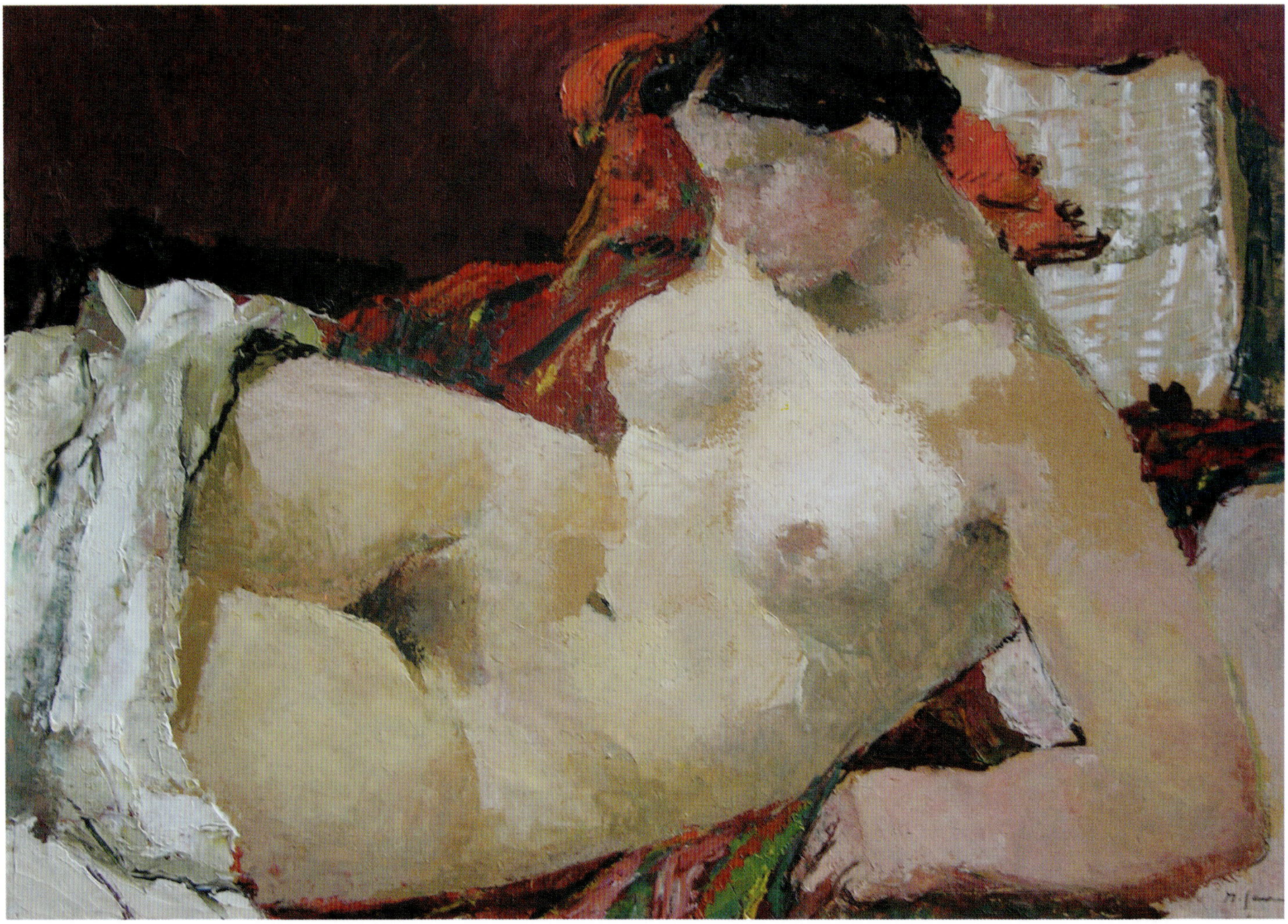

Nanette Genoud
Nu Allongé, c.1920
Papillon Gallery, Los Angeles, California

Jacques Geuens
1910-1991

Jacques Geuens was born in Brugges in 1910. He studied at l'Académie de Bruxelles and at the Hoger Institute. Geuens, however, was more influenced by visiting artists' studios around Paris and viewing their work rather than his formal education. He was married to Marguerite Aers, also a successful artist.

Geuens' models have a sculptural quality; his use of color and shadow display an intimate understanding of the form. His composition is reminiscent of many French artists of the School of Paris. Geuens' first exhibition was at Galerie Breughel in Anver and he exhibited in Paris through the 1960s.

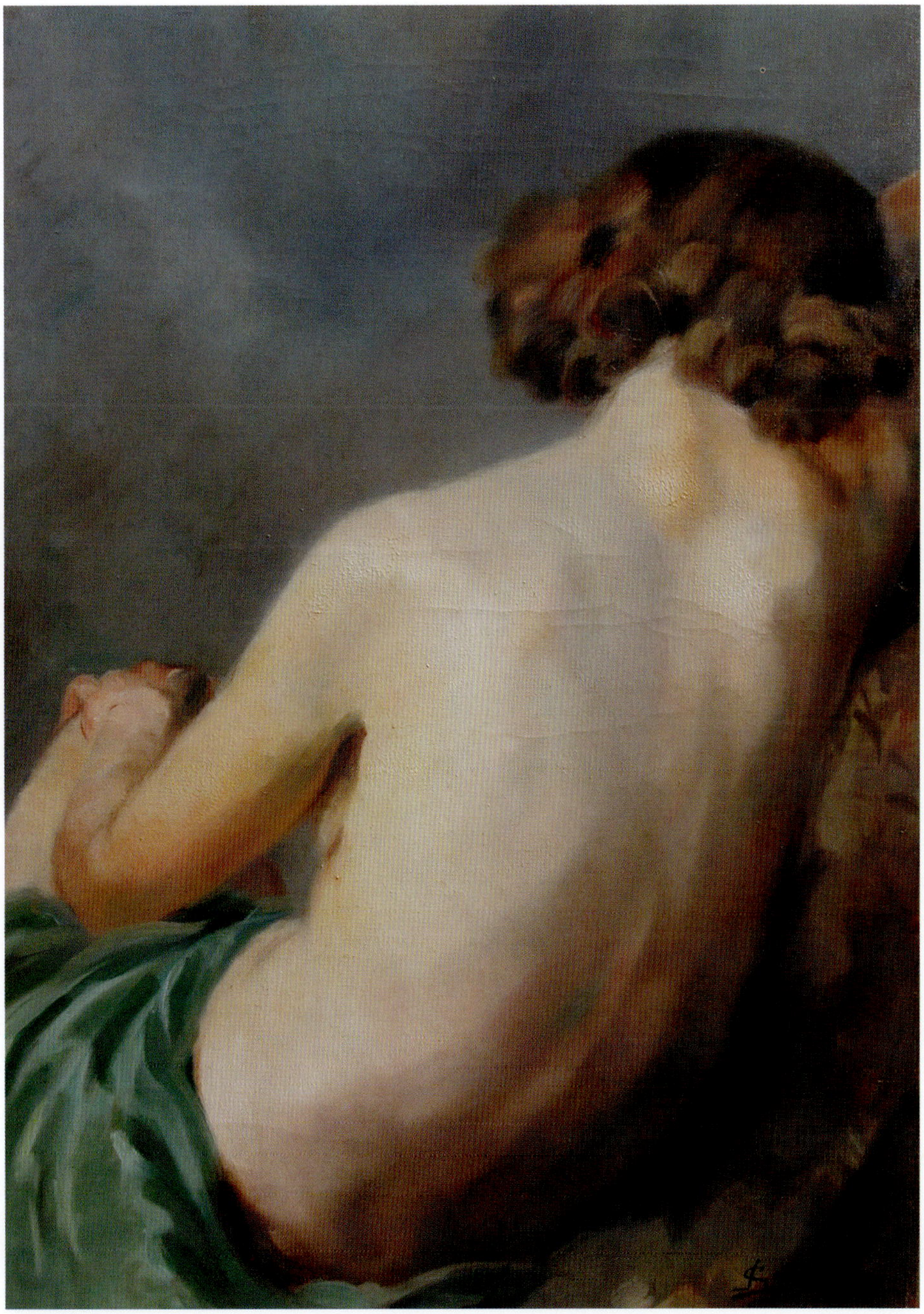

Jacques Geuens
Nu en Repose, c.1940
Private Collection

Robert Giron

1897-1967

Robert Giron was born in Brussels in 1897. He attended l'Académie de Bruxelles from 1919 to 1920 and later at l'Académie Libre Labor.

Giron exhibited with Belgian Surrealist Paul Delvaux in 1925. From 1931 to 1967 he was the director of exhibitions of painters at the Palais des Beaux-Arts de Bruxelles. He was also the vice president of La Jeune Peintre Belge.

Giron is known for his expressionistic compositions of cafés and theatres. Typical of the Belgian modernists, he used cubist elements combined with a technique that exaggerates the features of his subjects.

There is an award named after Robert Giron that is presented to outstanding artists that exhibit at the Palais des Beaux-Arts de Bruxelles. Giron died in 1967 in Sao Paulo, Brazil.

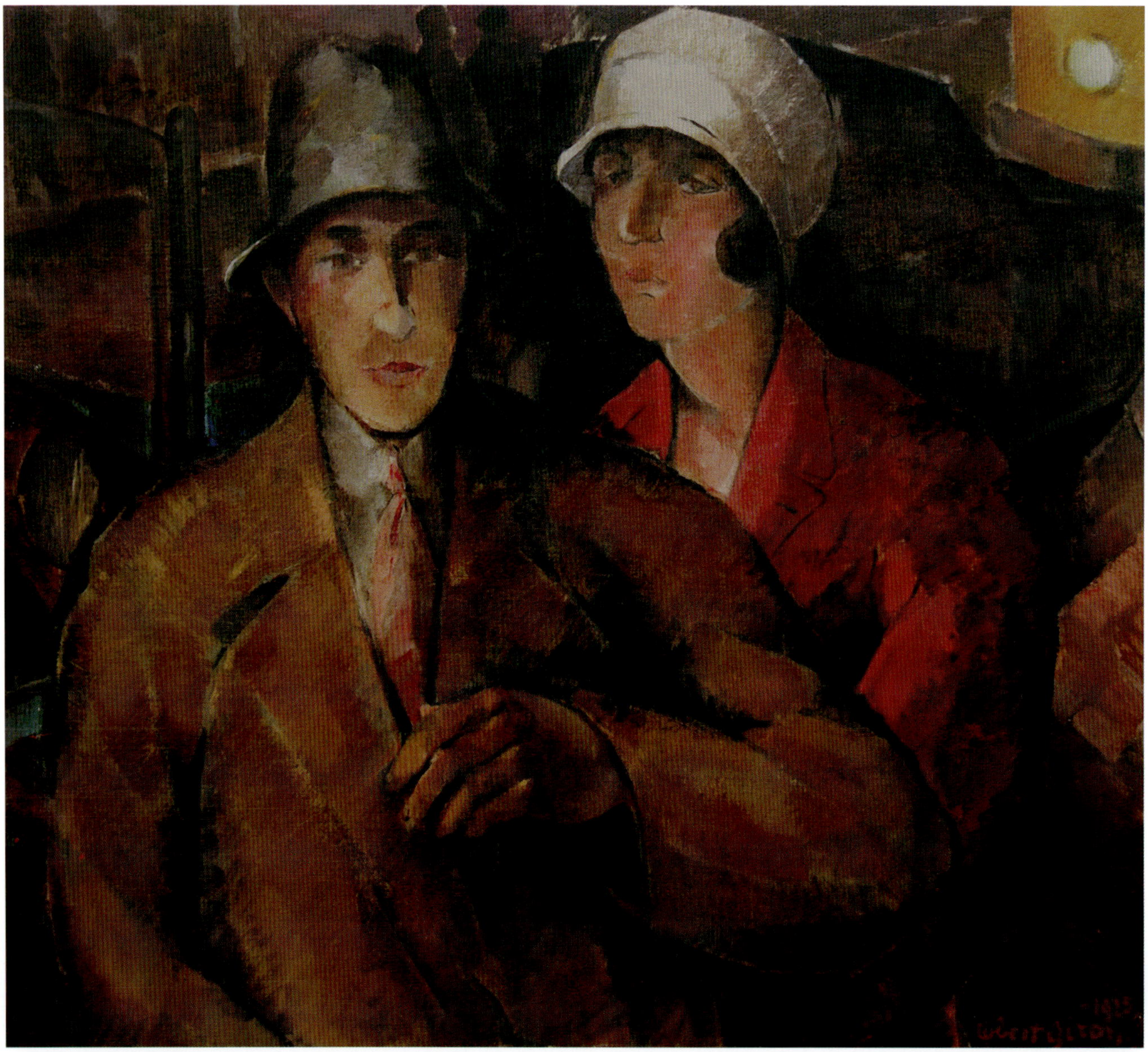

Robert Giron
Le Couple Moderne, Dated 1925
Skaar Collection, Winston Salem, North Carolina

Simon Glatzer

1890-1945

Simon Glatzer was born in 1890 in Russia and settled in Paris in 1914. Before joining the armed forces he attended l'Académie des Arts de Vilnius and later enrolled in the atelier of Cormon while at l'Académie de la Grande Chaumière. He fought with the French army in World War I and in 1920 received French citizenship.

After his military service Glatzer enjoyed success at the Salon d'Automne, Indépendants, Surindépendants and Nationale des Beaux-Arts. He was granted solo exhibitions in Cleveland, Chicago, New York and Johannesburg in South Africa.

With the coming of the Gestapo in World War II he went into hiding with a friend at l'Hôpital Sainte-Anne in a psychiatric ward. He took on a false name and continued to paint for three years with materials provided by a doctor at the hospital. After the war he moved to Aix-en–Provence and much of his work was dispersed.

Glatzer's paintings are filled with humor; he depicted the lighter side of café life in Paris. His technique is unusual and is not easy to categorize though the softness of his palette is distinctive. Glatzer died in 1945 in Aix-en-Provence.

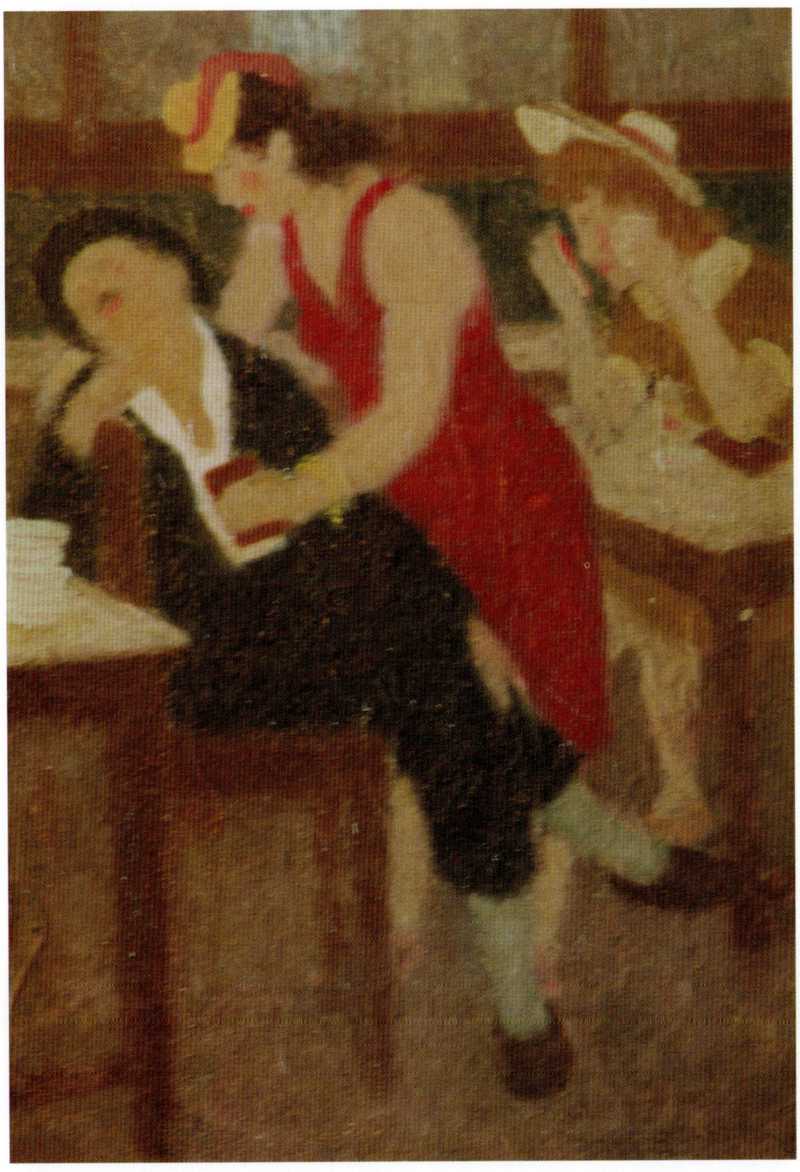

Simon Glatzer
Dormeur, c.1935
Richard and Jan Schlesinger,
Alameda, California

Nicolas Gloutchenko

Born 1902

Nicolas Gloutchenko was born April 17, 1902, in the Ukraine. He exhibited widely in Europe and often in the major Parisian Salons.

Gloutchenko's work was influenced more by the Parisian society than his Eastern European background. He gained a reputation for paintings, watercolors and pastels of nudes and beautiful women in modern interiors. The date of his death is unknown.

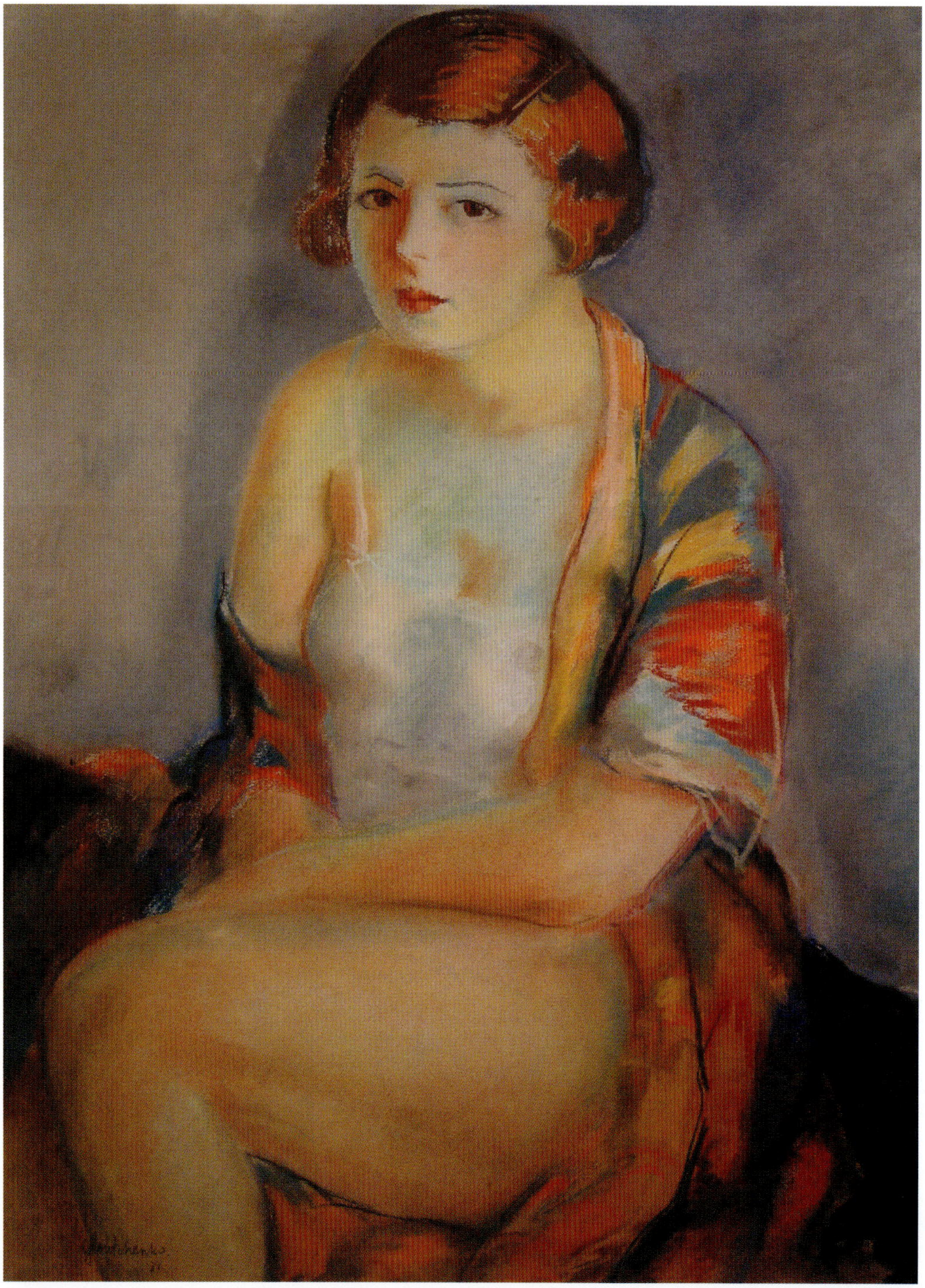

Nicolas Gloutchenko
Femme au Kimono, c.1930
Kathleen Avery Fine Art, Palo Alto, California

Maurice Goossens
1877-1938

Maurice Goossens was born in Belgium and attended l'Académie de Bruxelles where he studied painting, engraving and sculpture. He focused on the science of anatomy and the sculpture of portraits at the encouragement of J. Delville. Goossens exhibited in the Salon d'Art Idéaliste alongside Montald, Rousseau and Lenoir among other notable artists of the time.

Goossens was a Symbolist in the tradition of Khnopff and Toorop. Like his fellow Symbolists his paintings are poetic and romantic. By combining the Beaux-Arts discipline in painting with the mystical subjects, he created intriguing and enduring fantasies.

In 1907 he moved to Paris where he collaborated with diverse literary and artistic figures before returning to Belgium in 1927.

Works by the artist have been acquired by the Cabinet des Estampes de Bruxelles. Maurice Goossens died in 1938.

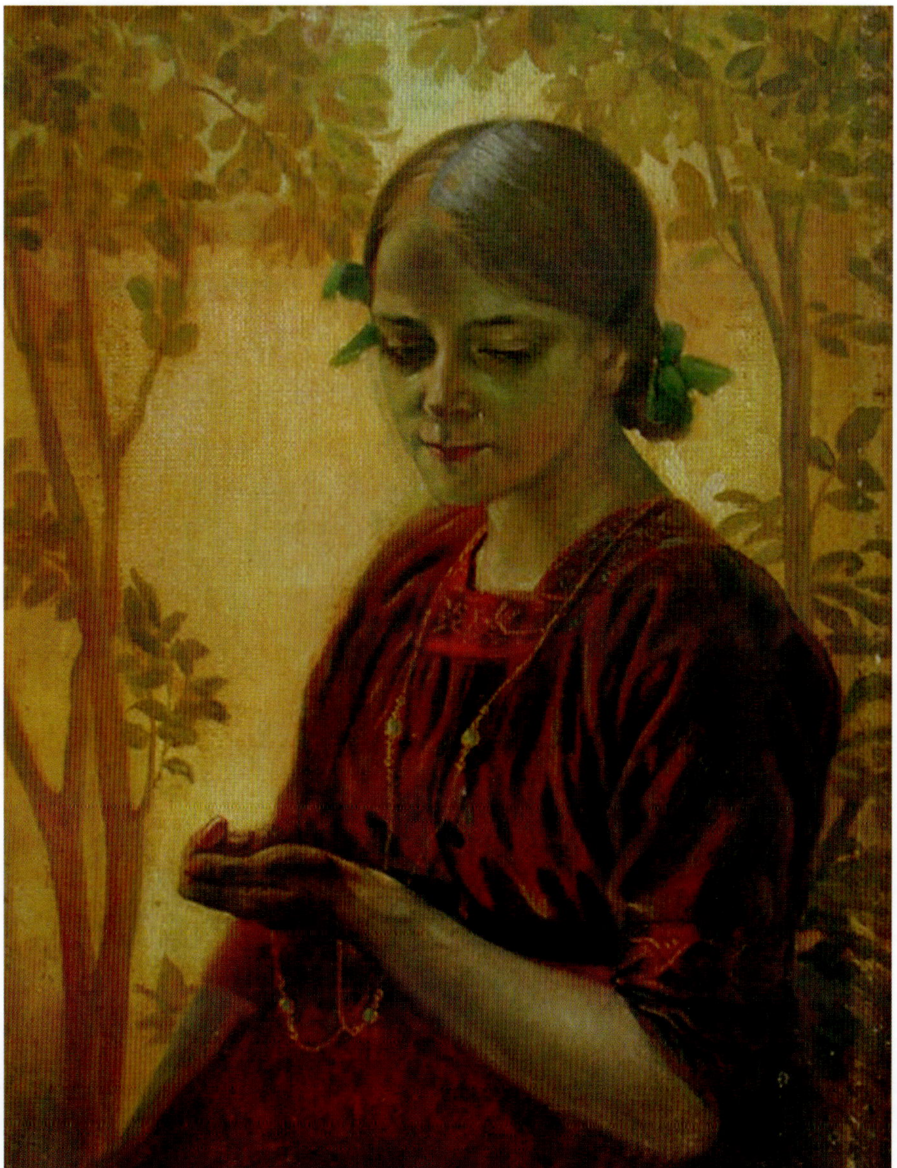

Maurice Goossens
Le Médallion, c.1925
Papillon Gallery, Los Angeles, California

Imre Góth
1893–1982

Imre Góth was born in Szeged, Hungary in 1893, and in 1912 he went to Budapest. While in Budapest he attended the Academy of Fine Arts. He went to Berlin 1920 where he studied with Arthur Kampf and he exhibited and worked as a portrait painter and illustrator. He painted portraits of film stars and one of his patrons was the Nazi Hermann Goering.

In the 1930s he moved to London where he had a successful career as a portrait painter and exhibited at the Royal Academy and the New Grafton Gallery Birmingham in 1935. He befriended Hungarian film director Alexander Korda who used Góth's work in film productions. In 1939 he received an exhibition at Ferens Art Gallery and continued to exhibit into the 1940s in England with such galleries as the Grundy Art Gallery in Blackpool, the Hull and the Russell Cotes Museum and Art Gallery in Bournemouth.

Góth's eyesight began to fail and he returned to a career as an inventor, which he had first pursued in Berlin. He had worked on inventions for parachutes and automobile headlights and in London he formed a company to market his creations.

With renewed interested in Hungarian artists, Imre Góth is sure to find his place in history. His paintings have the precision of many of the German Realists of his era and his fashionable subjects are pleasure to observe.

Góth is listed in *Magyar Festokés Grafikusok Életrajzlexikona*, an encyclopedia of Hungarian artists, and in the book *Art Deco Paintings* by Edward Lucie-Smith. He died in London in 1982.

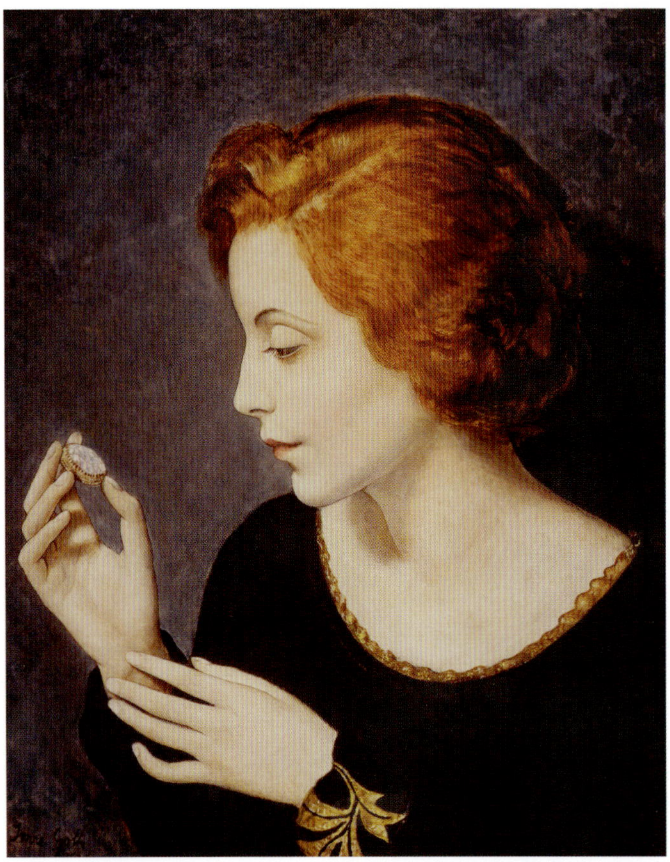

Imre Góth
Petit Cadeau, c.1930
Private Collection

Imre Góth
Femme dans la Robe Élégante, c.1930
Private Collection

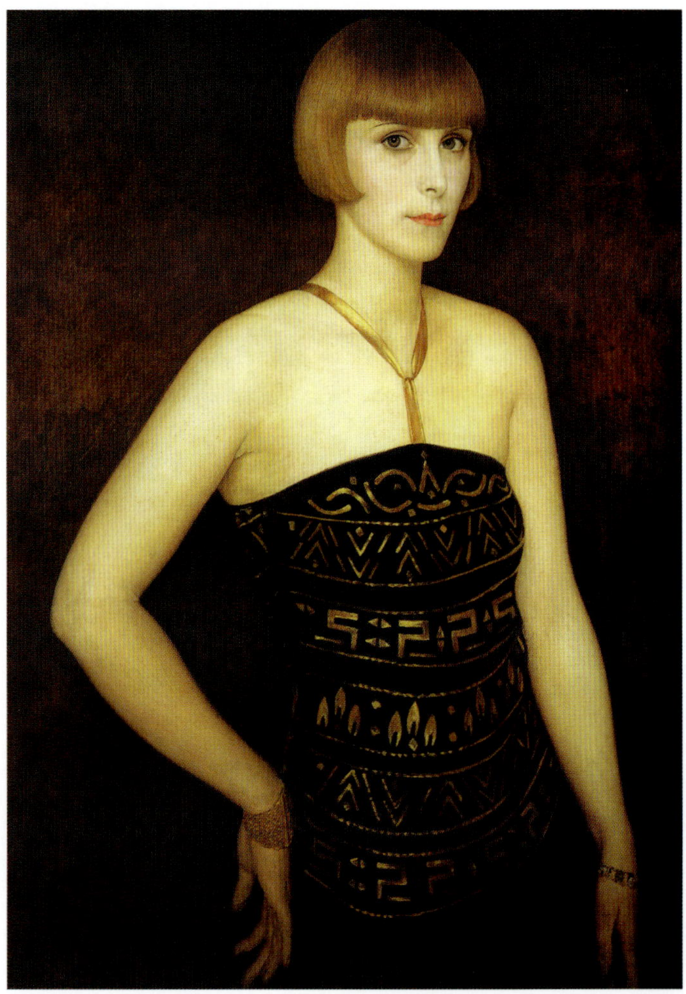

Jean Léon Henri Gouweloos

1868-1943

Jean Léon Henri Gouweloos was born in Anderleht, Belgium in 1868 and spent a good deal of time working in Brussels as a muralist and decorative artist. He is best known for his paintings of genre scenes, nautical scenes, figures, nudes, portraits and landscapes. Notable among his works is the portrait of Reine Élisabeth de Belgique. He was also commissioned to paint murals for the Masonic Lodge in Brussels and the ceilings of the Ostend casino.

Gouweloos worked for decorator Chambon and studied lithography in his uncle's studio. He later traveled to Paris to live and work as a lithographer, painter and decorative artist. Upon returning to Brussels he enrolled in l'Académie des Beaux-Arts de Bruxelles where he studied under J. Portaels. He is also credited for leading and exhibiting with the artistic group the *Voorwarts* (Forwards). During World War I, he was in exile in the Netherlands.

Gouweloos' paintings are similar to the Belgian artist Henri Thomas. Both artists depicted beautiful modern women in a variety of environments; they employed traditional technique unlike many of the Belgian moderns.

Exhibitions include the Brussels Triennial Salon, Salon de Société des Beaux-Arts and the Cercle Artistique et Littéraire de Bruxelles. He received a Médaille d'Argent in the Exposition Universelle in Paris 1900. Gouweloos' work is collected in the museums of Brussels, Antwerp, Bergen and Saint-joost-ten-Node. Jean Gouweloos died on May 5, 1943 in Uccle, Belgium.

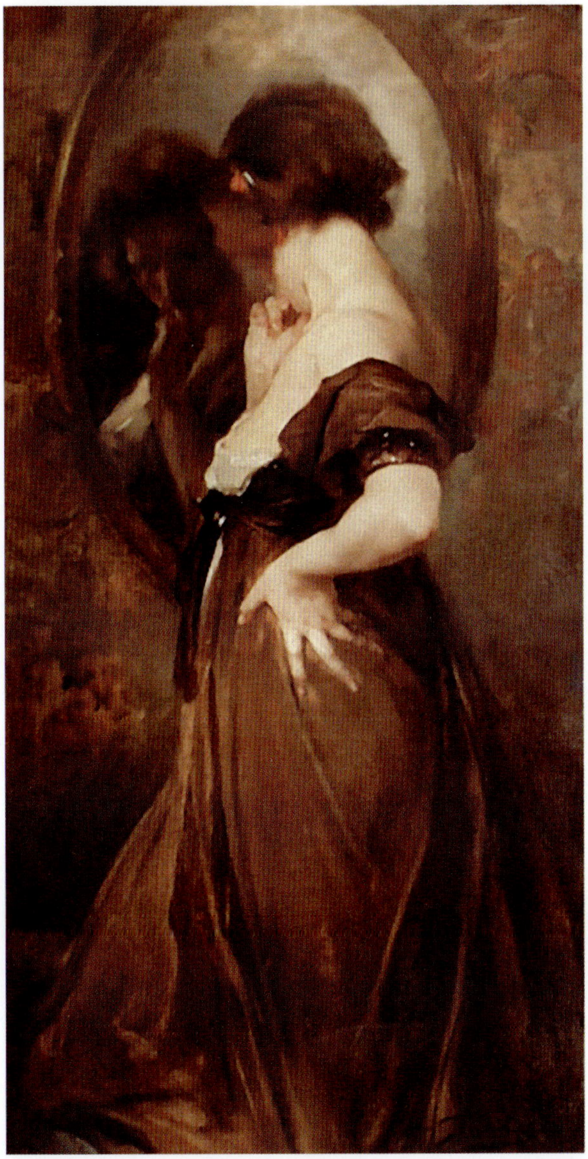

Jean Gouweloos
Au Miroir, c.1920
Los Angeles Fine Art Gallery, Los Angeles, California

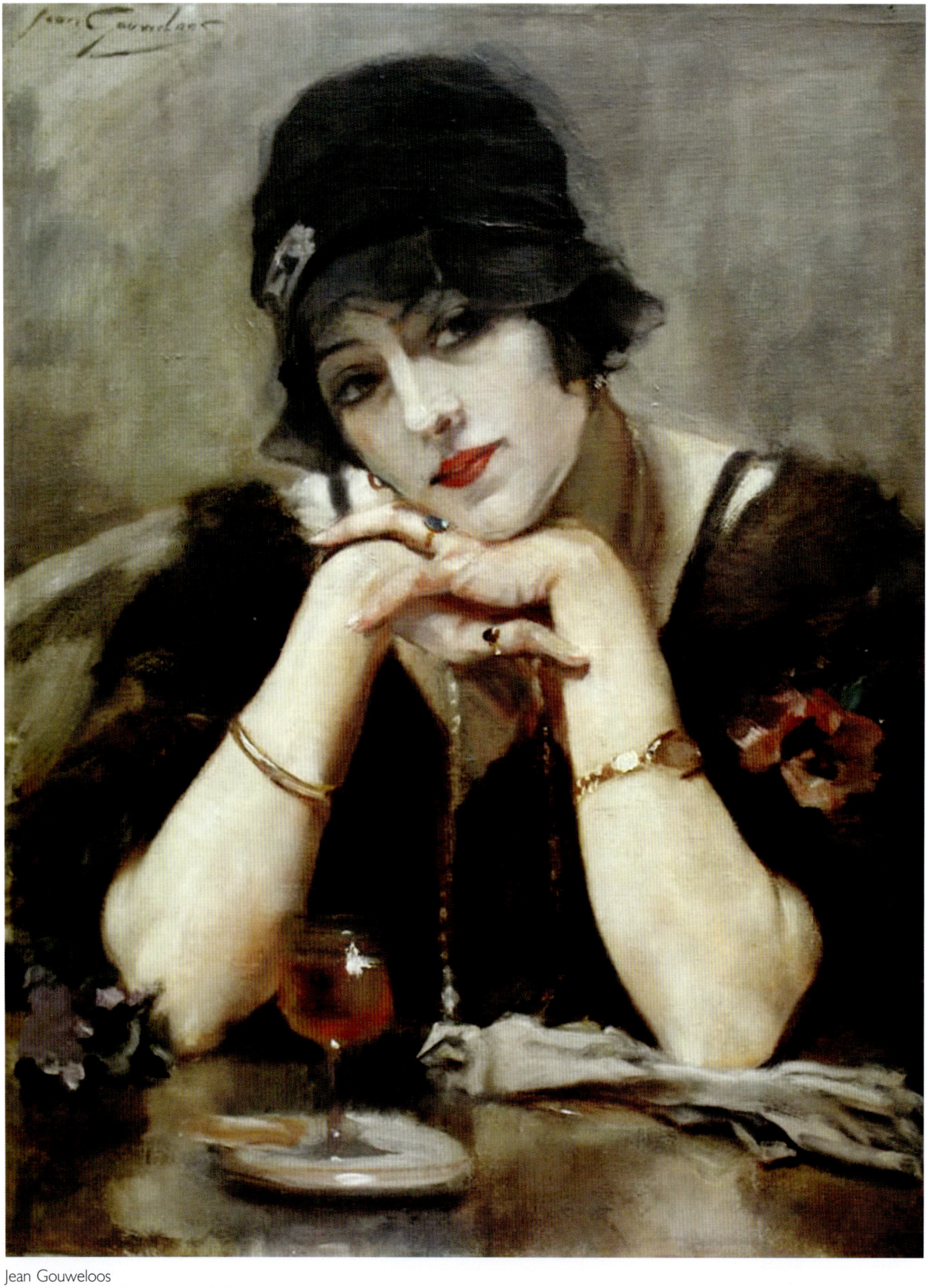

Jean Gouweloos
Jeune Femme au Chapeau, c.1925
Private Collection

Lucien-Henri Grandgérard
1880-1970

Lucien-Henri Grandgérard was born November 1, 1880 in Nancy, France. He studied under Bonnat, Jules Lefebvre and Luc-Olivier Merson.

Grandgérard was best known for his nudes and female figures and exhibited at the Salon des Artistes Français. In 1912 he received a Médaille de Troisième Classe. His works have been exhibited additionally in Rouen, Madrid and London and his atelier was sold at auction in Paris in six sales from 1964 to 1967.

In Montreal in 1945, Grandgérard published a book *L'Art de Peintre: Confidences d'un Artiste* in which he discusses technique, color palettes, exhibitions and other observations. Grandgérard died June 16, 1970 in Perreux-sur-Marne, France.

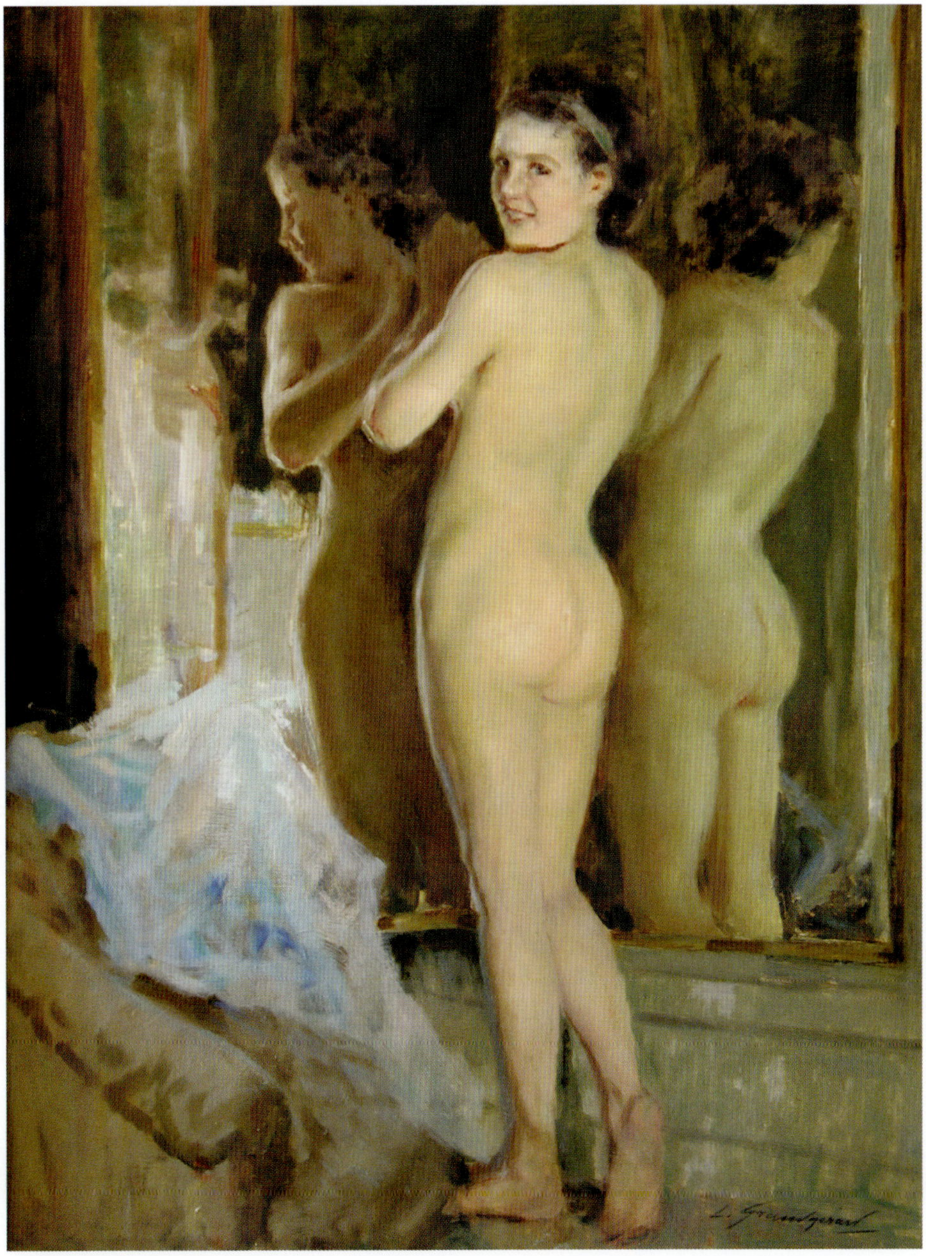

Lucien-Henri Grandgérard
Jeu de Glace, c.1930
Ronald J. Gillio, Santa Barbara, California

Marcel Gromaire
1892-1971

Marcel Gromaire was born in Noyelles-sur-Sambre, France. After first pursuing a legal career, he studied painting under Henri Matisse and printmaking under Felix Vallot at l'Académie Ranson.

He first exhibited at the Salon des Indepéndants in 1911 with a total of six paintings. Gromaire went on to study in various ateliers in Montparnasse before joining the French Army during World War I.

After the War he exhibited frequently at the Salon d'Automne, Salon des Indépendants and in several dozen group exhibitions in Paris, Brussels, London, Liverpool, Venice, Munich, Berlin, Grenoble, Oslo, Tokyo and Kyoto.

In 1921 Gromaire received a solo exhibition at the Galerie La Licorne. This was the first of several solo shows in Paris (including one in 1963 at the Musée National d'Art Moderne), Charleroi, Toulouse, Amsterdam, London, Luxembourg, Geneva and New York.

Gromaire was well recognized for his work in etching, lithography, figure studies and nudes, illustration and tapestry design. In 1947 he was made Officier de la Légion d'Honneur and in 1952 received the Carnegie International Prize for Art. In 1954 he was made Commandeur de la Légion d'Honneur.

In 1956 Gromaire received the Guggenheim National prize for his painting *La Cité* and the same year warranted the first retrospective of his work in Besançon. Later retrospectives were hosted by the Musée de Saint-Denis and in Charleroi. Gromaire also held a position on the jury the Carnegie Prize and was a professor of mural art at l'École Normal Supérieure des Arts Décoratifs.

Gromaire was a prolific artist whose career spanned several decades. Purely modern, he captured the spirit and romance of the era in his rich canvases.

A comprehensive and illustrated catalogue raisoné of his work by François Gromaire and Françoise Chibret-Plaussu was published in 1993 by the Bibliothèque des Arts, Paris with a forward by Bernard Dorival.

Institutions that have acquired work by Gromaire include the Musée d'Art Moderne de la Ville de Paris, Musée Carnavalet in Paris, Fine Arts Museum San Francisco and the Oglethorpe University Museum, Georgia. Marcel Gromaire died in Paris in 1971.

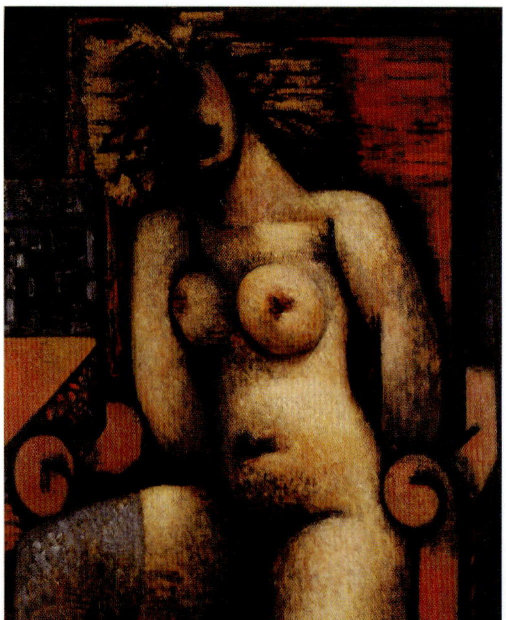

Marcel Gromaire
Nu Rouge et Or, 1937
Galerie de la Présidence, Paris, France

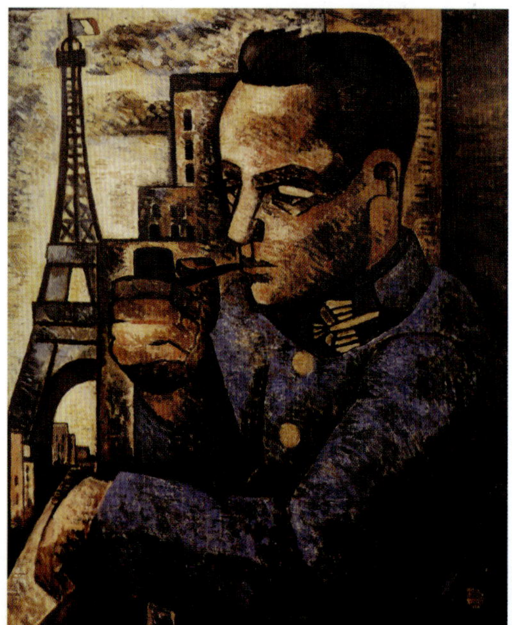

Marcel Gromaire
Monsieur Perdriel, 1925
Galerie de la Présidence, Paris, France

Marcel Gromaire
Les Ballons, 1930
Galerie de la Présidence, Paris, France

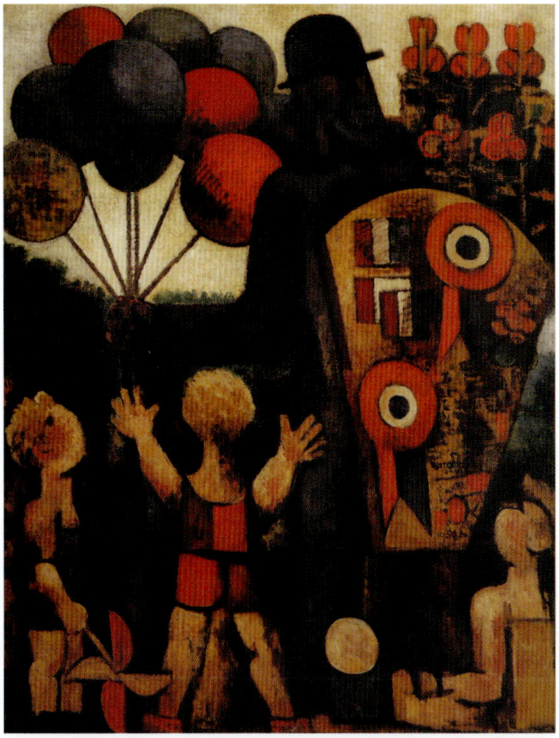

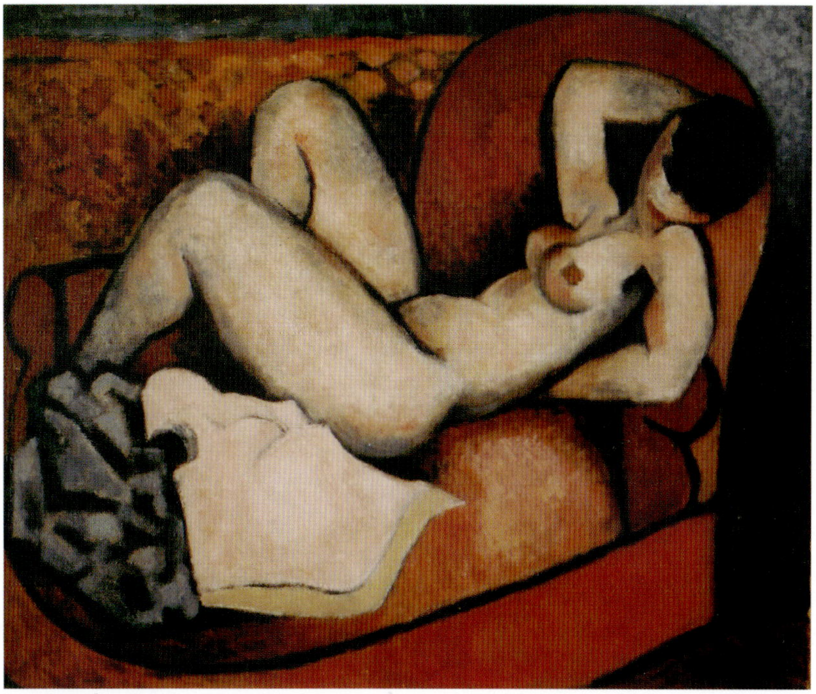

Marcel Gromaire
Nu Allongé, c.1930
Galerie de la Présidence, Paris, France

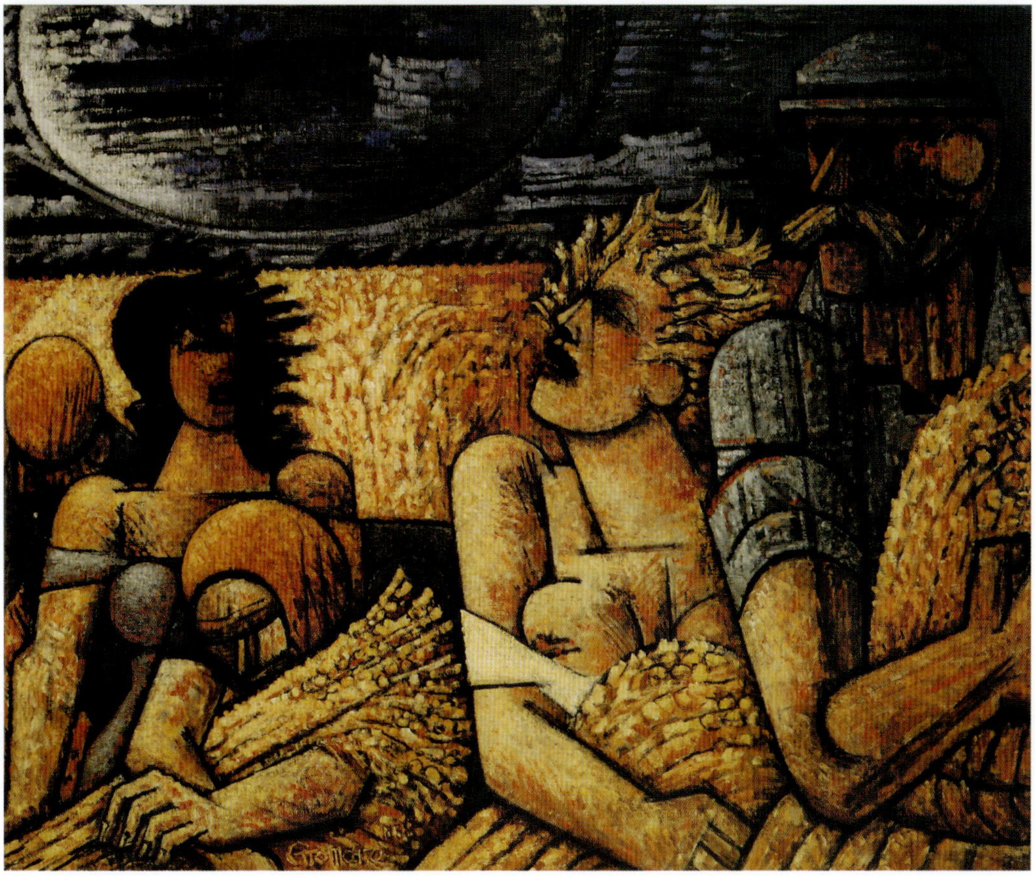

Marcel Gromaire
Orage Sur le Blé, 1938
Galerie de la Présidence, Paris, France

Nathan Grunsweigh
1880-1943

Nathan Grunsweigh was born April 2, 1880, in Krakow, Poland. During World War I he established himself in Paris and was part of the community of Russian artists.

He exhibited genre paintings and suburban scenery at the Salon des Indépendants, Salon d'Automne 1921-1936 and the Salon des Tuileries, 1921. Grunsweigh was granted a solo exhibition by Galerie Pierre in Paris, 1924.

Grunsweigh, like many Eastern European artists defined as working within the School of Paris, had a unique vision of his adopted city. With clever humor he documented Parisian lifestyles.

In 1943 Grunsweigh was deported and assassinated by Nazi officials. The University of Haifa in Israel held two exhibitions in which Gunsweigh was included: *Memorial in Honour of Jewish Artist Victims of Nazism*, 1978, and *Eighteen Artists who Perished in the Holocaust*, 1996.

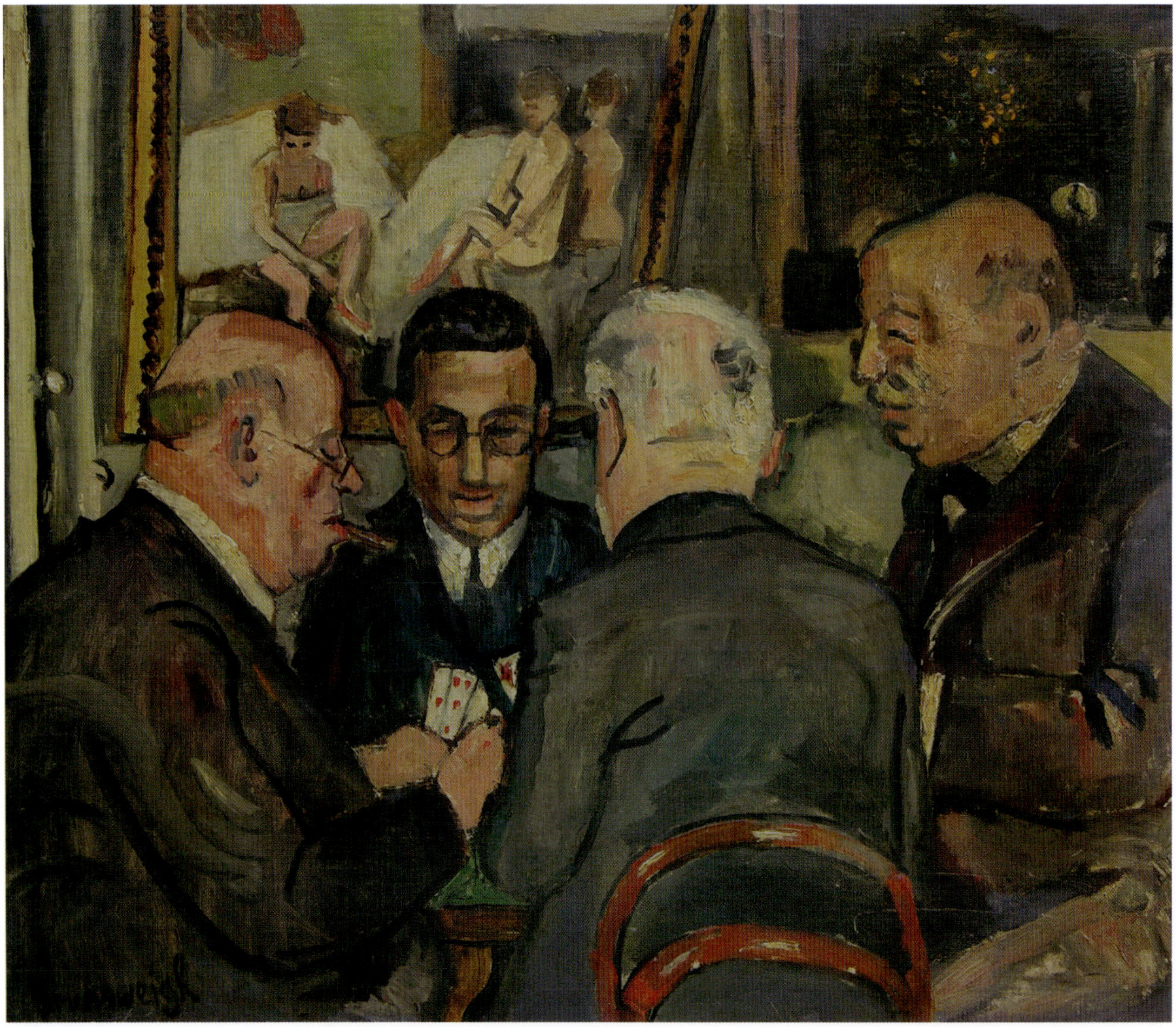

Nathan Grunsweigh
Joueurs de Carte, c.1930
Papillon Gallery, Los Angeles, California

Adolfo Guiard y Larrauri

1860-1916

Adolfo Guiard y Larrauri was born in Bilbao, Spain, in 1860. He studied in Barcelona and later worked in Paris. While in Paris, he befriended Edgar Degas and it is believed he was Degas' only student. After a trip to London he returned to Bilbao, where he was continually inspired by scenes of modernity in the city. Guiard settled in Paris in 1878 and contributed drawings and illustrations to the weekly publication *La Vie Moderne*.

Guiard was an Impressionist at the height of the movement, he specialized in images of women in beautiful costumes experiencing modern life. His tonality was rare and impressive and gave his canvases a distinctive atmosphere. He exhibited in diverse individual and collective exhibitions. The Bilbao museum has collected *Un Faubourg* and Miguel de Unamuno highly praised his work. Guiard died in 1916.

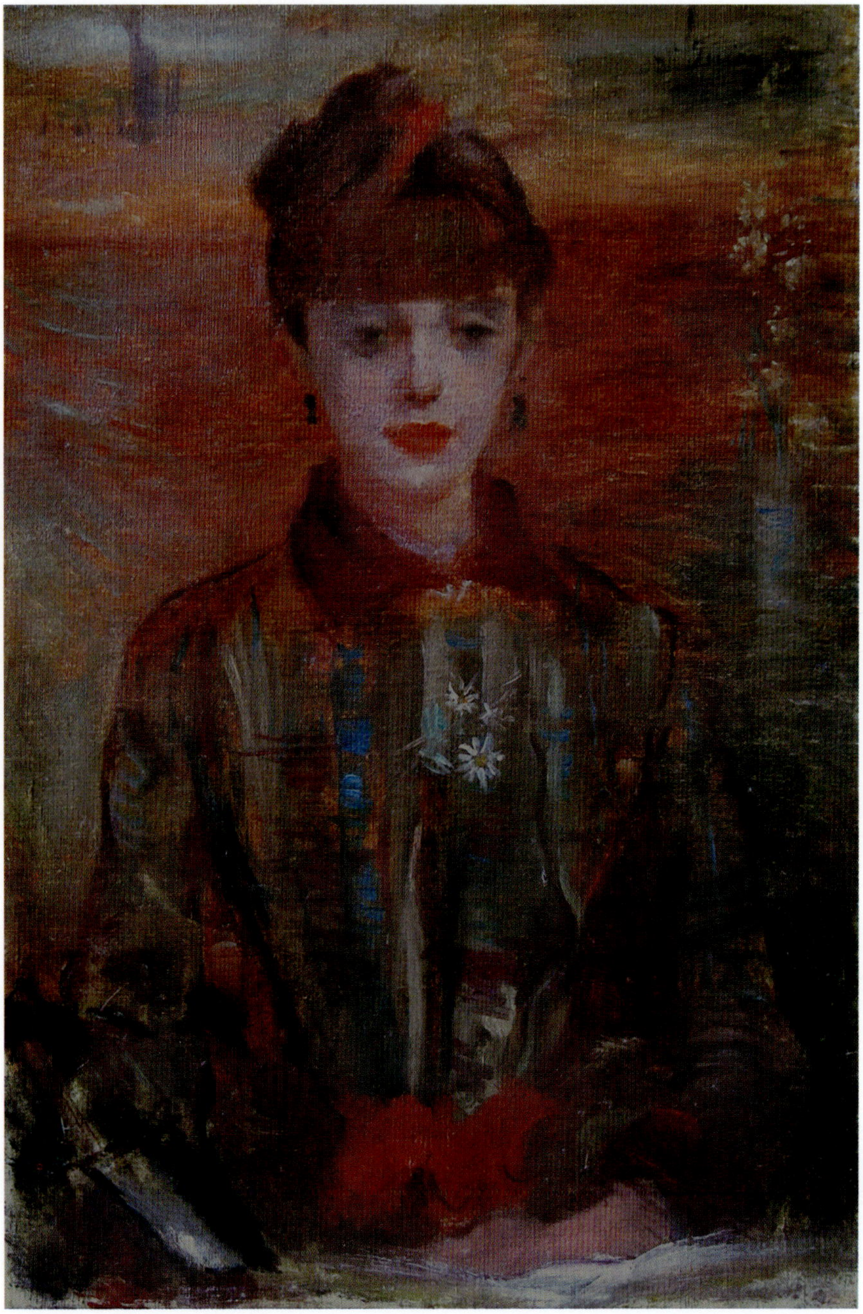

Adolfo Guiard y Larrauri
Femme Assis, c.1910
The Parrish Collection, San Francisco, California

Paul Louis Guilbert

Born 1886

Paul Louis Guilbert was born December 20, 1886 and in 1923 dedicated his life and work to fine art and illustration. He was a student of Manuel Robbe and Ligeron and exhibited at the Salon des Indépendants. Guilbert illustrated *La Fille Elisa* by Edmond de Goncourt and *Le Curé de Village* by Balzac, among other works.

Guilbert's was a romantic storyteller and his paintings are extremely detailed even with his heavy application of paint. The date of his death is unknown.

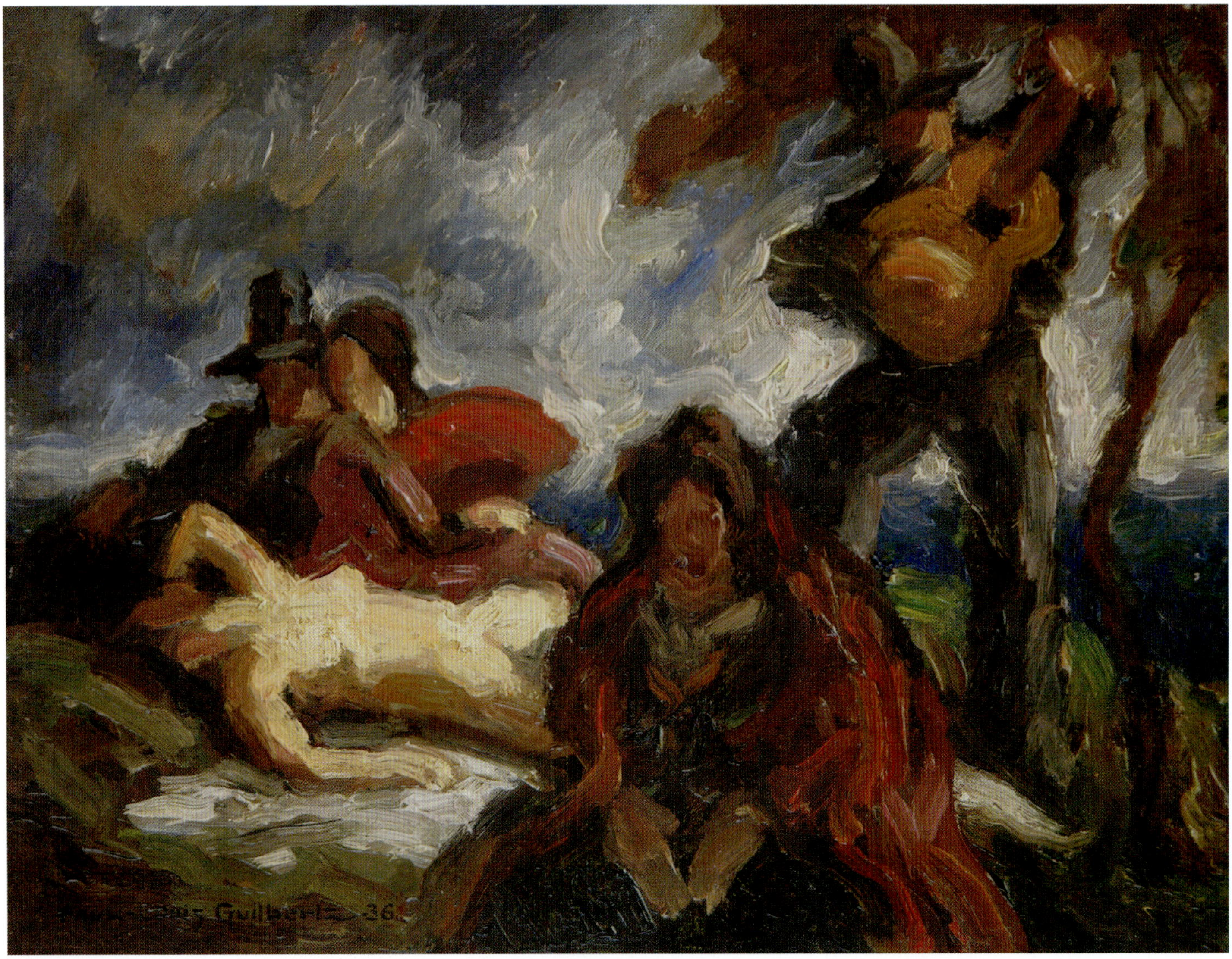

Paul Louis Guilbert
Fête dans le Fôret, Dated 1936
Dulcy Rogers Bader, Los Angeles, California

Alice Halicka

1895-1975

Alice Halicka was born December 20, 1895 in Krakow, Poland. The artist was born to a wealthy family and, after her mother's death, was raised predominantly by her grandparents in Tyrol.

Following her formative education, she moved to Munich to study painting under Hungarian artist Simon Hollosy. She studied in the ateliers of Wyczolkowski and Pankiewcz as well. In May of 1912 Halicka moved to Paris where she continued her studies at l'Académie Ranson under Sérusier and Maurice Denis. During this time she also met renowned Cubist Louis Marcoussis.

Halicka and Marcoussis eventually married and befriended many artists and writers who were instrumental in the early movements of Parisian society and culture including Apollinaire, Braque, Gris, Dufy and André Salmon. Apollonaire subsequently reviewed Halicka's first exhibition at the Salon des Indépendants in *Soirées de Paris*.

Halicka began to work under the influence of Zborowski, who was a strong proponent of Cubism. He represented her work, though Marcoussis discouraged it. As a result Halicka destroyed much of her cubist work and, in 1919 focused on collage and fabric design. In 1920 she exhibited at the Salon des Indépendants, Salon d'Automne, Salon des Tuileries and the Salon Surindépendants.

In Paris in 1922, Galerie Bernheim-Jeune presented an exhibition of a group of significant modern artists including Henri Matisse, Alice Halicka, Auguste Herbin, Pierre Hode, Marie Laurencin, Henri Lebasque, Fernand Léger and Moise Kisling.

Galerie Druet held a successful exhibition of her work in 1924 and she went on to exhibit at the Galerie Georges Petit in Paris in 1930 and 1931, Leicester Gallery in London, 1934, and M. Harriman Gallery and Galerie Levy in New York in 1936 and 1937.

Other exhibitions include *Art Polanais*, Société Nationale des Beaux-Arts, Musée du Grand Palais, 1921; the International Exhibition of Modern Art, Brooklyn Museum,1927; Galerie Bonjean, Paris,1931; *From Impressionism to Abstraction : 13 Women Painters*, AWA Club House, New York, 1934; *Les Dames de Montmartre*, Musée de Montmartre, Paris, 1966; *Les Cubistes, Musée d'Art Moderne*, Paris, 1973; *The Circle of Montparnasse Jewish Artistes in Paris 1905-1945*, Jewish Museum, New York, 1985. Halicka also exhibited frequently with the esteemed Bernheim-Jeune and Berthe Weill galleries among many others in Paris, Brussels, London, Zurich and New York.

In 1925 Halicka illustrated *Enfantines* by Valery Larbaud and *Les Enfants du Ghetto* by Israel Zangwill. She also created set designs for several ballets while in the United States, one of which was performed at the Metropolitan Opera, New York, and Covent Garden, London.

Halicka spent the duration of World War II in Normandy and in 1946 she published a book of memoirs, *Hier*. She continued to exhibit her work in France and travel abroad in the 1950s and 1960s. Her works are held by the Barnes Foundation, the Museum of Modern Art in Paris, the Yale Museum, the Cincinnati Museum, the Museum of New Delhi and the Museum of Warsaw in Poland.

Her biography has been written in *Peintres Juifs à Paris* by Nadine Nieszawer, Marie Boyé and Paul Fogel, *L'École de Paris* published by the Paris Museum of Modern Art, *Modern French Painters* by Maurice Raynal and in 1962 Pierre Cailler published a catalogue of Halicka's exhibitions and collections in an edition of *Documents*, an encyclopedia of fine arts. In 2002 the Musée du Montparnasse held an exhibition, *Elles de Montparnasse*, in which Halicka's work and biography were included. Her work is represented in virtually every modern exhibition of Cubism and The School of Paris.

Also of note, renowned painter and muralist Diego Rivera painted a portrait of Halicka in 1915. Alice Halicka died in Paris in 1975.

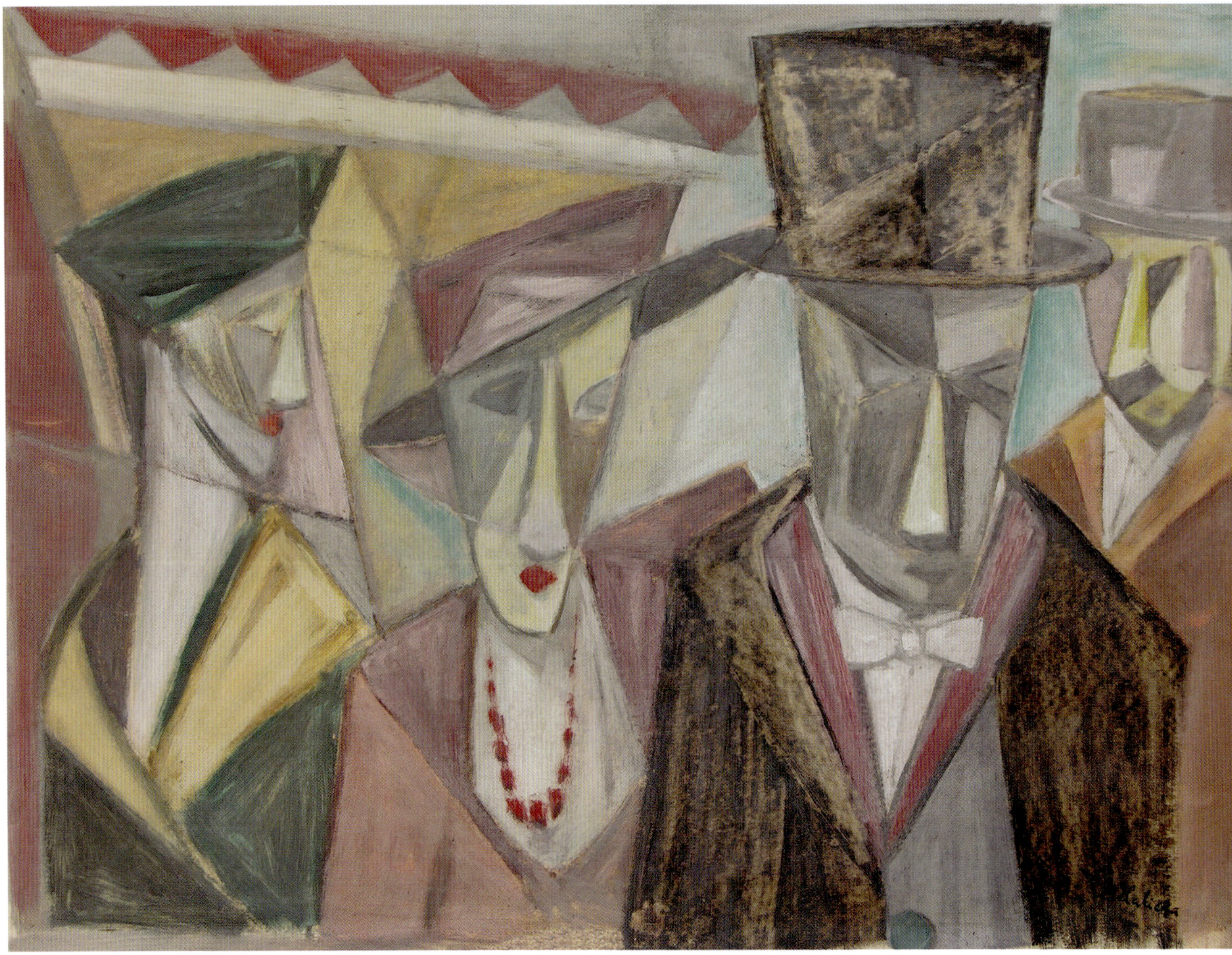

Alice Halicka
Les Élégantes, c.1916
Papillon Gallery, Los Angeles, California

Jean Hanau

Born 1899

Jean Hanau, though Parisian born, traveled and worked in New Mexico in 1928. Considered an Art Deco artist, he began exploring American Southwestern subjects; mostly Pueblo Indians and landscapes, in a unique expressionistic manner. This work was exhibited in Paris in 1929.

Hanau was recognized as an accomplished artist extremely early in his career with his premier exhibit at age thirteen at the Salon des Indépendants in 1913. He received his education at l'École des Beaux-Arts under the instruction of Fernand Cormon and in the atelier of sculptor Filippo Colarossi in Paris and Rome. He participated as well at the Salon des Tuileries and Salon d'Automne, and exhibited in the Devambez, Drouant and Simonson galleries.

Contemporaries with whom Hanau exhibited include Matisse, Roualt, Marquet, Bonnard, Louis-François Biloul, Bernard Naudin, Charles Guerin and C.A. Picart Le Doux.

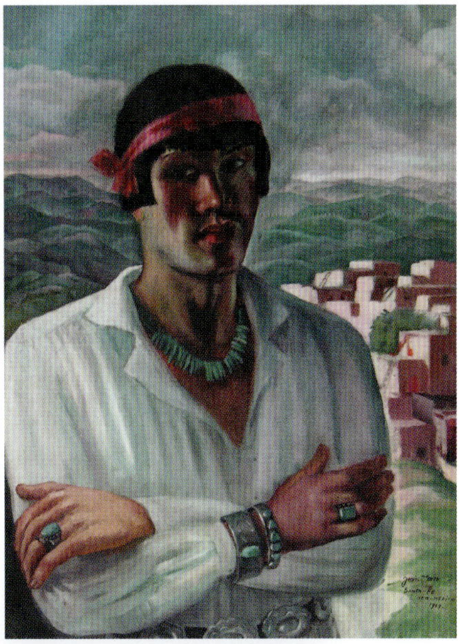

Jean Hanau
Portrait of a Pueblo Indian Man, Dated 1929
Galerie A-B, Paris, France

Jean Hanau
Pueblo Indian Group, New Mexico, Dated 1928
Fred & Jann Kline, Santa Fe, New Mexico
Photo Copyright 2004

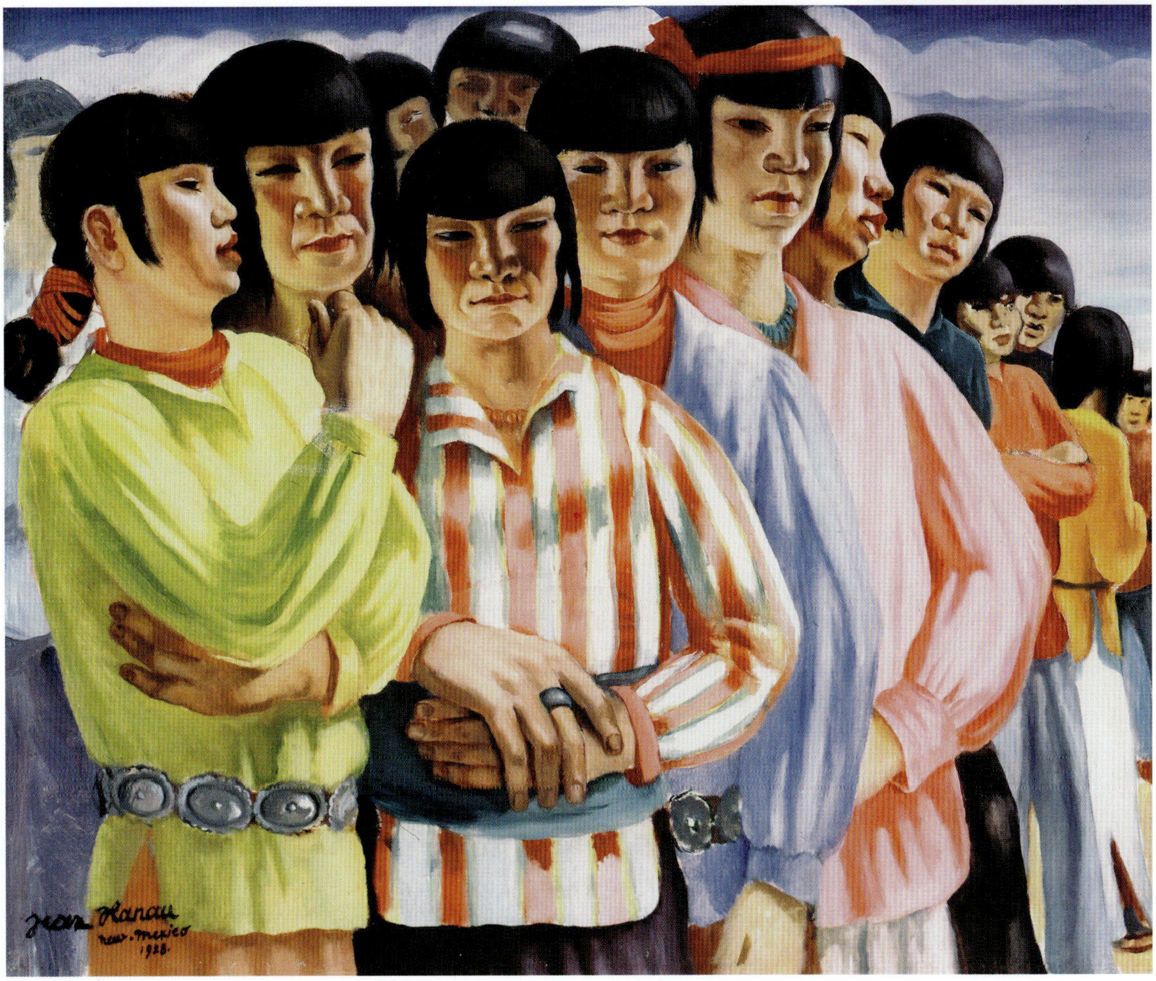

Gaston Haustrate

1878-1949

Gaston Haustrate was born in Brussels in 1878 where he attended l'Académie des Beaux-Arts. He is best recognized for landscapes, urban scenery and still lifes.

Haustrate paintings are reminiscent of many of his contemporaries. The female forms he painted are romantic compositions in the tradition of the Belgian moderns. Wide brush strokes, profound colors and intelligent construction bring excellent balance to his canvases. Haustrate exhibited frequently in Brussels, Anvers and Lokeren. He died in 1949 in Brussels.

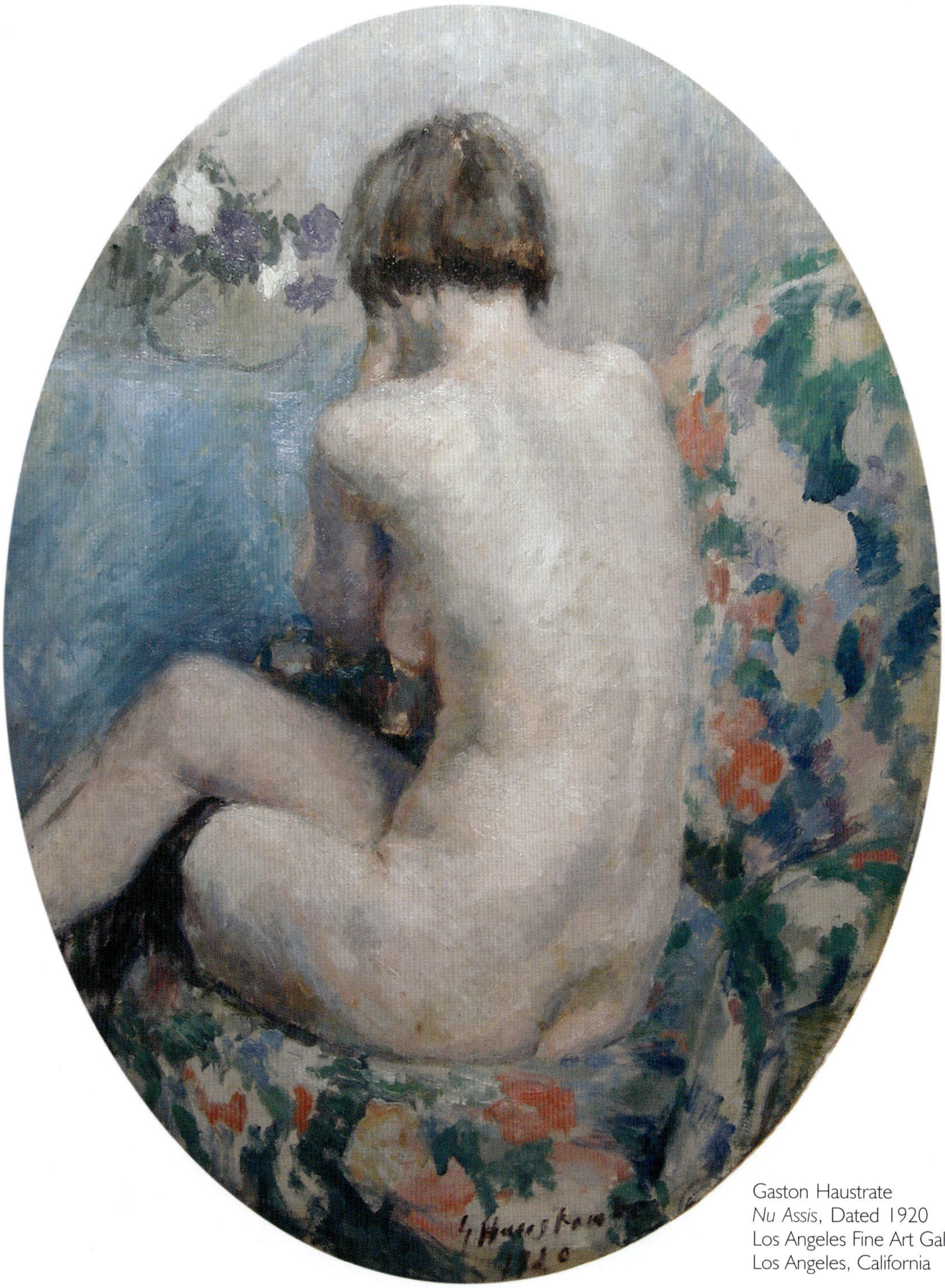

Gaston Haustrate
Nu Assis, Dated 1920
Los Angeles Fine Art Gallery,
Los Angeles, California

Maurice Henri Hensel

Born 1890

Maurice Henri Hensel was born in Montmartre in 1890. He was an artist of l'École de Montmartre and best is known as a watercolorist and painter.

Beginning in 1920, Hensel was associated with the Salon des Artistes Indépendants. He also exhibited regularly at the Salon d'Automne. In 1925 he received a solo show called *Figures de Montmartre* in Paris at Galerie Bernheim-Jeune. The following year at Galerie Bernheim-Jeune, he exhibited a group of paintings called *Femmes du Sud-Algérien*. In 1928 he exhibited at Galerie Barreiro a group of works called *Femmes de Paris* and *Femmes d'Afrique du Nord*.

Hensel traveled to Africa shortly after World War I. In keeping with his interests in Montmartre, he painted the local courtesans.

Hensel's style is in the taste of the Postimpressionists, similar in technique to Jacque-Émile Blanche. Like many of his contemporaries, including Toulouse-Lautrec, he romanticized the darker side of the Bohemian life.

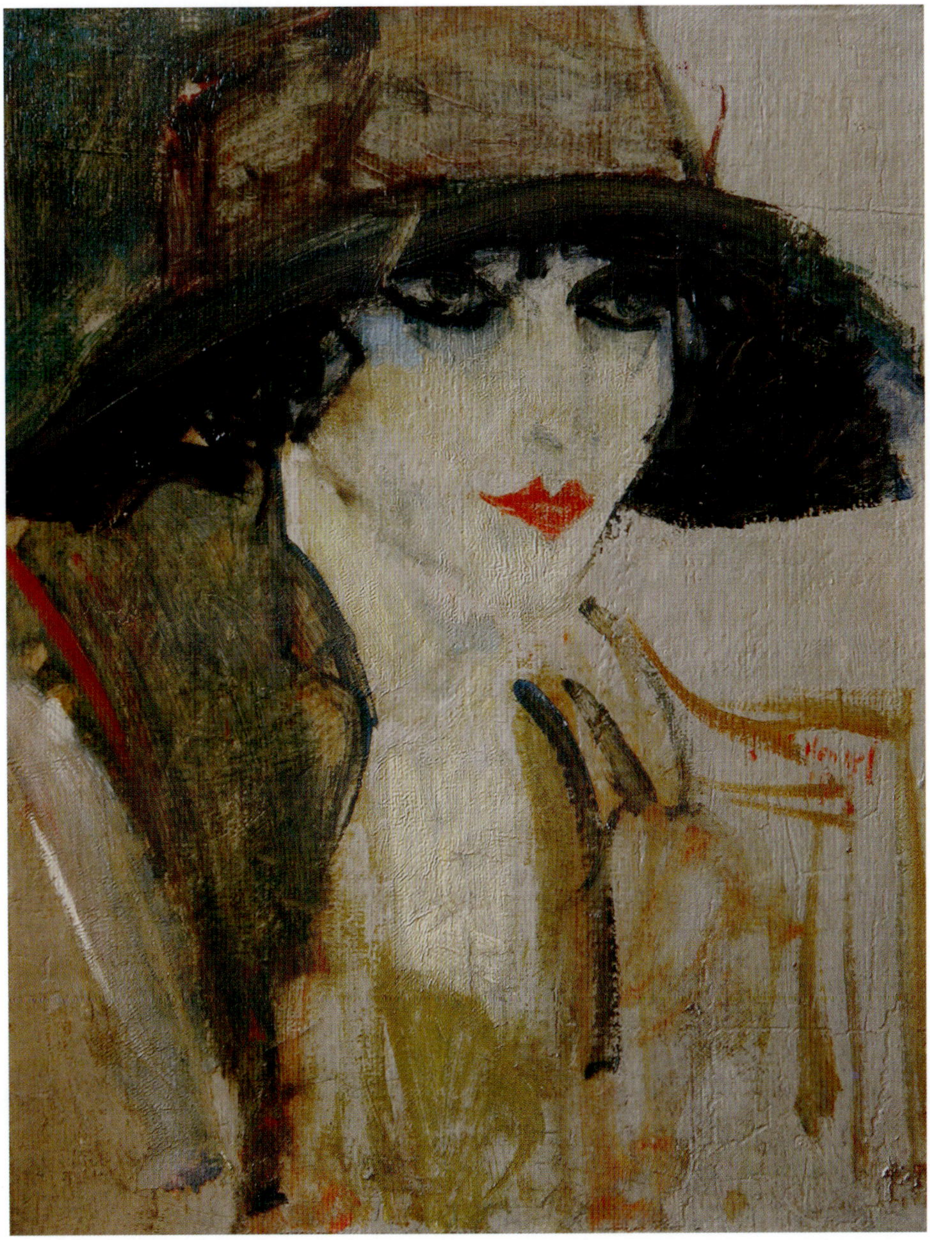

Maurice Henri Hensel
Femme au Chapeau, c.1920
The Parrish Collection,
San Francisco, California

René Georges Hermann-Paul

1864-1940

René Georges Hermann-Paul was born in Paris and studied at l'École des Arts Décoratifs and the Académie Julian. He studied under Henri Lerolle and Gustave Colin and came to be known as a painter, printmaker, prolific illustrator and draftsman. His illustrations maintained a politically satirical nature while his paintings were greatly influenced by Cézanne.

Positions Hermann-Paul held include professor at l'École des Beaux-Arts in Paris and an elected membership to the Salon d'Automne. He also exhibited with Bonnard, Vuillard and Denis.

Two well known albums of black and white lithographs were published in 1894 and 1895; *La Vie de Monsieur Quelconque* and *La Vie de Madame Quelconque,* among others. Hermann-Paul also belonged to a group of French artists who utilized a combination of traditional printmaking methods with new photomechanical relief-printed images, which allowed for substantial distribution of their work. This group included Toulouse-Lautrec, Vuillard, Bonnard and Vallotton.

Several leading Paris journals supported Hermann-Paul's illustrations including *L'Assiette au beurre, Le Canard Sauvage, Candide, Le Courrier Européen, Le Courrier Français, Les droits de l'Homme, L' Escarmouche, L'Homme Libre, La Vie Parisienne, Le Rire, Le Figaro* and a number of others. Among the books he illustrated were works by Gabriele d'Annunzio, Émile Zola, François Villon, Gustave Flaubert and Rabelais.

Fletcher Copenhaver Fine Art of Fredericksburg, Virginia , provided this biographical information.

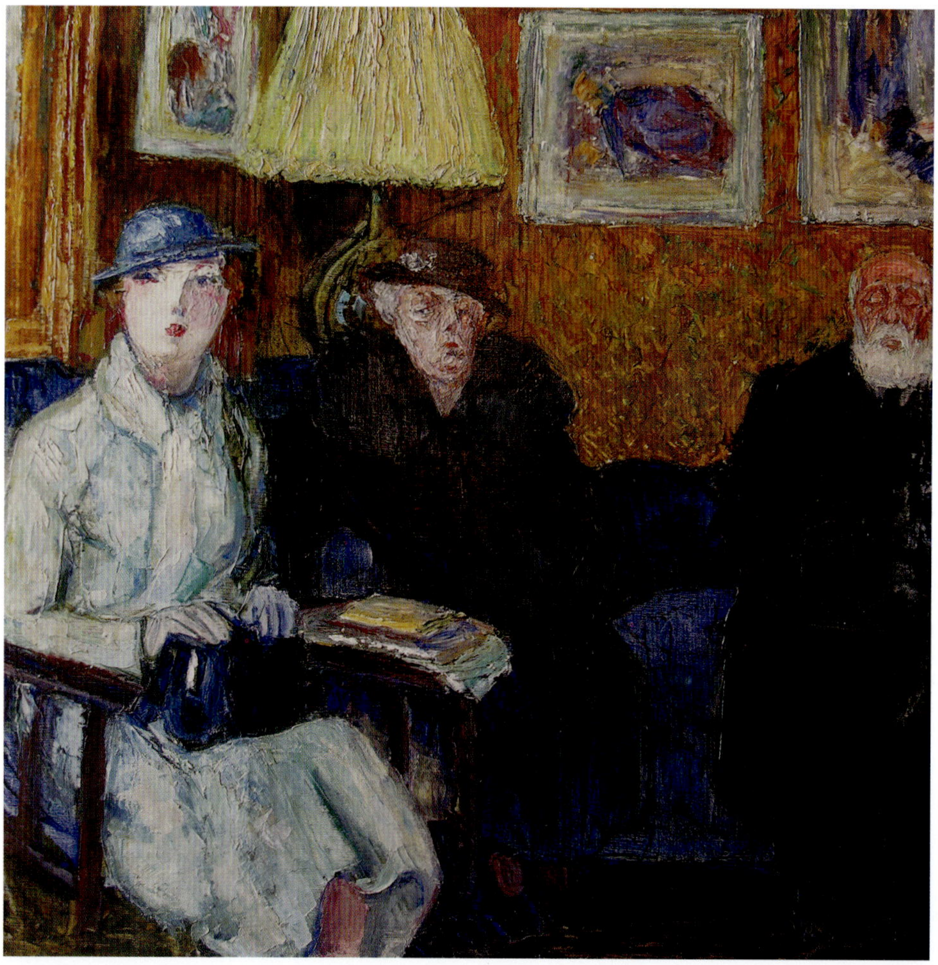

René Georges Hermann-Paul
Attente, c.1925
Ernie and Ronna Vigil, Aptos, California

André Hofer
20th century

André Hofer was born in Autun, Saône-et-Loire, France. He is known as a 20th century French painter and illustrator. He began exhibiting his paintings in 1912, frequently at the Salon des Indépendants.

His style is typical of many artists of his time; his vivid colors and creative composition made his works commercially successful. Hofer illustrated Kipling's *Des Voyages et Parfums* and Buck's *Le Patriote*.

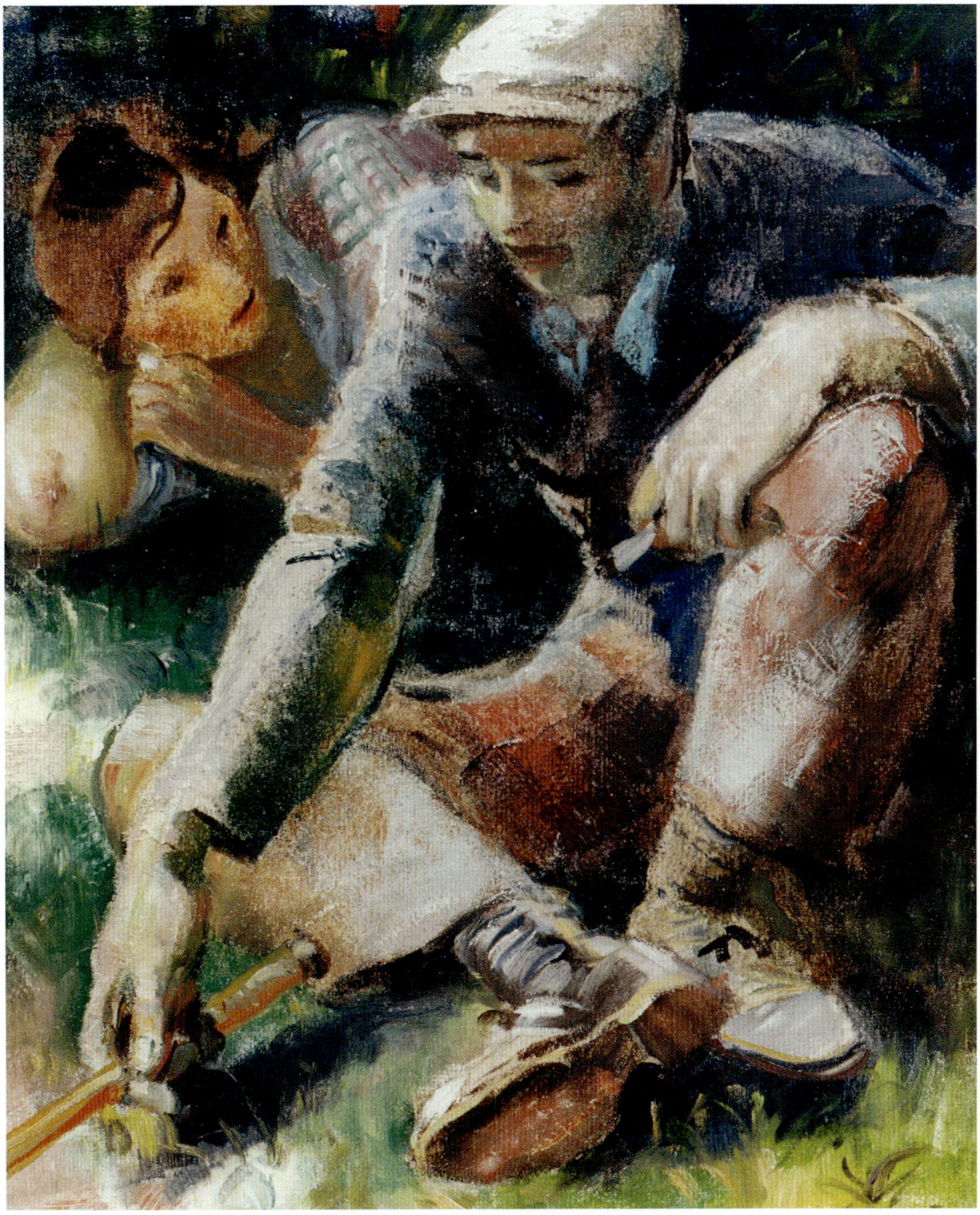

André Hofer
Au Parc, c.1930
Los Angeles Fine Art Gallery, Los Angeles, California

André Louis Maxime Humbert

Born 1879

André Louis Maxime Humbert was born on November 27, 1879 in Paris. Humbert studied with Léon Bonnat and exhibited regularly at the Salon des Artistes Français. He earned a Médaille de Troisième Classe in 1901, a Médaille de Deuxième Classe in 1904 and a travel scholarship in 1907. Humbert's painting *La Lapidation de saint Étienne* is part of the permanent collection of the Musée Périgueux.

Humbert painted symbolist subjects typical of La Belle Époque. His beautiful maidens standing pensively in the forest were subjects of immense popularity at the turn of the 20th century.

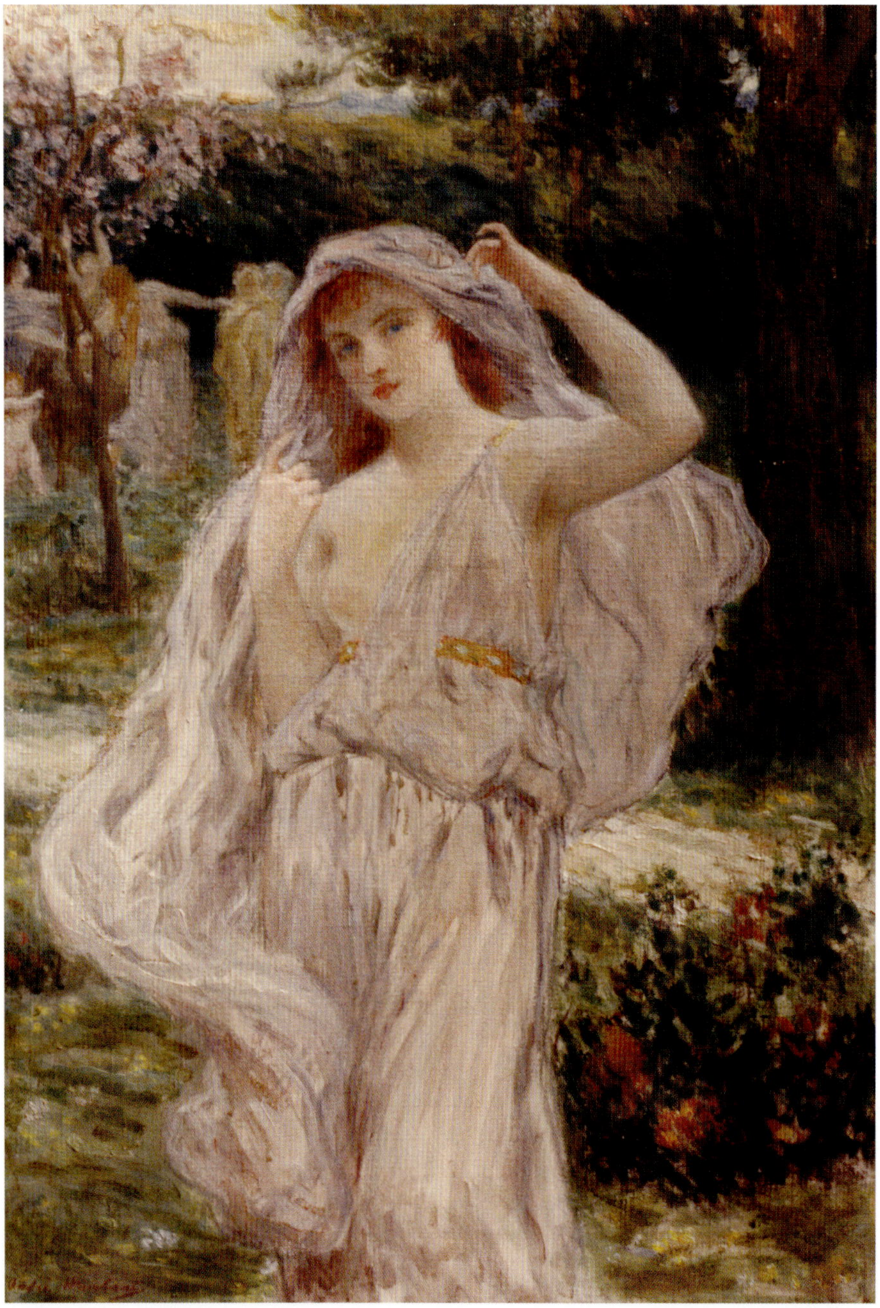

André Louis Maxime Humbert
Nu Symboliste, c.1900
Los Angeles Fine Art Gallery, Los Angeles, California

Léonie Humbert-Vignon

Born 1878

Léonie Humbert-Vignon was born February 16, 1878 in Lyon where she attended l'École des Beaux-Arts and was instructed by Alexandre Bonnardel and Édouard Toudouze.

Her first exhibition at the Lyon Salon was in 1896 where she received the Médaille de Deuxième Classe in 1901. Léonie received first prize in 1908 as well as an honorable mention at the Salon des Artistes Français the same year. In 1910 she received a Médaille de Troisième Classe at the Salon.

Humbert-Vignon's paintings demonstrate an Orientalist influence. Stylistically a realist, she incorporated interiors and costumes that make her painting rich and appealing.

Her work has been collected by the Digne Museum and has been exhibited in Paris in 1990 and 1993. The date of her death is unknown.

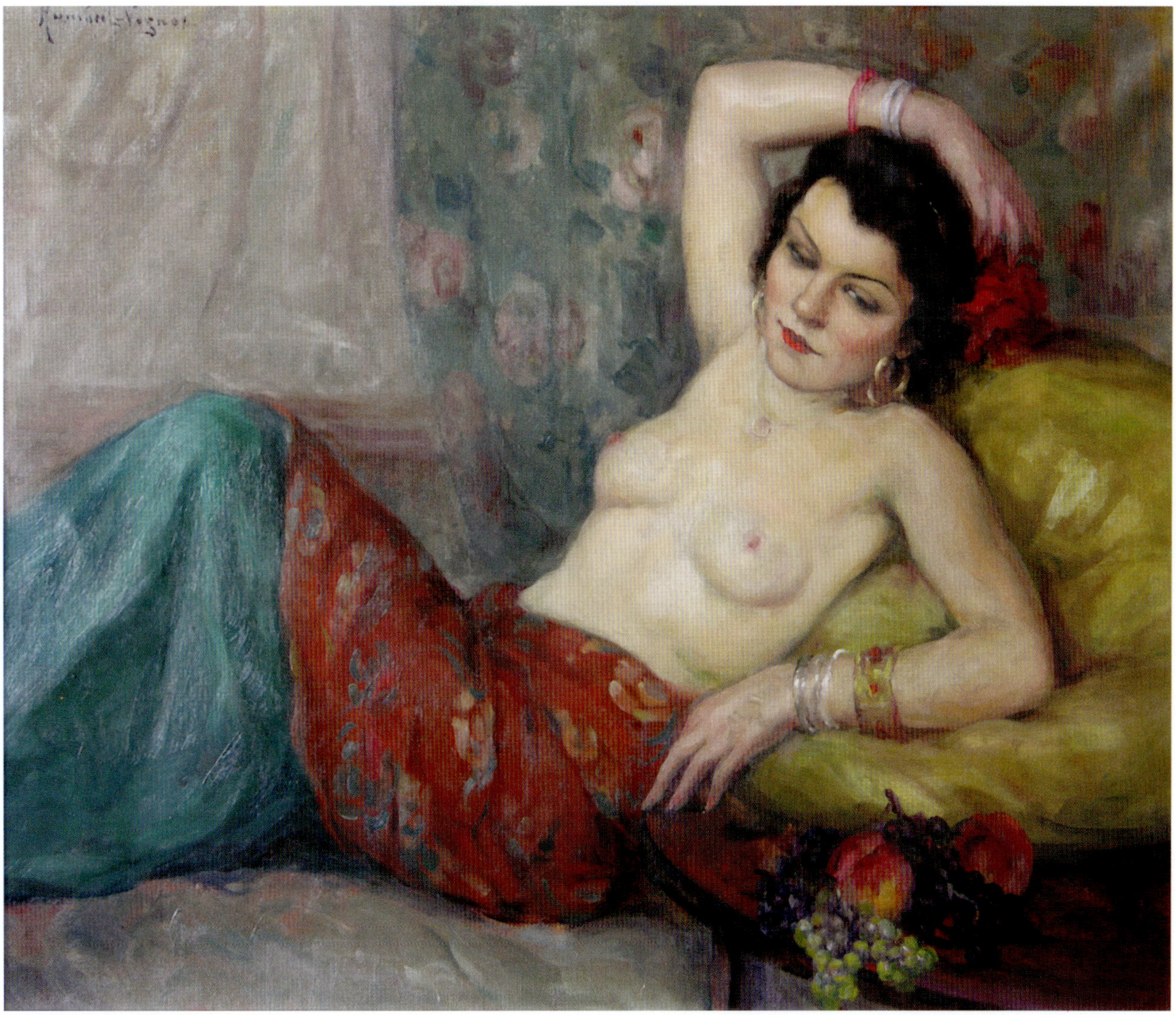

Léonie Humbert-Vignon
Nu Orientaliste, c.1925
Tracey Jacobs, Los Angeles, California

Jean Jannel

Born 1894

A native Parisian, Jean Jannel studied under Luc-Olivier Merson. Jannel exhibited at the Salon des Artistes Français and Salon des Artistes Indépendants. Jannel was a prolific painter of realistic nudes and charming nymphs that may have graced the walls of many Art Deco apartments in Paris.

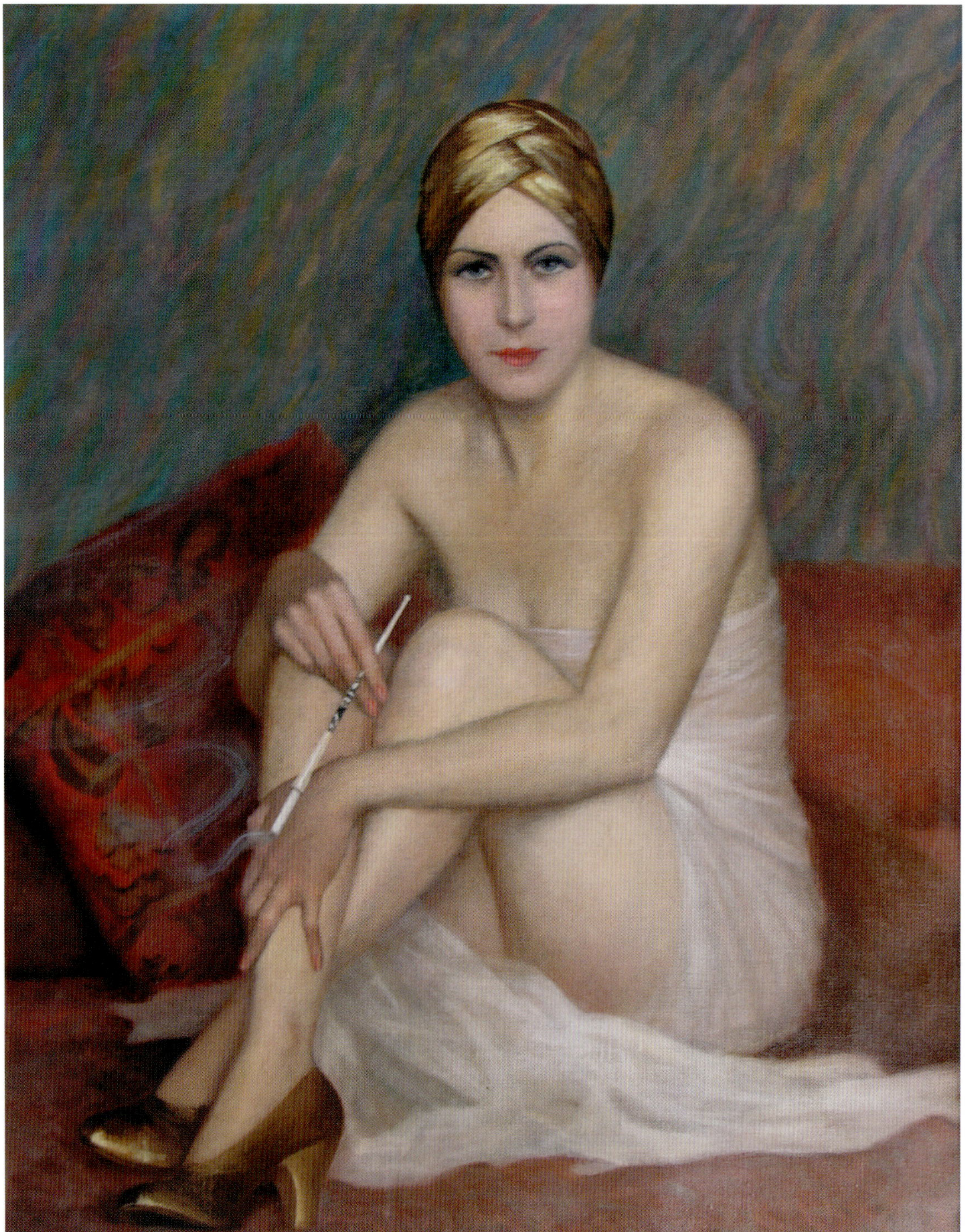

Jean Jannel
Femme au Turbin, c.1925
Andrew Herrera II, San Francisco, California

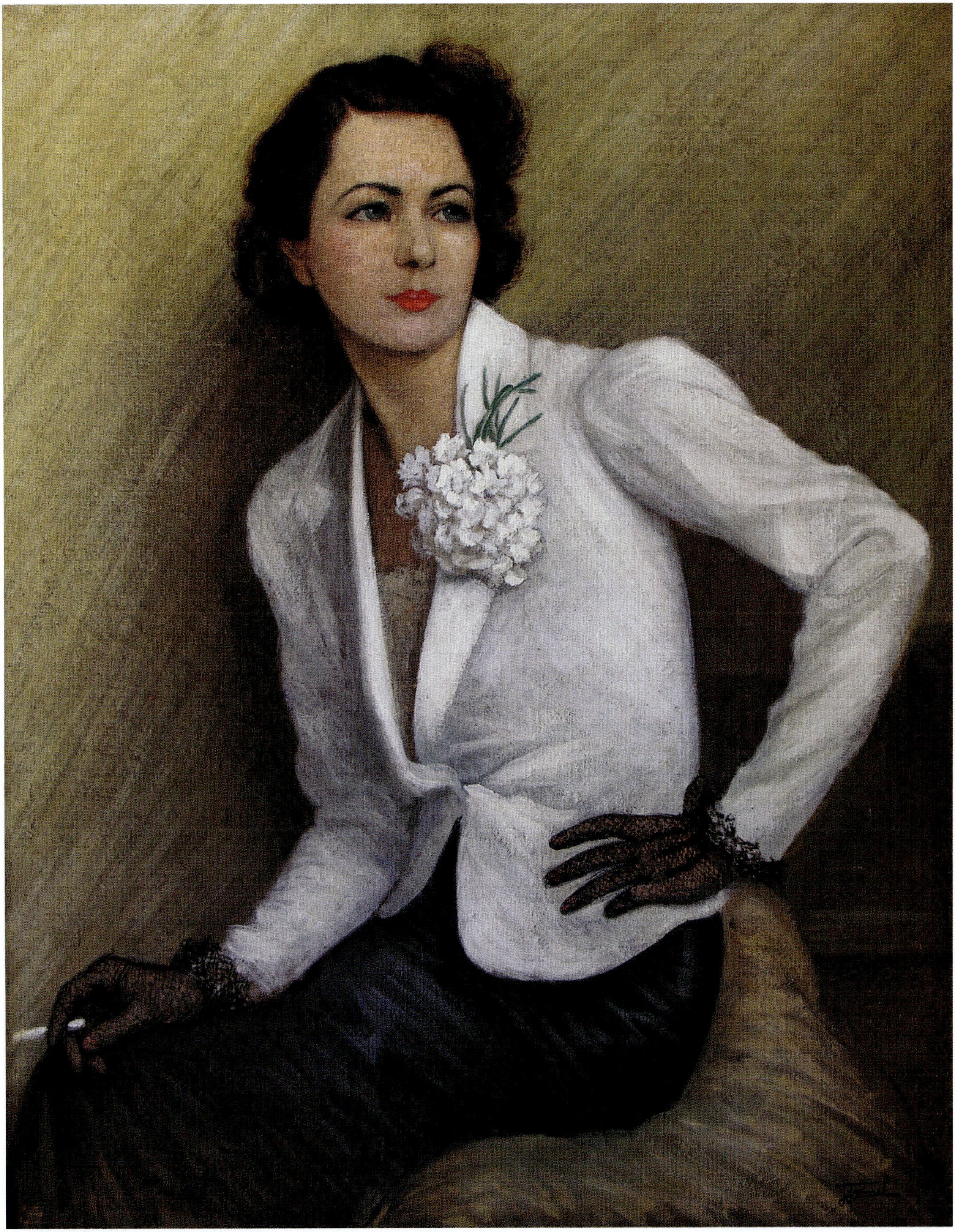

Jean Jannel
Portrait de Madame Jannel, c.1925
Martin and Marsha Brander, Brentwood, California

Romain Jarosz
1889-1932

Romain Jarosz was born in January 29,1889. The artist studied under Charles Guérin, during which time he worked primarily in still lifes of flowers and landscapes. Jarosz exhibited at the Salon des Indépendants 1922, Salon d'Automne 1924 and Salon des Tuileries 1930.

A talented draftsman, Jarosz worked in pencil drawings of horses and riders and is also known for his studies and paintings of nude figures. Jarosz died in 1932.

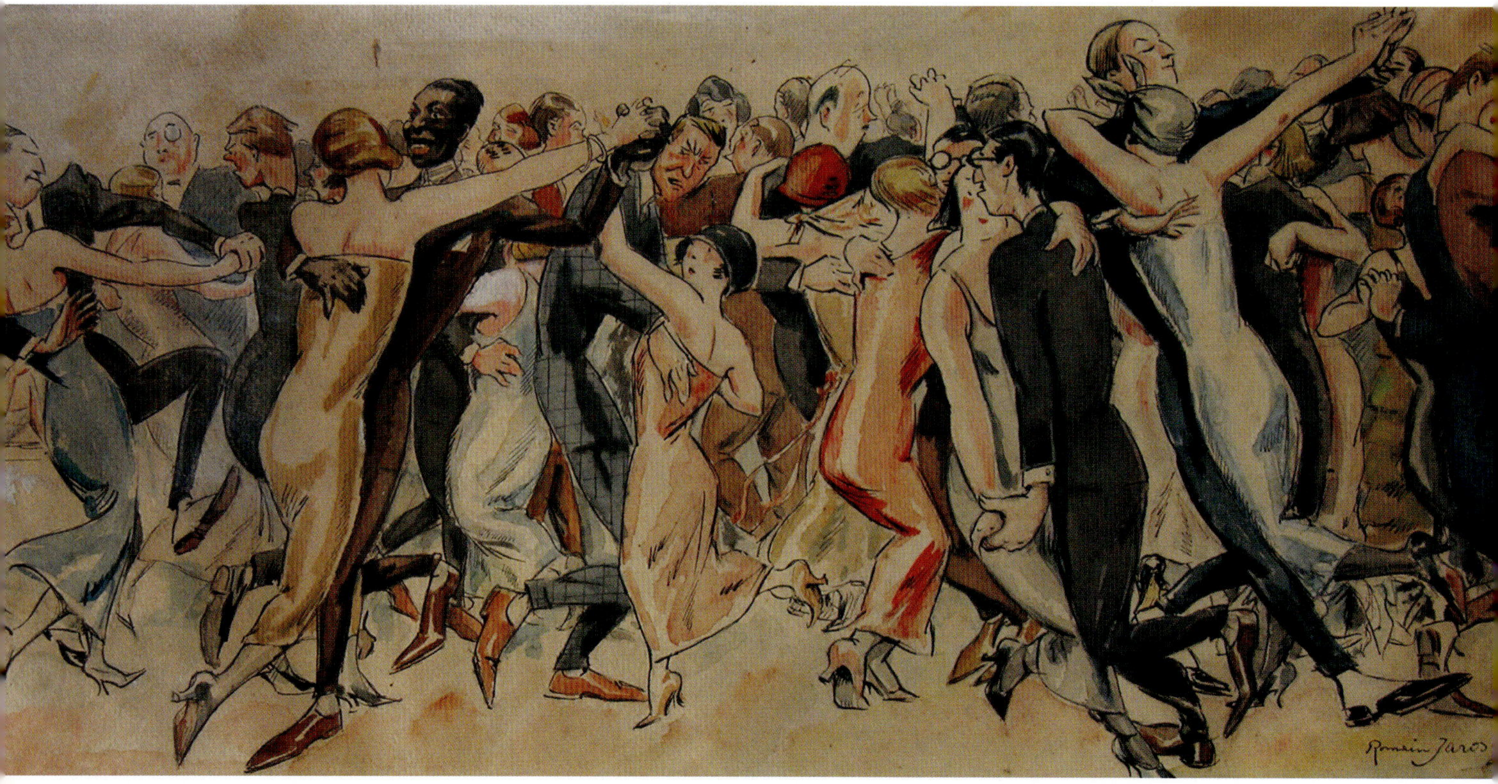

Romain Jarosz
Les Danseurs, c.1925
Carol Lopilato, Los Angeles, California

Mainie Harriet Jellett

1897–1944

Mainie Harriet Jellett was born in Dublin, Ireland, in 1897. She studied in the atelier of André Lhote in Paris and in 1921 became the student of Albert Gleizes.

From 1910 to 1938 she exhibited with the Salon des Surindépendants in Paris and was a member of the group *Abstraction-Création* from 1931 to 1936. Along with another student of Gleizes, Evie Hone, Jellett founded l'Exposition Irlandaise d'Art Vivant, which became the principal annual exhibition of Irish avant-garde painters.

Three retrospectives have been held at the Dublin Municipal Gallery in 1962, the Neptune Gallery 1991-1992 and the Museum of Modern Art in Dublin. Jellett died in 1944.

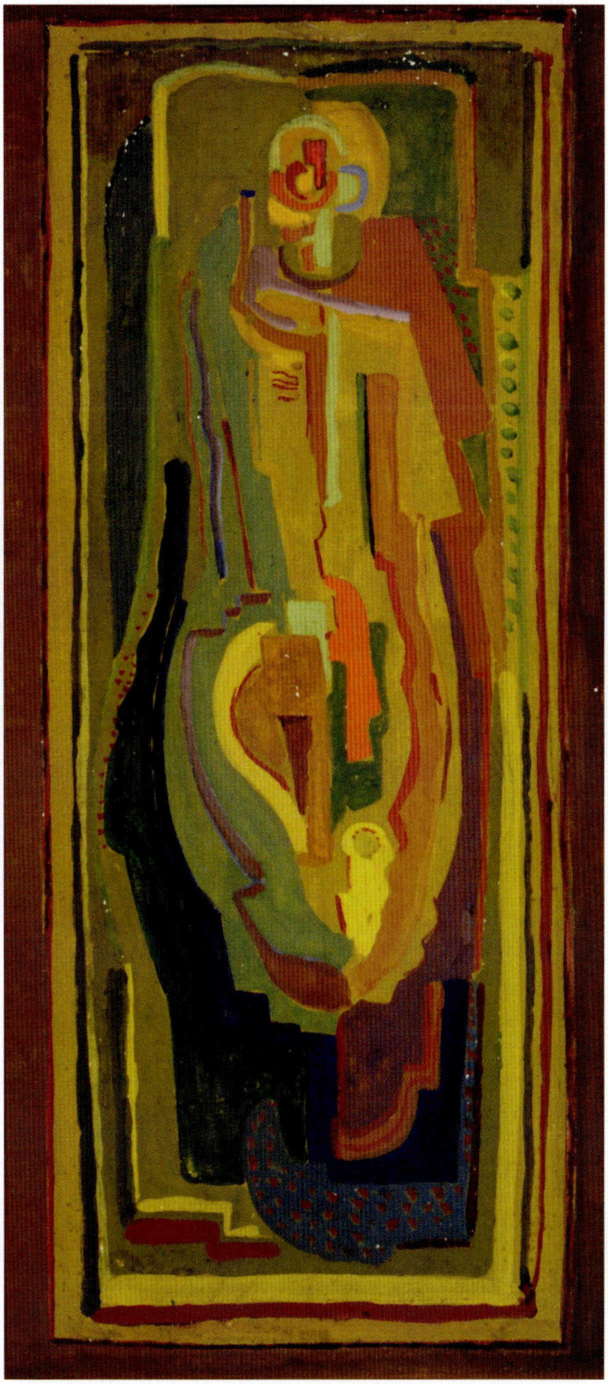

Mainie Harriet Jellett
Nu Abstrait, c.1930
Courtesy of the Jeri L. Waxenberg Collection, USA

Lucien Hector Jonas

1880-1947

Lucien Hector Jonas began his studies at Valenciennes under the instruction of Layraud before attending l'École dès Beaux-Arts in Paris. There he studied with Maignan, Bonnat and Harpignies.

Jonas exhibited at the Salon des Artistes Français, of which he was also a member and received; the Deuxième Prix de Rome in 1905, a Médaille d'Or in 1907, the Prix National du Salon in 1911, the Légion d'Honour in 1929 and a Médaille d'Honour each for engraving and painting in 1945. Jonas also served as jury member for paintings and engravings.

Jonas decorated many churches, specifically in the north of France between 1920 and 1925, and was commissioned for illustrations of several publications including *Le Prince Charmant* by Gaston-Charles, *César Birotteau* by Balzac, *Tartuffe* by Molière, *L'Arlésienne* by Daudet and *Chloé* by Longus.

Jonas died in Paris in 1947. His work has been collected by museums in Paris, Dijon, Grenoble, New York, Versaille and Montréal. A retrospective was held in Paris in 1992.

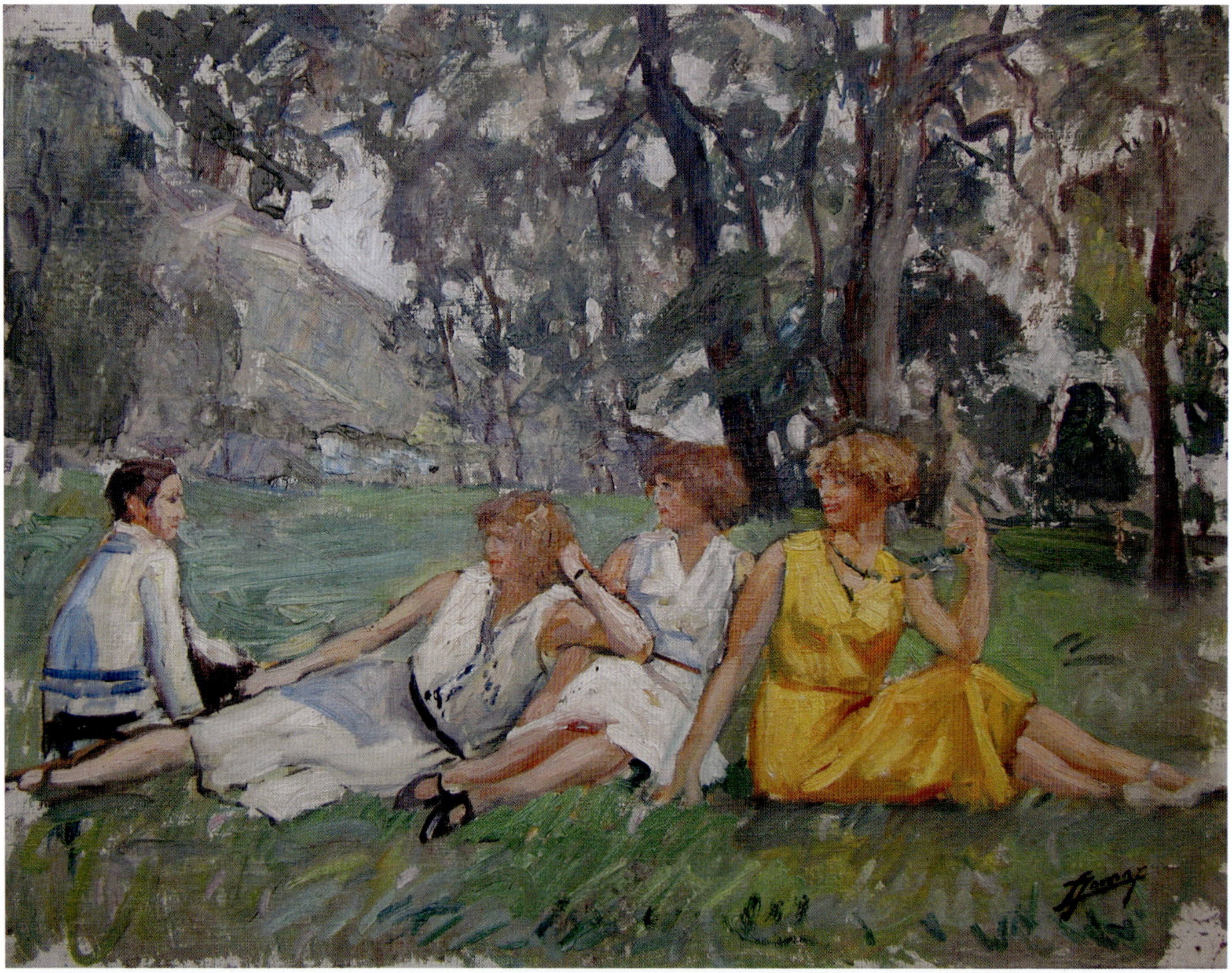

Lucien Hector Jonas
Au Parc, c.1930
Kathleen Avery Fine Art, Palo Alto, California

George M. Josimovich
1895-1986

George M. Josimovich was born on May 3, 1895 in Sremska Mitrovica, Serbia. From 1914 to 1919 Josimovich studied with George Bellows and Randall Davy at the Art Institute of Chicago. After graduating, Josimovich studied crafts for a year with Herman Sachs.

Josimovich is best known as a painter specializing in still lifes and worked in oils, watercolors and acrylics. Additionally, he worked as a designer, lithographer and craftsman. He was a member of the Chicago Society of Artists where he served as Vice President of the organization from 1942 to 1943 and President from 1943 to 1944. Josimovich was a member of the No-Jury Society of Artists, serving as Vice President in 1929, and a member of the Society of Independent Artists.

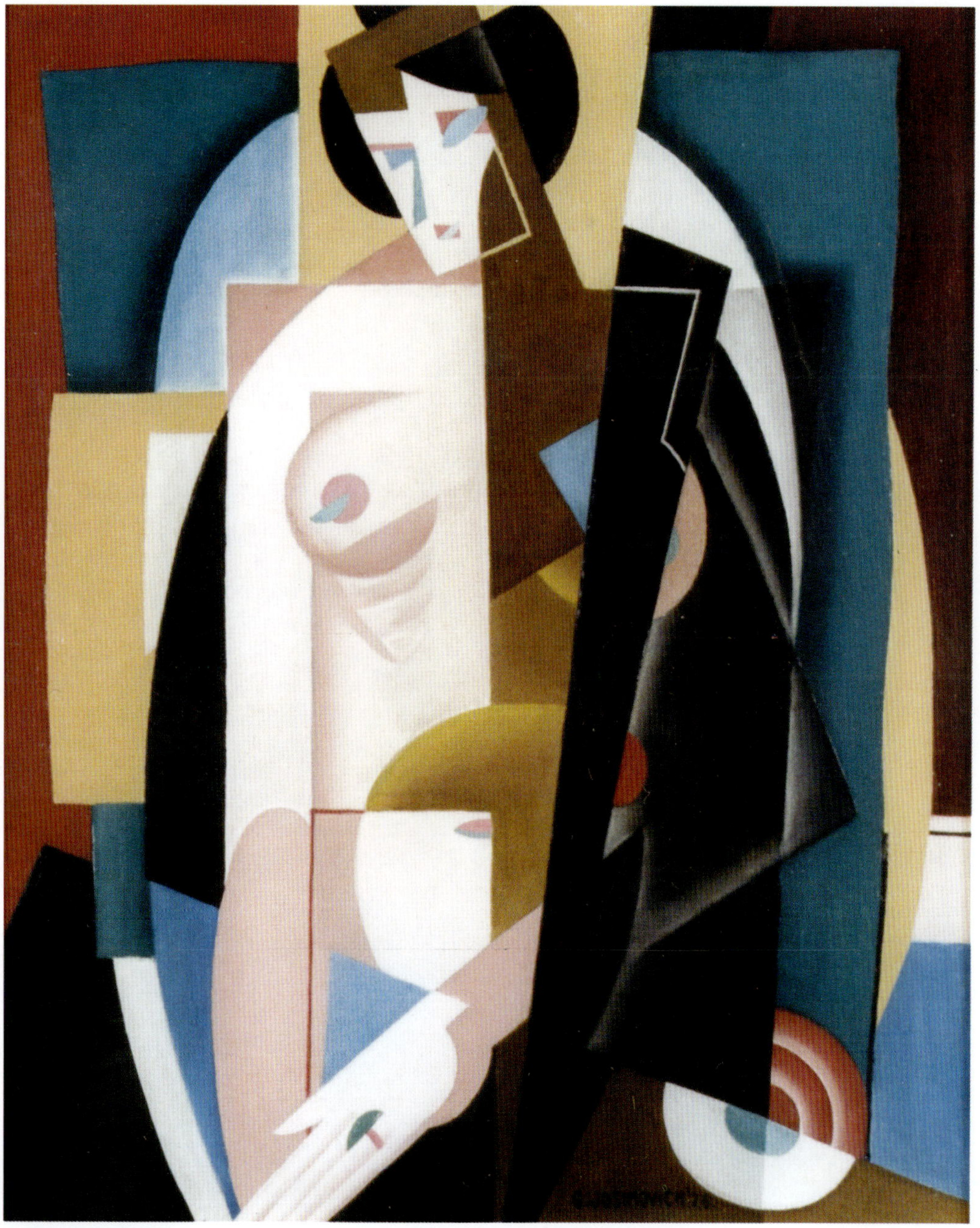

George M. Josimovich
Cubist Nude, Dated 1926
Robert Henry Adams Fine Art, Chicago, Illinois

Josimovich amassed an extensive exhibition record during his long career. In 1927 he showed at the Galerie du Contemporain in Paris. The following year, Josimovich showed at the Salons Américains. In 1928, he exhibited at the Salon des Indépendants. His work was included in the twenty-eighth annual International Exhibition at the Carnegie Institute, 1928-1929. He won a sliver medal at the 1929 Chicago Society Artists exhibition. The following year he was in a group exhibition of paintings at the Tweed Museum of Art at the University of Minnesota, Duluth. In 1931 he exhibited a solo show at the Knoedler Gallery in Chicago. Twelve years later in 1943, Josimovich had a solo exhibition at the University of Chicago. In addition to these exhibitions, Josimovich participated in many different annual exhibitions. During the 1930s and 40s, he showed in the Chicago and Vicinity artist exhibition organized by the Art Institute of Chicago. In 1949, 1951, 1953 and 1955, Josimovich exhibited at the North Mississippi Valley Artists show. Additionally, he participated in the Three Rivers Arts Festival in 1968 and 1970.

Josimovich's work is included in the permanent collection at the Joslyn Art Museum in Omaha, Nebraska and Mattoon, Illinois, High School.

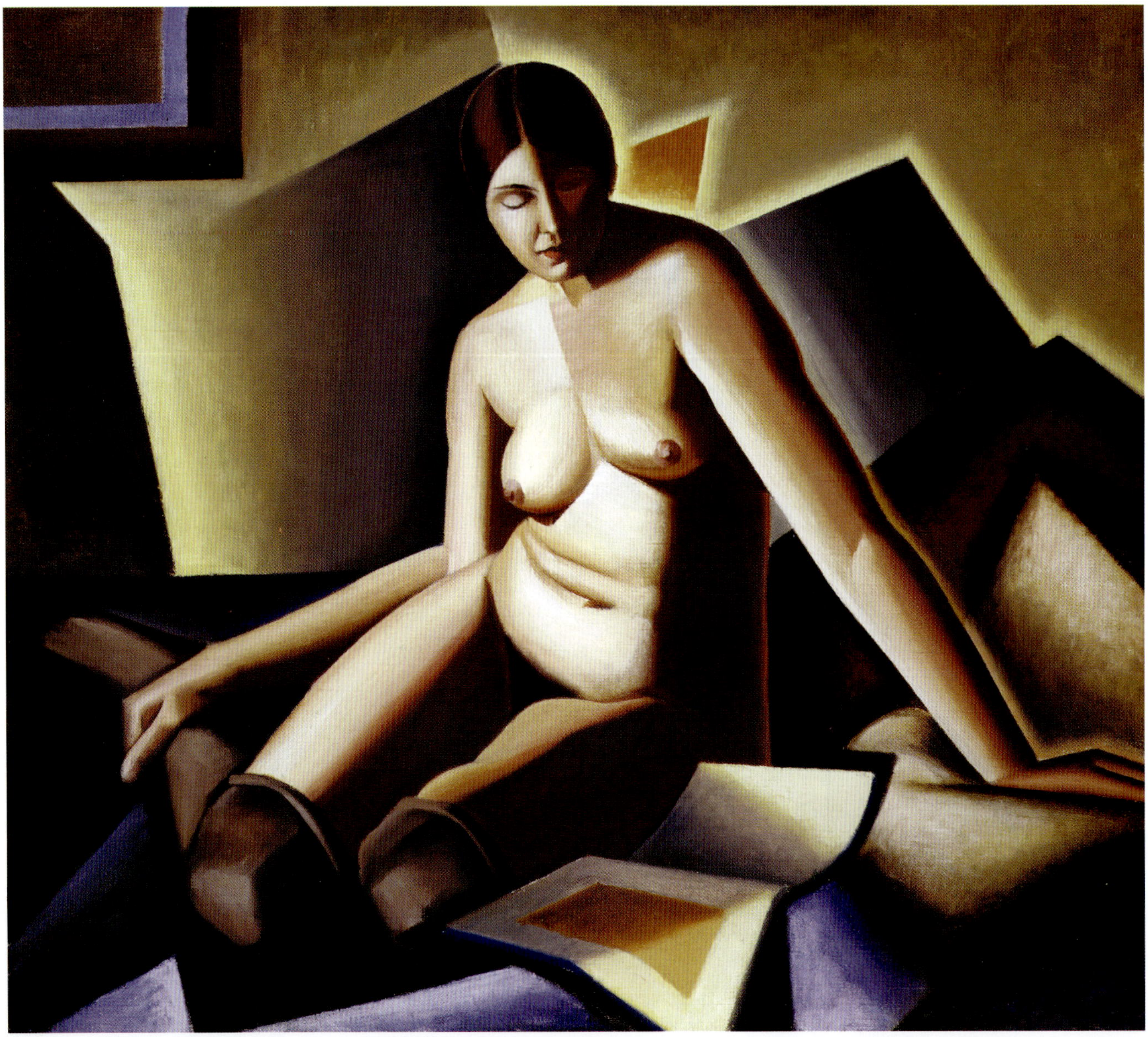

George M. Josimovich
Nude Reading, c.1926
Robert Henry Adams Fine Art, Chicago, Illinois

Josimovich's paintings of the 1920s demonstrate influences of the masters of Cubism and Purism. One can see elements of Valmier, Lhote and Le Corbusier in his work. His use of geometry, color and composition give his canvases an unusual brilliance.

Working with the family of the artist, the Robert Henry Adams Gallery in Chicago has brought to the attention of a new generation of collector this extraordinary body of work. Josimovich died in September 1986, in Newark, New Jersey.

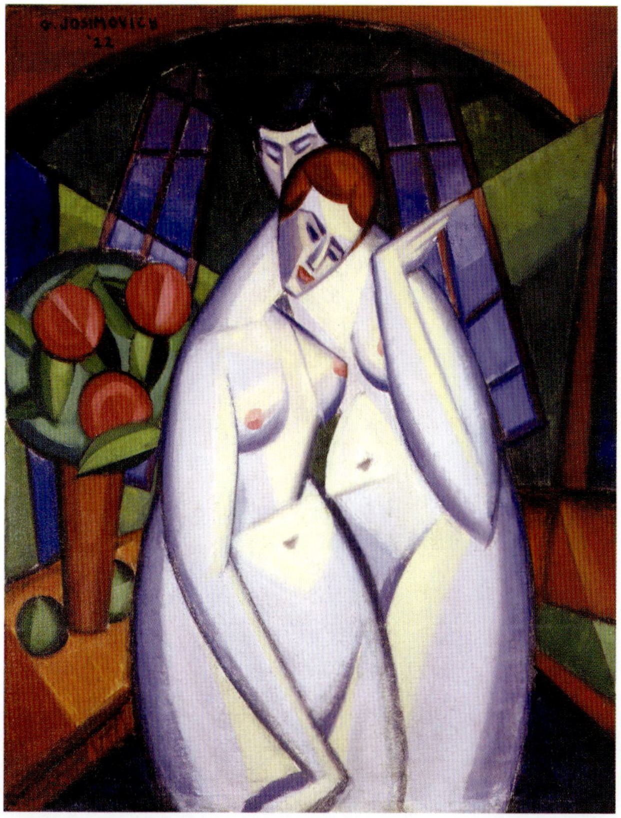

George M. Josimovich
Two Nudes, Dated 1922
Robert Henry Adams Fine Art, Chicago, Illinois

George M. Josimovich
Housekeeper, Dated 1928
Robert Henry Adams Fine Art, Chicago, Illinois

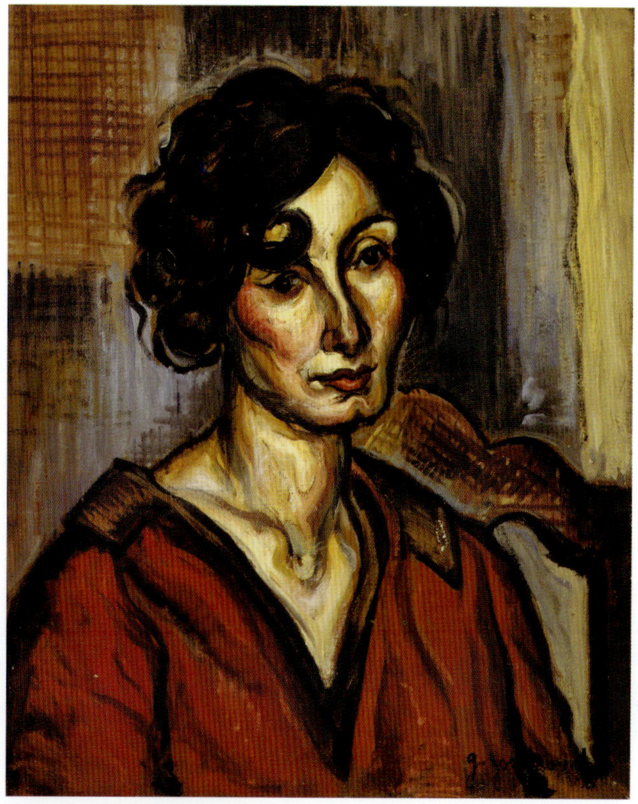

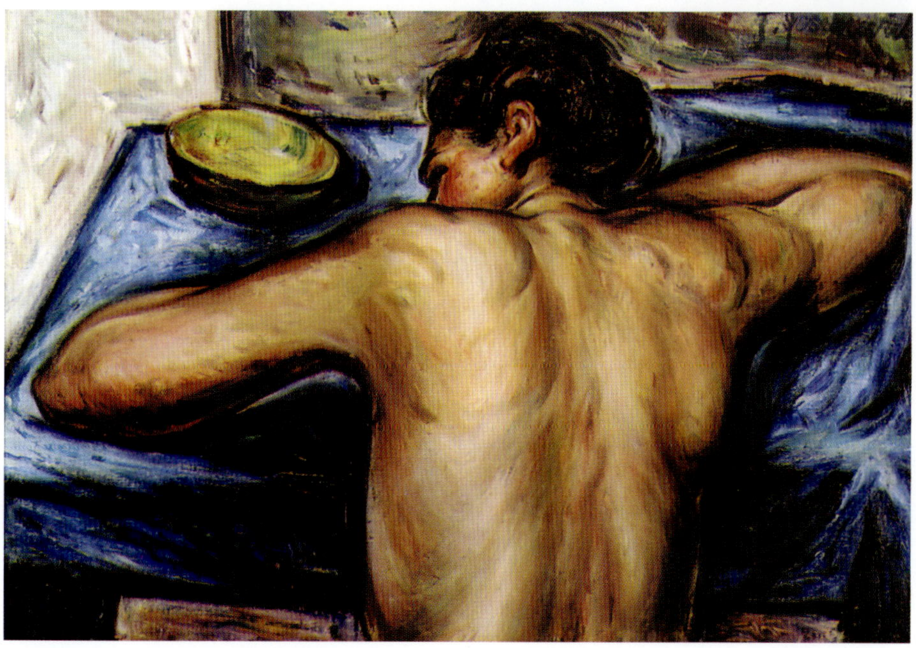

George M. Josimovich
Asleep, Dated1942
Robert Henry Adams Fine Art, Chicago, Illinois

Chrysis Jungbluth
Born 1907

Chrysis Jungbluth was born January 23, 1907 in Boulogne-sur-Mer. She studied under Humbert and exhibited at the Salon Nationale and Salon des Indépendants.

Jungbluth was an expressionist painter; she used decisive color and composition to illustrate the seedier side of the nightlife in the bars and cafés of France. She also painted nudes and portraits. The date of her death is unknown.

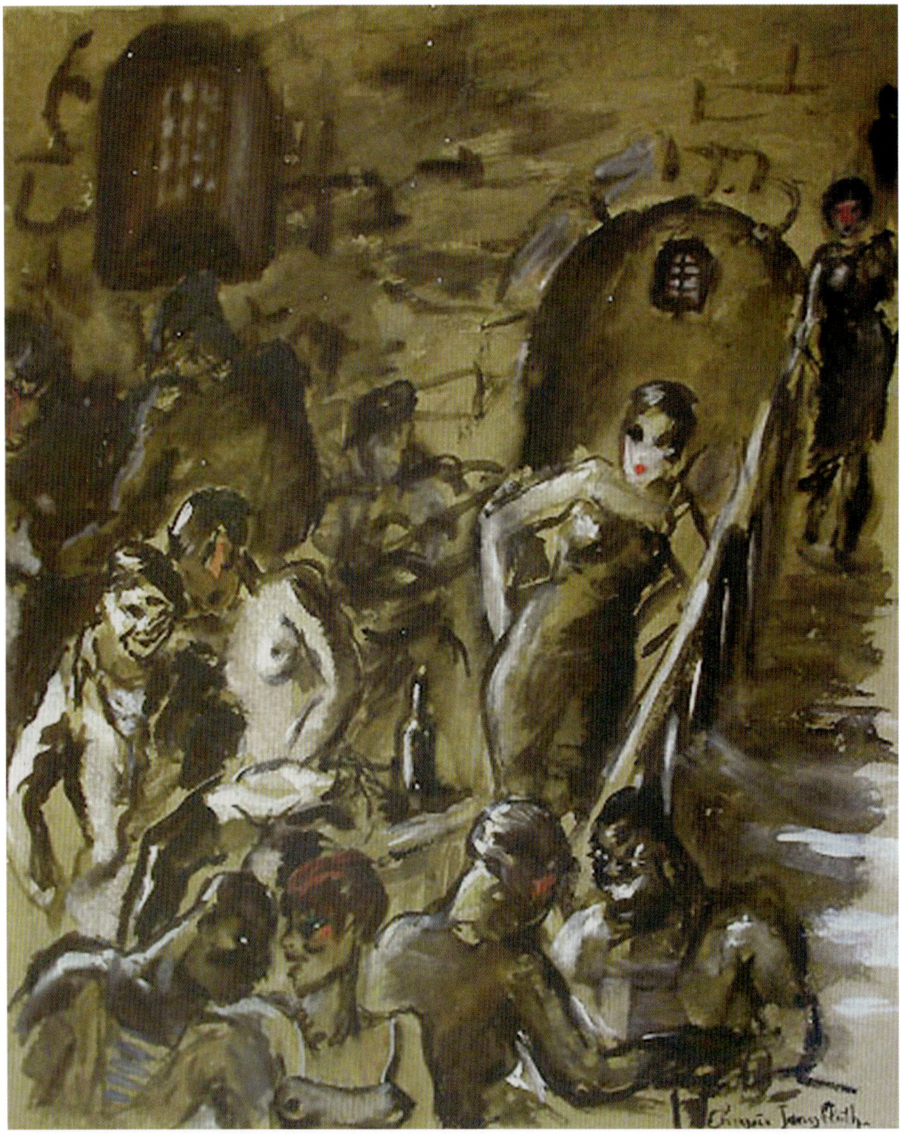

Chrysis Jungbluth
Café des Gitanes, c.1930
Papillon Gallery, Los Angeles, California

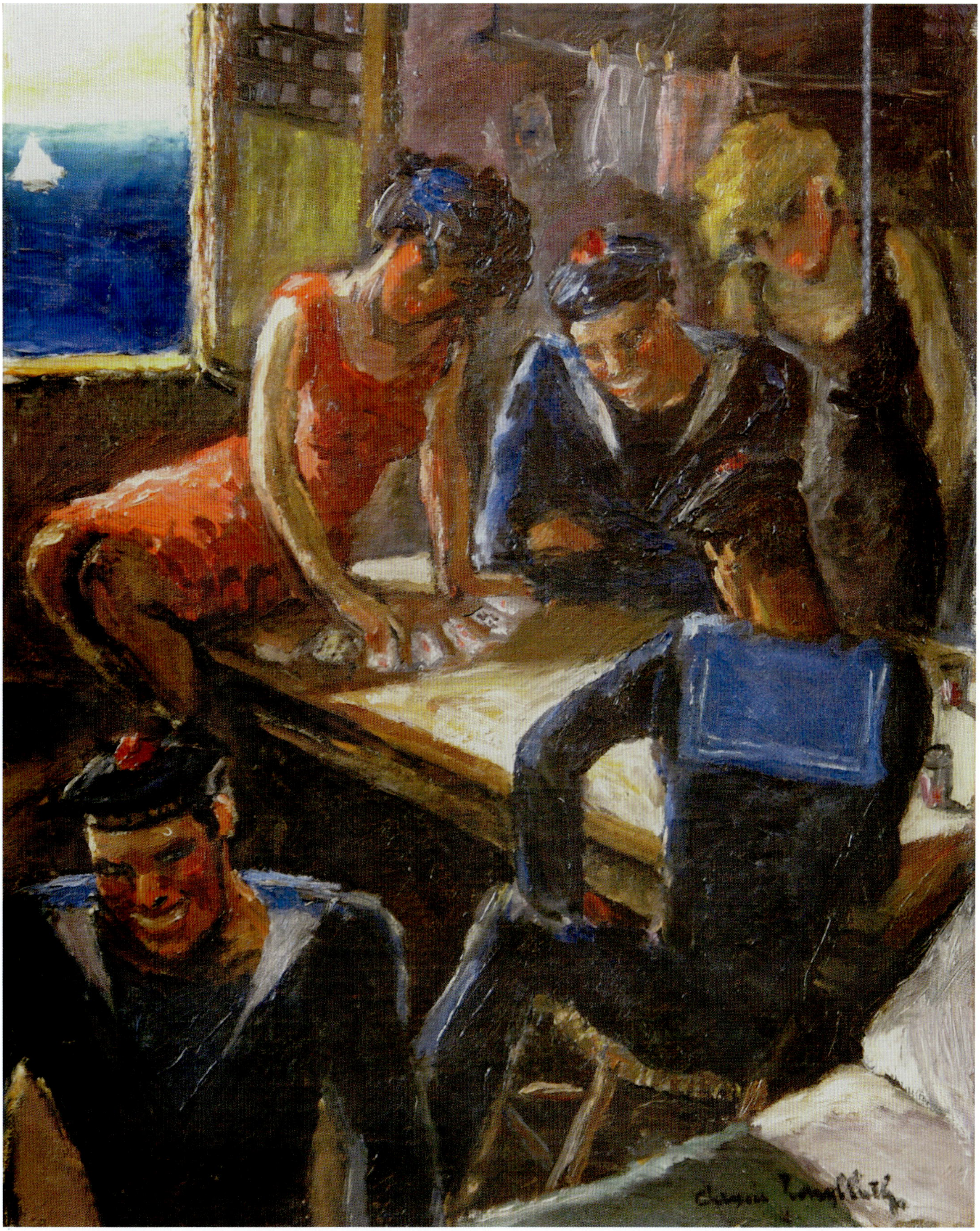

Chrysis Jungbluth
Le Jeu, c.1930
Jeffrey Winter Fine Arts, Long Beach, California

Morris Kantor
1896-1974

Morris Kantor was born in 1896 in Minsk, Russia. He moved to New York in 1906 where he lived and worked for the majority of his career. He studied at the Independent School of Art in New York under Homer Boss.

Kantor exhibited prolifically in salons, biennials and traveling exhibitions in the United States and received awards at the Art Institute of Chicago, Pennsylvania Academy of Fine Arts, Corcoran Gallery Biennial and the University of Illinois. The Metropolitan Museum, Phillips Memorial Gallery, Chicago Art Institute, Detroit Museum, Pennsylvania Academy of Fine Arts and the Whitney Museum have collected his work.

For a short period he lived in Paris where he was greatly influenced by Futurism and Cubism. He returned to New York where his inspiration carried over to a realist approach to street scenes and city life. Kantor went on to teach at the Art Students League, Cooper-Hewitt, University of Michigan, Michigan State University, University of Colorado, University of Illinois, University of Minnesota in Duluth and the University of New Mexico.

Kantor is mentioned in many books on American modern art and many of his paintings are illustrated. Over his long and productive career his style evolved but always he remained a committed modernist. The artist died in 1974, in Nyack, New York.

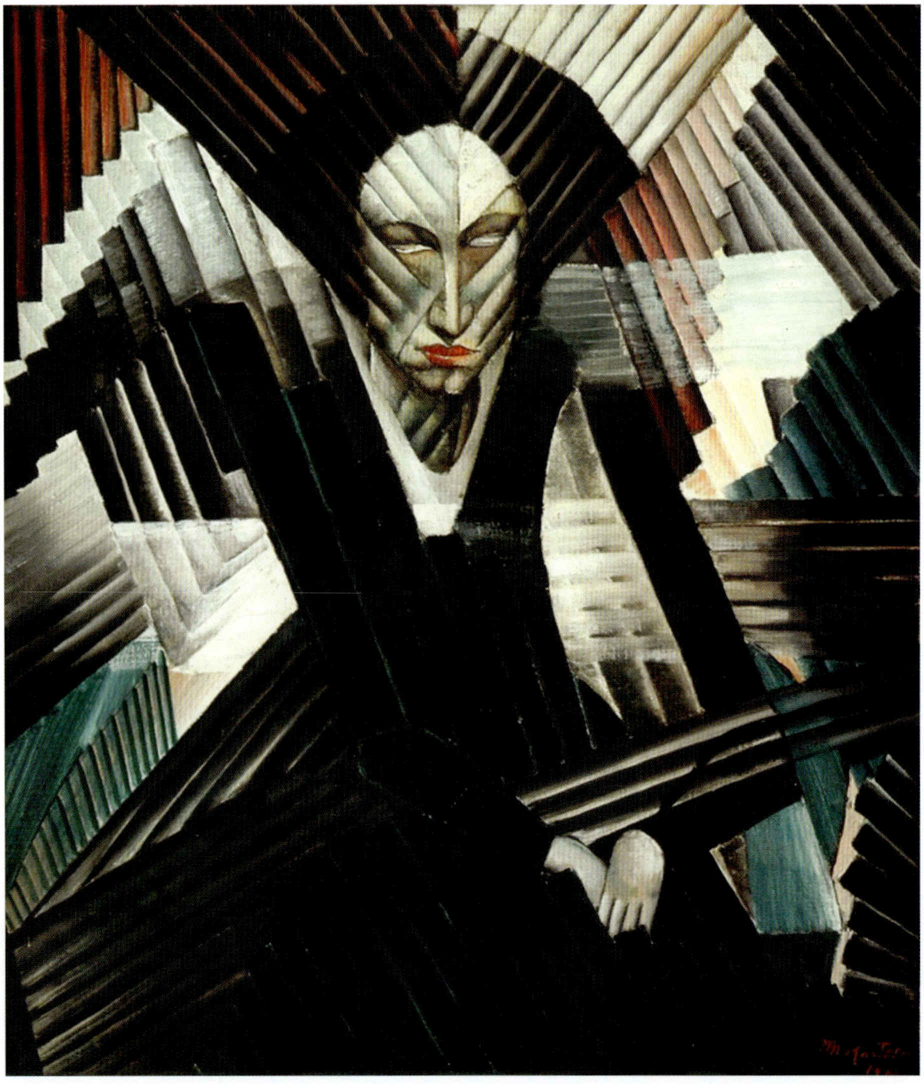

Morris Kantor
Portrait of the Artist's Mother,
Dated 1922
Private Collection

Andrée Karpelès
Born 1885

Andrée Karpelès was born in Paris. She was influenced by the Hindu poet, Rabindranath Tagore. She is best known for her paintings and illustrations, including a children's book *Maman, dis-mois,* written by Germain Montreuil-Straus in 1927. Karapelès studied under René Ménard and Lucien Simon.

Karpelès idealistic paintings can be considered traditionally Art Deco. The date of her death is unknown.

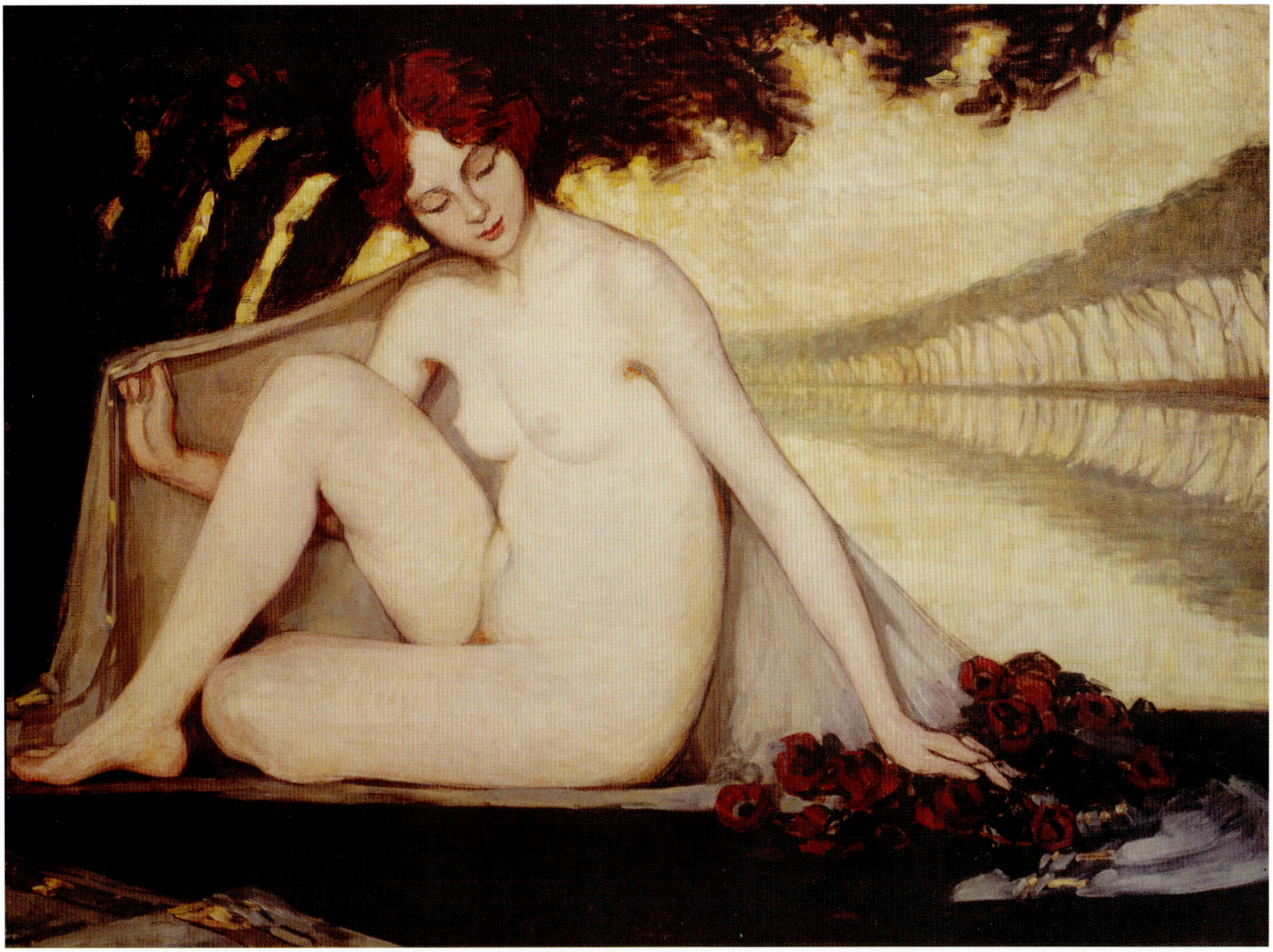

Andrée Karpelès
Jeune Femme au Bord du Lac, c.1925
Private Collection

Vital Keuller
1866-1945

Vital Keuller was born in 1866 in Lille, France. He was a student of Stallaert and Portaels. Until 1914 Keuller lived in Ostende; at the onset of World War I he moved to England.

He worked in France and Belgium and is known for his portraits, landscapes and nautical paintings. Keuller also painted cityscapes and patriotic images. At the end of the war he returned to Belgium and lived near Anvers. In 1991 the Musée des Beaux-Arts d'Ostende organized a comprehensive retrospective of Keuller's work.

Keuller's work is typical of the Beaux-Arts style; elegantly painted and composed. Keuller died in Schaerbeek, Belgium, in 1945.

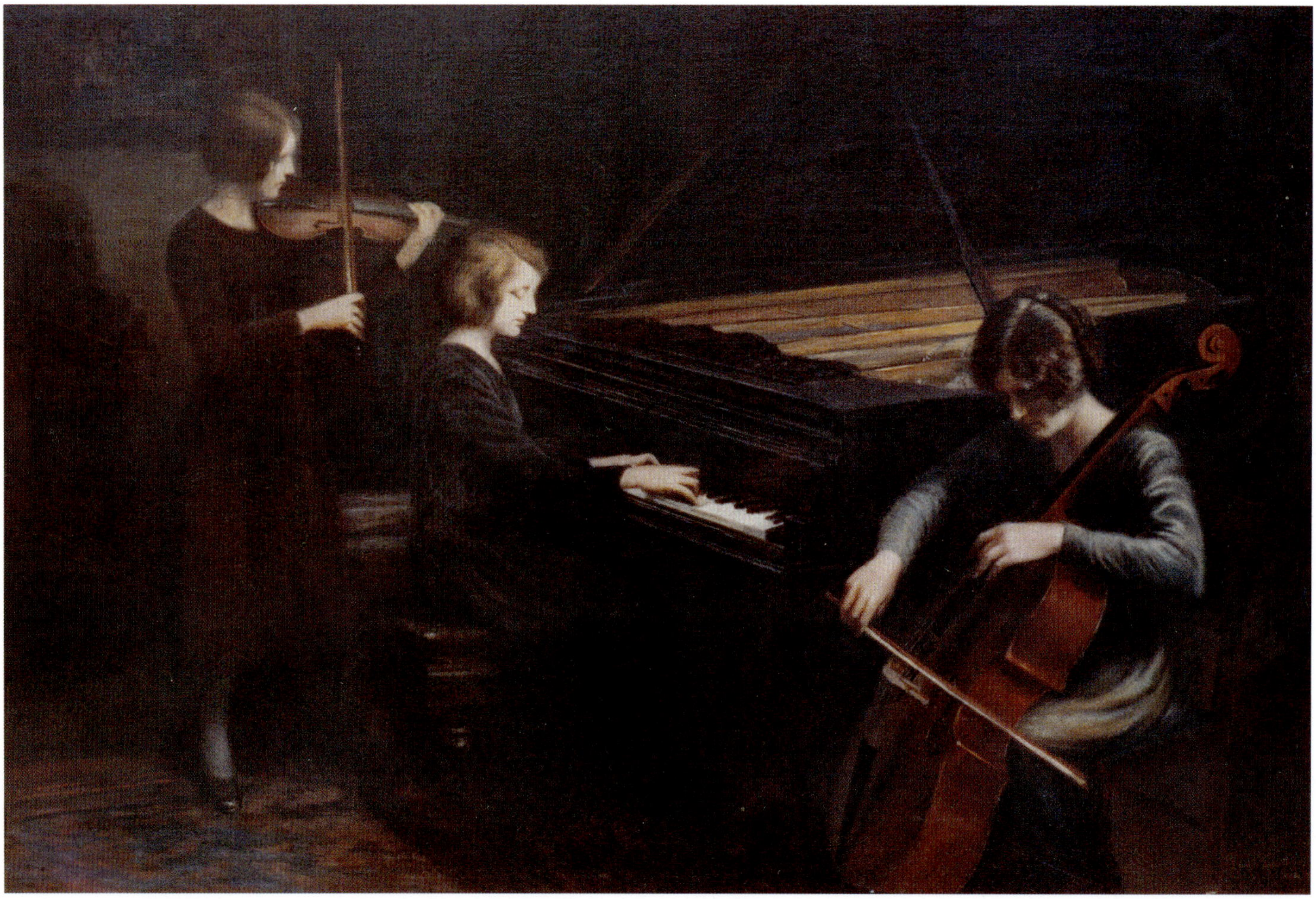

Vital Keuller
Concert, c.1910
Los Angeles Fine Art Gallery, Los Angeles, California

Reimond Kimpe

1885–1970

Reimond Kimpe was born on December 8, 1885, in Gent, Belgium. He began his career as an engineer. From 1918 to 1923 he worked on building projects in Middelburg, a town in the southern province of Zeeland, the Netherlands. Kimpe and Albert Servaes were childhood friends, and it was Servaes who introduced Kimpe to the St. Martens Laethem School. Kimpe, together with Frits Van Den Berghe and Gustave de Smet, wrote the manifesto *Vie et Lumière* in protest to the Luminists.

In 1923 Kimpe became ill and consequently abandoned his work as an engineer. While in recovery he dedicated himself to painting, which became his life's work.

Kimpe's most prolific period was during World War II, between 1939 and 1945. This productivity was a result of the early bombings that devastated the town of Middelburg including his studio and over 200 hundred paintings. After the bombings he became more and more reclusive. This solitude was of great artistic benefit to Kimpe, as he escaped the cruel restrictions that the Nazis imposed on other artists. As a result of the Nazi's regulations, several of Kimpe's friends deserted their artistic practices.

Many of his paintings illustrate his interest in the sea and seafaring paraphernalia. All of his paintings are deeply symbolic. Kimpe's style brings together all of the romance, mystery and technical excellence of the Belgian Expressionists.

Kimpe's paintings were first shown in 1922 at the Den Haag Kunstzaal Toorop and then in 1924 at the Middelburg Kunstmuseum. Kimpe exhibited his works almost every year in Belgium and the Netherlands. He showed his work in 1930 at La Galerie Themis in Belgium. Kimpe lived in Paris for a time beginning in 1929, in1931 and 1932 he exhibited with the Surindépendants. It was in this period he met Picasso and Chagall. In 1942 he exhibited at the Frans Hals Museum in Haarlem and in 1962 in Antwerp at the C.A.W. aan de Meir. He exhibited throughout his career in his hometown of Middelburg, including many exhibitions at the Middelburg Kunstmuseum. He also showed his works at the Middelburg Vleeshal and the Middelburg Studio.

Kimpe's exhibitions in Holland included the Amsterdam Stedelijk Museum and the Amsterdam Rijksmuseum. He also exhibited at the Het Prisonhof in Delft in 1952. In 1951 Winants HeerlenIn published an illustrated monograph on Kimpe and in 1972 Joos Florquin published a finely illustrated book on Kimpe's work. A 1997 major retrospective held at the Singer Museum in Laren traveled to the Zeeuws Museum in Middelburg and an extensive catalogue with many color illustrations complemented the exhibit.

Kimpe's works have been acquired by many museums including the Musée d'Art Moderne in Paris, Museum Boymans in Rotterdam, Museum voor Schone Kunsten in Antwerp, Zeeuws Museum in Middelburg and the Museo dell'Arte Moderno in Caracas. After a career that spanned four decades Kimpe died in 1970.

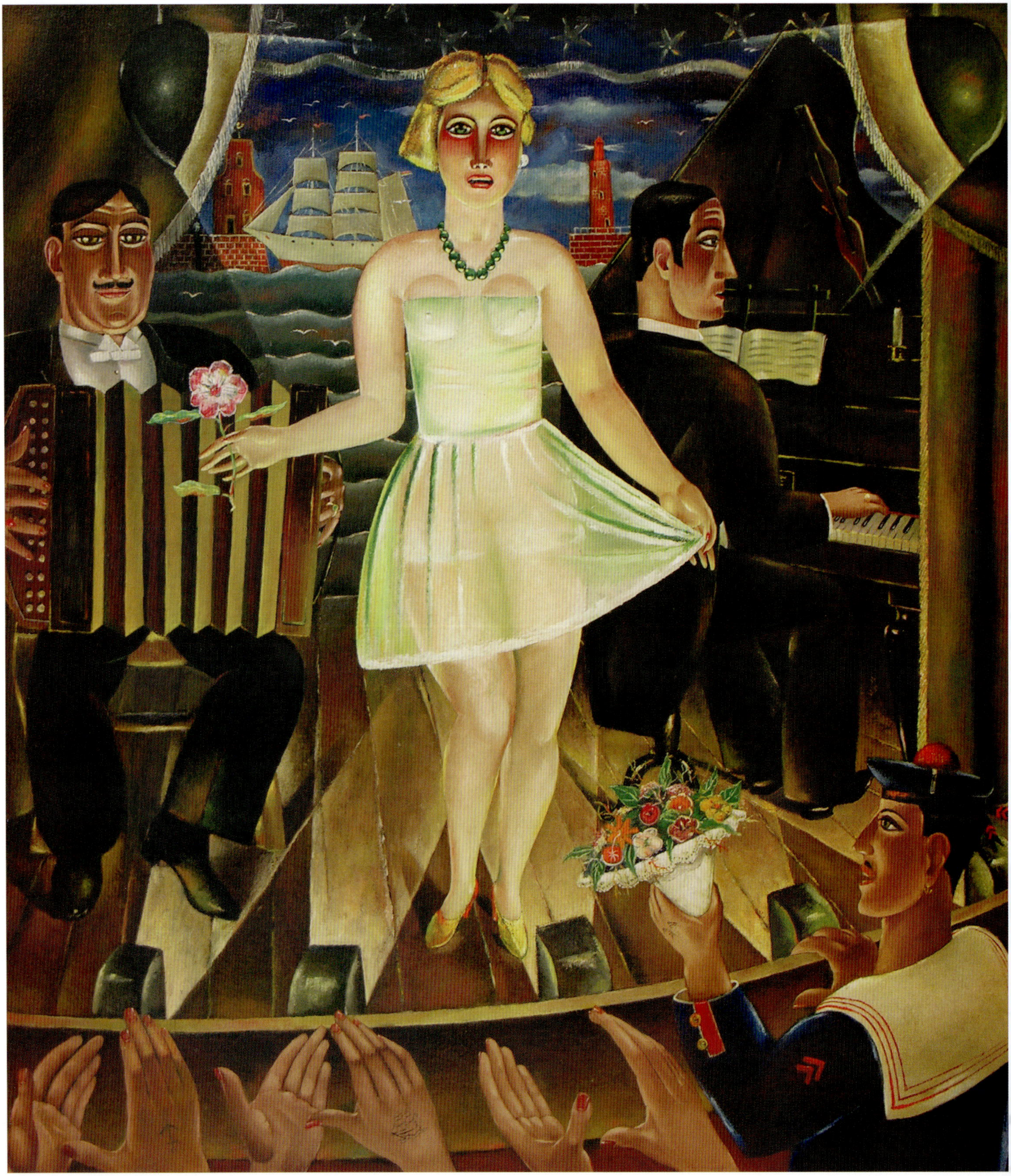

Reimond Kimpe
Cabaret, Dated 1944
Mark and Marina Plon, Henderson, Nevada

Raphaël Kirchner
1876-1917

Raphaël Kirchner was born in 1876 in Vienna, Austria. He attended the Akademie der Bildenden Kunste in Vienna before moving to Paris at the turn of the century. Kirchner exhibited at the Salon des Artistes Français and collaborated with several Parisian journals and magazines including *La Vie Parisienne*. In August of 1914 Kirchner moved to the United States. He died in New York in 1917.

Kirchner was an extremely prolific illustrator, having produced over 1,000 original postcards. The most popular of his work is a series of postcards depicting geishas, which was reprinted four times for a total of 40,000 copies.

The Cabinet des Estampes in Paris has a series of three postcards by Kirchner and his works have been included in several exhibits in Paris, Versailles and London since his death.

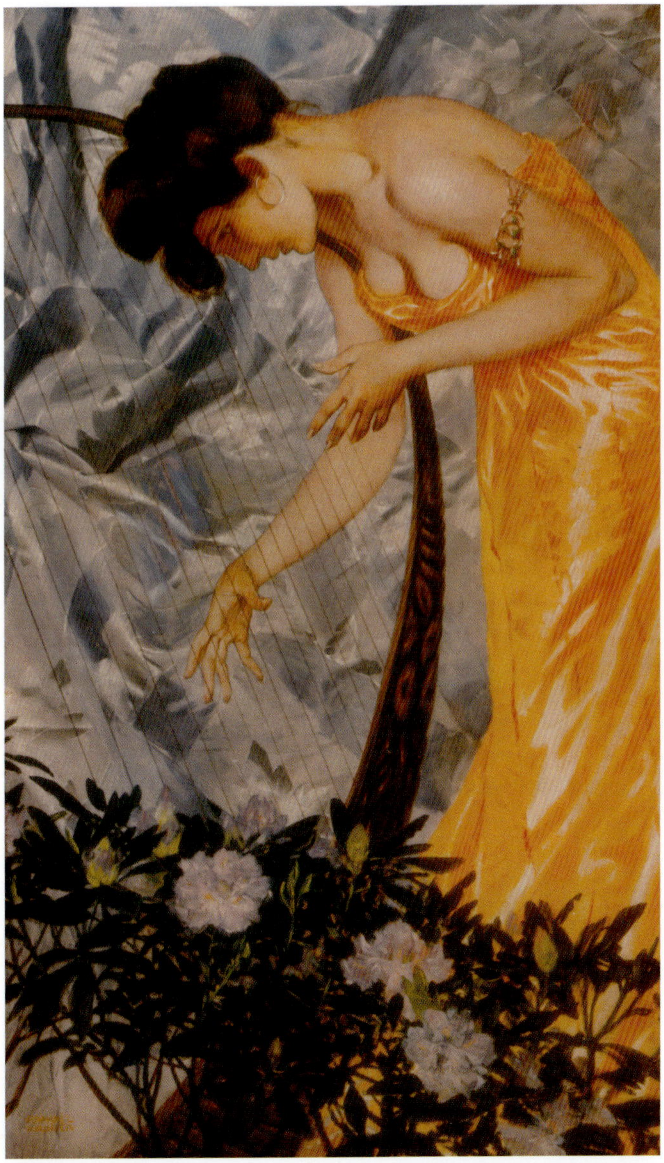

Raphaël Kirchner
Dans le Jardin, c.1900
Private Collection

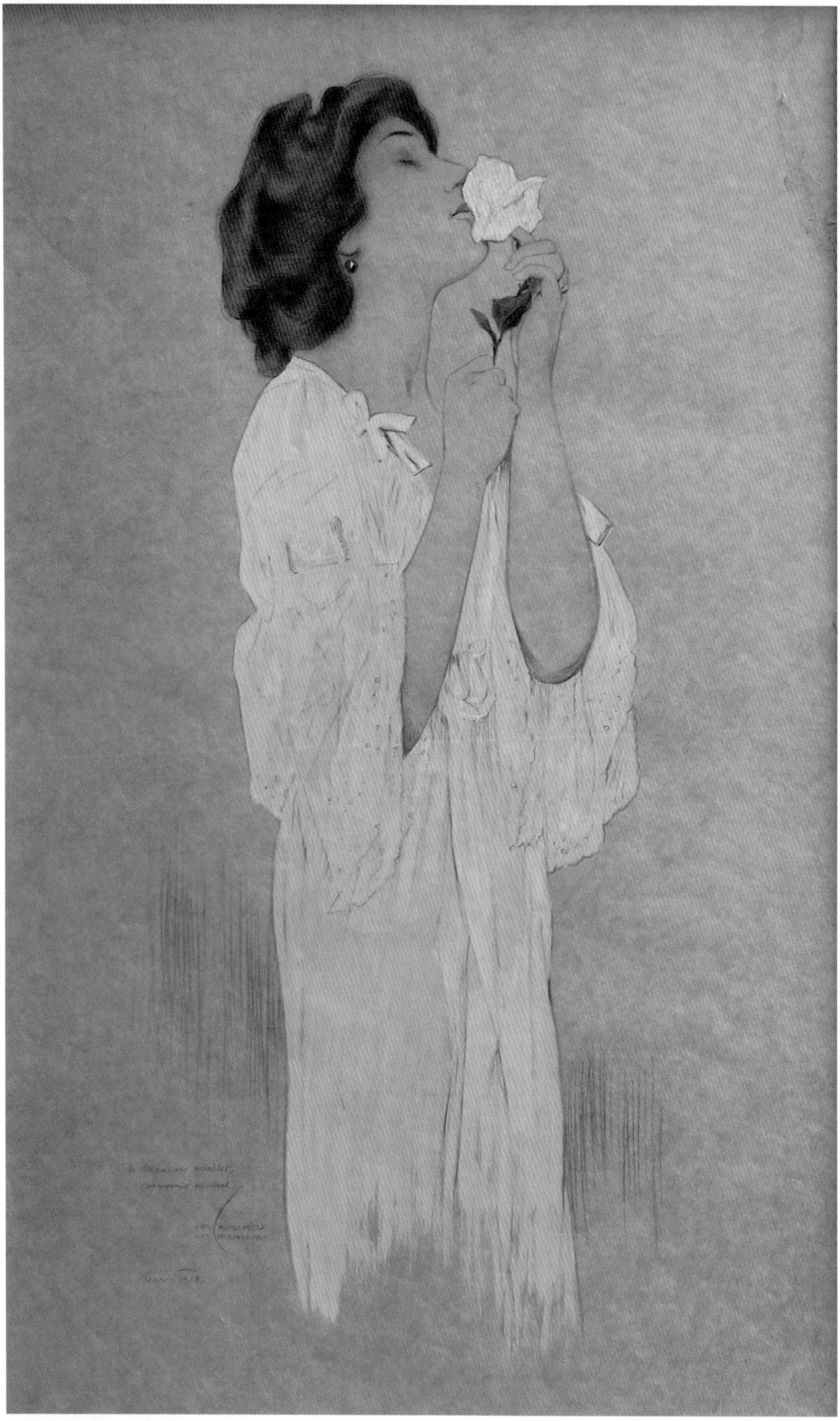

Raphaël Kirchner
Femme au Rose, Dated 1910
Papillon Gallery, Los Angeles, California

Alice Kohn

1902-1990

Alice Kohn was born in 1902 in Lyon, France. She was a painter, actress and set designer. Kohn was a student of Madeleine Plantey and later studied at l'École des Beaux-Arts de Lyon. Around this time she befriended René Dumas, Pierre Pelloux, Antoine Chartres and Henri Vieilly, all of whom exhibited together as *Les Nouveaux*.

Kohn exhibited as early as 1926 at the Salon du Sud Est. She also exhibited at the Galerie Pouillé-Lecoutre and Galerie des Archers.

Les Nouveaux first exhibited together in 1931 at the Saint-Pierre gallery. Critics greatly praised Kohn's works, which were shown at the 1931 Salon d'Autonme de Paris as well as the Salon du Sud Est. The Galerie Saint-Pierre in Lyon organized her first solo exhibition in 1933.

In 1936 Kohn met Pierre Bonnard and Foujita. She became friends with the artist Salvado, who was Picasso's model for his painting *l'Arlequin*. Kohn also modeled for Picasso. In 1941 she exhibited at Galerie Roger in Lyon.

Kohn became a member of the French Resistance during World War II. She changed her name to "Marie-Claude" and worked as the secretary for the Regional State Major of Combat.

Kohn received a solo show at the Galerie des Jacobins in Lyon in 1948.

Having given up theater early in her life to pursue painting, Kohn returned to found her own company called *Tréteaux de Bellecour*. In 1951 she quit painting and opened an antique shop in Lyon.

Kohn was a bold painter and an innovator in the tradition of Expressionism. Her use of vibrant colors mystified critics. Kohn's subjects are always contemplative almost to the point of sadness.

Patrick Pons, a gallery owner in Lyon, recently rediscovered Kohn's paintings. He restored and exhibited a large group of her canvases, the exhibition of which was so impressive that an illustrated article was written in the prestigious French magazine *AZART*. Alain Vollerin's new book, in which he documents the history of *Les Nouveaux,* further documents Kohn's oeuvre, with many illustrations and a bi-lingual French and English text. Kohn died in 1990.

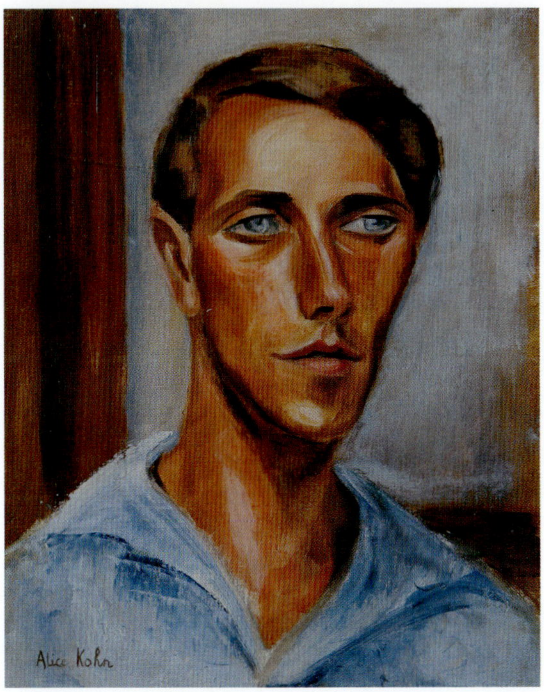

Alice Kohn
Portrait de Jeune Homme, c.1930
Private Collection

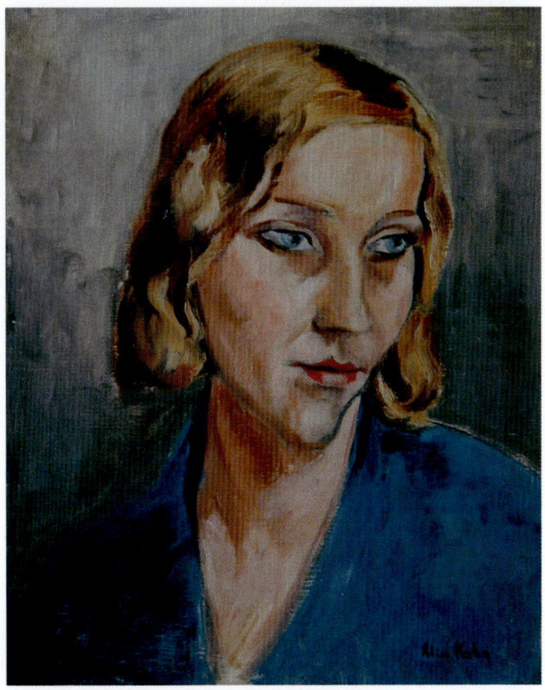

Alice Kohn
Portrait de Femme Blonde, c.1930
Papillon Gallery, Los Angeles, California

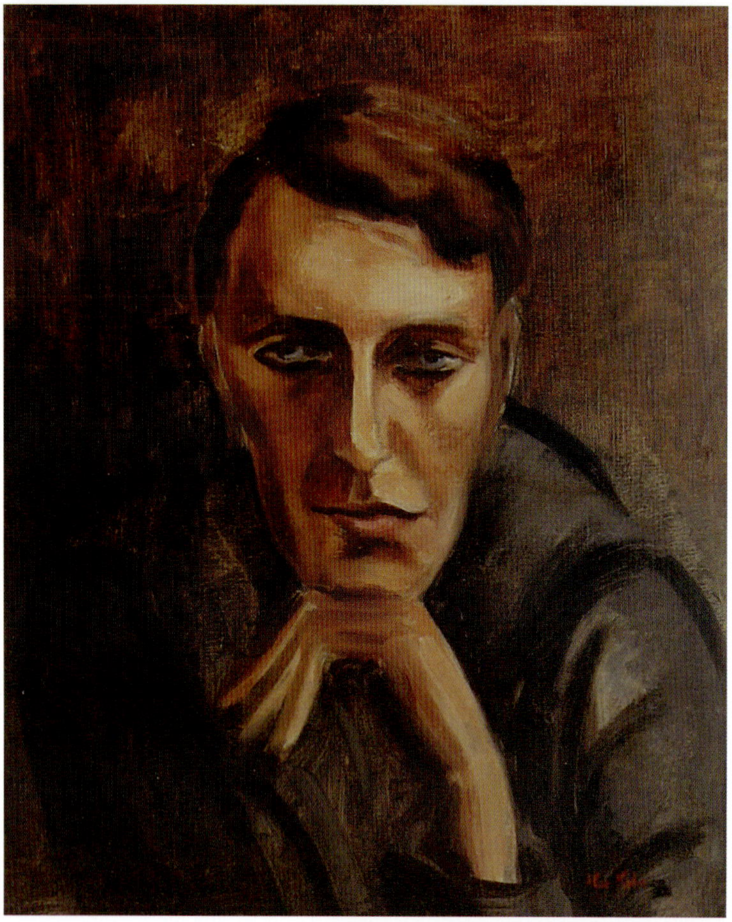

Alice Kohn
Portrait d' Henri De Lubac, c.1930
Jeffrey Winter Fine Arts, Long Beach, California

Alice Kohn
Nu Assis, c.1930
Papillon Gallery, Los Angeles, California

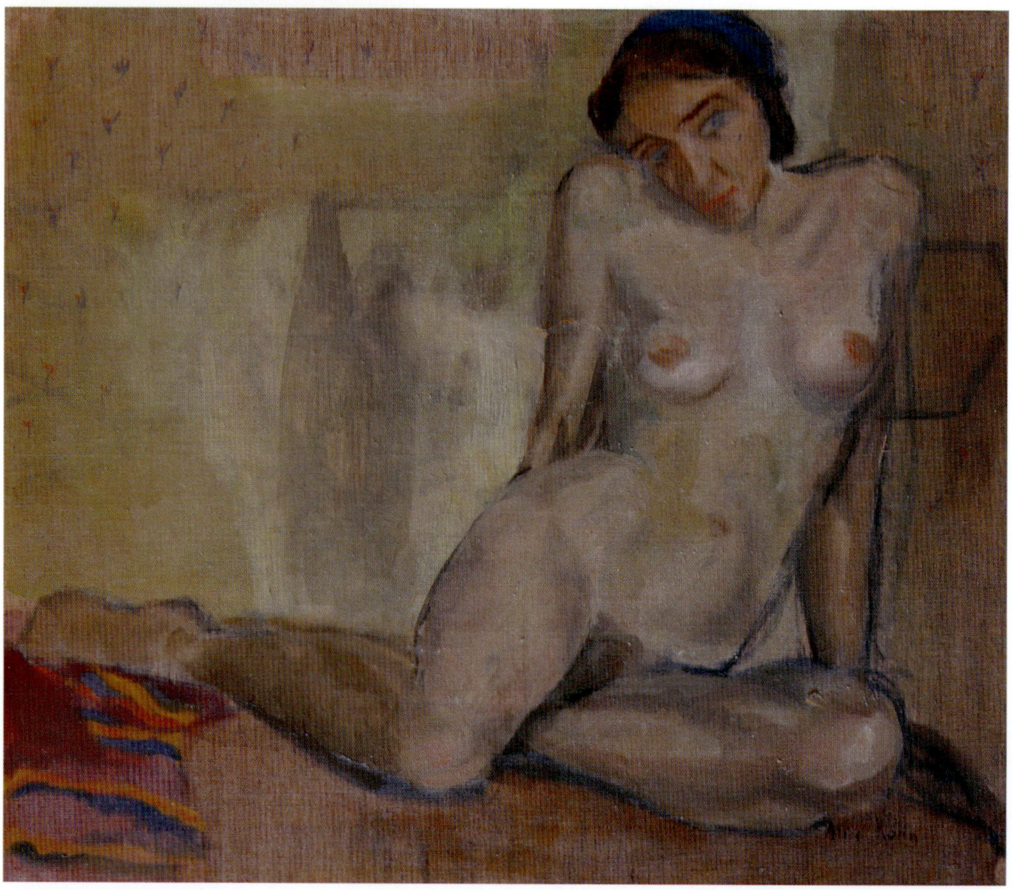

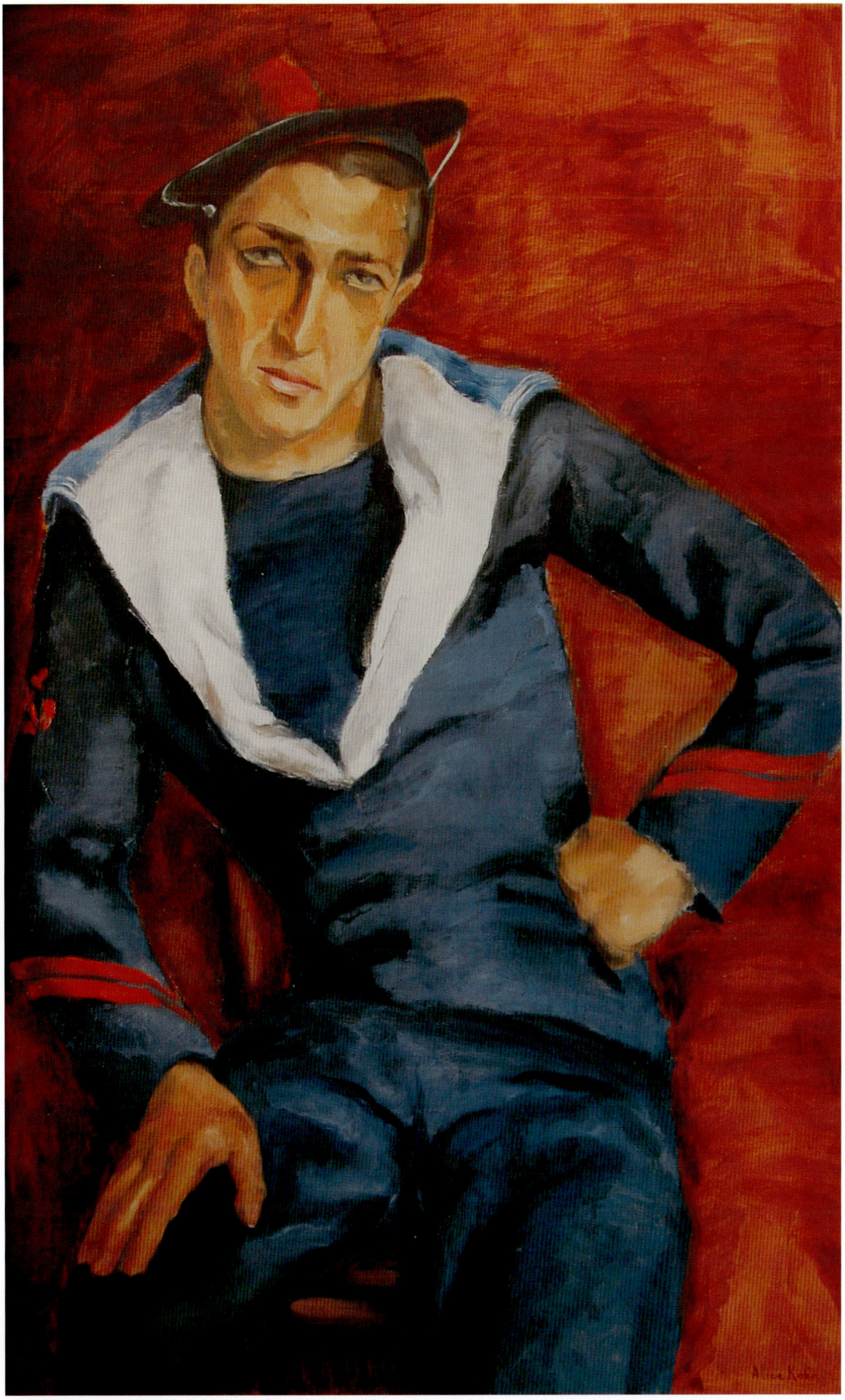

Alice Kohn
Portrait de Marin, c.1930
Papillon Gallery, Los Angeles, California

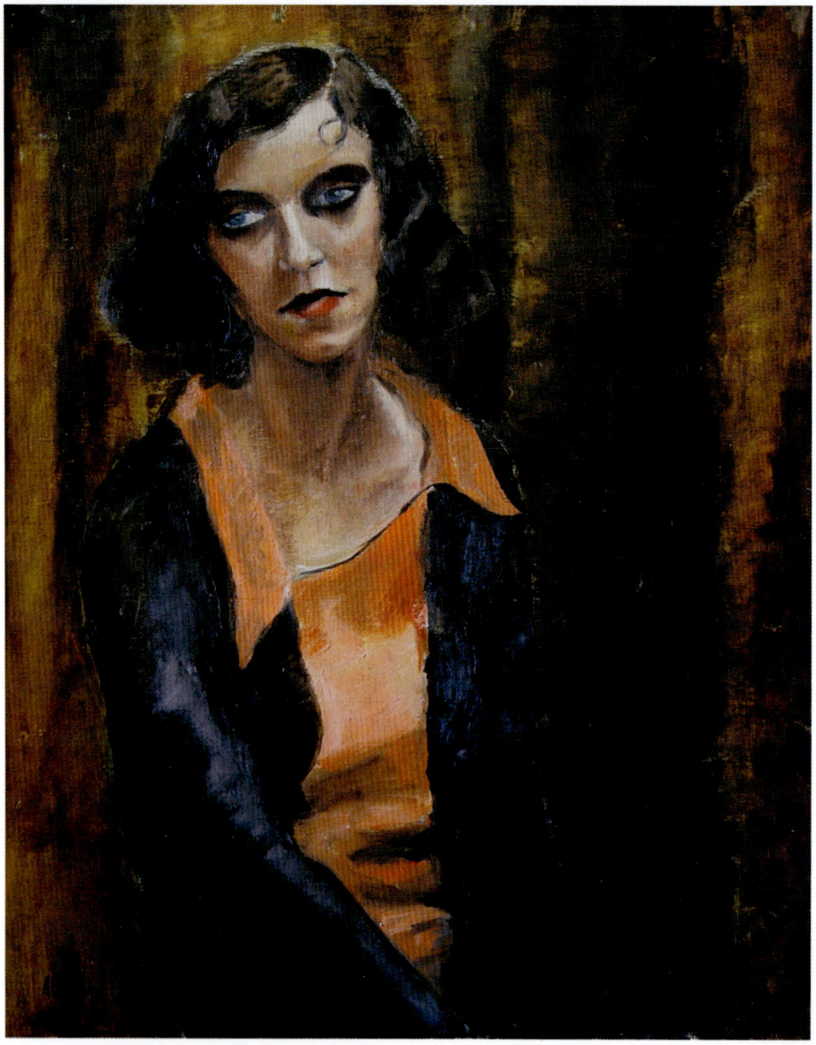

Alice Kohn
Femme Assis, c.1930
Papillon Gallery, Los Angeles, California

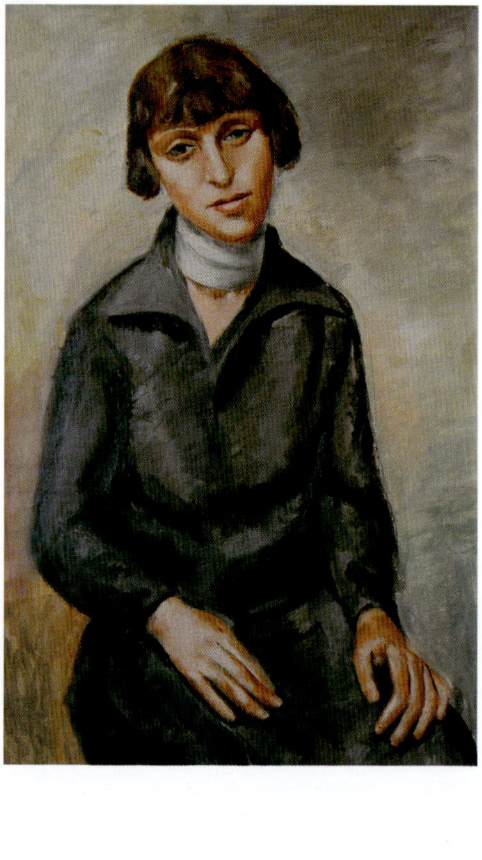

Alice Kohn
Portrait de Femme, c.1930
Papillon Gallery, Los Angeles, California

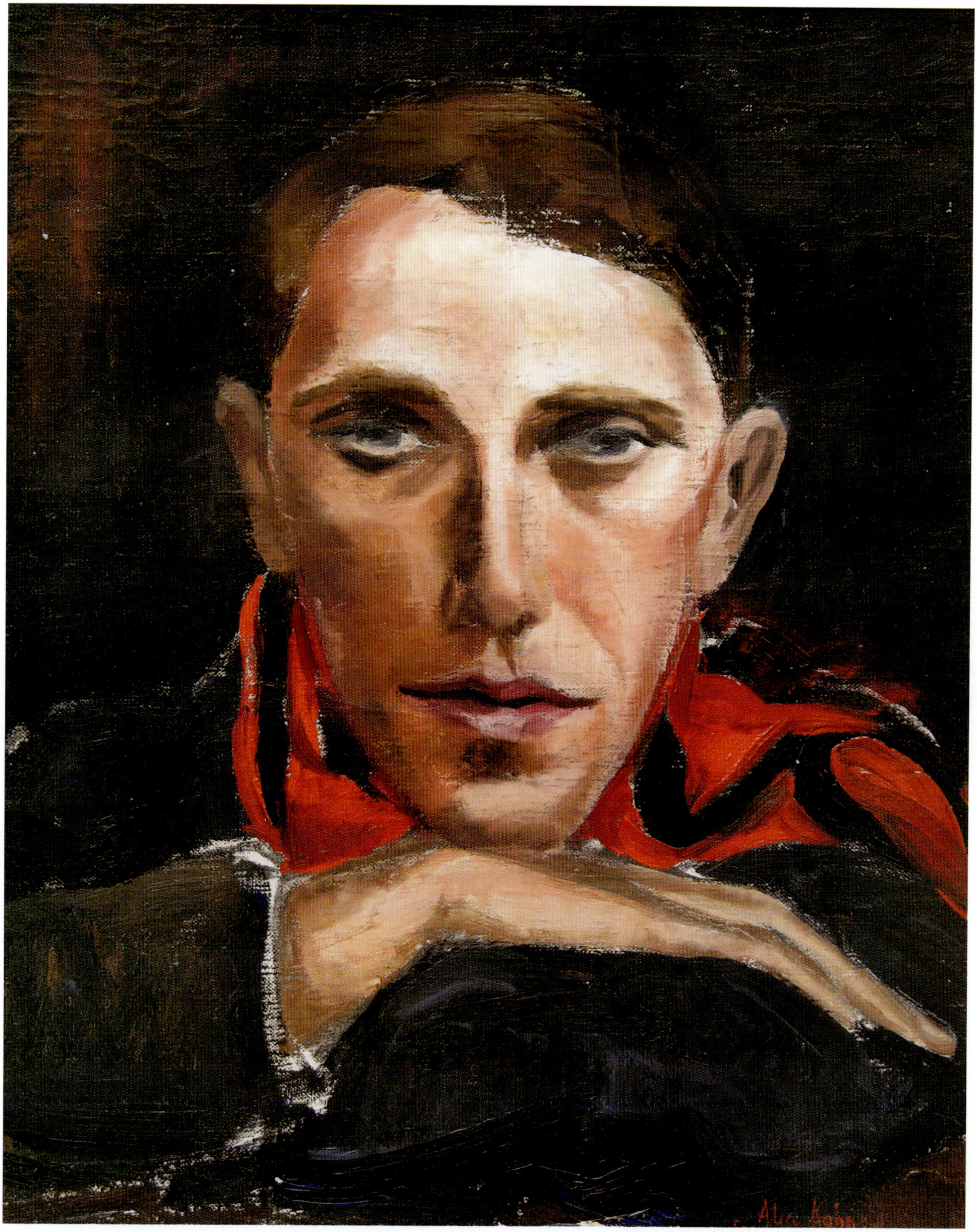

Alice Kohn
Portrait de Jeune Homme, c. 1930
Jeffrey Winter Fine Arts, Long Beach, California

Richard Kollorsz

1900-1983

Richard Kollorsz was born near Breslau, Germany in 1900. Both his father and brother Franz were artists. Kollorsz studied at the Academy of Art in Breslau. After World War I he attended the Kunstakademie in Dresden for seven years. The academies of this period taught traditional techniques though the students also learned about New Realism in German painting. Kollorsz won a scholarship to study in Rome and after his study abroad returned to Dresden.

The turning point in Kollorsz's education came when he studied with renowned 20th century painter Otto Dix who was one of the most important proponents of the new direction in German Realism. He responded favorably to Kollorsz's work and the artist later directed Dix's master painting class.

Kollorsz traveled to the United States in 1929 where he began a long career as an art director in Hollywood movies. Kollorsz was the protégé of director Josef Von Sternberg, a successful film director who worked with Marlene Dietrich in many films during the 1920s and 1930s. Kollorsz became Von Sternberg's principal set director.

Von Sternberg was an avid art collector and Kollorsz no doubt had significant input on his collecting. Among Von Sternberg's collection were several works by Kollorsz.

Kollorsz's career in films precluded him from pursuing a thriving art career in Los Angeles. In 1932 he worked with esteemed Mexican muralist Alfonse Siquerios on a mural on Olivera Street. Kollorsz and his friends in the film industry helped Siquerios gain attention in the Los Angeles art community. Also, in 1932 Kollorsz loaned his painting *Street Musicians* to an exhibition at the Palace of the Legion of Honor in San Francisco. In the early 1930s Von Sternberg sponsored an exhibition of Kollorsz's work at the Plaza Art Center on Olivera Street. This exhibition drew attention to the work of Kollorsz and Peter Ballbusch.

Kollorsz employed a painting technique not often used by American painters. He built his surfaces through the time consuming process of layering oil glaze over tempera. This method of painting developed from the tradition of Holbein and Dürer. The technique lends itself to the portrayal of extraordinary realism with rich colors and exquisite detail.

Though Kollorsz did not exhibit, he continued to paint. The passionate expression of realist subject matter in Kollorsz's early works suggests the influence of Dix. His early style of German Realism gave way to a more postimpressionist method. His subjects remained figurative as well and analytical of the human condition but were lighter and more cheerful. He also painted many watercolors of beaches, workers, cityscapes and nudes.

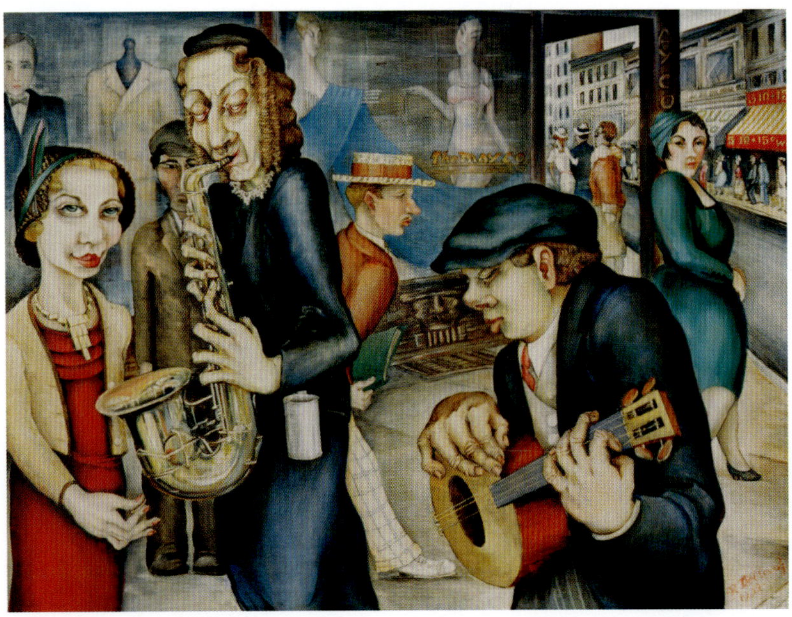

Richard Kollorsz
Street Musicians, Dated 1932
Private Collection

Peter Krasnow

1886–1979

Peter Krasnow was born on August 20, 1886, in a small village in the Ukraine. He was the son of an interior decorator who taught him to make his own paint and mix colors.

Krasnow moved to the United States in 1908 and studied at the Art Institute of Chicago. In 1919 he moved to New York and then in 1922 he and his wife moved to California. He worked with an independent group of California modernists including Stanton Macdonald Wright. The artist lived continually in Los Angeles, except from 1934 to 1939 when his resided in the South of France. While in France, he worked in a studio in the village of Cazillac, in the Dordogne valley and exhibited in Paris.

Krasnow was both a sculptor and a painter. His early work was figurative and always modernist, with some influences from the Impressionists and German Realists. Like many of the artists of his generation, Krasnow's work after 1940 became increasingly more abstract. As a sculptor he carved fantastic, abstract expressionist images directly into the wood. Krasnow was creative and prolific for many decades; his works are unique and immediately recognizable.

Krasnow was a member of the California Art Club. He exhibited at the Los Angeles County Museum of Art in 1922 and 1927, Oakland Art Gallery in 1928, Scripps College in 1929 and 1964, and Stendahl Art galleries in 1930 and 1940. Additionally, he showed work at Galerie Pierre in Paris in 1934, UCLA in 1935 and 1940, and the San Diego Fine Art Gallery in 1939. His later exhibitions include the Pasadena Art Institute in 1954, the L.A. Municipal Art Gallery in 1975, and the San Francisco Museum of Art in 1976. Moreover, Krasnow participated in many group exhibitions.

Krasnow's work is represented in the Oakland Museum, Pasadena Art Museum, Student Union at the University of Southern California, and San Francisco Museum of Art. He also carved the altar at the Temple Emmanuel in San Francisco. Krasnow died in Los Angeles on October 30, 1979.

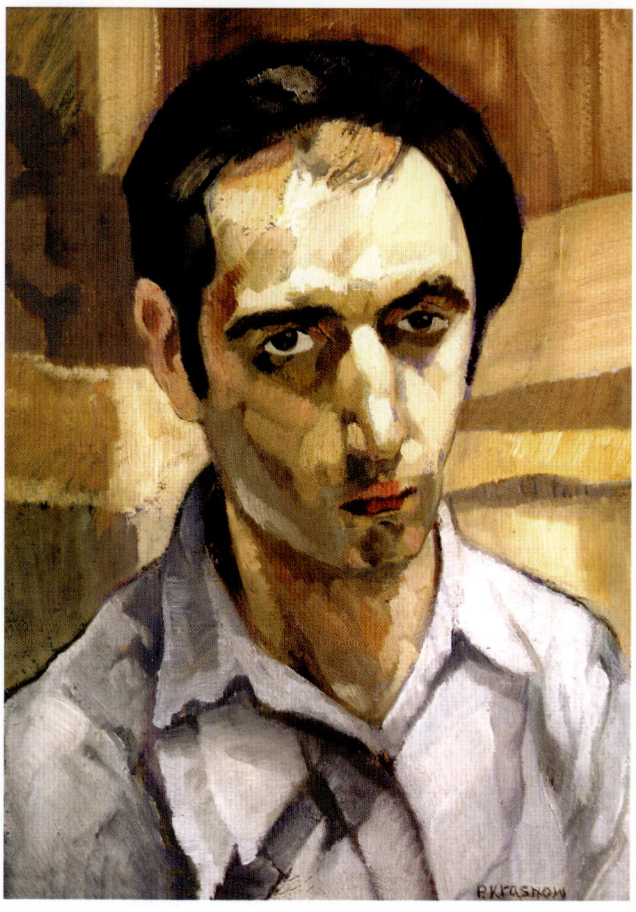

Peter Krasnow
Self-Portrait, c.1930
Photo courtesy of Tobey C. Moss Gallery, Los Angeles, California

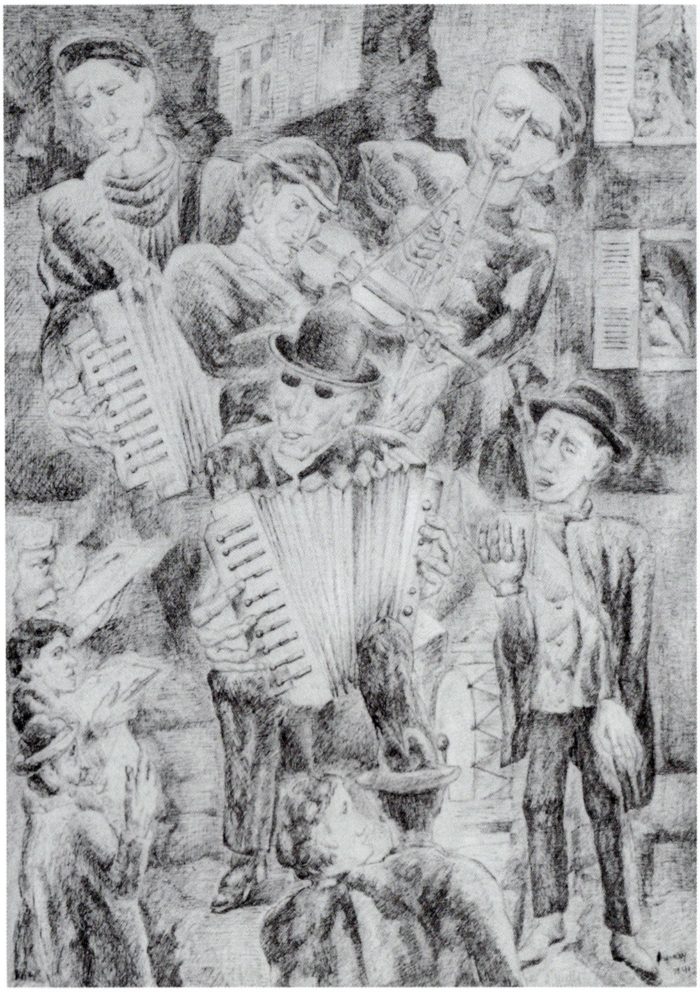

Peter Krasnow
Street Musicians, Dated 1941
Julia Evershade and Mark Smith, Los Angeles, California

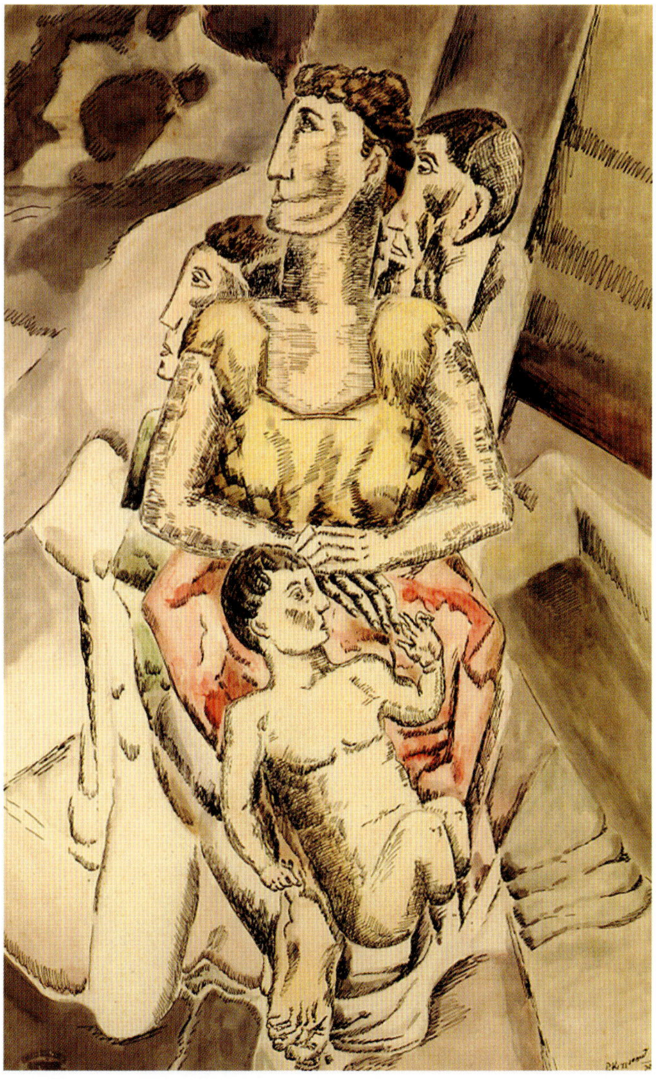

Peter Krasnow
The Family, Dated 1930
Photo courtesy of Spencer Jon Helfen Fine Arts, Beverly Hills, California

Luc Lafnet

1899-1939

Luc Lafnet was born in Liege, Belgium in 1899. He studied at l'Académie des Beaux-Arts in Liege under A. de Witte, F. Marchal, Ubaghs and E. Berchmans. In 1917, Lafnet formed *Les Hiboux* and was active in *Le Cénacle*, *L'Aspic* and *La Caque*. He moved to Paris in 1923 where he worked under several pseudonyms until his death in 1939.

Lafnet was known for his paintings, watercolors, illustrations, printmaking and poster designs, which often came under the influence of Oriental mythology and legends of the Middle Age. He received commissions by the Chapelle Saint-Pierre in Billancourt, l'Eglise Saint-Charles de Montreuil, l'Église de Nanterre and la Chapelle des Péres Assomptionnistes.

Illustrated works include *Une Courtisane Romantique* and *Marie Duplessis* by J. Gros in 1929, *Le Pied de Fanchette* by Restif de la Bretonne in 1932. In 1930 Lafnet's illustrations were published in an essay by Michel Seuphor in the publication *Cercle et Carré*. The artist died in 1939, and in 1956 a retrospective was held in Liege.

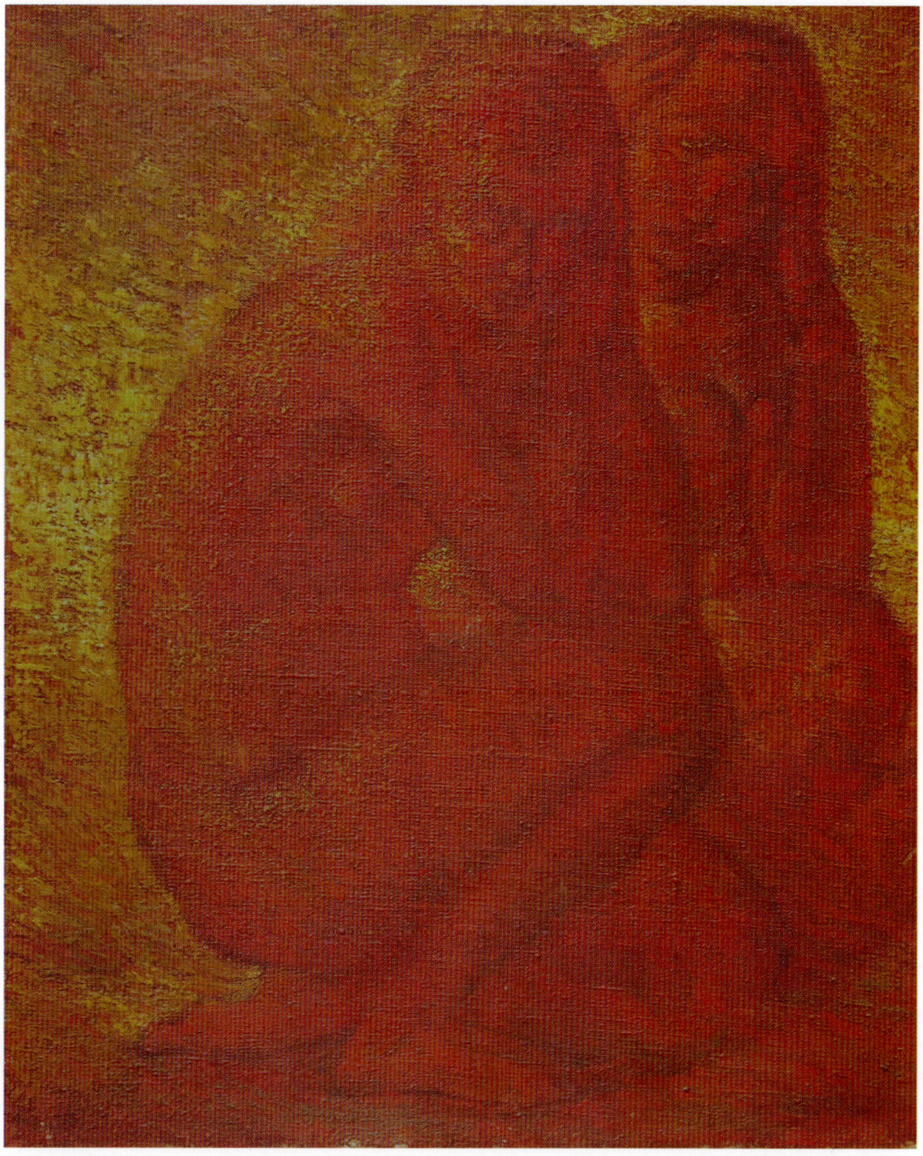

Luc Lafnet
La Toilette, c.1922
Jeffrey Winter Fine Arts, Long Beach, California

Jean Francis Laglenne

1899-1962

Jean Francis Laglenne was born on June 23, 1899 in Paris. He entered l'École des Arts Decoratifs in 1916, but left almost immediately to work away from the influences of Montmartre artists. Laglenne resumed his studies in 1919.

Beginning in 1920, Laglenne exhibited in Paris at the Salon des Indépendants, Salon d'Automne and the Salon des Tuileries. In 1924 he participated in the first Exposition des Néo-Humanistes.

Laglenne had a unique style; he combined elements of Cubism, Postimpressionism and Expressionism. His canvases were bold and figurative, with a significant use of abstraction.

Many important collectors, including Paul Rosenberg and Jacqueline Marval, acquired Laglenne's works. He was included in Maurice Raynal's book *Modern French Painters,* published in 1935. Laglenne is represented in the Musée d'Art Moderne in Paris. He died in 1962.

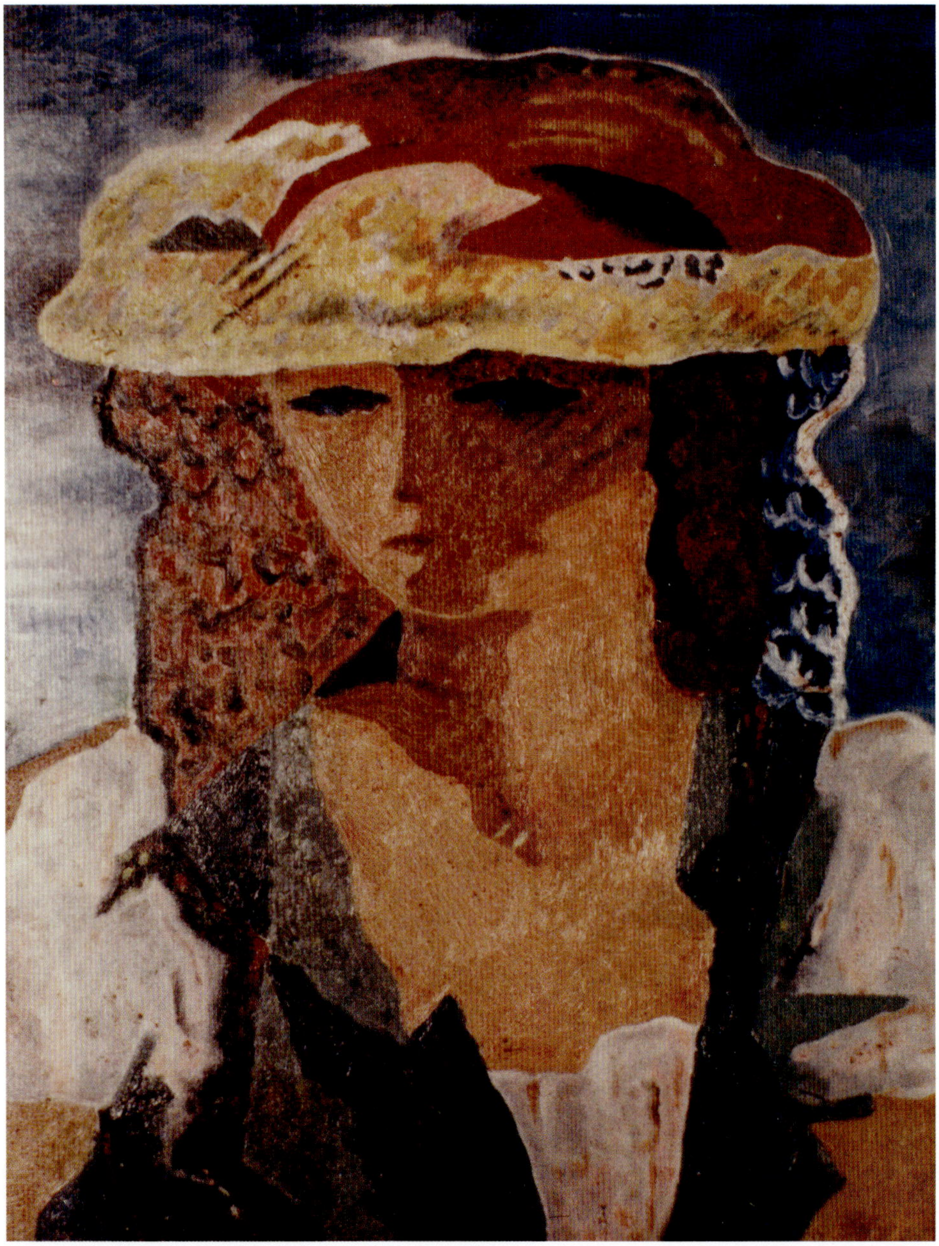

Jean Francis Laglenne
Femme au Chapeau, c.1930
Private Collection

Anne-Marie Lagrange

20th century

Ann-Marie Lagrange was born in Montceau-les-Mines and was a student of de Decote. She began exhibiting paintings at the Salon in 1928.

Lagrange composed her nudes at the waters edge in the style of her contemporaries like Charles Kvapil. She filled her large canvases with life and activity that could only be experienced in those years at the French countryside. The dates of her birth and death are unknown.

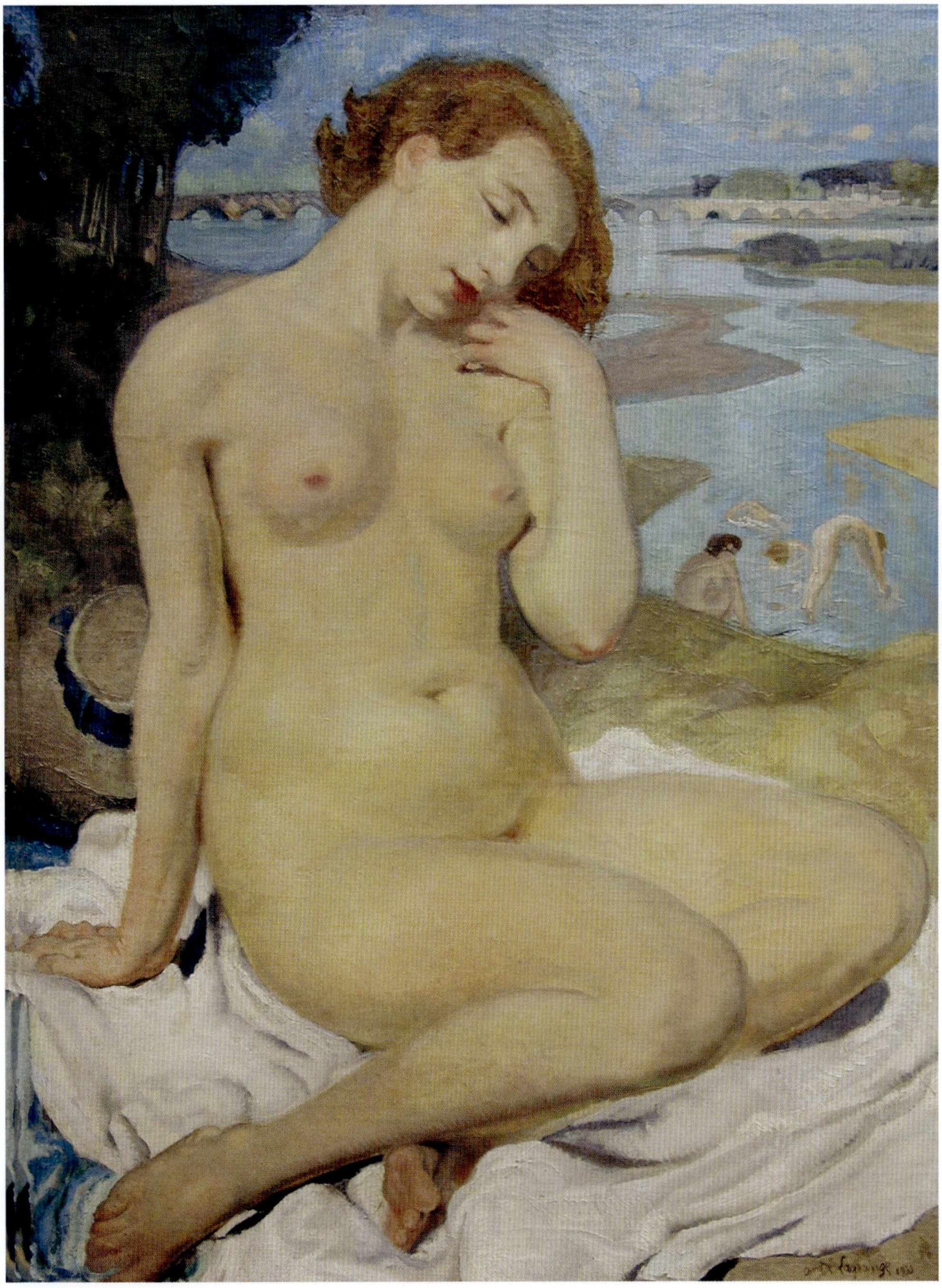

Anne-Marie Lagrange
La Femme du Lac, Dated 1933
Kathleen Avery Fine Art, Palo Alto, California

Adolphe La Lyre
1848-1935

Adolphe La Lyre was born in Rouvres, France and studied at l'École des Beaux-Arts. He exhibited at the Salon de Paris in 1876 and was a member of the Société des Artistes Français. He received two Médailles de Deuxième Classe in 1900 and two medals at the Expositions Universelles in 1889 and 1900.

He is best known for his religious and mythological subjects. He often painted large works in a classical style but with themes popular with modern Parisians. He often painted seaside scenes with nymphs and sirens frolicking in the surf.

La Lyre's works have been collected by museums in Chartres and Montbaun. He died in 1935.

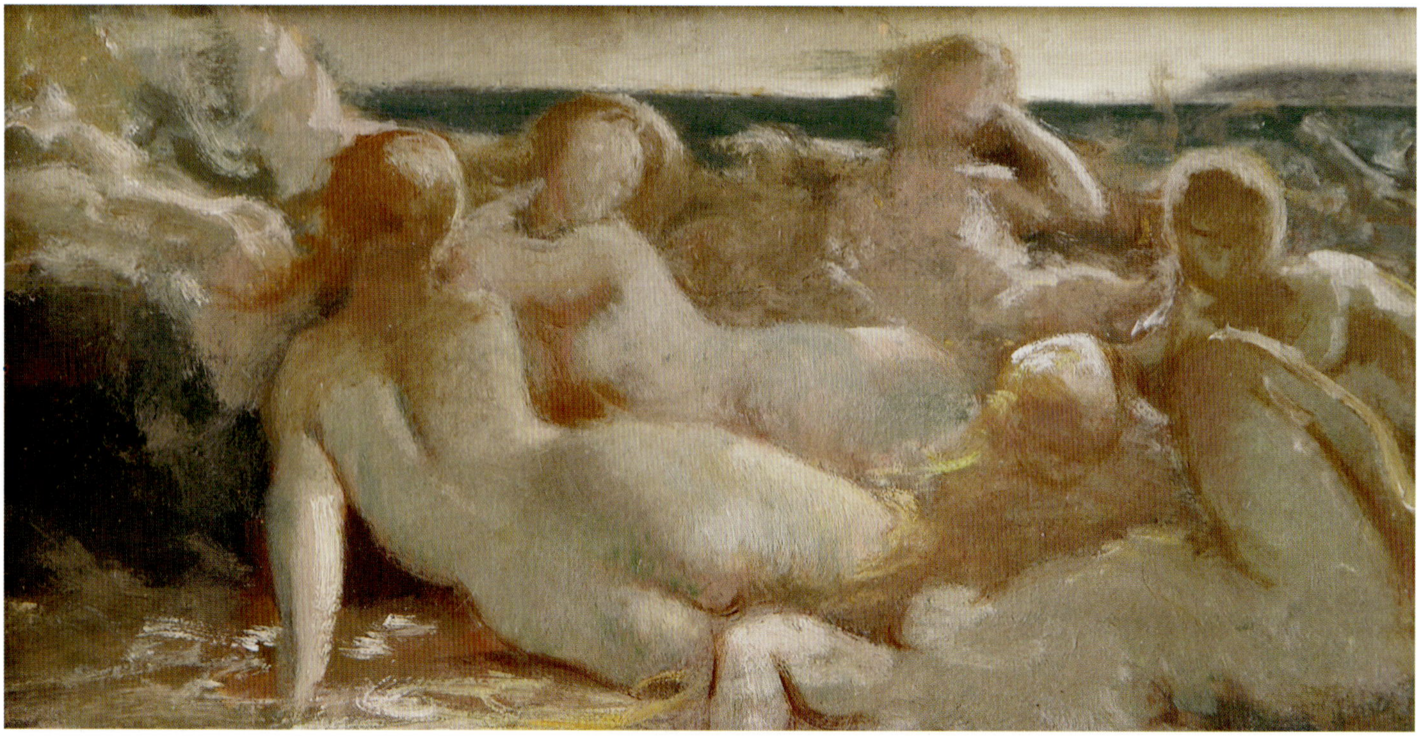

Adolphe La Lyre
Sirèns, c.1910
Jeffrey Winter Fine Arts, Long Beach, California

Bernard Lamotte

1903–1983

Bernard Lamotte was born and educated in Paris where he beautifully captured modern-day Parisian city life and street scenes. Lamotte had been bedridden for a period as a child and spent his time studying the color and textures of the cityscape below his window, which would later greatly influence his artistic style and passion.

Lamotte received his formal training at l'École des Beaux-Arts under Fernand Corman and Lucien Simon. Lamotte's travels took him to New York City in 1932, where he settle in 1935 and became a naturalized U.S. citizen in 1951. His atelier was located above the restaurant *La Grenouille* where fellow expatriate French artists and famed New York personalities congregated including Greta Garbo, Charlie Chaplin and Marlene Dietrich. The studio, which he and his wife shared, became a bohemian haven and was known as *Le Bocal* (The Fishbowl).

While in New York, between travels to Tahiti and Paris, Lamotte received several mural commissions and exhibitions including a solo show at the Wildenstein Gallery within one year of his arrival. Other exhibits included the Art Institute of Chicago in 1941, the Carstairs Gallery in New York City annually from 1941 through the 1950s and a solo show at the Palm Beach Gallery in 1965. Like Pierre Sicard and Grigory Gluckmann, Lamotte was represented by the Dalzell-Hatfield Gallery in Los Angeles and received an exhibit there in 1975.

Lamotte also created a mural for the swimming pool room of the White House in 1961, which now is preserved in the John F. Kennedy Library and Museum in Boston. Other commissions include businesses, restaurants, corporations and private collectors. Lamotte was an illustrator and theatre designer as well and created the illustrations for *Flight to Arras* by Antoine de Saint-Expuréry. In 1945 an illustrated book, *Bernard Lamotte, Oil Painting and Brush Drawing,* was written by Louis Gauthier. In 1948 his work was reviewed in *Time* magazine.

Lamotte's style is reminiscent of other artists of the School of Paris; modern with a flare for the romantic. His technique gives his oil paintings the look and texture of a watercolor.

Museum collections of Lamotte's work include the Tokyo Museum, Luxembourg Museum, Musée d'Art Moderne in Paris, and the French Embassy in Finland. Private collections include Joseph P. Kennedy and Alfred Barnes among several others. Bernard Lamotte died in 1983 and The Vose Gallery of Boston has since hosted several exhibitions from his estate. Lamotte died in 1983.

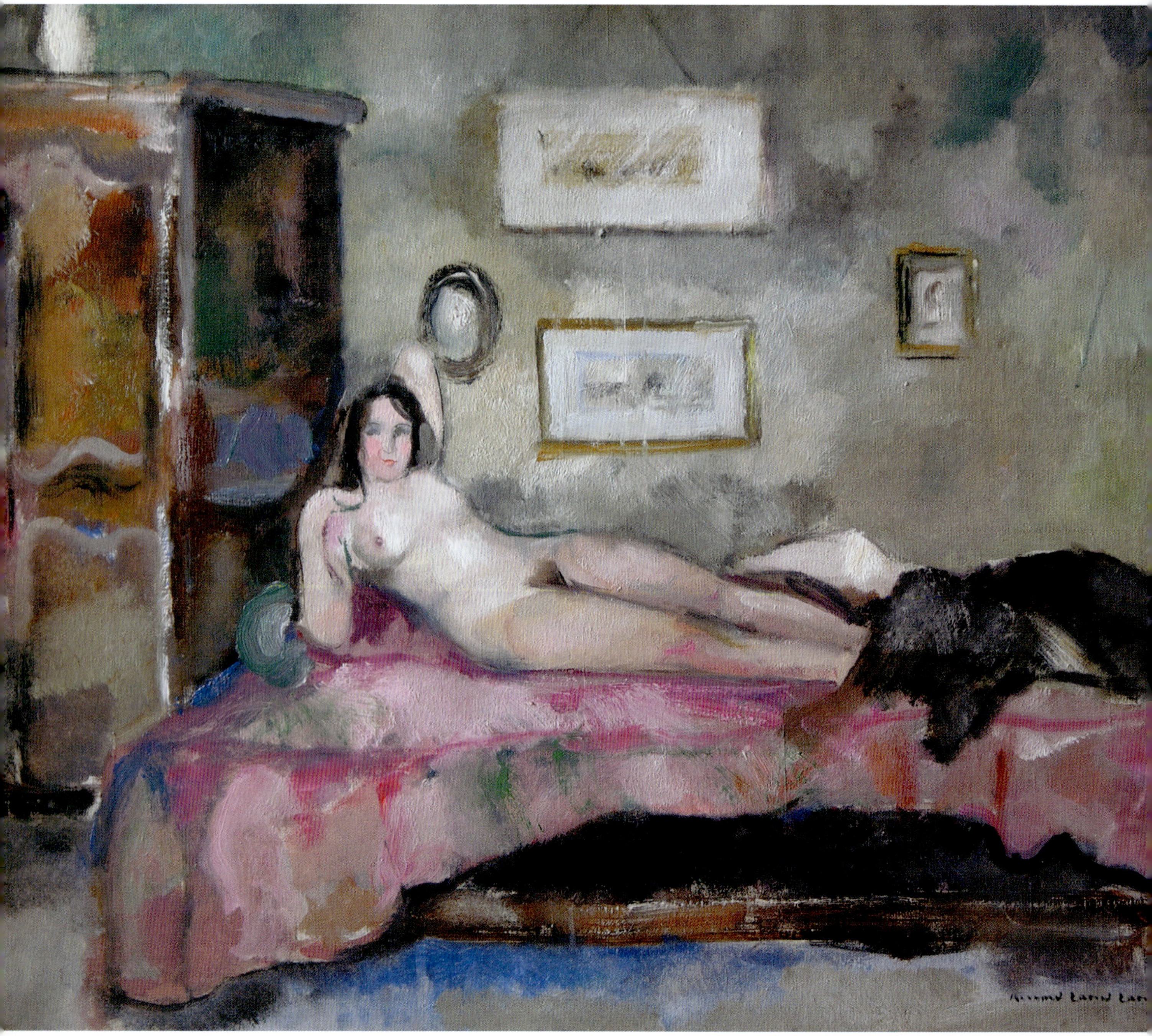

Bernard Lamotte
Chambre á Coucher, c.1930
Papillon Gallery, Los Angeles, California

William Julien Émile Édouard Laparra
1873-1920

William Julien Émile Édouard Laparra was born November 25, 1873 in Bordeaux. He began his studies at l'École de Dessin de Bordeaux before moving to Paris where he enrolled at l'Académie Julian. At the academy Laparra was a student of Jules Lefebrve, William Bouguereau and Tony Robert-Fleury. He lived for three years at the Villa Medicis in Florence before returning to Paris.

Laparra exhibited in Paris at the Salon des Artistes Français where he became a member in 1905. He received the Prix de Rome and Médaille de Troisième Classe in 1898 and the Médaille de Deuxième Classe in 1903. Additional exhibitions include the Galerie Georges Petit in 1903 and a private show in Bordeaux in 1908. He received several public and private commissions, including notable mural decorations created for the 18th century Chateau de la Plaze in Auvergne.

Laparra painted many charming women and girls in elaborate interiors. His style was very popular during La Belle Époque and typically French. He also painted some symbolist works.

Laparra died at the age of 47 in 1920. In 1997 the Musée des Beaux-Arts de Bordeaux hosted a retrospective of the artist's work. The Basilica of Saint-Seurin in Bordeaux and the Musées de Beaux-Arts de Bordeaux, Chateau-Thierry, Nantes and Musée d'Orsay in Paris have also collected Laparra's work.

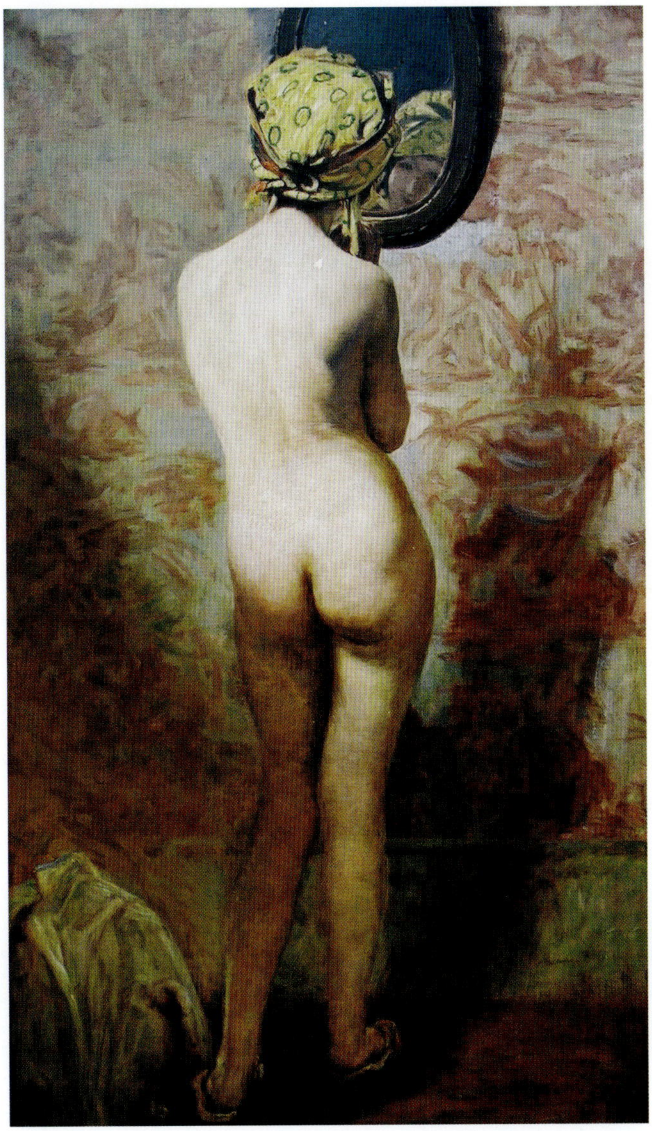

William Julien Émile Édouard Laparra
Dame avec Turbin Jaune, c.1900
Private Collection, Paris

Edmond Édouard Lapeyre

1880-1960

Edmond Édouard Lapeyre was born in Reims. He studied with Cormon, Boutigny and Larteau and was a member of the Salons des Artistes Français where he exhibited beginning in 1906.

Lapeyre enjoyed considerable success in the Paris Salons. His subjects were provocative in the tradition of French aesthetics, though the lush interiors that framed his coquettes may have shocked gallery visitors in London and New York in the early 1900s. Lapeyre died in Paris in 1960.

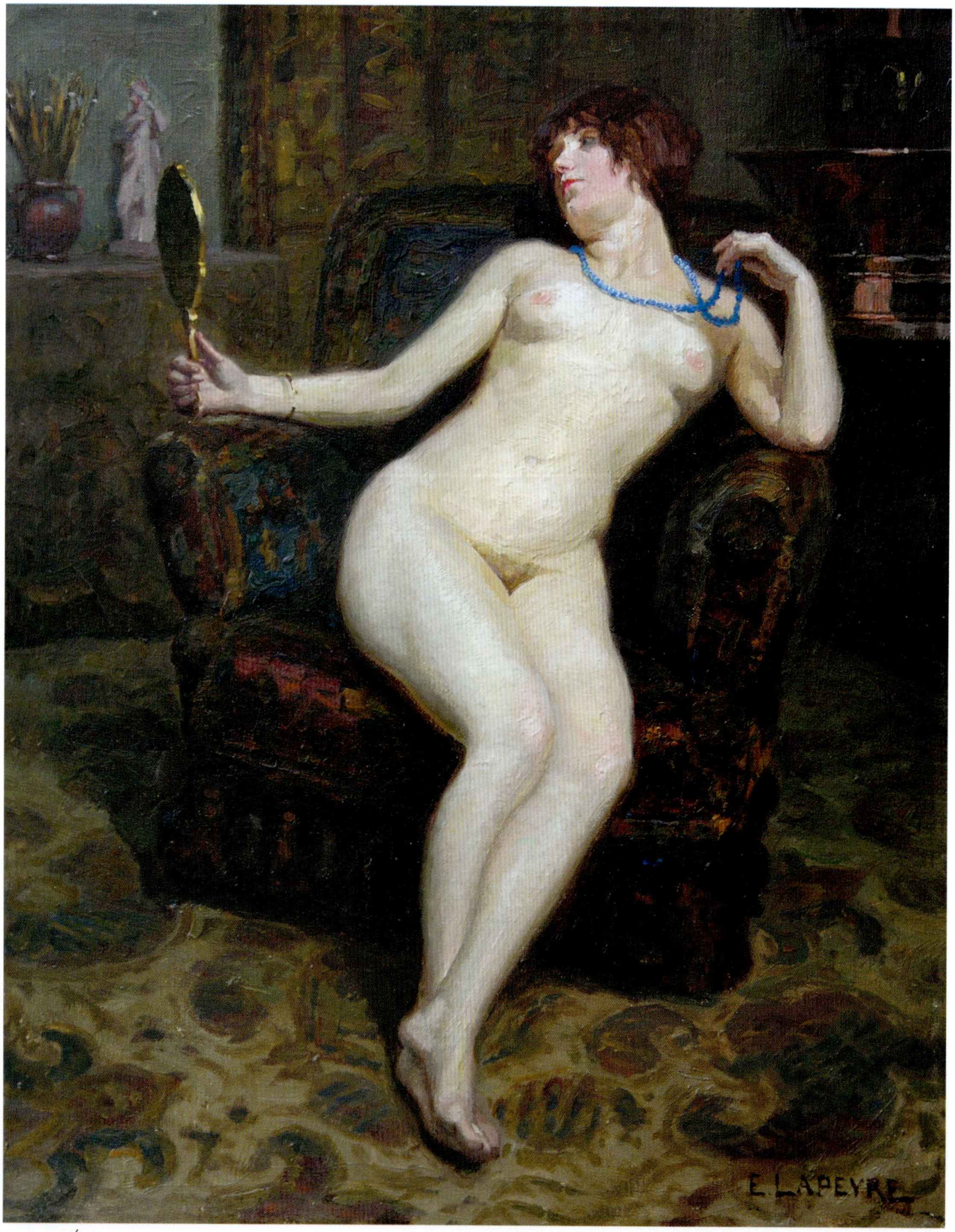

Edmond Édouard Lapeyre
Admiration, c.1900
Papillon Gallery, Los Angeles, California

Jean Laudy

1877-1956

Jean Laudy was born in the Netherlands in 1877; in 1893 he moved to Belgium. He is considered a 20th century Belgium painter noted for his nudes, portraits and floral still lifes. He studied at the Brussels Academy under the famed Isidore Verheyden from 1894 to 1895, and at the Antwerp Academy where he met his friend and fellow artist Alfred Bastien. Laudy became a member of two prominent Belgian artists' societies, *L'Effort* and *La Patte de Dindon* and the Belgian Royal Academy as well in 1954.

Laudy was a prolific artist. He employed an expressionistic method popular with the Belgian artists of his generation. Laudy died in 1956.

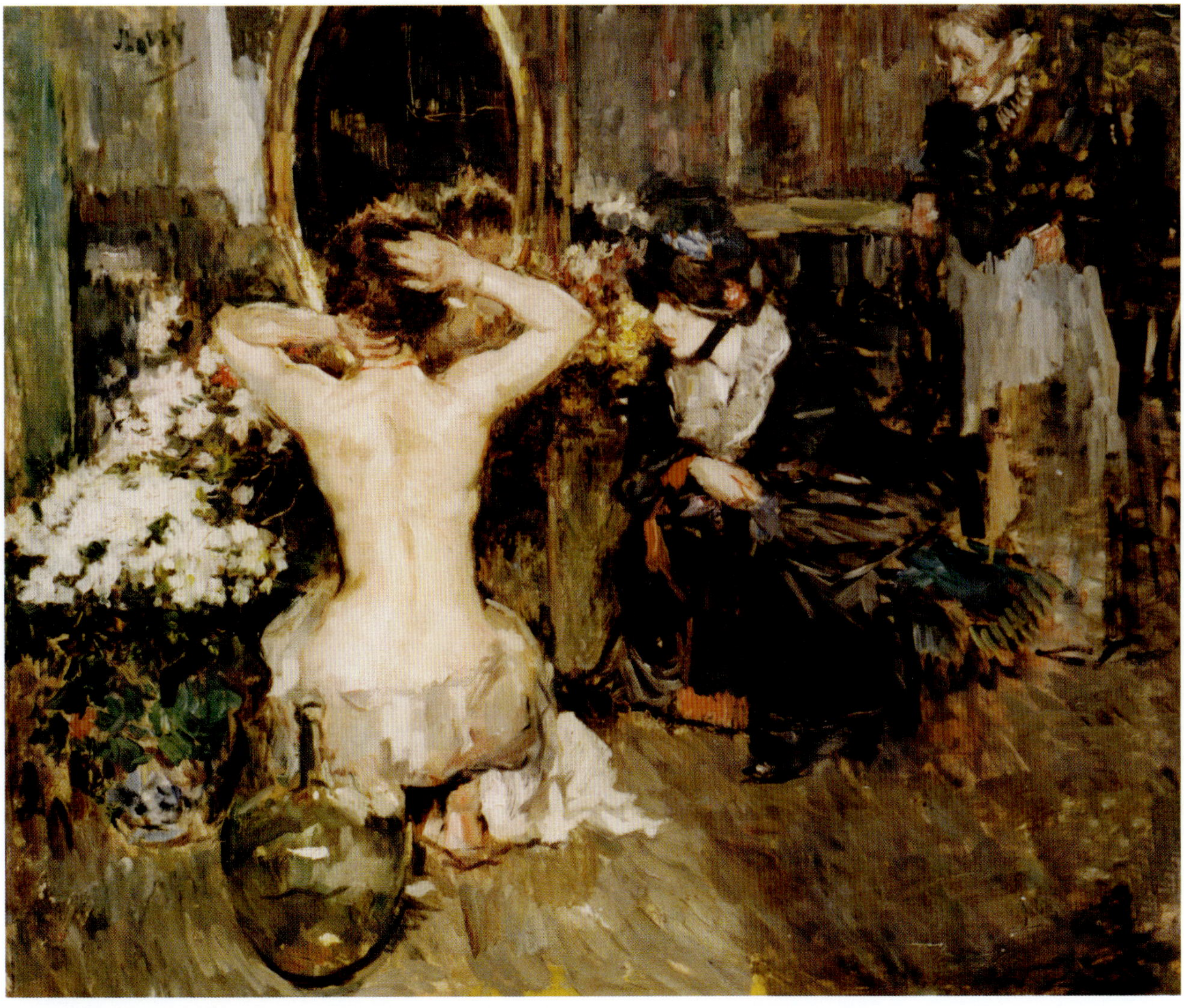

Jean Laudy
Avant le Bal, c.1915
Los Angeles Fine Art Gallery, Los Angeles, California

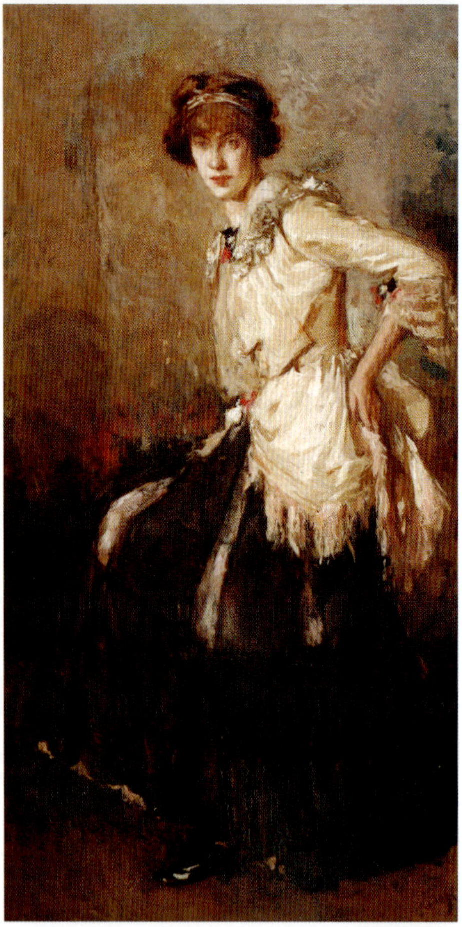

Jean Laudy
Femme Élégante, c.1915
Los Angeles Fine Art Gallery, Los Angeles, California

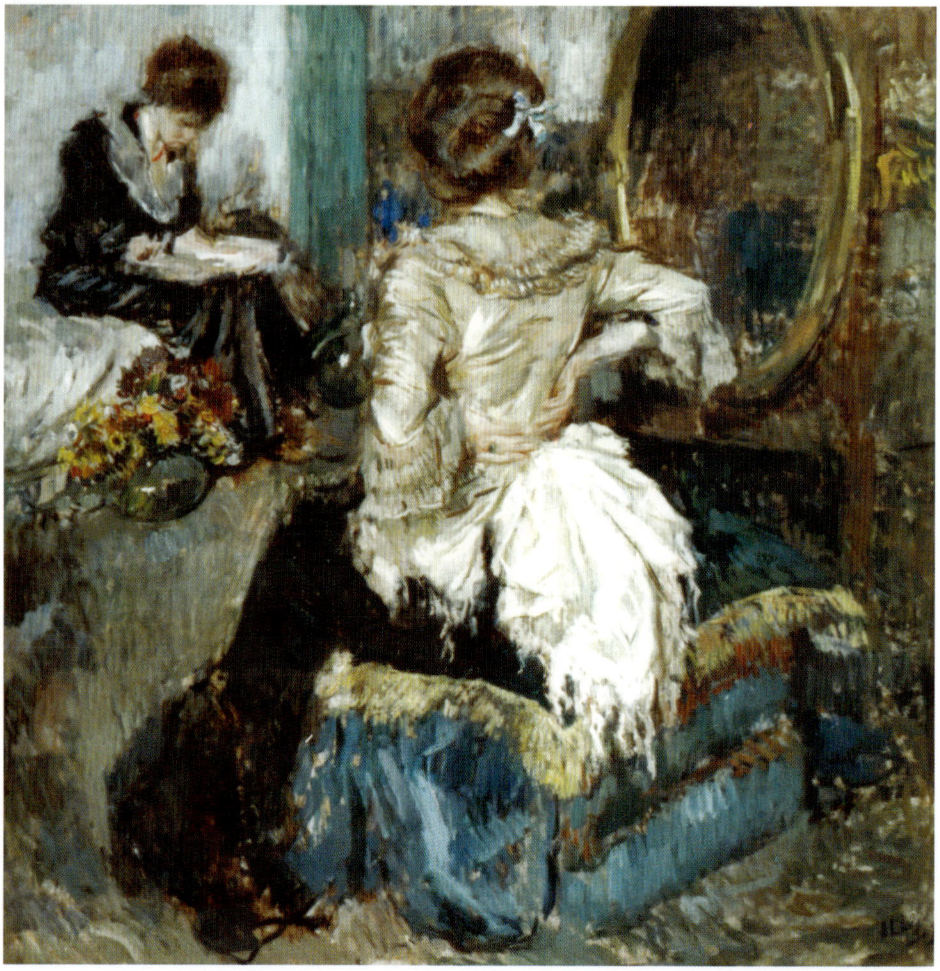

Jean Laudy
Au Boudoir, c.1915
Los Angeles Fine Art Gallery,
Los Angeles, California

Paul Émile Lecomte

1877-1950

Paul Émile Lecomte was born in Paris on October 29, 1877. He was the brother and student of Paul Lecomte and also studied with Cormon at l'École des Beaux-Arts de Paris.

Lecomte is best known for his landscape, portrait, and nautical paintings and also worked as a watercolorist. Lecomte exhibited at the Salon des Artistes Français in 1902 where received a Médaille d'Or and painted the Ministère de la Marine.

Lecomte used symbolist subjects painted with the boldness of the Expressionists. His use of strong brush strokes and bold colors gave his canvases a striking presence. He died in 1950.

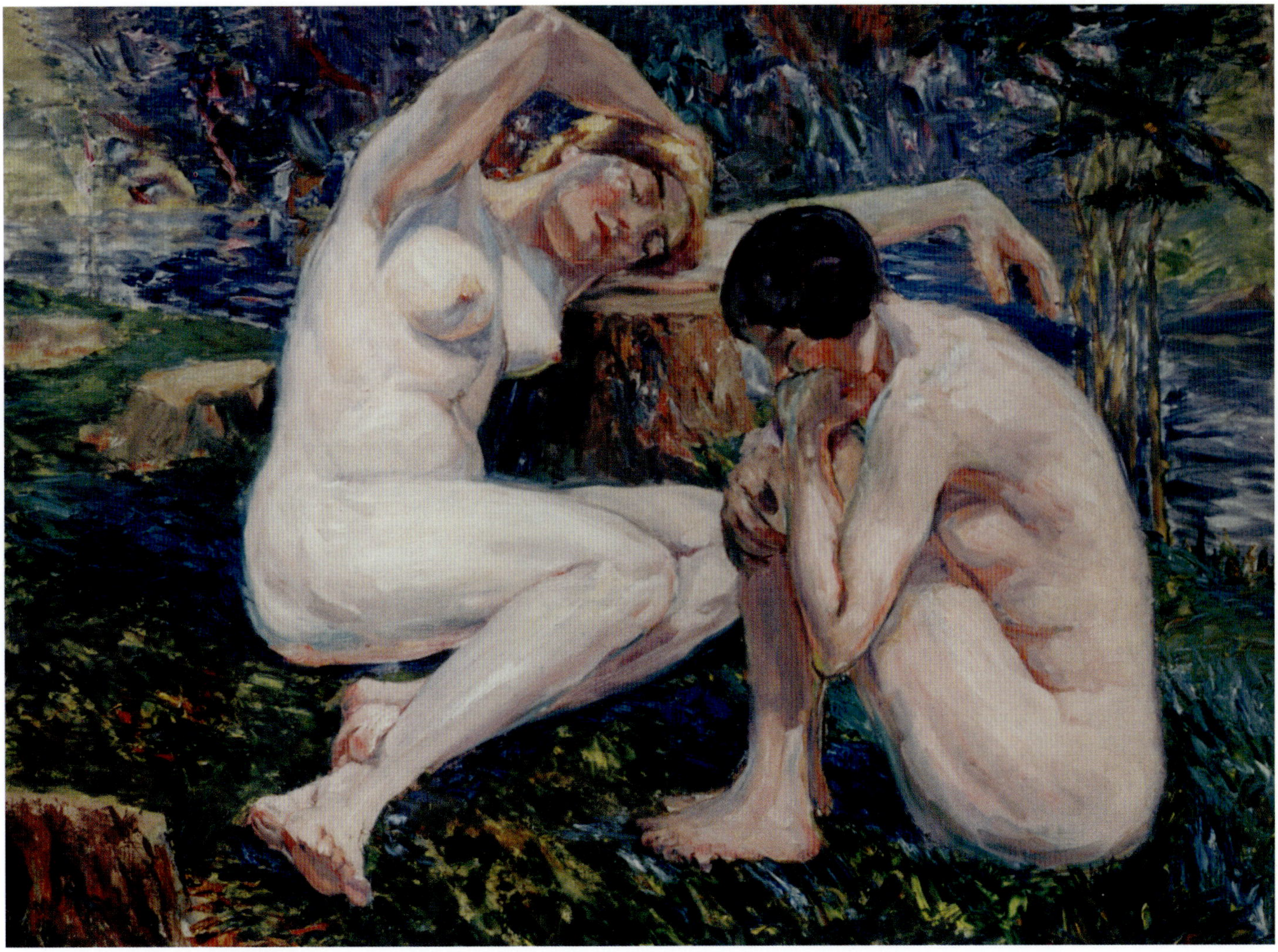

Paul Émile Lecomte
Deux Nus, c.1910
Los Angeles Fine Art Gallery, Los Angeles, California

Mercedes Legrand

1893-1945

Mercedes Legrand was born in Almodavar-del-Campo, Spain, to Belgian parents. Legrand spent her first years in Spain though she went on to study in Brussels, England and Germany. Legrand attended l'Académie des Beaux-Arts de Bruxelles from 1916 to 1919.

Legrand married painter and art critic Roger van Gindertael. She participated in the development of the avant-garde magazine *Héliante* and beginning in the early 1920s made her home in Paris.

Legrand exhibited at the Salon des Tuileries, Salon d'Automne, and in various group shows at Parisian galleries. She also exhibited in several galleries in Brussels while living in Paris. In 1924 she worked as a designer for the French newspaper *Le Matin*.

Legrand exhibited with many avant-garde artists of her generation such as Mané Katz, Pougny, Dufy, Friez, Lhote, Vuillard and Rouault. She also had several solo exhibitions in Paris, including the Galerie Zak in 1935 for which Eugenio d'Ors wrote the catalog essay for her exhibition. André Salmon also wrote an essay for another exhibition.

In 1937 she remarried to the painter Edmond Kayser who, in 1938, became the director of l'École des Arts Décoratifs de Limoges. The couple moved to Limoges and Legrand began to work with ceramics and enamels. In 1941 she fled Nazi-occupied Limoges because of her Jewish heritage and took refuge near Avignon. It is believed that she died at the age of 52 in 1945, from acidic chemical poisoning, a result of the production of enamels.

Very few of Legrand's works are known to exist. She was influenced by Cubism and the starkness of Paris after World War I and her paintings have a superbly modern and mysterious quality that may come from being well traveled at a young age.

Legrand's work, like many of her contemporaries, has almost fallen into obscurity, yet recently sophisticated collectors are becoming more interested in her oeuvre. Legrand is represented in several museums, including those in Liège and Mons.

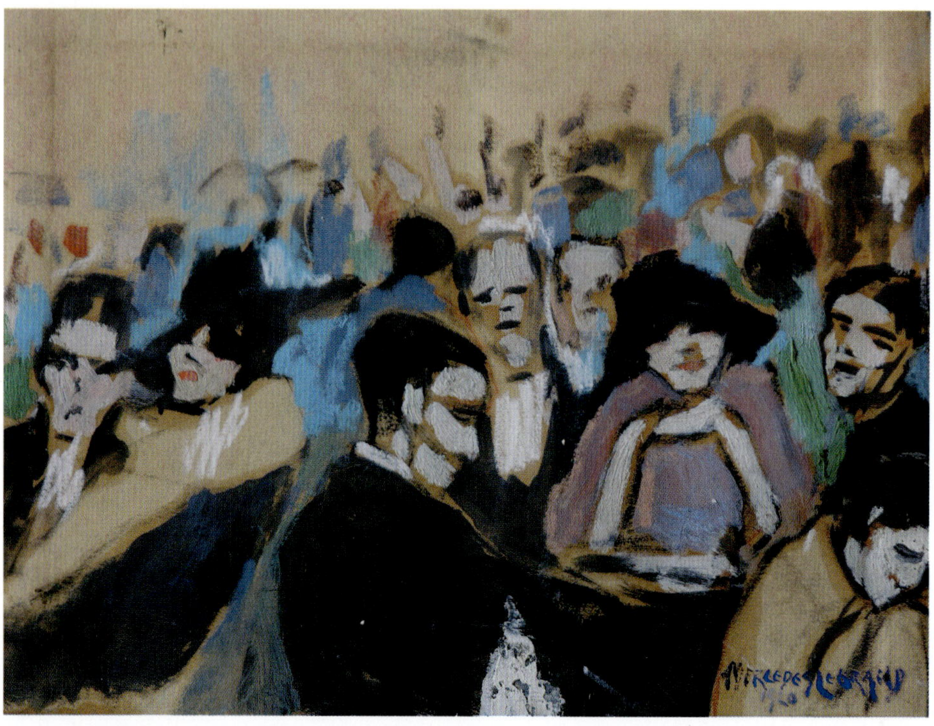

Mercedes Legrand
Au Bar, c.1925
Max Ember, Los Angeles, California

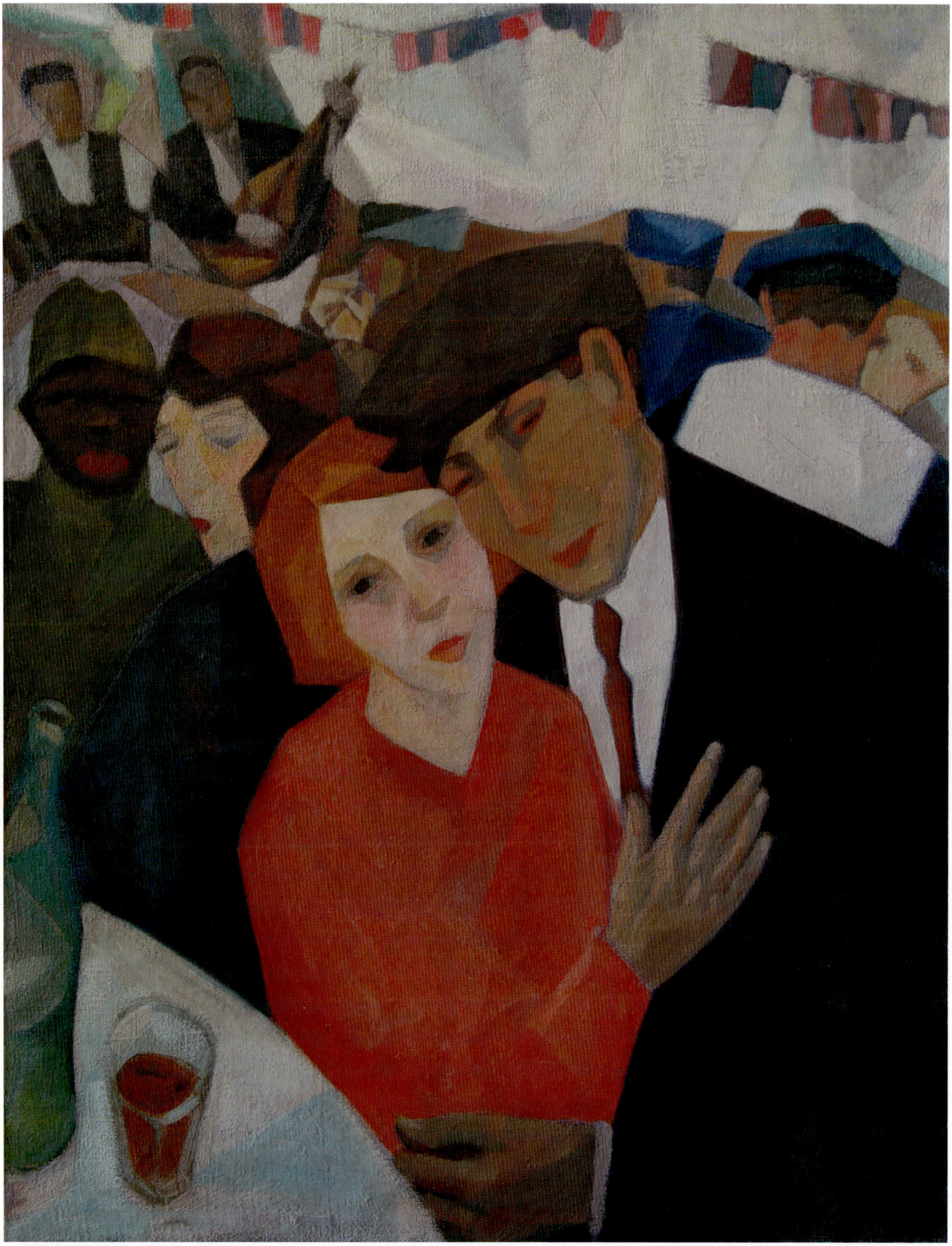

Mercedes Legrand
Bal Musette, Dated 1923
Papillon Gallery, Los Angeles, California

Pierre Lelong

1908-1984

Pierre Lelong was born in Paris in 1908. After living in Antilles, Lelong began to paint, pursuing his career in art relatively late in life.

Lelong is known for his lively and charming paintings. He portrayed contemporary life in his colorful drawings, while his paintings are more elegant and display a refined understanding of light and its reflective qualities. He also worked as a lithographer and illustrator.

Lelong exhibited at many different Salons including, Salon des Indépendants, Salon d'Automne, Salon de Mai, Salon Comparaisons, and in the exhibitions of the Secessionists in 1972.

Lelong exhibited in several solo shows: New York in 1967, Paris Galerie Carlier in 1969, Chicago in 1971, Tokyo and Paris in 1971, and Cannes in 1973 among others. Lelong created paintings, decorative drawings and lithographs for literary works including publications of Shakespeare's and Colette's work. He died in 1984.

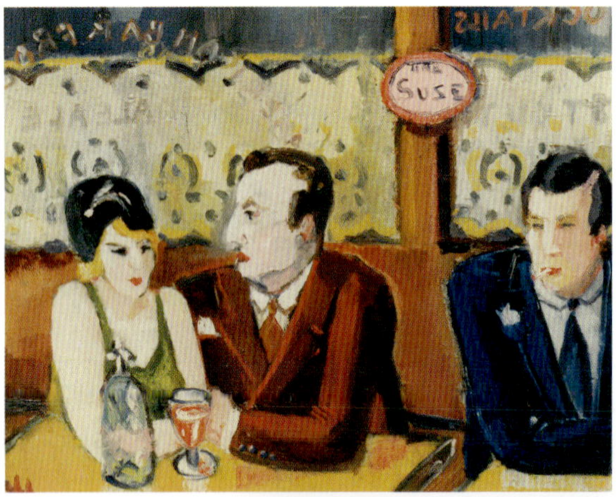

Pierre Lelong
Au Bar, c.1930
Los Angeles Fine Art Gallery,
Los Angeles, California

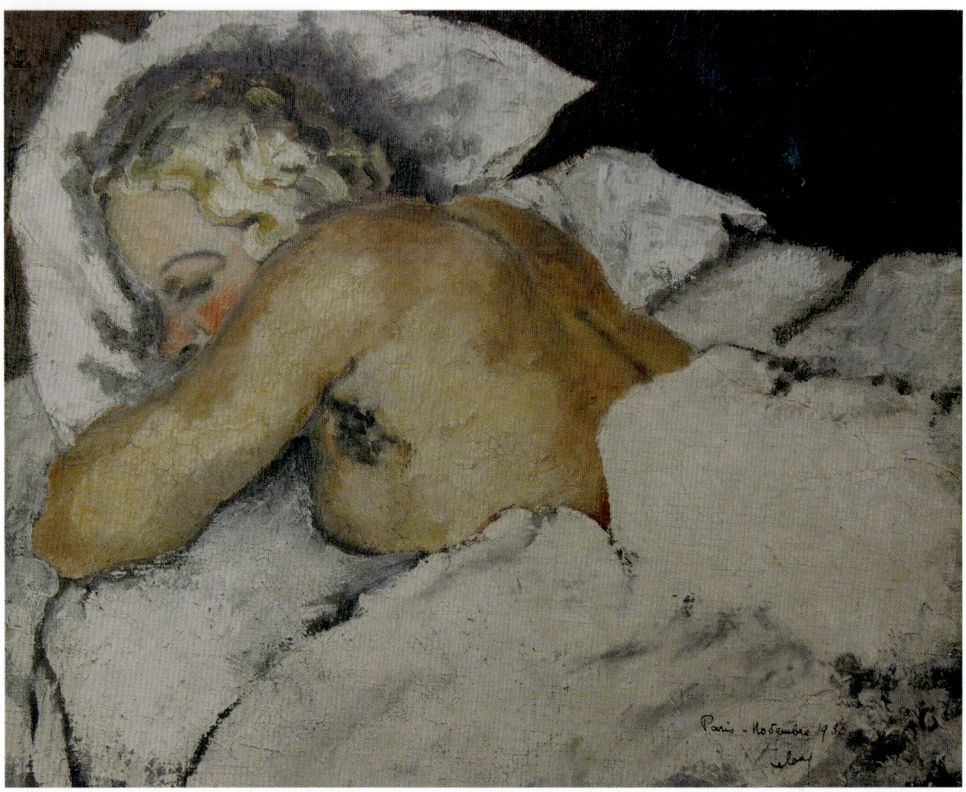

Pierre Lelong
Coucher, Dated 1933
Jim and Linda Ries,
Beverly Hills, California

René Lelong
20th century

René Lelong was born in Arrou, France, and was known as an illustrator and painter. He exhibited at the Salon des Artistes Français of which he was a member and where he received the Médaille de Troisième Classe in 1895. Lelong also illustrated several works by Hervieu, Richepin, Diderot, Maupassant and Marcel Prévost. The dates of his birth and death are unknown.

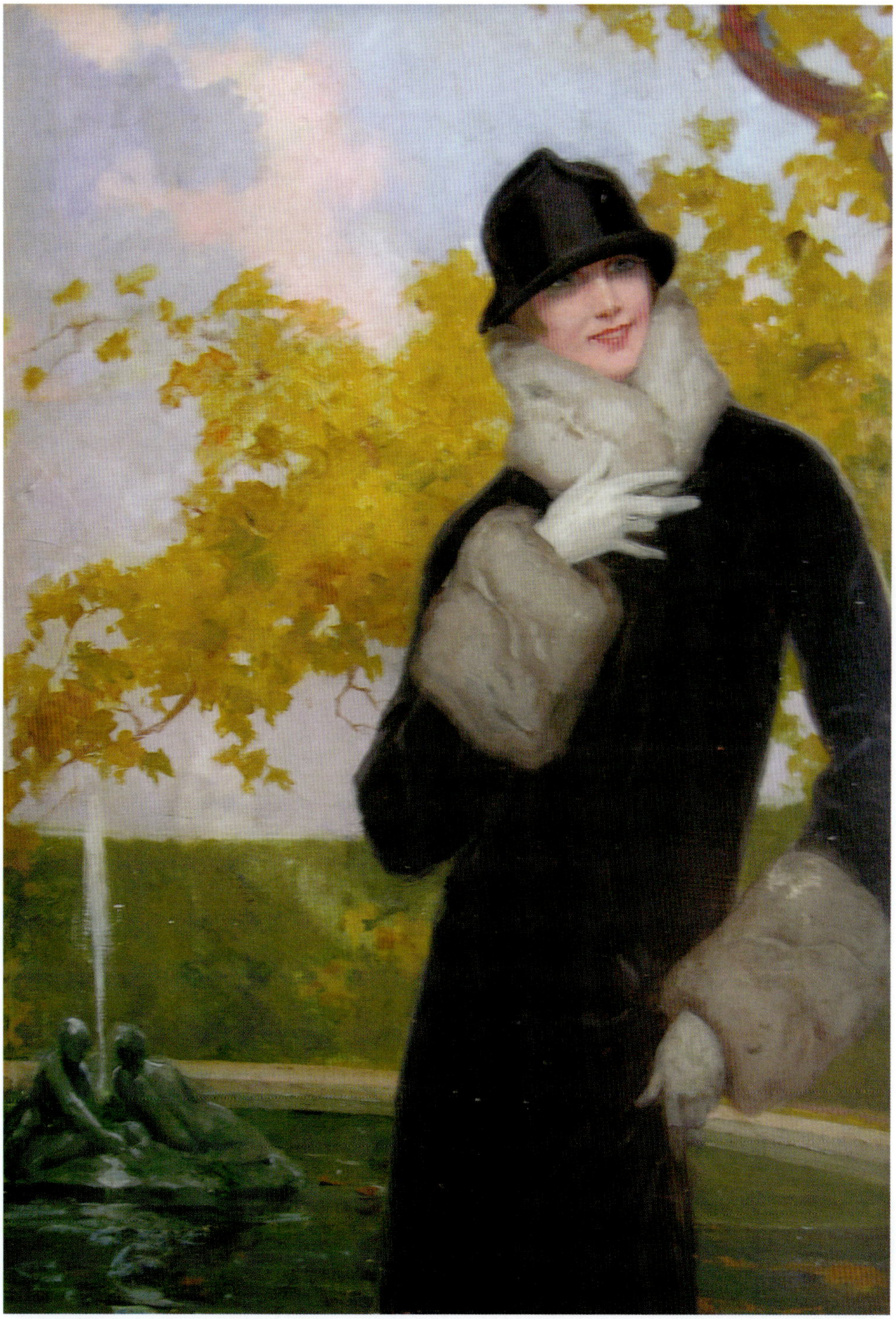

René Lelong
Élégante dans le Parc, c.1925
Andrew Herrera II, San Francisco, California

Edmond Lempereur
1876-1909

Edmond Lempereur was born in Ouillins in 1976. He was a member of the Salon des Artistes Indépendants with whom he exhibited.

Lempereur was known for diverse styles and subjects. He was largely influenced by Claude Monet's paintings and worked in realms of Impressionism and Realism depicting landscapes, the Seine and Marne coasts, gardens, bar scenes, cafés and concerts. He died in 1909. In 1929 a retrospective of his work was held.

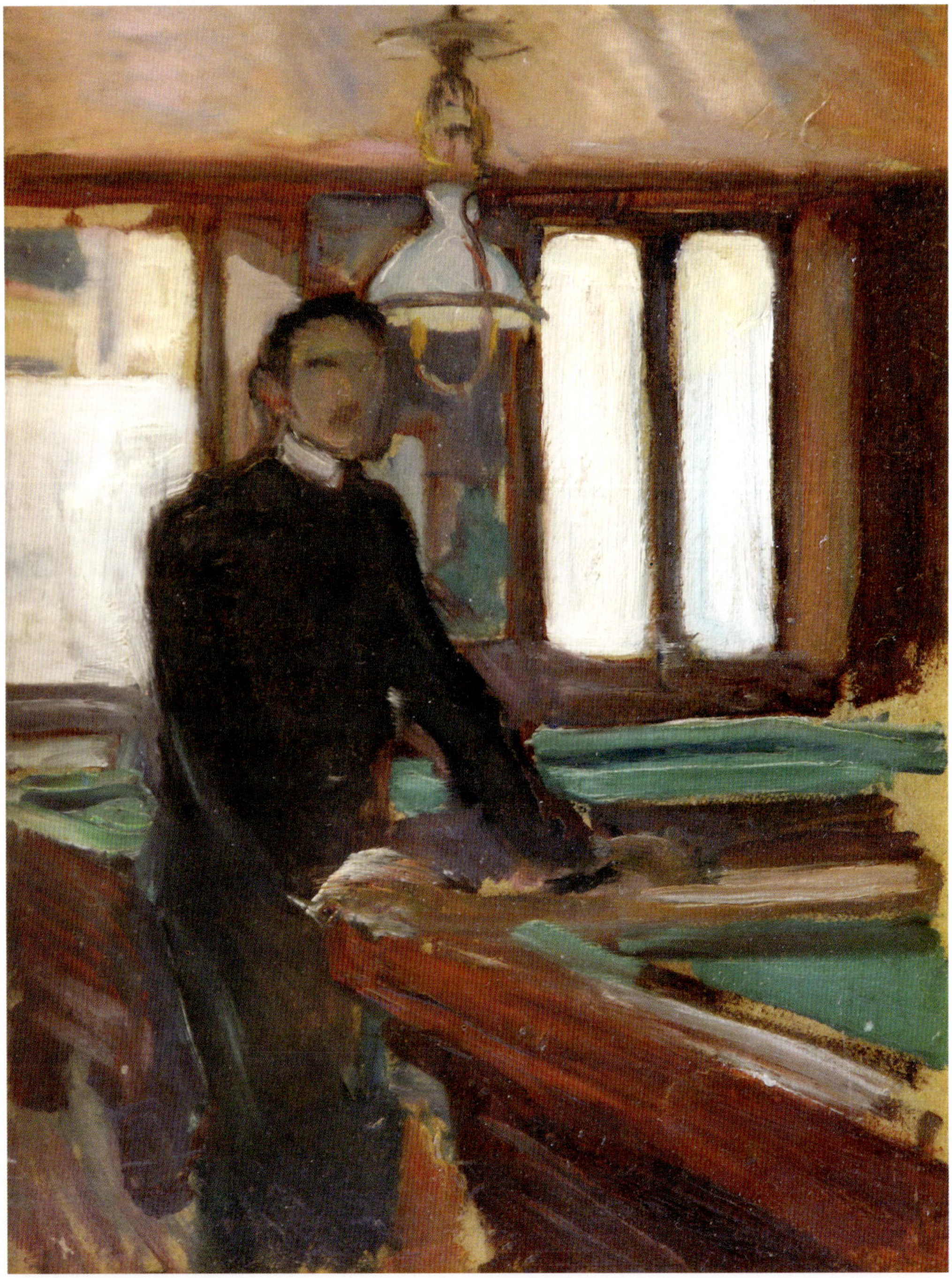

Edmond Lempereur
Salon de Billiards, c.1900
Papillon Gallery, Los Angeles, California

Georges Lépine

20th century

Georges Lépine was born in Latronquière, France. He exhibited at the Salon des Indépendants in 1905 and was known for his paintings and pastels.

Lépine's work has a mystical quality usually associated with Symbolist artists and there is a softness to his subjects that creates intrigue for the viewer.

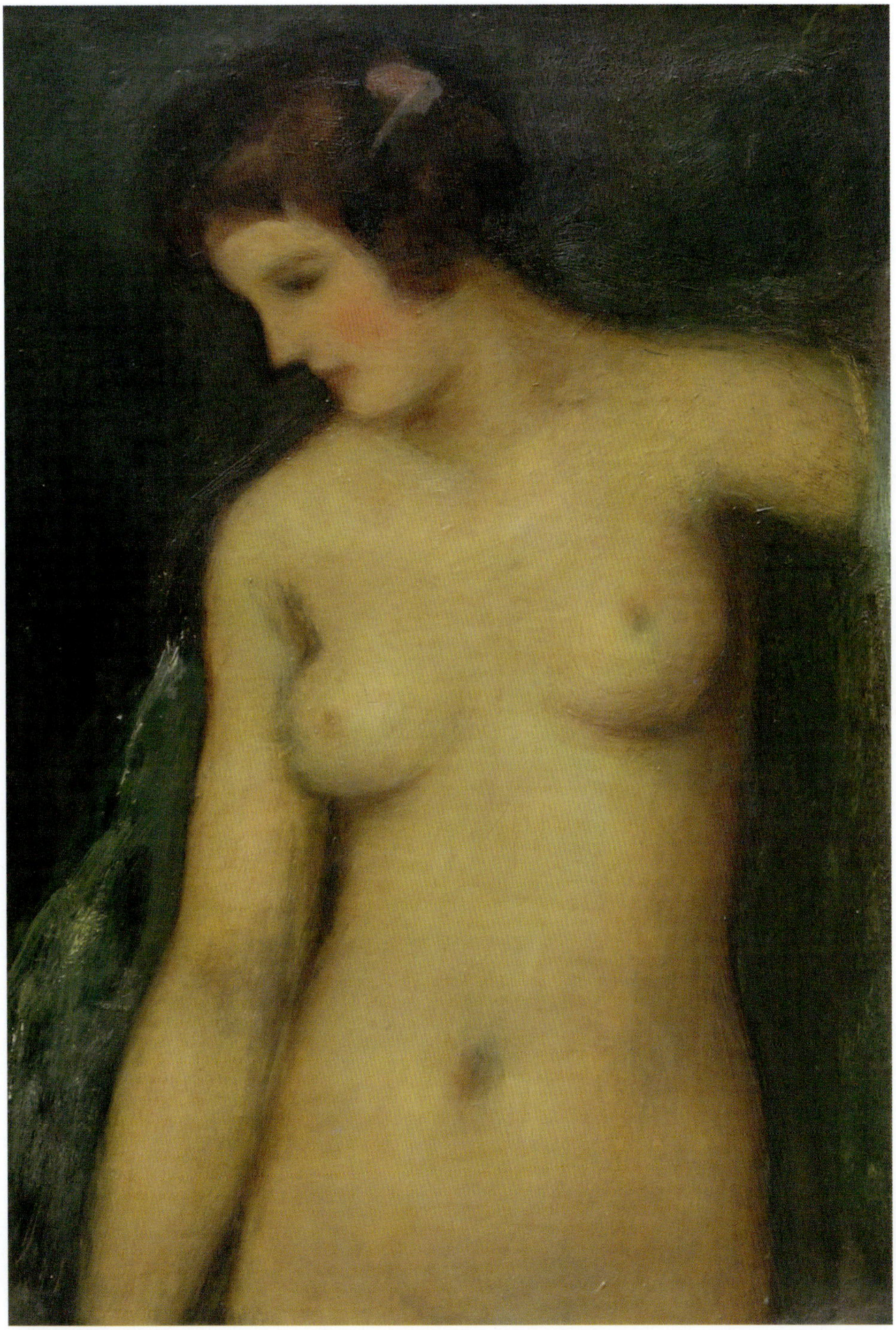

Georges Lépine
Jeune Femme, c.1920
Ernie and Ronna Vigil, Aptos, California

Axel Linus
1885-1980

Axel Linus was born in Öreboro, Sweden in 1885. He attended the Royal Academy of Arts in Stockholm, Académie Colorossi and Académie Moderne in Paris. He subsequently moved to Chicago where he received commissions for portraits such as Carl Sandberg and Charles Lindbergh and murals including one for the Chicago World's Fair in 1933.

Linus had the opportunity to travel the United States on his honeymoon during which time he painted the countryside and various landscapes in the South and Southwest. He and his wife eventually settled in Palm Springs, California where they purchased a hotel and set up a studio in Snow Creek Canyon.

Linus became a member of the Desert Art Center and Palm Desert Palette Club where he exhibited. He also participated in exhibitions held by the Scandinavian Artists of the West in Los Angeles 1939 and the Society for Sanity in Art in 1941. Linus died in Palm Springs in 1980.

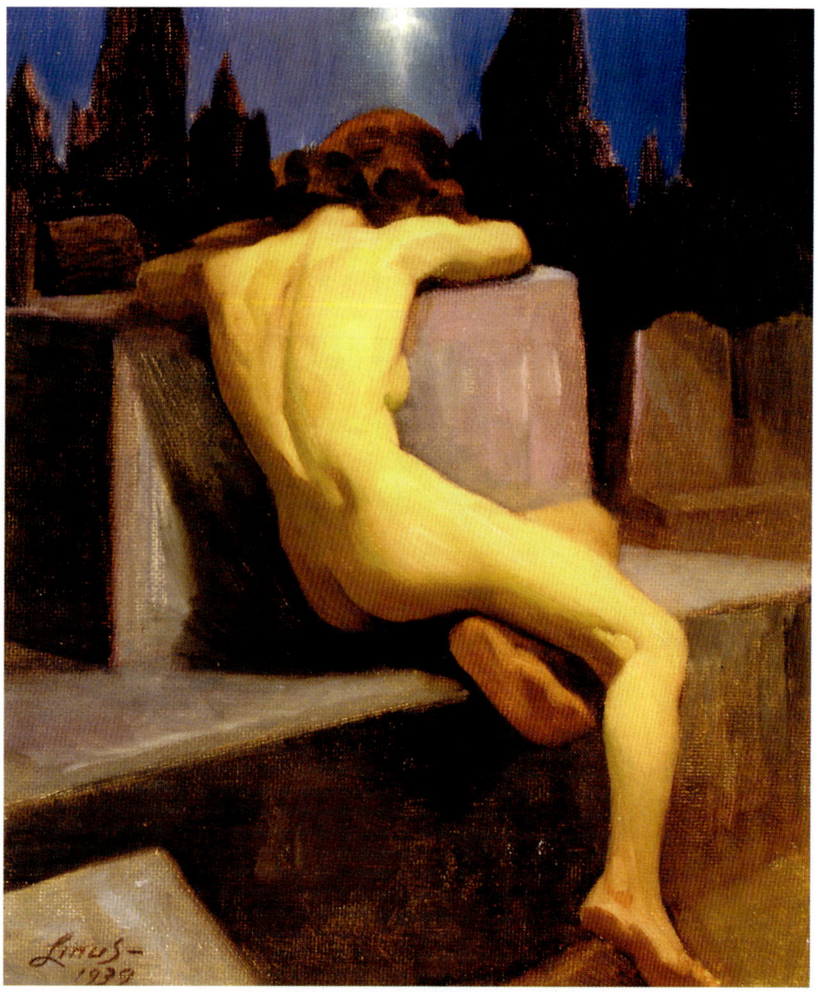

Axel Linus
Evening Star, Dated 1939
Photo courtesy of Spencer Jon Helfen Fine Arts, Beverly Hills, California

Almery Lobel-Riche
1880-1950

Known also as Riche Alméric, Lobel Riche was a prolific artist and illustrator in Paris. He was most recognized for his depictions of Morocco and scenes of war. He illustrated several books by well known authors such as Oscar Wilde, Charles Baudelaire and others.

Lobel-Riche exhibited in Paris, London and Switzerland. He published a book of ten original etchings, *Moeurs, Costumes & Attitudes,* for the Société des Amis de la Petite Estampe Moderne in 1913. He died in 1950. In 1992 his work was included in the exhibition *De Bonnard à Baselitz,* at the National Library in Paris, for which his biography was written in the exhibition catalogue.

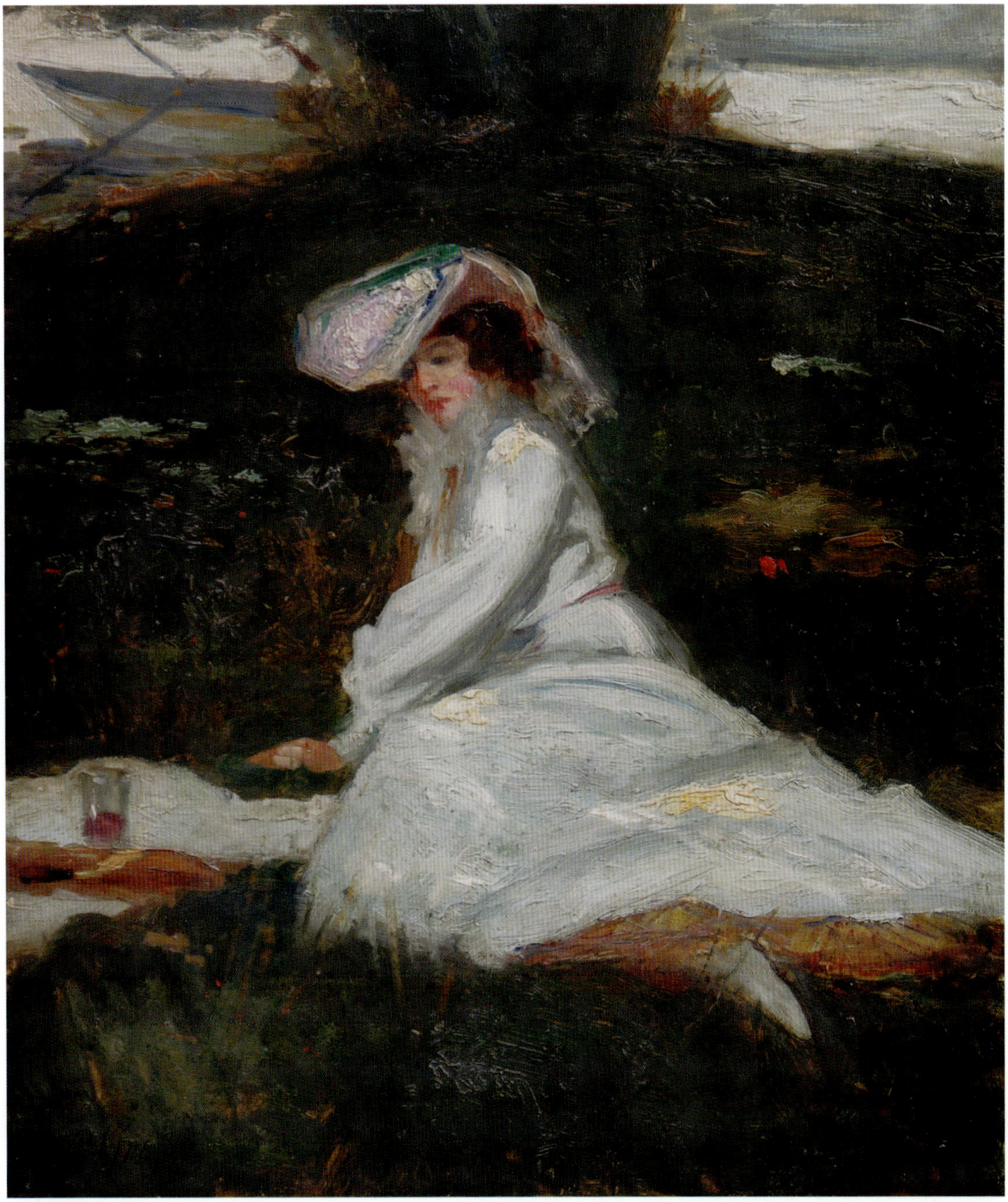

Almery Lobel-Riche
Prés du Fleuve, c.1910
Irene Slade, Los Angeles, California

DeWitt McClellan Lockman

1870-1957

A New York native, DeWitt McClellan Lockman established himself in both the United States and Europe as a talented painter of landscapes, genre scenes, historical events and most significantly portraits. He began painting at the early age of four and continued to be self-taught until, as a teenager, he received instruction from James N. Beard, Nathan Bickford and William Sartain. Several distinctions were given extremely early in Lockman's career, such as the youngest artist to exhibit at the National Academy and as one of the youngest artists to exhibit in Paris. Lockman continued his studies abroad in Paris from 1891-1892 and in Holland from 1901-1902.

Lockman held numerous prominent positions throughout his career; as full Academician to the National Academy in 1917; Founder and Vice-President of the National Association of Portrait Painters (1912-1925) and President (1925-1957), President of the Allied Artists of America (1945-1946); President of the National Academy of Design (1949-1950); trustee of the New York Historical Society (1925-1957);Secretary of the Committee (1929- 1957); Chairman of the Society's Committee on Fine Arts (1930-1948); and Treasurer of the American Artists Committee of One Hundred La Fraternité des Artistes, Paris France (1915-1919). He also served the School Art League of New York and the Metropolitan Museum of Art as trustee, as Director of the Municipal Art Society (1933-1935) and as board member of the American Artists Professional League.

Awards and medals Lockman received for his talent and commitment include; the Panama-Pacific International Exposition Silver Medal, 1915; the Pennsylvania Academy of Fine Arts Lippincott Prize, 1918; La Fraternité des Artistes Gold Plaque for Officer of Soldier-Artistes Relief Fund, the National Academy of Design Isaac N. Maynard Portrait Prize, 1922; and Gold Medals from the New York Historical Society, 1933; the Allied Artists of America, 1936; the Hudson Valley Art Association, 1957 and the University of Tampa, 1957. Lockman's work has been widely collected by institutions such as The Metropolitan Museum of Art, National Academy of Design, New York Historical Society, Pennsylvania Academy of Fine Arts, Portland Museum of Art, Newport Historical Society, West Point Military Academy and Yale University. Lockman died in 1957.

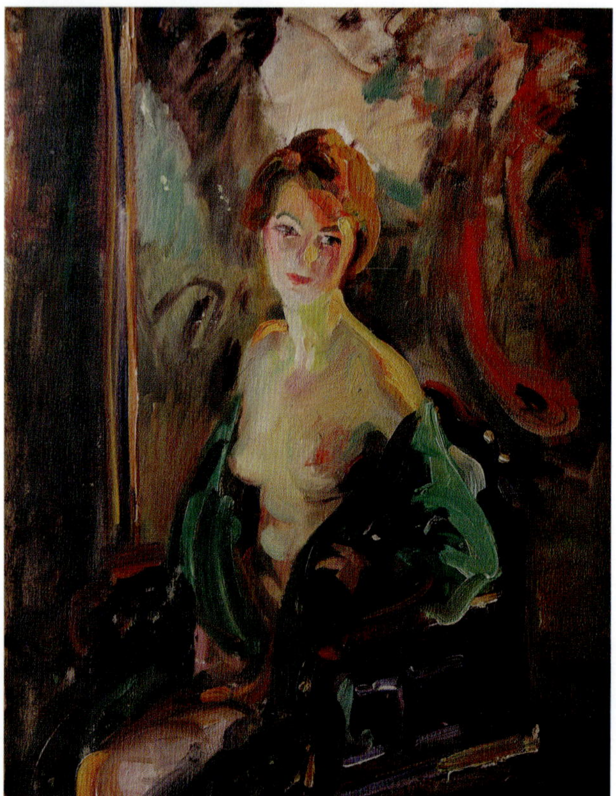

DeWitt McClellan Lockman
Seated Nude, c.1920
Papillon Gallery, Los Angeles, California

René Charles Eugène Longa
Born 1878

René Charles Eugène Longa was born on April 11, 1878 in Paris. He studied with Raphaël Collin and Octave Guillonnet.

Longa is best known as a painter of portraits, landscapes and flowers but his most interesting works are symbolist fantasies. His depiction of nymphs in dreamy fields is characteristic of the utopian ideals expressed by many artists of his generation. He exhibited regularly at the Salon des Artistes Français; in 1922 he won a monetary award and in 1924 he received a Médaille d'Or and high honors.

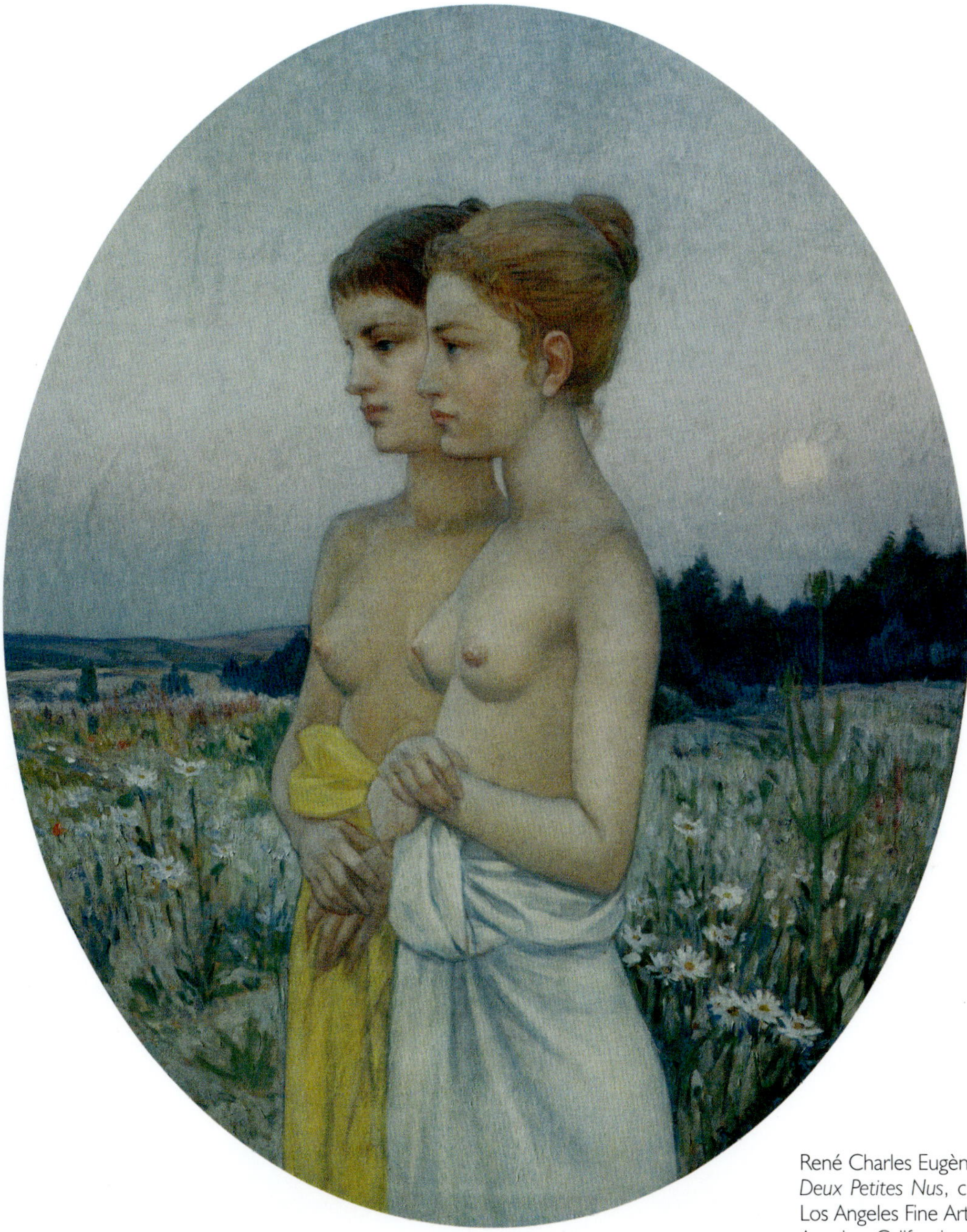

René Charles Eugène Longa
Deux Petites Nus, c.1910
Los Angeles Fine Art Gallery, Los Angeles, California

Jean Lurçat
1892-1966

Jean Lurçat was born July 1st 1892 in Bruyères. He entered the atelier of Victor Prouvé and in 1912 he moved to Paris where he attended l'Académie Colarossi and studied under Bernard Naudin.

Lurçat had an affinity for Surrealism and became acquainted with the circles of artists of similar taste and influence. He exhibited at the Salon des Indépendants and the Salon des Tuileries and illustrated several books.

Travel became a passion for Lurçat after the war and he journeyed through Germany, Austria, Italy, Spain, Greece, Asia, Morocco, the Sahara and the United States. His experiences added another dimension to his paintings and tapestries having been exposed to unfamiliar techniques and aesthetics. Like Picasso and Jean Cocteau he produced editions in ceramic.

Museums that have collected his works include the Musée d'Art Moderne, Paris; Musée d'Art Occidental, Moscow; the Barnes Foundation, Philadelphia; Musée de Petit Palais, Paris; Musée de Nancy, Strasbourg, Grenoble and Limoges; and museums in Amsterdam, Dublin, Düsseldorf, Chicago, Los Angeles, New York, Sidney, Tokyo, Sao-Paulo, Zurich, Stockholm and Johannesburg.

Lurçat died in 1966. In October, 2004, Galerie Zlotowski and Galerie Jacques de Vos coordinated an exhibit, *Jean Lurçat: Les Années Lumière 1915-1935,* in Paris.

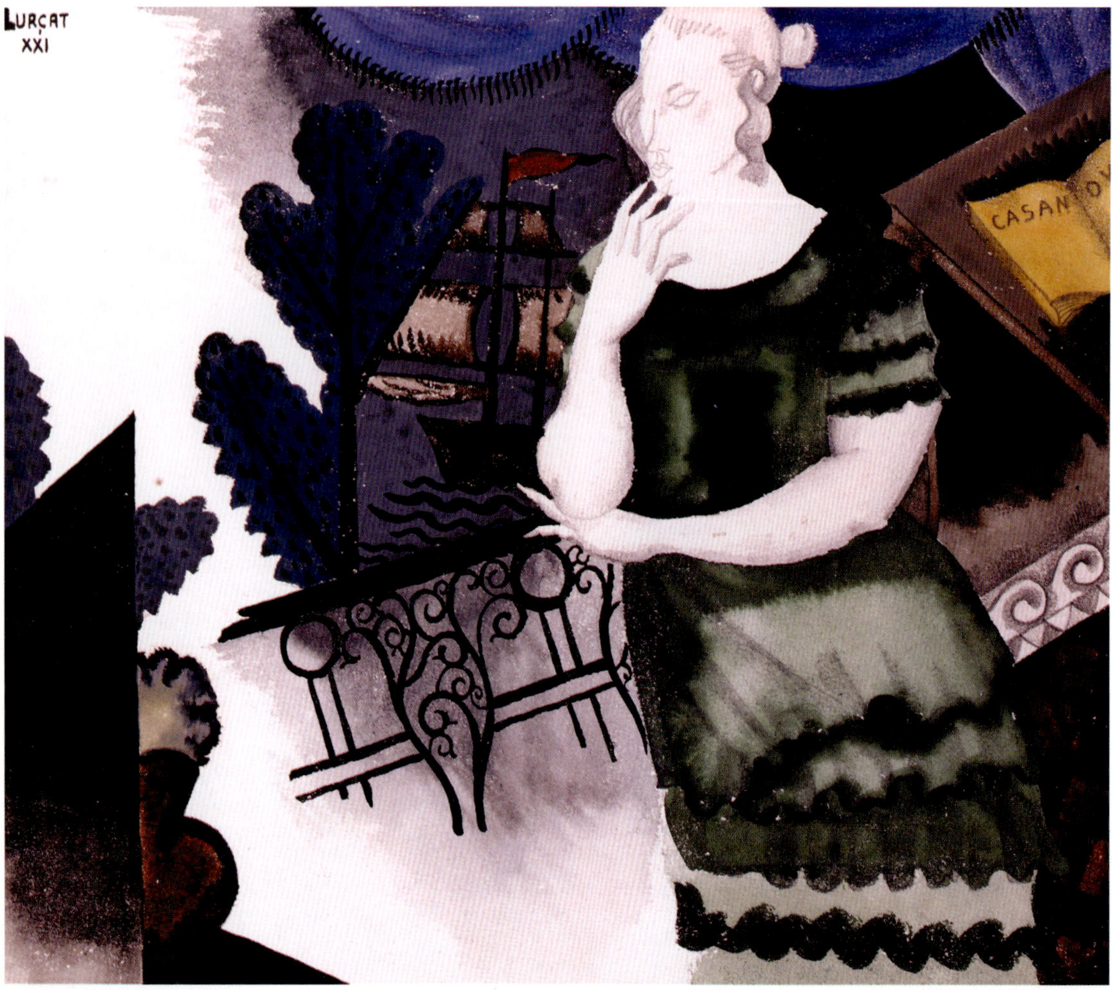

Jean Lurçat
Au Balcon, Dated 1921
Whitford Fine Art, London, England

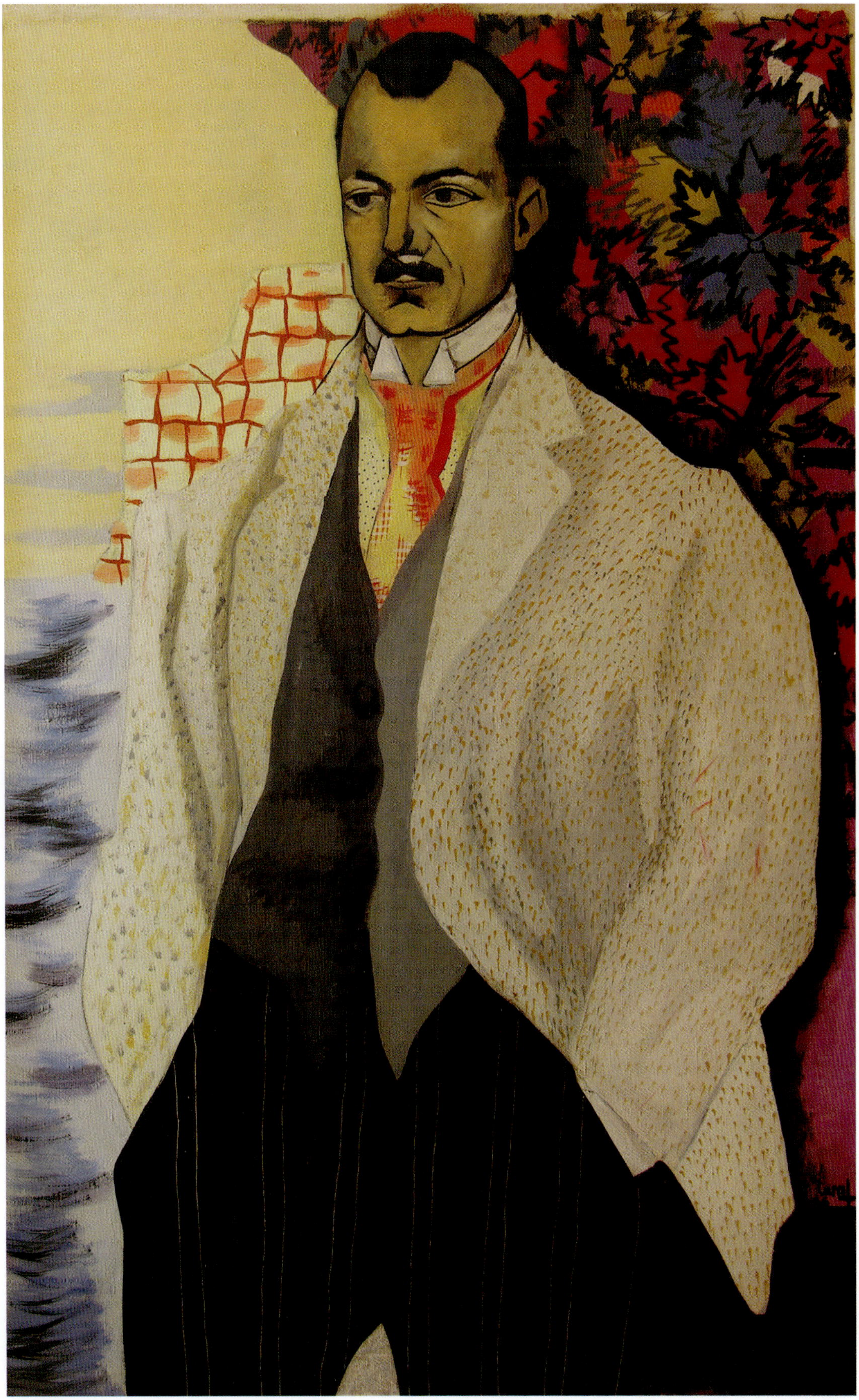

Jean Lurçat
Portrait d'Etienne Bignou, Dated 1926,
Mark and Marina Plon, Henderson, Nevada

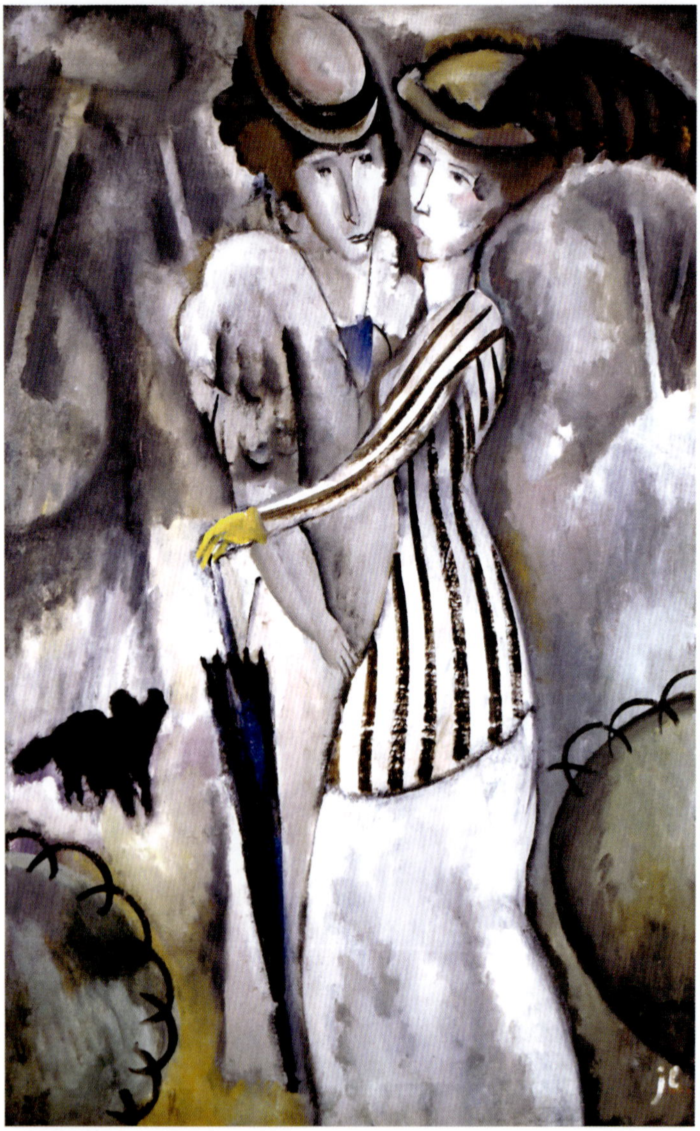

Jean Lurçat
Promenade, c.1920
Whitford Fine Art, London, England

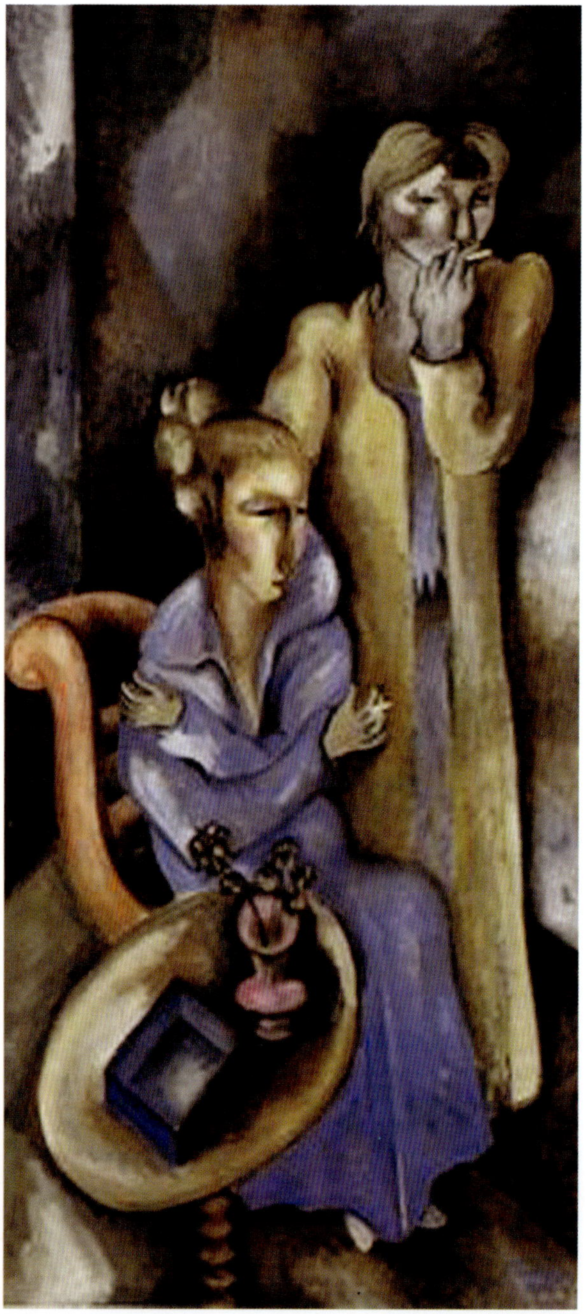

Jean Lurçat
La Table Mise, Dated 1925
Whitford Fine Art, London, England

Mariette Lydis
1890-1970

Mariette Lydis was born in Vienna. She moved to Paris in 1927 after having traveled extensively in Russia, England, Italy, Greece, Egypt and the United States.

Lydis illustrated several works by Baudelaire, Mirbeau, Lucien, Henri de Monthlerlant, Paul Valéry, Jane Régny and Pierre Louy among many others. She published a book of original lithographs, *Criminelles*, as well. In 1938 Henri de Monthlerlant published the catalogue *Mariette Lydis,* which includes fifty-five reproductions and features *Le Cirque* on the front cover.

She was best known as a painter, printmaker and illustrator, and exhibited at the Salon d'Automne in Paris. Lydis exhibited in Milan, Florence, Amsterdam, Vienna and London as well and her works have been collected by the national libraries of Paris and Berlin, the Albertina library in Vienna and the Art and History Museum library in Geneva. Museum collections include Amsterdam, Florence, Geneva, London, Milan, Paris, Vancouver and Vienna.

Lydis's work has a surreal quality that comes from unususal composition. Even her most simple works seem to have something unworldly happening that invites the viewer to look more deeply. Mariette Lydis died in 1970.

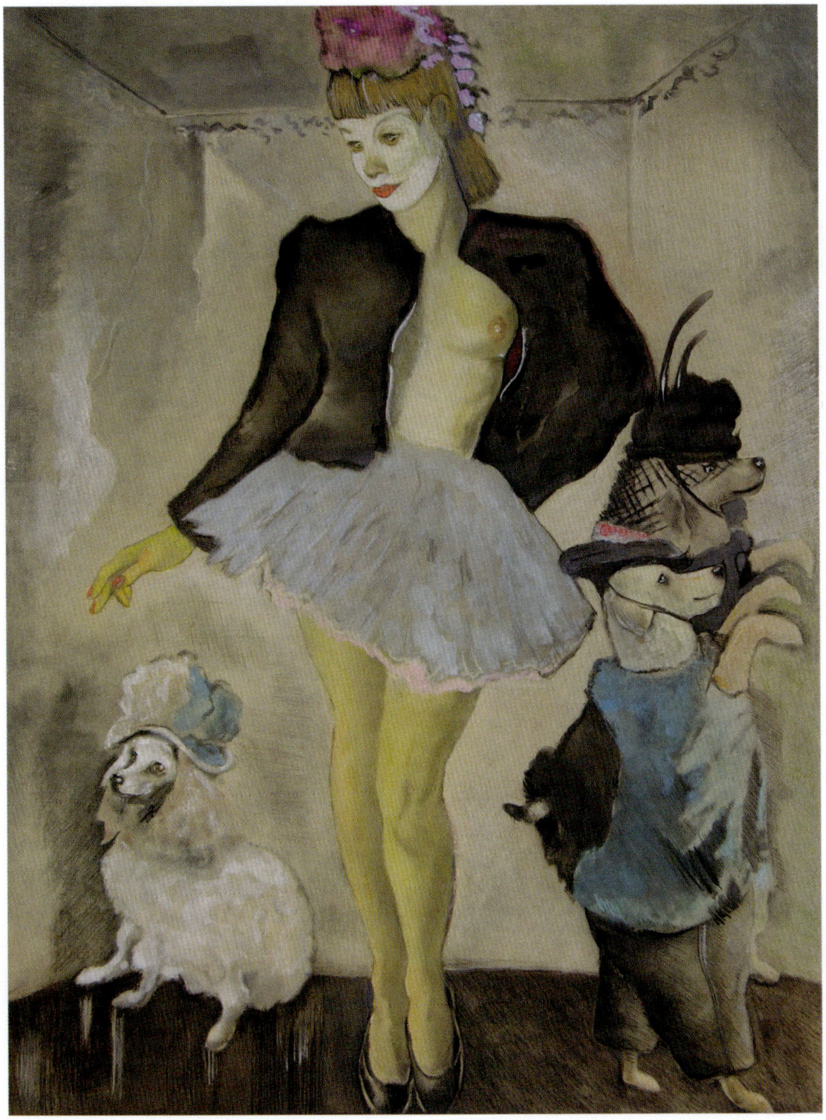

Mariette Lydis
Le Cirque, c.1935
Susan Kay, Ross, California

Marcel-Lenoir
1872-1931

Marcel-Lenoir was born Jules Oury on May 12, 1872 in Montauban, France. He moved to Paris in 1889 and attended l'École des Arts Décoratifs for six months. He was greatly influenced by Italian painters represented at the Louvre and by works from the Middle Ages at the Cluny museum.

Marcel-Lenoir's highly stylized symbolist works came before the turn of the 20th century. He participated in the Salons de la Rose-Croix, which began in 1892. This group of artists used Catholic symbolism and symbols from the occult in their paintings. The Salons de la Rose-Croix were conceived and presented by Péladan as *gestes esthétiques*; it was to be a synthesis of the visual arts, literature and music. He also produced beautiful lithographs including one published by *l'Estampe Moderne*.

In 1902 he returned to Montauban and began to write poetry and paint landscapes. As early as 1912 he incorporated cubist elements in his technique. With his roots in Symbolism and modern style he produced allegorical paintings of beautiful god-like people playing in forests, which were typical of the Art Deco movement. In the 1920s he began to employ a pointillist technique, though his subjects remained consistent. Marcel-Lenoir was also known for his frescoes, some with religious symbolism.

Marcel-Lenoir died in 1931, at the age of 59, in Montricoux. He left almost 700 paintings and drawings. His work is collected in the museums of Vienna and the Musée Marcel-Lenoir in Montauban.

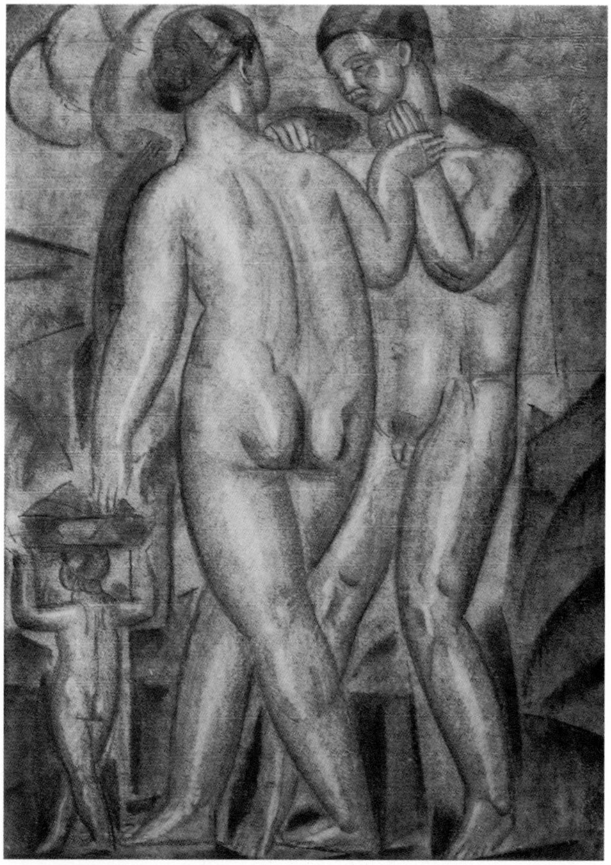

Marcel-Lenoir
Promenade, c.1911
Papillon Gallery, Los Angeles, California

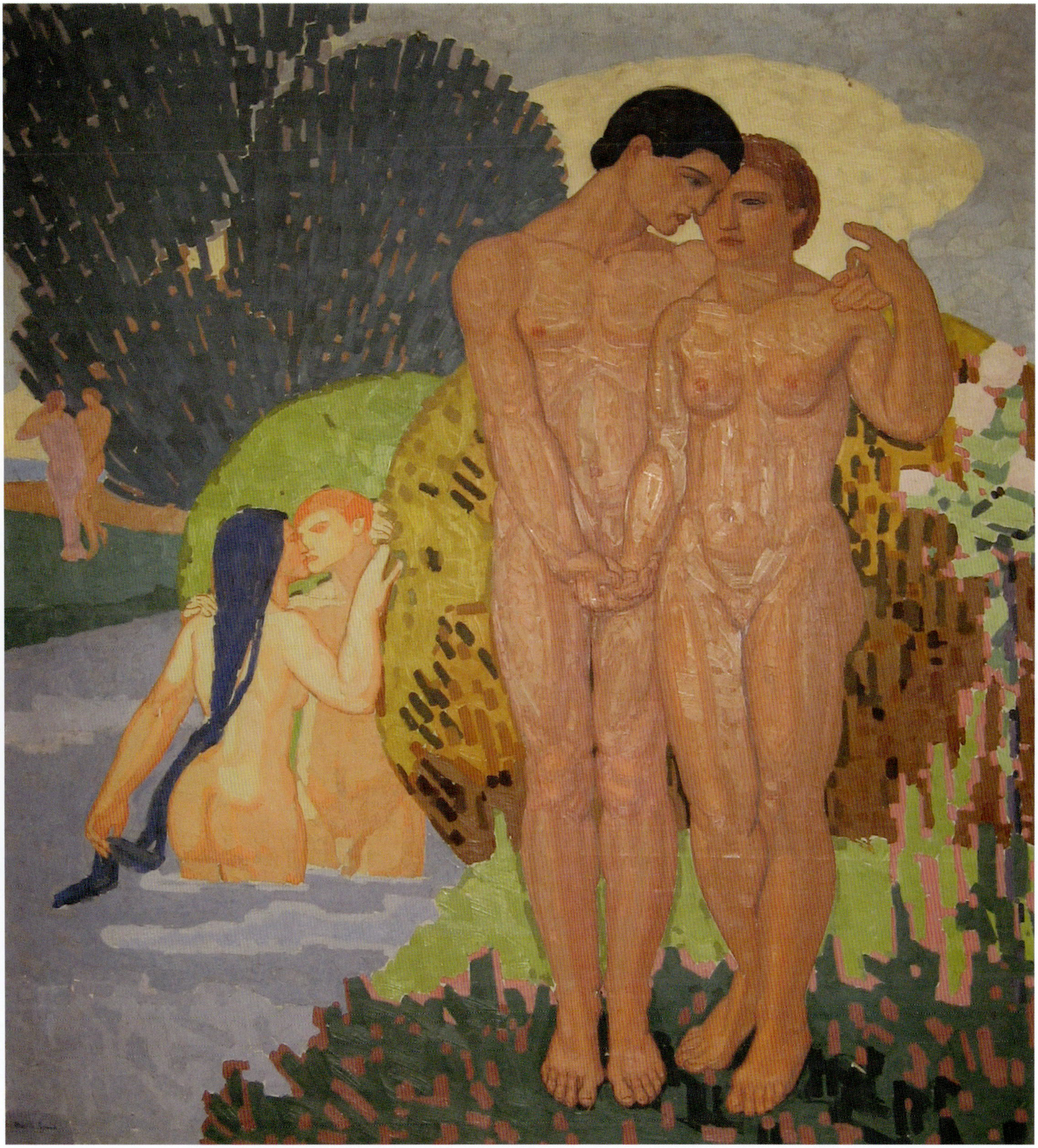

Marcel-Lenoir
Au Jardin, c.1925
Per Fruergaard, Copenhagen, Denmark

Georges Maresté
1875-1940

Georges Mareste was born in 1875 in Cognac, Charente. He is known primarily as a landscape painter. Mareste's use of expressionistic colors and clear tones exemplify Postimpressionism.

Like many artists of his generation, he painted nightclub scenes as well as more traditional subjects. He captured the ambience of the period with fine detail and composition. Mareste is included in the permanent collection of the Musée de Cognac.

Mareste died in 1940. His work is discussed in Gérald Schurr's *Les Petits Maîtres de la Peinture 1820-1920,* t. IV, published by Les Editions de l'Amateur, Paris, 1979.

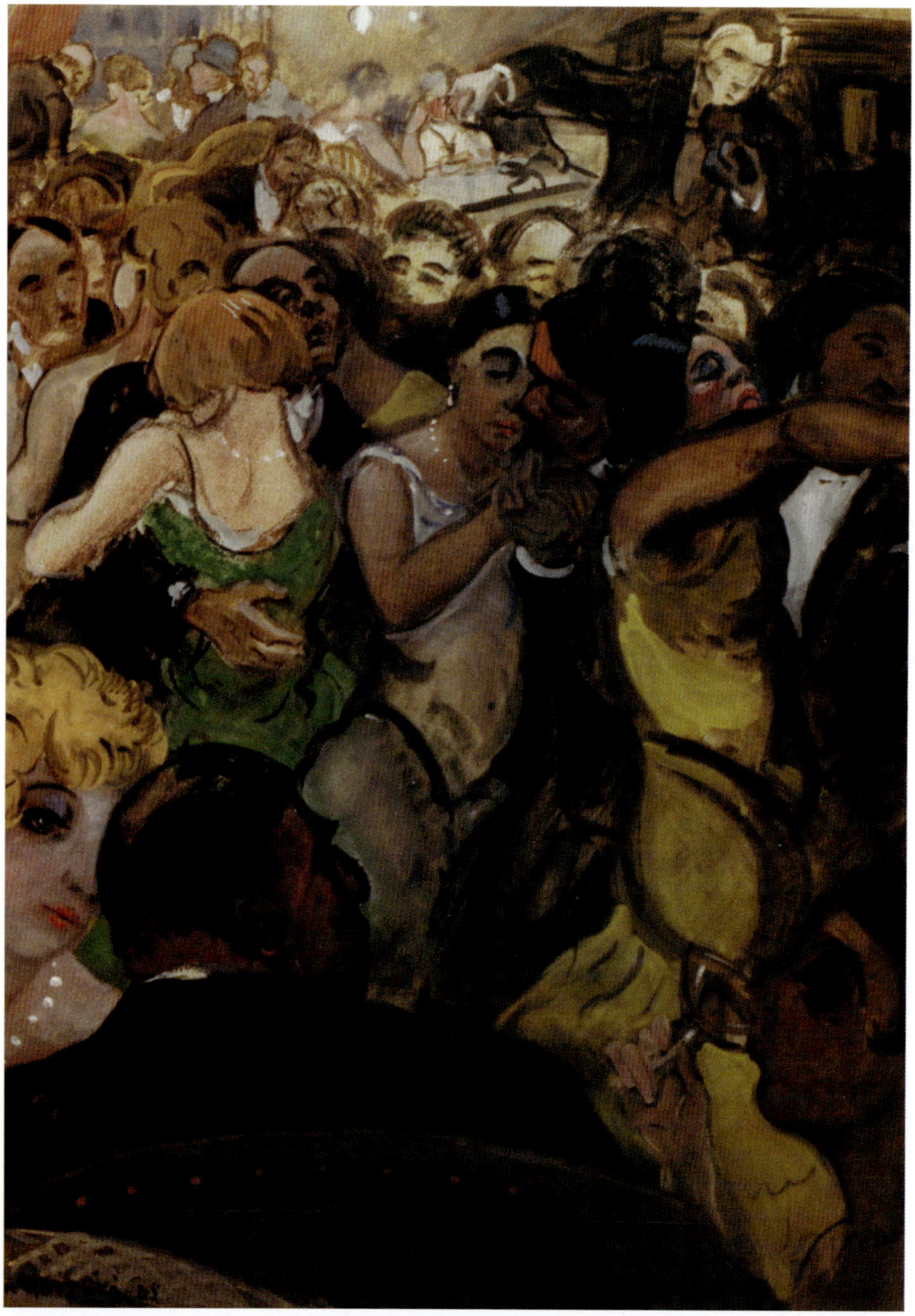

Georges Mareste
La Vie Nocturne, c.1925
Private Collection

Mania Mavro

Born 1889

Mania Mavro was born August 24, 1889 in Odessa, Ukraine. She was a professor of art and known for her portraits, nudes and landscapes.

Mavro exhibited at the Salon de Tuileries, Salon d'Automne, Salon des Artistes Français and the Groupes Peintures et Littérateurs of Brittany, Creuse and Greece. She held a large exhibition of 100 paintings and 75 drawings which traveled to the Feuillets d'Art in 1919, Galerie Georges Petit in 1924, Galerie André in 1925, Galerie Bernheim-Jeune in 1929 and Loup Blanc in 1930.

Mavro was a bold expressionistic painter; her lively colors and modern technique afforded her great success. She exhibited extensively in the years between the wars. Her works can be compared to other Russian women artists that came to Paris, like Vera Rockline and Polish artist Mela Muter. The date of her death is unknown. Mavro's atelier was recently sold at auction in Paris.

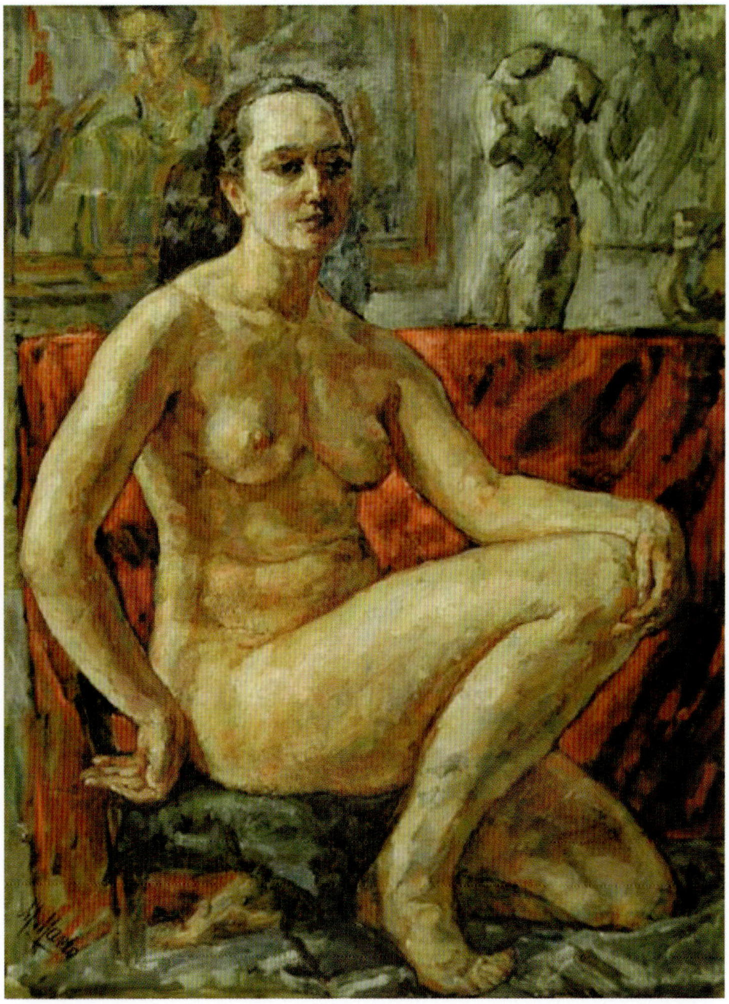

Mania Mavro
Nu Assis, c.1925
Unknown

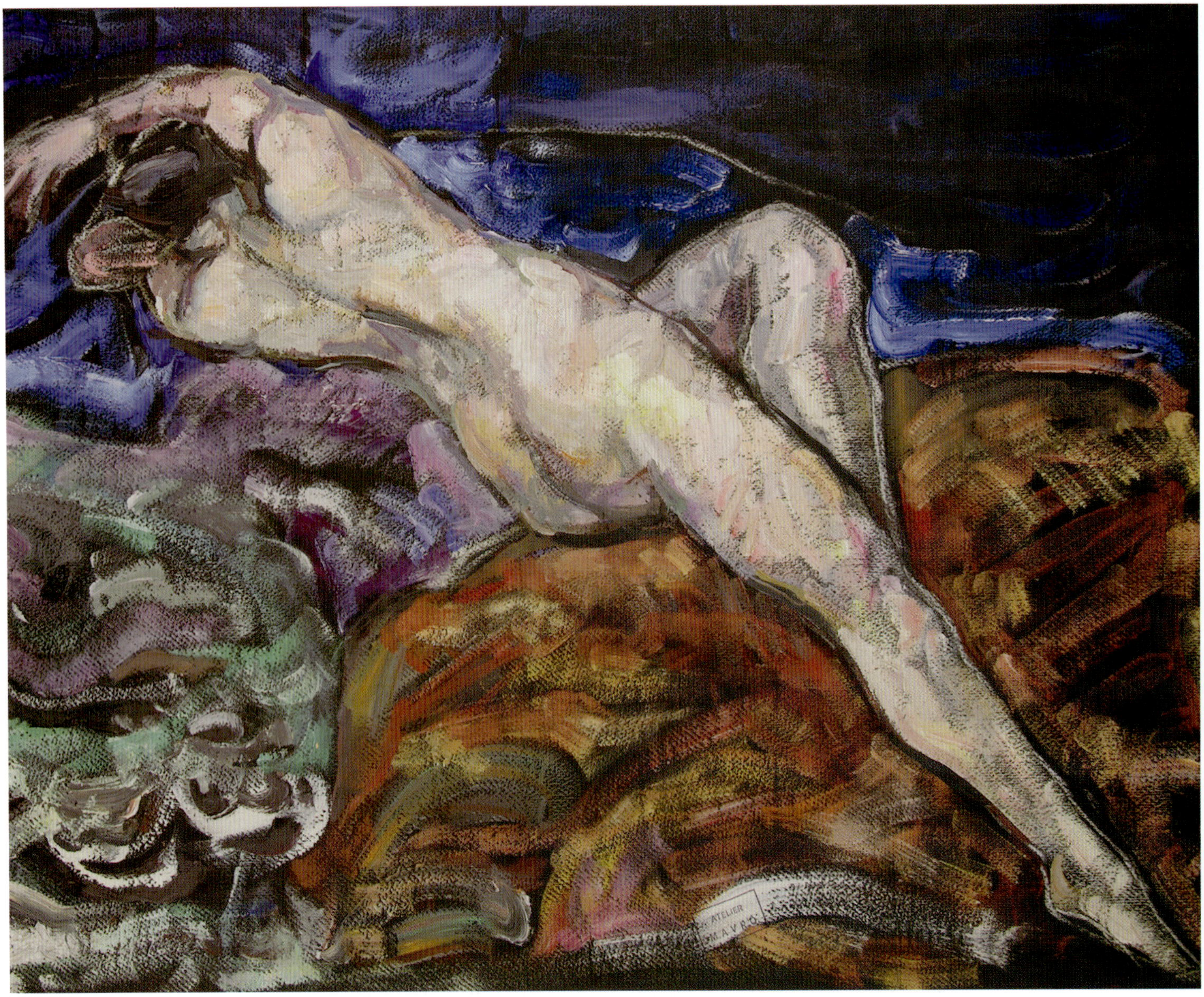

Mania Mavro
Nu Allongé, c.1930
The Parrish Collection, San Francisco, California

Mayo
1905-1990

Mayo was born Antoine Malliarakis in 1905, in Port Saïd, Egypt. His father was Greek and his mother was French. He moved to Paris in 1924 and met Man Ray, Desnos, Tzara and Salmon in Montparnasse. In 1927, René Crevel introduced him to André Breton, a leader of Surrealism, but Mayo had no interest in participating in a collaborative movement. Two years later, Mayo exhibited with Chirico at the Galerie des Quatre Chemins.

During the 1934 economic crisis in France, Mayo returned to Egypt where he continued to work though he eventually moved back to France. Mayo spent the six years of the French occupation in Cannes with Prévert where he designed theatre costumes among other work. At the end of the war, Mayo continued to develop his oeuvre, painting expressionistic works of realistic images as well as still lifes and images of fishes and bottles. Mayo traveled extensively in Greece and Spain where he discovered luminescent, iridescent colors and the importance of light.

In 1966, Mayo moved his soon-to-be demolished Paris studio to Rome at Via Magutta. Following this move, Mayo began a new body of work of historic ruins from antiquity, which is known as his *Période Romaine*. In 1983 the Centre Cultural Français de Rome exhibited a retrospective of Mayo's work, including the recent images of historic ruins. In 1985 Mayo returned to France. He received the Grade de Commandeur de L'Ordre des Arts et des Lettres. Mayo died in 1990 on his houseboat at Seine Port.

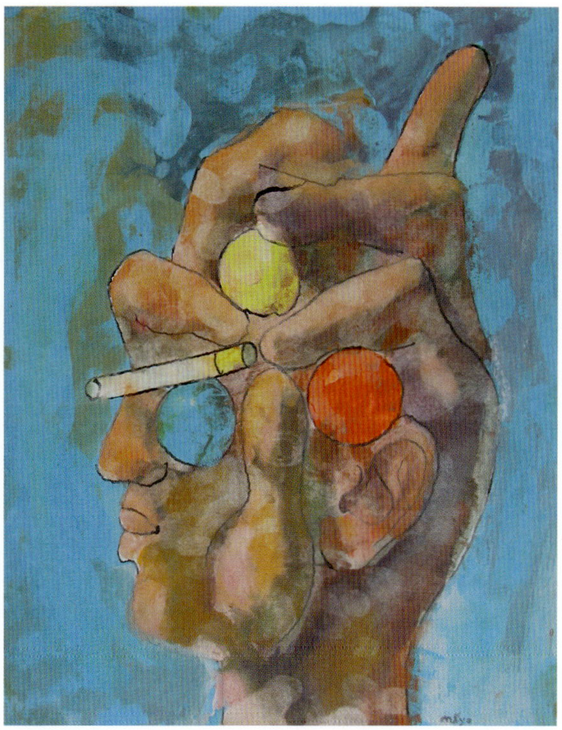

Mayo
La Tête, c.1950
Gary Berkowitz, West Hollywood, California

Mayo
Deux Nus, Dated 1929
Gary Berkowitz, West Hollywood, California

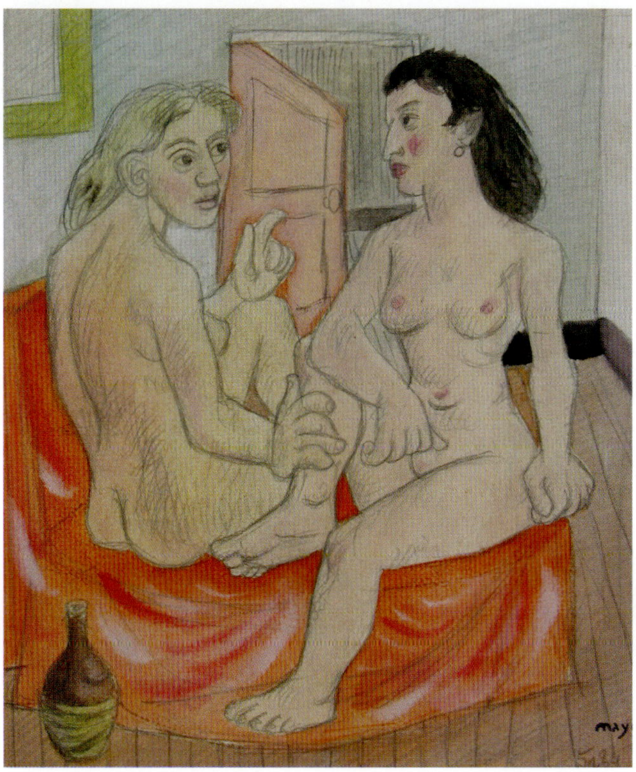

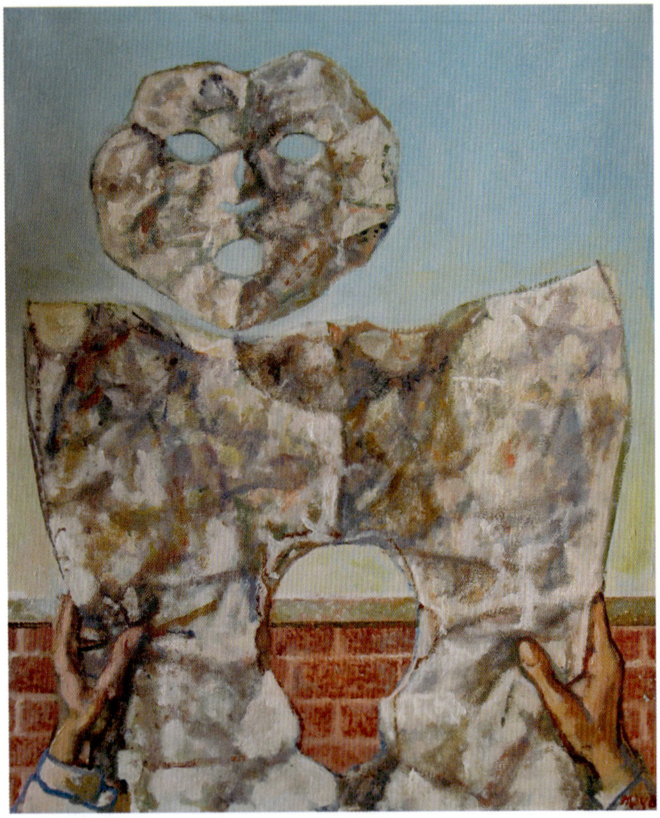

Mayo
Figure Surrealiste, c. 1950
Barry Friedman Ltd., New York, New York

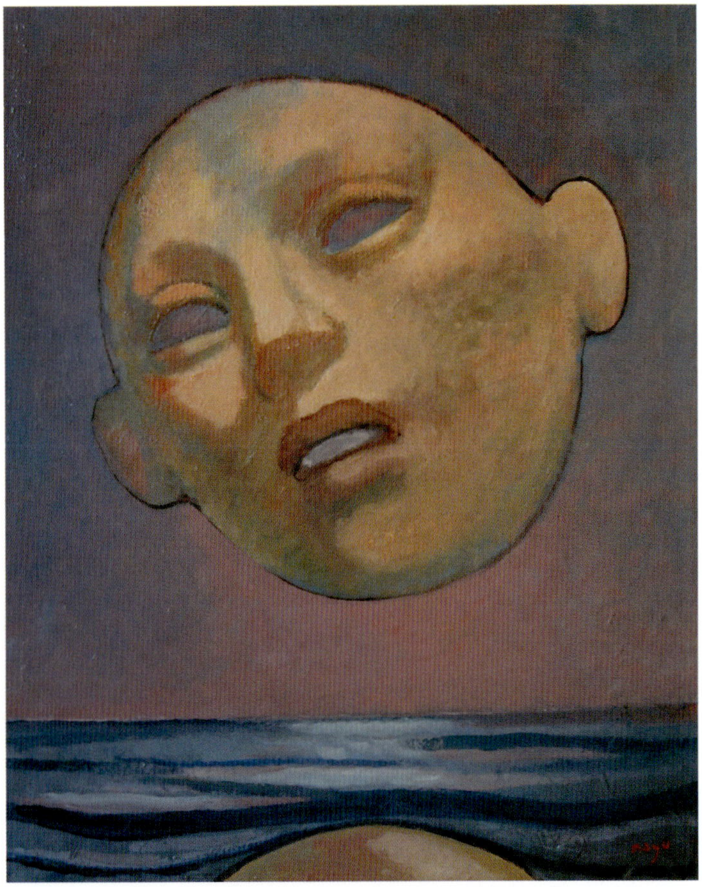

Mayo
Visage Surrealiste, c. 1950
Barry Friedman Ltd., New York, New York

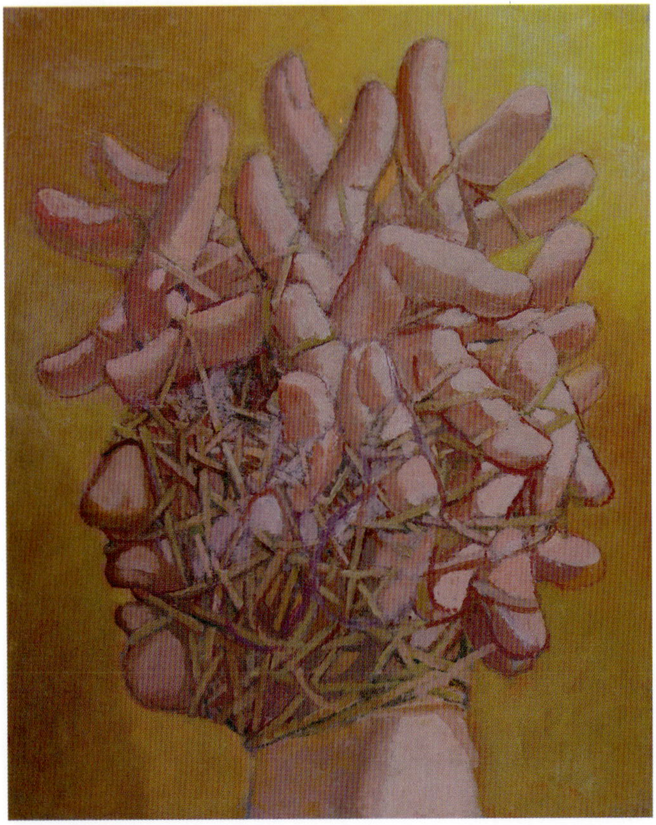

Mayo
Tête des Mains, c.1960
Gary Berkowitz, West Hollywood, California

Marie August Émile René Ménard

1862–1930

Marie August Émile René Ménard was born in Paris, on April 15, 1862. He was the son of René Joseph Ménard and the nephew of Louis Ménard. He was known as René Ménard. He is noted for his character compositions, mythological subjects, portraits and landscapes.

Ménard's landscapes illustrate his superb workmanship and understanding of composition. He worked in pastels with a typically warm palate. Ménard's style is considered symbolist and neo-classical.

Ménard debuted in the art world in the 1883 Paris Salon des Artistes Français. He also showed in the Société Nationale des Beaux-Arts. Ménard participated in a group called the *Bande Noir*, which focused around the artist Cottet. He received a Médaille de Troisème Classe in 1889, the Chevalier de la Légion d'Honneur in 1900 and Officer de la Légion d'Honneur in 1910. He also was a member of l'Institute. Ménard's works can be found in museums in Anvers, Brussels, Helsinki, Luxemburg, Munich and Stockholm. He died in 1930.

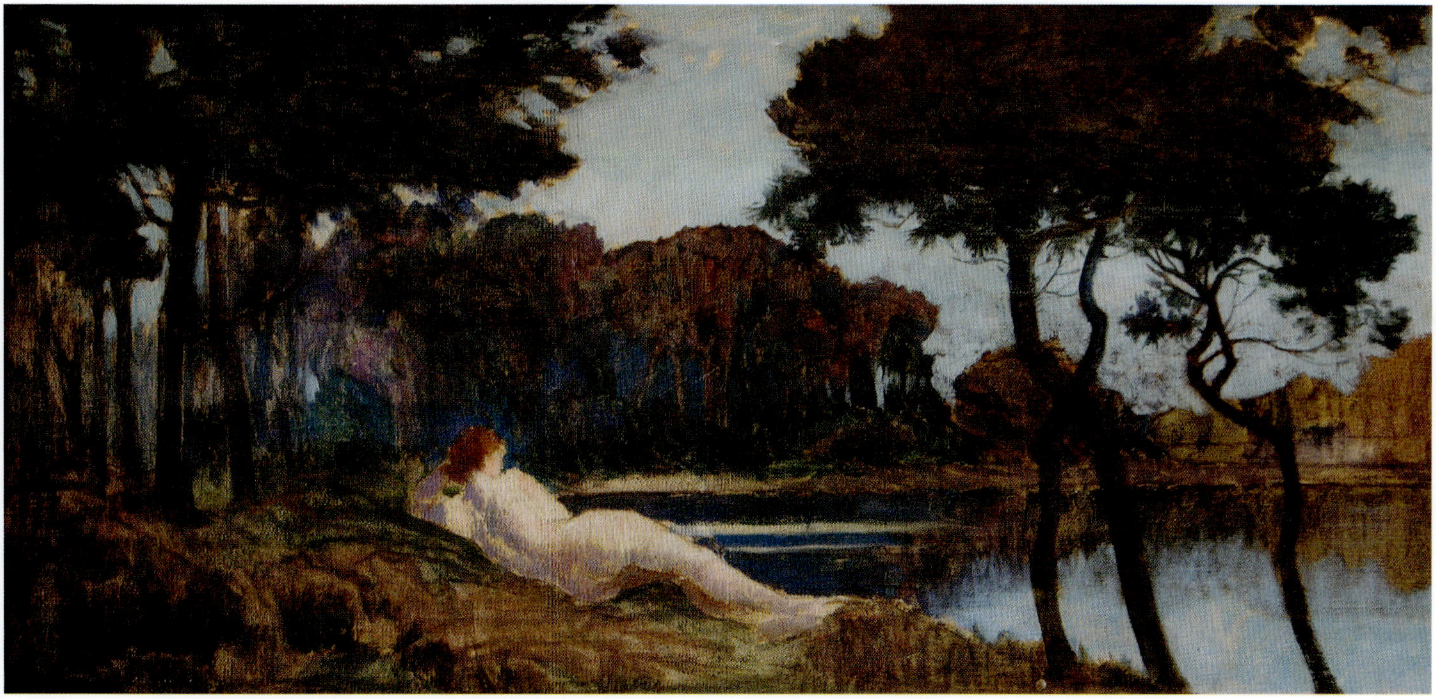

Marie August Émile René Ménard
Nu au Bord de Lac, c.1900
Bill and Jo LaMond, Los Angeles, California

Maurice Jean Micha

1890-1969

Maurice Jean Micha was born in Spa, Belgium in 1890. He painted genre and urban scenes, figures, portraits, landscapes, still lifes and frescoes. Micha studied at l'Académie de Bruxelles and traveled to Italy to see the great masterpieces of art and architecture.

Initially, Fauvism influenced Micha's style but as his work matured his pallet became more somber. Micha's boldest paintings are typical of the Belgian Expressionists, including cubist elements and brush strokes that create angular movement. He created a fresco for the Belgian pavilion at the 1939 New York World's Fair and the Musée d'Ixelles has collected Micha's work. He died in 1969.

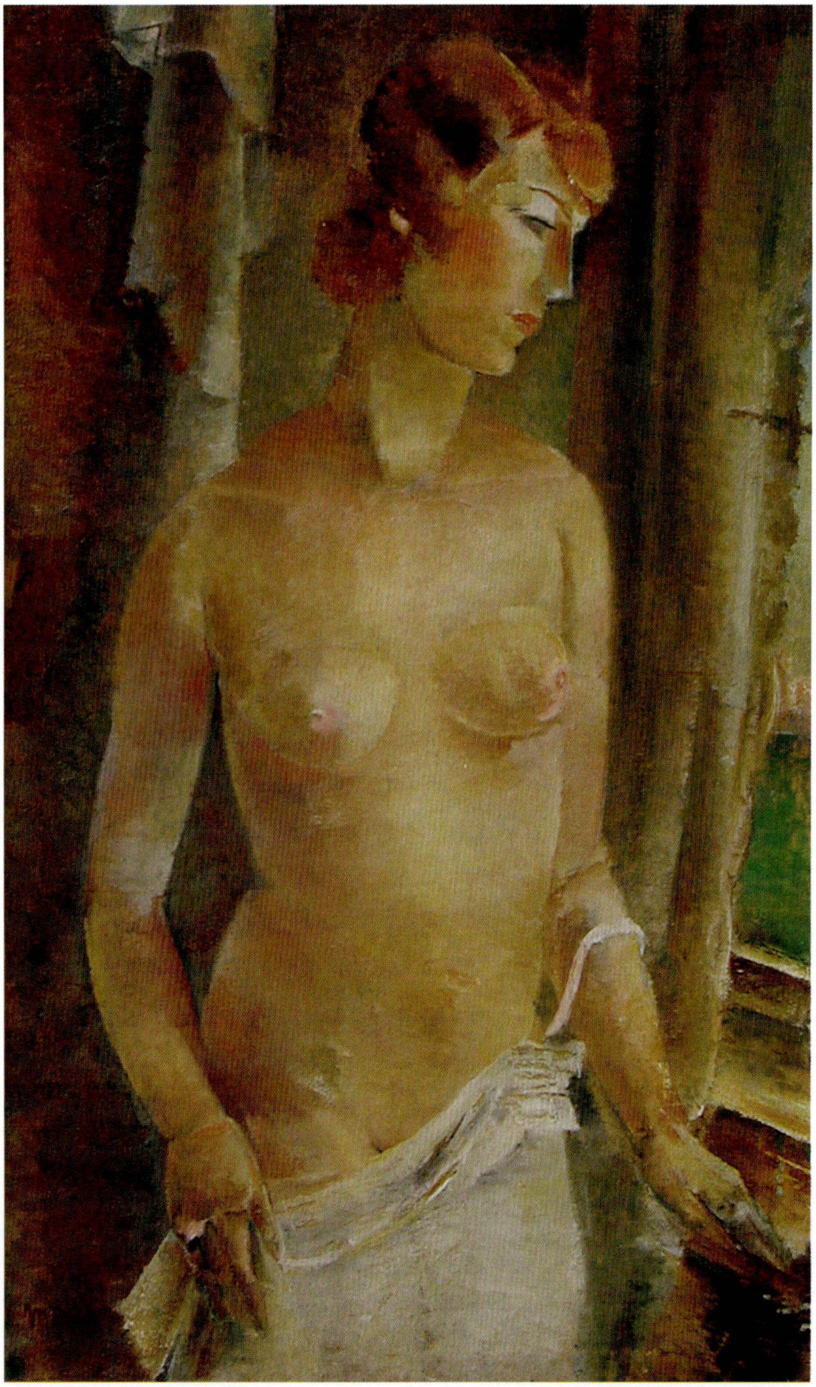

Maurice Jean Micha
Femme á la Fenêtre, c.1930
Private Collection

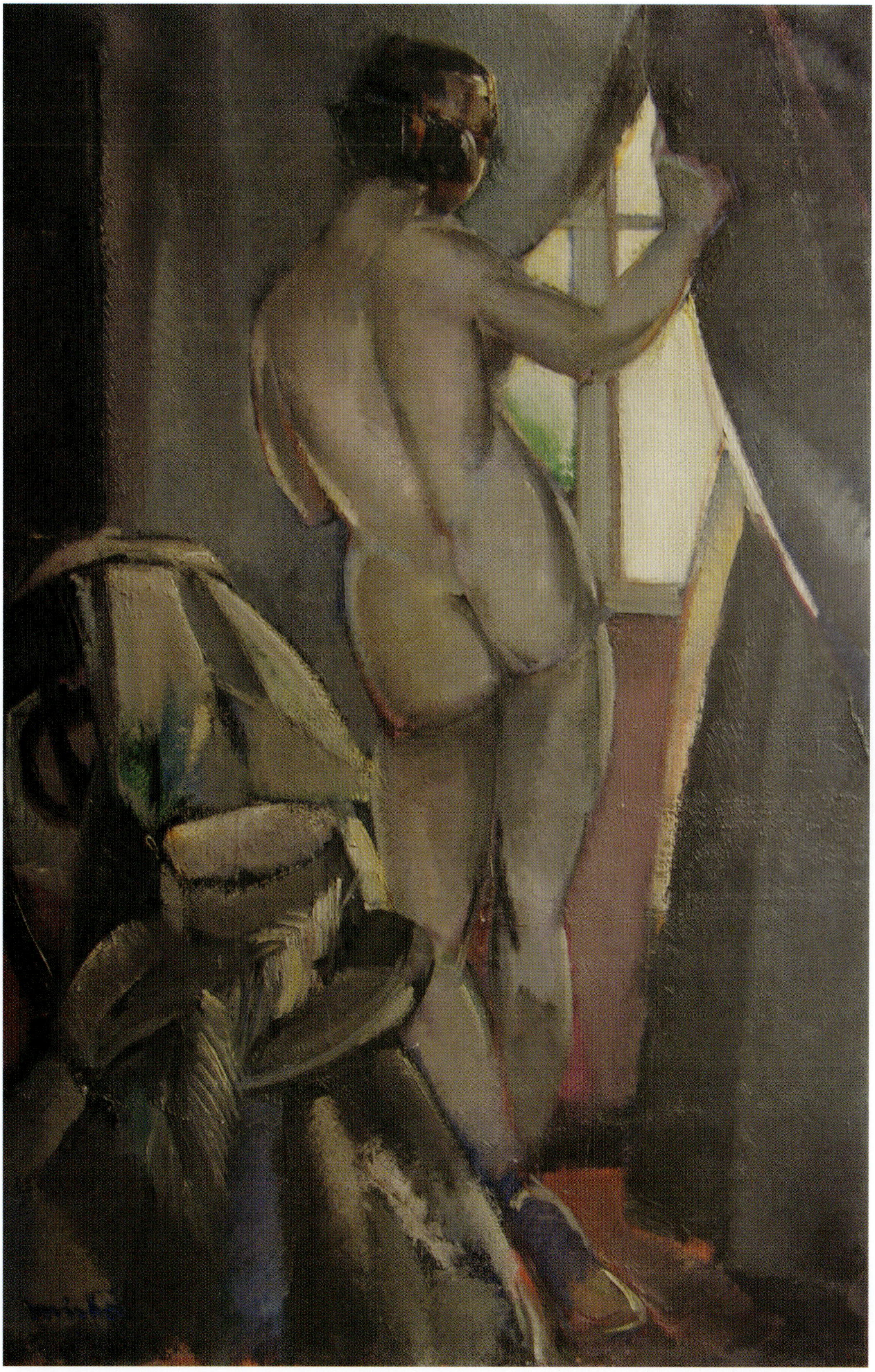

Maurice Jean Micha
Avant le Bal, c.1925
Gary Bleiberg, New York, New York

Maurice Millière
1871-1946

Maurice Millière was born December 12, 1871. He was a student of Bonnat at l'École des Beaux-Arts and l'École des Art Decoratifs and became known for his drawings of nudes. He collaborated with the publications *La Vie Parisienne* and *Fantasio,* and illustrated works for Gyp and Maurice Vaucaire. Millière exhibited at the Salon des Humoristes and the Salon des Artistes Français. He received the Médaille d'Or at the Exposition Coloniale in 1931 and the Chevalier de la Légion d'Honneur.

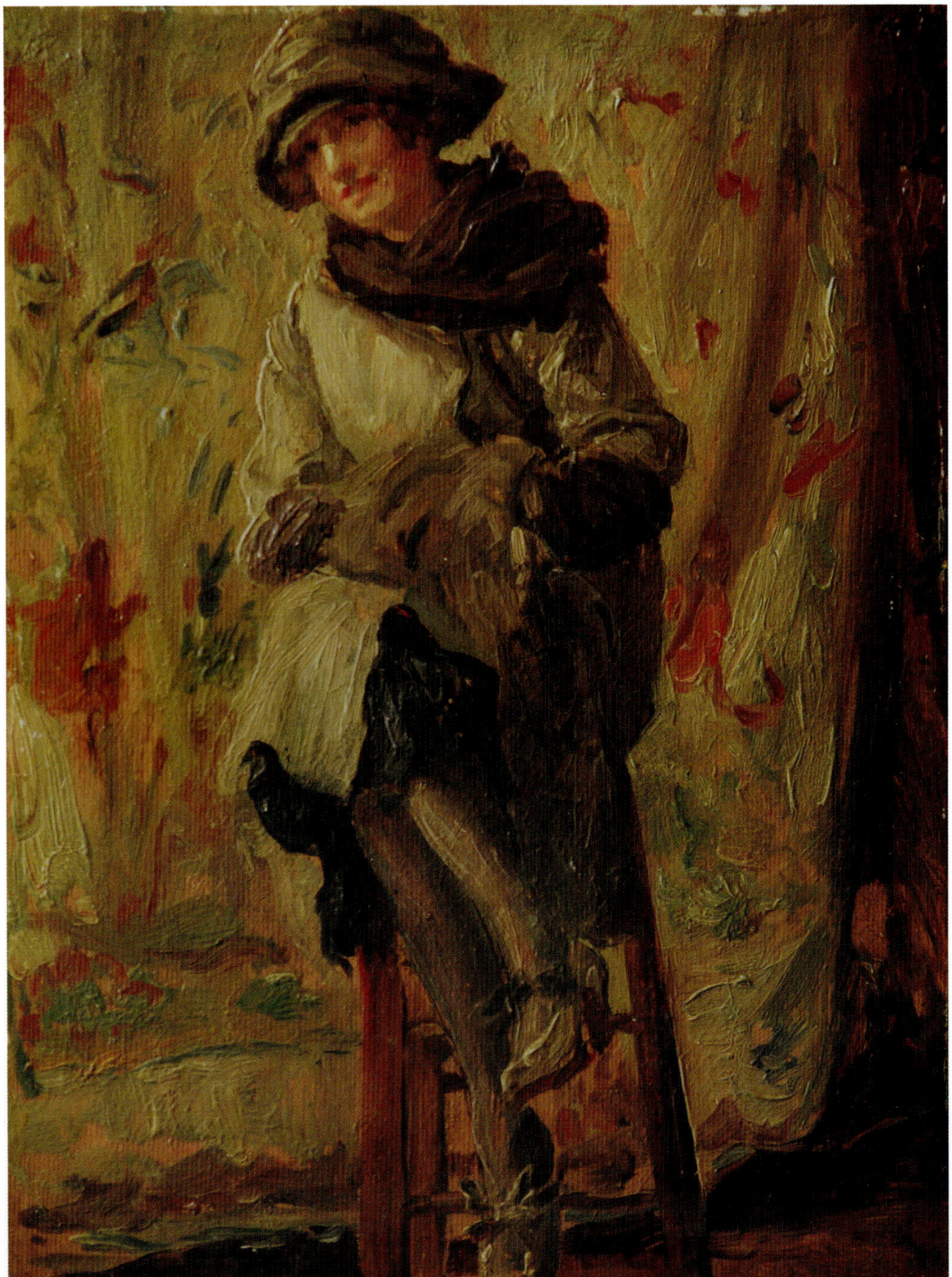

Maurice Millière
Femme Assis, c.1910
Private Collection

Alfred Moitroux

1886-1938

Alfred Moitroux was born in 1886 in Binche, Hainaut, Belgium. He studied at l'Académie des Beaux-Arts de Mons and Bruxelles. Moitroux's work is characteristic of 20th century Belgian painting. His use of color gives the impression that light is coming through the painting itself, complimenting the brush technique and application of the paint. He is best known for his figures, portraits, and landscapes and also worked as a watercolorist and engraver. Moitroux died in 1938.

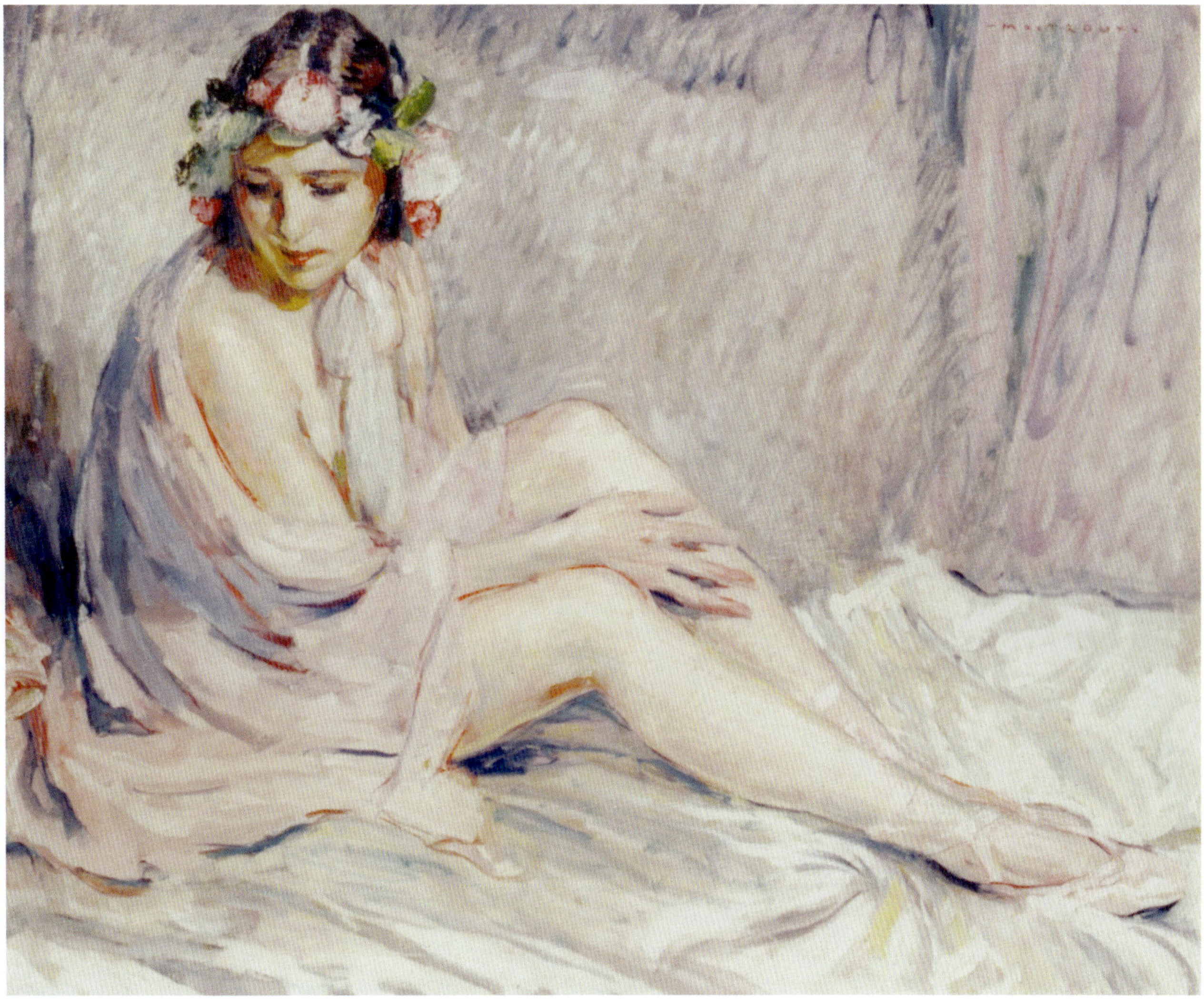

Alfred Moitroux
Jeune Femme en Blanche, c.1920
Los Angeles Fine Art Gallery, Los Angeles, California

Émile-Pierre de la Montagne
1873-1956

Émile-Pierre de la Montagne was born in 1873 in Antwerp, Belgium. He studied painting at l'Académie d'Anvers, de Malines and at l'Académie de Bruxelles. He attended the workshops of J. Callot in Paris, where he studied as a portraitist.

De la Montagne lived for five years in England and exhibited throughout Europe and the United States. He is best known for his drawings, murals and sculptures. De la Montagne died in 1956 in Brussels.

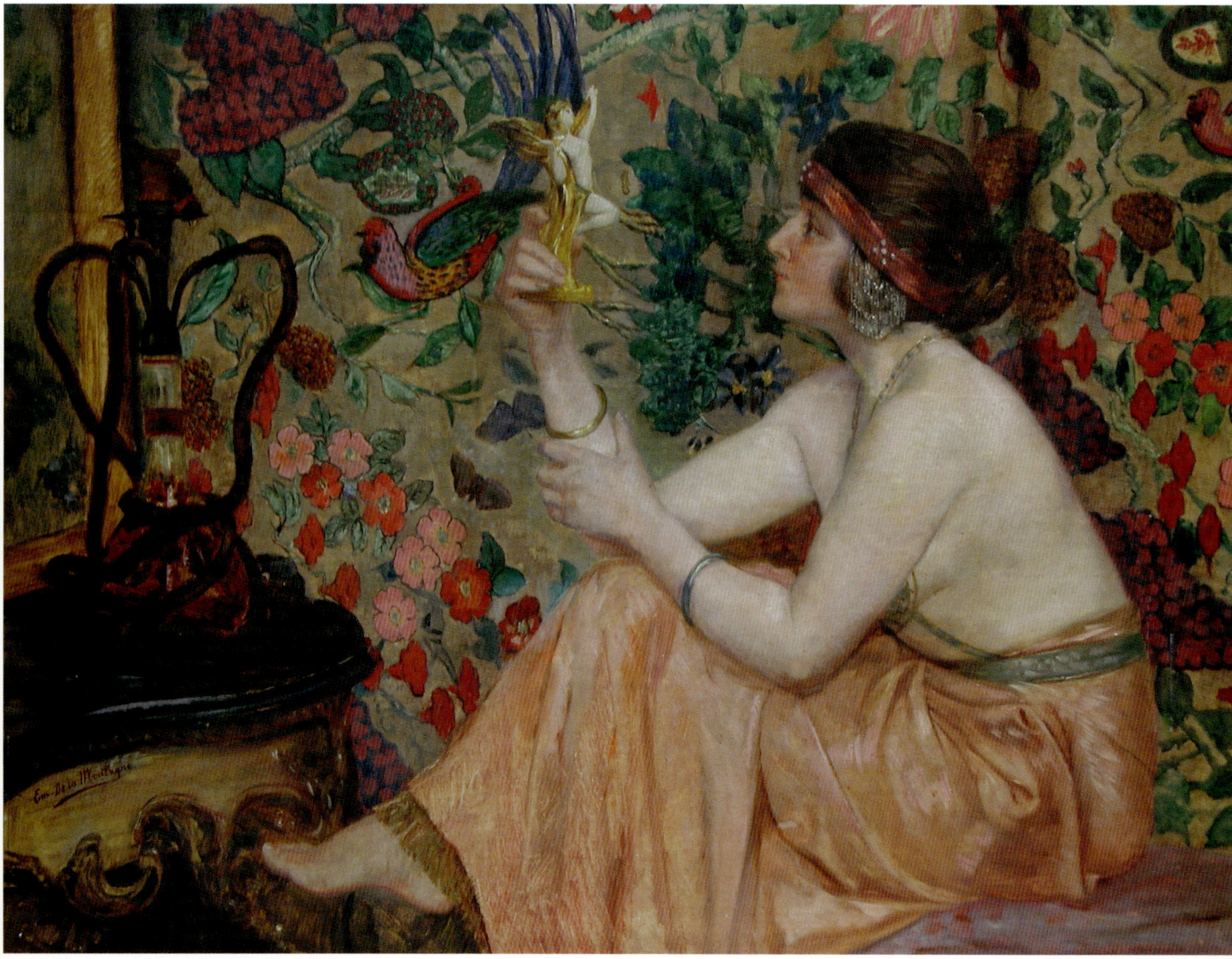

Émile-Pierre de la Montagne
La Danseuse a l´Étude, c.1910
Ron and Barbara Sickmen, New York, New York

Max Moreau
1902-1992

Max Moreau received much of his artistic education from his father Henry Moreau. At the Musée Royal des Beaux-Arts in Brussels Moreau studied under Hals and Vélasquez before traveling in Tunisia where he drew much of his inspiration. Moreau lived in France during World War II and in 1947 left for Marrakech where he spent three years. Moreau returned to reside in France in 1950 though he continued to travel extensively through the Bahamas, United States, Spain and Portugal.

In 1965 Moreau settled in Granada with his wife where he spent time writing poetry, theater pieces and composing music.

Moreau's early works exhibit an exuberance that embraced the atmosphere of the 1920s. He however became best known for his celebrity portraits of Jules Romains, Bernanos, Paul Robert, Michel Simon and Anthony Quinn in addition to many others. He exhibited his portraits, figures and still lifes in Tunisia, Algiers, Casablanca, Brussels, Arlon, Charleroi, Anvers and Luxemburg. There is now a Max Moreau Museum in Granada and his works can be viewed in museums in Luxemburg, Nimes, Tournai and Tunis. He died in 1992.

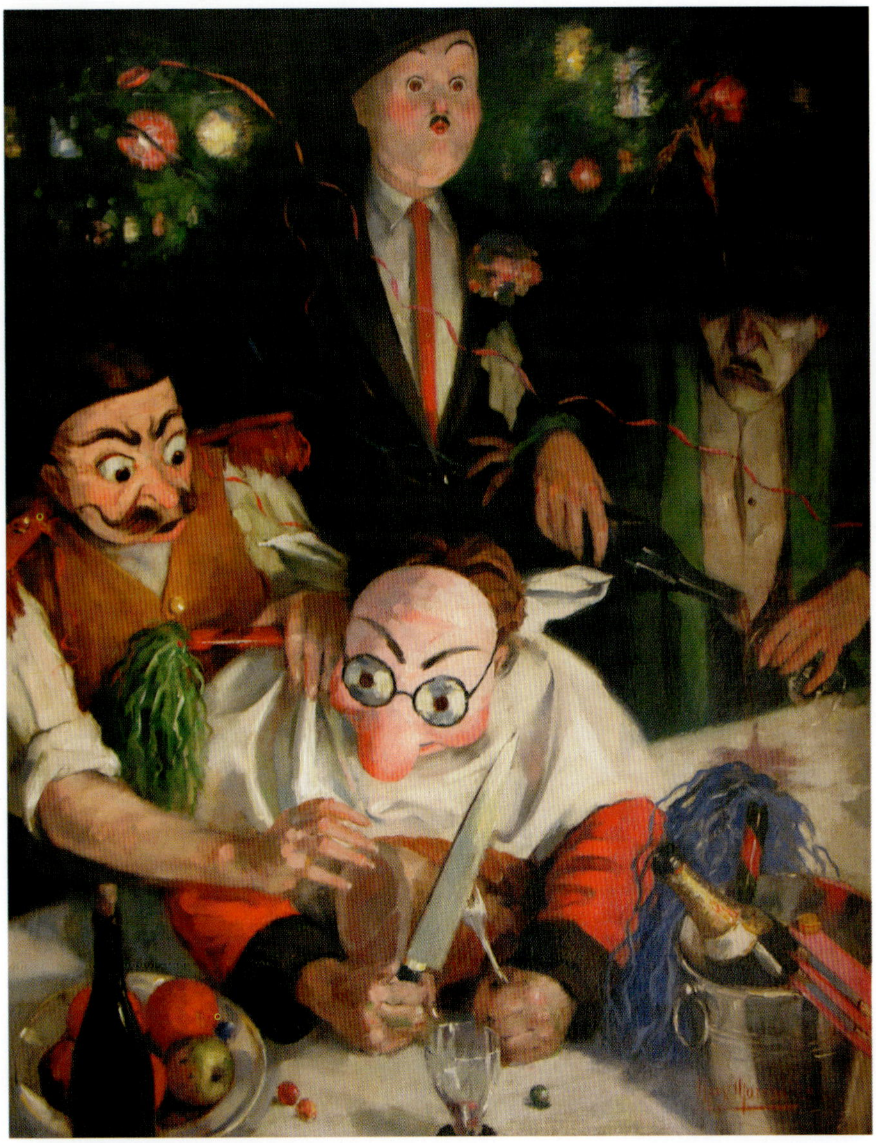

Max Moreau
Les Cavaliers de L'Apocalypse, Dated 1928
Andrew Herrera II, San Francisco, California

Adrien Moreau-Neret

1860-1940

Adrien Moreau-Neret was born on November 13, 1860 in Paris. He was a student of Luc-Olivier Merson, Léon Galland and Albert Maignan. Moreau-Neret exhibited frequently as a member of the Salon des Artistes Français.

Moreau-Neret received many medals and awards, among them an Honorable Mention in 1894, Médaille de Troisiéme Classe in 1899, Médaille de Bronze in 1900 at l'Exposition Universelle de Paris and the Médaille de Deuxième Classe in 1903.

Public decorative works include le Crillon, le Palais d'Orsay, l'Hôtel du Louvre, l'Université de la Sorbonne and Le Marais du Xe arrondissement.

Moreau-Neret was a Symbolist and his subjects were popular with the avant-garde around the turn of the 20th century. In his work nymphs and fairies play in idealized settings tempting the imagination of the viewer. Adrien Moreau-Neret died in 1940.

Adrien Moreau-Neret
Nymphes Symbolistes, c.1900
Rudy and Alice Cicatelli, Encino, California

Mela Muter

1876-1967

Mela Muter was born in Warsaw, Poland in 1876. She studied for a year at the School of Painting and Drawing for Women under Milosz Kotarbinski. In 1901 Muter left Poland for Paris. She studied sporadically at l'Académie Colarossi and l'Académie de la Grand Chaumière. She exhibited at the annual Paris salons and also in group shows throughout Poland. Muter was granted her first solo exhibition in 1912 at the Dalmau Gallery in Barcelona and received membership to the Société Nationale des Beaux-Arts the same year. Other solo exhibitions include the Galerie Cheron, Galerie Druet and the Société pour l'Encouragement des Beaux-Arts Zacheta in Warsaw in 1923.

French citizenship was granted to Muter in 1927. She remained closely associated with Polish born artists living in Paris at the time and was greatly influence by her travels in Spain and Britain. She was married to Michal Mutermilch, a Parisian correspondent for the Polish press, until 1922.

Muter continued to exhibit in Paris, Munich and Pittsburg. She became well acquainted with her contemporaries and was greatly influenced by Leopold Gottlieb, Gauguin, Cézanne, Vuillard, van Gogh and Dufy. She drew inspiration form the Pont-Aven school as well. She often used fauvist color combined with impeccable brushwork and was able to create a singular beauty in her paintings.

Her work was praised by Mieczyslaw and André Salmon, and in 1953 a retrospective of 120 works was held in Paris. Muter died in 1967. In 1994 a large exhibition of her work from the Boleslaw and Lina Nawrocki Collection was held by the Warsaw National Museum.

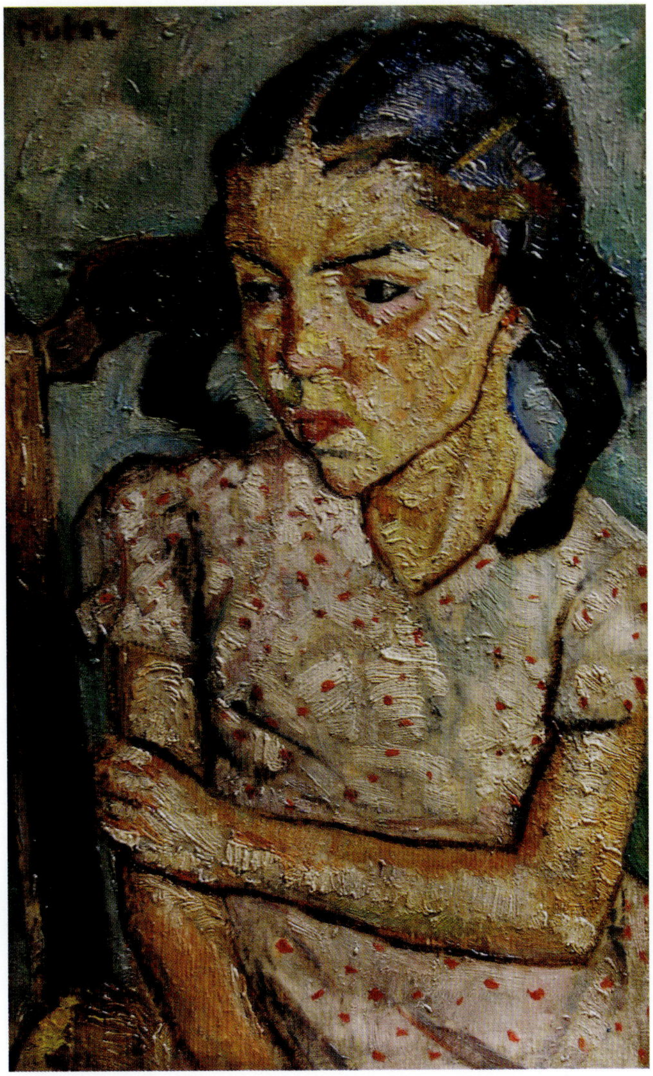

Mela Muter
Petite Fille Assis, c.1920
Galerie des Modernes, Paris, France

Charles Naillod

Born 1876

Charles Naillod was born on June 6, 1876 in Paris. He is known for his portraits, nudes and paintings of sailors. Naillod participated in many Parisian Salons including the Salon des Indépendants beginning in 1906. He also exhibited in the Salon des Artistes Français and in 1920 became the secretary of the organization.

Naillod was primarily a painter, but he also produced many fine aquatint etchings in the fashion of Louis Icart. His paintings can be compared to the neoclassical style of Jean Dupas.

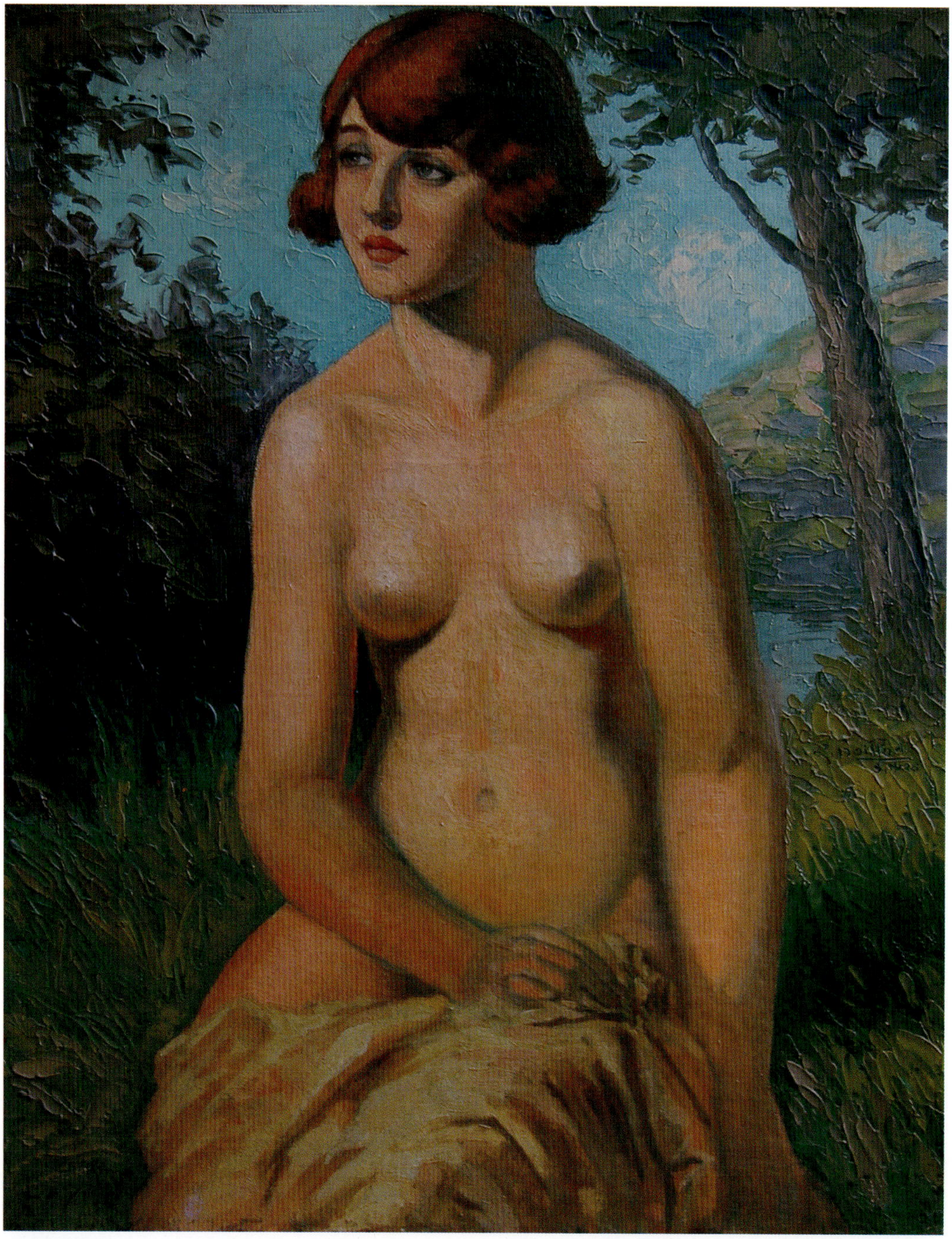

Charles Naillod
Nu au Bord du Lac, Dated 1925
Papillon Gallery, Los Angeles, California

Warren A. Newcombe

1894-1960

Warren A. Newcombe was born in Waltham, Massachusetts in 1894. He studied, worked and exhibited as a painter and set designer in the United States, though a substantial Parisian influence is evident throughout his work.

Newcombe studied under Joseph de Camp at the Boston Normal Art School in 1914. He went on to teach drawing in Massachusetts before moving to New York in 1918, where he supported himself as a commercial artist and portraitist.

Cinema and set design became an alluring career path as Newcombe joined Selznick Co. in 1920. Shortly after, he built his own special effects production company and in 1923 produced *The Enchanted City* and *The Sea of Dreams*, both drawing high acclaim.

In 1924 and 1925 Newcombe worked for D.W. Griffith, designing sets and developing advanced mechanics for filming difficult shots and scenes. In 1925 he moved to California where he became the head of the special effects department for MGM Studios and developed the widely used "Newcombe Process."

Newcombe is also credited for having designed brilliant sets, such as the Emerald City in *The Wizard of Oz,* and was awarded two Academy Awards for his work in special effects.

In the fine arts world, Newcombe continued to paint and exhibit regularly in Los Angeles and Carmel, where he received two solo shows. He exhibited with the Society of Independent Artists and in galleries and museums in California, Texas, New York and Colorado. Newcombe contributed as well to various national art magazines and newspapers in the United States. The artist died 1960 in Taxco, Mexico.

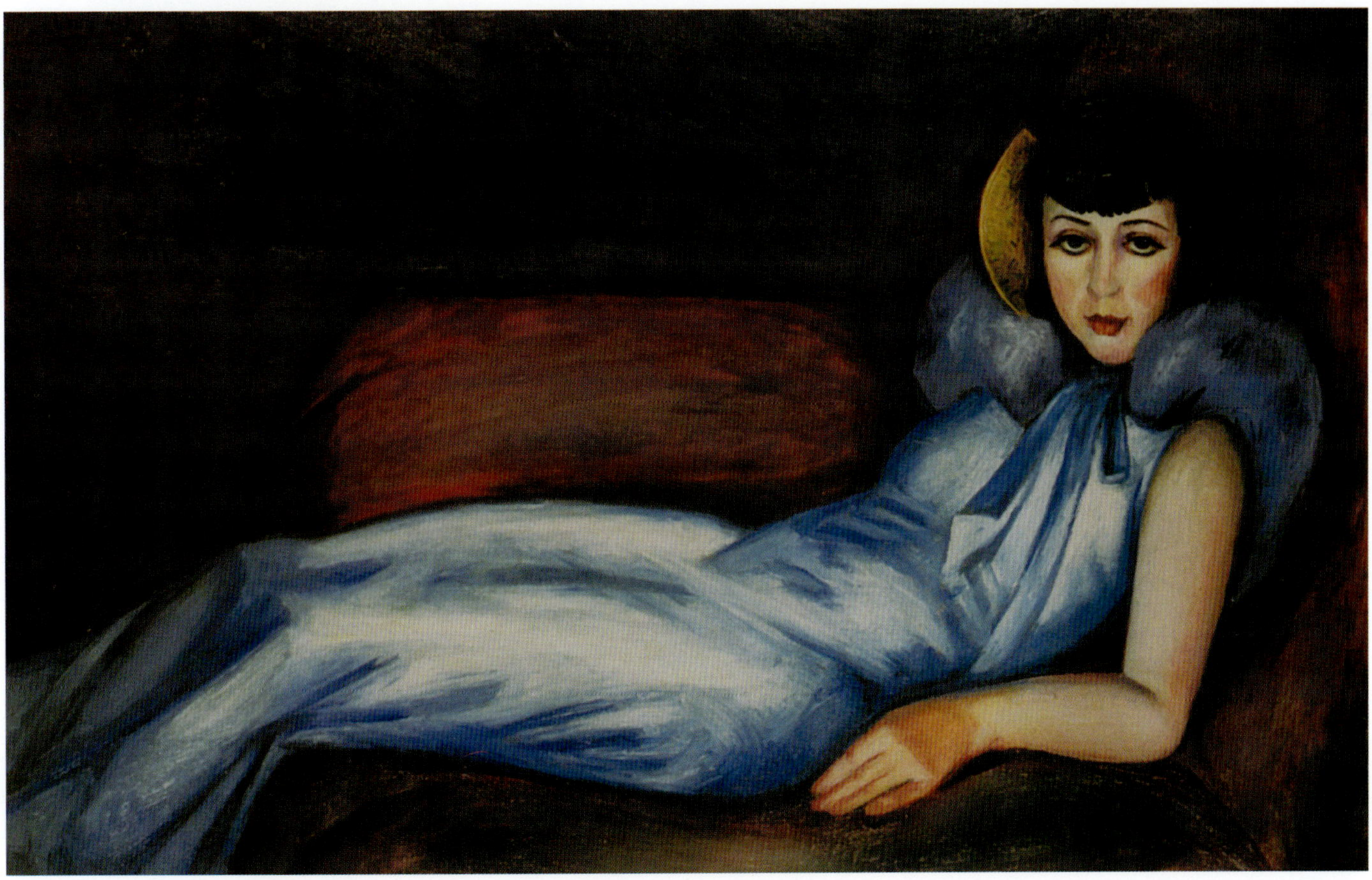

Warren Newcombe
Hazel in Blue, Dated 1932
Ron and Barbara Sickmen, New York, New York

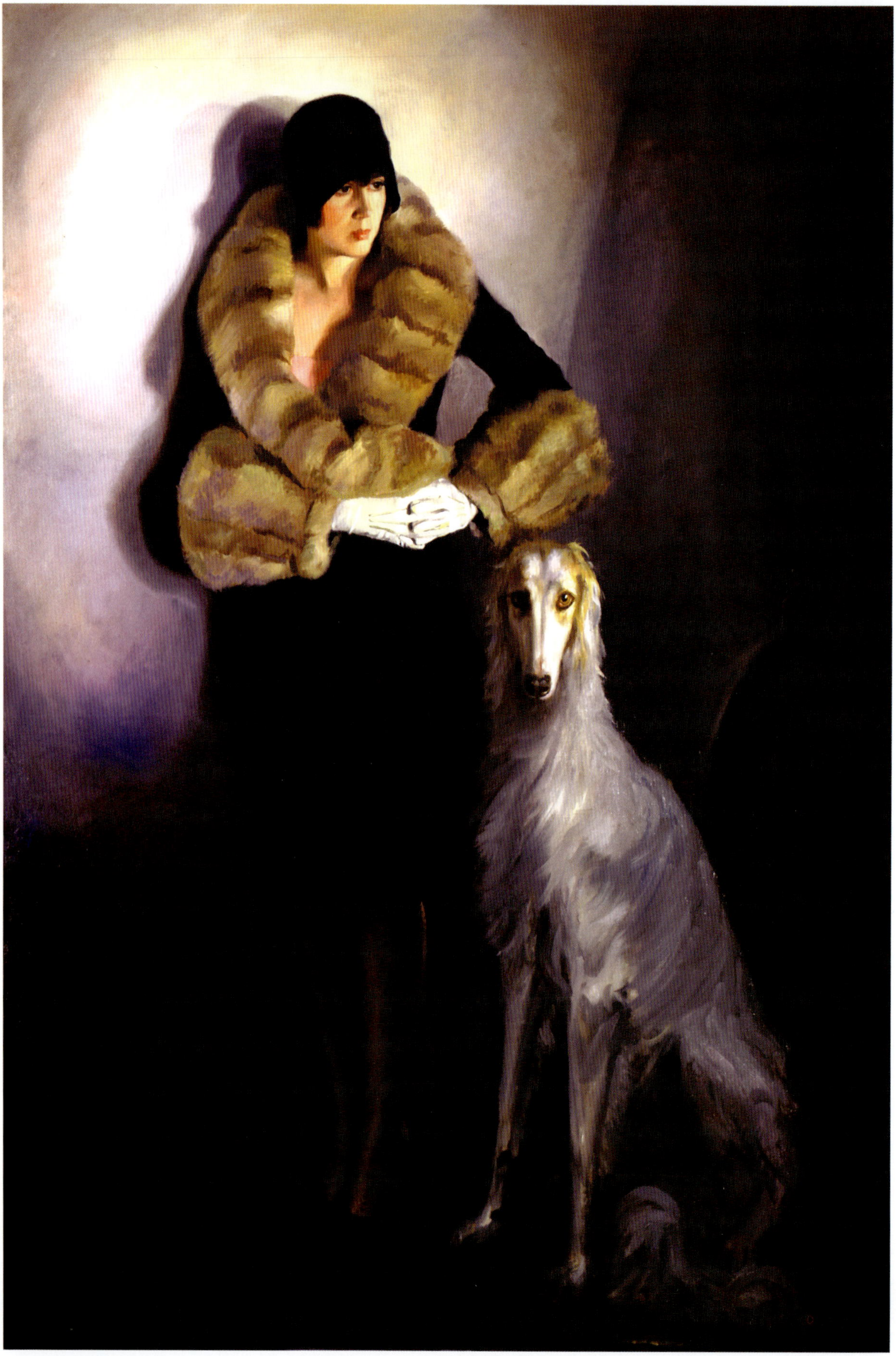

Warren Newcombe
Hazel and Big Boy, c.1928
Adamson-Duvannes Gallery, Los Angeles, California

Robert (Salmon Ernest) Noir

1864-1931

Robert Noir was born in 1864 in Paris, and was known also by the pseudonym Salmon Ernest. Noir was the nephew of journalist Victor Noir, who was killed by Prince Pierre Bonaparte in 1870. Robert Noir worked in Paris as a painter; his first works were signed Ernest Noir and after 1912, Robert Noir. Influences were derived from friendships with Étienne de Martenne and sculptor Louis de Monard. In Paris, he exhibited at the Salon des Artistes-Français, Salon des Humoristes and the Société Nationale des Beaux-Arts. Noir received an honorable mention from the Salon des Artistes Français in 1903. In 1918 Noir Also exhibited at the Devambez Gallery in Paris.

Retrospectives of his work have been hosted by the Société Nationale des Beaux-Arts in 1981 and by the Musée de Vernon in 1984.Noir's works are moody and often fairly bizarre. He used somber colors and haunting characters to draw the viewer into his world.

Museums that have collected his work include the Bois-le-Rois, Musée du Petit Palais, Paris and Musée Poulain, Vernon. Robert Noir committed suicide in 1931 after suffering from an incurable disease.

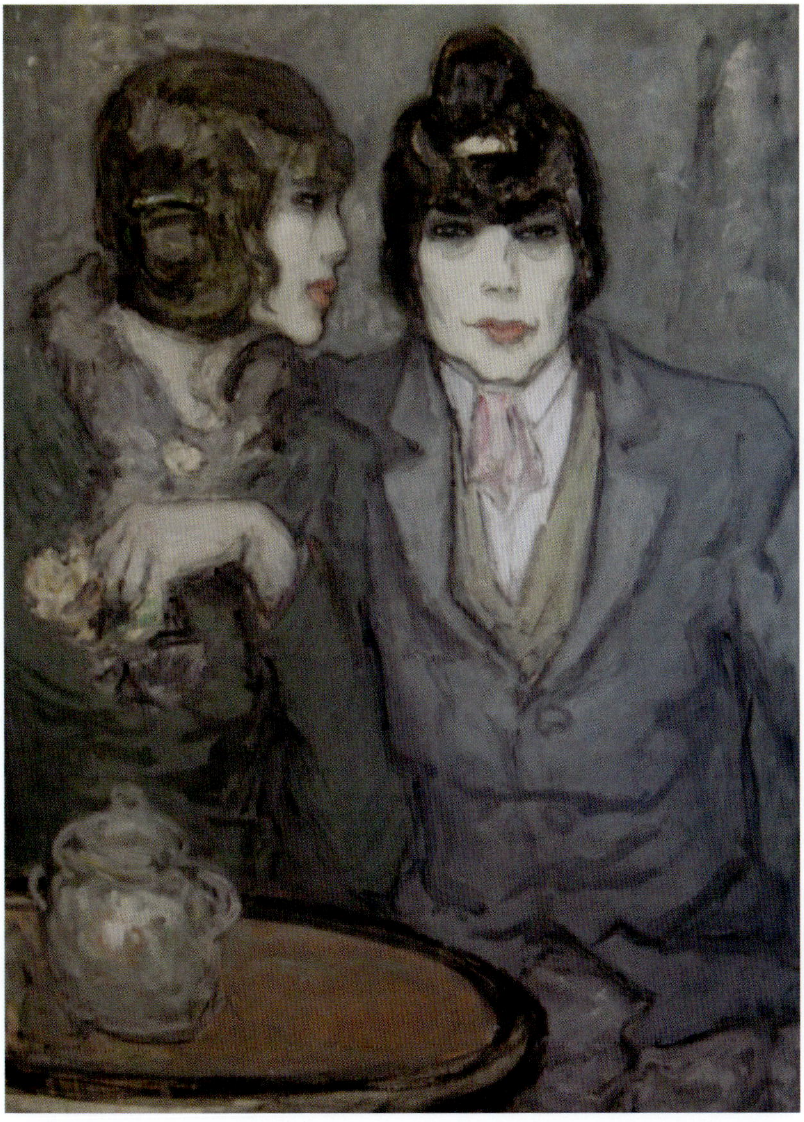

Robert Noir
Les Deux Amis, c.1925
Christine Thorailler, Paris, France

Carl (Charles) Nys
Born 1858

Carl Nys was born in Antwerp, Belgium, in 1858. In Paris he was a student of J. Gérôme and William Bouguereau. He exhibited among the Salons in Paris and Anvers. Nys received an honorable mention in 1888. The date of his death is unknown.

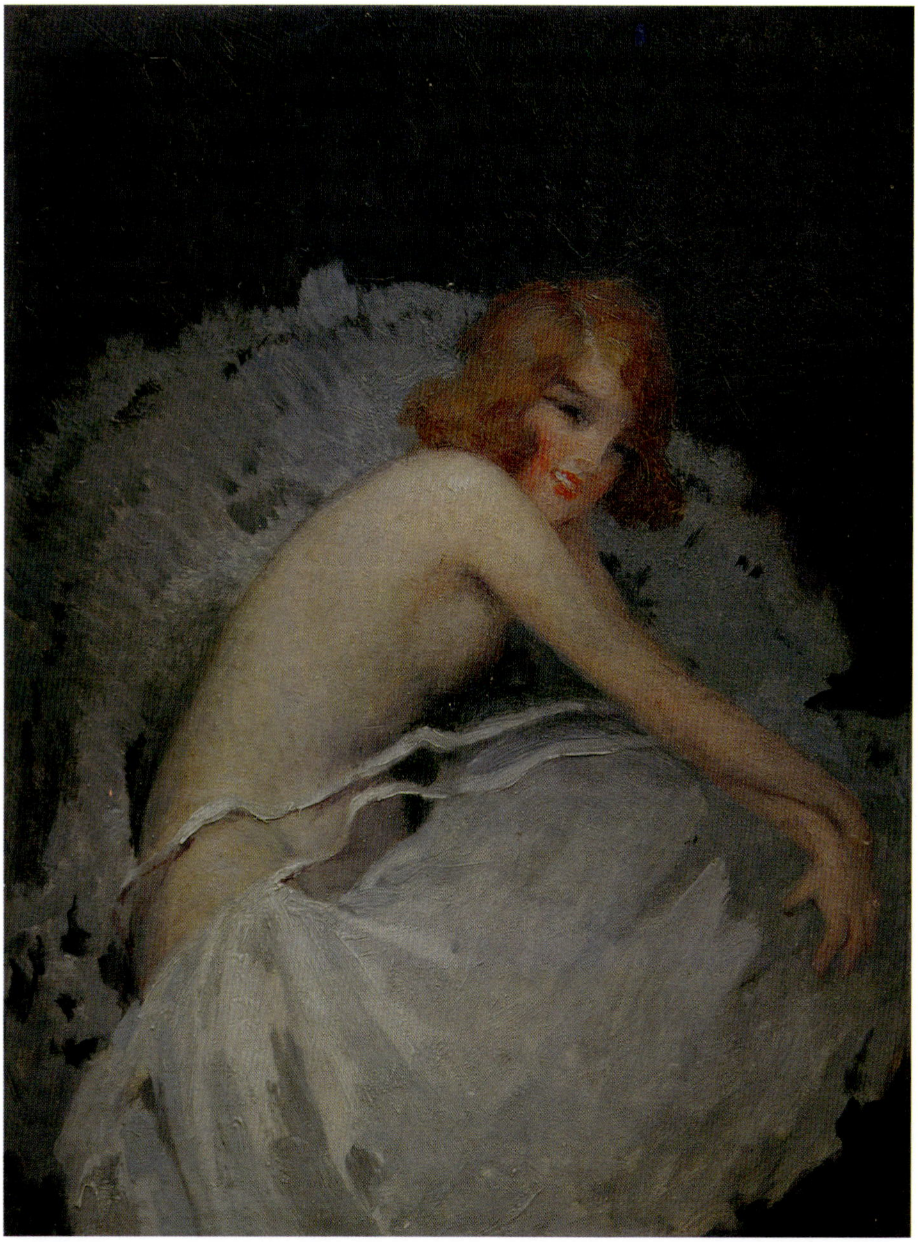

Carl (Charles) Nys
Petite Danseuse, c. 1920
Tracey Jacobs, Los Angeles, California

Jean Oberlé

1900-1961

Jean Oberlé was born on January 12, 1900, in Brest, Finistère. Oberlé is known for his paintings, drawings and illustrations. He worked for a long time drawing images for major Parisian newspapers and magazines. Oberlé illustrated the books of contemporary writers including Colette, Cendrars, Anatole France, Courteline, Carco and Galtier-Boissère, among many others.

In 1934, Oberlé received the Blumenthal prize. During World War II, Oberlé worked for France Libre à Radio in London. He worked as a theater set decorator, most notably *L'Île des Esclaves de Marivaux* and *Tartuffe* by Molière. In 1956 Oberlé published his memoirs *La Vie d'artiste*.

Oberlé exhibited regularly in well established Parisian galleries. His work is included in the permanent collection of the Musée Nationale d'Art Moderne. Oberlé died on March 2, 1961, in Paris.

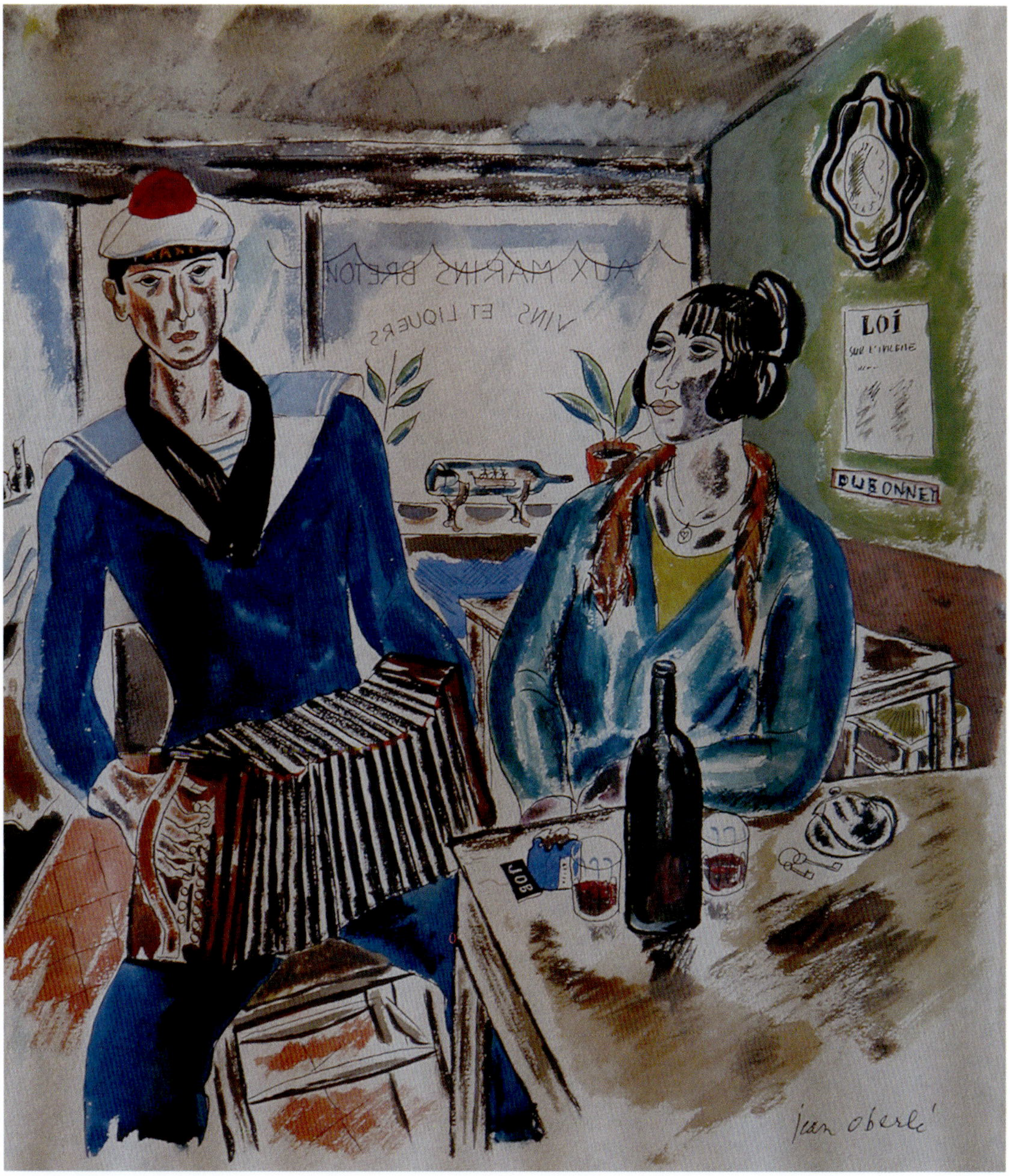

Jean Oberlé
Le Marin au Bar, c.1925
Lara Lowan, New York, New York

Otis Oldfield
1890 - 1969

Otis Oldfield was born in Sacramento, California, and worked primarily in oils, watercolors, lithographs, etchings and as a muralist. In 1906 he apprenticed in a local print shop before traveling through Nevada, Montana and Idaho, moving from job to job. In 1909 the artist enrolled in Best's Art School in San Francisco, and in 1911 left to study at l'Académie Julian in Paris.

During World War I Oldfield resided in Bouffemont, where he learned the art of bookbinding. He returned to Paris in 1919 and began exhibiting at the Salon d'Automne and Société des Artistes Indépendants.

In 1924 Oldfield returned to the United States where he taught a course at the California School of Fine Arts. Two solo exhibitions were granted at the Galerie Beaux-Arts for which he was awarded the Gold Medal for Graphic Arts by the San Francisco Art Association. Shortly after Oldfield became a full-time professor at the California School of Fine Art. He received two solo exhibitions at the Montross Gallery in New York in 1929 and 1930 which were followed by solo exhibitions at the Harriman, Lambertson-Brownell and Downt-Town galleries. Oldfield exhibited a group of watercolors at the Galerie Beaux-Arts in 1931 and in 1933 was included in the *Exhibition of American Art* at the Whitney Museum in New York.

In San Francisco he continued to gain recognition through WPA commissions, a solo exhibition at the San Francisco Museum of Art in 1936 and an exhibit at the Art Center. Other awards include the Governor Olsen Medal and the Anna Klumpe Portrait Award in addition to memberships with the California Guild of Book Binders, Artist's Council of the San Francisco Art Association and the Federation of Western Artists in Los Angeles. Oldfield died in 1969.

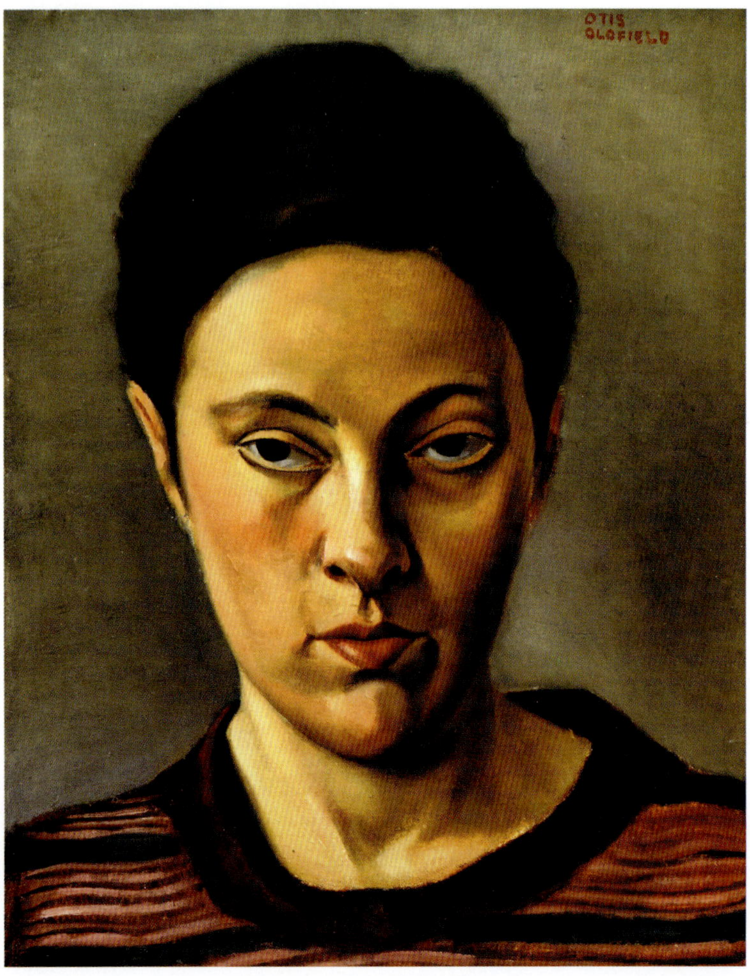

Otis Oldfield
Purple Sweater, Dated 1933
 Photo courtesy of Spencer Jon Helfen Fine Arts, Beverly Hills, California

Oldfield was best known in San Francisco for his depictions of Telegraph Hill, the Embarcadero and San Francisco Bay. Among his influences were Lucien About, Maynard Dixon, Ansel Adams, Edward Weston, Ralph Stackpole, Beniamino Bufano and Timothy Pfluger.

The artist's work can be found in the following collections: Achenbach Foundation of the California Palace of the Legion of Honor; the Brooklyn Museum of Art; W.L. Smith Memorial Gallery, Shasta State Park; Oakland Museum; M.H. deYoung Memorial Museum, Harrison Museum of Art, Utah State University; Cantor Arts Center, Stanford University and the National Museum of American Art, Washington D.C. Spencer Jon Helfen Fine Arts in Beverly Hills, California currently represents the artist.

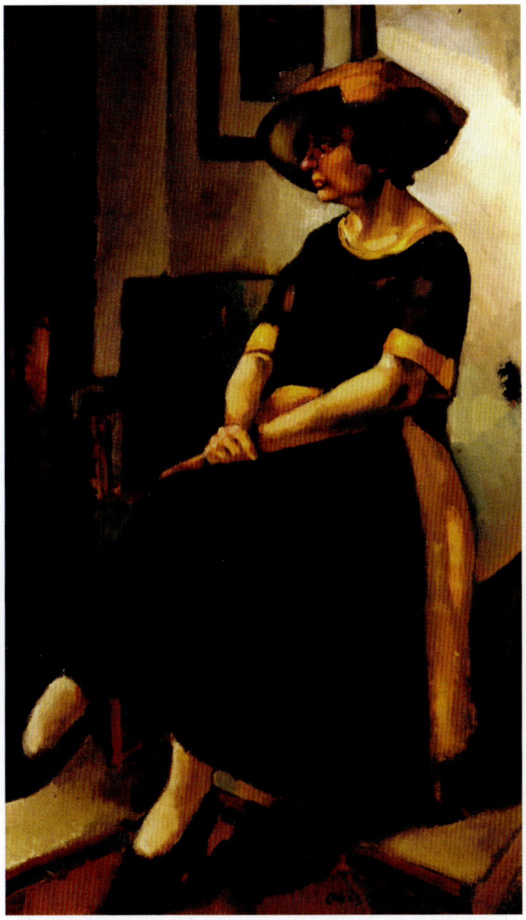

Otis Oldfield
Woman in Black, Dated 1922
© Jayne Blatchly Trust/Otis Oldfield Estate, San Francisco, California. Photo courtesy of Spencer Jon Helfen Fine Arts, Beverly Hills, California

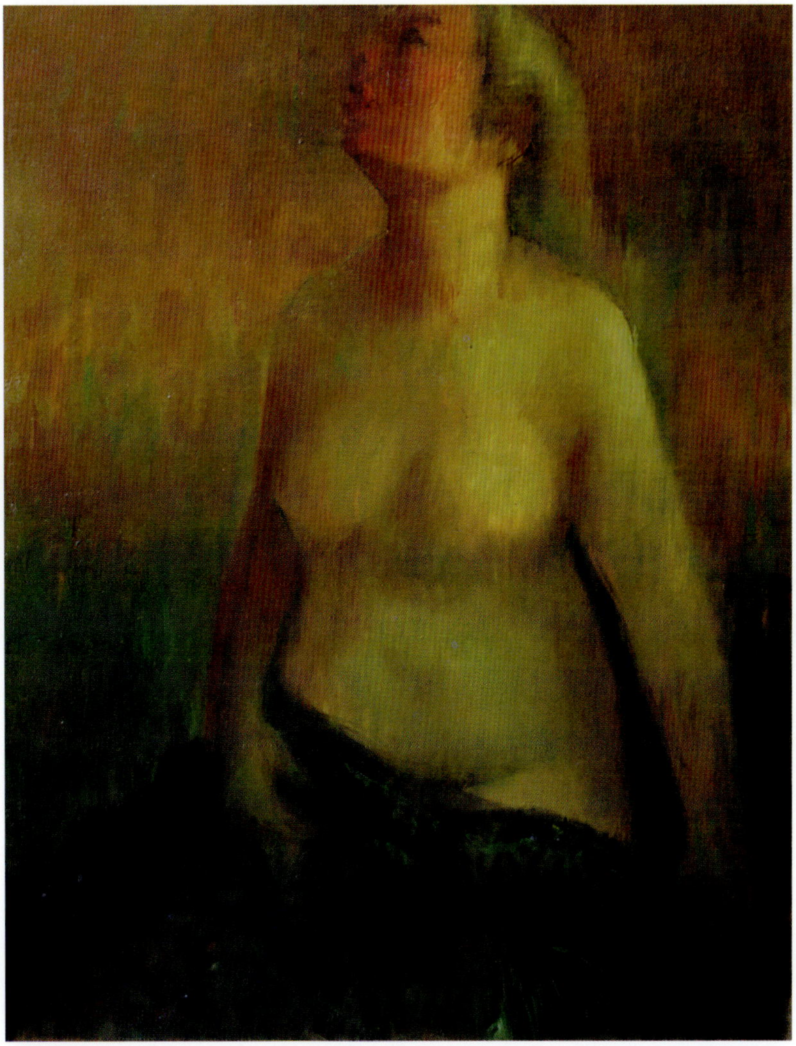

Otis Oldfield
Seated Nude, c.1940s
Papillon Gallery, Los Angeles, California

Philippe Parrot
1831-1894

Philippe Parrot was born in Saint-Martin d'Excideuil. He studied at l'Académie Suisse in Paris and exhibited at the Salon de Paris.

Parrot is known for his drawings and pastels of mythological figures, portraits and nudes. His work has been collected by the Musée des Beaux-Arts in Bordeaux.

In the last decades of the 19th century many classically trained artist like Parrot painted subjects that were in vogue in the age of La Belle Époque. His paintings are personal and accessible and rich with the history of that period. Parrot died May 15, 1894.

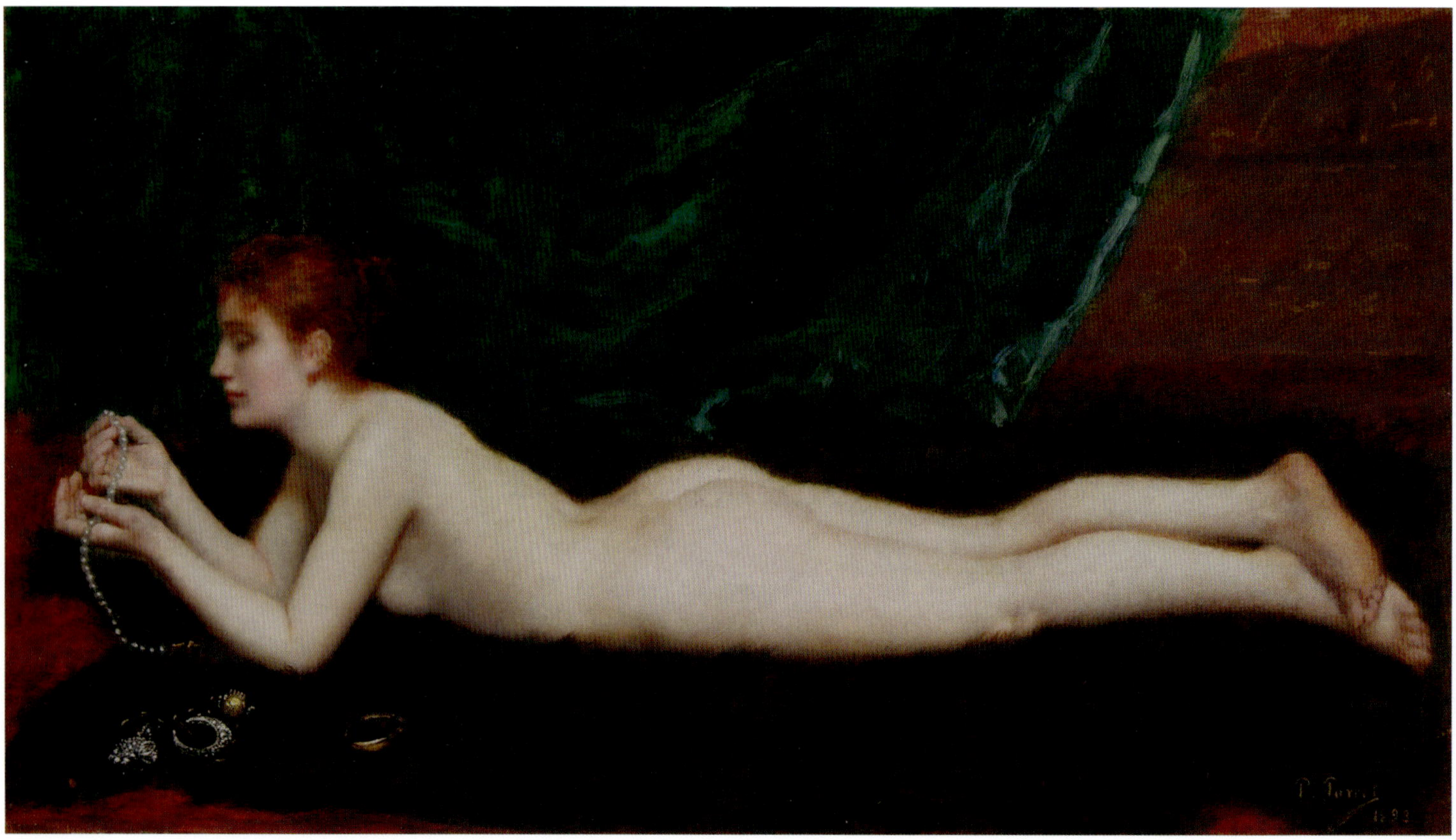

Philippe Parrot
Bijoux, Dated 1893
Papillon Gallery, Los Angeles, California

Albert Joseph Penot

Born 1870

Albert Joseph Penot was born in 1870 in Xermamenil, France. He studied with Gabriel Ferrier. Penot exhibited regularly at the Salon des Artistes Français. In 1903 he received an honorable mention and in 1908 the Médaille de Troisième Classe.

Penot was an academic painter in the grand tradition of the French Academy, but his subjects transcended that tradition; he painted vivacious women in opulent interiors which were ideal subject matter for French collectors at the beginning of the 20th century.

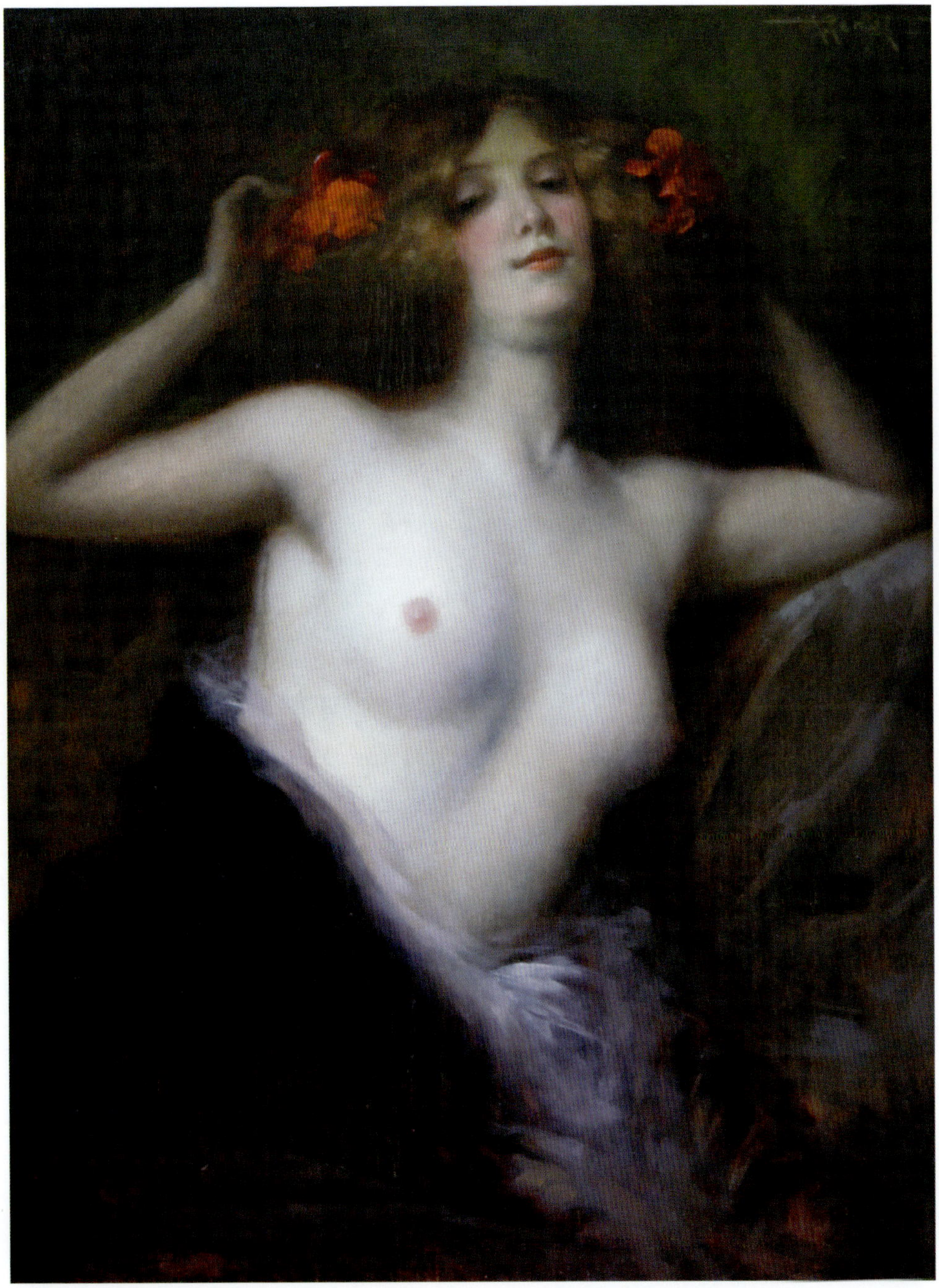

Albert Joseph Penot
Du Fleuve, c.1910
Galerie de l'Elysee, Paris, France

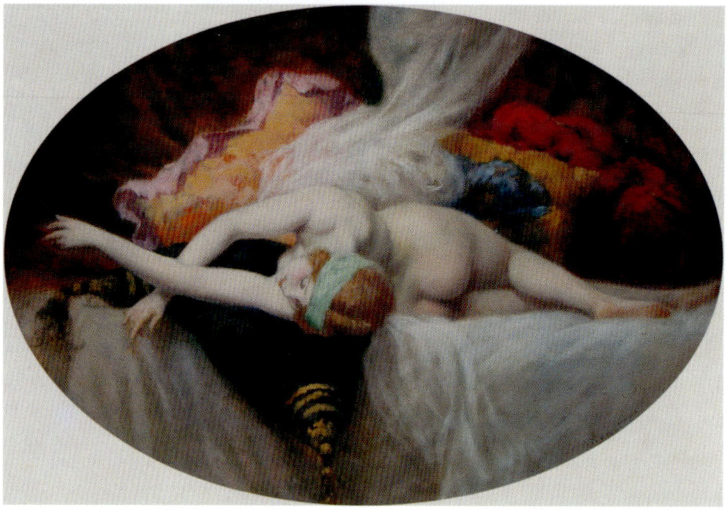

Albert Joseph Penot
En Repose, c.1920
Private Collection

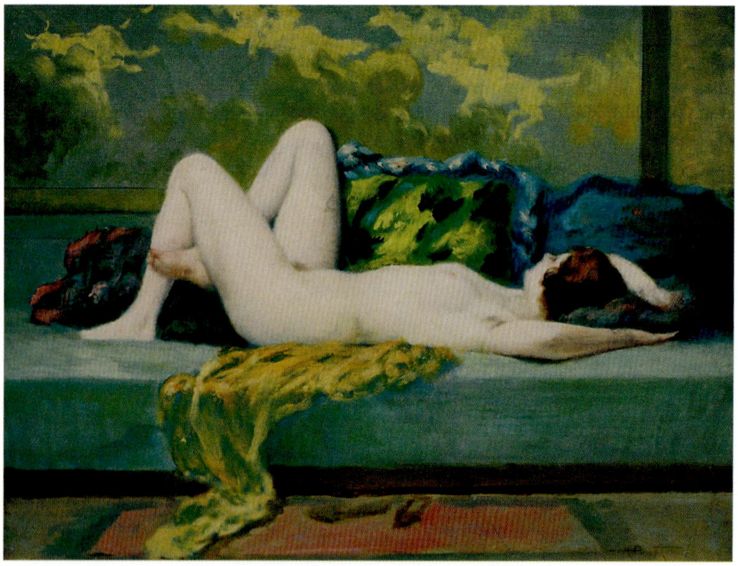

Albert Joseph Penot
Le Chaleur de l'Eté, c.1920
Galerie de l'Elysee, Paris, France

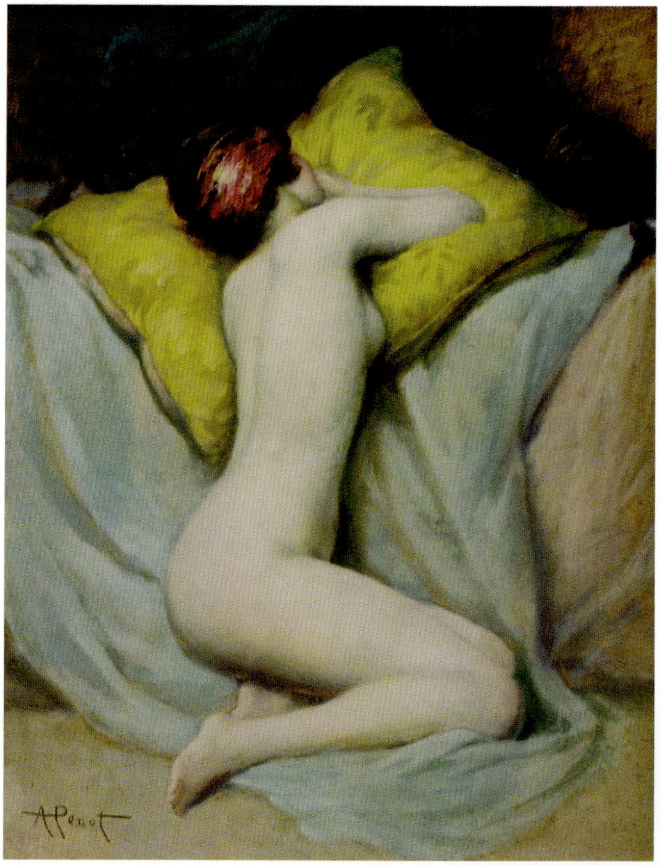

Albert Joseph Penot
Le Coussin Jaune, c.1920
Galerie de l'Elysee, Paris, France

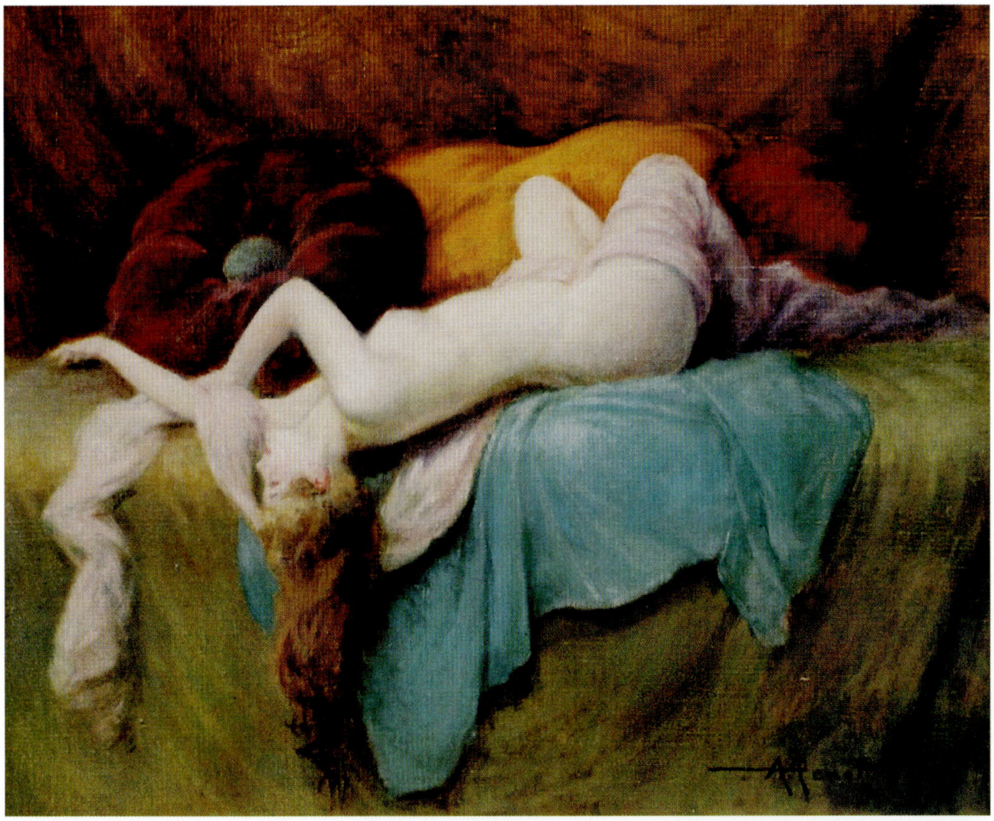

Albert Joseph Penot
Volupté, c.1920
Galerie de l'Elysee, Paris, France

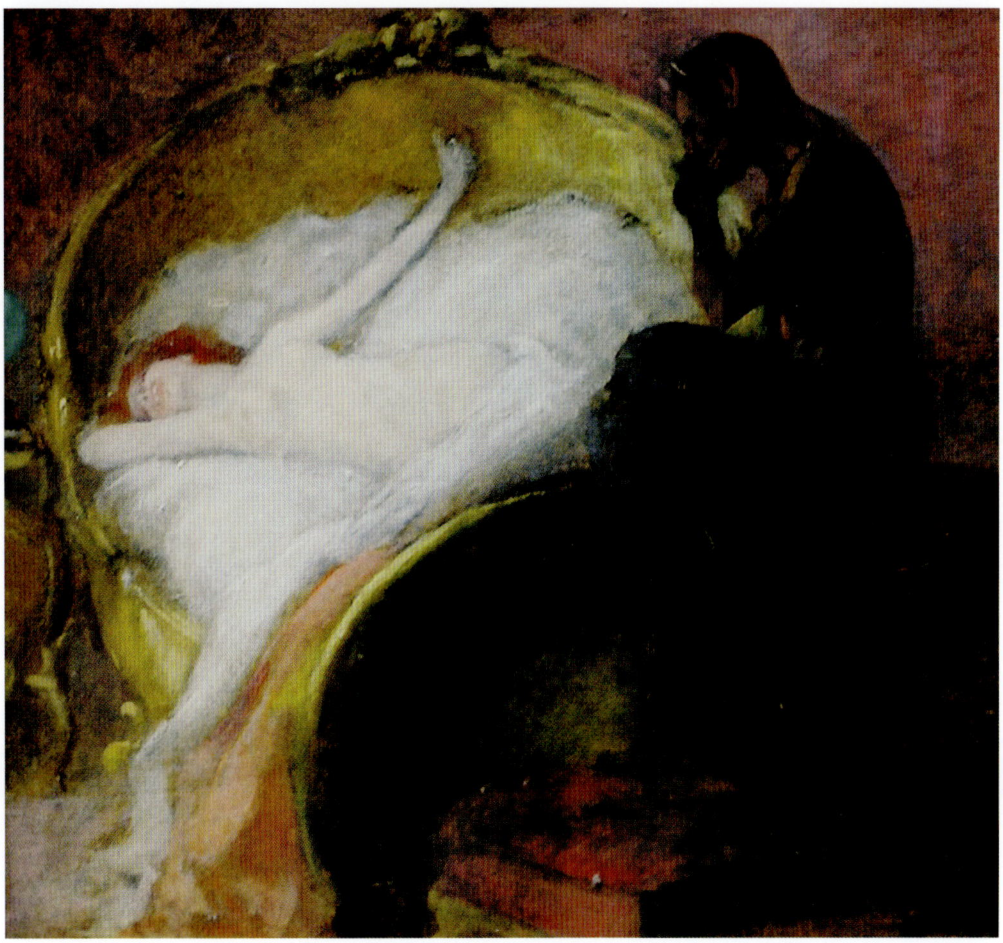

Albert Joseph Penot
Je n'ose pas la Réveiller, c.1920
Galerie de l'Elysee, Paris, France

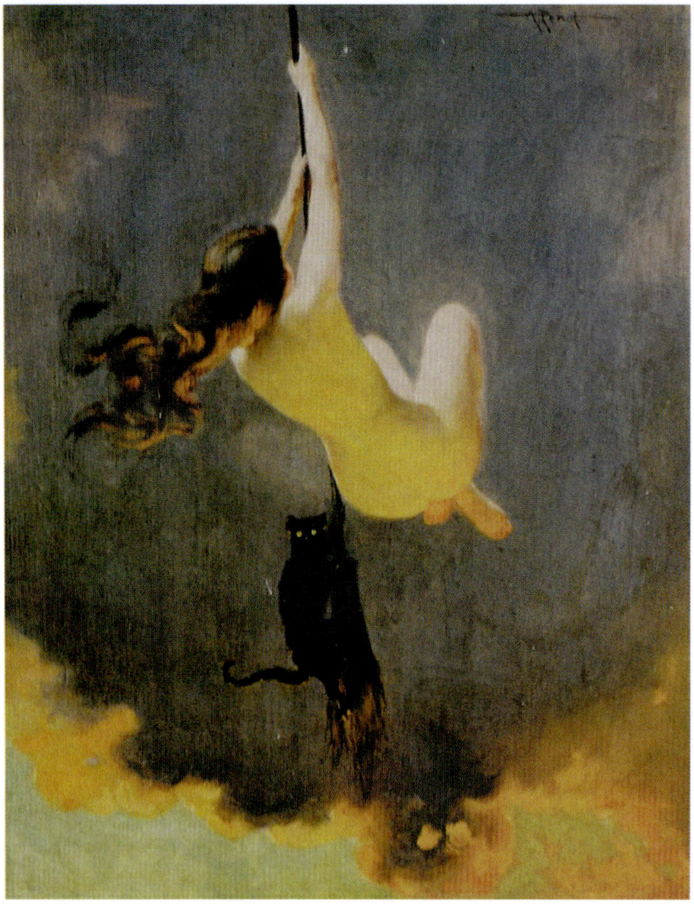

Albert Joseph Penot
En Route pour le Sabbat, c.1915
Galerie de l'Elysee, Paris, France

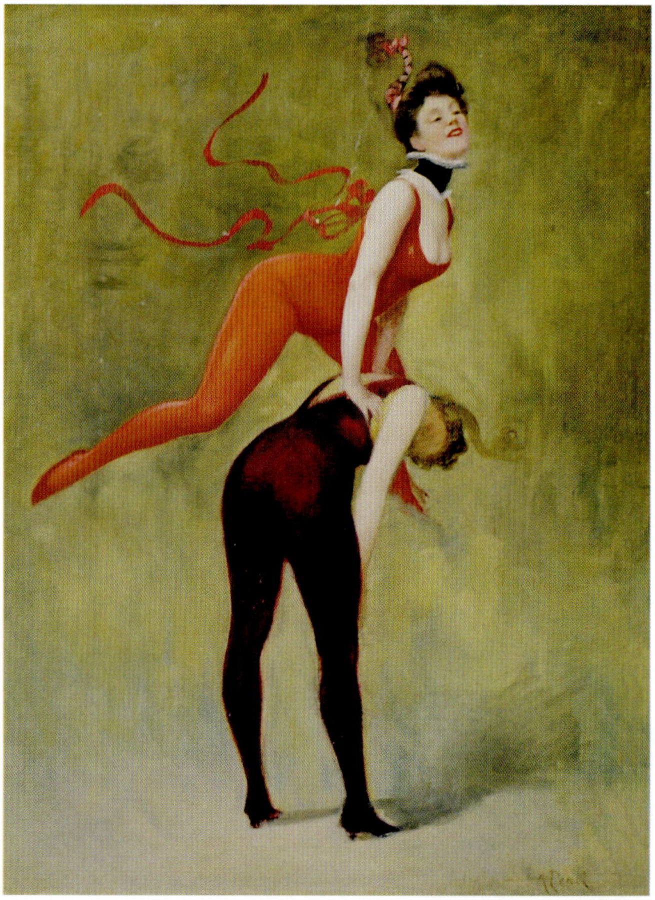

Albert Joseph Penot
Le Saut, c.1910
Galerie de l'Elysee, Paris, France

Robert Philipp

1895-1981

Robert Philipp was born on February 2, 1895 in New York City. His name at birth was Moses Soloman Philipp. His father was born in Hamburg, Germany and was a painter in England before moving to New York. His mother was Hungarian.

He studied with Frank Vincent DuMond and George Bridgman at the Art Students League and between 1914 and 1917 he studied with Volk and Maynard at the National Academy of Design. Art historians believed that he lived in Paris for ten years; unfortunately the dates of his sojourn are unknown. It is thought that he supported himself in Paris by selling paintings. He had also been a relatively successful tenor in his uncle's opera company.

Philipp has been called "America's Last Impressionist." He painted diverse subject matter, genre scenes, clowns, flowers, portraits, and coastal areas. He also painted scenes of the Netherlands and Paris.

Philipp received numerous awards for his paintings. In 1922 he won the third Hallgarten prize and in 1936 he won awards from the Art Institute of Chicago and Laguna Beach Art Association. He received a silver medal at the 1937 Carnegie Institute's International Exhibition. Two years later in 1939 he won an award from IBM. He was awarded prizes from the National Academy of Design in 1947 and 1951. In 1958 he won a third place medal from the Allied Artists of America.

Philipp's work is included in the permanent collections of the Metropolitan Museum of Art, Whitney Museum of American Art, Brooklyn Museum of Art, Corcoran Gallery of Art, Dallas Museum of Art and Museum of Fine Arts Houston.

In addition to a successful professional career, Philipp also had a distinguished teaching career. During the 1940s, Philipp taught at the High Museum of Art, University of Illinois, Art Students League of New York, and National Academy of Design. Philipp was elected an associate of the National Academy of Design in 1935 and a full member in 1945.

The Impressionists, particularly Renoir, influenced Philipp's style. His early work had more deliberate brush strokes and a deeper color palate. Philipp died in New York City in 1981.

In 1985 a large retrospective of Philipp's work was organized by the Grand Central Galleries in association with the Art Students League of New York. The exhibition included eighty paintings that spanned his sixty-year career.

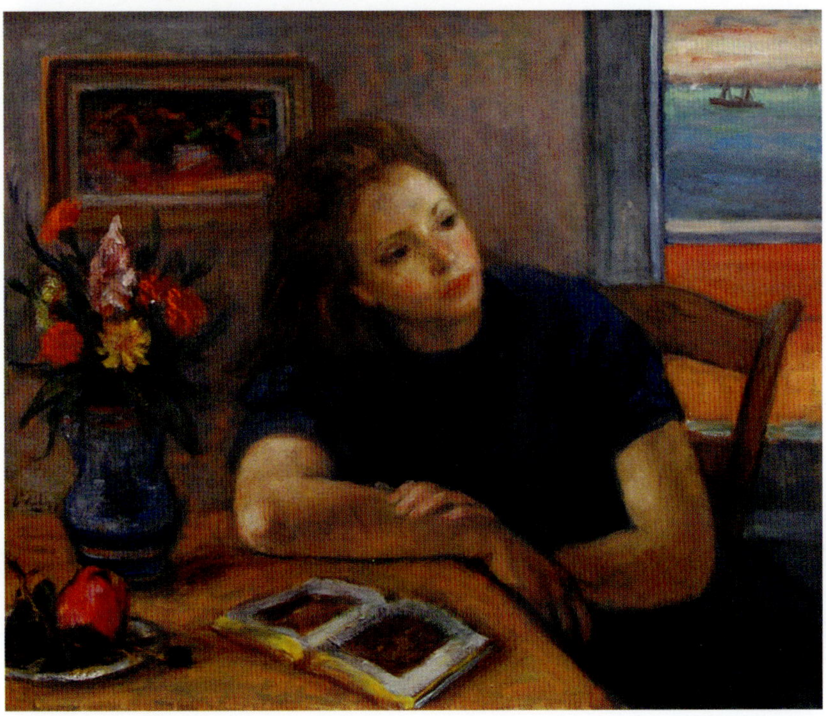

Robert Philipp
Portrait d'une Jeune Fille, c.1940
Private Collection

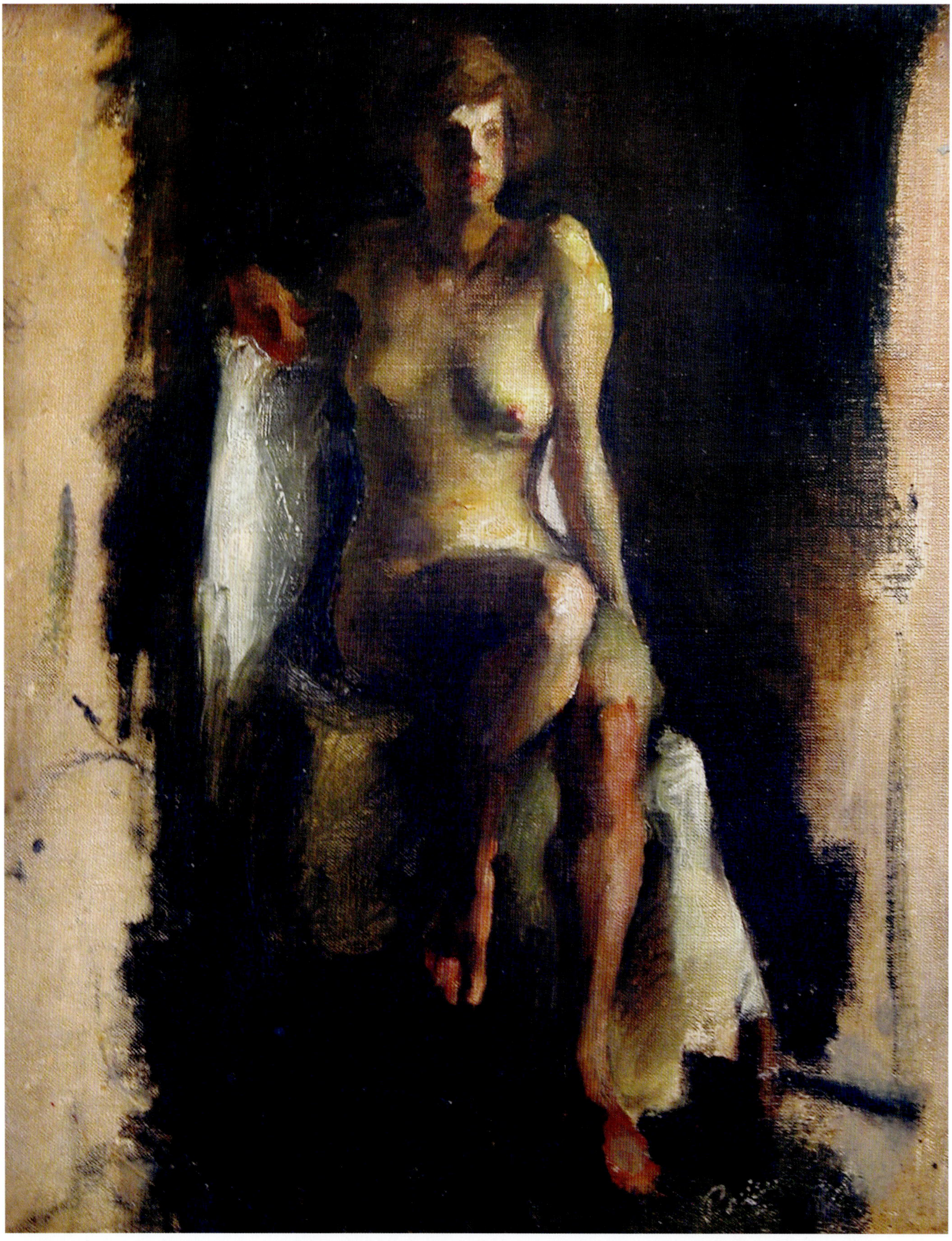

Robert Philipp
Nu Assis, c.1930
The Parrish Collection, San Francisco, California

Louis Picard
Born 1861

Louis Picard was born on September 10, 1861 in Paris. He was the younger brother of notable French artist Georges Picard; both artists studied with Gérôme.

Louis Picard exhibited regularly at the Salon des Artistes Français. He received an honorable mention in 1887, Chevalier de la Légion d'Honneur in 1900, as well as the Médaille d'Argent that year. Beginning in 1890, Picard exhibited with the Nationale des Beaux-Arts.

Many of Picard's paintings are ethereal and whimsical nymphs that are typical of the Art Nouveau and Symbolist tradition in France around 1900.

Le Musée de Nancy purchased *Femme près d'une fenêtre,* 1894. A museum in Luxembourg purchased *La femme qui passe,* while *A sa toilette* was bought by a museum in Göteborg.

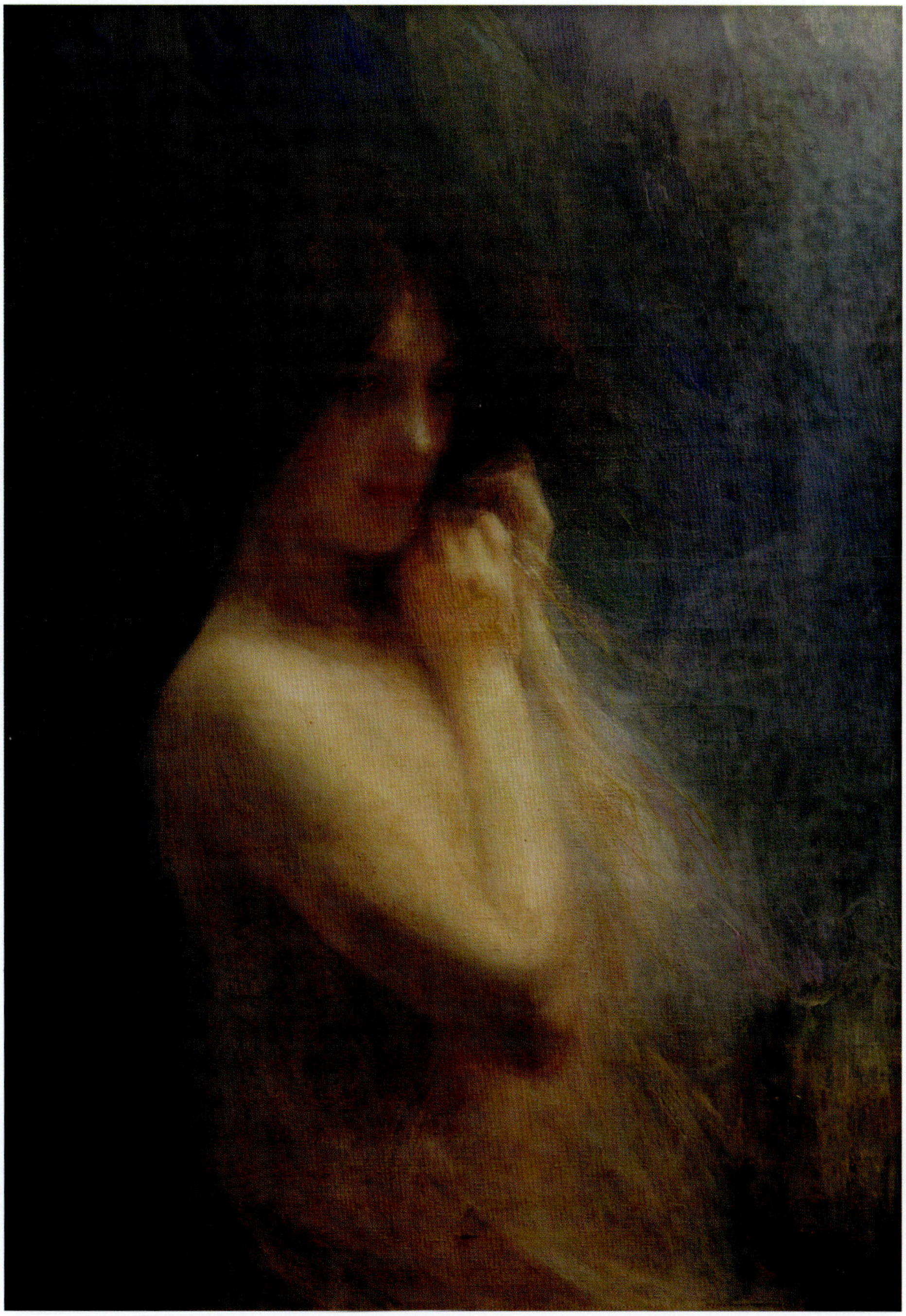

Louis Picard
Nu Tranquille, c.1900
Julia Evershade and Mark Smith, Los Angeles, California

Fernand Piet

1869-1942

Fernand Piet was born to painter Charles Mozin the 26th of August, 1869 in Paris. Piet studied at the Lycée Chaptal in Paris and attended the workshops of academic painter Fernand Cormon. He worked with French Symbolist Eugène Carrière and took courses at l'École des Beaux-Arts in Paris. Piet also attended l'Académie de la Grande Chaumiére throughout his life.

Piet exhibited at the Salon des Artiste Français, Salon d'Automne and the Salon des Artistes Indépendants, where he also served as a member of the jury in 1902. Piet served on the jury of the Société Nationale des Beaux-Arts as well. Piet was awarded the Médaille de Bronze at l'Exposition Universelle in Paris, and in 1910 the Palmes Académiques. In 1911 Piet refused the Légion d'Honneur.

Piet approached his canvases with the mind of a Postimpressionist. He used wide brushwork but was able to express fine detail and bring the viewer into his warm interiors. Piet was known to frequent cabarets, bars and breweries representing Parisian youth of the time.

Piet died February 24th, 1942 in Paris. His atelier sold at auction in Paris in 1987.

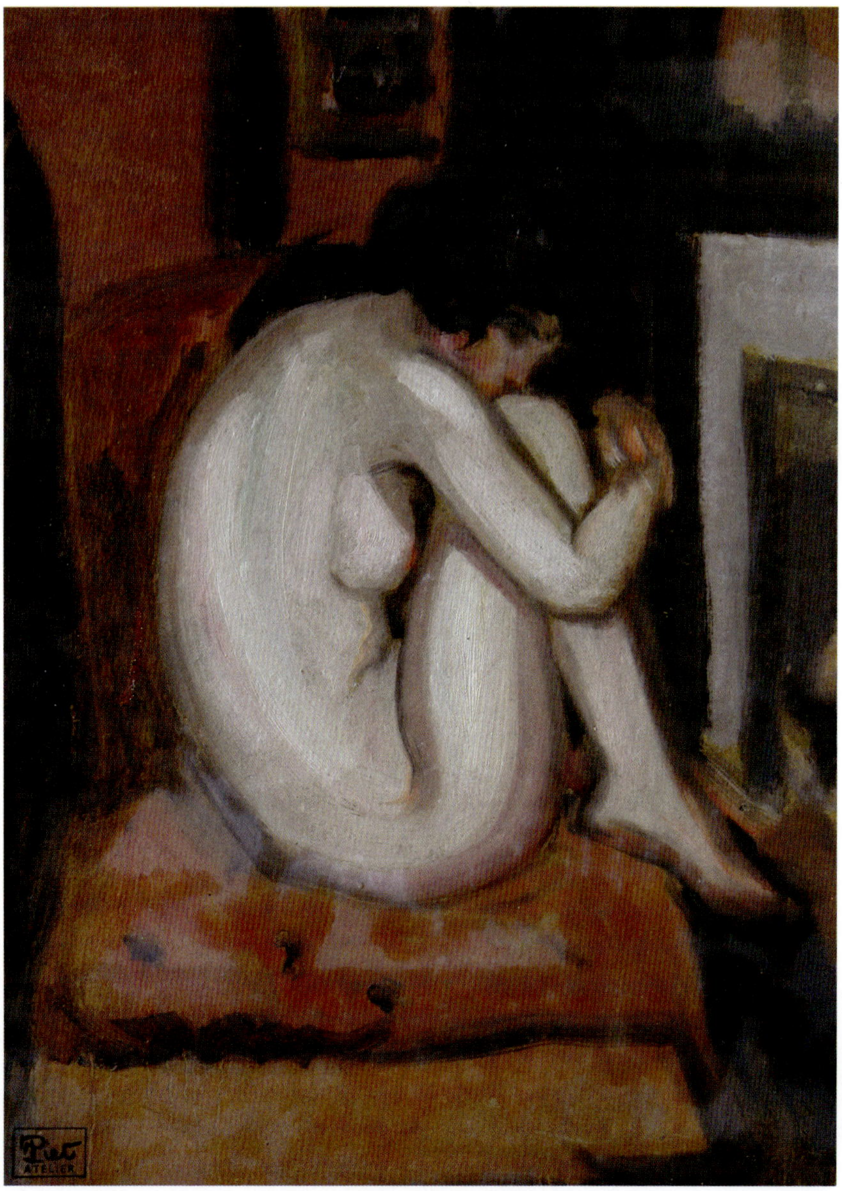

Fernand Piet
Nu sur un Coussin, c.1930
The Parrish Collection, San Francisco, California

Edgar Pillet

1912-1996

Edgar Pillet is considered a pioneer of geometric abstraction in post-war Paris with influence from Kandinsky, Mondrian and Delaunay. Though his career spanned from literature to film, his education began at l'École des Beaux-Arts in Bordeaux and continued at the same institution in Paris in 1931 where he studied painting and sculpture.

Pillet became Secretary General of the publication *Art d'Au Jourd'hui* in 1949 and in 1950 founded the *Atelier d'Art Abstrait* in Montparnasse. He later traveled to the United States where he took on teaching positions at the University of Louisville, Kentucky and the Art Institute of Chicago. Pillet lived for a time in New York as well, where he directed the film *Genesis* before returning to Paris.

Exhibiting abroad, specifically in Scandinavian countries, became opportune for Pillet at this time. He continued to paint, sculpt and create architectural monuments and ensembles. He exhibited at the Galerie Loeb in Paris as well. Pillet rarely painted figures though, like other artists that are known primarily for their abstract works, he did occasionally paint a representational work.

Collections of Pillet's work include the National Museum in Algiers, National Museum in Djakarta, Museum of Modern Art in Eilat, Museum of Painting and Sculpture in Grenoble, the Museum Ateneum in Helsinki, the Museum of Modern Art in New York and the Musée d'Art Moderne in Paris. In 1990 Martine Arnaul of Galerie Claude Lemand published a catalog of Pillet's painting and sculpture. Pillet died in 1996.

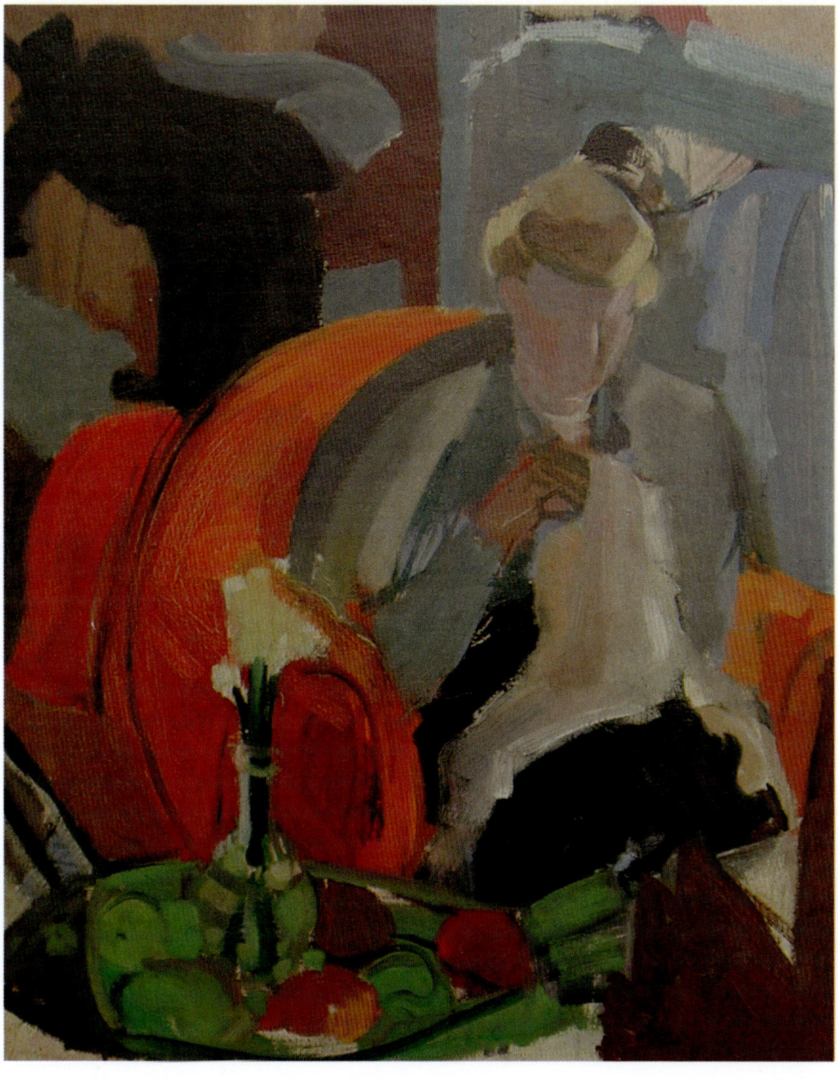

Edgar Pillet
Portrait d'une Femme, c.1945
Papillon Gallery, Los Angeles, California

Marcel Pouget

1923–1985

Marcel Pouget was born August 15, 1923 in Oran, Algeria. In 1943 he studied at l'École des Beaux-Arts in Oran and in 1946 he briefly attended l'École des Beaux-Arts de Paris. After school he remained in Paris and befriended many avant-garde artists from his generation. He associated himself with the Expressionists, including Alenchinsky, Appel, Lindström and Maryan.

Pouget painted figurative works early in his career and later turned to more abstract images. The color compositions of his paintings evoke Expressionism and his technique is bold and modern. Beginning in 1947 he participated in many of the Paris salons including the Salon des Indépendants and Salon d'Automne. He also showed in the Salon de Mai and occasionally in the Salon des Réalités Nouvelles.

Pouget participated in individual and group exhibitions in many Paris galleries including Denise Breteau, Arnaud, Art Vivant, Claude Bernard and Ariel. Pouget died on December 5,1985, in Paris.

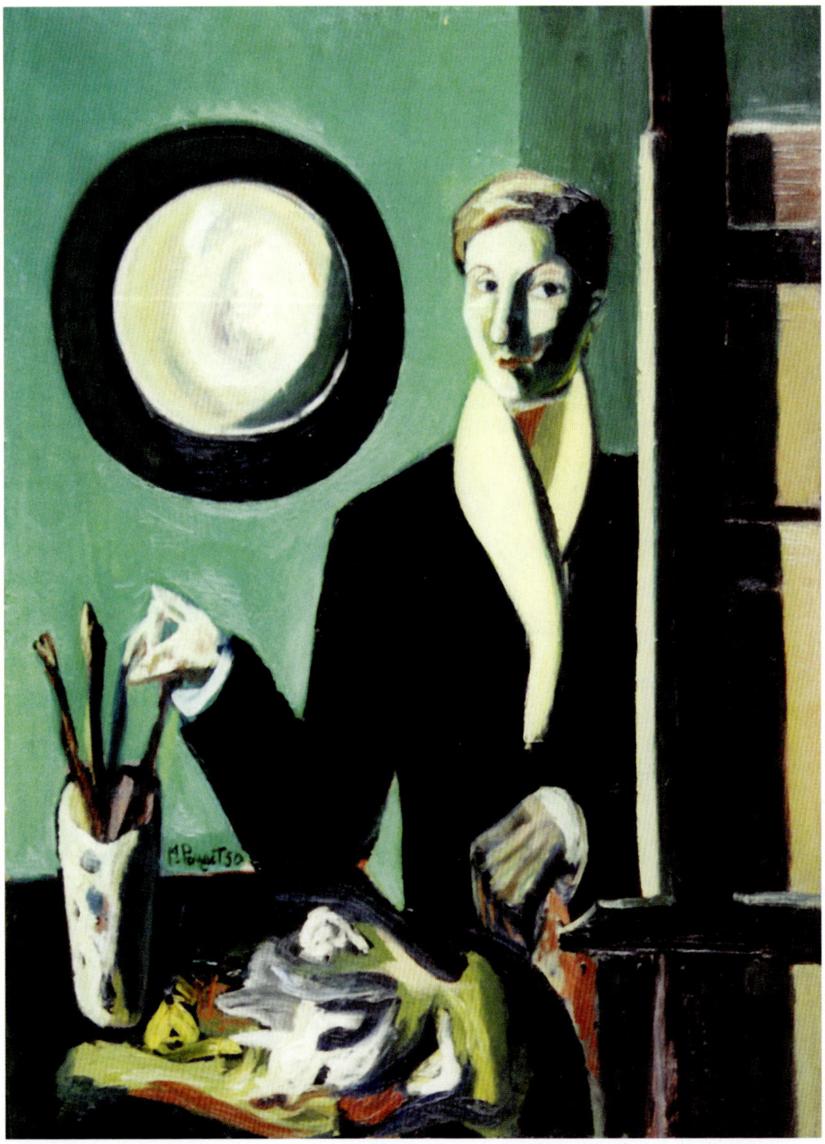

Marcel Pouget
Dans l'Atelier, c. 1950
Mike Werb and Brian Roskam, Los Angeles, California

Gaston Prunier
1863-1927

Gaston Prunier was born in Havre, France in 1863. He studied under Lhuillier before moving to Paris in 1887. Prunier began exhibiting at Galerie Bing in 1889 and later exhibited at the Société Nationale des Beaux-Arts, where he became a member in 1903.

He is best known for his paintings and watercolors of modern city scenes, architecture and cathedrals. Prunier had a superb command of the effect of light on his subjects. He painted familiar scenes and captured the essence with use of color and interesting composition. His works have been collected by museums in Dijon, Le Havre, Limoges, Toulouse and Paris. Prunier died in 1927.

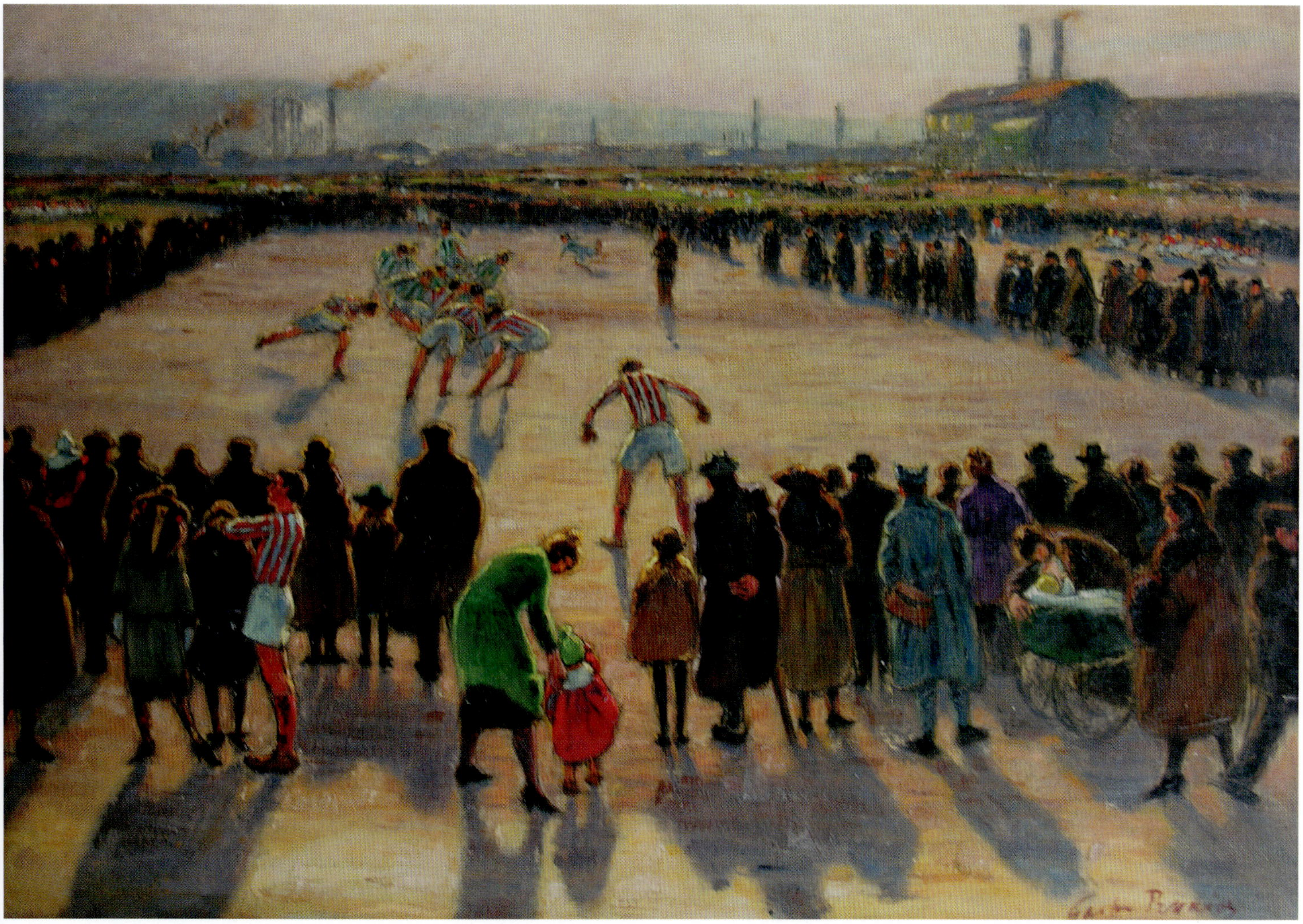

Gaston Prunier
Rugby, c.1910
Andrew Herrera II, San Francisco, California

Marcel Prunier

20th century

Marcel Prunier exhibited at the Salon d'Automne and the Salon des Indépendants in 1941. His atelier was located in Monmartre on rue Damrémont and he died sometime around 1980. Prunier worked for the most part in watercolors and gouaches, depicting night clubs, café scenes and nude figures.

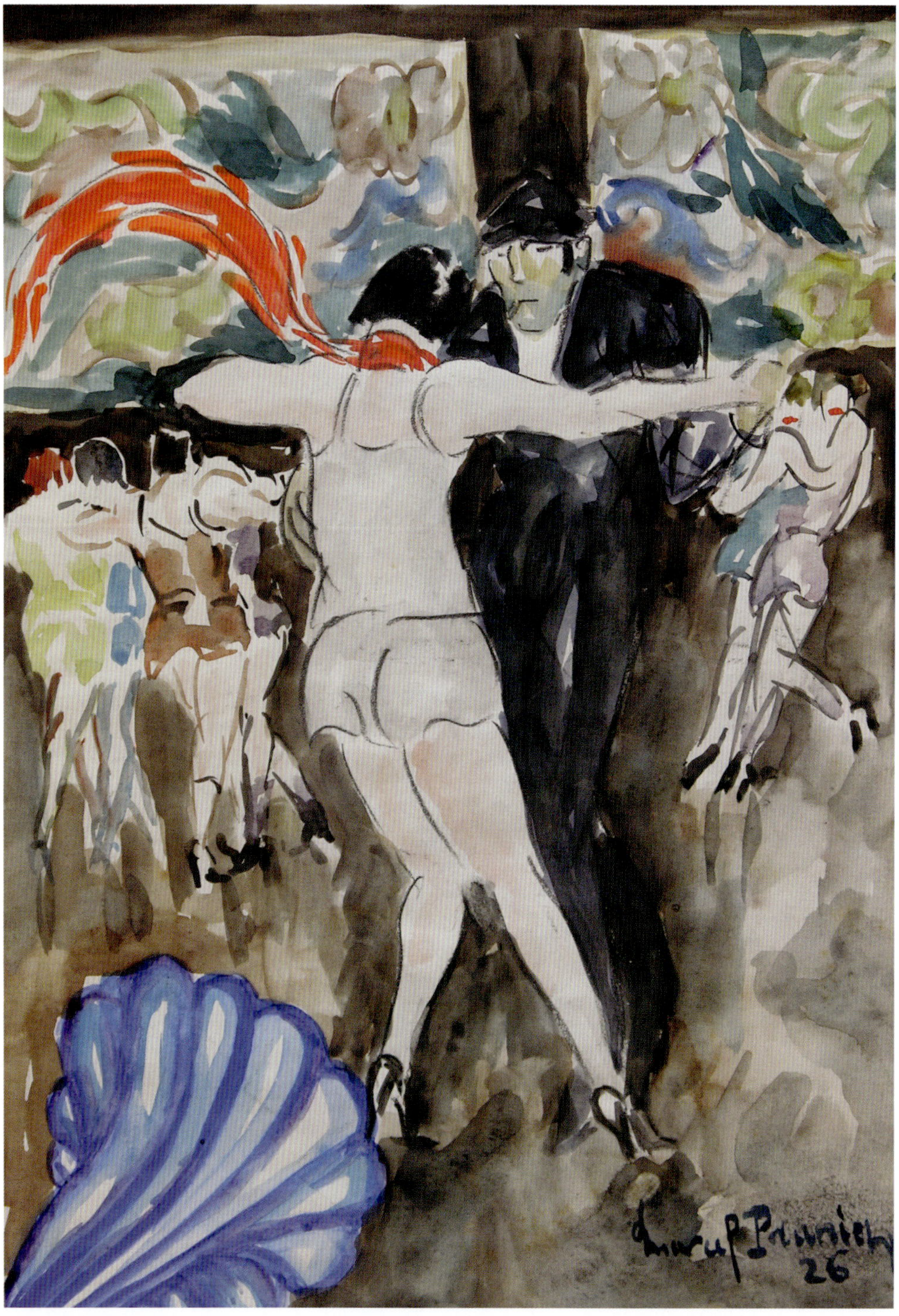

Marcel Prunier
Danseurs d'Apache, Dated 1926
Private Collection

Jules Rambo

20th century

Jules Rambo is known for his lively landscapes, cityscapes, portraits and figures. He exhibited at the Galerie G. Giroux in Brussels in 1945, 1947 and 1950, and at the Galerie Rubens in 1956.

Rambo's paintings are rich with exciting and bold brush strokes which are seen in the works of many Belgian artists of this period. Strong colors and interesting subjects are combined for an ageless appeal. His work is mentioned in the *Dictionnaire des Artistes Plasticiens de Belgique des XIX*$_e$ *et XX*$_e$ *Siecles* by Paul Piron and the *Arto Dictionnaire Biographique des Arts Plastiques en Belgique*.

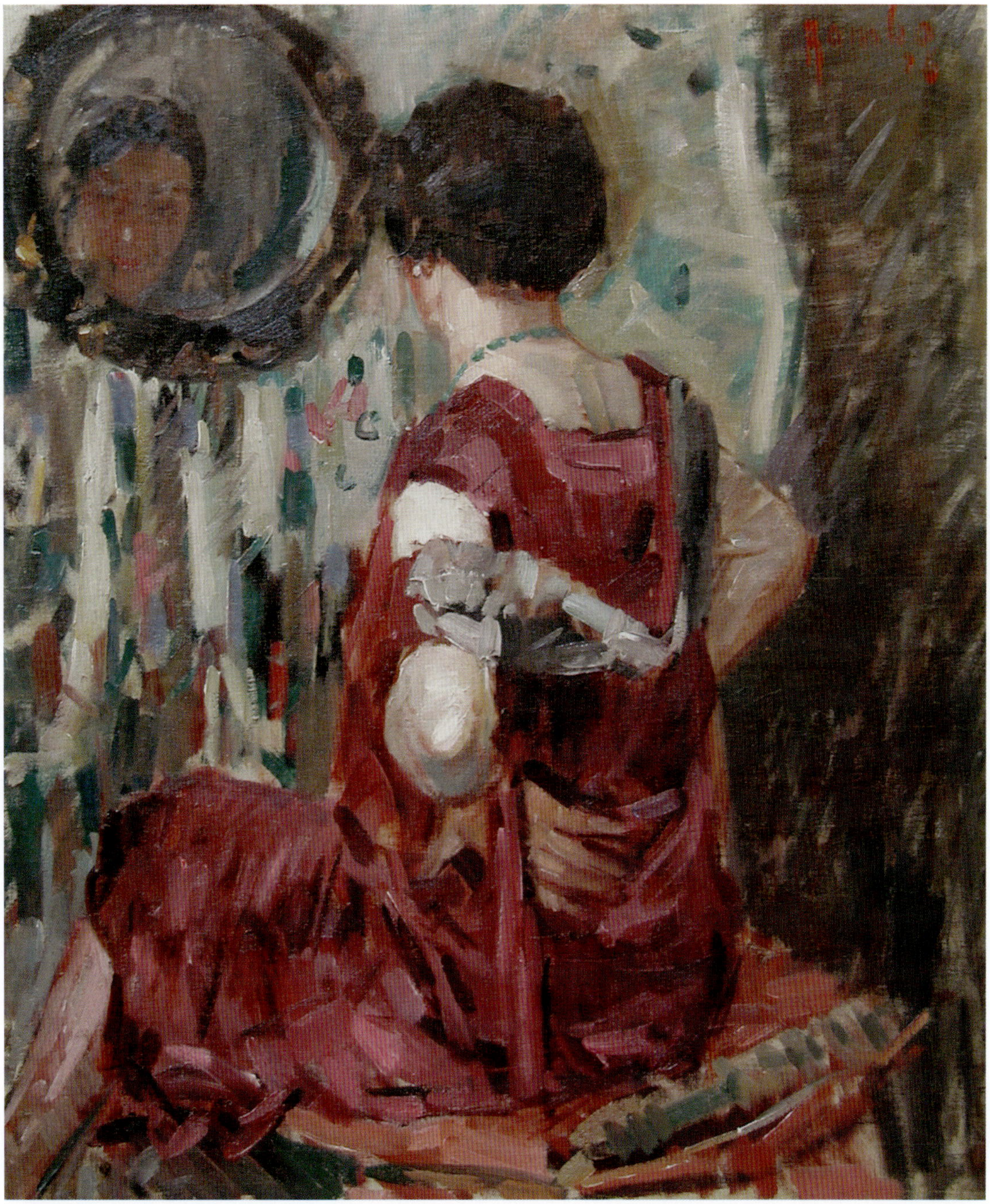

Jules Rambo
Femme Assis au Miroir, c.1920
Los Angeles Fine Art Gallery, Los Angeles, California

Lucie Ranvier-Chartier

1867-1932

Lucie Ranvier-Chartier was a student of Baschet and Paul Thomas. She exhibited in Paris at the Salon des Artistes Français and became a member in 1912. Her figures and landscapes display a predominantly Orientalist influence. Ranvier-Chartier died in 1932.

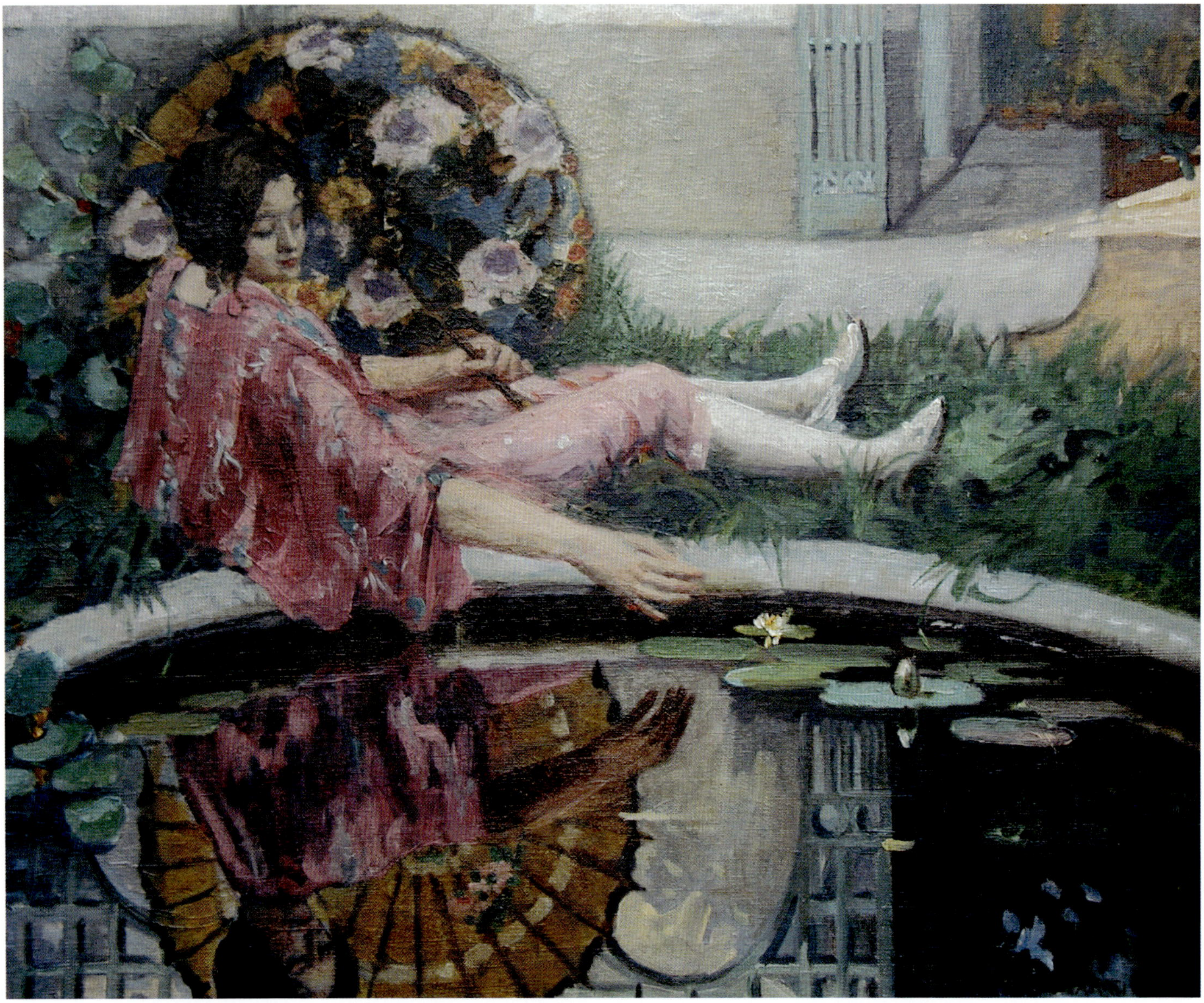

Lucie Ranvier-Chartier
Les Réflexions, c.1925
Kathleen Avery Fine Art, Palo Alto, California

Antoine Marie Raynolt

Born 1874

Antoine Marie Raynolt was born on July 10, 1874 in Toulouse, Haute-Garonne. He is best known as a painter, illustrator and decorator. Raynolt studied with Benjamin Constant and Jean-Paul Laurens. He exhibited at the Salon des Artistes Français in Paris. Raynolt received an honorable mention in 1897 and the Médaille de Troisième Classe in 1902. Raynolt's paintings are distinctively Art Deco with a blend of allegorical subjects and modern style.

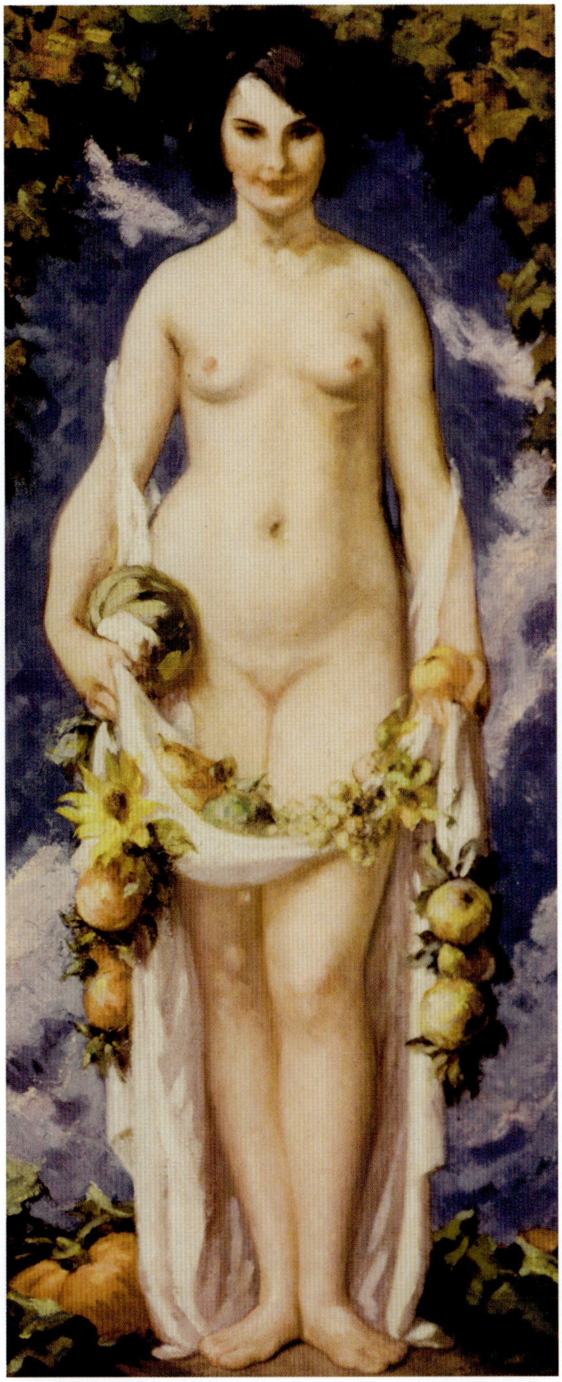

Antoine Marie Raynolt
Femme du Fleurs, c.1925
Private Collection

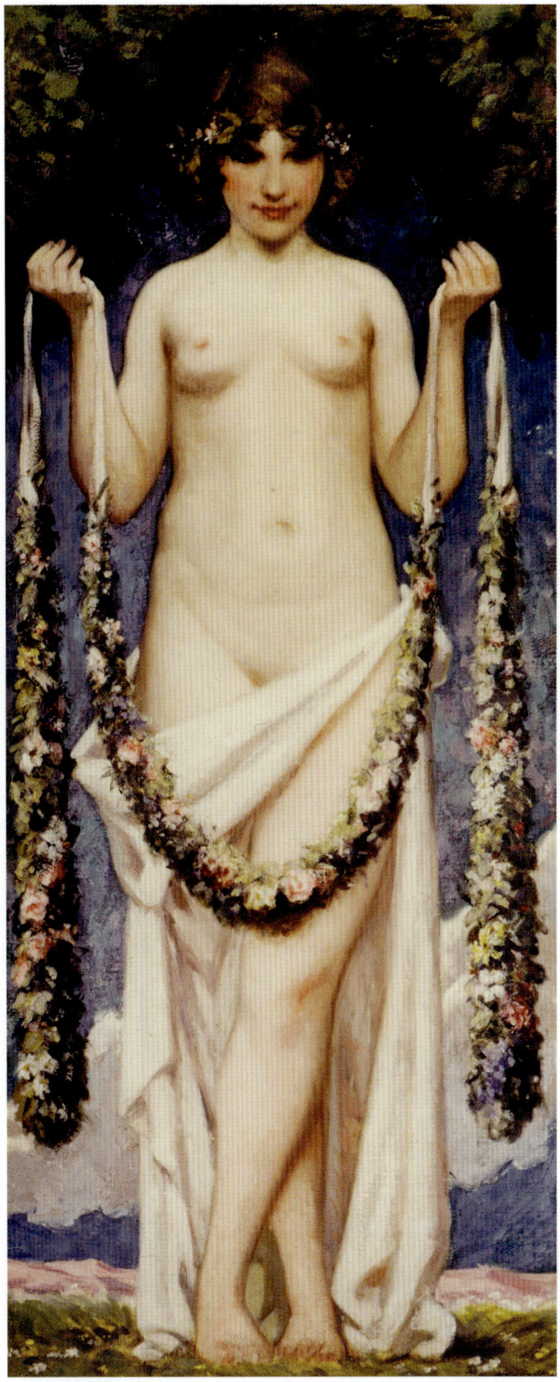

Antoine Marie Raynolt
Femme Art Deco, c.1925
Private Collection

Paul Renaudot
1871 - 1920

Paul Renaudot was born in Rome to French parents November 29, 1871. He exhibited from 1907 to 1914 at the Salons des Indépendants and participated at the Salon de la Société Nationale des Beaux-Arts. Renaudot received the Chevalier de la Légion de Honneur.

Renaudot was a Postimpressionist; his use of color, brush technique, composition and treatment of light gives his paintings outstanding warmth and beauty. Though he was known for paintings landscape and nudes his most striking works are attractive women in period dress in richly decorated interiors, he mostly painted medium and small format works.

The Musée d'Orsay and the Musée de Rouen have collected Renaudot's works. Gérald Schurr writes of the artist's life and work in *Les Petits Maîtres de la peinture valeur de demain*. Paul Renaudot died in 1920 in Paris.

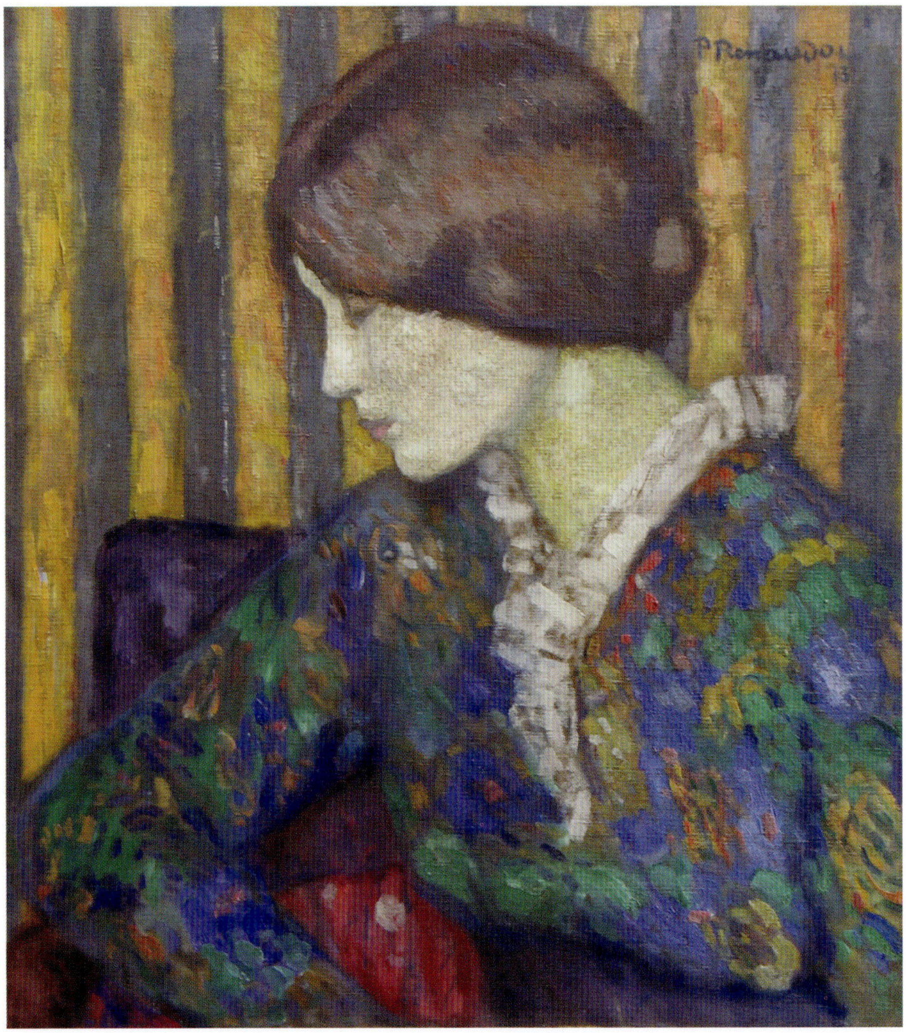

Paul Renaudot
Femme Pensive, Dated 1913
Patricia Timsit, Paris, France

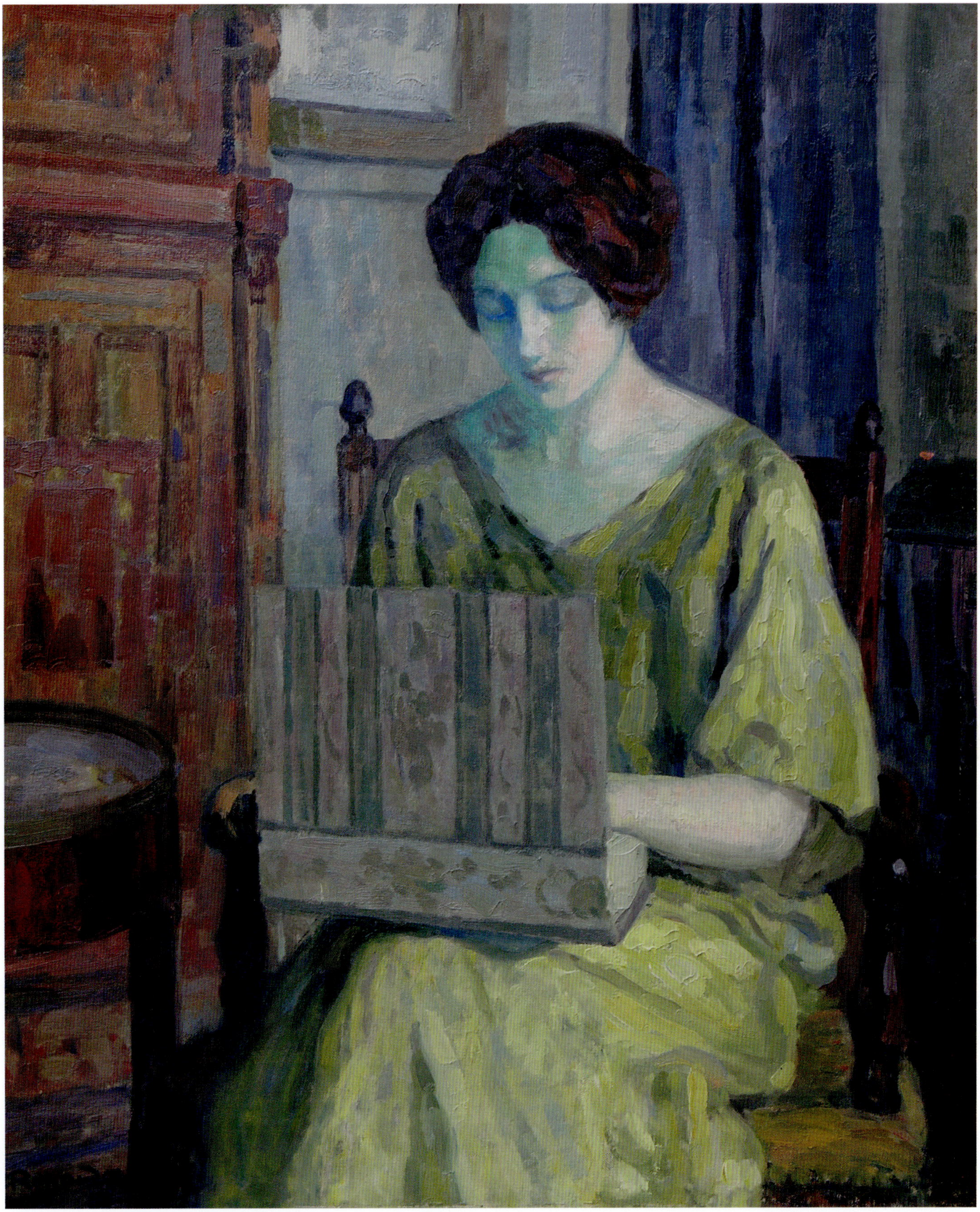

Paul Renaudot
Coffre de Bijou, Dated 1910
Papillon Gallery, Los Angeles, California.

Alfred Reth

1884-1966

Alfred Reth was born February 29, 1884, in Budapest. He worked within the artists' colony Nagbanya, known as the "Barbizon of Hungary," before traveling to Paris in 1903 and then throughout Italy. Reth attended the Academy of Fine arts in Florence and later the Academy of Fine arts in Budapest.

He was influenced greatly by Paul Cézanne, Paul Gauguin and Georges Roualt. Reth moved to Montparnasse permanently in 1905. He attended several schools and academies in Paris while continuing to exhibit his work in Budapest. He eventually exhibited at the Salon d' Automne alongside Matisse and Roualt. Reth subsequently joined the Société des Artistes Indépendants in 1911 and continued to exhibit with the annual Salon until 1914, playing an active role in the Cubist movement during this time.

After being imprisoned for several years during the war, Reth started experimenting with line and color as means of a more pure abstraction in his work. He continued to exhibit prolifically in Paris, exploring different materials and their relationships to nature. He continued to face adversity in Paris during wartime years but was able to maintain a committed and passionate career throughout.

A well illustrated book was released in 2003 titled *Alfred Reth, 1884-1966,* published by Maklary Artworks. Alfred Reth died in his Montparnasse studio on September 15, 1966.

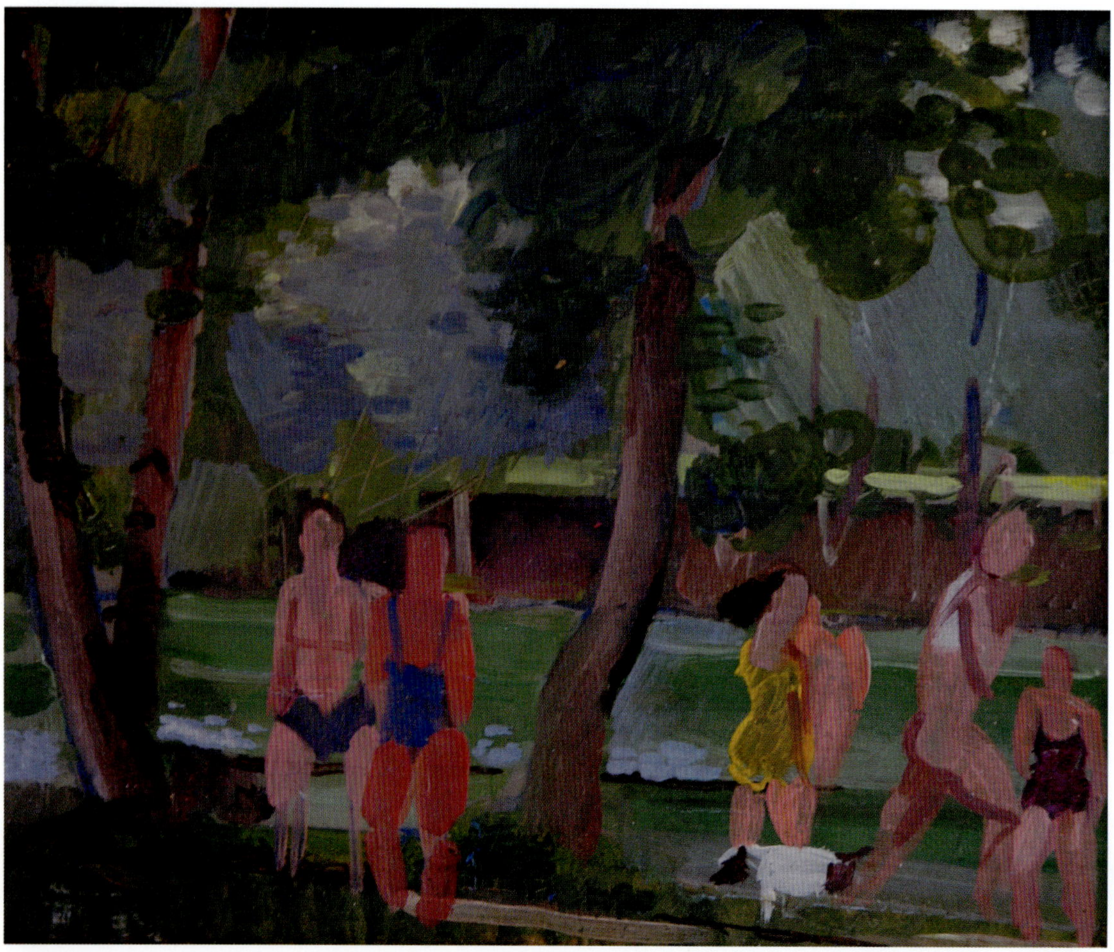

Alfred Reth
Fête dans le Parc, c.1925
Jeffrey Winter Fine Arts, Long Beach, California

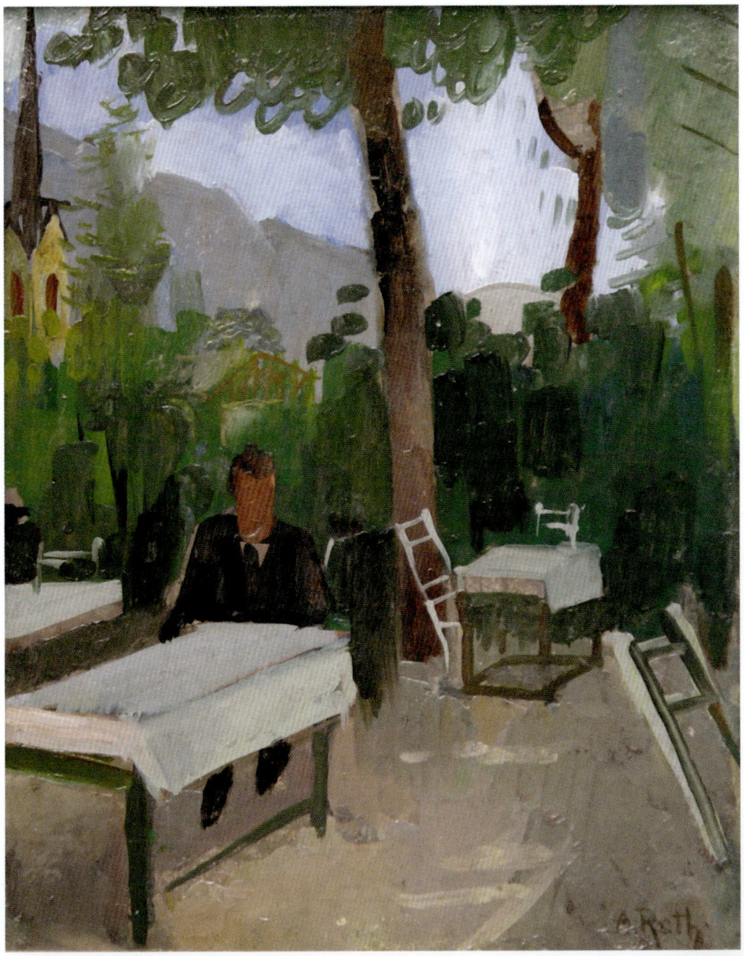

Alfred Reth
Au Café c.1925
Jeffrey Winter Fine Arts, Long Beach, California

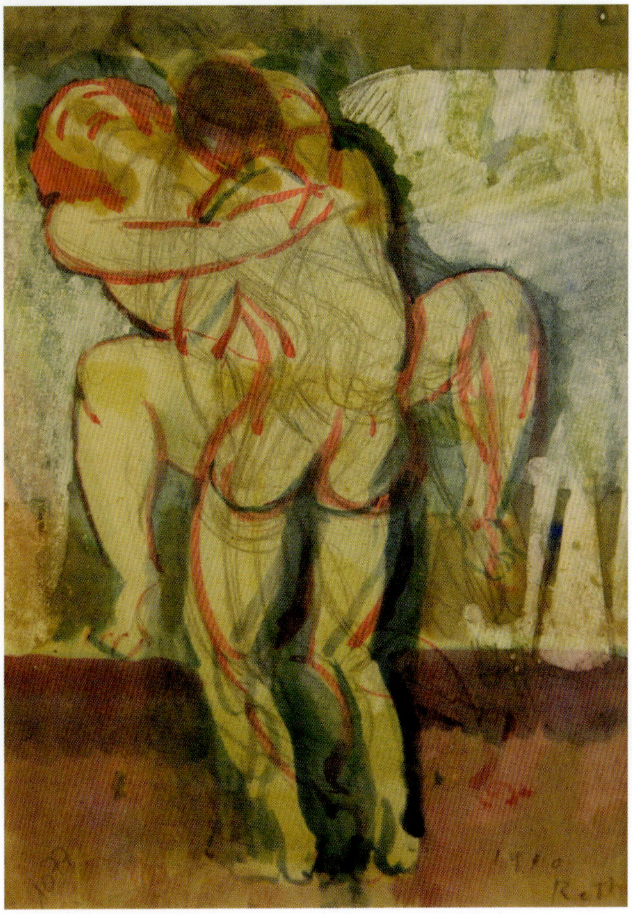

Alfred Reth
Les Amoureaux, dated 1910
Jeffrey Winter Fine Arts, Long Beach, California

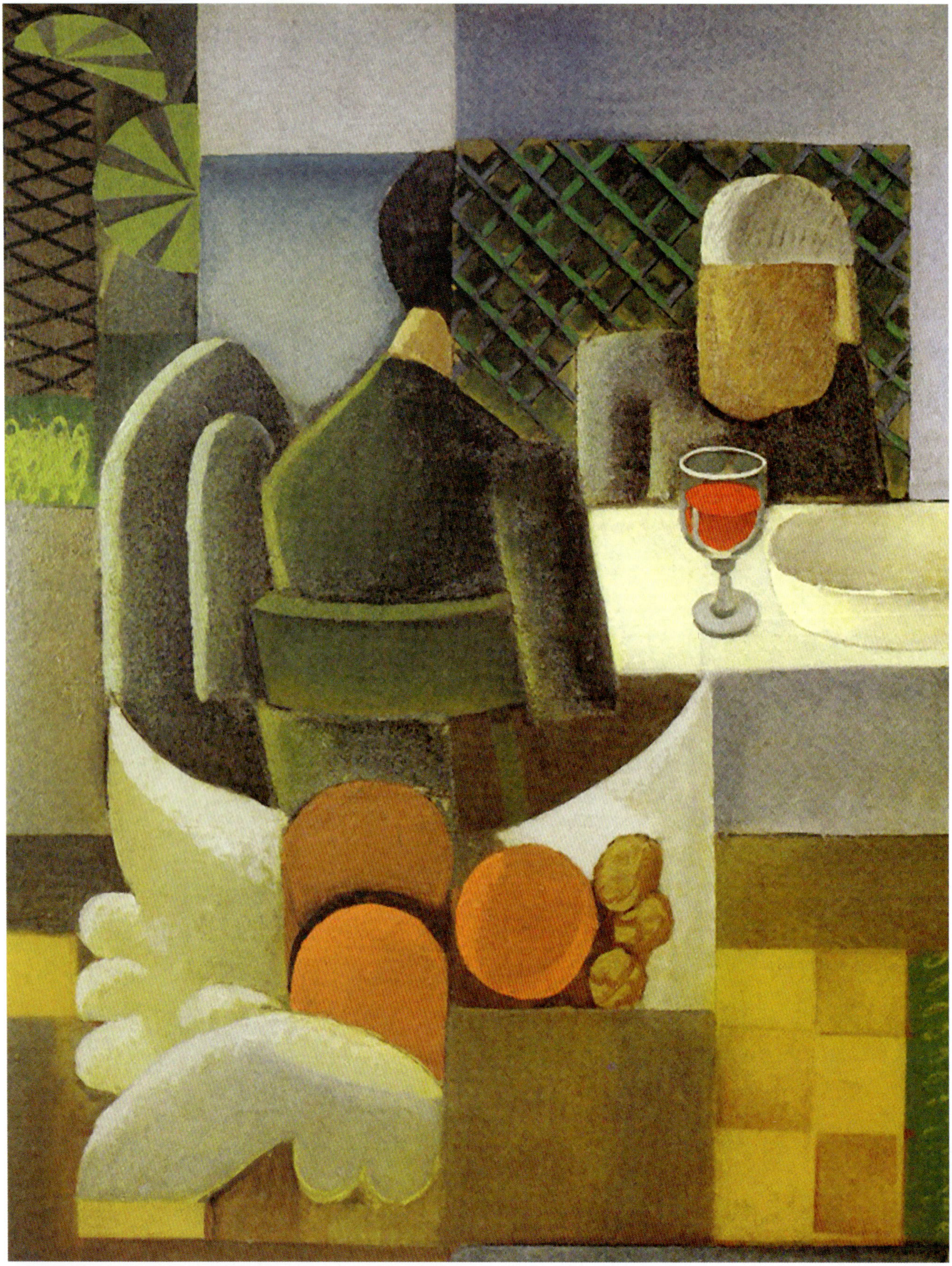

Alfred Reth
Terrase d'un Restaurant à Antibe, dated 1926
Art K, Paris, France

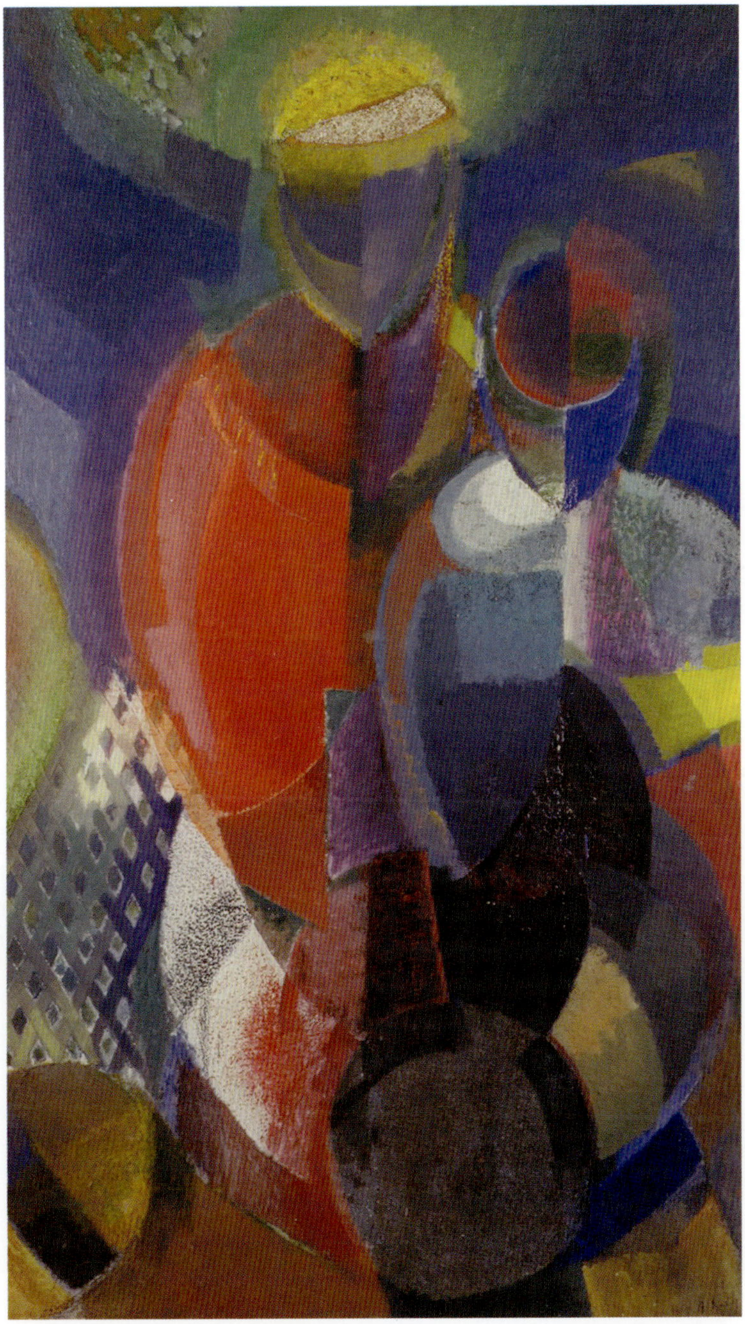

Alfred Reth
Chantilly, Dated 1939
Art K, Paris, France

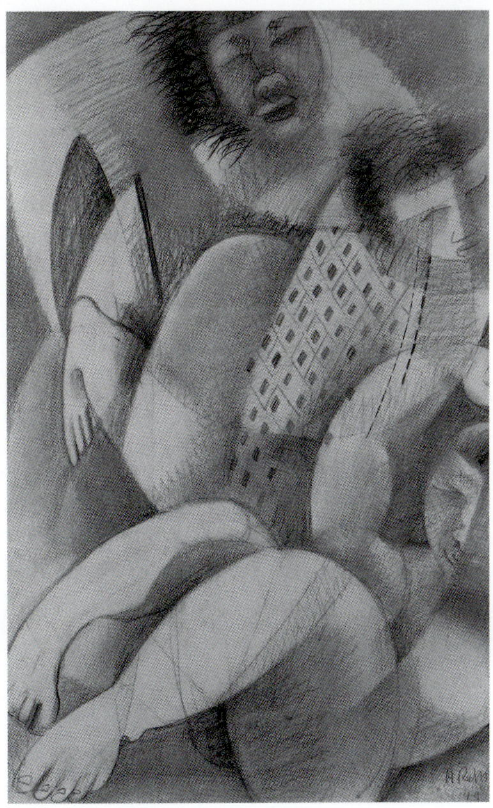

Alfred Reth
Figures Cubistes, Dated 1955
Papillon Gallery, Los Angeles, California

Georges Antoine Rochegrosse

1859-1938

Georges Antoine Rochegrosse was born August 2, 1859 in Versailles, France. Rochegrosse was abandoned by his father and his artistic talents flourished under the guidance of his stepfather. At the age of twelve, Rochegrosse began his education at l'Académie Julian in Paris where he studied with Gustave Boulanger and Jules Lefebvre. He later studied at l'École des Beaux-Arts.

In 1883 Rochegrosse received the Prix du Salon which enabled him to travel to Italy. He also visited Belgium, the Netherlands and Germany. In 1890 Rochegrosse met Marie Leblond who became the love of his life as well as a model for many of his paintings. Beginning in 1900 they spent their winters in Algeria where Rochegrosse was influenced by local culture, architecture and design.

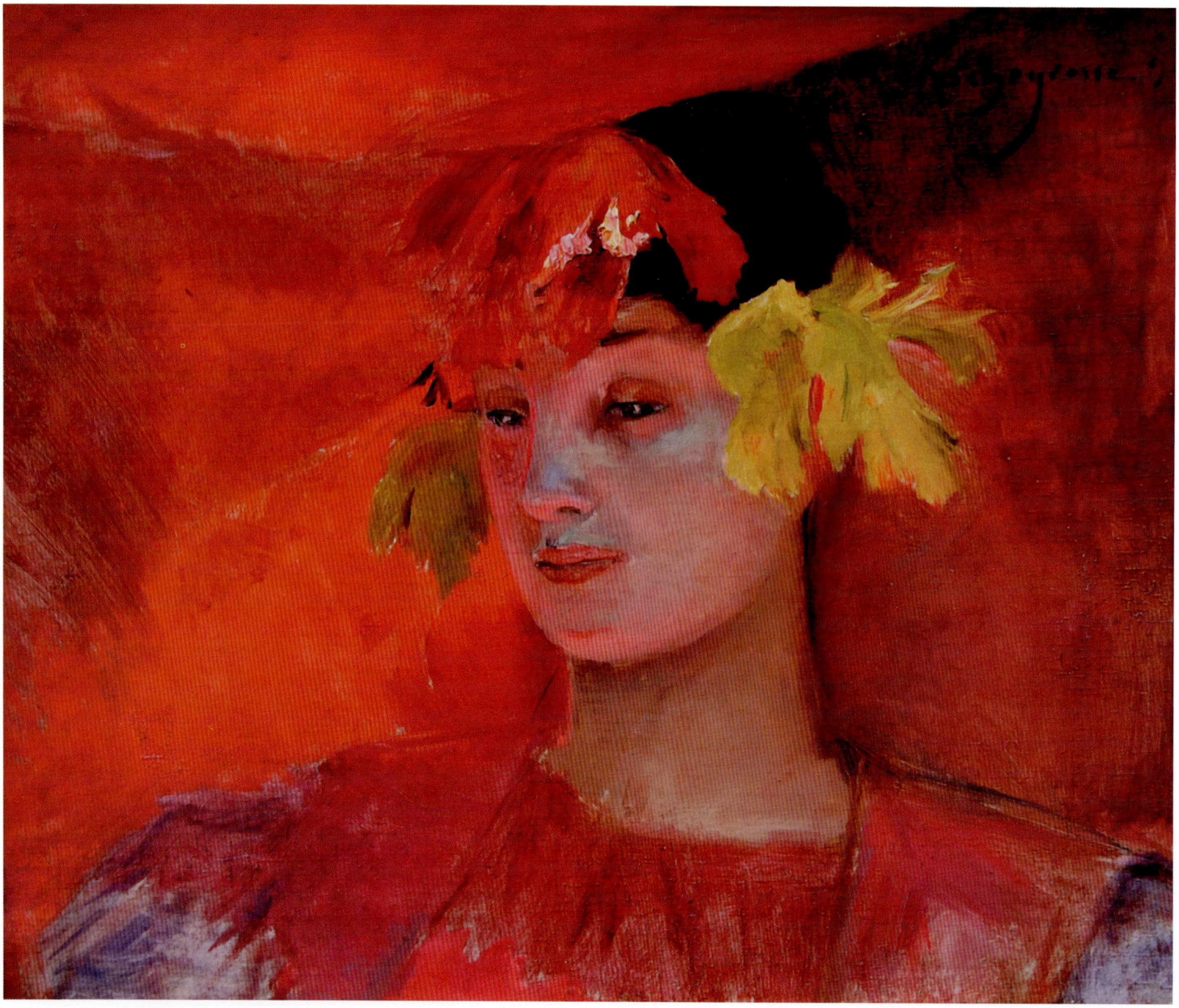

Georges Antoine Rochegrosse
Danseuse, Dated 1894
Jeffrey Winter Fine Arts, Long Beach, California

Rochegrosse is well known for his paintings however, he also worked as a watercolorist, illustrator, poster designer, decorator, theater set painter and muralist. The subject matter of his work is equally diverse including historic events, mythological figures, allegorical scenes, genre, figures, nudes, portraits, interiors and landscapes. Rochegrosse exhibited regularly at the Salon des Artistes Français where he became a member in 1887. He received a bronze medal in 1889, a Medal of Honor in 1906 and became Officier de la Légion d'Honneur in 1910. He also exhibited at the Salon de la Société des Aquarellistes Français.

In Algeria he participated in Salon des Artistes Algériens et Orientalistes, the Union Artistique de l'Afrique du Nord and Syndicat Professionnel des Artistes Algériens. His wife, Marie Leblond, died in 1920. In 1937 Rochegrosse married Antoinette Arnau, and he died the following year.

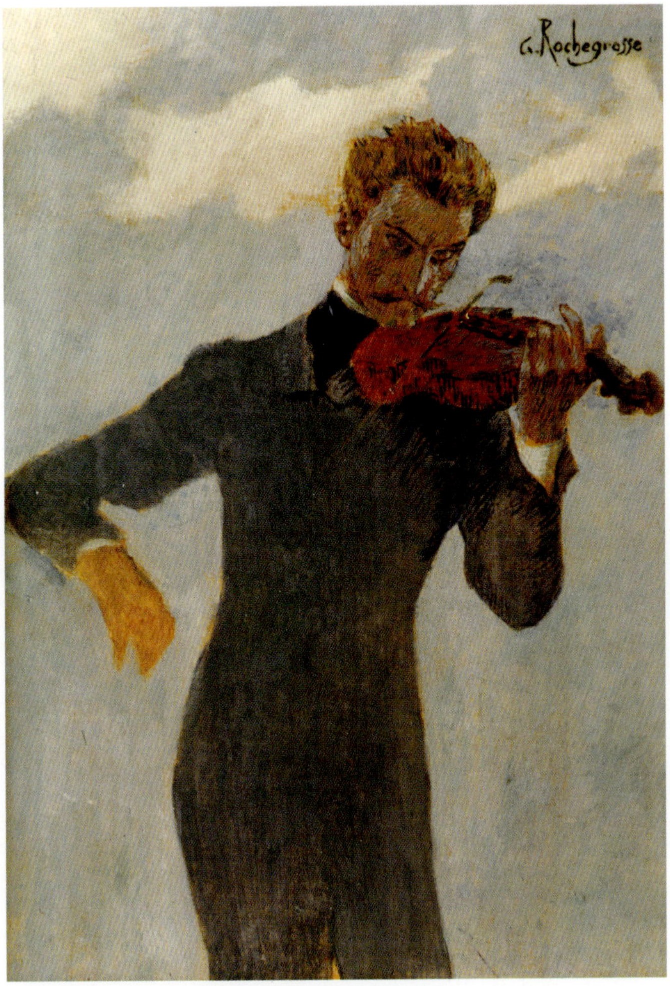

Georges Antoine Rochegrosse
Violiniste, c.1900
Christine Thorailler, Paris, France

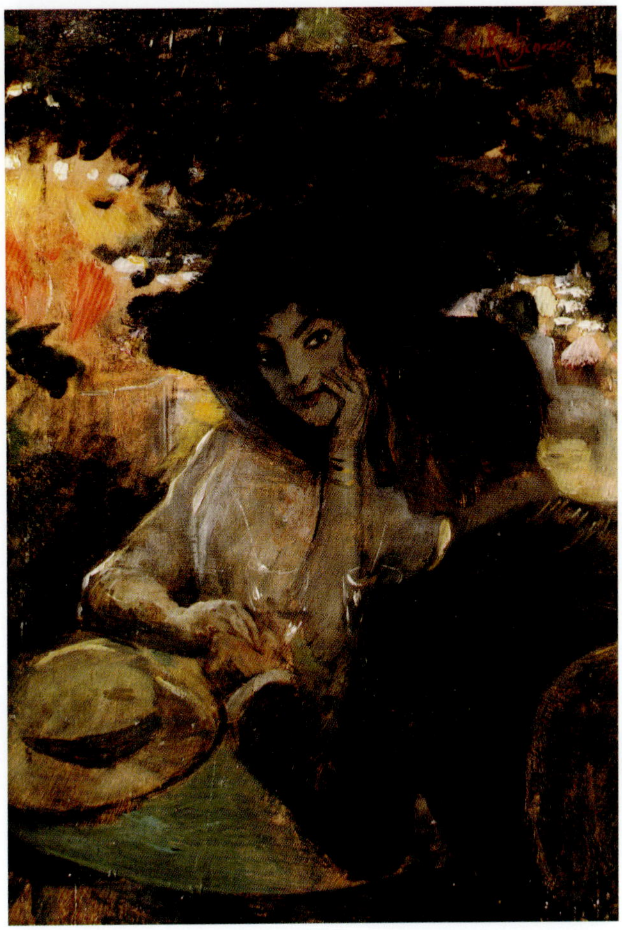

Georges Antoine Rochegrosse
Petite Déjeuner, c.1900
Christine Thorailler, Paris, France

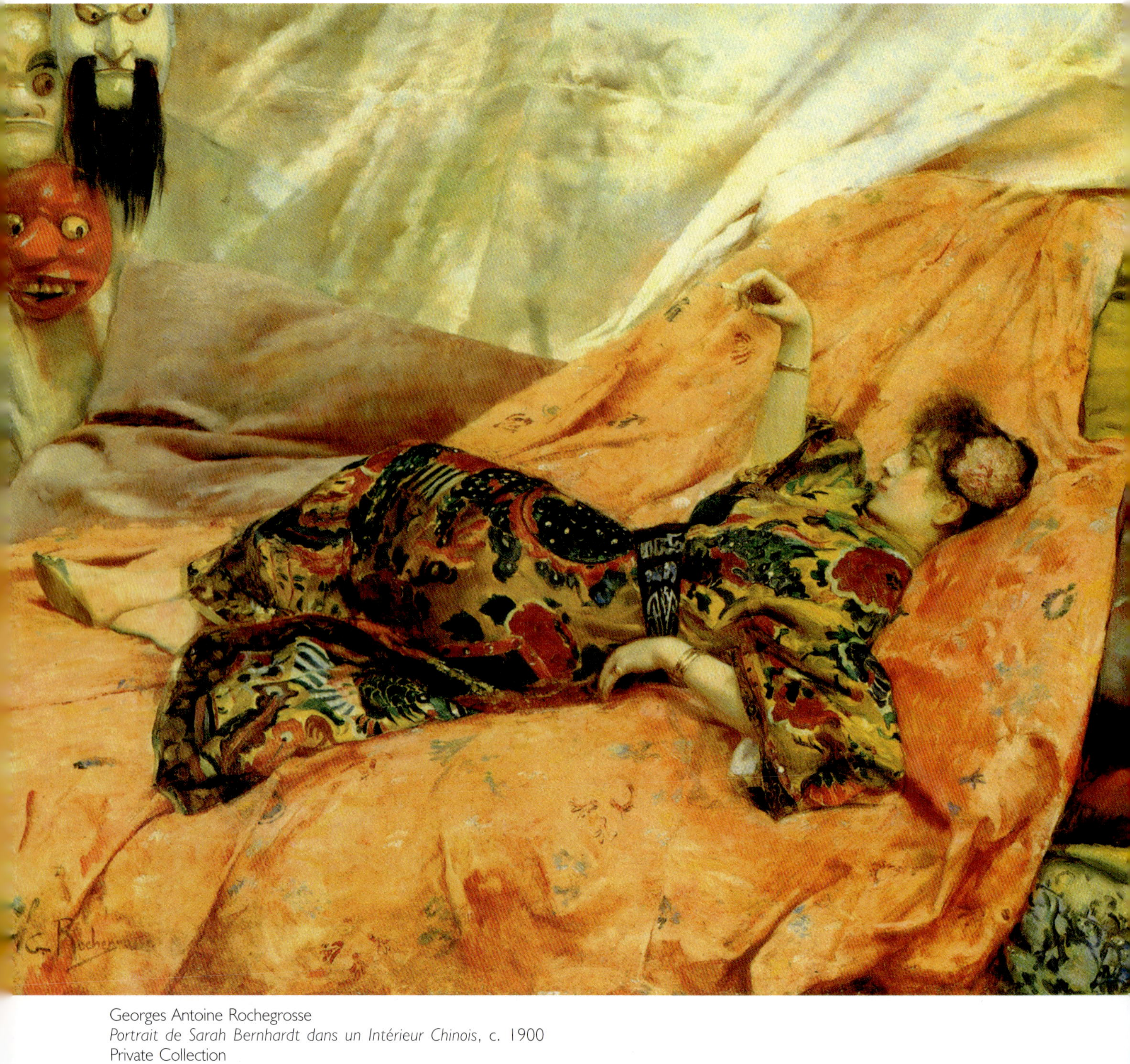

Georges Antoine Rochegrosse
Portrait de Sarah Bernhardt dans un Intérieur Chinois, c. 1900
Private Collection

Vera Schlesinger Rockline

1896-1934

Vera Schlesinger Rockline was born in Moscow in 1896. Her mother was French and her father was Russian. In Moscow she studied at the atelier of I. Machkoff, and while in Kiev she continued her education with Alexandra Exter.

She married in 1918 and in 1919 Rockline used the pseudonym "Schlesinger" to exhibit her work at the Union of Russian Painters' *Exhibition of Jewish Painters and Sculptors*. She exhibited at the fifth annual national exhibition *Impressionism and Abstraction* as well, and designed decorations for the anniversary of the Revolution.

Rockline fled Moscow in 1919 and took refuge in Georgia. She arrived in Paris in 1921 and settled in the Montparnasse district. In 1922 she exhibited at the Salon d'Automne where Paul Poiret bought several of her paintings. Poiret was an influential designer and serious art collector whose private collection was exhibited at Galerie Barbazanges, including works by Rockline, alongside van Dongen, Modigliani, Picasso, Matisse, Marval and many others.

Rockline also exhibited at the Salon des Indépendants and Salon des Tuileries. She received a solo exhibition at Galerie Vildrac in Paris in 1925 for which Poiret wrote the catalogue preface. The following year she exhibited at Galerie Bernheim-Jeune and in 1929 she exhibited at Galerie le Studio and in 1930 at Galerie Barreiro, where she exhibited for the following four years. She exhibited at l'Éxposition Coloniale in 1931. Galerie Barreiro held a retrospective exhibiting drawings, pastels and paintings done between 1919 and 1934. Rockline was a member of the l'Union Russe des Arts as well. Rockline died in 1935 at the age of 38.

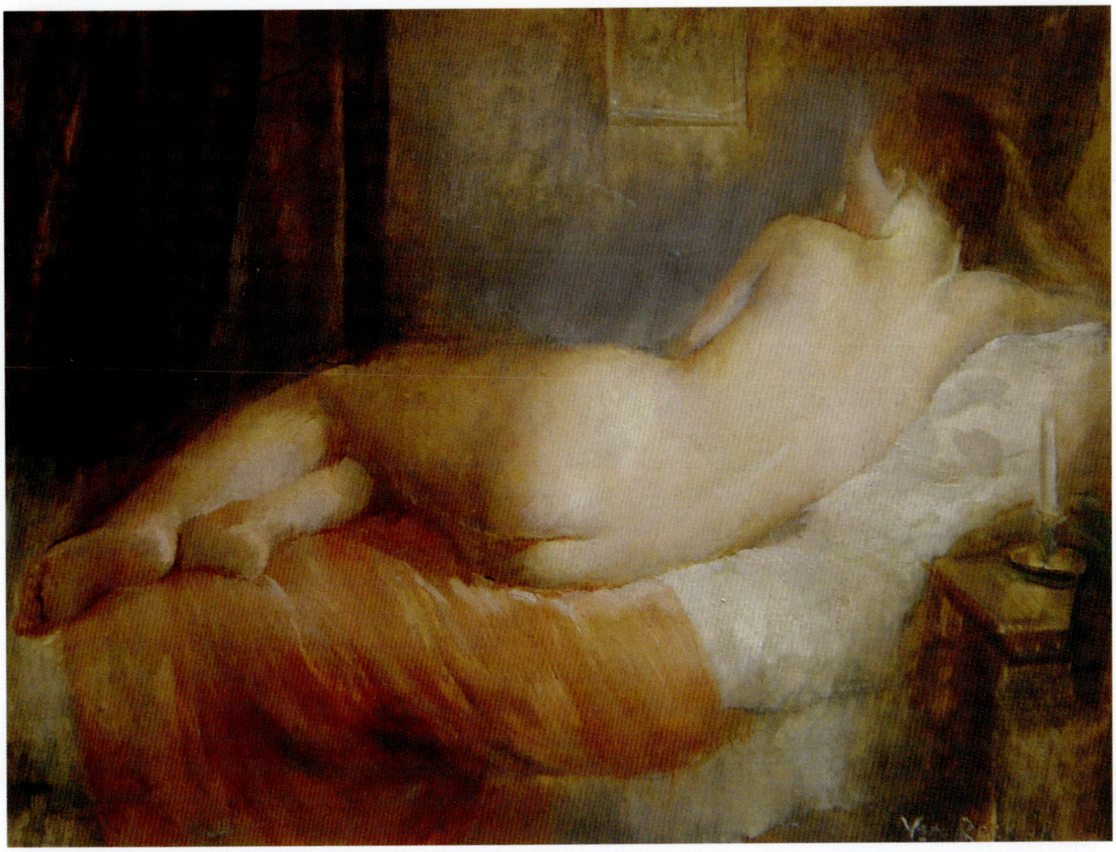

Vera Rockline
Nu en Repose, c.1925
Galerie Agnes Thiebault, Paris, France

Over the years there have been several retrospectives of Rockline's work at Parisian galleries; in 1965 at Galerie Balzac and 1975 at Galerie Battais, with a catalogue essay by Gérald Schurr. To mark the anniversary of her death Galerie Drouart held a retrospective in 1954.

Rockline's early work conveys the influence of Cubism and of her mentor Alexandra Exter. The subtler color composition of her works, however, refers more to Cézanne. Rockline is best known for painting nudes and a few portraits. She incorporated her cubist tendencies into her unique postimpressionist style, including use of bold brush strokes and rich colors thereby creating stunning works of modern beauty. In Montparnasse there was a large Russian community with which Rockline was certainly familiar. She died at the young age of 38, cutting short a brilliant career.

As with many women artists of her generation, Rockline is becoming recognized. In 1991 there was a major exhibition of her paintings at Galerie Makassar in Paris. Rockline's work was included in *Elles de Montparnasse*, 2002, at the Musée du Montparnasse. Her paintings were exhibited alongside Tamara de Lempicka, Jacqueline Marval, Maria Blanchard, Natalia Gontcharova, Lioubov Popova, and many other of her contemporaries. At the Musée Montmartre in 2003, she was included in a major exhibition of Russian artists that worked in Paris, including Marie Vassilieff, Sonia Delaunay, Lioubov Popova, Mikhail Larionov, Serge Tchekhonine and Léon Bakst.

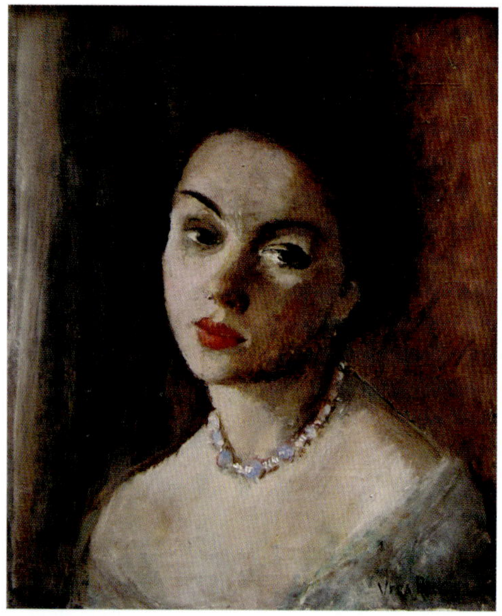

Vera Rockline
Femme Élégante, c.1925
Galerie Agnes Thiebault, Paris, France

Vera Rockline
Nu Allongé, c.1925
A.B.A. Gallery, New York, New York

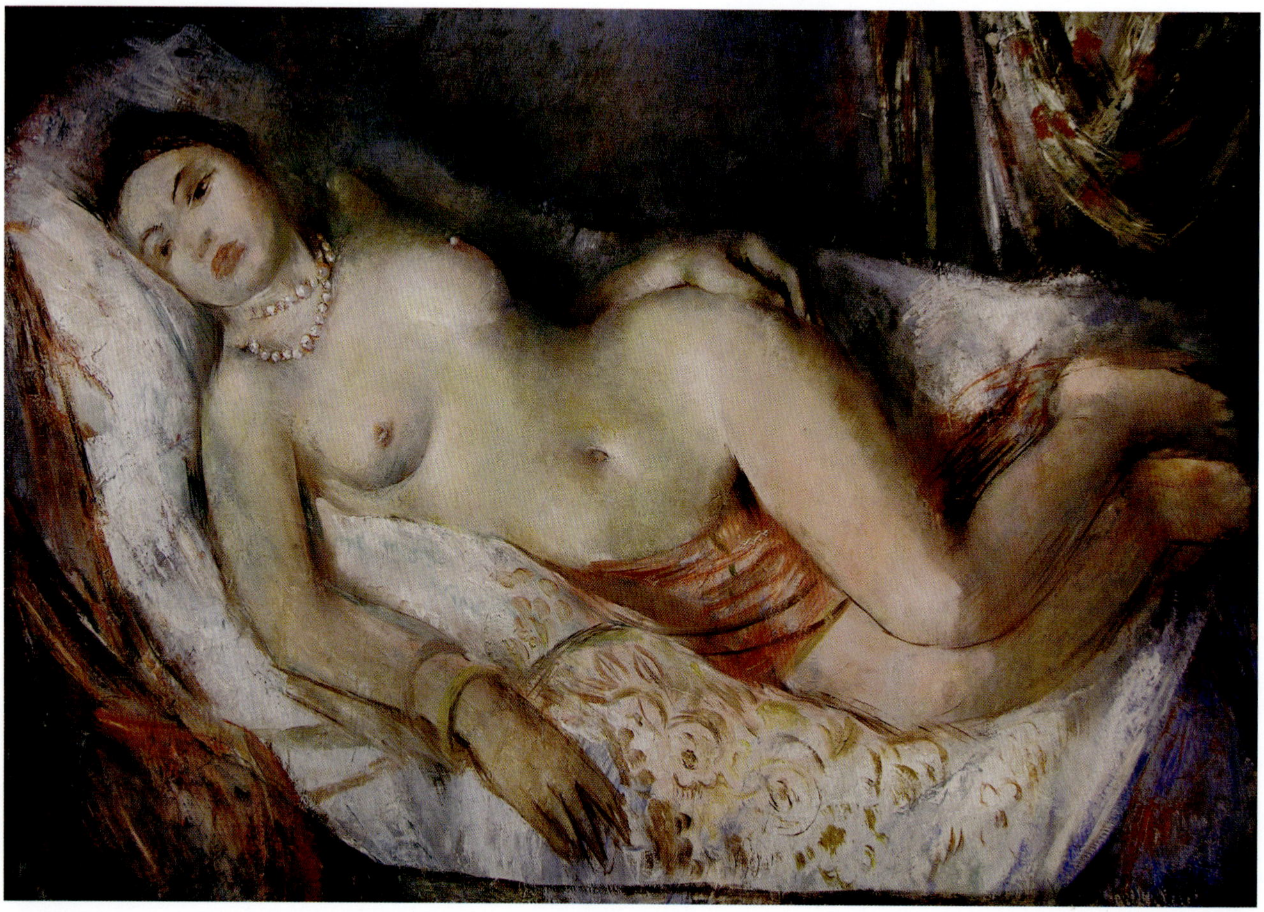

Georges Rogy
1897-1981

Georges Rogy was born on November 26, 1897 in Etterbeek, Belgium. In 1915 he entered l'Académie des Beaux-Arts de Bruxelles to study architecture. Two years later he chose an art major and received high honors and a private studio in the advanced painting class.

Rogy was an art professor at l'École des Arts et Métiers d'Etterbeek. He was reclusive and not overly interested in exhibiting his work. Nonetheless, he began exhibiting in 1927 and during the following years participated in several of the Belgian Salons. His paintings received notice at the 1930 Centenary of National Independence exhibition and the 1935 Brabant Pavilion at the Universal and International Exhibition.

Rogy painted many portraits utilizing modern techniques. Clever and creative, his scenes of parks and cafés show his mastery of light and composition.

In a 1936 edition of *Le National Belge* Charles Bernard wrote about Rogy's portraits commenting that "beneath their visible appearance, he displays the hidden side, mysterious, it is this which particularly explains the charm of his portraits...." Richard Durrieux wrote in 1948 in *Le Soir*, "[Rogy] wants to go beyond, to surprise the spirit beyond psychological exactitude and let the subject live in its atmosphere, in its light...."

Rogy's work is included in museums and private collections. In 1955 the Belgian Embassy in Moscow purchased several of his works. A book on the artist was published in 1993 by Patrick and Vivian Berko with an introduction by Ernest Van Buynder. Rogy died August 28, 1981.

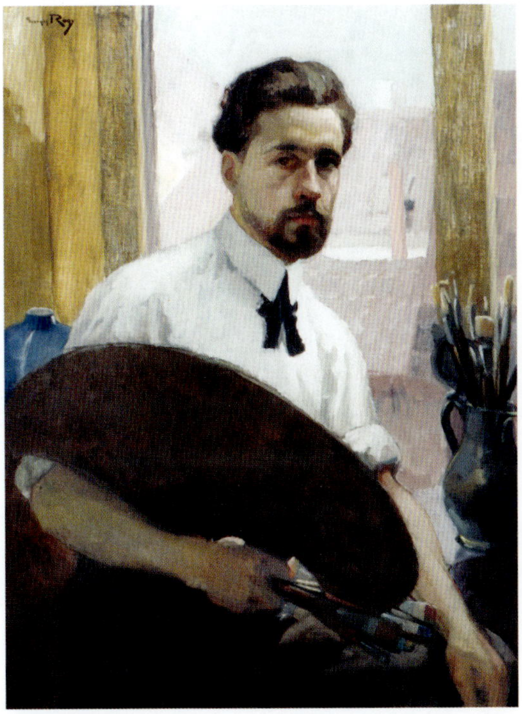

Georges Rogy
Dans l'Atelier, c.1920
Los Angeles Fine Art Gallery, Los Angeles, California

Georges Rogy
Nu au Boudoir, c.1920
Los Angeles Fine Art Gallery, Los Angeles, California

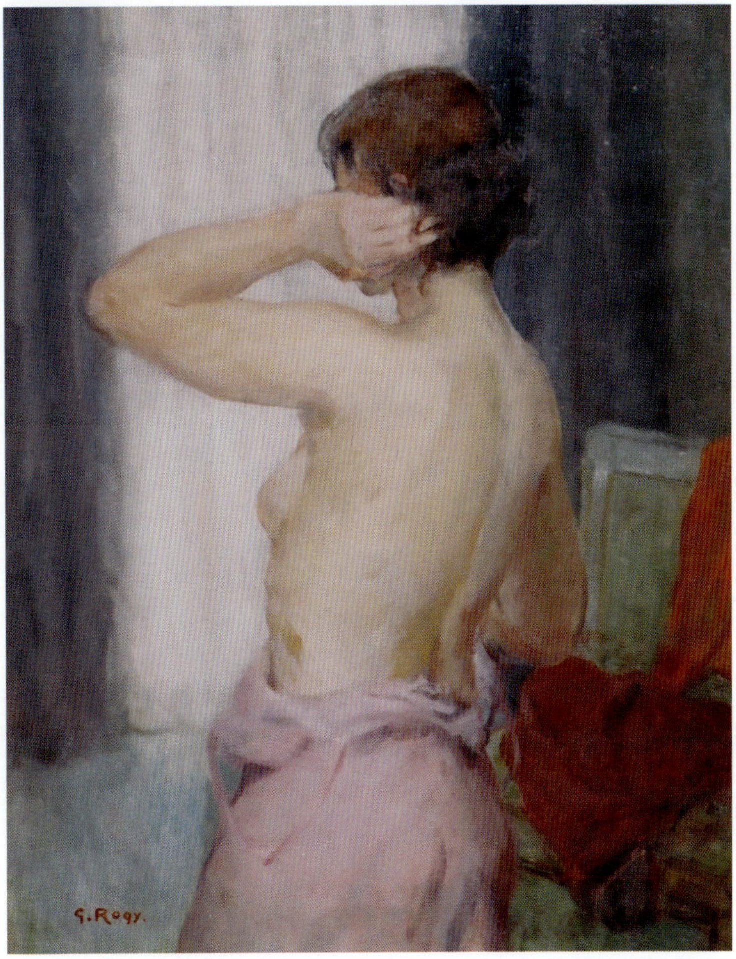

Walter Louis Émile Sauer

1889-1927

Walter Louis Émile Sauer was born February 12, 1889 in Saint-Gilles-les-Bruxelles to parents of German descent. Having been frequently home bound due to childhood illnesses he was surrounded by the family library, which was full of books and references on music and the arts.

In 1903 he attended l'École des Beaux-Arts in Brussels under the tutelage of Moonens, van Damme-Sylva, Montald, Delville and Fabry. He exhibited at the Triennial Salon, Brussels in 1914 and 1921 illustrated *Symphonie Macabre* by Limbosch.

Sauer produced a large body of work in his short life. His earliest paintings are typical of the Belgian Postimpressionists but he came to adapt a style more associated with the German and Viennese Secessionists. Around 1917 Sauer began a series of extraordinary watercolors and paintings that truly set him apart from other Belgian artists. Combining fine graphic technique and an emotional connection with his subjects Sauer created works with a rare and refined beauty. He portrayed beautiful and intriguing men and women in exquisite detail, incorporating costumes of the period. These works provide a glimpse of the era. Sauer can be compared stylistically with the Viennese artist Raphaël Kirchner, who died in 1917 at the age of 41. Sauer died on September 6, 1927 in Algiers.

In 1974 Galerie l'Ecuyer in Brussels organized an exhibition of Sauer's work. Since then his work has been included in many exhibitions of Belgian artists. In 2001 a well illustrated book, *Walter Sauer, 1889-1927,* was published by Bern'art.

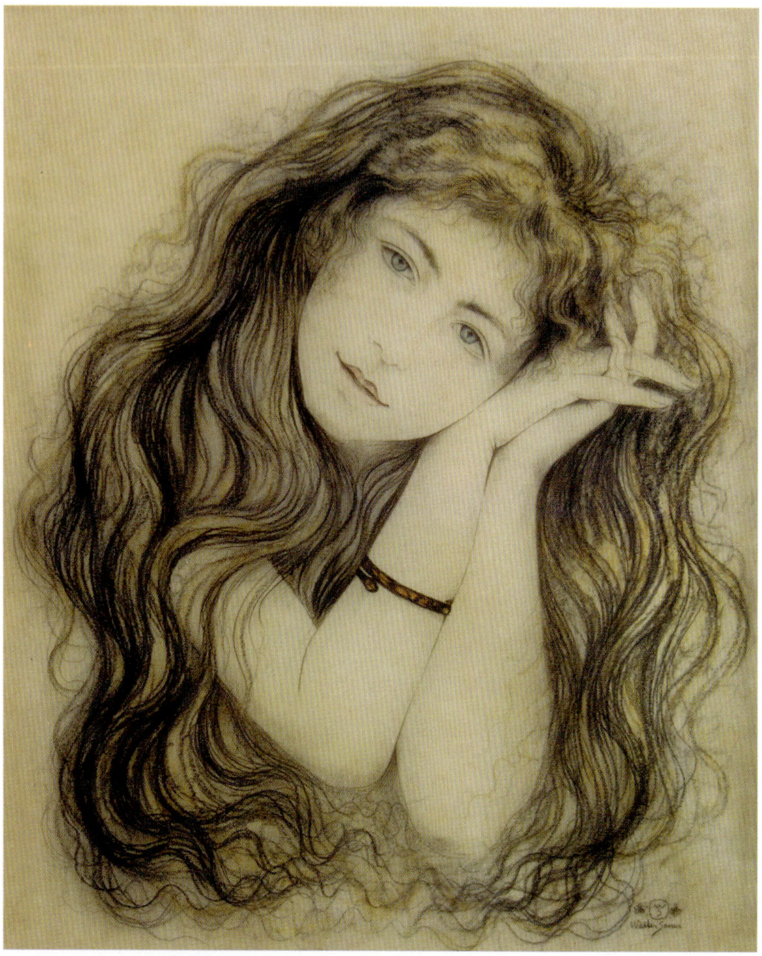

Walter Louis Émile Sauer
Jeune Femme, c.1910
Julia Evershade and Mark Smith, Los Angeles, California

Edgar Scauflaire

1893–1960

Edgar Scauflaire was born in Liège in 1893. The painter Daco, for whom he was a model, inspired Scauflaire to become an artist. He studied at l'Académie des Beaux-Arts de Liège where he was a student of Auguste Donnay, Adrien de Witte and François Maréchal, Émile Berchmans and Ludovic Bauès.

Scauflaire exhibited often in Paris and Brussels. He participated in most of the official exhibitions of Belgian artists in foreign countries. Scauflaire's work was included in the following exhibitions: La Biennale de Venise in 1924, 1938, and 1948; La Biennale de Sao Paulo in 1951 and 1953; Biennale de Menton in 1953; Salon des Tuileries in 1949; and l'Exposition Universelle in Brussels in 1958. His works can be found in the collections of museums in Brussels, Liège, Verviers, Seraingm La Louvière, Strasbourg, Montbar, Bale and Buenos Aires.

Scauflaire was awarded le Prix de l'Association Industrielle de Santa-Margarita Ligure in 1950. He was the founding member of l'Association pour les Progrès Intellectuels et Artistiques de la Wallonie.

Scauflaire was a brilliant draftsman: his drawings are finely detailed and his early paintings, from the period just after World War I, convey a strong cubist influence that carries through his entire oeuvre. His subjects became more romantic and surreal in the 1920s. The style of the Belgian Expressionists, a style unique to the region, emerged in Scauflaire's works. Exaggerated and expressive, geometric and colorful, these paintings communicated his confidence. Scauflaire's style changed in the 1940s and 1950s: he flattened the forms but continued to use strong colors; the effect of which gave these paintings a more graphic aesthetic. His canvases tended to be large, some as much at two and a half meters wide. Scauflaire executed many paintings on glass, frescos, tapestries and other decorative murals as well.

Scauflaire was a very prolific artist whose career spanned many decades. He recently has been recognized for his contribution to 20th century art and in 1994 a major retrospective sponsored by the Générale de Banque was organized in Liege. The exhibition catalogue includes extensive color illustrations and an essay by Delphine Quirin and Louis Maraite. Scauflaire died in Liège in 1960.

Edgar Scauflaire
Portrait d'une Femme, c.1930
The Parrish Collection, San Francisco, California

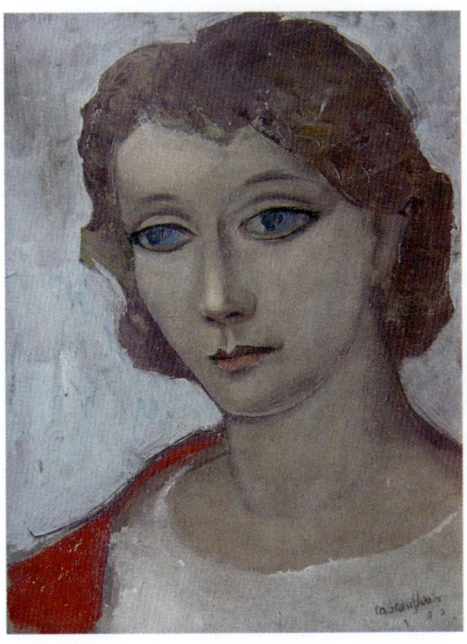

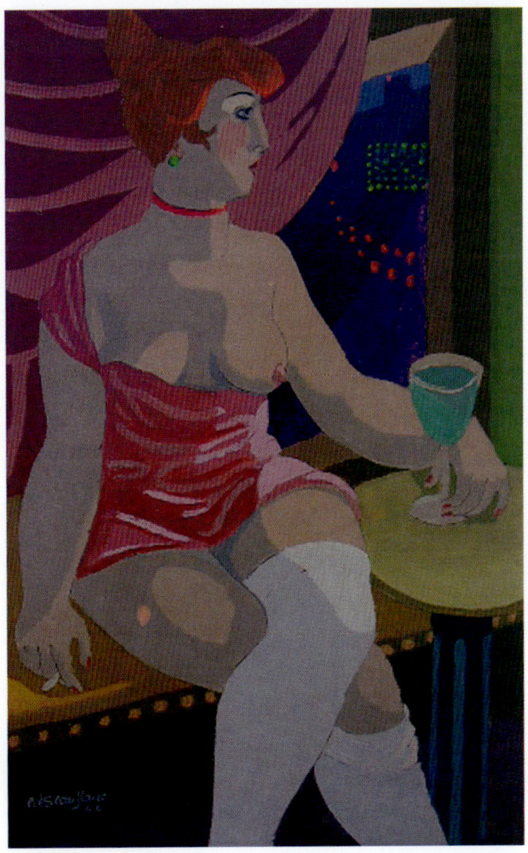

Edgar Scauflaire
Au Bordello, Dated 1937
Anil and Christine Singh, Hillsborough, California

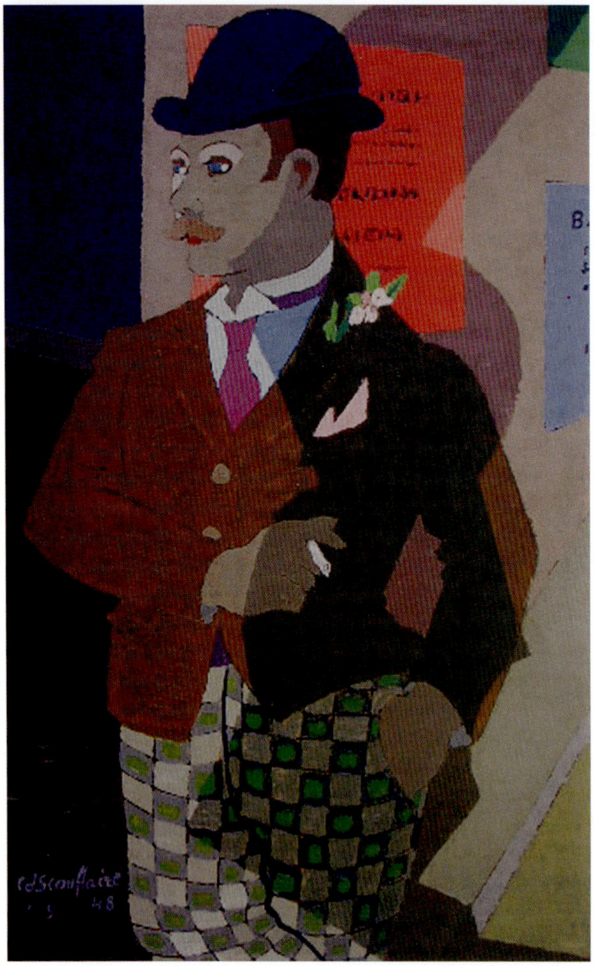

Edgar Scauflaire
Chapeau Violet, c.1940
Anil and Christine Singh, Hillsborough, California

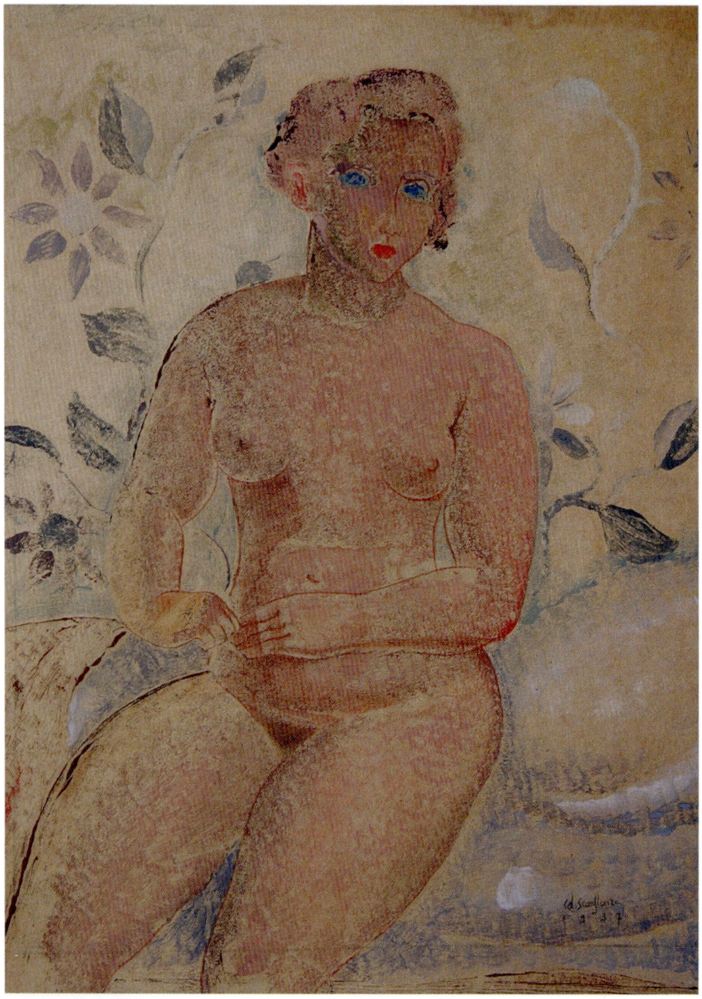

Edgar Scauflaire
Nu Assis, c.1940
Parrish Collection, San Francisco, California

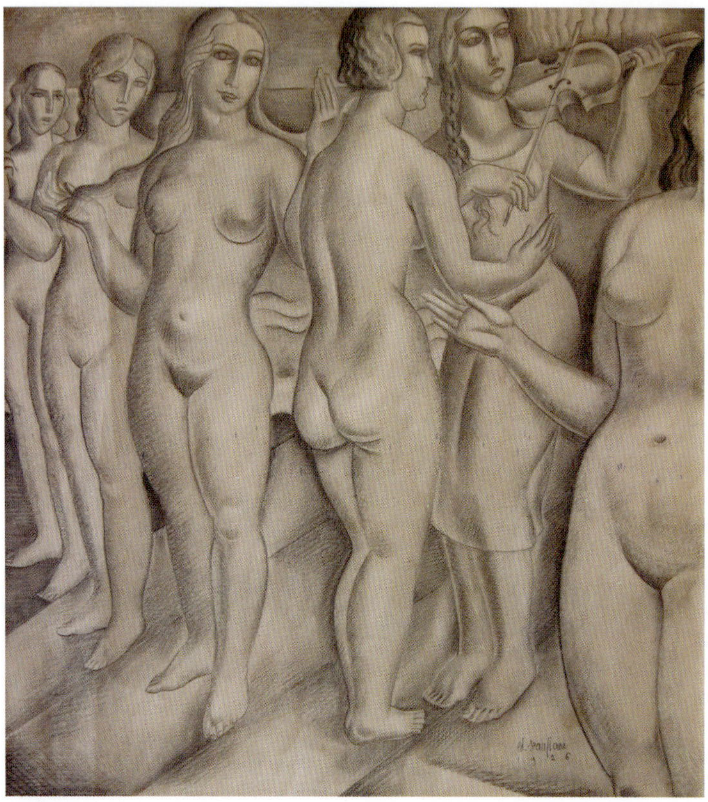

Edgar Scauflaire
Danseuses Nus, Dated 1926
Private Collection, Los Angeles, California

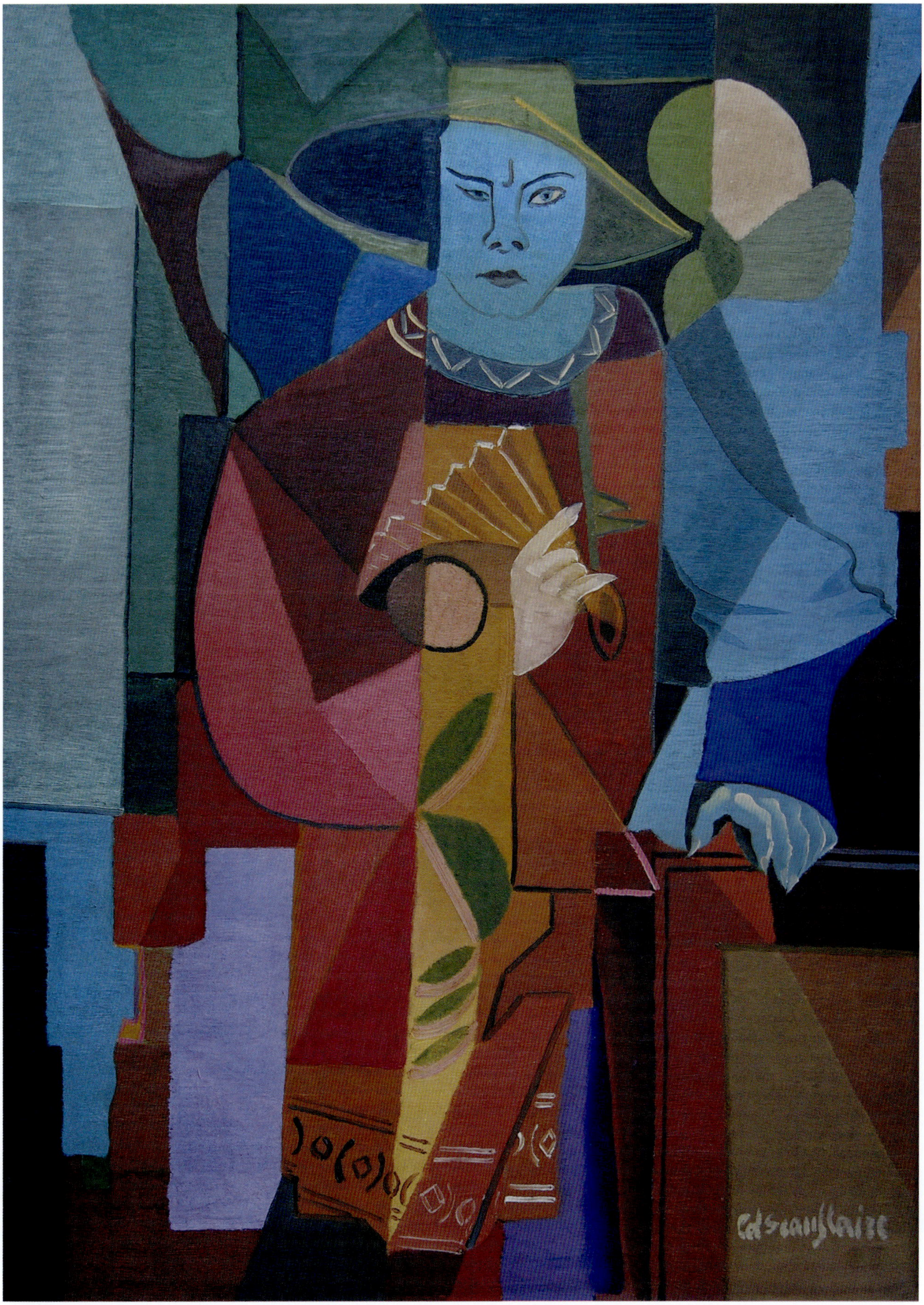

Edgar Scauflaire
Mikado, c.1940
The Parrish Collection, San Francisco, California

Lucien-Victor Guirand (Guérand) de Scévola

1871-1950

Lucien-Victor Guirand de Scévola was born November 14, 1871. As a painter and watercolorist he studied under Cormon at l'École des Beaux-Arts in Paris. Among his exhibitions were the Société des Artists Français from 1889 to 1897 and the Société Nationale des Beaux-Arts, of which he was a committee member. He also exhibited frequently at the Galerie Mona Lisa. An Honorable Mention in 1897, a Bronze Medal in 1900 and the Légion d'Honneur in 1914 were among his awards and honors.

His work is found in the collections of the Musée de Mulhouse and the Musée d'Art Moderne de la Ville Paris. Guirand de Scévola died March 29, 1950 in Paris.

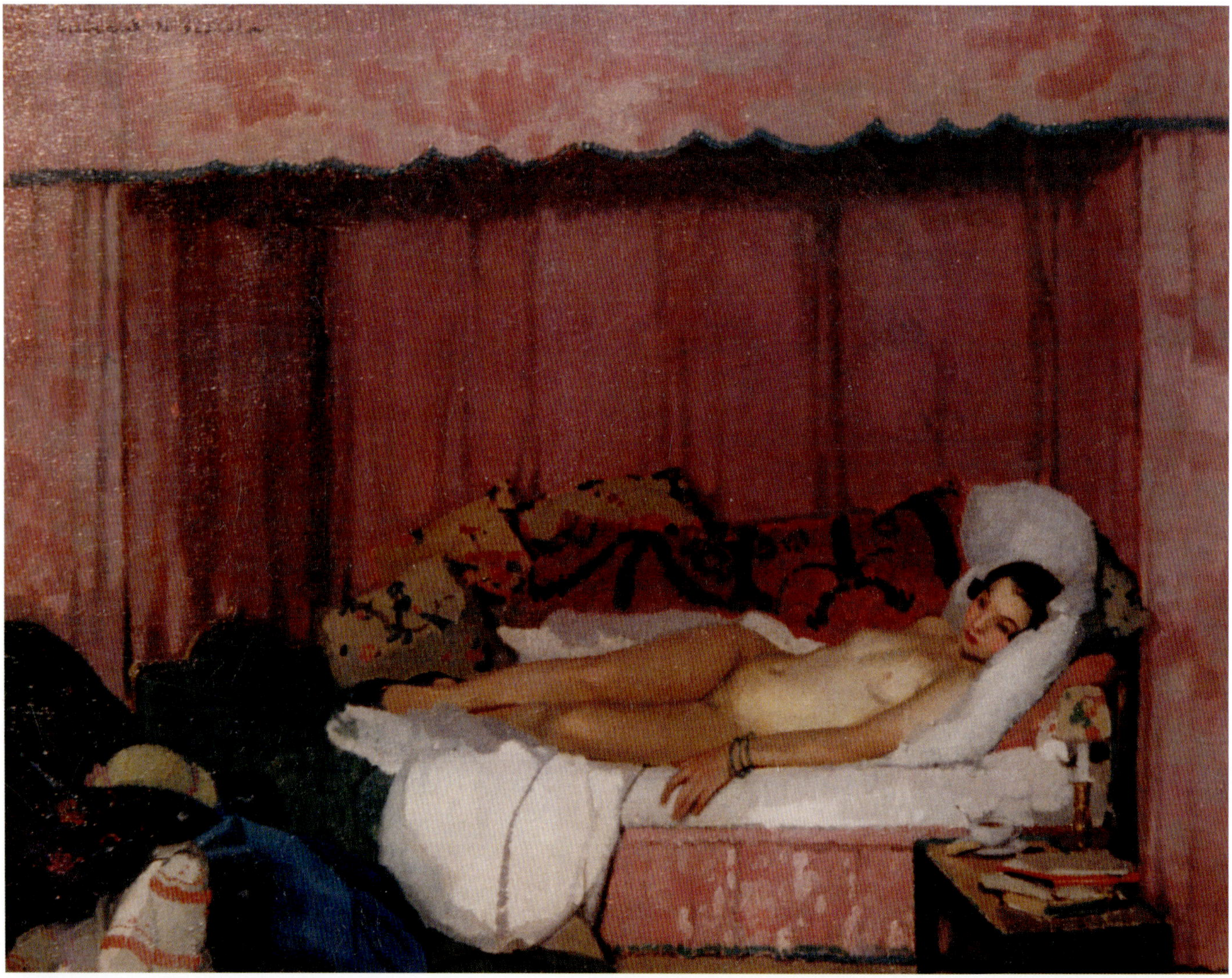

Lucien de Scévola
Á la Chambre à Coucher, c.1920
Kathleen Avery Fine Art, Palo Alto, California

Hugo Schimmel
Born 1869

Hugo Schimmel was born September 9, 1869 in Chemnitz, Germany. He was a student of Bantzer in Dresden and, while in Paris, studied under Morisset. His most notable achievement is his contribution to the Landestheater in Neustrelitz, Germany where six of his paintings hang.

Schimmel's paintings were influenced by the Vienna and Berlin Secession; rich in feeling, color and texture. His work while in Paris had considerable success. The date of his death is unknown.

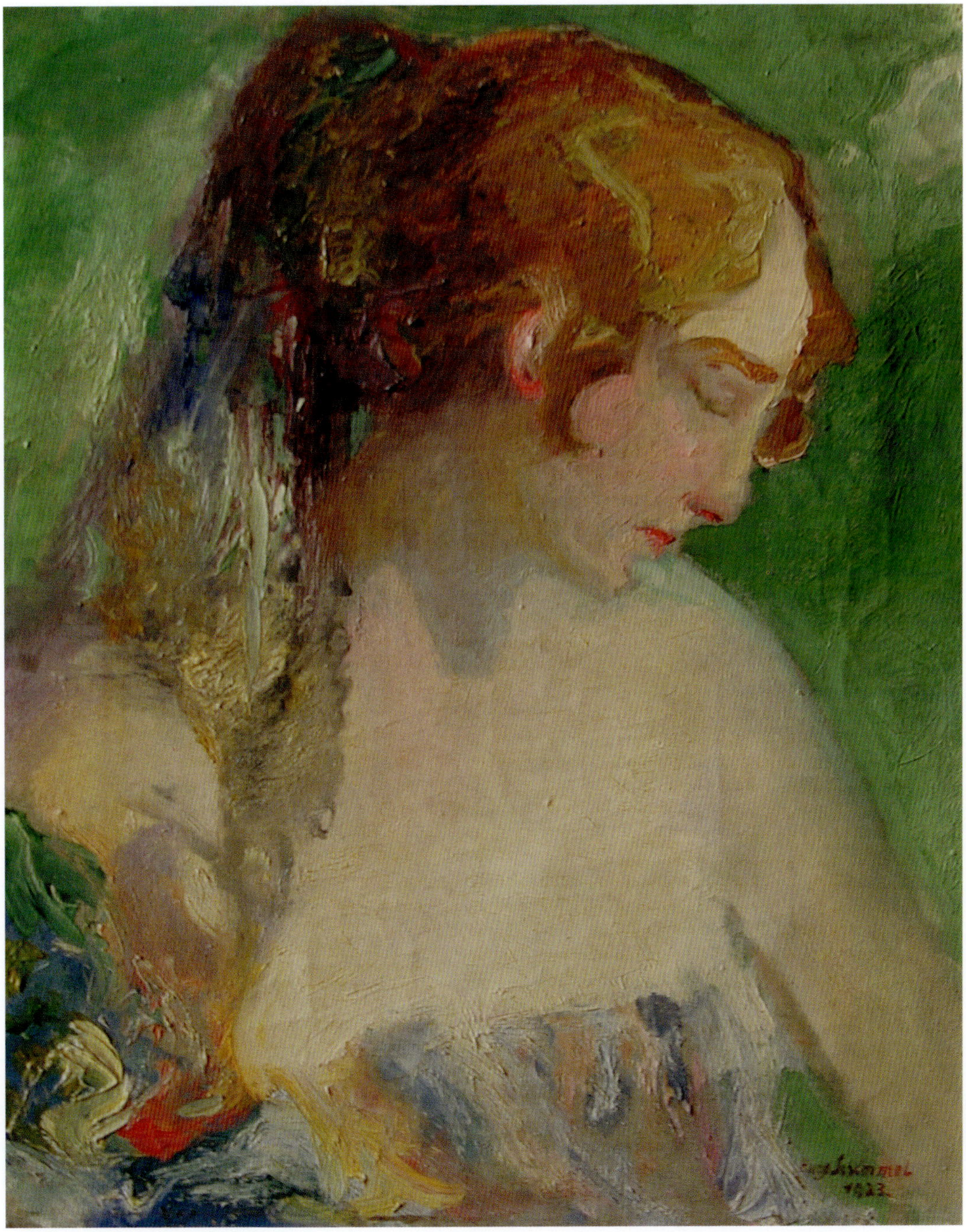

Hugo Schimmel
Portrait of a Young Woman, Dated 1923
Jeffrey Winter Fine Arts, Long Beach, California

Rodolphe Schönberg

1901-1944

Rodolphe Schönberg was born in Brussels in 1901. He studied with Kurt Peiser and Gérard Jacobs at l'Académie des Beaux-Arts de Bruxelles. He was known for his paintings, watercolors and aquatints of urban scenes. He was a sensitive painter who exhibited the technique of traditional academy artists, yet his subjects are of modern life.

In his short career he traveled to England, Denmark and Central America. Schönberg was a leader in the Resistance during World War II and was killed by the Nazis in May of 1944.

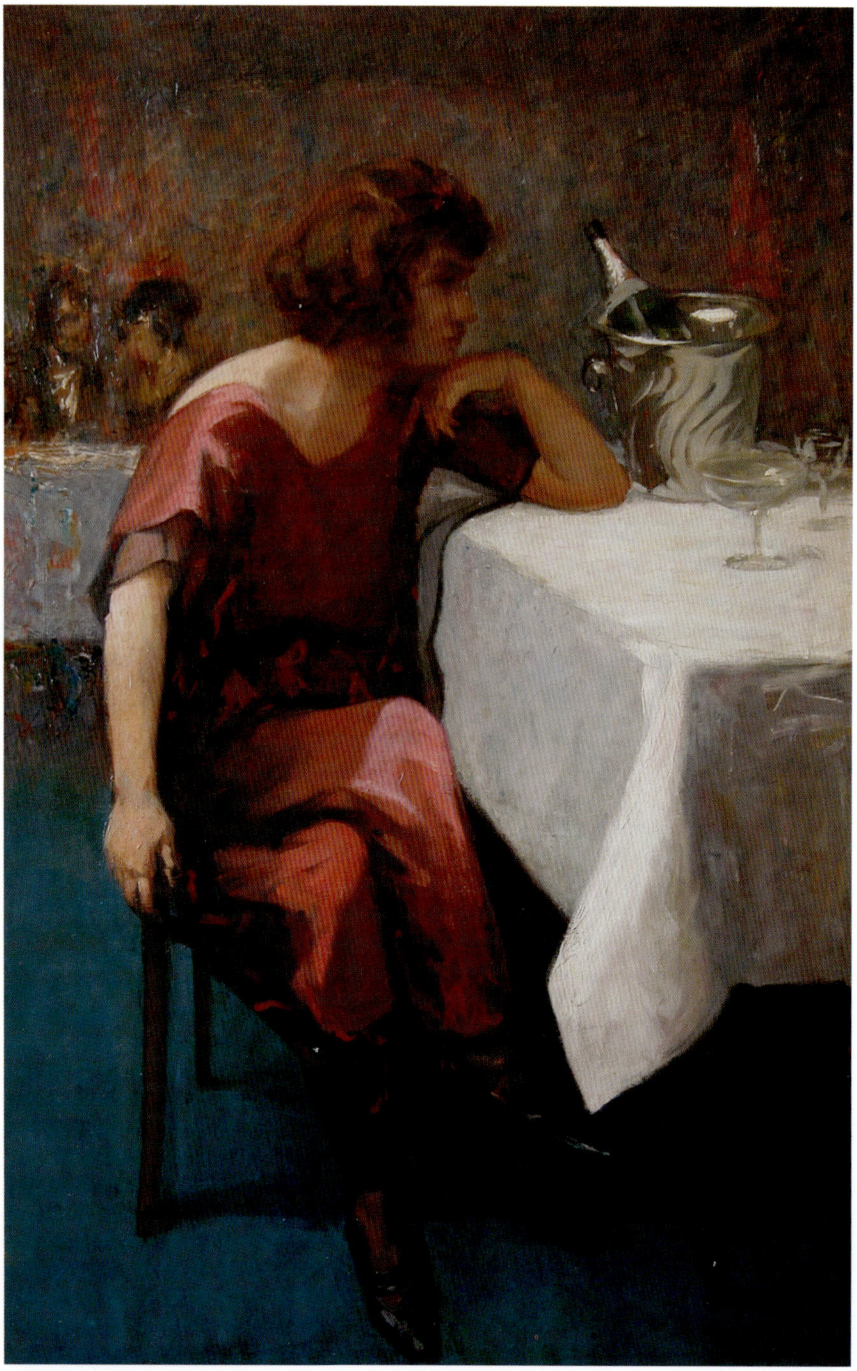

Rodolphe Schönberg
Au Café, Dated 1924
Papillon Gallery, Los Angeles, California

William Samuel Schwartz

1896-1977

William Samuel Schwartz was born in Smorgon, Russia, on February 23, 1896. His studies and travels were extensive as were his body of work and his musical endeavors.

Schwartz studied at the Vilna Art School in Russia with a four year scholarship before immigrating to the United States at the age of 17. He lived with his sister in New York for eight months before joining his brother in Omaha. There he became a housepainter and continued his fine art studies at the Kellom School. Under the instruction of J. Laurie Wallace, Schwartz studied life drawing, portraiture and painting.

He later moved to Chicago where he continued his lessons at the Art Institute and assumed the role of principle tenor in various vaudeville, radio, concert and operatic performances. His musical career supported his tuition at the Institute throughout the 1920s when he became a well-recognized painter. Schwartz's musical career continued to influence his works of abstract compositions, most notably in his series *Symphonic Forms*. His paintings have been closely sourced to the writings and philosophies of Wassily Kandinsky who explored the relations of music, spirituality, color and abstract form.

After graduating from the Art Institute, Schwartz continued to exhibit there annually in group shows until, in 1926, he received his first solo exhibition at the Institute. He continued to exhibit extensively in Chicago, Madison, Dallas, New York, Detroit and at the Pennsylvania Academy of Fine Art. Schwartz received numerous awards and prizes throughout his career across the United States.

In 1930 Manuel Chapman published an extensive study, *William S. Schwartz* and In 1984, Hirschl & Adler Galleries Inc. held an exhibition of Schwartz's work for which Doug Dreishpoon wrote an eloquent introduction to the catalogue, *The Paintings, Drawings, and Lithographs of William S. Schwartz*.

There is no evidence that Schwartz ever exhibited or studied in Europe, but recently several of his works have been found in Paris. Work from every period of his long career is decidedly modern, he used the discipline of the Cubists and Futurists and molded it with his unique colorization. His use of color ranges from brilliant to somber often in similar compositions; he filled his canvases with passion. Schwartz was also meticulous in numbering, dating and titling his paintings. He died in Chicago in 1977.

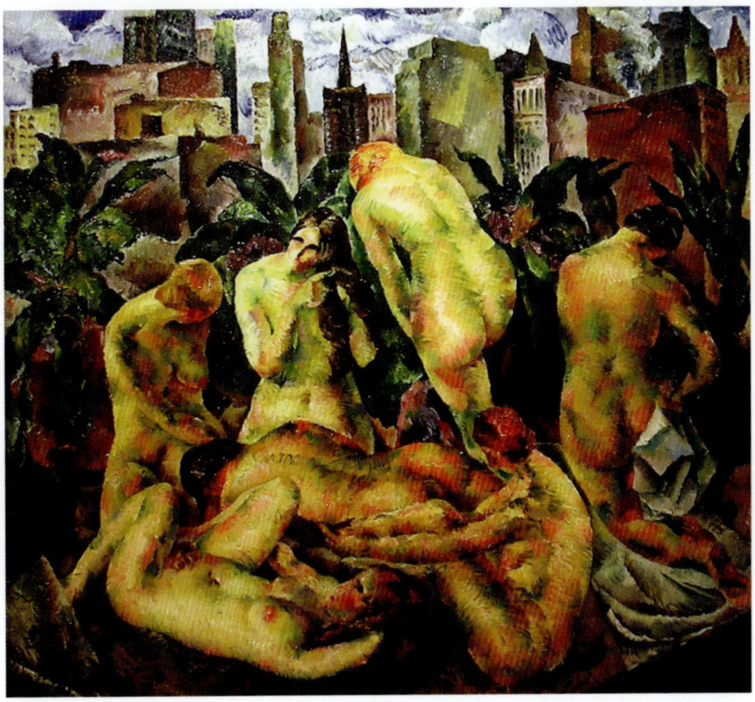

William S. Schwartz
Sun Bathers, Dated 1930
Madron LLC, Chicago, Illinois

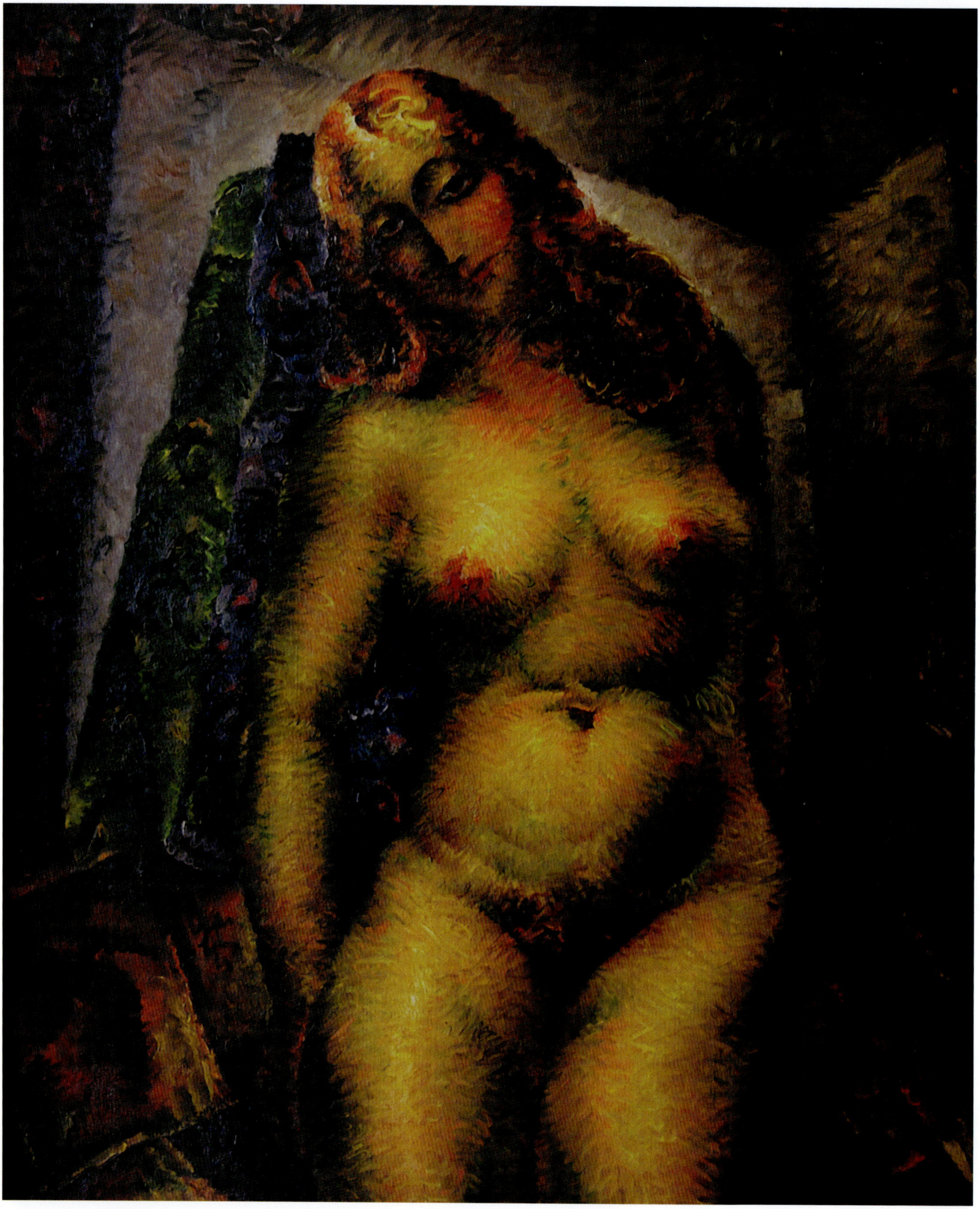

William S. Schwartz
Judith, Dated 1930
Papillon Gallery, Los Angeles, California

Lucien Seevagen

1887-1959

Lucien Seevagen was born January 29, 1887, in Chaumont. He was a student of Eugène Charvot and attended l'École des Arts Décoratifs in Paris. Seevagen worked frequently on the island of Bréhat and exhibited often at the Salon des Indépendants, the Salon d'Automne and the Salon des Tuileries.

Seevagen is known for his paintings and engravings of small villages, urban landscapes and seascapes. His nudes however have a special quality bordering on the erotic. His composition and use of color bring his exotic subjects to life. Seevagen died on June 25, 1959.

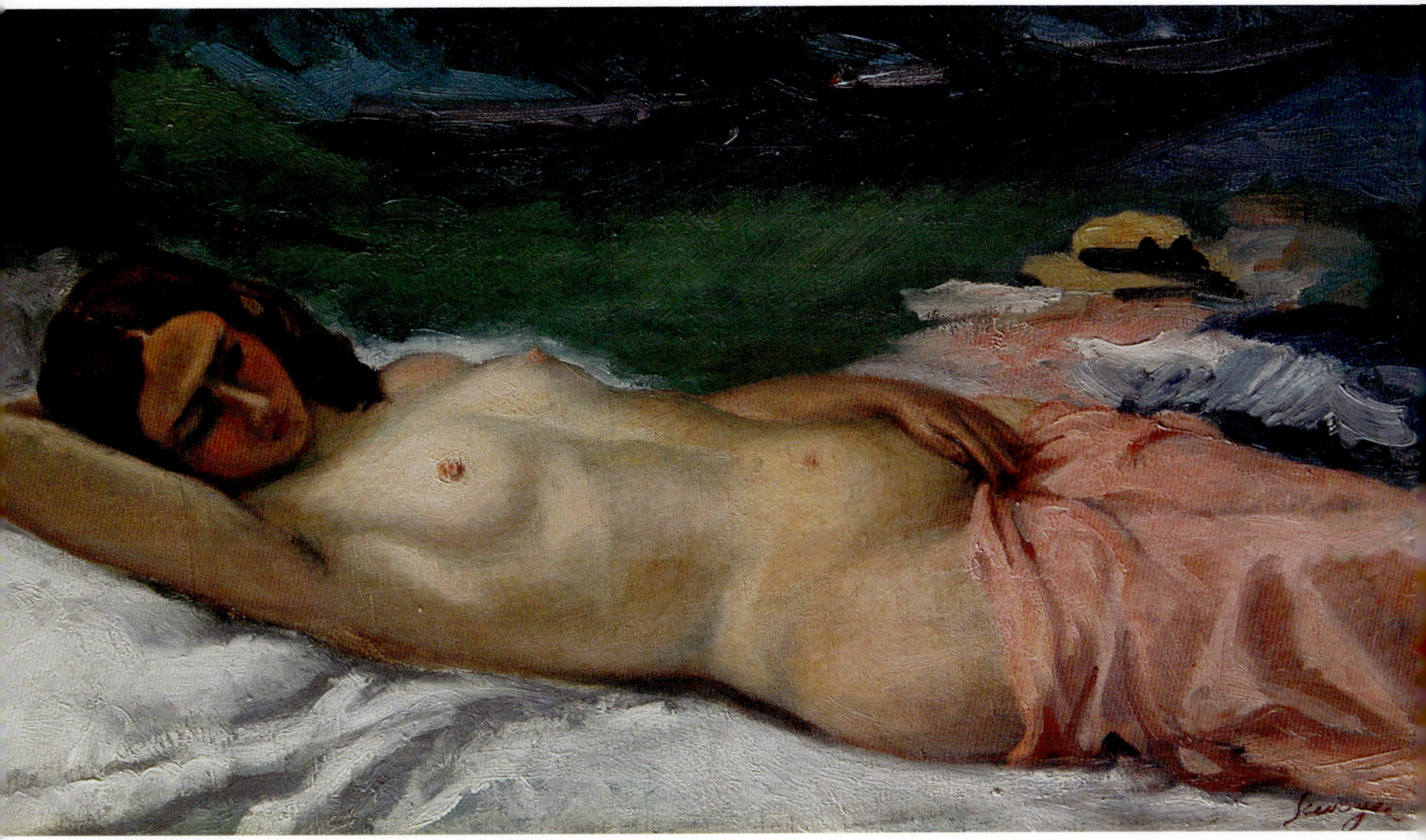

Lucien Seevagen
Nu Allongé, c.1930
Papillon Gallery, Los Angeles, California

Boris Smirnoff

20th century

Boris Smirnoff was born at the end of the 19th century of French nationality. He studied in the studio of Lucien Simon at l'École des Beaux-Arts in Paris.

Smirnoff exhibited extensively in Paris, London, Lisbon, New York, Stockholm, Berne, Geneva, Claire, Palermo, Rome, Nice and Cannes and in Cagnes-sur-Mer where he usually resided. The dates of his birth and death remain undocumented, though his major body of work was created in the 1920s and through the 1940s.

Smirnoff's work is subtle and sensual and it is believed that he worked closely with Foujita as their pastels are similar in technique. He painted many portraits including Hollywood actors and actresses along with many nudes and semi-erotic works.

Smirnoff created some of the decorations for the Italian Embassy in Tokyo and his works can be found in the art museums of Cagnes-sur-Mer, Claire, Grenoble, Moscow and Prague.

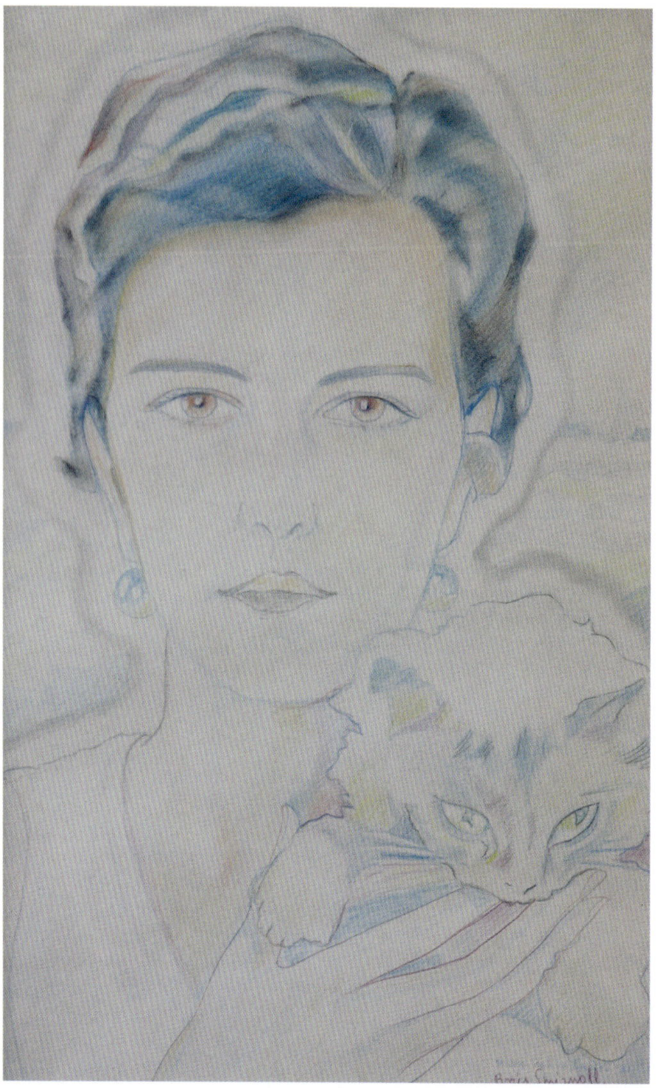

Boris Smirnoff
Femme au Chat, c. 1930
Papillon Gallery, Los Angeles, California

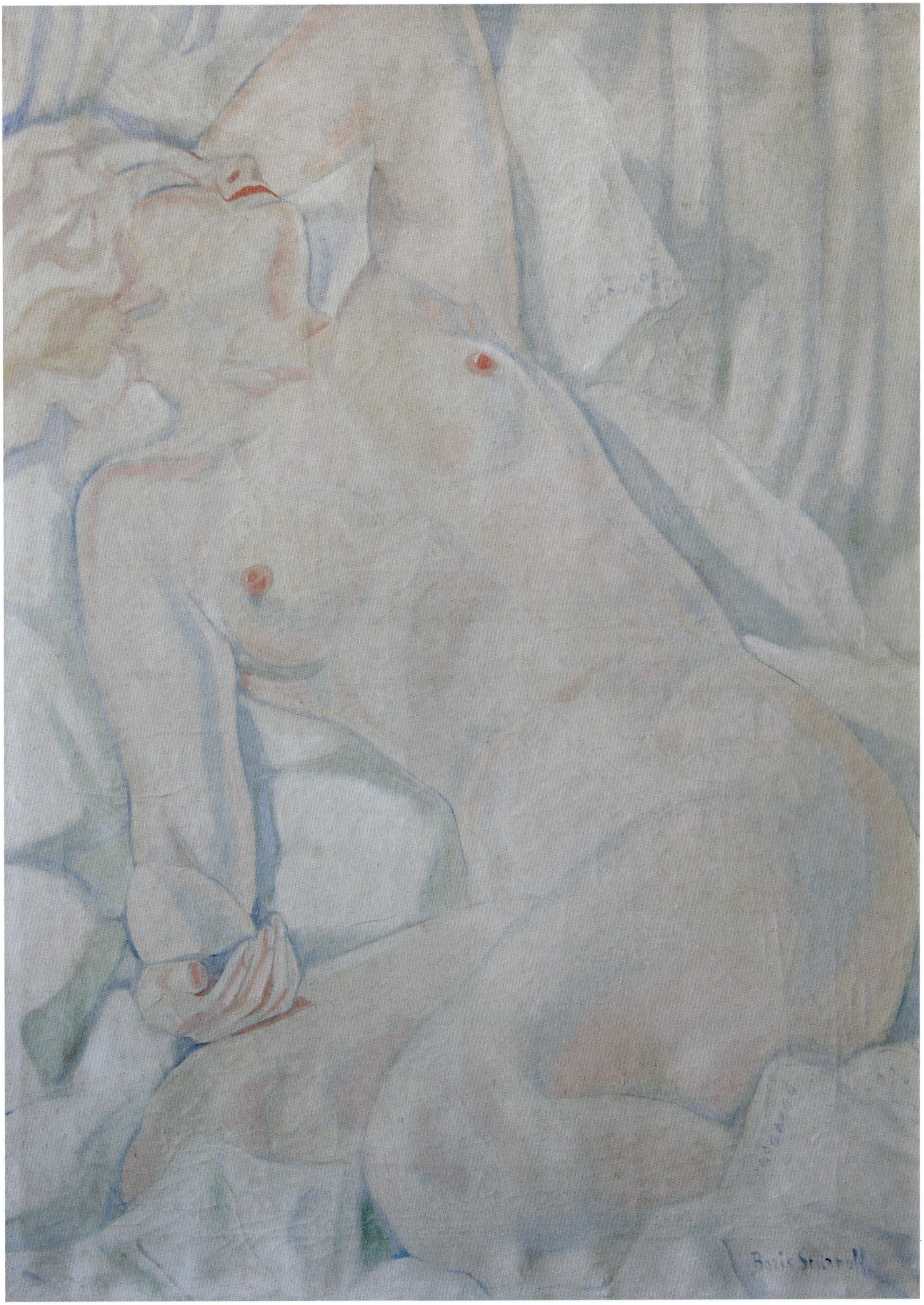

Boris Smirnoff
Repose, c.1930
Papillon Gallery, Los Angeles, California

Henri Alexandre Sollier

1886-1966

Henri Alexandre Sollier was born December 7, 1886 in Bagnolet, Seine-Saint Denis. He worked for three years in Dakar where he studied the local architecture and fine arts. Noted for his painting skills, Sollier studied with Flammeng, Fr. Schommer and J. Adler.

Sollier exhibited frequently in Paris and in 1914 he began participating with the Salons des Artistes Français. He received a notice in 1920 and two years later in 1922, Sollier won the Prix de l'Afrique Occidentale Française. He won a monetary ward in 1930 and at l'Exposition Internationale in 1934 and 1937 he received the Médaille d'Or twice. After 1957 Sollier worked in many locations, including Auvergne, Haute-Savoie, Provence and Italy.

Sollier was a committee member of the Jury des Artistes Français in 1937. L'ex-Musée des Colonies in Paris owns several of his works. Sollier's paintings of nudes, with his bold and sensuous brush strokes, were popular among the French collectors of the years between the wars and are equally sought after today. He died in 1966.

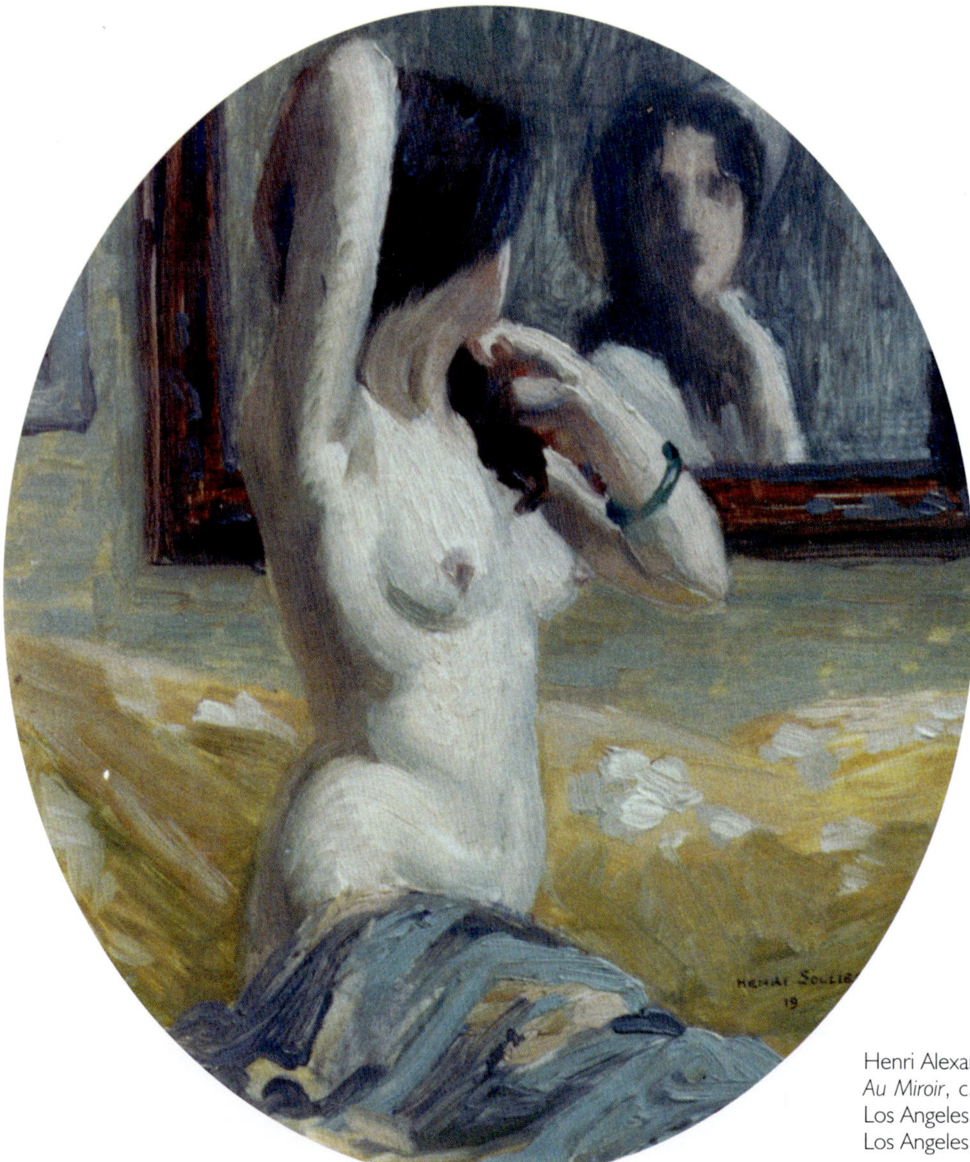

Henri Alexandre Sollier
Au Miroir, c.1925
Los Angeles Fine Art Gallery,
Los Angeles, California

Simeon Solomon

1840-1905

Simeon Solomon was born in London in 1840 to a large Jewish family. He was a prolific painter of Pre-Raphaelite influence and befriended many artists of the same school including Rosetti, Burne-Jones and the poet Algernon Swinburne while attending the Royal Academy in 1855. His first painting exhibition was at the Academy in 1860.

In 1856 Solomon formed a sketching group with fellow students and in 1859 joined the Artists' Rifle Corps. He continued to exhibit at the Academy for several years in addition to Gambart's French Gallery and the Dudley Gallery. In 1862 Solomon moved into his first studio near Middlesex hospital; he later moved to Fitzroy Square.

Solomon illustrated Swinburne's unpublished novel *Lesbia Brandon* in 1865 and later published his own prose poem, *A Vision of Love Revealed in Sleep* in 1871, which was written while traveling in Italy.

Simeon's last exhibition was held in 1872 at the Royal Academy. In 1873 he was arrested with George Roberts on charges of indecent exposure and attempted acts of sodomy and was arrested yet again in 1874.

He published a one-act satire entitled *Cleopatra's Needle* in 1877. Solomon was eventually admitted to St. Giles Workhouse where he lived on and off until his death in 1905 from heart failure due to alcoholism.

After his death Solomon's work was exhibited in a retrospective at Baillie's Gallery in 1905; the 37th Winter Exhibition of the Old Masters and Deceased Masters of the British School of the Royal Academy in 1906; the Whitechapel Art Gallery and in 1908 Julia Ellsworth Ford published a monograph, *Simeon Solomon: An Appreciation.*

His paintings are in the collections of the National Gallery of Art Washington D.C., Aberdeen Art Gallery and Museum in Scotland, Delaware Art Museum, National Portrait Gallery in Delaware and the Tate Gallery in London. Awards and medals include a bronze at the Exposition Universelle in Paris, 1871 and a monetary award in 1900.

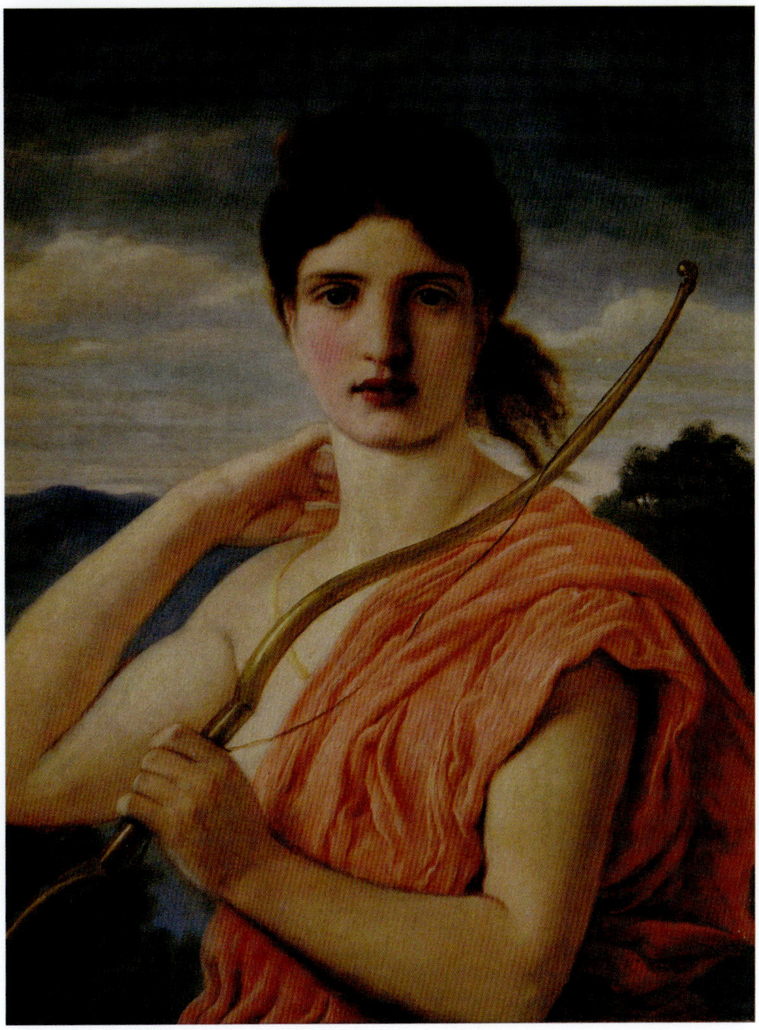

Simeon Solomon
Diana, c.1900
Bill and Jo LaMond,
Los Angeles, California

Henri Somm (François Clément Sommier)

1844–1907

Henri Somm, born François Clément Sommier, established himself in Paris in the 1860s after completing his studies at l'École Municipale de Dessin in Rouen under Gustave Morin.

Between 1879 and 1889 Somm participated in the exhibitions of the Impressionists at Durand-Ruel in Paris. As his recognition grew, Somm exhibited with several galleries in Paris including the Galerie Berth Weill in 1911 and others in London and Dusseldorf.

Working to supplement his career, Somm became a prolific illustrator collaborating with such publications as *Le Chat Noir, La Charge, La Cravache, Chronique Parisienne, High-Life, Frou-Frou, L'Inutile, Courrier Français* and *Le Rire.*

Paintings, drawings, illustrations and prints of Henri Somm can be found at the Musée d'Orsay, Louvre, Rouen Musée des Beaux-Arts, Daubigny Museum, Cleveland Art Museum, the Museum of Rockhill Nelson in Kansas City, San Francisco Art Museum and the Washington D.C. Museum of Fine Art. Somm died in 1907.

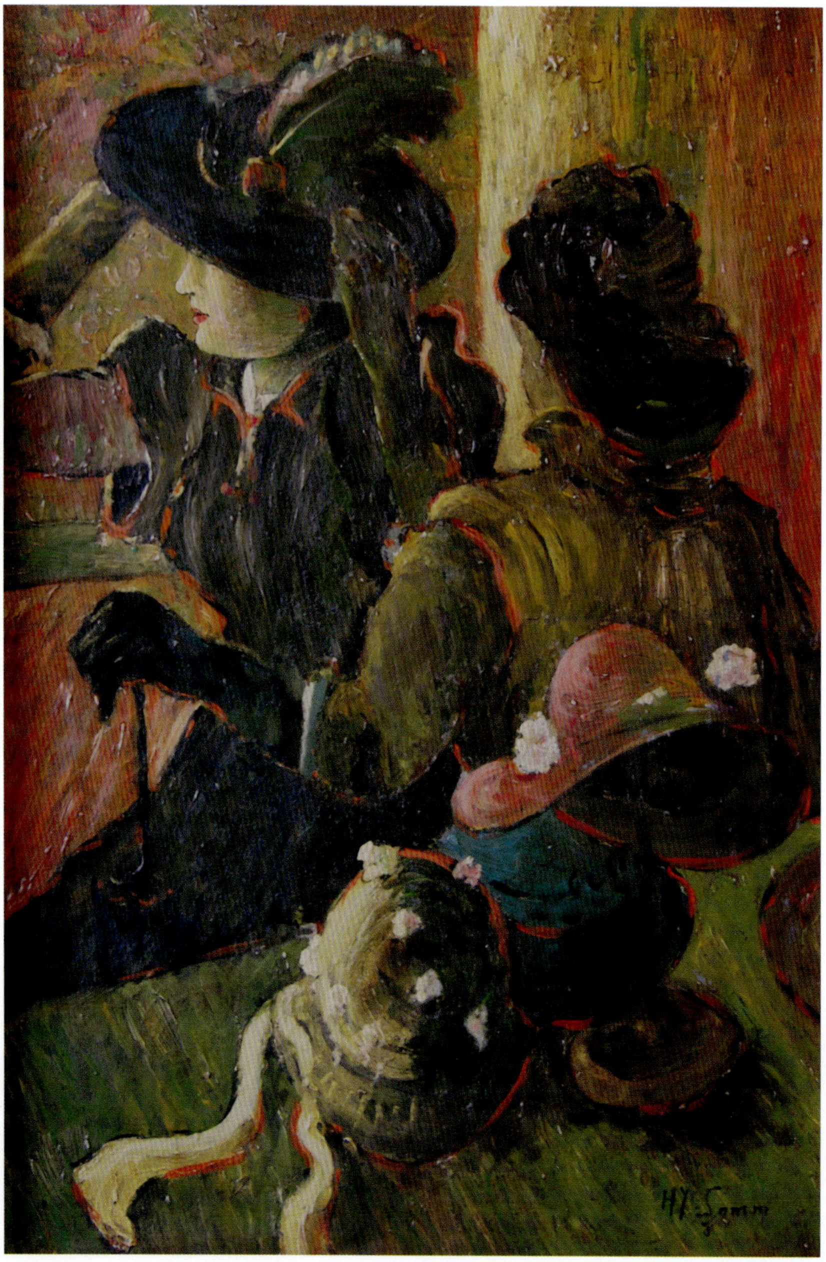

Henri Somm
Sur la Chapeliere, c.1890
Irene Slade, Los Angeles, California

Elisabeth Sonrel
Born 1874

Elisabeth Sonrel was born on May 17, 1874, in Tours, France. She studied with Jules Lefebvre. Sonrel created beautiful Art Nouveau paintings and watercolors and many of her works were printed as high quality lithographs. The narrative compositions of her works are typical of Art Nouveau and Symbolist artists. Beauty and decadence personified La Belle Époque making Sonrel's works very popular.

Sonrel exhibited in the Salon des Artistes Français where she received an honorable mention in 1893 and a Médaille de Troisième Classe in 1895. In 1900 she was awarded a bronze medal at the l'Exposition Universelle. Sonrel was also awarded the Henri Lehmann prize.

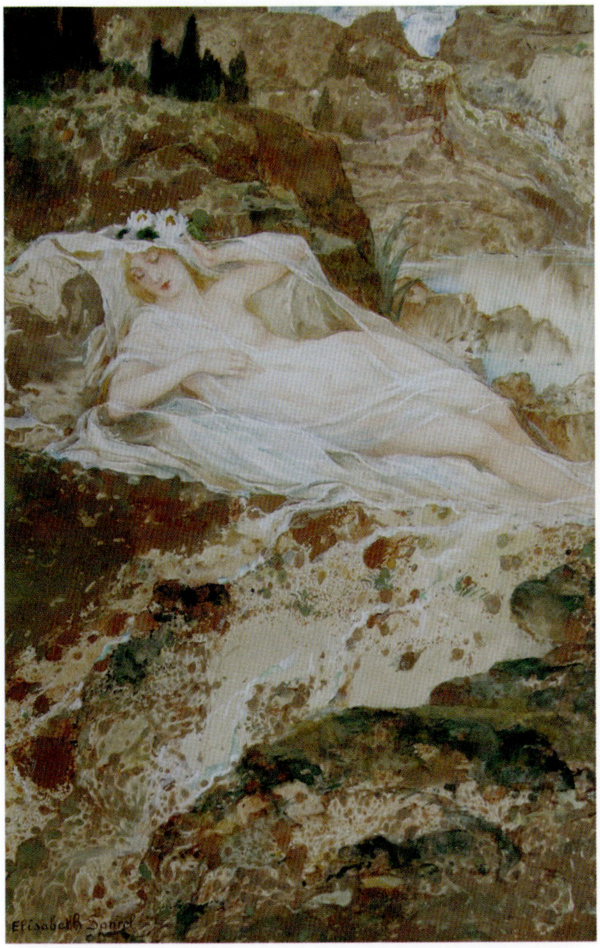

Elisabeth Sonrel
Nymph, c.1900
Jeffrey Winter Fine Arts,
Long Beach, California

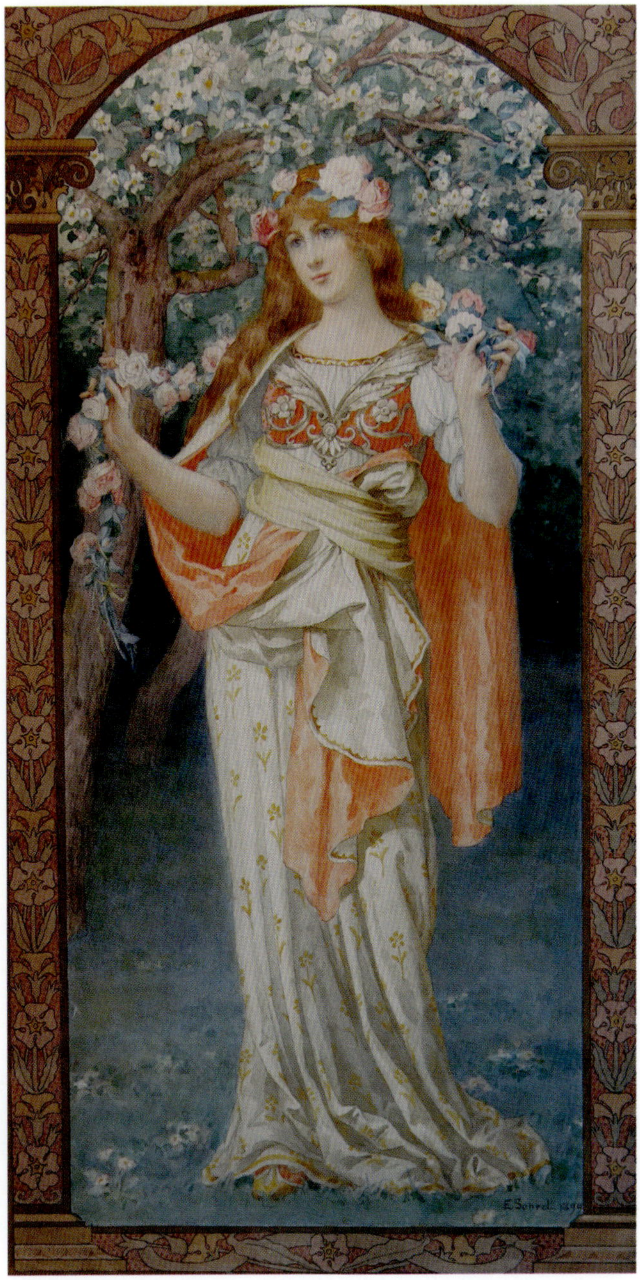

Elisabeth Sonrel
Dans le Jardin, c.1900
Mark Smith and Julia Evershade, Los Angeles, California

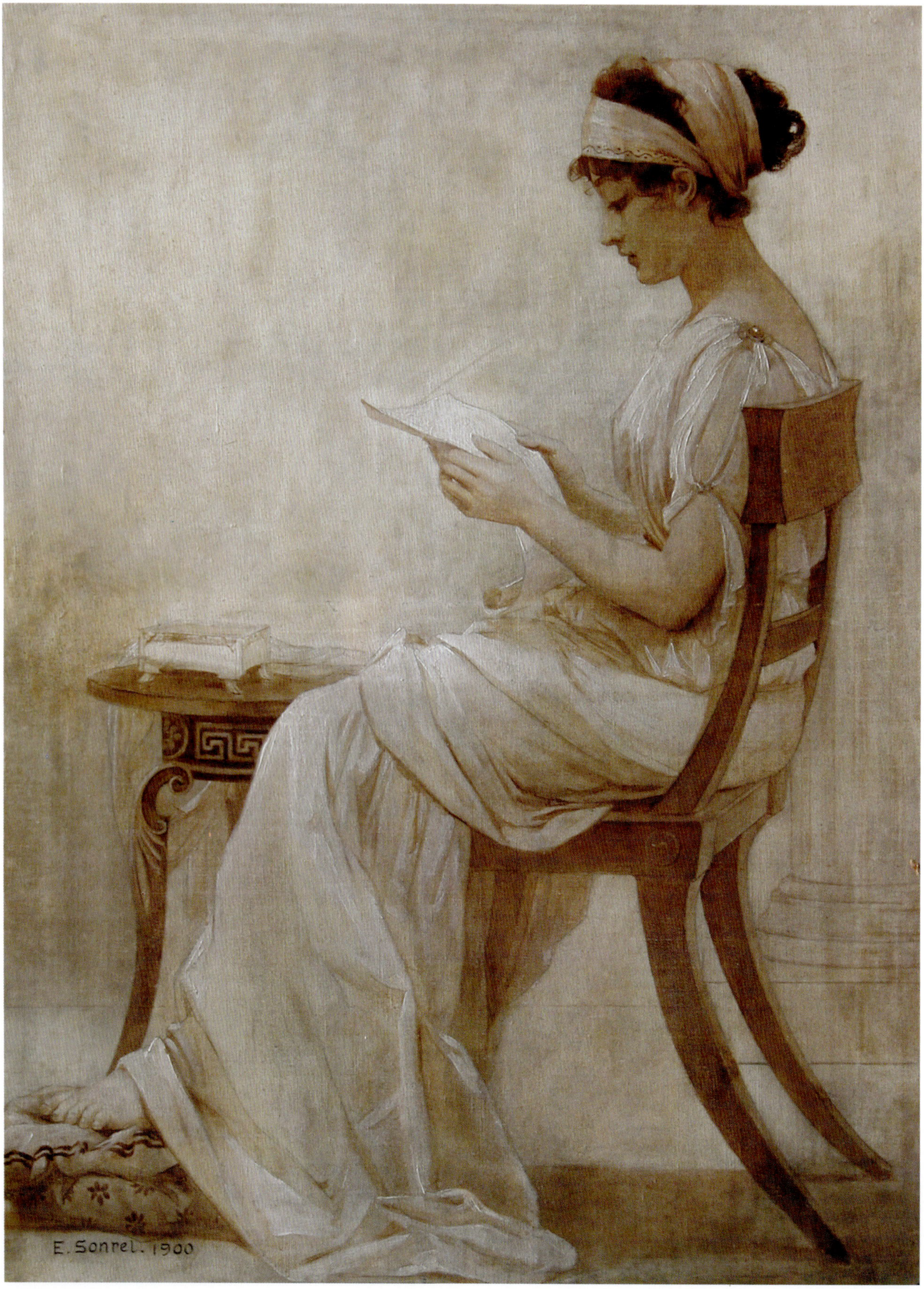

Elisabeth Sonrel
Femme avec un Livre, Dated 1900
Seligman Family Collection, Los Angeles, California

Jean Souverbie
1891-1981

Jean Souverbie was born March 21, 1891 in Boulogne-Billancourt. Souverbie studied with Jean-Paul Laurens. In 1916 two members of the Nabis group, Maurice Denis and Paul Sérusier, encouraged him to enroll in l'Académie Ranson where he befriended Bonnard, Vuillard and Vallatton.

Other influences in Souverbie's career include Georges Braque and the French classical painter Poussin. His wife, his principal model and muse, also greatly influenced his work.

Souverbie exhibited at the Salon d'Autome from 1923 and the Salon des Tuileries in 1925 and 1926. The Galerie Vavin-Raspail who, in 1925 hosted the Section d'Or, put Souverbie in close contact with Lhote, Gleizes, Picasso and Marcoussis among others. He had his first solo exhibition at Galerie Vavin in 1926 and again in 1929. Galerie Bernheim-Jeune held an exhibition of fifty-four cubist works in 1931. In 1932 he had a solo exhibition at Galerie Danthon. In 1945 Souverbie began teaching at l'École des Beaux-Arts in Paris.

Souverbie was a prolific artist and enjoyed a long and successful career. He painted highly stylized allegorical scenes incorporating many modern techniques including cubism and surrealism. Souverbie's approach is similar to that of Jean de Botton and Roger Bissière who painted bold and powerful works that were modern in every sense. Their fantastic canvases combined well with the decorative arts and furniture of the Art Deco era.

Souverbie is represented in many museums including the Musée National d'Art Moderne in Paris and museums in Boston, Philadelphia, Geneva and Luxemburg. Jean Souverbie died in February, 1981.

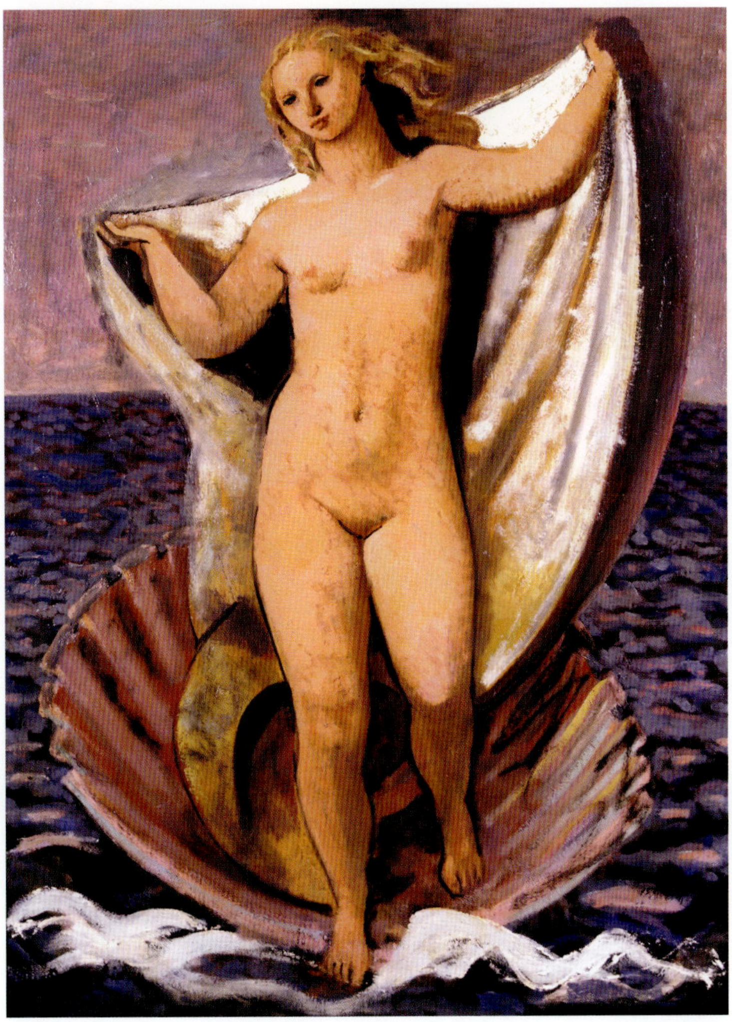

Jean Souverbie
Venus, c.1930
Whitford Fine Art, London, England

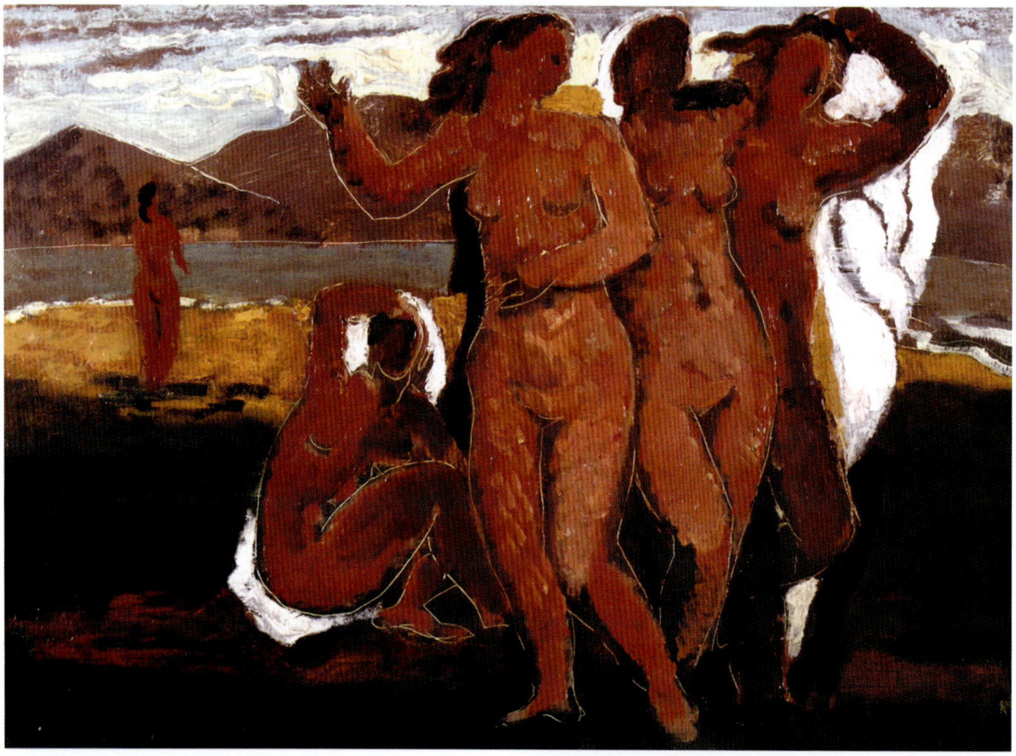

Jean Souverbie
Les Trois Graces, c.1935
Whitford Fine Art, London, England

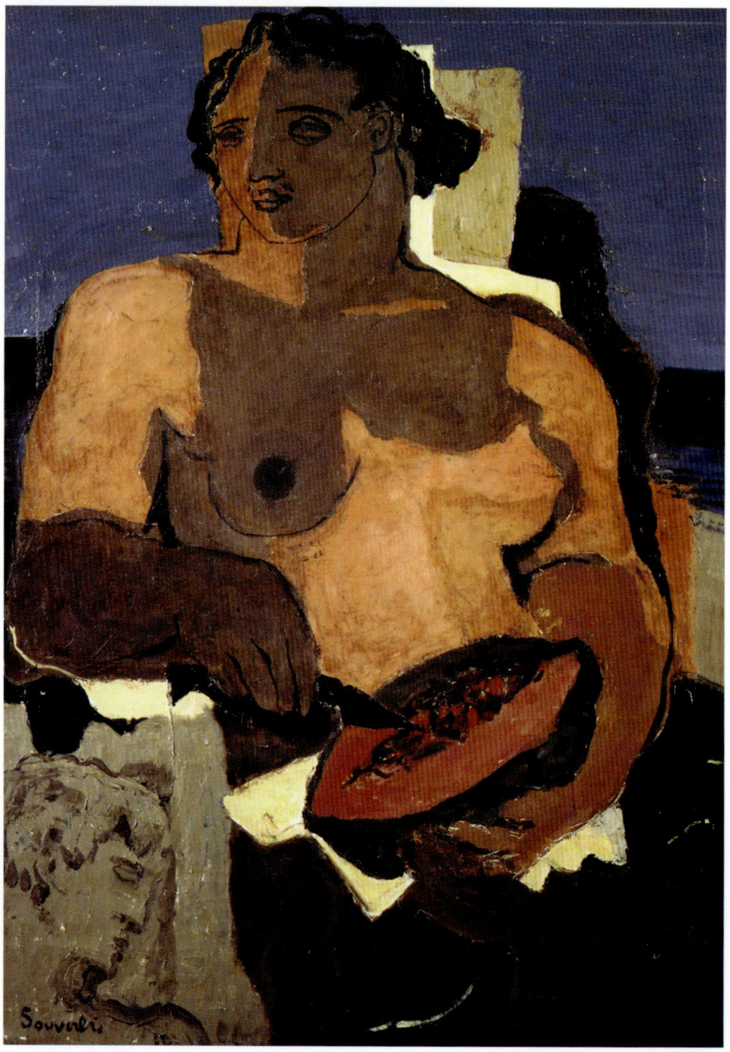

Jean Souverbie
Femme à la Pastèque, c.1927
Whitford Fine Art, London, England

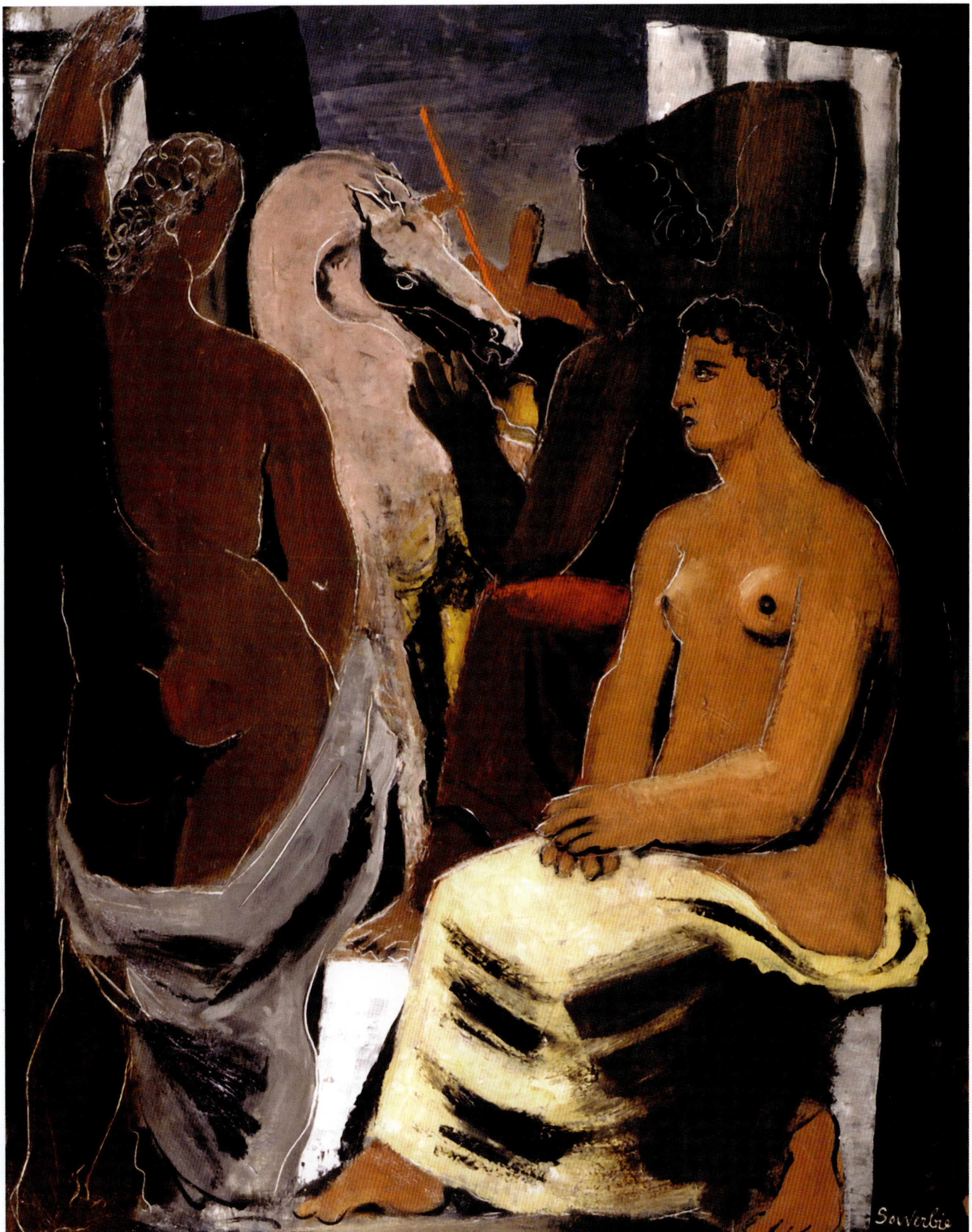

Jean Souverbie
La Couple, c.1920
Whitford Fine Art, London, England

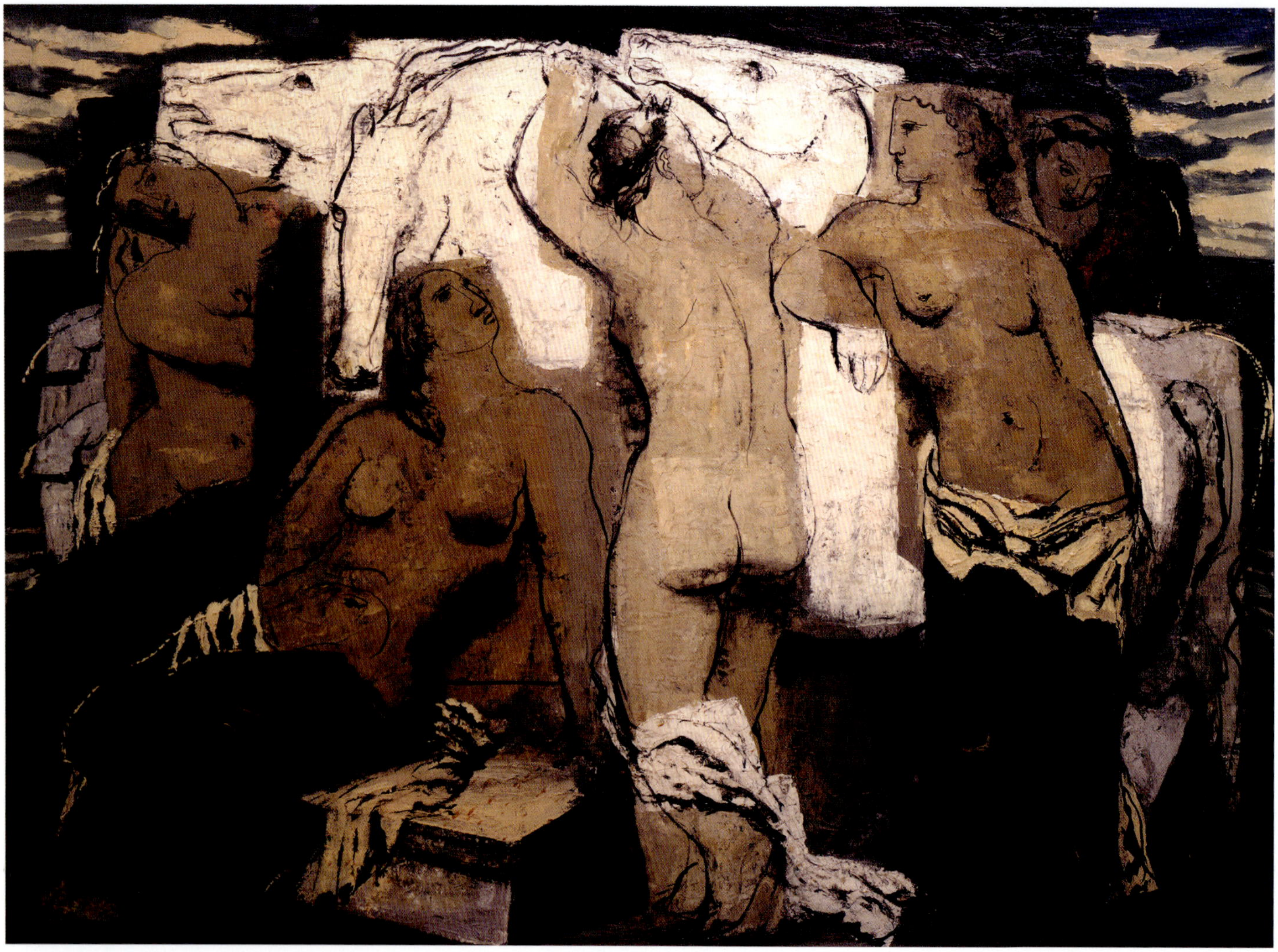

Jean Souverbie
Femmes et Chevaux, c.1930
Beverly Sacks Fine Art Inc., New York, New York

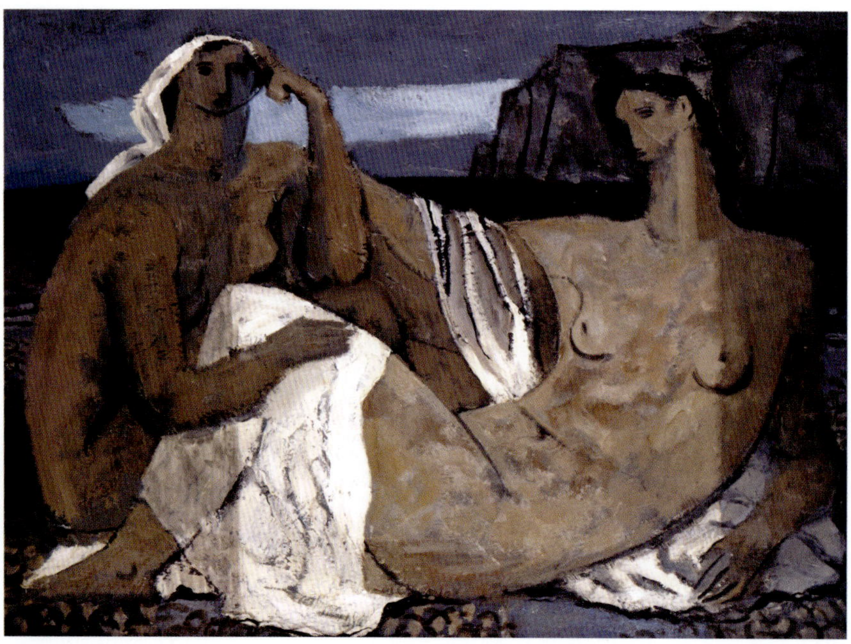

Jean Souverbie
Les Deux Baigneuses, Dated 1963
Whitford Fine Art, London, England

Frantisek Srp

1895-1943

Frantisek Srp was a Czechoslovakian painter in the 1920s and 1930s. Little is known about the artist, but from the few known paintings it can be said he was certainly accomplished. His paintings have the feeling of Parisian influence; very modern, attractive and serious. His work is occasionally sold at auction houses in Prague. Srp died in 1943.

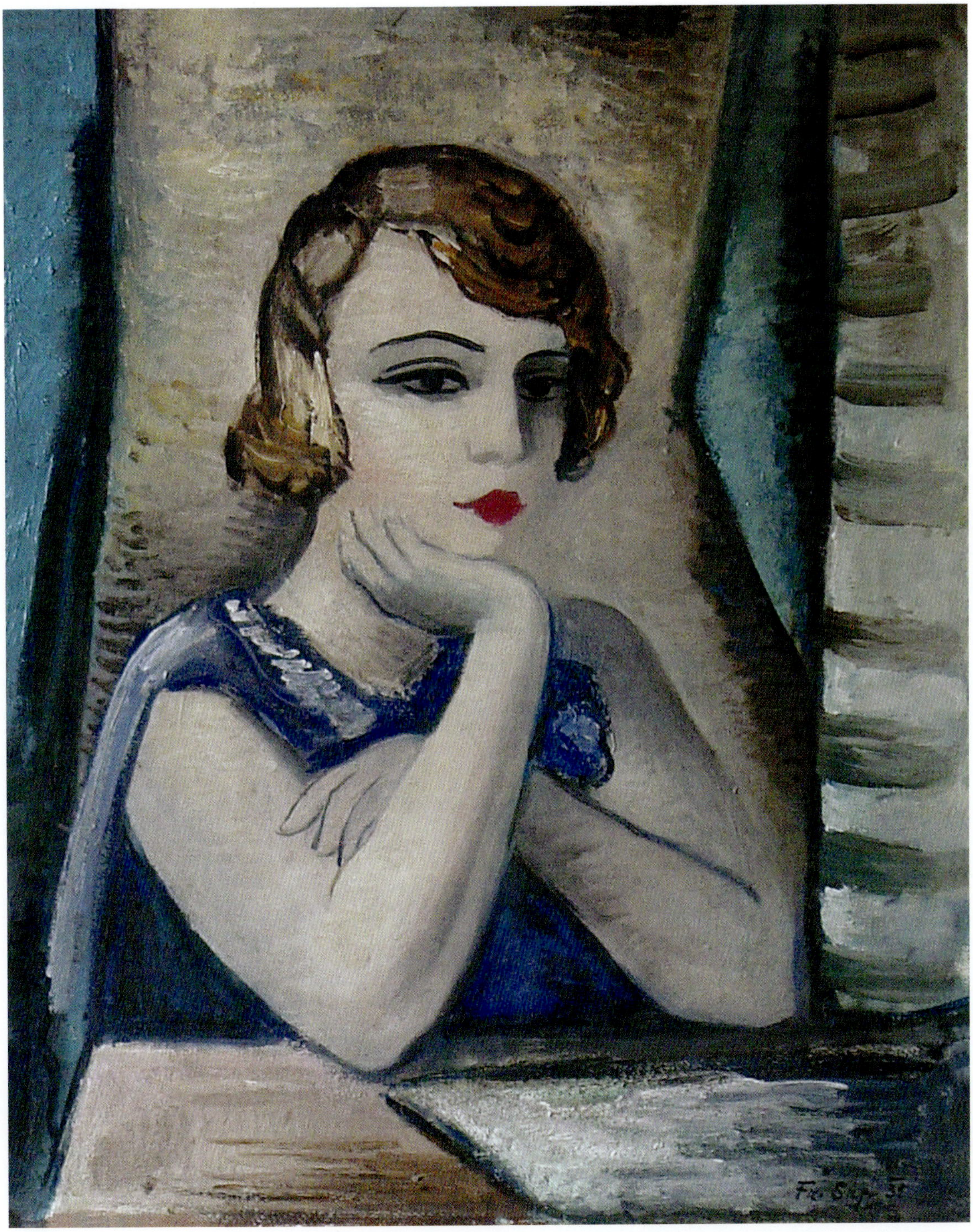

Frantisek Srp
Femme Assis, Dated 1939
Private Collection

Nicolas Sternberg

Born 1901

Nicolas Sternberg was born in 1901. He worked as an illustrator of books and magazines such as *Elle* in France. In 1930 in *L'Art et les Artistes* André Warnod published a review of an exhibition by Sternberg at the Galerie Georges Petit in Paris.

In October of 2003 a Paris auction company sold his estate, which included mostly portraits of women and circus performers. Sternberg's work shows the influence of the German Realists. His subjects though often humorist are just as often strange and dark. He did not paint many oils, but he was a very prolific watercolorist and a fine draftsman. Sternberg executed many self-portraits over the years as well as many portraits of beautiful women and scenes of Parisian lifestyle.

Like many Hungarian artists that came to Paris his work is unknown in Hungary, which will change as it has for many artists when a body of work surfaces. Sternberg died in the 1960s.

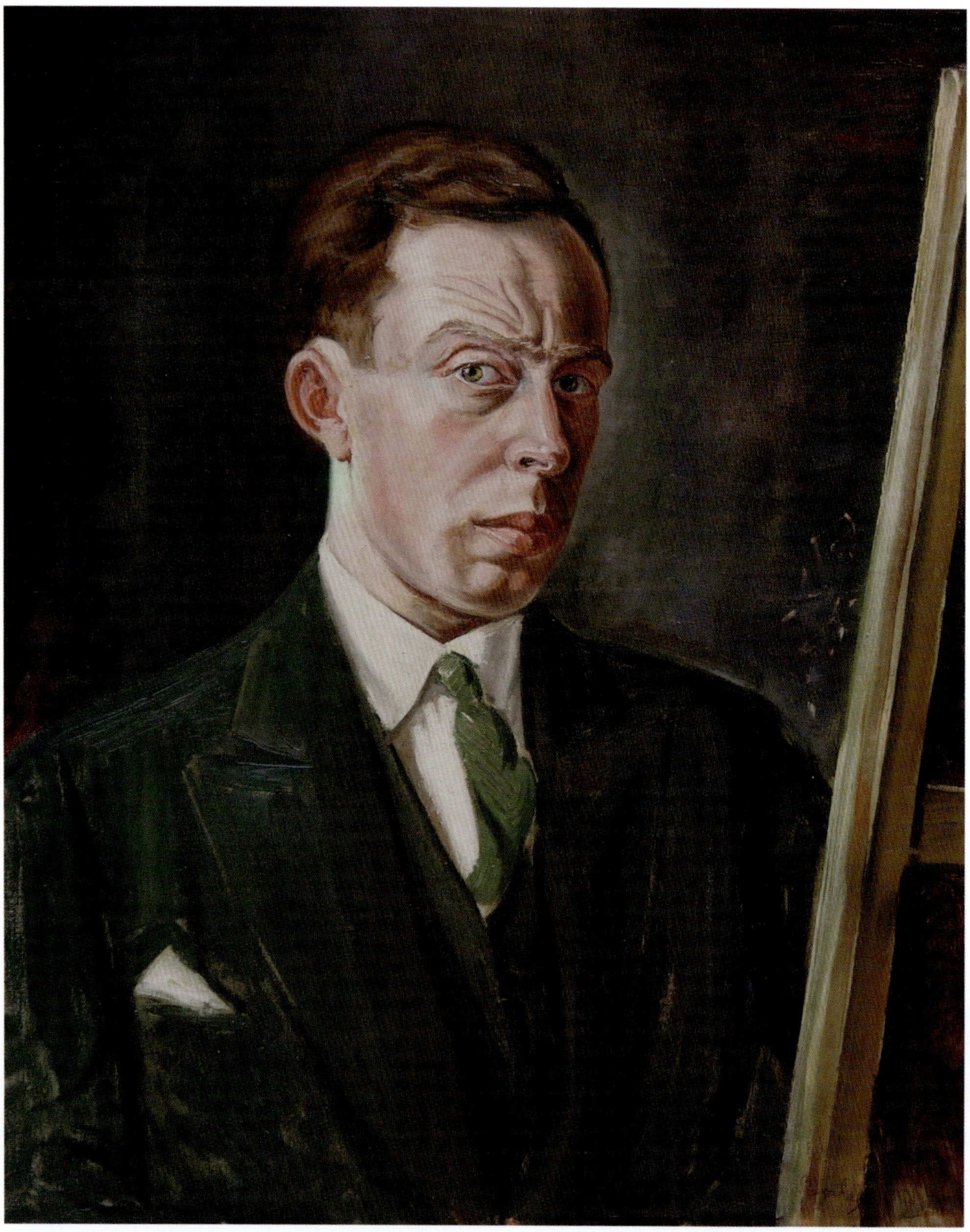

Nicolas Sternberg
Autoportrait, c.1925
Mark and Marina Plon,
Henderson, Nevada

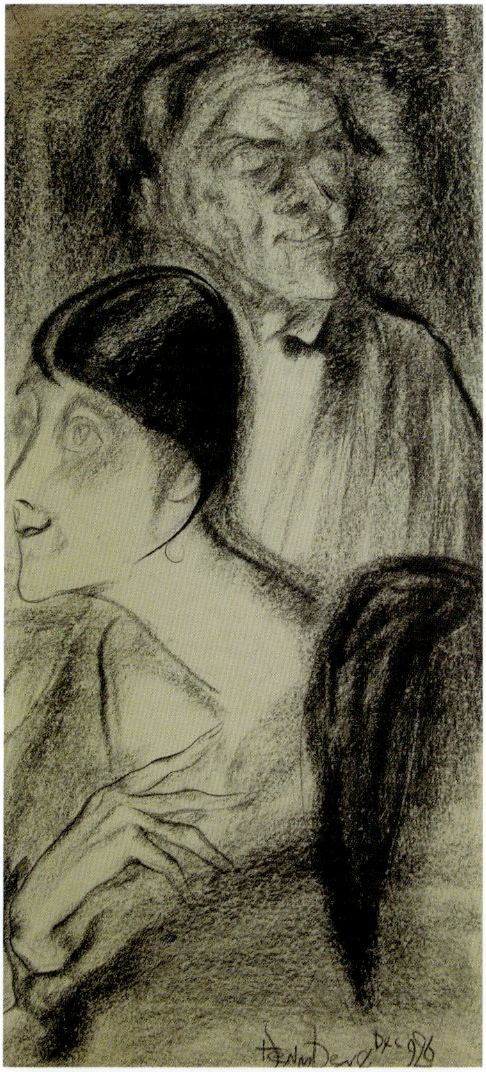

Nicolas Sternberg
Le Couple, c.1925
Papillon Gallery, Los Angeles, California

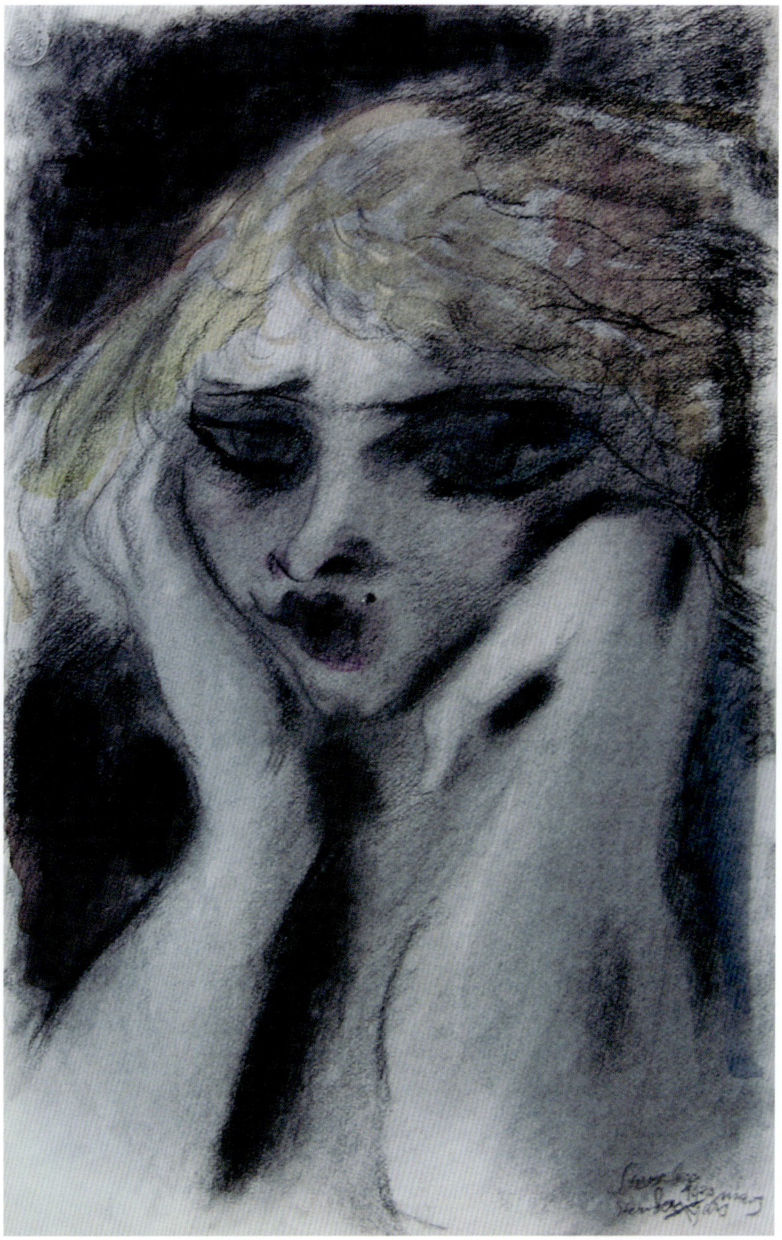

Nicolas Sternberg
Vamp, c.1925
Papillon Gallery,
Los Angeles, California

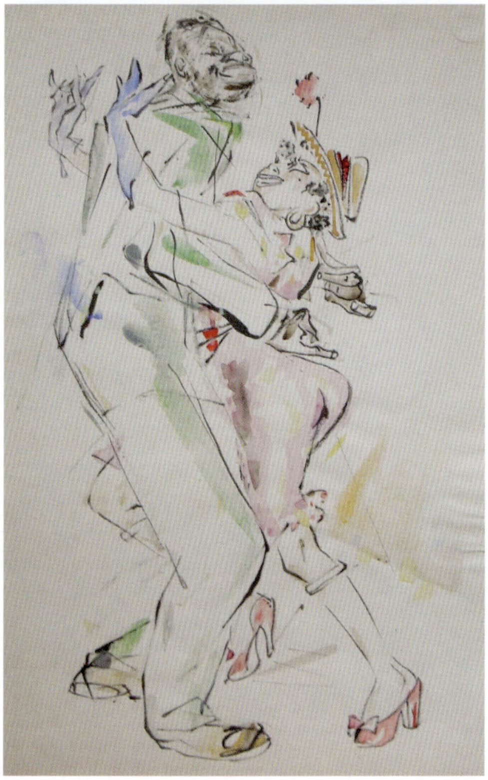

Nicolas Sternberg
Dance, c.1925
Papillon Gallery, Los Angeles, California

Walter Stiner
Born 1909

Walter Stiner was born in Palatinate, Germany in 1909. His brother Sigfried was a well-known graphic artist and influenced Walter from an early age. Stiner immigrated to the United States in 1929. He received formal training from George Grosz and Kuniyashi in addition to his studies at the Art Students League in New York from 1935 to1936 and the Académie Julian in Paris under Cavailles and Sabouraud from 1946 to1948. Stiner was a member of the Silvermine Guild where his paintings were exhibited and received many favorable reviews. He continued to have solo exhibitions in New York, where he also received fine reviews.

Stiner served in World War II with the United States Army's Fine Art, Monument and Archives Division. He was stationed in Morocco and made many drawing of his experiences. Being a German born American officer and fluent in French, Stiner had a unique perspective on the societies and cultures to which he was exposed. After the war he exhibited at the Carnegie Institute, in Pittsburg, the National Gallery in Washington D.C., the Foyer Montparnasse exhibition of American painters in Paris and at Pershing Hall in an exhibition titled *Paintings by American Veterans*.

Stiner had many exhibitions in his lifetime. He exhibited at the Montrose Gallery in New York several times, beginning in 1937. In 1938 he was an instructor for the WPA and exhibited at the Society of Independent Artists, he also exhibited at the Crespy Gallery through the 1950s in New York. Stiner did cartoons for Paris newspapers and had an academic article published in the German magazine *Der Standpunkt*.

Stiner exhibited as late as 1988 in New York with Art Studio Club and West Side Art Coalition. His later work shows influences of the Surrealists, though it eventually became totally abstract.

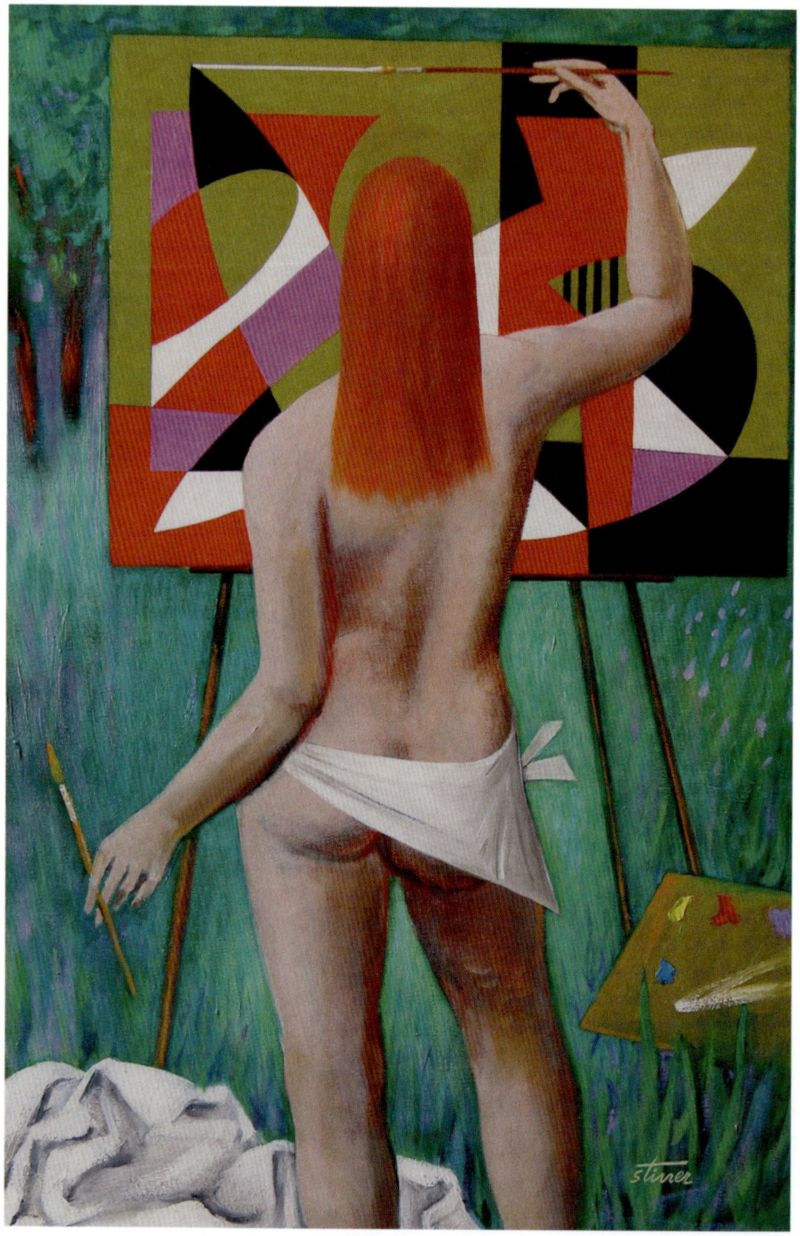

Walter Stiner
The Abstractionist, Dated 1940
Seligman Family Collection,
Los Angeles, California

Yasushi Tanaka

Born 1886

Yasushi Tanaka was born May 13, 1886, in Saitana, Japan. In 1904 he moved to Seattle, Washington. After graduating high school in Seattle he studied at the Seattle Fine Art Association where he exhibited and taught from 1901to 1920. His first exhibition was at the Washington Museum in Seattle in 1912. In 1914, he had his first solo show where he exhibited Cubist- and Futurist-influenced works.

In 1917 Tanaka married American author Louise Gebhard Cann who published several books and articles on French artists. Cann was also acquainted with James Joyce, Ezra Pound and Ernest Hemingway. In 1920 Tanaka had a farewell exhibition and moved to Paris. It is not known whether he ever returned to Japan or the United States.

Tanaka exhibited often in Paris at the Société Nationale des Beaux-Arts, Salon d'Automne and Salon des Tuileries. In 1922 and 1924 Tanaka had a solo-exhibition at the Galerie de Marsan for which an illustrated catalogue was produced with a biography by Émile Henriot. Other exhibits include the Galerie Bernheim-Jeune, Galerie Simonson, Galerie Devambez, Galerie Carmine and Galerie Druet. He also exhibited at the Japanese-Club in London in 1924.

His work consists of landscapes, still-lifes and portraits, but he became most well-known for his nudes. French photographer Imogen Cunningham created a platinum print portrait of Tanaka around 1915.

The Tokyo Museum has acquired one of his paintings.The date of his death is unknown.

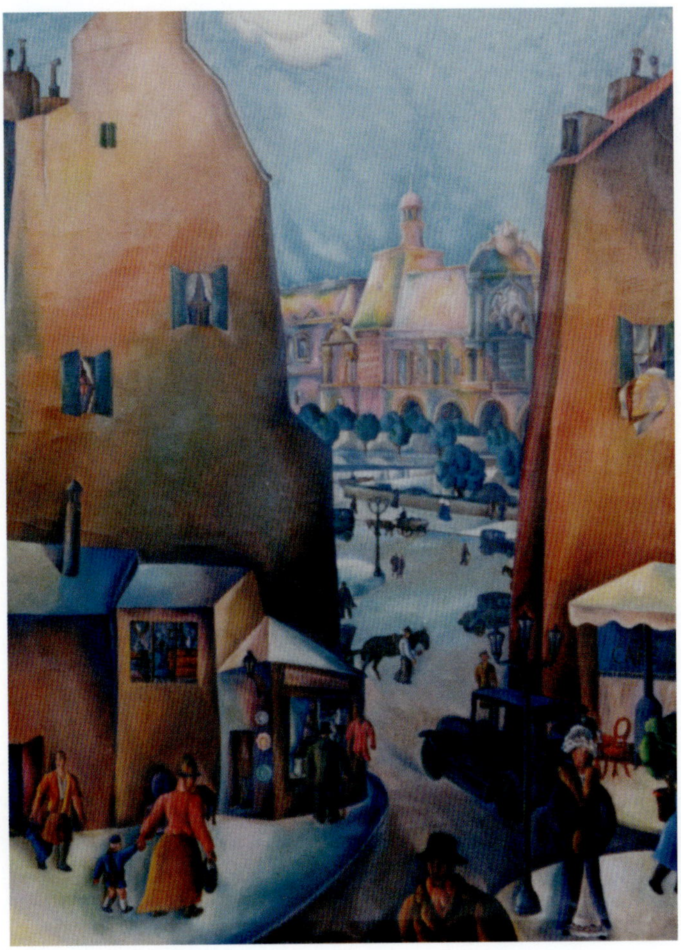

Yasushi Tanaka
Dans la Ville, c1925
Mark Brock, Acton, Massachusetts

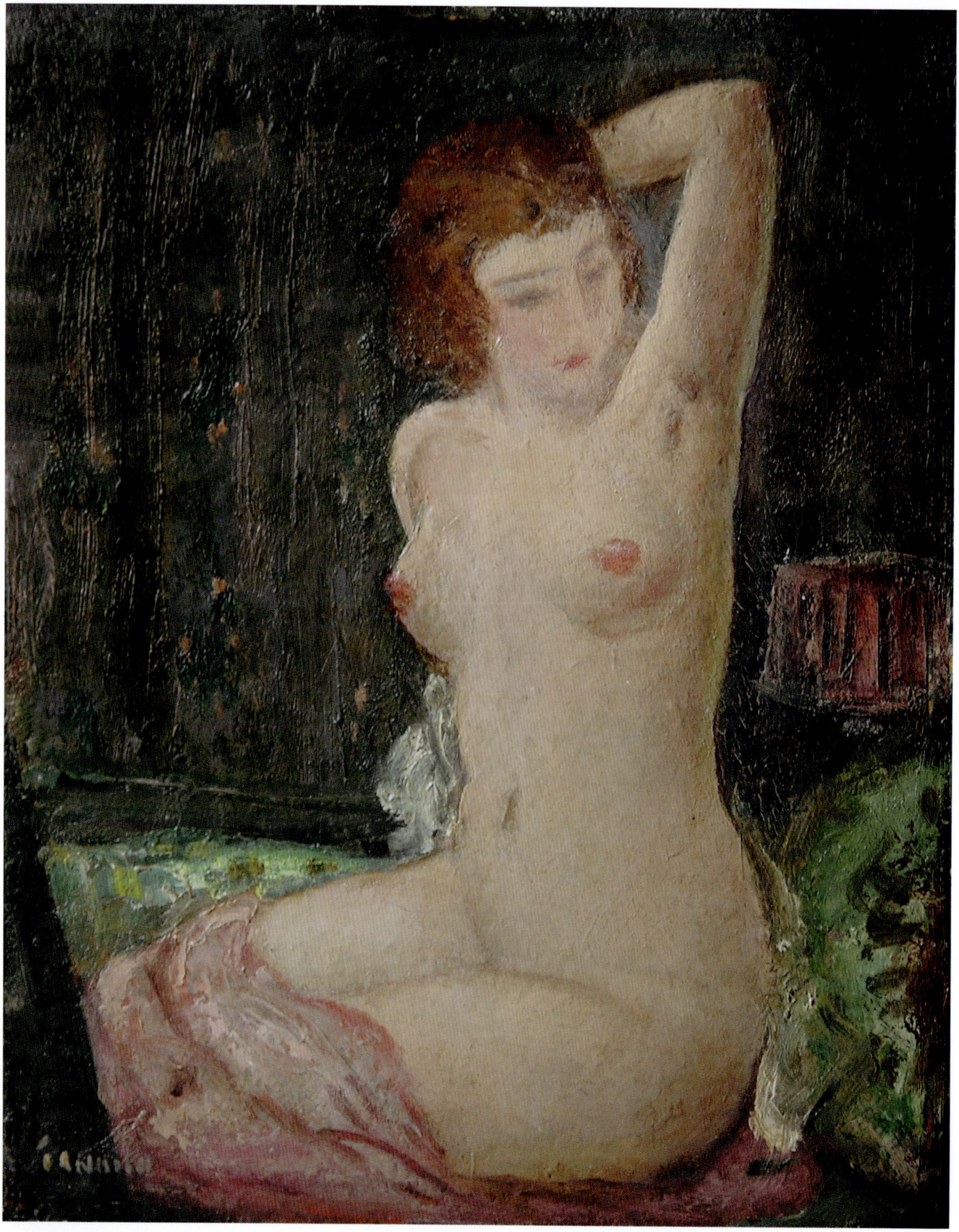

Yasushi Tanaka
Nu Assis, c.1925
Papillon Gallery, Los Angeles, California

Maurice Louis Tête
1880-1948

Maurice Louis Tête was born in 1880 in Roanne, France. He studied with William Adolphe Bouguereau and received a diverse education in the liberal arts and critical thinking.

Tête is known as a painter and pastel artist who worked in the styles of Neo-Impressionism and Cubism and exhibited his work at the Société Nationale des Beaux-Arts de Paris. His paintings have a soft yet colorful palate in the manner of André Lhote and Roger de la Fresnaye. Tête died in 1948.

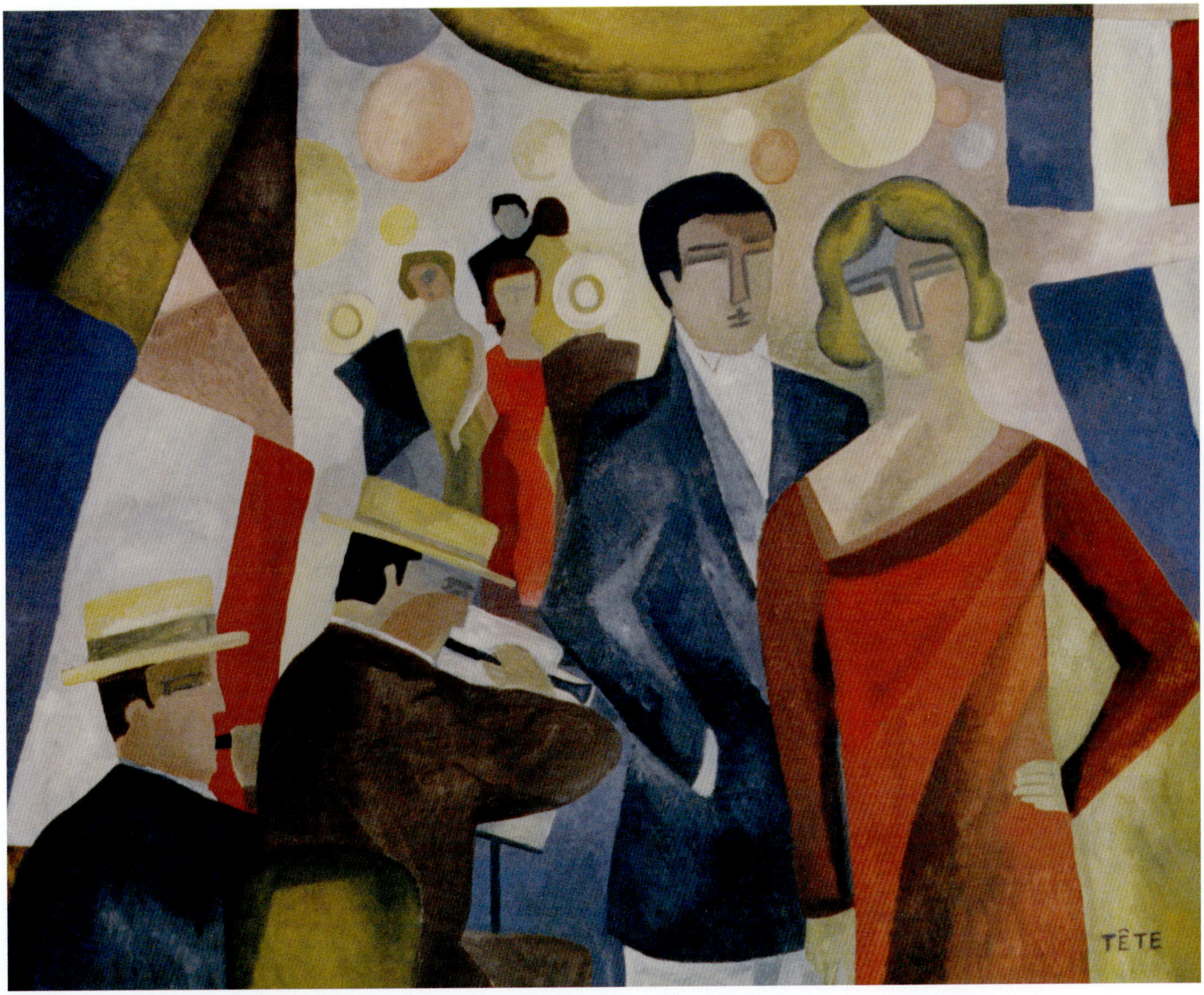

Maurice Louis Tête
Fête du 14 de Julliet, c.1925
Private Collection

Adrien Thevenot

20th century

Adrien Thevenot was born in Rougemont-le-Château, in the territory of Belfort, France. Thevenot exhibited in the 1929 Salon des Artistes Français. He received an honorable mention in the 1929 Salon and a Médaille d'Or in 1931.

Thevenot's paintings are exquisitely executed with the sensitivity of a classical painter. His subjects however are utopian Art Deco at their finest. His nudes and allegorical compositions have a similar presence as the artists of the Bordeaux School like Jean Despujols and Jean Dupas. There is very little known about this artist after the 1930s.

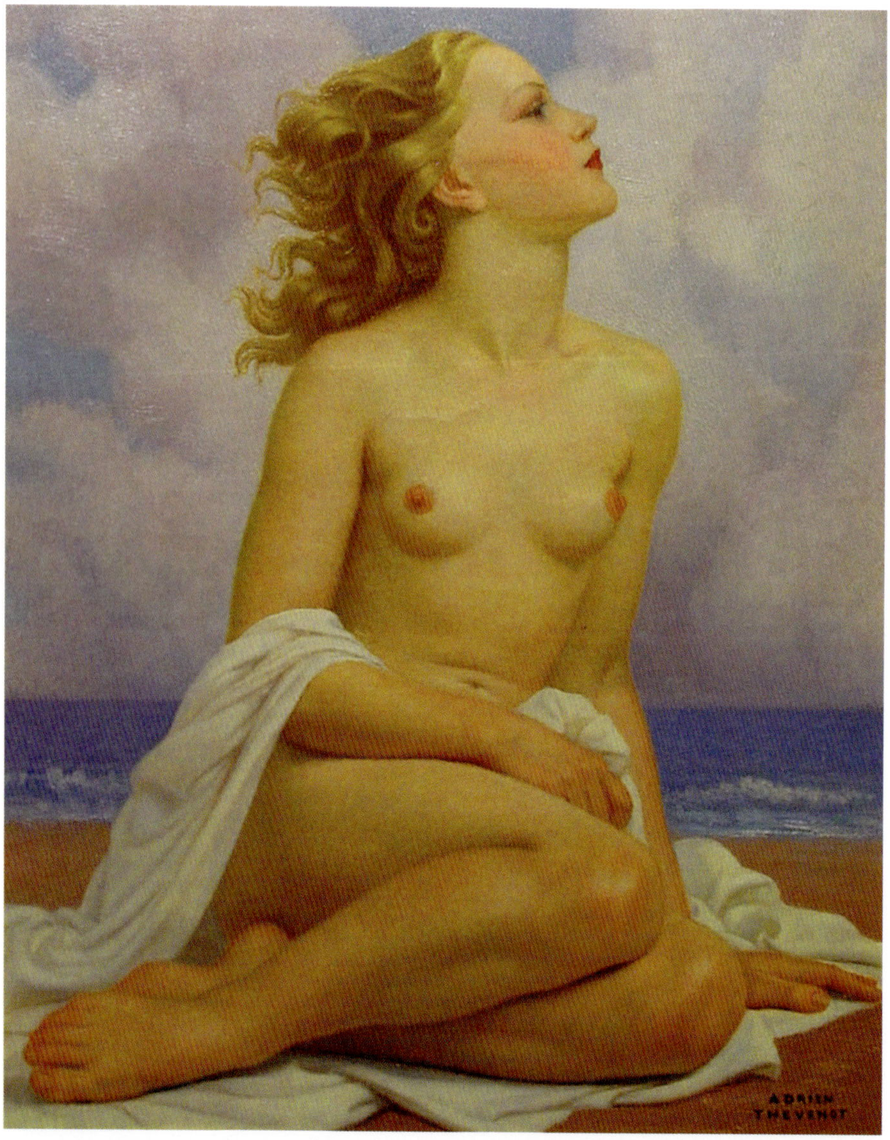

Adrien Thevenot
Nu au bord du Mer, c.1925
Galerie Chadelaud, Paris, France

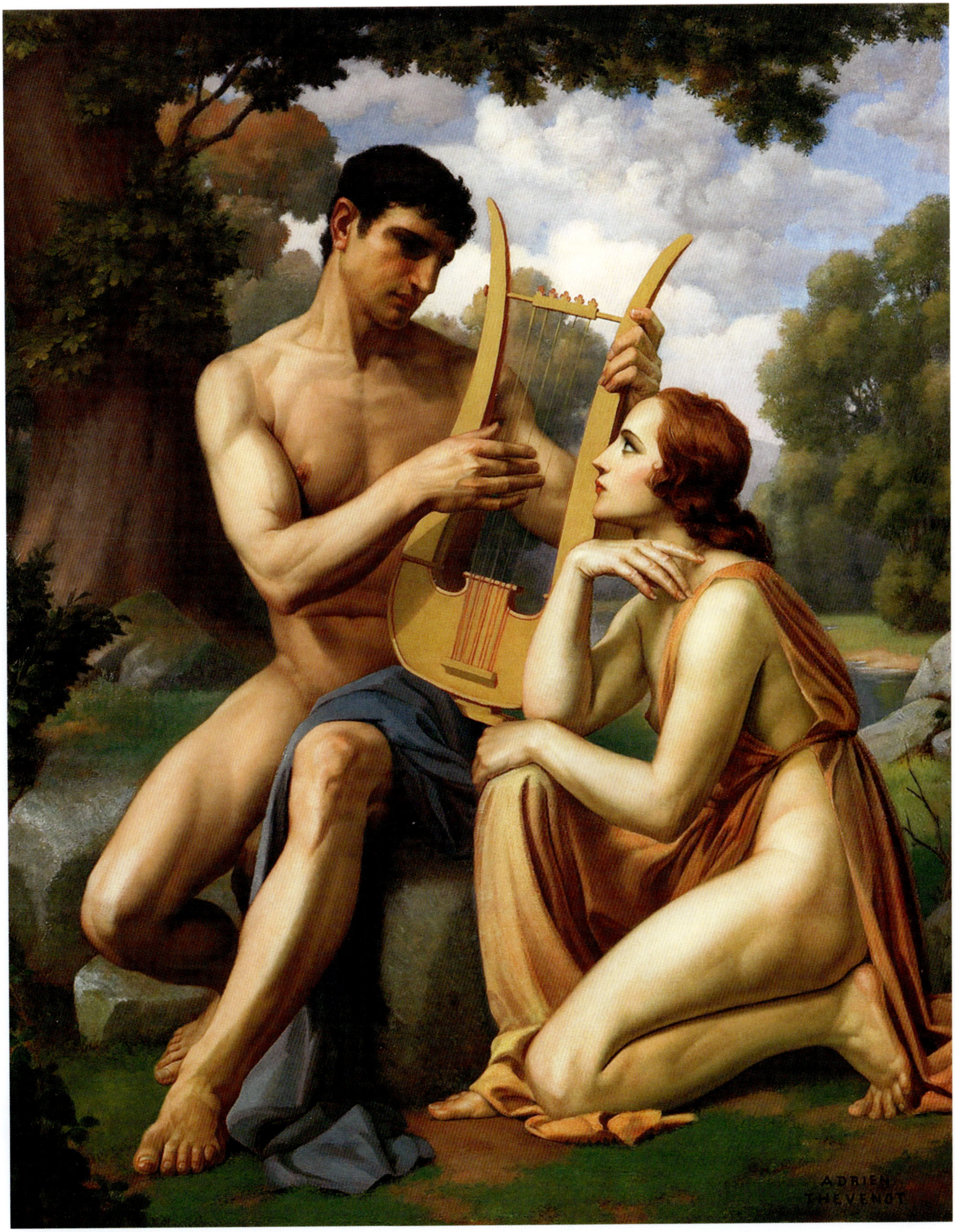

Adrien Thevenot
Sérénade, c.1925
Galerie Chadelaud, Paris, France

Léon Tirode

Born 1873

Léon Tirode was born March 30, 1873 in Besançon and was a student of Léon Bonnat. Tirode exhibited in Paris at the Salon des Artistes Français; he received an honorable mention1905 and a bronze medal in 1913. In 1937 he received a bronze medal at l'Exposition Internationale.

Tirode's paintings though classical in technique have some sensitivity toward the modern world. He was a fine and subtle artist that created beautiful and timeless images. The date of his death is unknown.

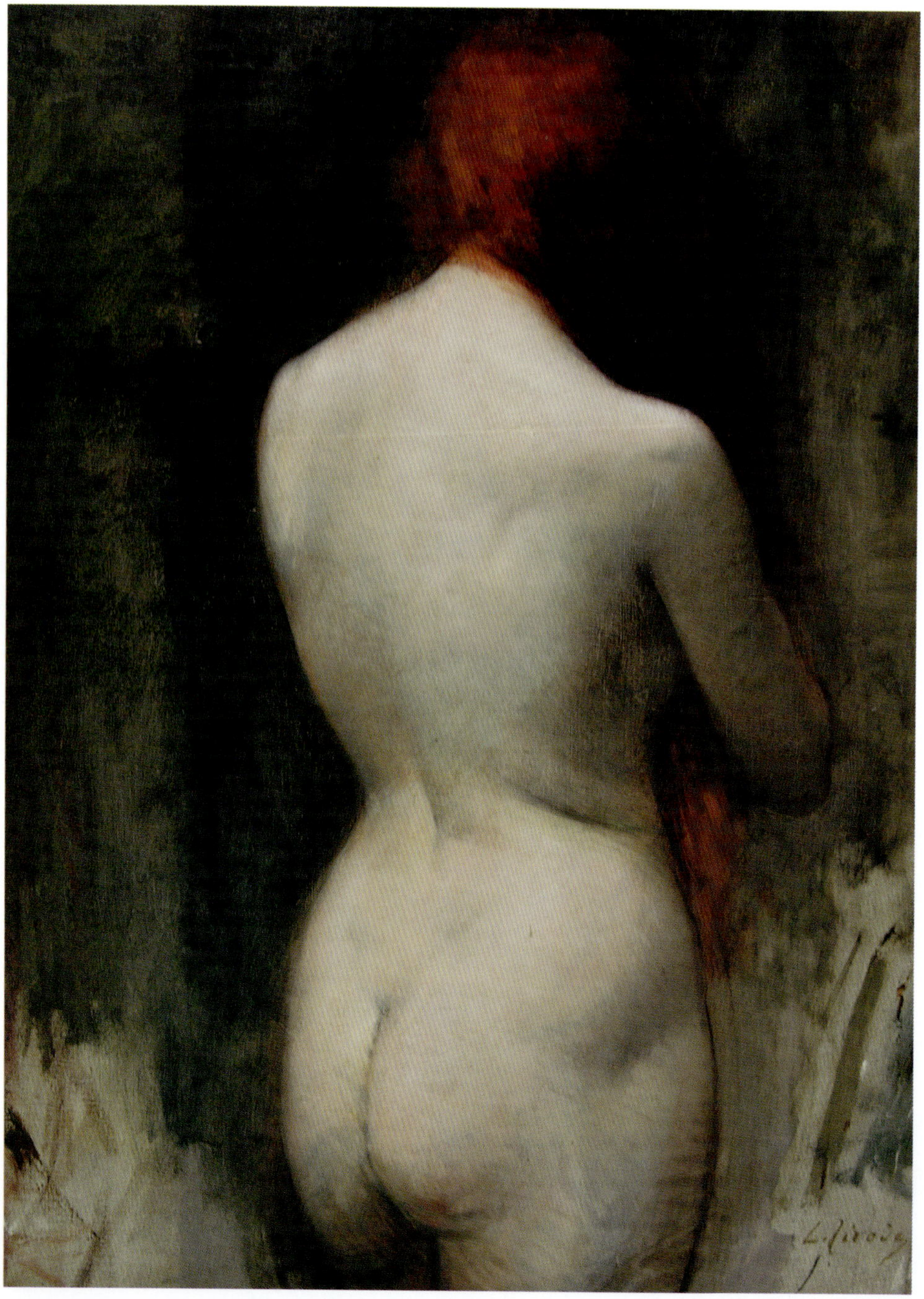

Léon Tirode
Nu avec des Cheveaux Rouge, c.1915
José and Carolyn Quant, Anaheim, California

André Paul Henri Tondu

1903-1980

André Paul Henri Tondu was born February 11, 1903. He studied the work of Cormon, Renard and J.P. Laurens at l'École des Beaux-Arts in Paris from 1920-1923. In 1931 he received the Prix de Rome. In 1987 a Parisian auction house sold his estate of hundreds of works.

Tondu was a prolific artist with a long and successful career. His subjects depict the lifestyle of Parisians of all classes. He used clever, modern techniques and unusual composition that make his paintings especially interesting; he was a storyteller with his paintbrush. Tondu died May 26, 1980.

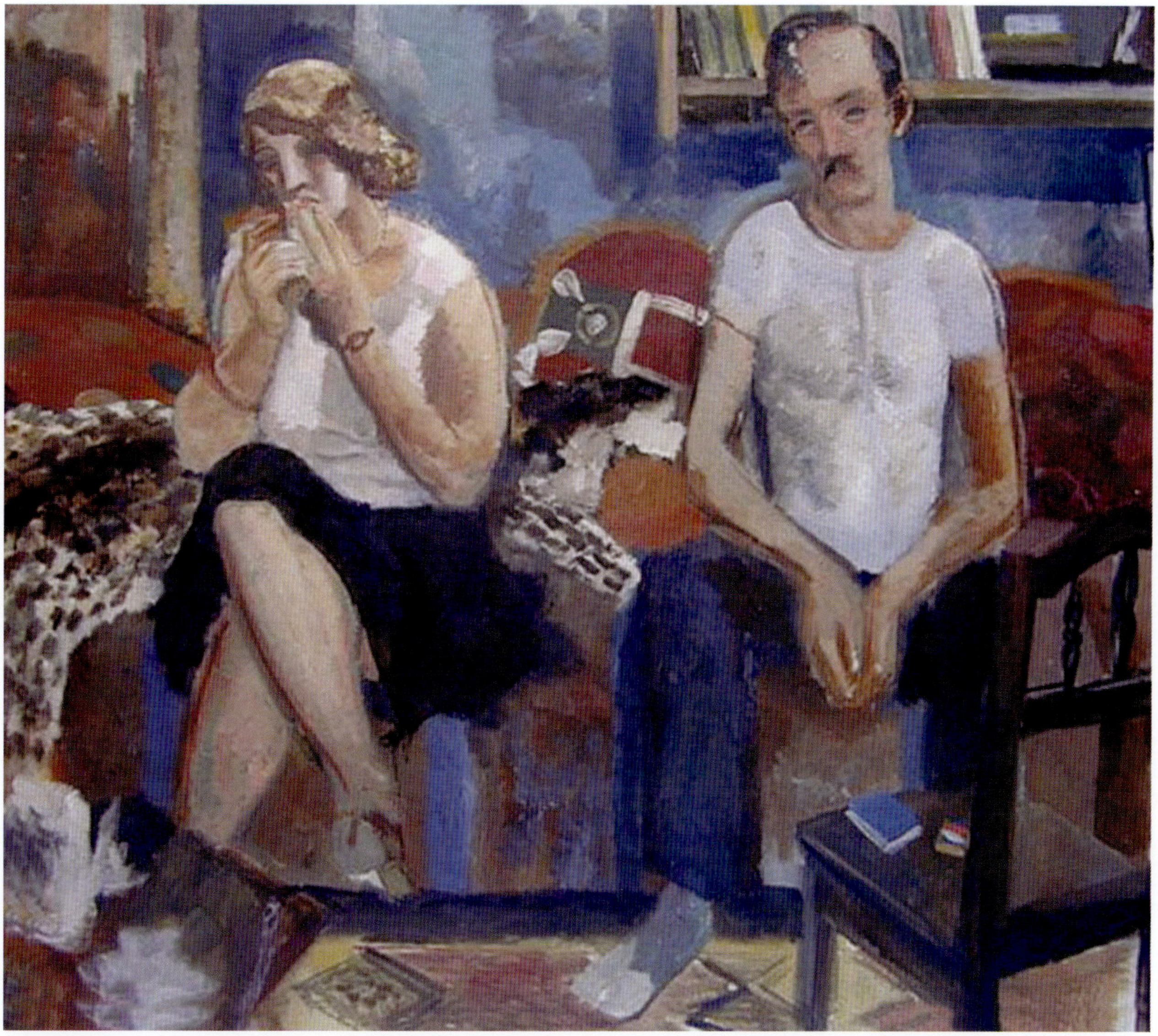

André Paul Henri Tondu
Couple, c.1930
Private Collection

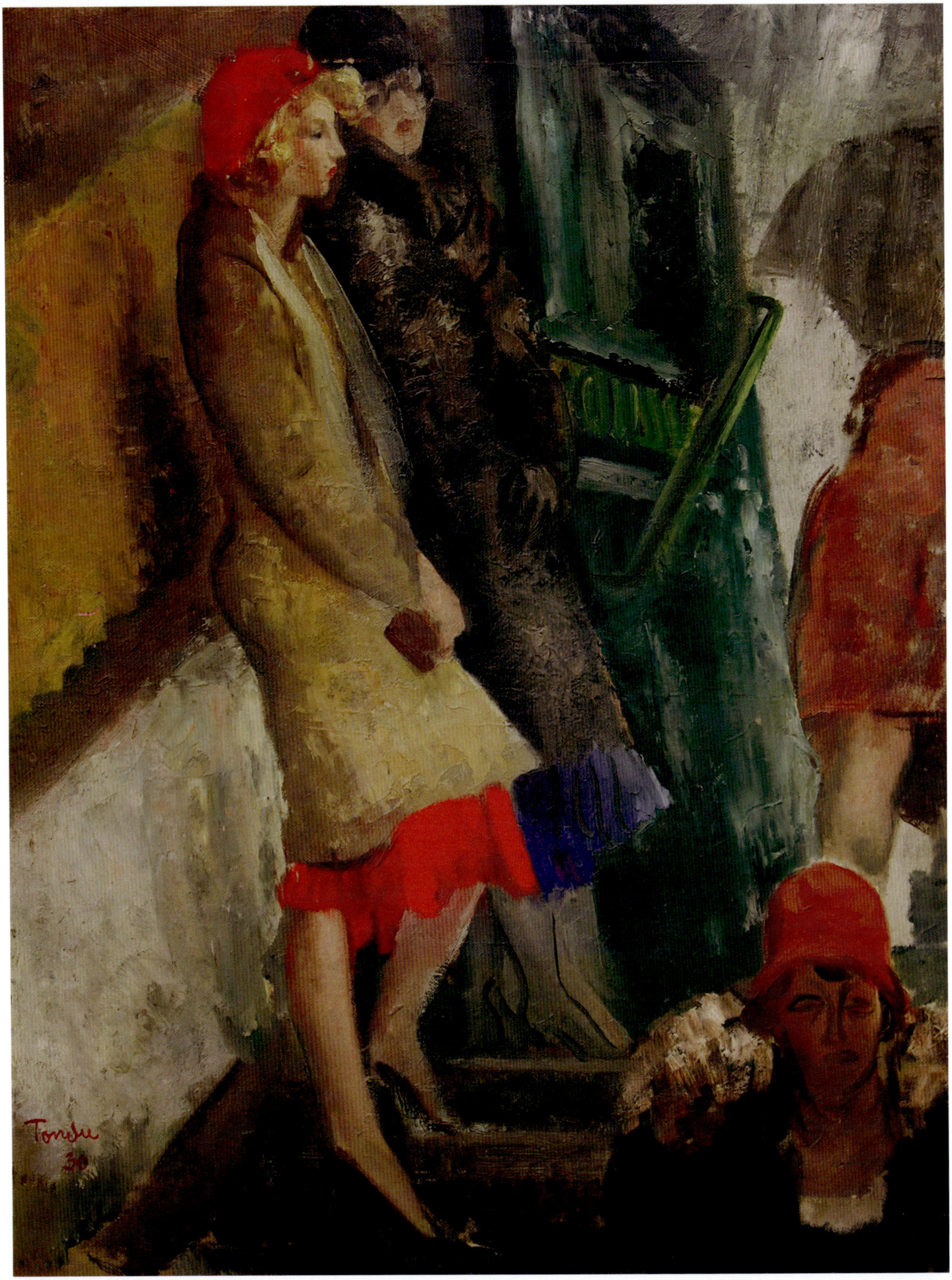

André Paul Henri Tondu
L'Entrée de la Metro, Dated 1930
Parrish Collection, San Francisco, California

Lucie Tullat

Born 1895

Lucie Tullat was born March 26, 1895 in Saint-Germain-en-Laye and studied at l'École des Beaux-Arts in Paris from 1919 to 1925. Though her style is realistic there is a hint of the surreal in her compositions that adds intrigue. Her sense of balance and composition results in especially pleasing paintings.

Tullat exhibited at the Salon des Tuileries, Salon du Dessin et da la Peinture à l'Eau and the Salon d'Automne, of which she was a member. The Musée d'Art Moderne in Paris has also collected her work. The date of her death is unknown.

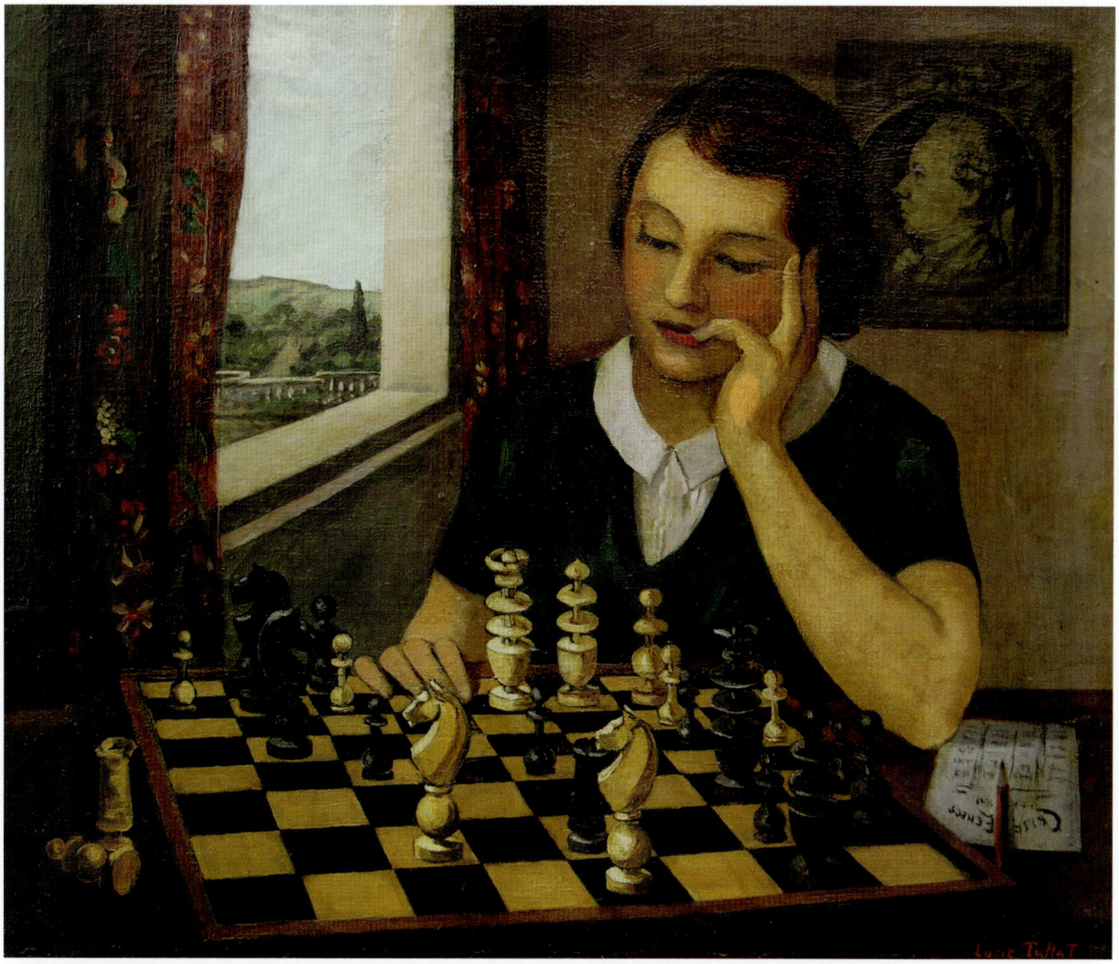

Lucie Tullat
Chess, c.1945
Ruth Marklowe, City Island, New York

Milivoy Uzelac

1897-1977

Milivoy Uzelac was born on July 27, 1897 in Mostar, Bosnia-Herzegovina, Yugoslavia. He studied with Jan Preisler at the Academy of Fine Art in Prague. Beginning in 1922, Uzelac exhibited at the Salons des Indépendants, Salons d'Automne and Salons des Tuileries. The French avant-garde artists with whom Uzelac exhibited influenced the development of his work. In 1946 he exhibited at the Musée d'Art Moderne de la Ville de Paris. This group exhibition was organized by the United Nations and traveled to museums in Brussels, London, Amsterdam, Zagreb and Belgrade.

Uzelac illustrated *Requiem* by Serge Essenine, *La Rencontre* by Pascal de François Maurice, *Le Moyen de parvenir* by Béroalde de Verville and many other publications. Uzelac is known for his figurative paintings as well as nudes. His style was appealing and purely modern. He did a series of lithographs depicting a variety of sports and also worked as an illustrator and sculptor.

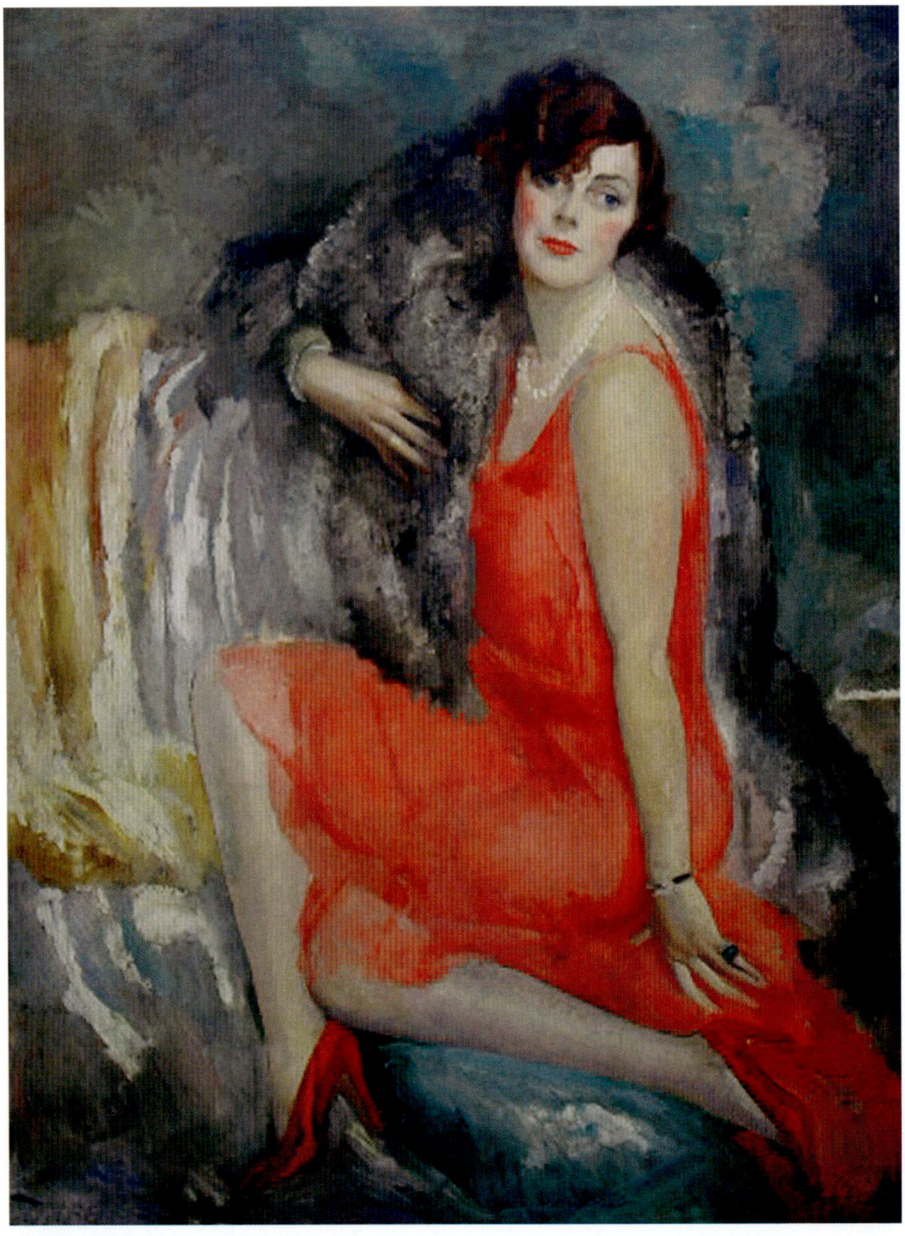

Milivoy Uzelac
Femme Élégante, c.1930
Private Collection

Prosper Louis Vagnier

Late 19th century

Prosper Louis Vagnier was born in Reims, France. He studied with Wiliam Bouguereau, J.P. Laurens, Toudouze and Baschet. Vagnier is considered a 19th and 20th century French painter of genre scenes. He exhibited regularly at the Salon des Artistes Français beginning in 1905 and received the Médaille de Troisième Classe the same year.

Vagnier painted in a traditional style. His subjects depict the modern lifestyle of his contemporaries and tend to be illustrative.

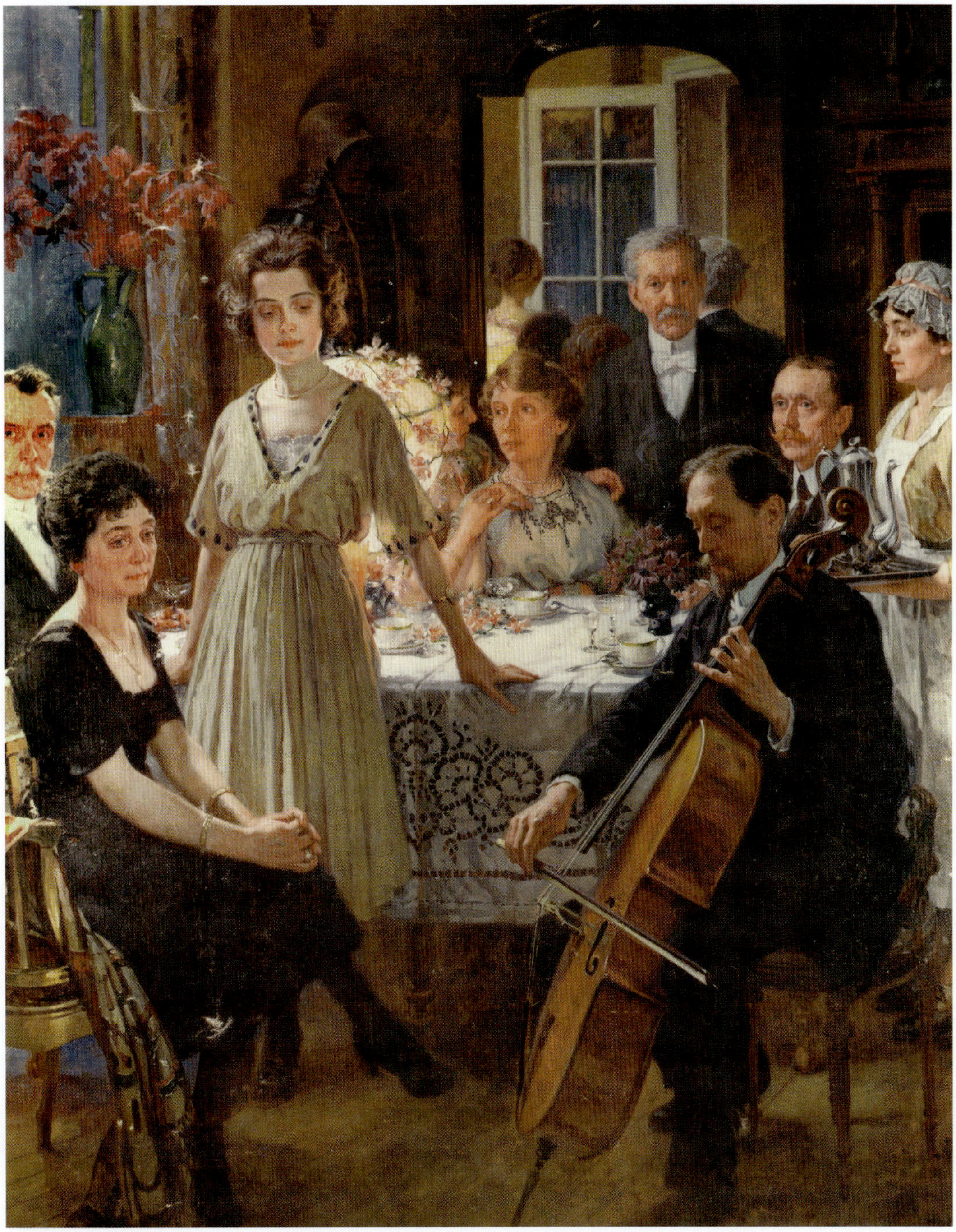

Prosper Louis Vagnier
Réfléchir, c.1915
Los Angeles Fine Art Gallery, Los Angeles, California

Karel van Belle

1884–1959

Karel van Belle was born in Gent, Belgium in 1884. She studied with Jean-Josef Delvin and Louis Tytgat at the Académie des Beaux-Arts de Gent. Karel van Belle painted genre scenes and nudes with poetic compositions that often glorified feminine beauty. She is best known for painting ethereal and mysterious subjects in a symbolist style. Karel van Belle was also a watercolorist in addition to working in oils.

In 1913 she received third place in painting in the Prix de Rome competition. Museums in Gent and Tournai have collected van Belle's work.

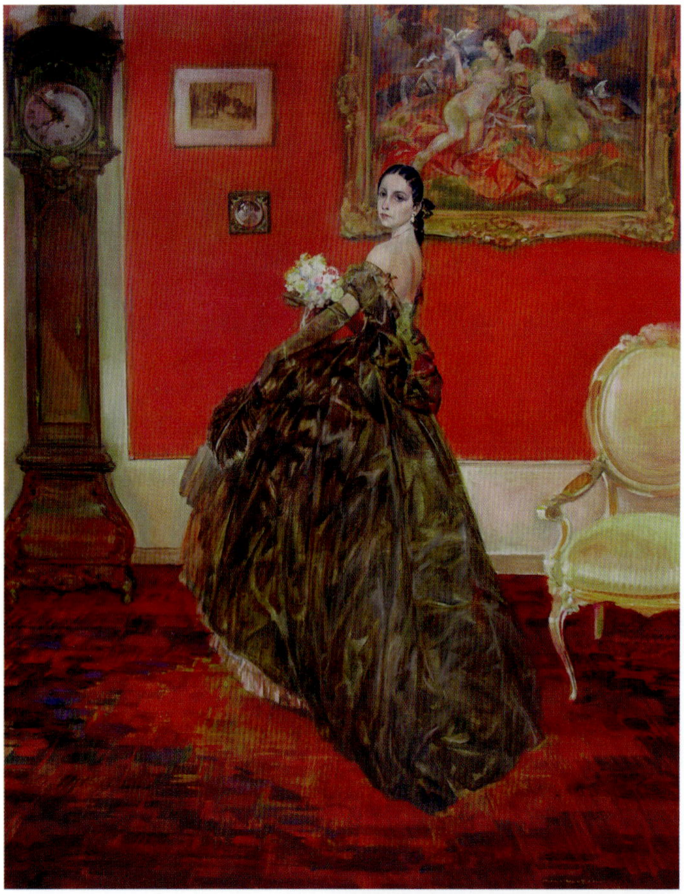

Karel van Belle
Portrait d'Élégante, c.1935
Papillon Gallery, Los Angeles, California

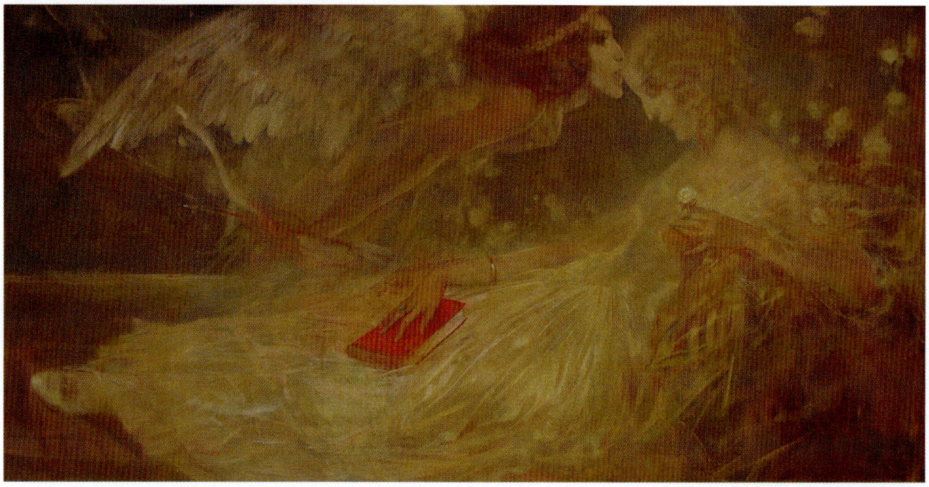

Karel van Belle
Rêverie, c.1920
Bill and Jo LaMond,
Los Angeles, California

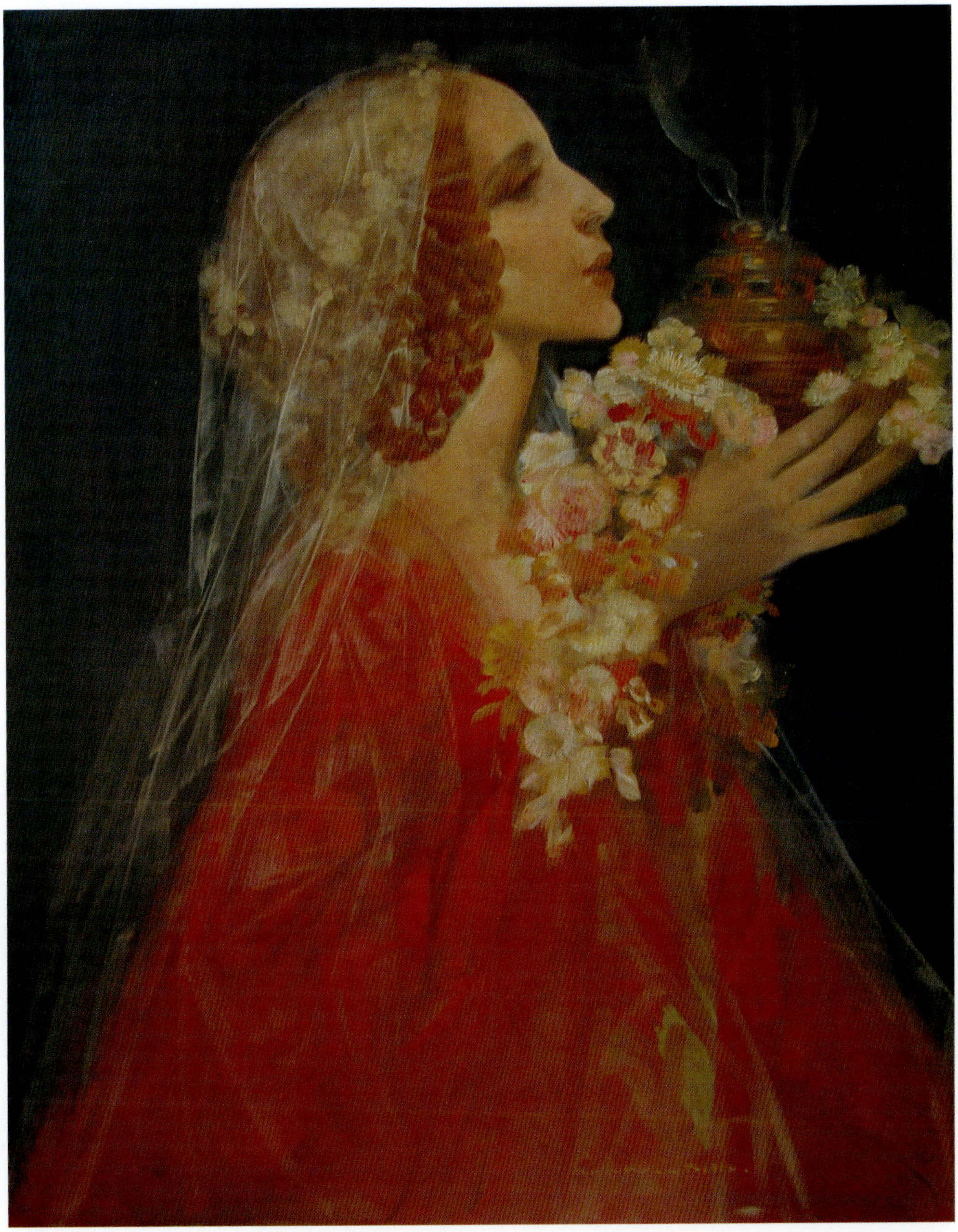

Karel van Belle
La Mariée, c.1920
Julia Evershade and Mark Smith,
Los Angeles, California

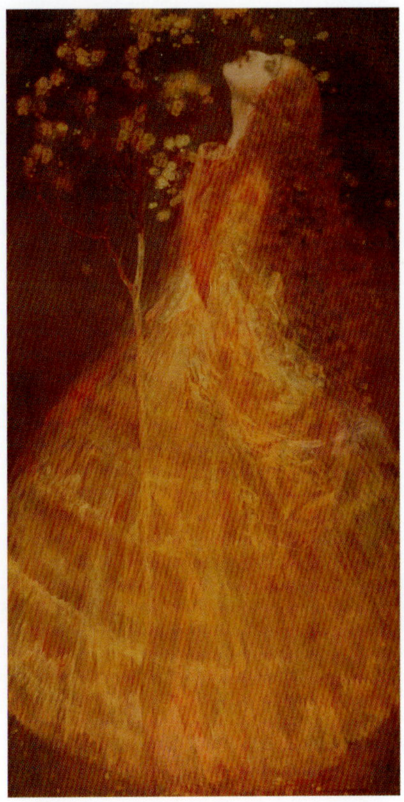

Karel van Belle
Juene Femme aux Fleurs, c.1920
Los Angeles Fine Art Gallery,
Los Angeles, California

Hugo van Beveren

1907-1985

Hugo van Beveren was born in Termonde, Belgium in 1907. At a young age he was encouraged by a close neighbor, L. Spanoghe, to study fine art and in 1926 he enrolled at l'Académie de Termonde and later at l'Académie de Gand and l'Académie de Malines. His final courses in sculpture, engraving and painting were finished at l'Institute Supérieur d'Anvers within the ateliers of E. Wijnants, J. De Bruycker and I. Opsomer.

Hugo van Beveren exhibited at *Vie Salon de Peinture Belge* at Galerie Georges Giroux in 1927 and the 45th Salon of the *Kunst en Kennis* in Gent, 1946. His paintings have a sculptural quality reminiscent of other Belgian Expressionists of the period. His brush technique is softer than most Belgians, his canvases give the feeling of a watercolorist.

He received the Belgian Second Prix de Rome in 1935. In 1941 he became a professor and from 1942 to 1970 acted as director for l'Académie de Termonde. The artist worked in an expressionist manner and worked primarily with cityscapes, still lifes and figures. The Musée de Termonde has collected his work. The artist died in Gent in 1985.

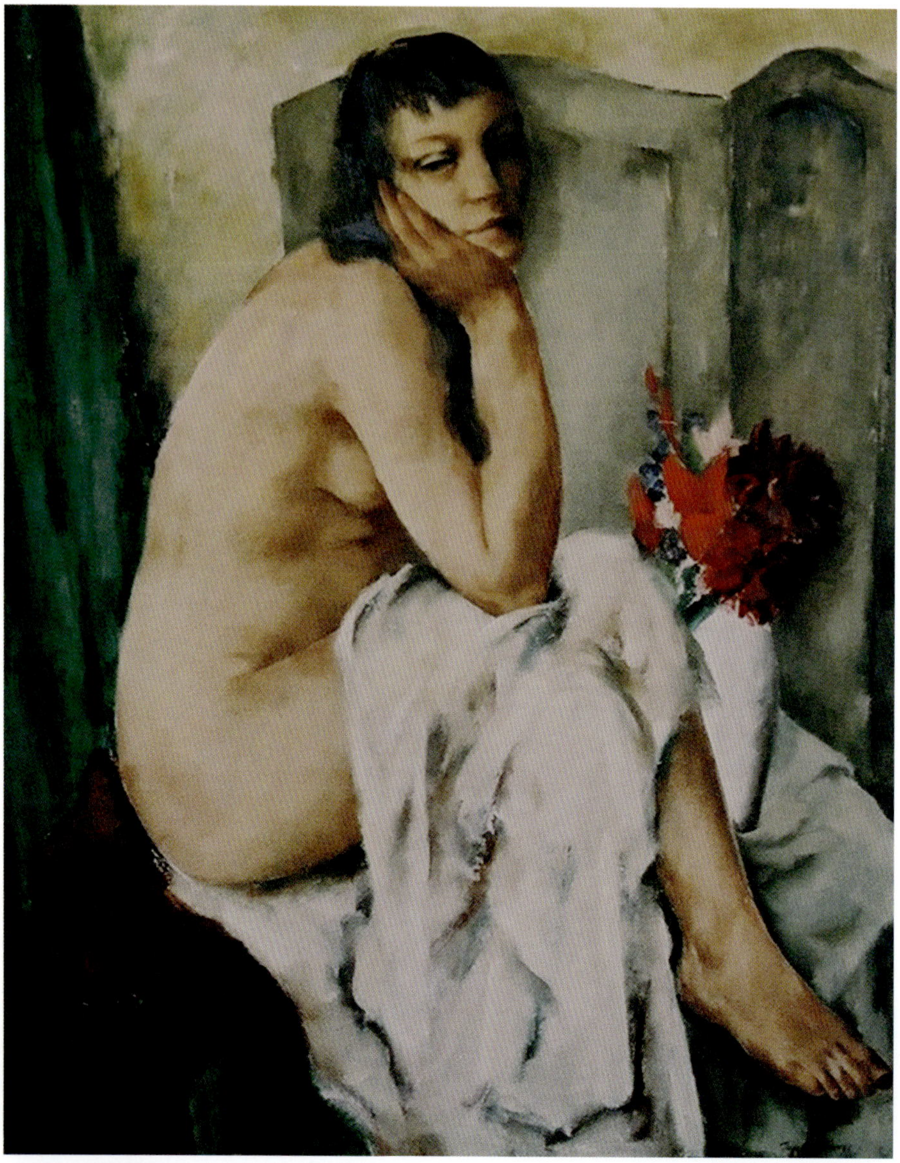

Hugo van Beveren
Nu Assis, c.1930
Private Collection, Paris

Carlo van Her

1884-1960

Carlo van Her was born Charles van Herbruggen in Brussels, Belgium in 1884. He studied with Delville at l'Académie de Bruxelles and also associated with Wagemans and Wouters.

The Brabançon artists greatly influenced the style and composition of Carlo van Her's work. He generally painted portraits and still lifes and is known for his paintings of Brussels as well as mysterious seascapes with monsters and sirens.

Carlo van Her was a professor at l'Académie de Saint-Josse-ten-Noode. His work is in the collections of the art museums in Antwerp and Doornik.

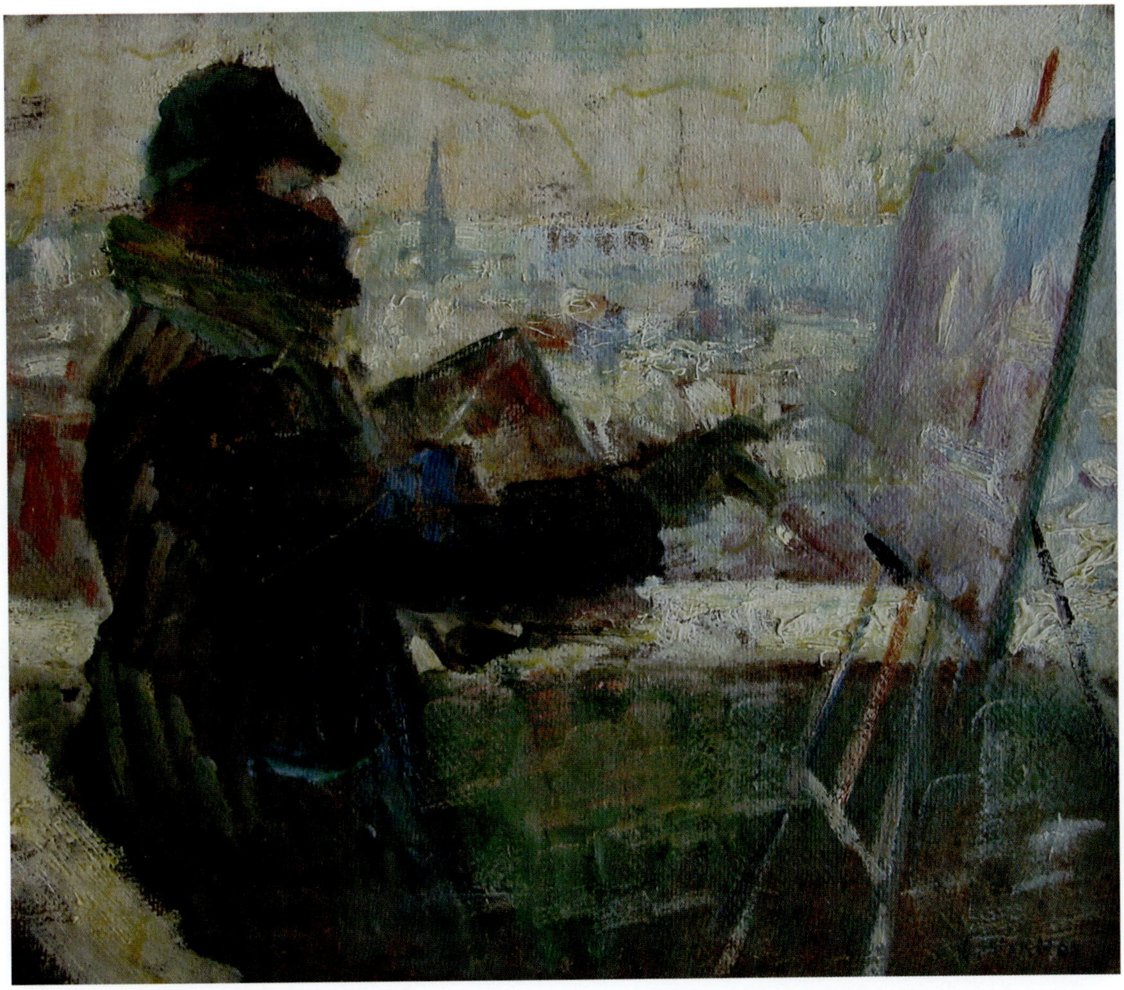

Carlo van Her
L'Artiste en Hiver, c.1920
The Parrish Collection, San Francisco, California

Georges van Nuffel
19th century

Georges van Nuffel was a figurative and portrait painter who worked in Antwerp, Belgium. He exhibited at l'Exposition d'Anvers in 1898 and Driejaarlijke Exhibition in Antwerp in 1901. The artist painted Art Nouveau scenes that rivaled those of the finest French artists and he often made intricate custom frames that complemented his paintings.

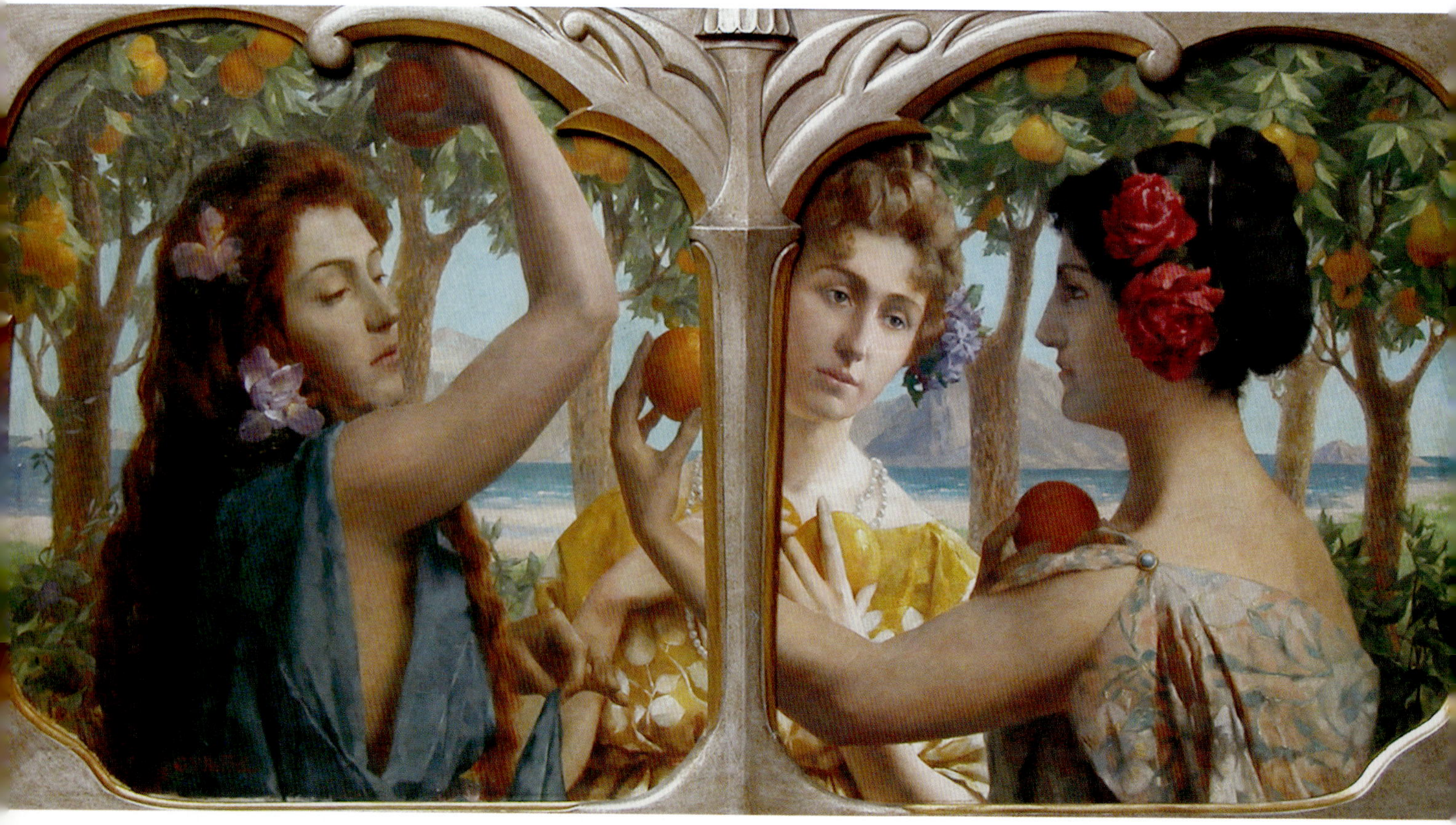

Georges van Nuffel
Le Jardin, c.1900
Allen and Mady Reid, New York, New York

Charles van Roose

1883-1960

Charles van Roose was born in Brussels in 1883 where he was a student at l'Académie des Beaux-Arts. He was a painter, illustrator and Art Nouveau draftsman. The artist painted charming and sensual feminine subjects and used the technique of the Belgian moderns of his time. He used lush interiors and furniture to frame his nudes and give them a place in time.

His work is collected by the Maison des Bouchers in Anvers and in Vleeshuis. Charles van Roose died in 1960.

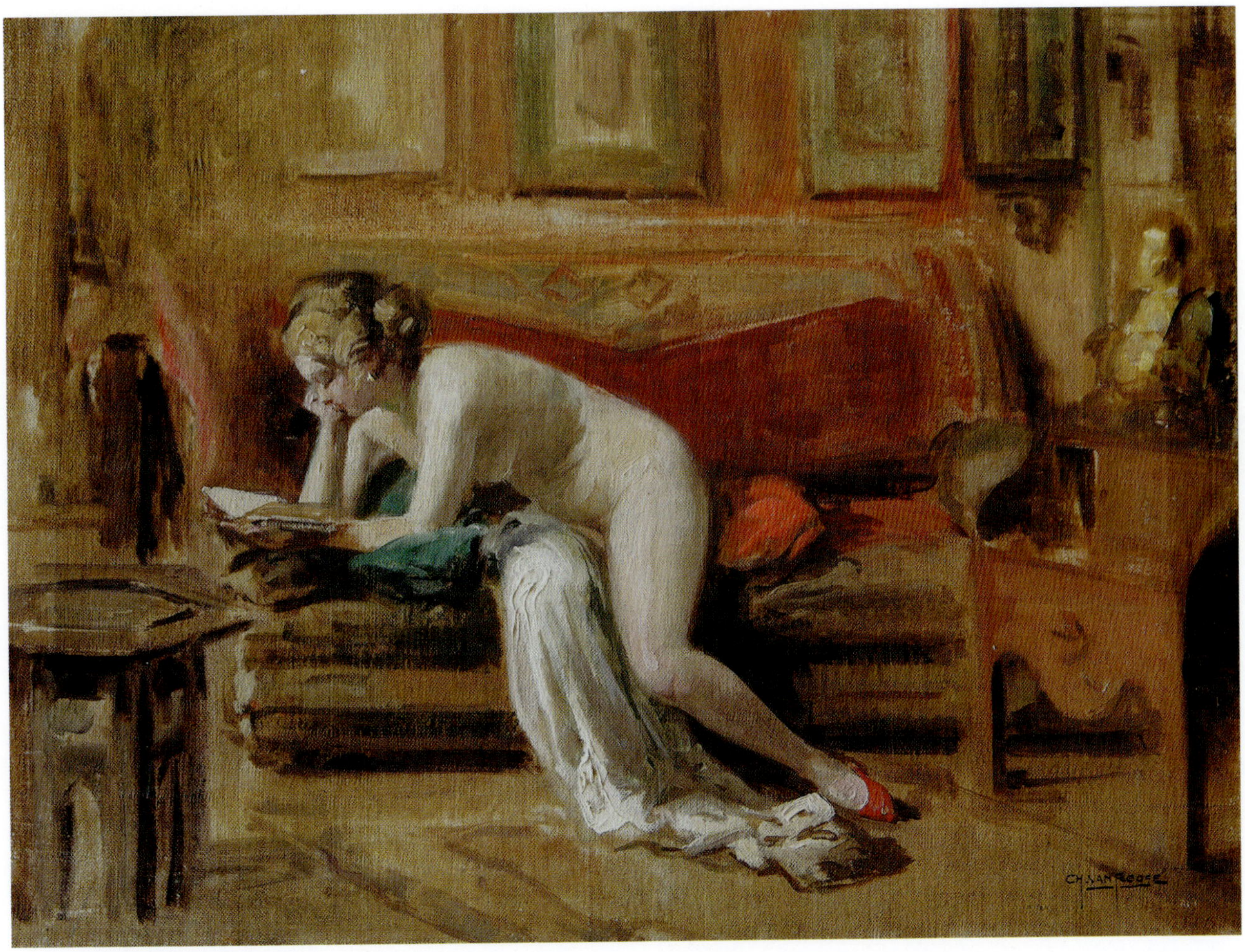

Charles van Roose
Femme au Livre, c.1925
David and Susan Levine, New York, New York

Georges Vanzevenberghen

1877-1968

Georges Vanzevenberghen was born in Molenbeek-Saint-Jean, Belgium in 1877. He studied at l'École de Dessin de Molenbeek and l'Académie des Beaux-Arts de Bruxelles then completed his studies with Jan Stobbaerts.

Vanzevenberghen began exhibiting in 1909 and participated in many salons, eventually receiving the Prix Émile Sacré. Later in his career he taught at l'Académie Royale de Belgique and in 1953 became a member of l'Académie Royale de Belgique.

Vanzevenberghen is known for his sensual and realistic nudes with warm colors and bold brush strokes. Vanzevenberghen painted genre scenes, nudes, portraits, landscapes and still lifes; his style is considered post-impressionist.

His work is mentioned in the *Dictionnaire et Biographie illustré des artistes en Belgique depuis 1830* published by Arto in Brussels, 1987. Vanzevenberghen's work is included in the permanent collections of numerous art museums including Anvers, Barcelona, Brussels, Mons, Riga and Saint-Josse-ten-Noode. Vanzevenberghen died in 1968 in Saint-Josse-ten-Noode.

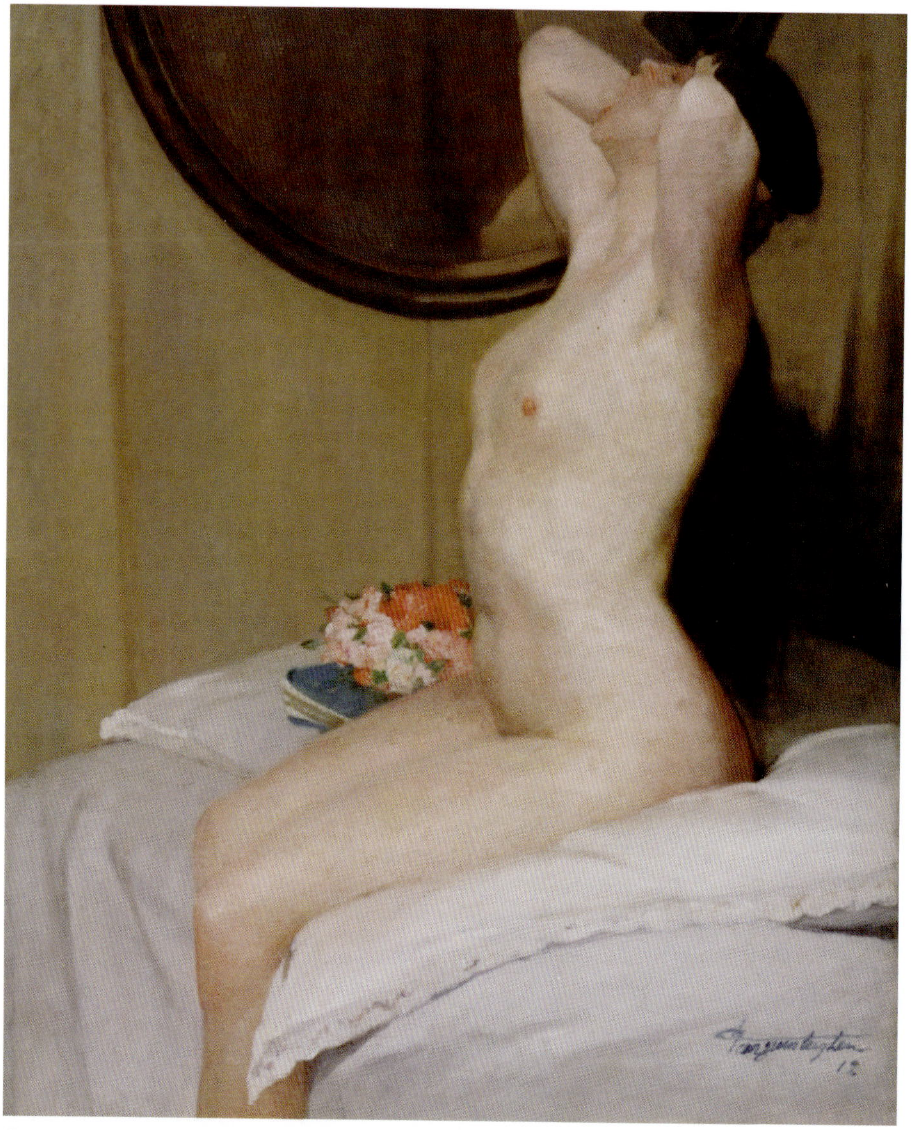

Georges Vanzevenberghen
Au Matin, Dated 1912
Los Angeles Fine Art Gallery, Los Angeles, California

Theodoor-Joseph Verschaeren
1847-1937

Theodoor-Joseph Verschaeren was born in Mechelen, Belgium in 1847 and attended l'Académie de Malines under W. Geets and W. Rosier.

Primarily known as a Belgian Expressionist painter he created a large body of portraits, specifically of women, mothers, soldiers and circus performers. Verschaeren was affiliated with the groups *De Distel* and *Van Onzen Tijd* and wrote several works for the theatre as well. Between 1906 and 1936 he exhibited with Salons in Brussels, Anvers, Liege and Malines. Verschaeren returned to l'Académie de Milanes to teach from 1921 until his death.

Verschaeren used the typical techniques and palette of many of the Belgian painters of his era; bold strokes and strong color enhanced the subjects he painted. His most interesting subjects are playful and humorous and depict the life and mood of his time. His works have been collected by the Malines Museum and the Musée Hof van Busleyden. Verschaeren died in 1937.

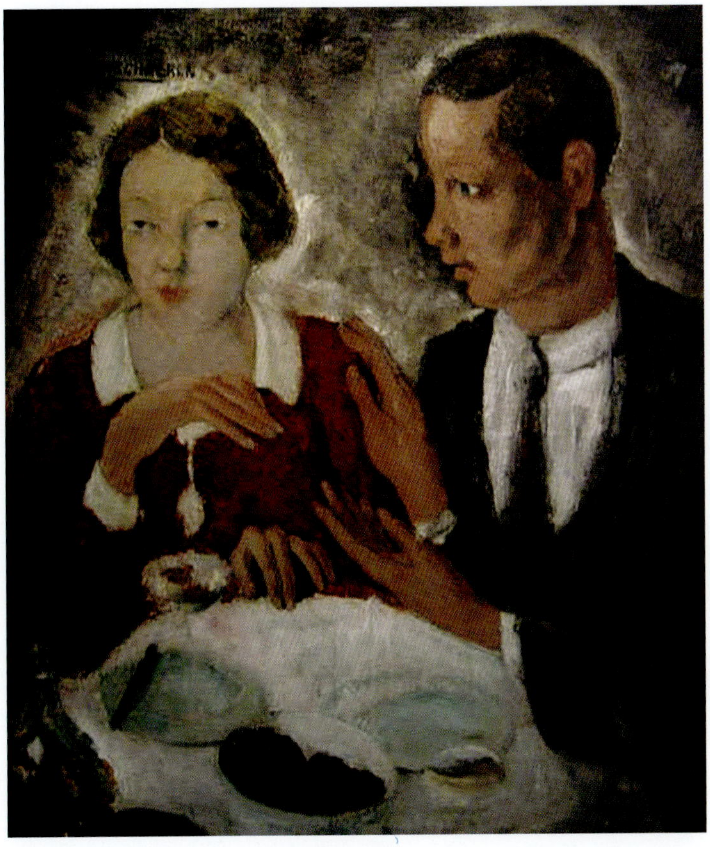

Theodoor-Joseph Verschaeren
Le Conversation, c.1930
Andrew Herrera II, San Francisco, California

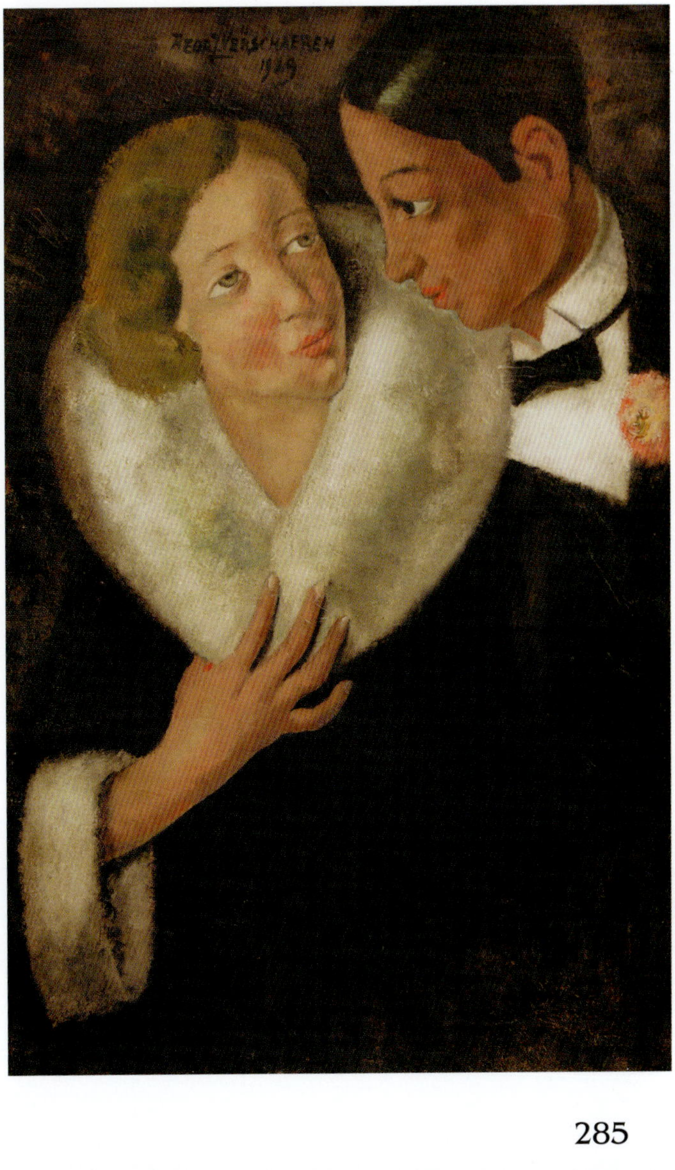

Theodoor-Joseph Verschaeren
Le Couple Élégant, Dated 1929
Martin and Marsha Brander,
Brentwood, California

Frede Vidar

1911-1967

Frede Vidar was born in Denmark. He initially attended the Royal Academy in Denmark and later the California School of Fine Arts in San Francisco, l'Académie Julian and l'École des Beaux-Arts in Paris, Academy of Fine Arts in Berlin and the American Academy in Rome with the support of the Caholner and Guggenheim Foundations. Vidar was best known for his figurative work and depictions of city scenes.

At the age of eighteen he received his first solo exhibition in Paris and participated in fifteen subsequent exhibits in Europe, the United States and Australia. In 1933 Vidar had the opportunity to study under Matisse and Dufy before returning to San Francisco. He was selected to create a mural for the Coit Tower project in 1934, for which he produced *Department Store*. It was a lively mural depicting all the texture and diversity of a bustling city life.

During World War II Vidar served as a combat artist and artist-correspondent for *Life* and *Fortune* magazines. He settled in New Jersey and taught at the New York School of Interior Decoration, Newark School of Fine and Industrial Art, University of Wisconsin, Washington University in St. Louis and University of Michigan. Spencer Jon Helfen Fine Arts Gallery currently represents the estate of Frede Vidar. Vidar died in 1967.

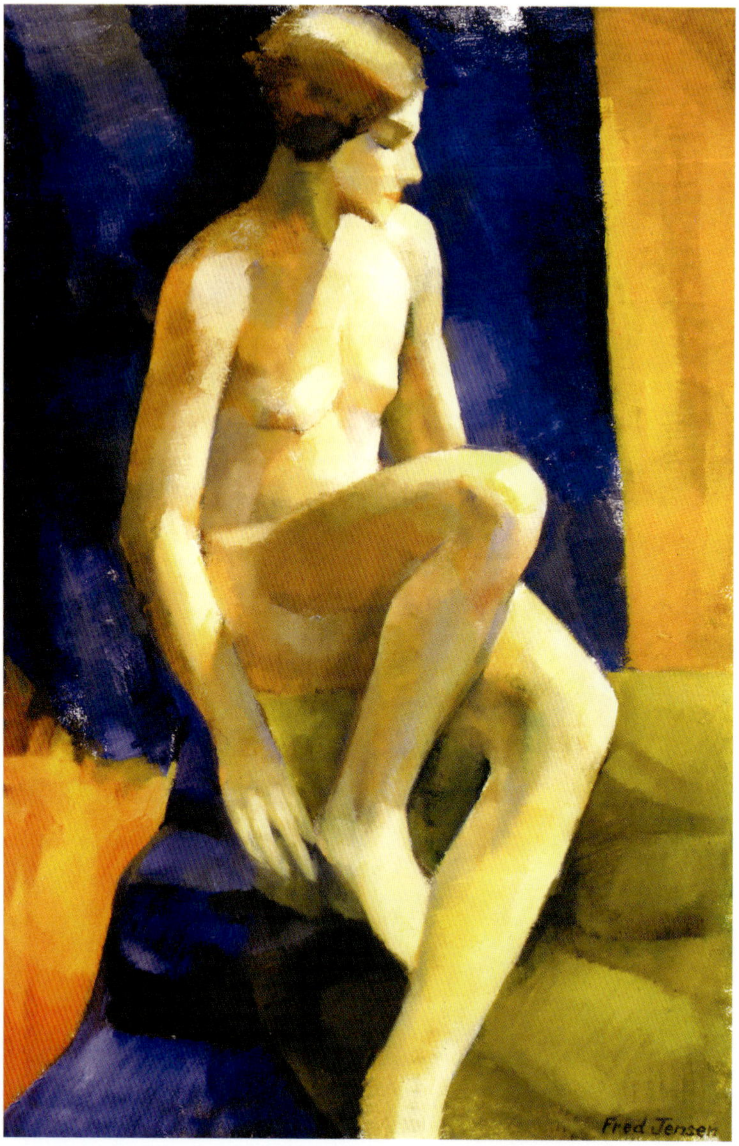

Frede Vidar
Beyond/Night , Signed Fred Jensen, c. 1930
Photo courtesy of Spencer Jon Helfen Fine Arts, Beverly Hills, California

Pierre Villain
1876-1936

Pierre Villain studied engraving at l'École des Beaux-Arts in Paris. While living in Paris and working professionally as an engraver he was largely influenced by Louis Anquetin and Toulouse-Lautrec.

Pierre Villain's style and technique show the influence of the Postimpressionists. He enjoyed the bars and cabarets of Paris and often depicted lively street and café scenes. Unlike most of his contemporaries Villain did not romanticize his subjects as reality seemed more his forte. Villain died in 1936. The family of the artist handles much of his estate to this day.

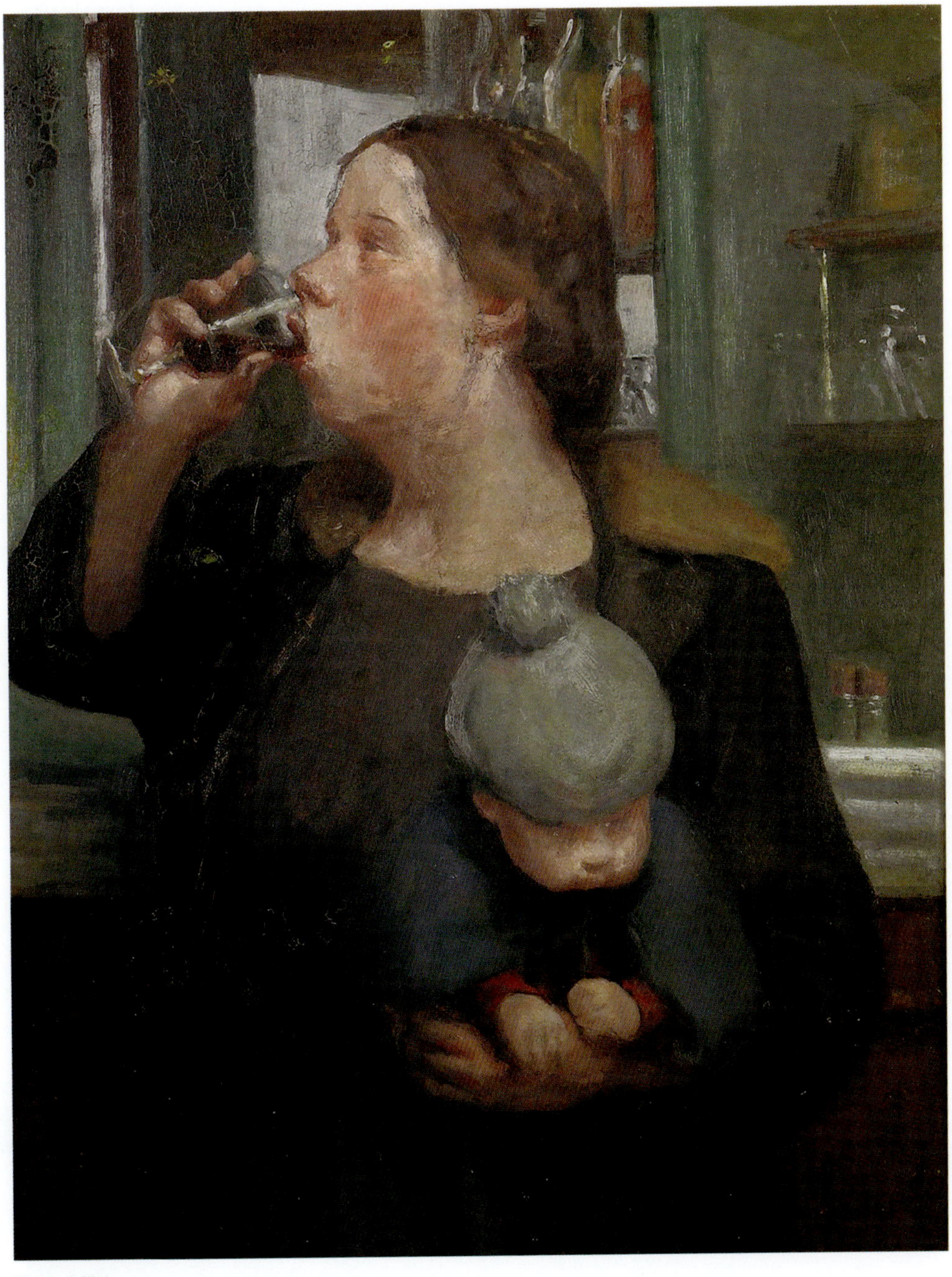

Pierre Villain
La Buveuse, c,1910
Private Collection, Paris, France

Léon Voguet

Born 1879

Léon Voguet was born May 14, 1879, in Paris. He participated frequently in group and solo exhibitions in Paris including those at the Salon des Réalités Nouvelles, Salon d'Automne, Salon des Artistes Décorateurs and the Musée de Rouen.

Voguet painted playful feminine subjects, his body of work reflects the tradition of Les Années Folles. Voguet illustrated several books including *L'Anglais Mangeur d'Opium* by Alfred de Musset and *Jadis et Naguère* by Paul Verlaine and in 1957 Voguet received the Prix Fénéon. The date of his death is unknown.

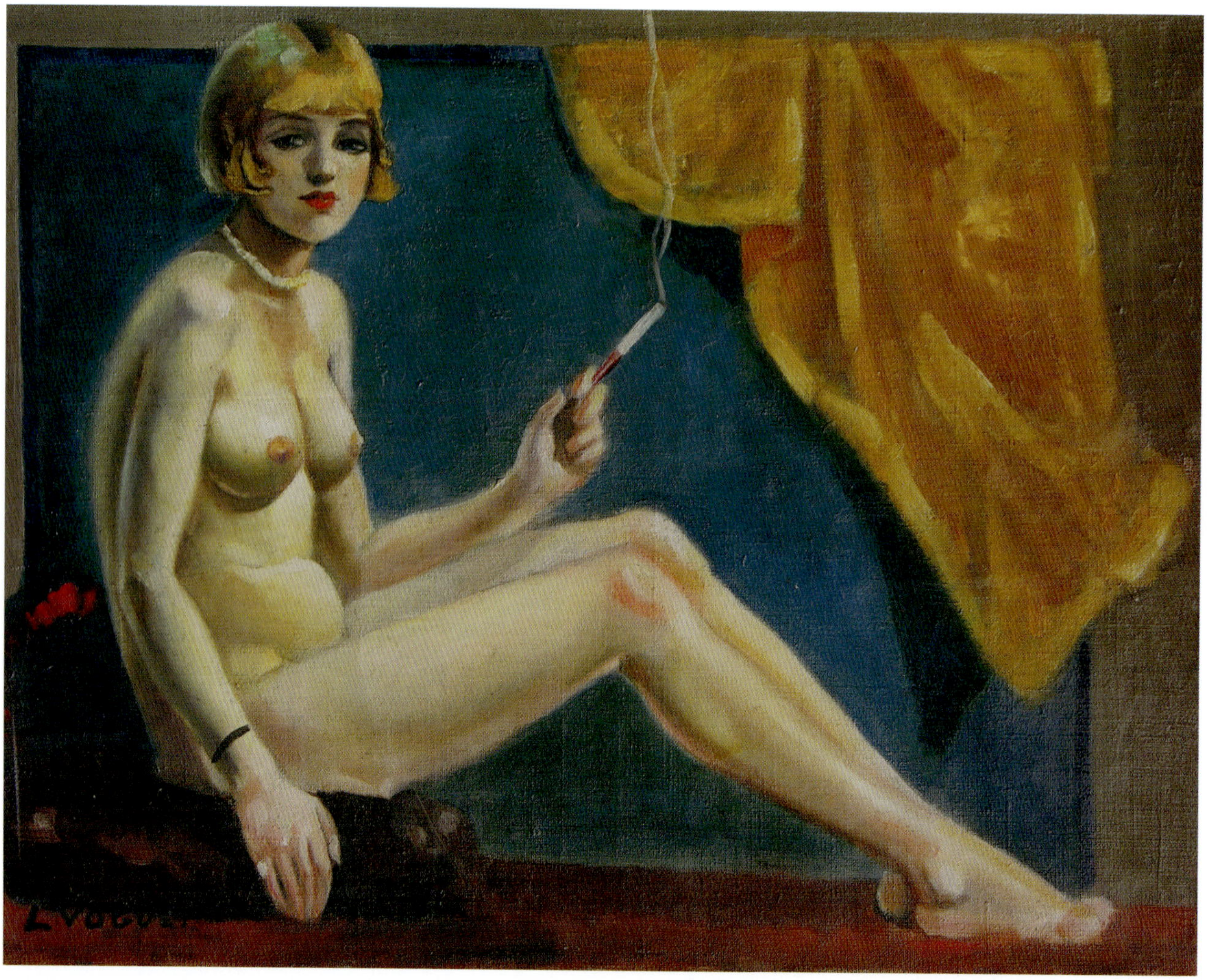

Léon Voguet
Nu Assis avec la Cigarette, c.1925
Papillon Gallery, Los Angeles, California

Maurice Wagemans
1877-1927

Maurice Wagemans was born in Brussels in 1877. He attended l'Académie de Bruxelles as a painting student of Jean Portaels and Joseph Stallaert. While attending the academy he befriended artists Alfred Bastien and Frans Smeers with whom he traveled to Paris in 1885. His influences came strongly from Frantin Latour and Édouard Manet during this time.

In 1900 he exhibited with the group *Le Sillon* after returning to Belgium. Two years later he exhibited with the Salon de Gands for the first time with the painting *Woman in Grey*. Wagemans' influences continued to change upon meeting Luminists Marcel Jeffreys and Rik Wouters in 1912 and he exhibited at the Galerie G. Giroux in Brussels with his new work. In Switzerland during the World War I, Wagemans exhibited between 1916 and 1917 and again in Brussels in 1919 at the Armistice. He became a member of the Société Nouvelle des Beaux-Arts and the Artists Association of London.

Wagemans' style and technique is in the tradition of Belgian painters of his era. His sensual subjects, use of color and composition come together to create a warm visual experience. The application of the paint, thick and bold gives a superb texture to his creations. Museums in Brussels, Ghent, Dublin and Johannesburg have collected his work. Wagemans died in 1927.

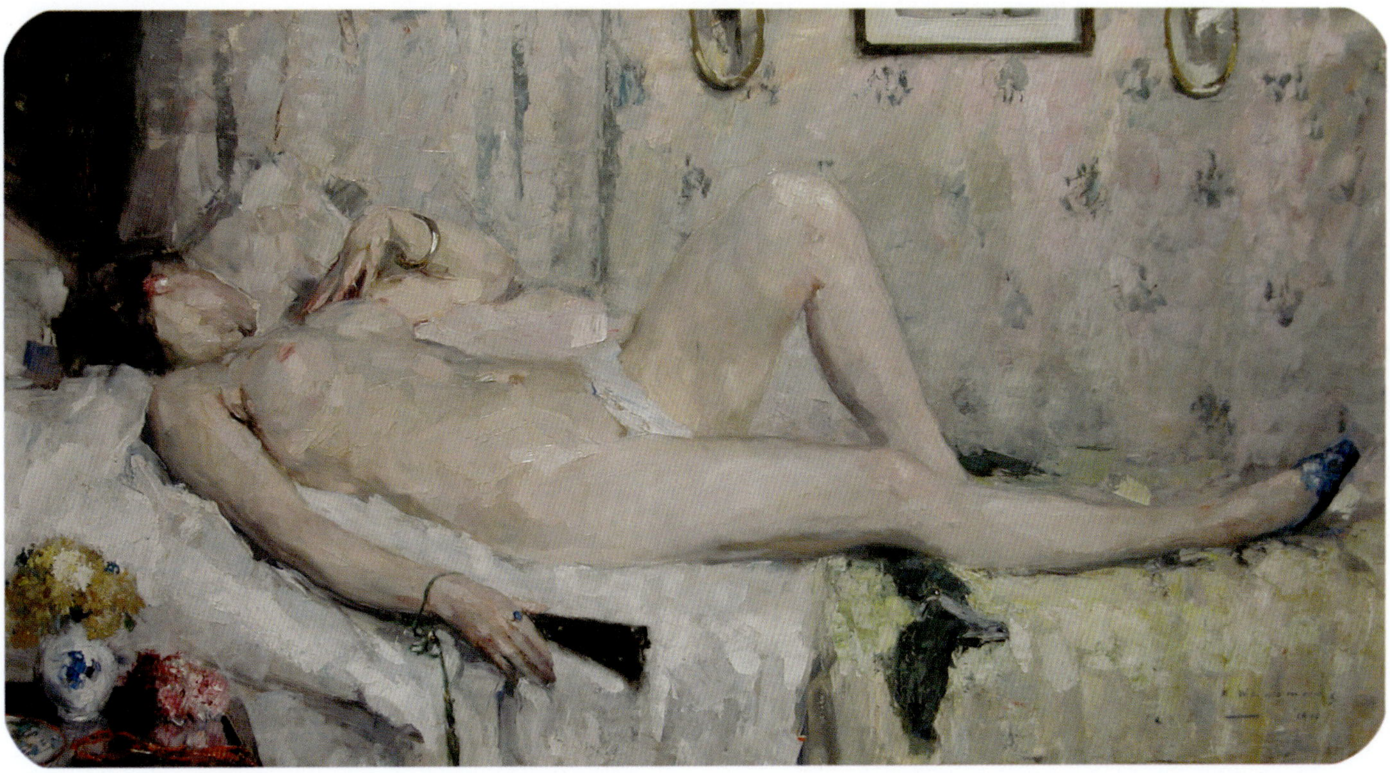

Maurice Wagemans
Nu Allongé, Dated 1910
Los Angeles Fine Art Gallery, Los Angeles, California

Charles Joseph Watelet
1867–1954

Charles Joseph Watelet was born in February, 1867 in Beauraing, Belgium. He studied under Jean Français Portaels at l'Académie des Beaux-Arts de Bruxelles and was also a student of Alfred Stevens. Watelet exhibited at the Salon des Artistes Français in 1902 and was awarded the Légion d'Honneur, the Médaille de Troisième Classe and the Médaille d'Or in 1925.

Known most widely for his depictions of female figures, Watelet also painted genre scenes, landscapes and created flyers and posters for theatre houses. Watelet's paintings of playful and charming women insured a long and successful career and are as popular now as when they were first exhibited.

Watelet is represented in several museums including Rochefort, Valenciennes, Versailles, Brussels, the Palace of Justice and Tournai. Charles Watelet died in 1954.

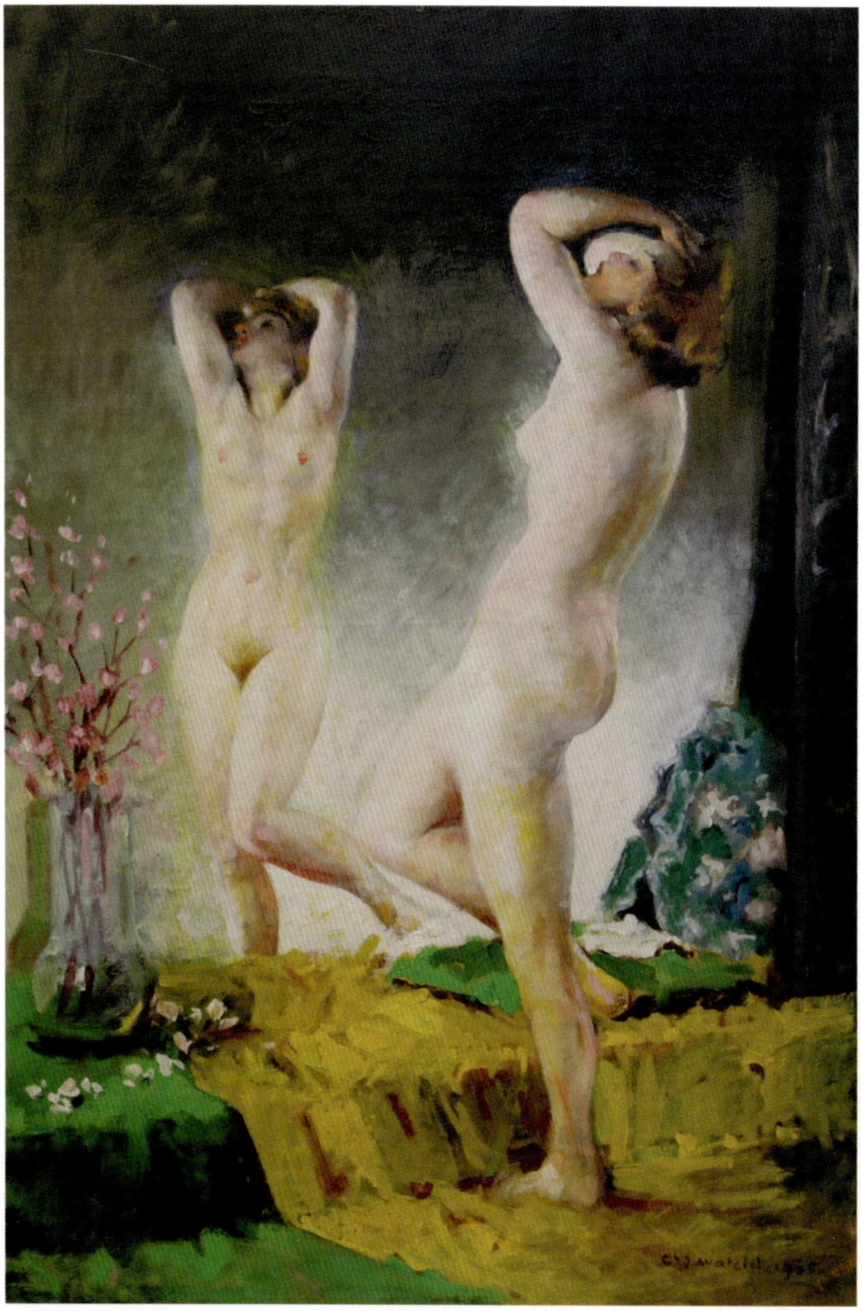

Charles Watelet
Au Miroir, Dated 1935
Andrew Herrera II,
San Francisco, California

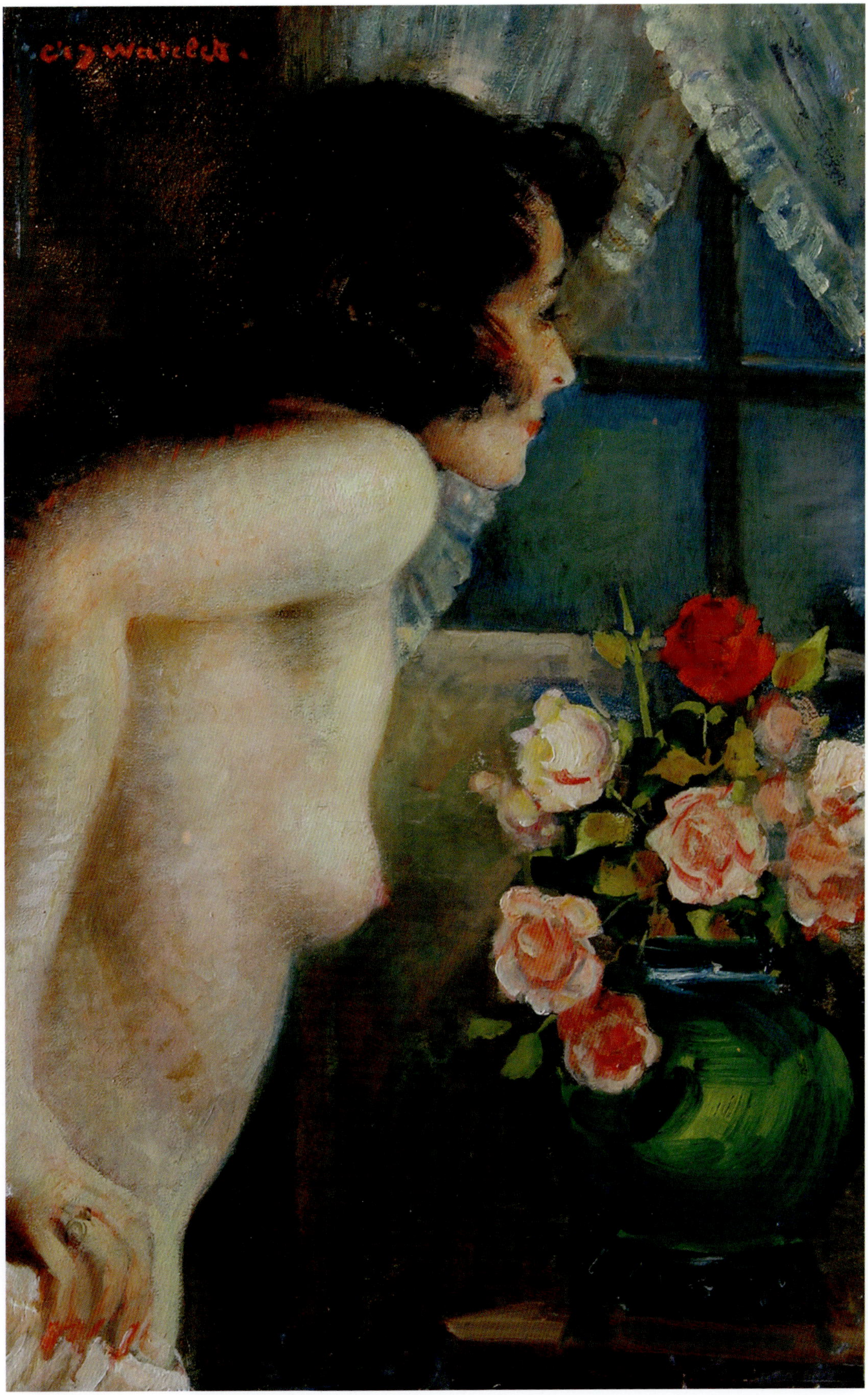

Charles Watelet
Au Fenêtre, c.1930
Seligman Family Collection, Los Angeles, California

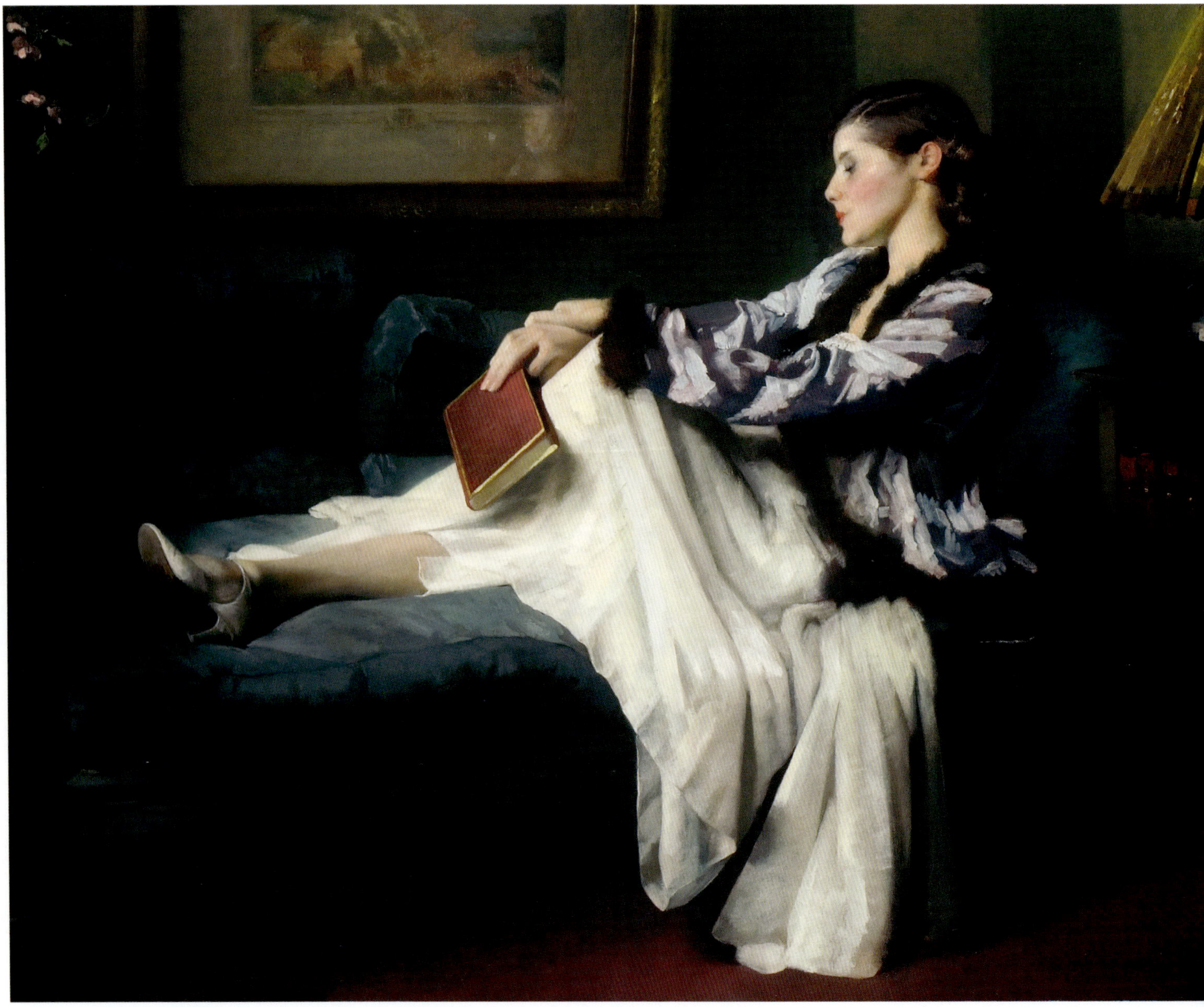

Charles Watelet
Jeune Femme Lisant, Dated 1938
Waterhouse and Dodd, London, England

Gerda Wegener
1885 or 1889-1940

Gerda Wegener was born between 1885 and 1889 in Copenhagen, Denmark. She was born Gerda Maria Frederikke Gottleib. Wegener was married to esteemed and notorious Danish painter Einar Wegener who underwent one of the first sex change operations in 1930 and became known as Lili Elbe. Wegener often used "Lili" as a model for her book and magazine illustrations.

Wegener studied at l'École des Beaux-Arts de Copenhague and traveled in Italy, England and France. She exhibited in several Parisian salons including the Salon d'Automne, Salon des Indépendants and Salon des Humoristes. Gérald Schurr discusses her work in *Les Petits Maîtres de la Peinture 1820-1920, Valeur de Demain*, 1976.

Wegener's exquisite watercolors of fashionable women are purely Art Deco. Her nudes set in modern interiors were a perfect addition to an Art Deco home. She is also known for erotic book illustrations and produced many pochoir prints. Among books she illustrated are *L'abdication de Ris-Orangis, Contes de Mon Père le Jars, Fortunio* and *Une Aventure d'Amour à Venise.*

A novel by David Ebershoff, titled *The Danish Girl,* was published in 2000. Though fictionalized it tells the story of Gerda and Einar Wegener. Wegener died in 1940.

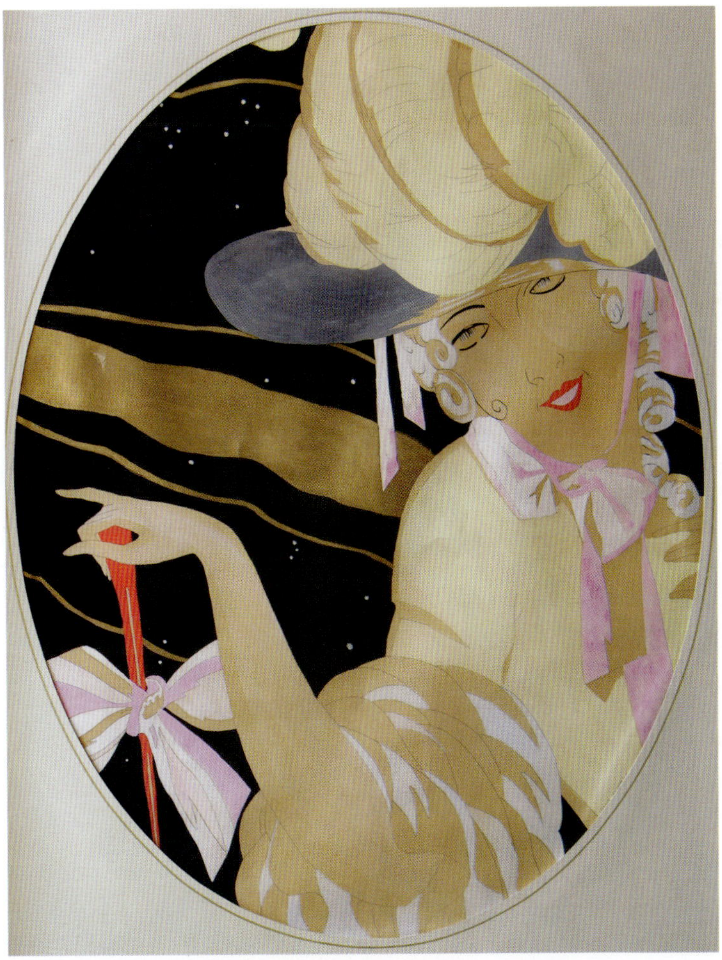

Gerda Wegener
Femme Élégante, c.1920
Papillon Gallery, Los Angeles, California

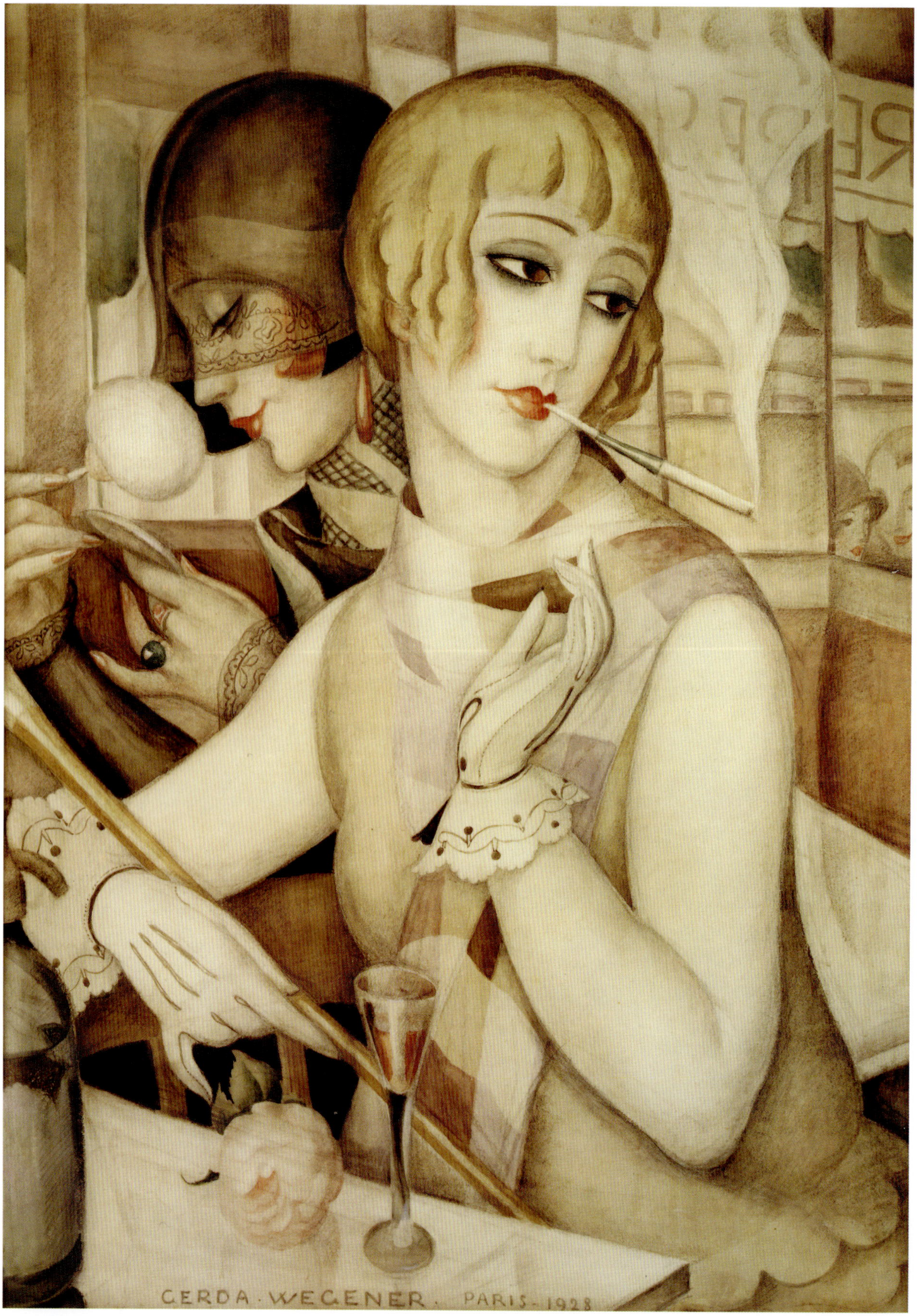

Gerda Wegener
Deux Femmes au Café, Dated 1928
Beverly Sacks Fine Art Inc., New York, New York

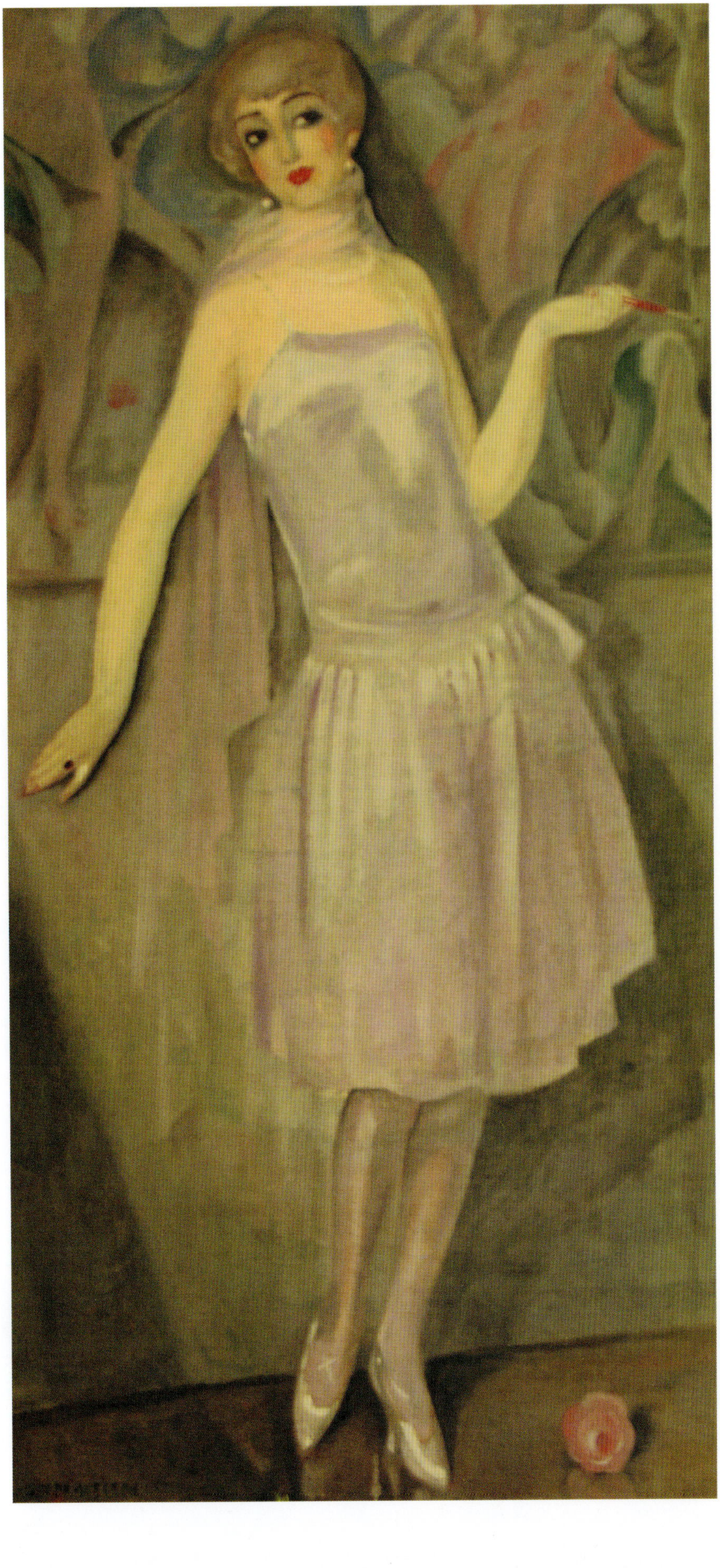

Gerda Wegener
Femme au Robe Rose, c.1925
Lisa Vanderpump, Beverly Hills, California

Muriel Wilson

Born 1892

Muriel Wilson was born in Chicago on July 21, 1892. She studied art at the Crystal Palace and the Central School of Arts and Crafts. Wilson was known as a watercolorist, painter and print maker. She exhibited at the Paris Salons, Royal Institute of Painters in Watercolor and the Royal Society of British Artists. She lived in London.

Wilson's paintings of the 1930s exhibited a strong influence of the Parisian moderns. The stylization of André Lhote, which was pervasive among young artists in Paris between the wars, is visible in Wilson's paintings. Her large bold canvases express the confidence of this accomplished artist.

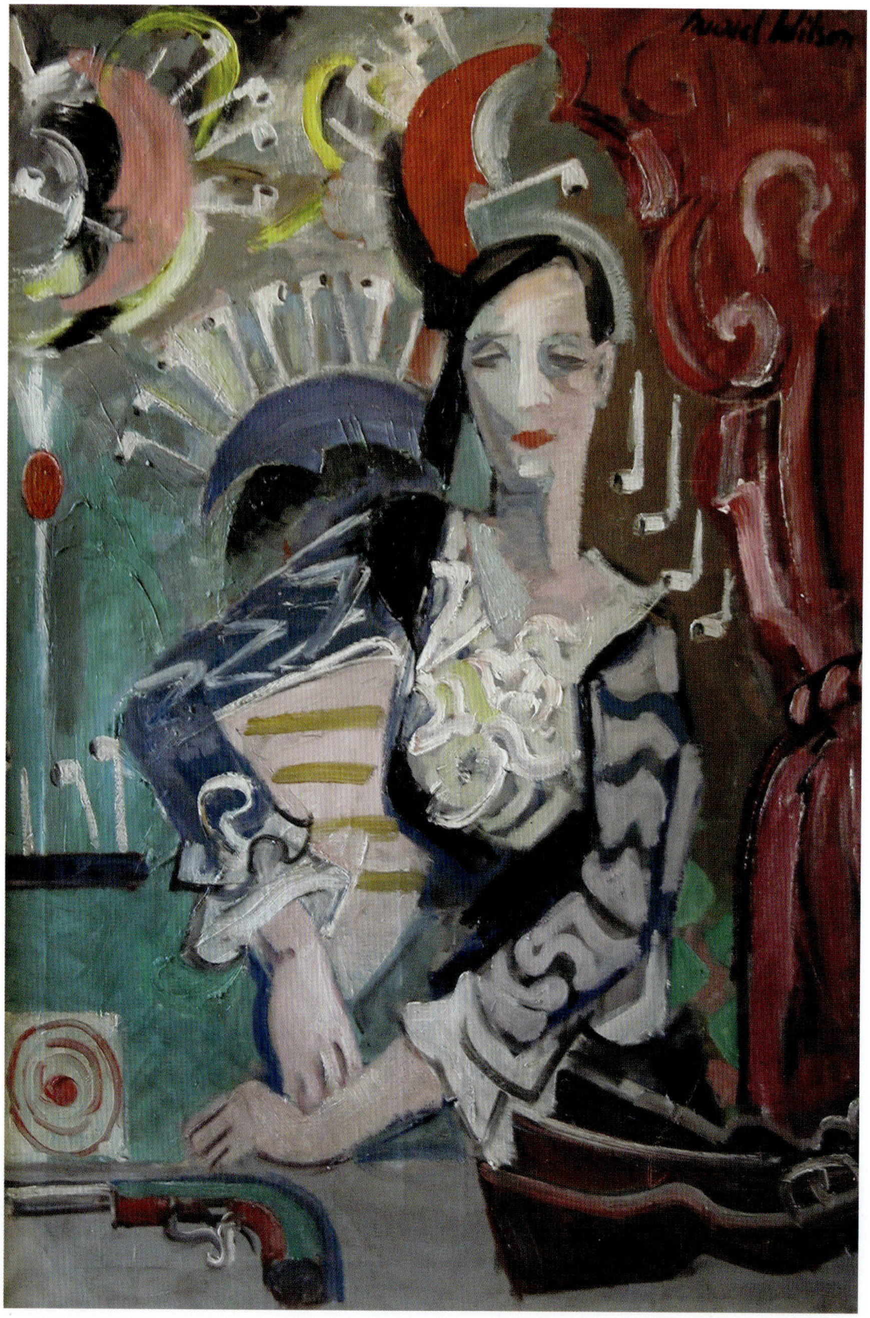

Muriel Wilson
Shooting Gallery, c.1940
Courtesy of the Jeri L. Waxenberg Collection, USA

Guy Brown Wiser

1895–1983

Guy Brown Wiser was born on February 10, 1895 in Marion, Indiana. Wiser graduated from Cornell University in 1917 and went on to serve as a pilot in the Air Force during World War I. After the war he returned to Indiana where he worked for several years as an architect.

Wiser traveled to Paris where he lived for almost two years and studied under Jean Despujols. When Wiser returned to the United States he studied in Cape Cod with Charles Hawthorne and later attended art classes at Ohio State University. In 1934 he moved to Los Angeles and taught at Scripps College for two years. Between 1935 and 1957 he illustrated close to 80 books for various publishing companies.

Wiser's figurative paintings of the 1930s are reminiscent of his teacher Jean Despujols. The works often portray utopian images similar to those found in the Art Deco paintings of the Bordeaux artists. His paintings combine classical technique and lyrical symbolism.

Wiser exhibited at the Painters and Sculptors of LA exhibition in 1935 and also at the Academy of Western Painters in 1936. The artist died in Fallbrook, California on March 30, 1983.

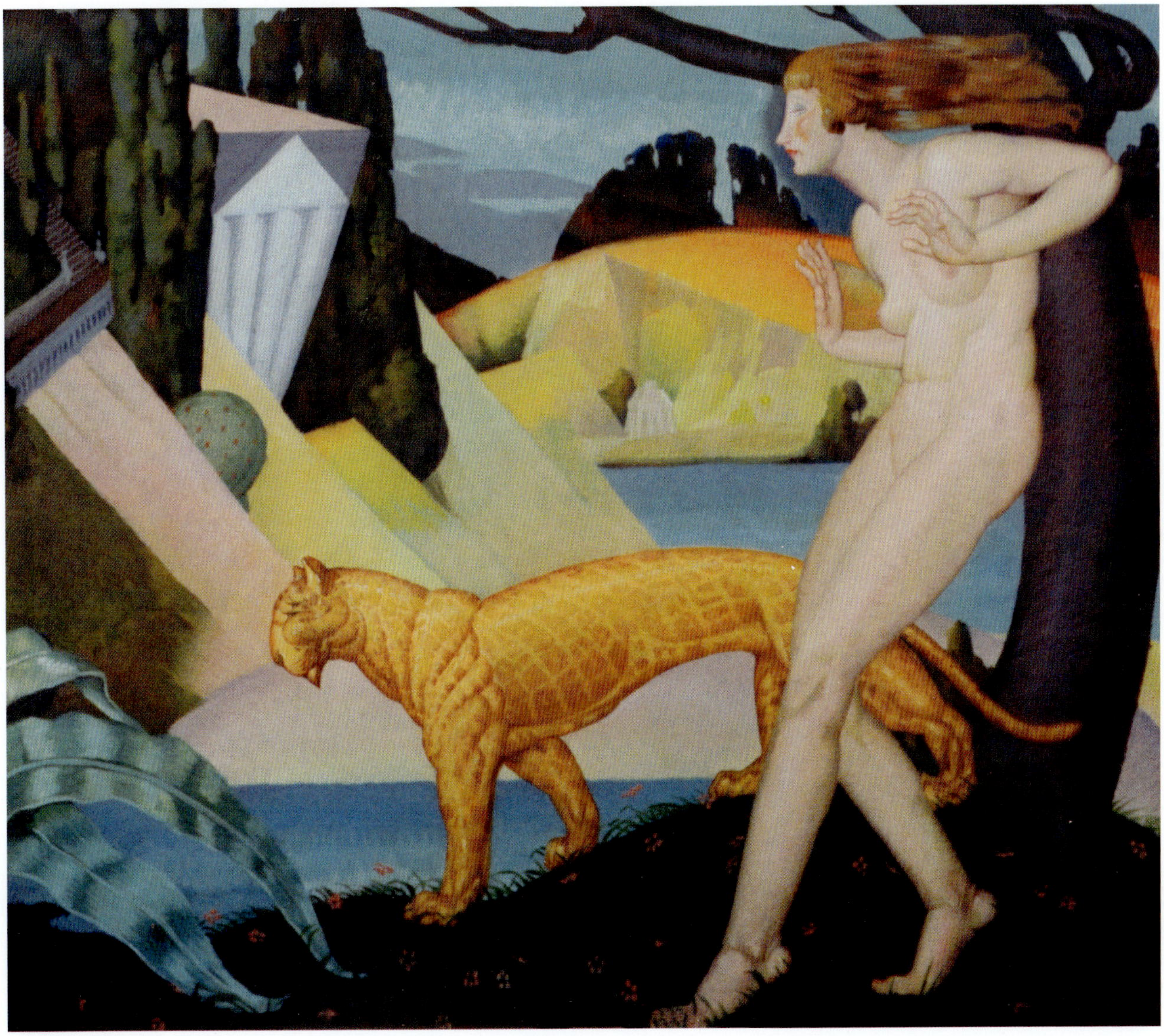

Guy Brown Wiser
Utopian Dream, c.1930
Private Collection

Edward Withers

1896-1964

Edward Withers was born in New Zealand. He studied at Wellington College, New Zealand; Royal Academy and Slade College in London, and at l'Académie Julian Paris. He is known for his figurative and portrait paintings.

Withers served as president and also as a member of the California Art Club. He exhibited widely in Southern California and has work in the permanent collection of the Museum of Archaeology and Art in Gunnison, Colorado. In addition to his fine art career, Withers worked as a calendar pin-up artist.

From 1921 through 1928 he worked in various roles in the film industry including Art Director, Writer and Special Effects Coordinator. Highlights from his film career include working as the Settings Writer on *The Wind*, 1928; Art Director on *The Frontiersman*, 1927 and Special Effects Coordinator on *The Girl I Loved*, 1923. Edward Withers died in 1964.

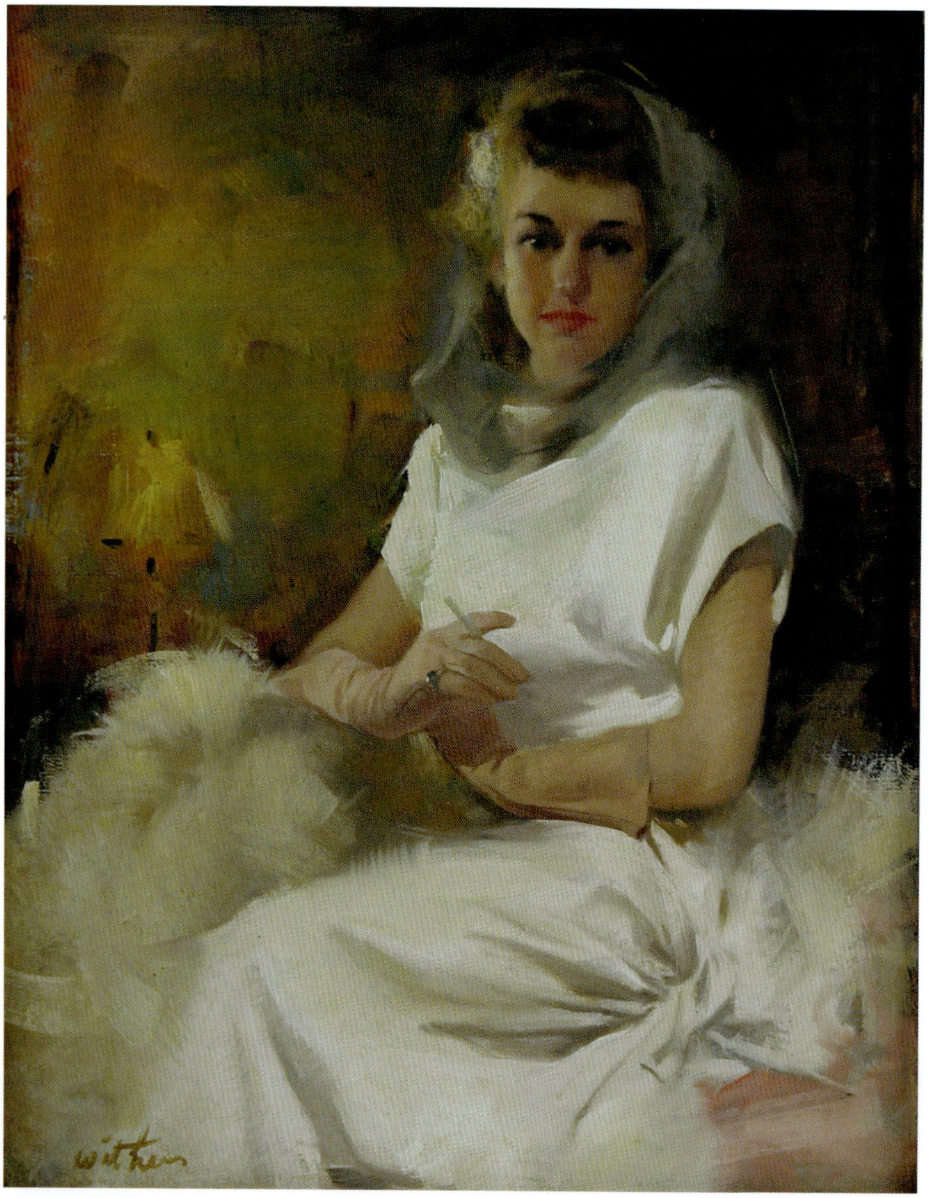

Edward Withers
Woman in White, c 1940
Ron and Barbara Sickmen, New York, New York

Henri Achille Zo

1873–1933

Henri Achille Zo was born in Bayonne on December 2, 1873. He was a genre scene painter and illustrator and worked for the most part in portraits, nudes and landscapes. He specialized as well in Spanish genre scenes, bull races, life in the Basque region and painted a number of portraits of theater and musical personalities. Zo studied with his father Achille, Léon Bonnat and Albert Maignan.

Zo first exhibited at the Salon des Artistes Français in 1895. He received many awards at the salon, including an honorable mention in 1897, Médaille de Troisième Classe in 1899, Médaille d'Or at l'Exposition Universelle in 1900 and Médaille de Deuxième Classe in 1901. Additionally, he received the Prix Rosa Bonheur in 1903 and the Prix National in 1905. In 1910 Zo was awarded Chevalier de la Légion d'Honneur. He also became a member of the Comité, the Jury and Sociétaire Hors-Concours. Zo was awarded the prix G. Ferrier in 1933.

He illustrated *Ramuntcho* by P. Loti and *A la Mer* by P. Margueritte. Zo also took part in decorating l'Opéra Comique and the chapel that was built for the victims of the Bazar de la Charité. Zo's work can be found in many museums including Bordeaux, Bayonne, Bucharest, London, Montauban, Nimes, Oran, Pau, Philadelphia, Saint-Quentin, Saint-Sebastian and Tourcoing. In Paris his work is part of the permanent collection at the Musée d'Art Moderne. Henri Achille Zo died in 1933.

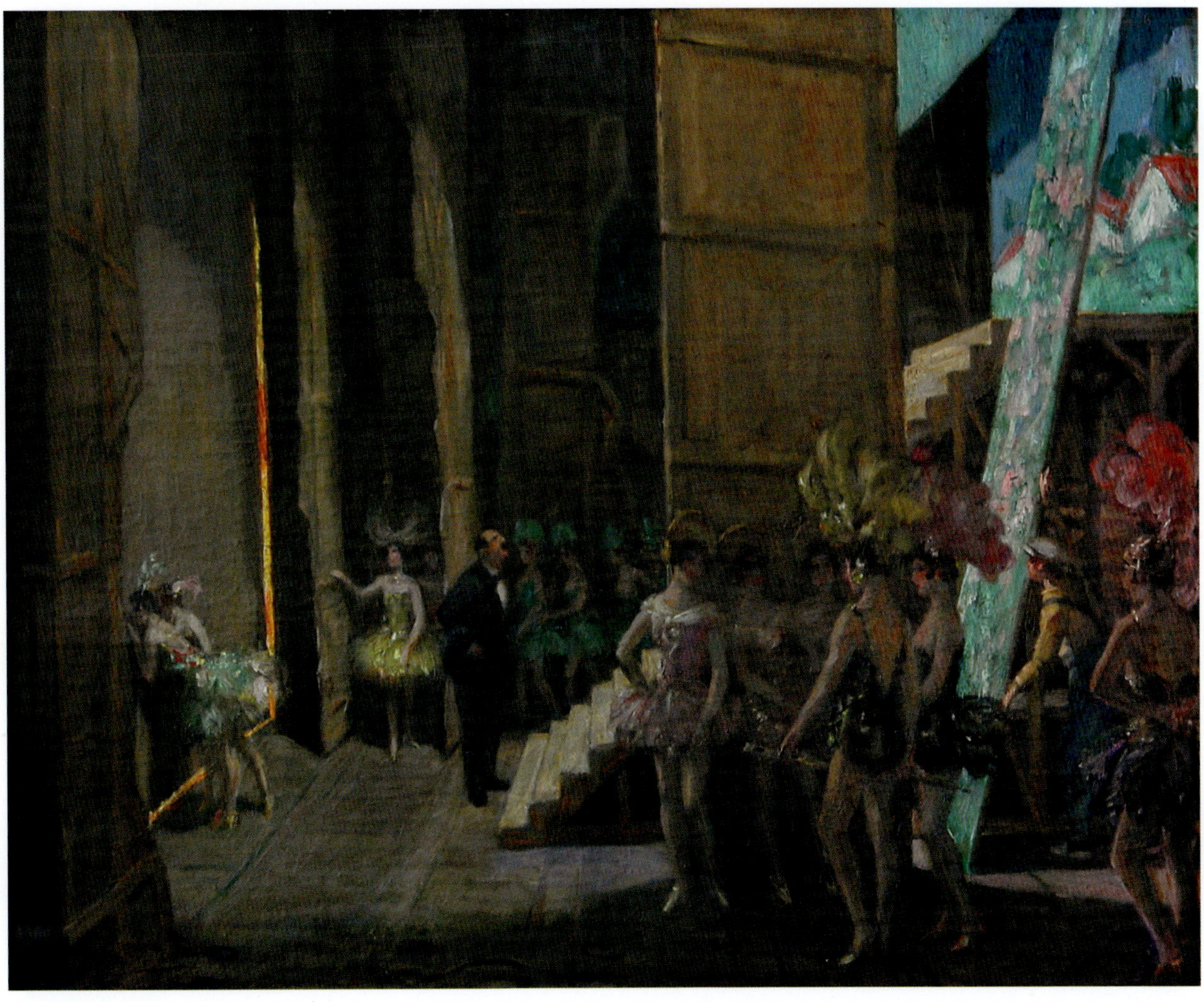

Henri Achille Zo
Le Première Nuit, c.1925
Axel d'Anthés, Santa Barbara, California

Selected Bibliography

Arnason, H.H. *History of Modern Art; Second Edition*. New York: Harry N. Abrams, Inc., 1977.

Baker, Phil. *The Book of Absinthe*. New York: Grove Press, 2001.

Bénézit. *Dictionnaire Critique et Documentaire des Peintres Sculpteurs Dessinateurs et Graveurs*. Paris: Gründ, 1999.

Berko, Patrick and Viviane and Rey, Stéphane. *Georges Rogy, 1897-1981*. Knokke-Zoute: Berko.

Booth, Martin. *Opium: A History*. New York: St. Martin's Griffin, 1996.

Bougault, Valerie. *Paris Montparnasse: The Heyday of Modern Art 1910-1940*. Paris: Terrail, 1997.

Boyé, Nadine; Fogel, Paul; Nieszawer, Nadine. *Peintures Juifs à Paris*: 1905-1939 École de Paris. Paris: Éditions Denouel, 2000.

Brecher, Edward, M. *Licit and Illicit Drugs*. Boston: Little, Brown and Co., 1972.

Buisson, Sylvie; Christian Parisot. *Paris Montmarte: A Mecca of Modern art 1860-1920*. Paris: Terrail, 1996.

Bulliet, C.J. *The Significant Moderns and Their Pictures*. New York: Covici-Friede Piublishers, 1936.

Cabanne, Pierre and Gérald Schurr. *Dictionnaire des Petits Maître de la Peinture 1820-1920*. Paris: Les Éditions de l'Amateur, 1996.

Clair, Jean editor. *The 1920s Age of the Metropolis*. Montreal: The Montreal Museum of Fine Art, 1991.

Clay, Jean. *From Impressionism to Modern Art*. New Jersey: Chartwell Books Inc., 1978.

Cserba, Júlia; Kopeczky, Csaba; Makláry, Kálmán; Passuth, Krisztina. *Alfred Reth 1884-1966*, Budapest: Makláry Artworks, 2003.

De Wilde, Elaine; Preface. *Le Dictionnaire des Peintres Belges du XIVe Siècle À Nos Jours*. Brussels: La Renaissance du Livre, 1995.

Escohotado, Antonio. *A Brief History of Drugs: From the Stone age to the Stoned Age*. Rochestor, Vermont: Park Street Press, 1996.

Gordon, Jan. *Modern French Painters*. Freeport, New York: Books for Libraries Press, 1923.

Gouttenoir, Bernard. *Dictionnaire des Peintures & Sculpteurs à Lyon au XIXe & XXe Siècles*. Lyon: La Taillanderie, 2000.

Chibret-Plaussu, Fançoise and François Gromaire. *Marcel Gromaire: La Vie et L'Oeuvre*. Paris: La Bibliothèque des Arts, 1993.

Hodgson, Barbara. *Opium: A Portrait of the Heavenly Demon*. San Francisco: Chronicle Books, 1999.

Klüver, Billy; Julie Martin. *Kiki et Montparnasse*. New York: Flammarion, 1989.

Langui, Emile. *Expressionism in Belgium, translation by Allistair Kennedy*. Brussels: Laconti, 1971.

Lanier, Doris. *Absinthe: The Cocaine of the Nineteenth Century*. Jefferson, North Carolina: McFarland & Company, Inc., 1995.

Lévêque, Jean-Jacques. *Les Années Folles 1918-1939 Le Triomphe de l'Art Moderne*. Paris: ACR Édition Internationale, 1992.

Lucie-Smith, Edward *Lives of the Great 20th Century Artists* published on www.artchive.com

Nacenta, Raymond. *School of Paris*. Greenwich, Connecticut: New York Graphic Society, 1960.

Nieszawer, Nadine; Marie Boye; Paul Fogel. *Peintres Juifs À Paris*. Paris: Denoël, 2000.

Paulvé, Dominique. *La Ruche: Un Siècle d'Art À Paris*. Paris: Gründ, 2002.

Perry, Gill. *Women Artists and the Paris Avant-Garde*. Manchester: Manchester University Press, 1995.

Petteys, Chris. *Dictionary of Women Artists*. Boston, Massachusetts: G. K. Hall & Co., 1985.

Piron, Paul. *De Belgische Beeldende Kunstenaars*. Brussels: Piron and Art in Belgium, 2000.

Piron, Paul. *Dictionnaire des Artistes Plasticiens de Belgique des XIX$_e$ et XX$_e$ Siècles*. Ohain-Lasne: Editions in Art, 2003.

Rudley, Richard. *Essential Substances*. New York: Kodansha America, Inc, 1993.

Roussard, André; *Dictionnaire des Peintres à Montmarte: Peintres, Sculpteurs, Graveurs, Dessinateurs, Illustrateurs, Plasticiens Aux XIX$_e$ & XX$_e$ Siècles*. Montmartre: Editions André Roussard, 1999.

Soyer, Gérard-Louis. *Jean-Gabriel Domergue: L'Art et La Mode*. Paris: Sous le Vent, 1984.

Tinterow, Gary; Geneviève Lacambre. *Manet/ Velázquez: The French Taste for Spanish Painting*. New York: The Metropolitan Museum of Art, 2003.

Warnod, Jeanine. *Les Artistes de Montparnasse*. Paris: Editions Mayer - Van Wilder, 1988.

Warnod, Jeanine. *Alice Halicka et ses Souvenirs*, La Revue *Terre d'Europe*, 1974.

Waters, Grant M. *Dictionary of British Artists Working 1900 – 1950*, Eastbourne: Eastbourne Fine Art, 1975.

Contemporary American Painting. Encyclopedia Britannica Collection, New York: Duell, Sloan and Pearce, 1945.

Dictionnaire Biographique des Artistes Contemporains. Paris: Edouard-Joseph, 1931.

Jean de Botton. San Francisco: The Museum o f California Palace of the Legion of Honor, 1944.

Jean Dulac: Artiste, Peinture-Statuaire 1902-1968, Paris: ADAGP, 2001

La Ruche. Paris: Musée du Montparnasse-Atlantica, 2002.

Le Dictionnaire des Peintures Belges du XIVe Siècle à nos Jours. Brussels: La Rennaissance du Livre, 1995.

L'École de Paris 1904-1929, la part de l'Autre. Paris: Musée d'Art moderne de la Ville de Paris, 2000.

Walter Sauer. Brussels: Bern'Art, 2001.

Index

Abadie-Landel, Pierre
Absinthe
Acrement, Jacques
Agutte, Georgette
Alleuame, Ludovic
Alvarez, Mabel
Arnautoff, Victor
Astoy, Gustave
Baes, Émile
Barbarite, James Peter
Beaupuy, Louis Jean
Bécat, Paul-Émile
Belair, Pierre de
Beltran-Masses, Féderico
Berjonneau, Jehan
Bertalan, Albert
Besserve, René-Pierre Louis
Biessy, Marie-Gabriel
Bisschops, Charles
Bissière, Roger
Bloch, Marcel
Bloos, Richard
Botton, Jean de
Bouchet, Robert
Boyé, Abel Dominique
Bréard, Henri Georges
Bussière, Gaston
Buzon, Frédéric Marius de
Calbet, Antoine
Camps, Gaspar
Carré, Ben
Chaliapin, Boris
Chambon, Émile
Chapin, Jean
Charmy, Emilie
Chavenon, Roland
Chepourkoff, Michael
Chimot, Édouard
Chistovsky, Lev
Cocaine
Cockroft, Edythe Varian
Compard, Émile
Costenoble, Anna
Courmes, Alfred
Courtens, Hermann
Cresswell, Albert
Creten, Georges
Dalbanne, Claude
Dayez, Georges
Daynes-Grassot, Susan
Decler, Ludmisla Ferri
Delalain, Henriette
Delescluze, Edmond
Delpech, Herman
Dequene, Jean-Pierre
Desmare, Lucien
Dierickx, Raymond
Domergue, Jean-Gabriel
Dormont, Jean
Dubois, Raphael
Dulac, Jean
DuMond, Frank
Dupagne, Adrien
Dupas, Jean
Durand-Rosé, Auguste
Edelmann, Charles-Auguste
Erdely, Francis de
Escribe, Ivan
Fernand-Renault, Albert
Fonseca, Gaston Simoes de
Fournier, Hippolyte
Frédéric, Baron
Fried, Pal
Fulop, Karoly
Galand, Léon
Geiger, Richard
Genoud, Nanette
Geuens, Jacques
Giron, Robert
Glatzer, Simon

Gloutchenko, Nicolas
Goossens, Maurice
Goth, Imre
Gouweloos, Jean
Grandgérard, Lucien-Henri
Gromaire, Marcel
Grunsweigh, Nathan
Guiard y Larrauri, Adolfo
Guilbert, Paul Louis
Halicka, Alice
Hanau, Jean
Haustrate, Gaston
Hensel, Maurice Henri
Hermann-Paul, René Georges
Hofer, André
Humbert, André Louis Maxime
Humbert-Vignot, Léonie
Jannel, Jean
Jarosz, Romain
Jellett, Mainie Harriet
Jonas, Lucien Hector
Josimovich, George M.
Jungbluth, Chrysis
Kantor, Morris
Karpelès, Andrée
Keuller, Vital
Kimpe, Reimond
Kirchner, Raphaël
Kohn, Alice
Kollorsz, Richard
Krasnow, Peter
Lafnet, Luc
Laglenne, Jean Francis
Lagrange, Anne-Marie
La Lyre, Adolphe
Lamotte, Bernard
Laparra, William Julien Émile Édouard
Lapeyre, Edmond Édouard
Laudy, Jean
Lecompte, Paul
Legrand, Mercedes
Lelong, Pierre
Lelong, René
Lempereur, Edmond
Lépine, Georges
Linus, Axel
Lobel-Riche, Almery
Lockman, DeWitt McClellan
Longa, René
Lurçat, Jean
Lydis,Mariette
Marcel-Lenoir
Maresté, Georges
Mavro, Mania
Mayo
Ménard, Marie
Micha, Maurice Jean
Milliere, Maurice
Moitroux, Alfred
Montagne, Émile-Pierre de la
Moreau-Neret, Adrien
Moreau, Max
Muter, Mela
Naillod, Charles
Newcombe, Warren A.
Noir, Robert (Ernest)
Nys, Carl (Charles)
Oberlé, Jean
Oldfield, Otis
Opium
Parrot, Philippe
Penot, Albert Joseph
Phillipe, Robert
Picard, Louis
Piet, Fernand
Pillet, Edgar
Pouget, Marcel
Prunier, Gaston
Prunier, Marcel
Rambo, Jules

Ranvier-Chartier, Lucie
Raynolt, Antoine Marie
Reth, Alfred
Rochegrosse, Georges
Rockline, Vera
Rogy, Georges
Sauer, Walter
Scauflaire, Edgar
Scévola, Lucien-Victor Guirand (Guérand) de
Schimmel, Hugo
Schönberg, Rodolphe S
Schwartz, William S.
Seevagen, Lucien
Smirnoff, Boris
Sollier, Henri
Solomon, Simeon
Somm, Henri (François Clément Sommier)
Sonrel, Elisabeth
Souverbie, Jean
Srp, Frantisek
Sternberg, Nicolas
Stiner, Walter
Tanaka, Yasushi
Tête, Maurice Louis
Thevenot, Adrien
Tirode, Léon
Tondu, André
Tullat, Lucie
Uzelac, Milivoy
Vagnier, Prosper
van Belle, Karel
van Beveren, Hugo
van Her, Carlo
van Nuffel, Georges
van Roose, Charles
Vanzevenberghen, Georges
Verschaeren, Theodoor-Joseph
Vidar, Fride
Villain, Pierre
Voguet, Léon
Wagemans, Maurice
Walloon Art
Watelet, Charles
Wegener, Gerda
Wilson, Muriel
Wiser, Guy Brown
Withers, Edward
Zo, Henri Achille